HANDBOOK ON GERMAN MILITARY FORCES

U. S. WAR DEPARTMENT

HANDBOOK
on
GERMAN
MILITARY
FORCES

With an Introduction by Stephen E. Ambrose

LOUISIANA STATE UNIVERSITY PRESS
BATON ROUGE

New material copyright © 1990 by Louisiana State University Press
All rights reserved

Louisiana Paperback Edition, 1995
04 03 02 01 00 99 98   5 4 3

Library of Congress Cataloging-in-Publication Data
United States. War Dept.
    Handbook on German military forces ; with an introduction by
Stephen E. Ambrose.
        p.   cm.
    ISBN 0-8071-2011-1 (pbk.)
    1. Germany—Armed Forces—Handbooks, manuals, etc.   2. Germany—
Armed Forces—History—World War, 1939–1945—Handbooks, manuals,
etc.   I. Title.
UA710.U587   1990
355′.00943—dc20   90-5954
                                                                              CIP

The paper in this book meets the guidelines for permanence and durability of the Committee on
Production Guidelines for Book Longevity of the Council on Library Resources.⊗

CONTENTS

INTRODUCTION

The republication of this volume is a major contribution to World War II scholarship. Without question, this is the authoritative work on the German army from 1939 to 1945. Its virtues are so many and so great that I can see no reason to restrain my enthusiasm. Originally issued in a limited and classified edition in March, 1945, this book has been generally unavailable and even unknown. Its availability in this edition is a blessing for which scholars and students will be thanking LSU Press for decades to come.

The virtues of the work are vast and far too many to cover here in any detail. Certain features demand some comment. There is, first of all, the sheer scope of the work. It covers everything from the high command to the lowest private. The organization of the German army is described better than it has been anywhere else; so too for its weapons, its tactics, its field equipment, its morale, its uniforms, and much else.

Second, there is the excellent writing and the clear, logical organization of the work. (The superb photographs speak for themselves.) War Department publications are not known for their sprightly writing, but this one is a joy to read. As an example, by no means unique, read the five paragraphs of "The German Army Today" on page 1. The movement of the work, from the German military system to the organization of field forces, on to tactics, fortifications and defense, the supply system, weapons, field equipment, uniforms, and finally the air forces, is as precise, well ordered, and sensible as it could possibly be.

Third, there is the depth of the work. It treats the psychology of the German soldier, his strengths and weaknesses. It covers the organization of the army in an objective and insightful manner. It lists the pluses and minuses of the army's weapons and equipment. It presents the best account I have ever seen on the tactical doctrines of the army. None of this is frozen in time; the work describes, accurately and understandably, the evolution of weapons, organization, and tactics from the offensive-minded, *blitzkreig* army of 1939 to the defensive-oriented army of March, 1945.

The broadness of the approach is exemplified by the section on the role of the *SS* in the army and in the nation. The *SS*, the book states, "is more than a state within a state; it is superior to both the Party and the government." The work goes on to show the truth of the assertion in a superb analysis of how Heinrich Himmler and his fellow gangsters took and held power in every aspect of German life. The section has a political sophistication to it one does not expect in a War Department study, along with an awareness of reality and a sensitivity to nuance that make it invaluable.

Fourth, the work is wonderfully up-to-date. Developments in January and February, 1945, are noted and commented upon, all within the context of explaining trends in the army since 1939. In general, the Germans believed that only the offensive could be decisive in war, a dogma that led to the *blitzkreig,* which featured close-in air support, light, fast tanks, rapid movements of infantry, and a relative neglect of artillery. But the lightning forces that had conquered much of Europe by 1942 were inappropriate to the defense of those conquests. Further, the Germans had major manpower problems and were forced to rely on old men, teenagers, and foreign conscripts. They met the new needs by improving their field and fixed fortifications, by switching to automatic weapons at the expense of accuracy, by building heavier but slower and less maneuverable tanks, and by adopting new tactical doctrines. Thus the general and accurate conclusion: "The primary goal of Germany today is to gain time and to achieve victory in a political sense, since the Germans are no longer capable of a military victory. Of necessity their military operations now supplement this effort and have become a large-scale delaying action."

Fifth, the work is realistic. While dispelling the myth of the German soldier as a superman, it avoids denigrating him. For example: "The belief of former years that the German Army was inflexible and lacking in initiative has been completely destroyed in this war, in which aggressive and daring leadership has been responsible for many bold decisions. Yet . . . the Germans . . . tend to repeat the same type of manouvers, a fact which has been fully exploited by Allied commanders." The work also points out that the German soldier of 1945 was one of several different types. The veterans were men "of many fronts and many retreats." They were "prematurely aged, war weary cynic[s], either discouraged and disillusioned or too stupefied to have any thoughts of [their] own." But they were also "seasoned campaigners" who performed their duties "with the highest degree of efficiency." By contrast, "the new recruit, except in some crack *SS* units, is either too young or too old and often in poor health [and] poorly trained. [But] he makes up for this by a fanaticism bordering on madness."

Sixth, the work is practical. Had I been a replacement officer on my way across the Atlantic in March, 1945, about to be thrown into the battle, I would have devoured it. The information it contains was exactly what men about to enter combat against the German army needed. As one example: "While scouting a woods, a favorite German ruse is to drive the leading car towards its edge, halt briefly to observe, and then drive off rapidly, hoping to draw fire that will disclose the enemy positions." For another, look at the illustrations of typical German defensive positions in the chapter "Fortifications and Defenses," especially the changing pattern of laying mine fields. Or glance at the chapter on weapons, where you will learn that the King Tiger, German's heaviest and latest tank, while fearful to behold and awesome in its firepower, had some significant weaknesses. The tank was "virtually invulnerable to frontal attack," but when "buttoned up" it was "extremely blind" and was vulnerable to flank and rear attacks. Best of all for the replacement officer, the work explains how to use captured weapons or other equipment.

In sum, this book is the last word on the most feared fighting machine the world has ever known. If that army was a long way from the one of 1939, which Hitler called "an army such as the world has never seen," it remained nevertheless a formidable force. It is described here accurately, dispassionately, fairly, and completely.

By 1945 U.S. Army Chief of Staff George C. Marshall may have known the German army better than Hitler did. This book convinces me that such was indeed the case. Although his name never appears in this book, Marshall's imprint is on every page. His thoroughness, his comprehensive mind, his objectivity, his realism, and his intelligence are evident throughout. He thought of doing this work and pushed it through to completion.

Where on earth did all this information come from? Part of it, obviously, was gleaned through the breaking of the German radio code, the so-called Ultra system (the one German communications system not mentioned in the book is the Enigma code; this was the most tightly held secret of the war), but most came from more mundane intelligence sources, primarily captured weapons and after-action reports. It was one of the features of Marshall's army that what was learned on the battlefield was quickly transferred back to units training in the States. The U.S. Army first entered combat against the German army in November, 1942, in North Africa; it then fought the Germans in Sicily, Italy, France, Belgium, and in Germany itself. The flow of information from the combat front back to the War Department was staggering; much of it is incorporated in this book.

Interrogation of prisoners is always a prime source of intelligence; clearly the results of those interrogations were flowing back to the War Department and contributed heavily to the analysis and description of the German army. Clearly, too, the men who put this work together were reading closely every bit of printed material they could get from inside Germany. On the other hand, there is relatively little in the book on lessons learned and information gleaned from experiences on the German Eastern Front, undoubtedly a reflection of how difficult it was for the Americans to get the Russians to reveal much of what was happening in their theater.

Who wrote this book? The title page gives no hint. Obviously it was a team effort, but there must have been one individual in charge of the whole project and probably its principal author.

My candidate is an obscure U.S. Army colonel named Truman Smith. He had been an instructor under Marshall at Fort Benning in the early thirties, then military attaché in Berlin. Marshall had depended on Smith for information about the development of the German army on the eve of World War II.

Smith fell afoul of President Franklin Roosevelt when he arranged for Charles Lindbergh to be received by German Air Marshal Hermann Goering; Lindbergh, a leading isolationist at that time, infuriated Roosevelt and much of the American public by accepting from Goering a German decoration for his air exploits. Smith, a right-winger and an isolationist in his politics, got some of the blame.

In 1940, Smith was discovered to have diabetes, which was cause for mandatory retirement. All the paper-work for his retirement was completed and went to Marshall's desk for his signature. Although ordinarily Marshall was a stickler for the rules, in Smith's case he just let the papers sit there. Day after day Smith came into the War Department expecting it to be his last day, but Marshall kept him on. Immediately after Pearl Harbor, Marshall ruled that the emergency overrode regulations, promoted Smith to colonel, and retained him at his side until the end of the war.

Marshall wanted to promote Smith to general officer rank, but Roosevelt would not allow it. Nevertheless, Marshall continued to look to Smith for insights into the German army. In the fall of 1943, when it appeared that Marshall would command Operation Overlord, he told Smith he intended to bring him to London to serve on his staff; Marshall was even ready to set up a special hospital for Smith outside his own headquarters.

At the end of the war, when Marshall learned that Smith could not earn proper retirement credit unless he served an additional year, Marshall arranged for Smith to stay on active duty until 1946. This was one of the few times that Marshall went against Roosevelt's known wishes.

Smith's reputation in the army was that of a brain, a writer, and an expert on the German army. If he was not the principal author of this work, he surely was one of the major contributors.

What impresses me most about this book is what it tells us about the U.S. Army and War Department in World War II. No other army in history has ever known its enemy as well as the American army knew the German army when the Americans crossed the Rhine River and began their final offensive. The British had fought the Germans longer, the Russians had fought more of them, so their collective experience was greater than that of the Americans. But they had not systematically gathered the information, put it in order, and published it. This volume is unique and valuable beyond measure.

STEPHEN E. AMBROSE

UNIVERSITY OF NEW ORLEANS

PUBLISHER'S NOTE

The *Handbook on German Military Forces* was one of a series of studies of foreign military forces prepared by the U.S. Army during World War II. When the need for these studies declined at the end of the war, a few copies of the *Handbook* were placed in military library collections and the remainder mostly discarded. The volume from which this facsimile edition was prepared came from the library of David I. Norwood III of Baton Rouge, a collector of World War II memorabilia.

The original volume was published in a loose-leaf format with each chapter conceived as a self-contained unit to which new material could be added as it became available. In preparing this edition, the publisher has added consecutive page numbers to permit easier cross-referencing than the original chapter references would allow and to facilitate the preparation of the comprehensive index that has been appended to the volume. The Introduction by Stephen E. Ambrose was commissioned especially for this edition. The text and illustrations appear exactly as they did in the original.

The volume has been officially released from restricted status by the U.S. Army Center for Military History.

HANDBOOK ON GERMAN MILITARY FORCES

WAR DEPARTMENT TECHNICAL MANUAL

TM-E 30-451

HANDBOOK ON

GERMAN

MILITARY FORCES

WAR DEPARTMENT • 15 MARCH 1945

United States Government Printing Office

Washington : 1945

(Facsimile of 1945 title page)

CHAPTER I

THE GERMAN MILITARY SYSTEM

Section I. INTRODUCTION

1. Total War

The Germans have long devoted a large part of their national energies to both the study and the application of the science of war. The German Army which was built up under the Nazi regime and which challenged the world in 1939 was the final product of this study. It represented the fruition of decades of long-range planning, organization, experimentation, and mechanical development directed toward the sole end of creating a military instrument which would be a match for any foreseeable combination of adversaries. Supported by the entire economic, political, and psychological resources of a totalitarian government, it was destined to overrun almost the whole of Europe in a series of victorious campaigns unequaled since the days of Napoleon. The three greatest nations on earth were forced to muster all their human and material power to crush the German military machine by the only possible method—overwhelming superiority of force.

Total war is neither a modern invention nor a German monopoly. But total mobilization, in the sense of the complete and scientific control of all the efforts of the nation for the purposes of war, and total utilization of war as an instrument of national policy have been developed to their highest degree by the German militarists. Central control and careful coordination, by qualified experts, of a military machine which is built with all the best available materials and put together for the highest efficiency of operation have been the secret of such military victories as the Germans have achieved.

It is the purpose of this Handbook to describe this military machine in all its aspects. No one of the supporting pillars of the German Army—its personnel, its High Command, its administrative structure, its unit organization, its weapons, its tactical doctrines—can stand or fall alone. The various chapters and sections which follow must be studied together as various facets of a whole.

2. The German Army Today

When the German *Panzer* divisions struck out across the Polish frontier at dawn on 1 September 1939, no one could predict the scope, intensity, and duration of the armed conflict which they were precipitating. The German Army then was fresh, vigorous, expansive, and obviously superior to its contemporaries. Its weapons were new and shiny; its tactics and techniques—the old doctrines adapted to the new conditions—were untried; its officers and men were young and full of enthusiasm. A career of easy conquest seemed to open up before it.

After five and a half years of ever growing battle against ever-stronger enemies, the German Army in 1945 looks, at first glance, much the worse for wear. It is beset on all sides and is short of everything. It has suffered appalling casualties and must resort to old men, boys, invalids, and unreliable foreigners for its cannon fodder. Its weapons and tactics seem not to have kept pace with those of the armies opposing it; its supply system in the field frequently breaks down. Its position is obviously hopeless, and it can only be a question of time until the last German soldier is disarmed, and the once proud German Army of the great Frederick and of Scharnhorst, of Ludendorff and of Hitler, exists no more as a factor to be reckoned with.

Yet this shabby, war-weary machine has struggled on in a desperate effort to postpone its inevitable demise. At the end of 1944 it was still able to mount an offensive calculated to delay for months the definitive piercing of the western bulwarks of Germany. Despite the supposed chronic disunity at the top, disaffection among the officer corps, and disloyalty in the rank and file, despite the acute lack of weapons, ammunition, fuel, transport, and human reserves, the German Army seems to function with its old precision and to overcome what appear to be insuperable difficulties with remarkable speed. Only by patient and incessant hammering from all sides can its collapse be brought about.

The cause of this toughness, even in defeat, is not generally appreciated. It goes much deeper than the quality of weapons, the excellence of training and leadership, the soundness of tactical and strategic doctrine, or the efficiency of. control at all echelons. It is to be found in the military tradition which is so deeply ingrained in the whole character of the German nation and which alone makes possible the interplay of these various factors of strength to their full effectiveness.

The German Army of 1939 was a model of efficiency, the best product of the concentrated military genius of the most scientifically military of nations. A study of the German Army of 1945, however, older and wiser, hardened and battle-tested, cornered and desperate as it is, will show best how this military science and military genius operate in the practical exigencies of long-drawn-out total war.

Section II. THE GERMAN SOLDIER

1. Fanatic or Weakling?

The German soldier who faces the Allies on the home fronts in 1945 is a very different type from the members of the Army of 1939 which Hitler called "an Army such as the world has never seen". The German soldier is one of several different types depending on whether he is a veteran of 4 or 5 years, or a new recruit. The veteran of many fronts and many retreats is a prematurely aged, war weary cynic, either discouraged and disillusioned or too stupefied to have any thought of his own. Yet he is a seasoned campaigner, most likely a noncommissioned officer, and performs his duties with the highest degree of efficiency.

The new recruit, except in some crack *SS* units, is either too young or too old and often in poor health.

He has been poorly trained for lack of time but, if too young, he makes up for this by a

fanaticism bordering on madness. If too old, he is driven by the fear of what his propagandists have told him will happen to the Fatherland in case of an Allied victory, and even more by the fear of what he has been told will happen to him and his family if he does not carry out orders exactly as given. Thus even the old and sick perform, to a certain point, with the courage of despair.

The German High Command has been particularly successful in placing the various types of men where they best fit, and in selecting those to serve as cannon fodder, who are told to hold out to the last man, while every effort is made to preserve the elite units, which now are almost entirely part of the *Waffen-SS*. The German soldier in these units is in a preferred category and is the backbone of the German Armed Forces. He is pledged never to surrender and has no moral code except allegiance to his organization. There is no limit to his ruthlessness.

The mentality of the German soldier of 1945 is the final result of that policy of militarism which, even in the 19th century, caused a famous German general to recommend that soldiers should be trained to ask of their superiors: "Master, order us where we may die."

2. Manpower Problems

a. ANNUAL CLASS SYSTEM. When Hitler reintroduced general conscription in 1935, the greatest possible care was taken to create a strong military force without disrupting the economic life of the nation. Men were registered by annual classes and during the years before the war those of the older classes were called only in small groups to attend training exercises of limited duration. Even for the younger classes, all feasible arrangements were made for the deferment of students and of those engaged in necessary occupations. Men accepted for active service were called to the colors by individual letter rather than by public announcement for their annual class. This system was continued in the gradual mobilization which preceded the outbreak of the war in such a way that the wartime Army could be built up organically and the normal course of life was not seriously upset.

b. WAR DEVELOPMENTS. As long as the war was conducted on a limited scale, the Armed Forces were very liberal in granting occupational and medical discharges. As the war progressed and grew in scope and casualties mounted, it became necessary to recall many of these men and eventually to reach increasingly into both the older and the younger age groups.

After Germany changed from the offensive to the defensive in 1943, it became both possible and necessary to transfer an increasing number of Air Force and naval personnel to the Army, to enforce "voluntary" enlistment in the *Waffen-SS,* and to commit line-of-communication units to regular combat not only against partisans but against regular enemy forces.

The increasingly heavy losses of the Russian campaign forced Hitler to cancel his order exempting "last sons" of decimated families and fathers of large families from front-line combat duty. Prisons and concentration camps were combed out for men who could be used in penal combat units with the inducement of possible later reinstatement of their civic rights.

Although a "total mobilization" was carried out in the spring of 1943, after Stalingrad, it became necessary by the end of that year to lower the physical classification standards drastically and to register men up to 60 years of age for military service. Even men with severe stomach ailments were drafted into special-diet battalions. During the summer of 1944, civilian occupations were reduced to an absolutely necessary minimum. Finally, the remaining male civilians from 16 to 60 were made liable for home defense combat service in the *"Volkssturm"* and even Hitler Youth boys and girls were called up as auxiliaries.

Along with these measures there went a continuous reorganization of combat as well as administrative units for the purpose of increasing efficiency and saving personnel.

The strength of divisions was lowered while their firepower was increased and their components were made more flexible. Severe comb-outs were made among rear-area personnel and technical specialists. The strongest possible measures were introduced against waste of manpower, inefficiency, and desertions, particularly after the Army was brought under the ever increasing control of the *SS,* in the summer and autumn of 1944.

After the Allied breakthrough in France, Himmler was appointed Commander of the Replacement Army and as such made the *Waffen-SS* the backbone of German national defense. Whole units of the Air Force and Navy were taken over and trained by the *Waffen-SS* and then distributed among depleted field units. The organi-

zation and employment of the *Volkssturm* is under Himmler's direct control.

The complicated record system of the Armed Forces was maintained in principle but streamlined for the sake of saving manpower.

c. FOREIGN ELEMENTS. (1) *Original policy.* In their attempts to solve their ever acute manpower problems, the Germans have not neglected to make the fullest possible use of foreign elements for almost every conceivable purpose and by almost every conceivable method. Originally, great stress was laid on keeping the Armed Forces nationally "pure". Jews and Gypsies were excluded from military service. Foreign volunteers were not welcomed. Germans residing abroad and possessing either German or dual citizenship were rounded up through the German consulates from 1937 on. When Germany set out to invade other countries, beginning with Austria, only the inhabitants of these countries who were held to be of German or related blood became liable to German military service; the Czech minority in Austria, for example, was exempted.

(2) *Recruiting of foreigners.* With the invasion of Russia in June 1941, German propagandists set themselves to the task of changing the whole aspect of the war from a national German affair to a "European war of liberation from Communism". In this way the Nazis were able to obtain a considerable number of volunteers from occupied and even neutral countries, who were organized in combat units of their own in German uniforms and under German training. The original policy was to incorporate racially related "Germanic" people, such as the Dutch and Scandinavians, into the *Waffen-SS* and non-Germanic people such as the Croats into the Army. When the failures in Russia and other increasing difficulties began to affect the morale of the foreigners, their "voluntary recruitment" became more and more a matter of compulsion and their service in separate national units had to be brought under more rigid supervision. The organization of such units, therefore, was turned over in increasing measure to the *Waffen-SS,* even in the case of racially non-Germanic elements.

At the same time, it became necessary for the Army to fill its own depleted German units by adding a certain percentage of foreign recruits. This was done partly by declaring the inhabitants of annexed territories, such as the Polish Corridor, to be "racial Germans" (*Volksdeutsche*), making them provisional German citizens subject to induction into the Armed Forces. A considerable source of manpower was Soviet prisoners of war of different national origins. Some of these were put into regular German units as "racial" Germans; others were employed in such units as "auxiliary volunteers". Separate national units also were created from Cossacks and from the numerous peoples who inhabit the Caucasus and Turkestan and are collectively referred to by the Germans as "Eastern Peoples" (Ostvölker). Every possible inducement has been used for the recruiting of foreigners, including their religion, as in the case of the Mohammedans in the Balkans. Only in the case of Jews and Gypsies was the original policy of exclusion not only upheld but extended during the war to include those of 50 per cent Jewish descent.

3. Duties and Rights of the Soldier

a. THE OATH. Every German soldier, upon induction, is compelled to affirm his legally established military obligation by means of the following *oath* (vow, for atheists): *"I swear by God this holy oath* (I vow) that I will render unconditional obedience to the Führer of Germany and of her people, Adolf Hitler, the Supreme Commander of the Armed Forces, and that, as a brave soldier, I will be prepared to stake my life for this *oath* (vow) at any time." If, because of an oversight, the oath has not been administered to a soldier, he is held to be in the same position as though he had sworn it; the oath is regarded only as the affirmation of an inherent legal duty.

b. MILITARY DISCIPLINE. The German system of military discipline is rigorous, and excesses are severely punished. In principle, absolute and unquestioning obedience towards superiors is required. However, since the summer of 1944, when the Army came under the political influence of the Nazi Party, new orders were issued providing that disloyal superiors not only need not be obeyed but in emergencies may be liquidated by their own men. Officers who do not lead their men into combat or show other signs of cowardice or who, for any reason, mutilate themselves, are normally condemned to death. Divisional commanders and other high-ranking combat officers are specifically ordered to set an example of leadership in the front lines; this explains the high casualty rate among German generals.

Traditionally, German superior officers were addressed only indirectly, in the third person, as "Herr Major is absolutely right." Hitler, however, is addressed directly as "My Leader". Therefore, the Nazis made use of the direct form of address toward superior officers at first optional, then compulsory. Superior officers and noncommissioned officers are addressed as "Mr." *(Herr)* followed by their rank; in the *Waffen-SS*, however, only by their rank: *"Herr Leutnant!"*, but *"Unterstürmführer!"*

Originally, a distinction was made between the regular military salute and the "German salutation" (*Deutscher Gruss*) which consists of saying "Heil Hitler!" with the right arm outstretched. In August 1944 the latter type of salute was made compulsory throughout. Everyone salutes his own superiors as well as others entitled to a salute according to the following general rules: Every officer is the superior of all lower-ranking officers and all enlisted men; every noncommissioned officer is the superior of all privates; every noncommissioned officer in one of the first three grades is the superior of lower-grade noncommissioned officers *in his own unit*. There is no general rank superiority otherwise among noncommissioned officers or among the various grades of privates; however, all members of the Armed Forces are obligated to "greet" one another as a matter of military etiquette.

Members of the Armed Forces are forbidden to associate with foreigners even if they are racially related; marriages between soldiers and non-German women are subject to approval, which is given only after a very thorough investigation; the offspring of such marriages are considered to be German. In the *Waffen-SS,* such marriages are entirely prohibited for German personnel.

Men who severely and repeatedly violate military discipline, but not to an extent that warrants a death sentence, are transferred to correction battalions for a probationary period and given arduous and dangerous assignments; if incorrigible, they are then turned over to the police for extreme punishment.

c. PRESERVATION OF HONOR. Honor is considered the soldier's highest possession. Except in extreme cases, he may be given the opportunity to redeem himself for a dishonorable action by a heroic death in battle or, in milder cases, by exceptionally brave and meritorious service in the lowest grade of private to which he is reduced from his former rank. However, there also exists a rigid personal honor code for officers. Under its provisions, they are obligated to defend their own personal honor as well as the good name of their wives by every possible means and are held to account for violations committed by themselves or their wives. According to the German conception, special honor rules apply to officers and those civilians who are socially their equals. These rules provide in extreme cases for settlement by duel with pistols until one of the two parties is fully incapacitated. This is a leftover from feudal times; before Hitler's assumption of power, a half-hearted attempt was made to outlaw duelling by officers, but the penalties provided were light and did not carry moral stigma. It is significant that under Hitler, duelling of officers was legalized in cases where all efforts at settlement by an officers' court of honor (appointed by a regimental or higher commander) fail; however, for duels between two officers, but not between an officer and a civilian, a decision must first be obtained from the Commander-in-Chief of the Army. Their medieval conception of honor has a strong influence on the mentality and actions of many German officers. An officer is obligated to react to deliberate insults instantaneously, in a positive and masterly fashion, and to protect other officers from becoming the object of public disgrace.

In the *SS*, "qualified" enlisted men (i.e. those who carry the dagger) are subject to the same honor rules as officers, being obligated to "defend their honor by force of arms".

4. Morale Factors

a. RELATIONSHIP BETWEEN OFFICERS AND MEN. The opening of the officer's career to the common German man of the people was a revolutionary change in the German social system brought about by Hitler. It has created an entirely different type of relationship among the ranks than existed in the armies of Imperial Germany.

No one can become an officer without being a certified Nazi, even if not a member of the Party, and without being considered capable of imbuing his men with the Nazi spirit. Thus, the social mingling between officers and men in off-duty hours, which has been encouraged by the Nazis to some extent, appears to have a strong propagandist purpose. A sincere personal interest of the officer in his men is encouraged, the all-important requirement being that he must have their confidence. In case of death, the soldier's next

of kin receive their first notification through a personal letter from his company commander, which is handed to them by the local leader of the Nazi Party.

b. POLITICS IN THE ARMED FORCES. Traditionally, all German military personnel is barred from all political activities including the right to vote. Hitler, when introducing general conscription, maintained this tradition in order to obtain the full support of the military and decreed that membership in the Nazi Party and all political activities would be dormant during the period of any man's active service. In the later stages of the war, however, serious reverses and the increasing danger of sagging morale caused the official introduction of politics into the German Armed Forces. This occurred progressively from the latter part of 1943 on, by appointment of National-Socialist guidance officers (*NS-Führungsoffiziere*) on all staffs, the organization of political meetings, and other efforts at raising morale, as well as through the merciless terrorization of wavering officers and soldiers by the "strong men" of the *Waffen-SS*.

c. AWARDS. A very extended and clever use has been made of honorary titles for units, medals and awards for individual achievements, and commemorative decorations for participation in outstanding combat engagements. It is significant, for instance, that because the German is basically averse to hand-to-hand combat, the golden close-combat bar was created in 1944, which is bestowed by Hitler personally at his headquarters, as the highest honor offered the German soldier. Himmler shortly thereafter created the golden partisan-combat bar which he bestows personally at his headquarters. The requirements for winning either bar are extremely severe so that soldiers will do their utmost. Awards and decorations may be held to have acted as very important morale-builders for the German Armed Forces.

5. Ranks

a. RANK GROUPS AND CLASSES. German soldiers are divided into the following four rank groups:

(1) *Officers* (*Offiziere*):
    1st rank class: general officers (*Generale*).
    2nd rank class: field officers (*Stabsoffiziere*).
    3rd rank class: captains (*Hauptleute und Rittmeister*).
    4th rank class: lieutenants (*Leutnante*).
(2) *Musicians* (activities suspended in November 1944).

(3) *Noncommissioned Officers* (*Unteroffiziere*):
  1st rank class: fortress shop-foremen and horseshoeing instructors (see table).
  2d rank class: noncommissioned officers of the 1st, 2d, and 3d grades. (*Unteroffiziere mit Portepee*)
  3d rank class: officer candidates and noncommissioned officers of the 4th and 5th grades. (*Fähnriche und Unteroffiziere ohne Portepee*)

(4) *Privates* (*Mannschaften*).

Figures 1 and 2 show tables of U. S. and German equivalent ranks.

b. OFFICERS. Nearly all German officer ranks correspond to U. S. Army rank, although their terminology differs for general officers, a *Generalmajor* being the equivalent of a brigadier general. The functions, however, do not always correspond. This is partly due to the fact that German wartime ranks are permanent, which makes it often impossible for German officers to be promoted to the higher rank which their wartime appointment actually would warrant.

c. NONCOMMISSIONED OFFICERS. The noncommissioned officer ranks are divided into two groups: the first group corresponds to the first three grades in the U. S. Army. There is no

rank of first sergeant; rather, this is a position usually held by a master sergeant or technical sergeant. A corporal in the German Army functions as acting sergeant and normally is promoted to the rank of staff sergeant rather than sergeant; as to the latter rank, see paragraph e.

d. PRIVATES. There are three grades in the group which correspond to U. S. privates first class, and a soldier may be promoted from any of them to become a corporal. They may be described as chief private first class in administrative position (*Stabsgefreiter*), senior private first class who functions as acting corporal (*Obergefreiter*), and ordinary private first class (*Gefreiter*). A soldier cannot become chief private first class without having been a senior private first class. In most branches there are senior privates first class (*Obergrenadiere* in infantry, *Oberkanoniere* in artillery; the *Oberjäger*, however, in the light, mountain, and parachute divisions, is a corporal) and ordinary privates (*Grenadiere, Kanoniere*, etc.).

e. PROMOTION OF ENLISTED MEN. In most branches, a soldier cannot become a private first class without having been a senior private and he cannot become a corporal without having been

U. S. Army Equivalent	German Basic Rank	Special Designation	Type of Personnel
General of the Army..	*Generalfeldmarschall*		
General	*Generaloberst*		
Lieutenant General ...	*General*	*General der Infanterie*, etc..	Infantry, etc.
		Generaloberstabs-	
		Arzt	Medical
		Veterinär	Veterinary
		Intendant	Administrative
		Richter	Judiciary
Major General	*Generalleutnant*	*Generalstabs-*	
		Arzt, etc. as above......	Medical, etc. as above
Brigadier General	*Generalmajor*	*General-*	
		Arzt, etc. as above......	Medical, etc. as above
Colonel	*Oberst*	*Oberst-*	
		Arzt, etc. as above	Medical, etc. as above
Lieutenant Colonel	*Oberstleutnant*	*Oberfeld-*	
		Artz, etc. as above.......	Medical, etc. as above
Major	*Major*	*Oberstabs-*	
		Arzt, etc. as above.......	Medical, etc. as above
Captain	*Hauptmann*	*Stabs-*	
	Rittmeister (cav)	*Artz*, etc. as above.......	Medical, etc. as above
First Lieutenant	*Oberleutnant*	*Ober-*	
		Arzt	Medical
		Veterinär	Veterinary
		Zahlmeister	Administrative
Second Lieutenant	*Leutnant*	*Assistenz-*	
		Arzt	Medical
		Veterinär	Veterinary
		Zahlmeister	Administrative

Figure 1.—Table of officer ranks.

U. S. Army Equivalent	German Basic Rank	Special Designation	Type of Personnel
none		Festungsober- Werkmeister	Fortress Chief Shop man
		Oberhufbeschlags- Lehrmeister	Chief Horseshoeing Instructor
none		Festungs- Werkmeister	Fortress Shop-Foreman
		Hufbeschlags- Lehrmeister	Horseshoeing Instructor
Master Sergeant	Stabsfeldwebel	Stabs—	
		Wachtmeister	Arty, Cav, AA
		Beschlagmeister	Horseshoeing
		Feuerwerker	Ordnance
		Schirrmeister	Supply
		Funkmeister	Signal
		Brieftaubenmeister	Pigeoneer
Technical Sergeant	Oberfeldwebel	Ober—	
		Wachtmeister etc., as above	Arty, Cav, AA as above
		Oberfähnrich	Senior Officer Candidate
		Unter—	
		Arzt	Medical
		Veterinär	Veterinary
Staff Sergeant	Feldwebel	Wachtmeister etc., as above	Arty, Cav, AA as above
		Fahnenjunker-Feldwebel	Advanced Officer Candidate
Sergeant	Unterfeldwebel	Unterwachtmeister	Arty, Cav, AA
		Fahnenjunker	Officer Candidate
Corporal	Unteroffizier	Oberjäger	Light and Mt Inf.
Private First Class (administrative)	Stabsgefreiter	Hauptgefreiter	Air Force
(acting corporal)	Obergefreiter		
(ordinary)	Gefreiter		
Private (Senior)	Obersoldat (collective term)	Obergrenadier (Oberschütze)	Infantry (rifleman)
		Panzer- Obergrenadier	Armored Infantry
		Oberschütze	Tanks, Antitank
		Ober-	
		Reiter	Cavalry
		Kanonier	Artillery
		Pionier	Engineers
		Funker	Signal
		Fahrer	Transport (horse-drawn)
		Kraftfahrer	Motor Transport
		Sanitätssoldat	Medical
(ordinary)	Soldat (collective term)	Grenadier (Schütze)	Infantry (rifleman)
		Panzer- Grenadier (Schütze)	Armored Infantry
		Jäger	Light Mountain Infantry
		Flieger	Air Force
		Reiter, etc. as above	Cavalry, etc. as above

Figure 2.—Table of enlisted ranks.

Promotions to all noncommissioned officer ranks except sergeant and master sergeant normally are dependent upon tables of organization, in addition to the following specifications:

From	To	After 4 months service in combat unit	other field unit	
		after:		
Private First Class (Ordinary, Senior, Chief)	Corporal	2 years total service	no limitation	
Corporal or Sergeant	Staff Sergeant	1 year in grade	2 years in grade	
Corporal or Sergeant or Staff Sergeant	Technical Sergeant in First Sergeant position	1 year in grade	2 years in grade	
Staff Sergeant	Technical Sergeant	1 year in grade	2 years in grade	

From	To	After 4 months service in combat unit	other field unit	Otherwise after
		after a total active service period of:		
Senior Private	Private First Class (Ordinary)	6 months	1 year	2 years
Private First Class (Ordinary)	Senior Private First Class	2 years	2 years	3 years
Senior Private First Class	Chief Private First Class	5 years (2 in grade)	5 years (2 in grade)	6 years (2 in grade)

at least an ordinary private first class (*Gefreiter*). Parachutists (*Fallschirmjäger*) may be privates to begin with, but the lowest rank provided for in their table of organization is corporal (*Oberjäger*), in lieu of a pay bonus. Otherwise, the designation (*Ernennung*) as senior private, which does not involve an increase in pay, is now automatic in principle upon completion of the basic training period. Promotions to any grade of private first class are dependent on time limits and merit, but not on tables of organization, as shown in the table above.

Promotions to the ranks of sergeant and master sergeant are not dependent on tables of organization; a corporal who has served the maximum time in grade without having been promoted to staff sergeant may be promoted to sergeant; having served the maximum time in that grade without having been promoted to technical sergeant, he may be promoted to master sergeant, as shown in table below.

After 4 months of service in a combat unit, privates of any rank who are squad leaders may be promoted to corporals and corporals who are platoon leaders may be promoted to staff sergeants, regardless of length of total service or service in grade.

Honorary promotions may be awarded for distinguished conduct in battle (posthumously to those killed in action).

From	To	After 4 months service in combat unit	other field unit	Otherwise after
		after a total active service period of:		
Corporal	Sergeant	6 years (3 in grade)	6 years (3 in grade)	6 years (4 in grade)
Sergeant or Technical Sergeant	Master Sergeant	12 years	12 years	12 years

6. Compensation

a. TABLE OF BASE PAY. Every member of the German Armed Forces in active wartime service (except when a prisoner of war) receives tax-free war service pay (*Wehrsold*), paid to him in advance, monthly or at shorter intervals of not less than 10 days, by his unit paymaster. If he has dependents, he receives (also when a prisoner of war) family support payable direct to his dependents through the civilian authorities.

A professional soldier receives, in addition to war service pay (but also when a prisoner of war) the equivalent of his regular peacetime pay (*Friedensbesoldung*) consisting of base pay (*Grundgehalt*), quarters allowance (*Wohnungszuschlag*), and allowance for children (*Kinder-zuschlag*), less a wartime deduction (*Ausgleichsbetrag*) which in the ranks from major upward cancels out the war service pay and in the lower ranks offsets it in part according to a sliding scale. This compensation is known as Armed Forces regular pay (*Wehrmachtbesoldung*); its recipients are not entitled to civilian family support. Payments, usually by check, are made by a local garrison administration in Germany (usually near the man's home) for two months in advance (until 1 January 1945 it was one month in advance) to the soldier's bank account or to his dependents, if any. These payments are subject to an income-tax deduction at the source according to a sliding scale based on the amount of pay and the number as well as category of dependents.

Rank	Column 1 Armed Forces (or Wartime) Regular Pay			Column 2 War Service Pay	
	Pay Group	Dollars	(Less Tax)	Pay Group	Dollars
General of the Army	W 1	1,120[1]	(438)	1a	120
(with official quarters)		1,008[1]	(394)		120
General	W 2	771	(295)	1b	108
Lieutenant General	W 3	705	(264)	2	96
Major General	W 4	560	(203)	3	84
Brigadier General	W 5	467	(164)	4	72
Colonel	W 6	372	(125)	5	60
Lieutenant Colonel	W 7	284	(87)	6	48
Major	W 8	237	(68)	7	43
Captain	W 9	171	(39)	8	38
First Lieutenant	W 10	109	(16)	9	32
Second Lieutenant	W 11[2]	80	(7)	10	28
Master Sergeant	W 19	70	(6)	11	24
Technical Sergeant	W 20	68	(5)	11	24
less than 12 yrs[3]	W 21	62	(4)		24
Staff Sergeant	W 22	64	(4)	12	21
less than 12 yrs[3]	W 23	60	(4)		21
Sergeant	W 24	63	(4)	13	18
less than 12 yrs[3]	W 25	55	(3)		18
Corporal	W 26	56	(3)	14	16
less than 12 yrs[3]	W 27[2]	46	(2)		16
Chief Private First Class	W 30	36	(½)	15	14
Senior Private First Class	W 31	31	(—)	15	14
Private First Class				15	14
Senior Private, or					
Private with				15	14
less than 2 yrs[3]				16	12

[1] Regardless of rank: Commander in Chief of a branch of the Armed Forces (Army, etc.); Chief of the Armed Forces High Command.
[2] Pay Groups W 12- W 16: Musicians; activities suspended in Nov. 44.
    W 17- W 18: Fortress Shop-Foremen and Horseshoeing Instructors.
    W 28- W 29: Navy only.
[3] Total length of active service.

Figure 3.—Table of base pay (per month).

Professional Armed Forces officials (*Wehrmachtbeamte*) receive, in addition to war service pay, their peacetime salaries and allowances (*Friedensgebührnisse*), less a wartime deduction offsetting their war service pay as a whole or in part in the same manner as for professional soldiers who receive Armed Forces regular pay.

Non-professional soldiers from the rank of senior private first class (*Obergefreiter*) upward may apply for wartime regular pay (*Kriegsbesoldung*). They are then paid exactly like professional soldiers and consequently are not entitled to civilian family support. Therefore, soldiers with dependents will not make this application if the amount of their civilian family support is higher than their wartime pay would be.

Armed Forces officials who have no peace time salary receive war time regular pay without having to apply for it.

In the foregoing table, column 1 shows the Armed Forces regular pay (*Wehrmachtbesoldung*) for professional soldiers or wartime regular pay (*Kriegsbesoldung*) for non-professional soldiers in ranks from senior private first class (*Obergefreiter*) upward and for wartime officials. The amounts quoted represent the minimum base pay for single men without dependents before deduction of the income tax, which is shown in parenthesis at the minimum rate applying when the soldier has no additional income. All figures are quoted according to the most recent revision, on 9 November 1944, of the Military War Compensation Law of 1939. The pay rises for men with dependents according to a scale which provides for additional amounts up to 10 children. Column 2 shows the war service pay (*Wehrsold*) for all members of the Armed Forces, including officials, regardless of whether they are also paid under column 1 or not. The amounts are shown in U. S. dollars at the basic rate of exchange (1 *Reichsmark* equal to $0.40).

b. ALLOWANCES. All soldiers in ranks from general to private receive $0.40 daily as combat area service compensation (*Frontzulage*). This is granted not because of the danger to life and limb but for the "more difficult living conditions". On trips taken in the line of duty, the soldier, regardless of rank, receives an allowance for overnight quarters and $2.40 per diem additional. Every member of the Armed Forces is entitled to free rations, quarters, and clothing; those who must or are allowed to take their meals outside receive $1.20 per diem as ration money. No

additional allowance is paid for living quarters in view of the fact that this is already included in the regular pay, whereas soldiers who receive only war service pay are entitled to civilian family support. Clothing is free except for officers, who receive a one-time clothing allowance of $180.00 ($280.00 for those wearing the blue naval uniform) and a monthly upkeep allowance of $12.00. Soldiers contracting for professional service receive a cash bonus, known as *Kapitulantenhandgeld,* of $120.00 (12-year contract) or $40.00 (4½-year contract).

c. PENSIONS. Regular officers and professional soldiers are entitled to various benefits upon their discharge; the extent of these depends on length of service. They include lump-sum compensations, unemployment assistance, and, in some cases, pensions. Discharged professional noncommissioned officers are encouraged to go into civil service or agriculture; particularly in the latter case they receive substantial cash sums for the purchase or lease of land. All honorably discharged soldiers receive a mustering-out pay of $20.00.

d. LEAVES, ETC. Leaves and furloughs are classified according to their purpose such as recreation, convalescence, occupational, bombing, or emergency. Transportation is free, in principle. The considerable liberality regarding leaves that was practiced in the early stages of the war was radically curtailed under the strain of the later emergencies, which in 1944 led to their complete freezing, except, possibly, in the case of convalescents.

7. Categories of Officers and Other Personnel

a. REGULAR OFFICERS (*aktive Offiziere*). The small corps of regular officers inherited by the Nazi regime from the pre-1935 German *Reichswehr* was substantially increased, before the war, by the recall of all suitable retired officers, the absorption of many police officers, and the creation of new officers from volunteer officer candidates and suitable noncommissioned officers and privates from the regular ranks. At the beginning of the war, suitable professional noncommissioned officers were given temporary officer ranks (as "*Kriegsoffiziere*"), which were made permanent in 1942.

Special categories of regular officers are medical officers (*Sanitätsoffiziere*), veterinary officers (*Veterinäroffiziere*), and ordnance officers (*Waf-*

fenoffiziere, commonly designated as *Offiziere (W)).*

After 1934, a number of First World War officers were recalled, mostly in administrative positions, as supplementary officers (*Ergänzungs-offiziere*) and designated as *aktive Offiziere (E);* the (E) has since been dropped and those who were qualified have been taken into the regular officer corps. Many officers who had been retired as "officers not in service" (*Offiziere ausser Dienst—a.D.*) as well as many regular officers eligible for retirement were designated as subject to active service in recalled status "at the disposal of a branch of the Armed Forces (Army, Air Force, or Navy)" (*Offiziere zur Verfügung eines Wehrmachtteiles—z.V.*). Retired officers designated *z.V.* were normally not recalled to active service before mobilization, but a number of them were appointed in peacetime to fill certain open officer positions as "officers recalled to service" (*Offiziere zur Dienstleistung—z.D.*). During the war, the designation *z.D.* has been used for certain officers whose qualifications are in doubt and whose final status (regular or reserve) is not determined. The designation of regular officers subject to retirement as *z.V.* continues in wartime, which means that such officers, immediately upon their discharge as regular officers, are retained in active service in recalled status in any position in which they may be needed.

b. GENERAL STAFF CORPS OFFICERS (*Generalstabsoffiziere, Offz.i.G.*). General Staff Corps officers are carefully selected and trained to represent the German General Staff Corps in both command and staff functions. On division staffs, as "*Ia*", they hold the position of operational chiefs of staff, and as "*Ib*" they are chiefs of the rear echelon. In the higher echelons, the intelligence and training staff sections are likewise in the personal charge of General Staff Corps officers.

c. RESERVE OFFICERS (*Reserveoffiziere*). The nucleus of the reserve officer corps consists of conscripts who because of their qualifications and performance during their first year of service were accepted in peacetime as reserve officer aspirants (*Reserve-Offizier-Anwärter—R.O.A.*), received special training in platoon-leadership during their second year, and were designated reserve officers after their discharge and subsequent recall for a four-week exercise period with their old unit. Suitable professional noncommissioned officers were made reserve second lieu-

tenants upon being discharged at the end of their contractual period.

In wartime, there cannot be any reserve officer candidates of the peacetime type, as conscripts are not being discharged upon completion of a compulsory two-year service period; instead, qualified volunteers and suitable conscripts from the ranks are designated as reserve officer applicants (*Reserve-Offizier-Bewerber—R.O.B.*).

Originally, there were two age groups of reserve officers, those of the reserve class under the age of 35, designated as *Offiziere der Reserve —O.d.R.*), and those of the *Landwehr* reserve class above 35, designated as *Offiziere der Landwehr—O.d.L.* Both types of officers, collectively, were called "officers in inactive status" (*Offiziere des Beurlaubtenstandes — O.d.B.*). During the war, the designation O.d.L. has been eliminated, so that all reserve officers are *O.d.R.* as well as *O.d.B.*

d. ARMED FORCES OFFICIALS (*Wehrmachtbeamte*). Officials in administrative, legal, and technical service positions are a category peculiar to the German Armed Forces. They consist of civil service personnel performing functions within the Armed Forces and are recruited, in part, from former professional noncommissioned officers who became military candidates for civil service (*Militäranwärter*) at the end of their 12-year contractual period of active military service. Until 1944, none of these officials were classified as soldiers, but certain groups have now been converted into officers in the Special Troop Service (*Truppensonderdienst—TDS*). These are the higher administrative officers (*Intendanten*) in ranks from captain to lieutenant general; the lower administrative officers (*Zahlmeister*) in the ranks of first and second lieutenant, and the judge advocates (*Richter*) in ranks from captain to lieutenant general. It was also made possible for reserve technical service officials to become reserve officers of the motor maintenance troops if qualified.

In addition to regular Armed Forces officials, there are the categories of reserve officials (*Beamte des Beurlaubtenstandes—B.d.B.,* also referred to as *B.d.R.*), officials in recalled status "at the disposal of the Army, etc." (*Beamte zur Verfügung—B.z.V.*), and officials appointed for the duration (*Beamte auf Kriegsdauer—B.a.K.*). These three categories are collectively referred to as supplementary Armed Forces officials (*Ergän-*

zungswehrmachtbeamte). Functionaries of the military administration in occupied areas (*Militärverwaltungsbeamte*) who are not civil service officials in peacetime are treated in the same manner as these three categories in matters of compensation.

e. SPECIALIST LEADERS. Certain positions in ranks from major to lieutenant and in all noncommissioned officer ranks except sergeant may be filled by specialists in foreign languages, propaganda work, and similar matters, who have been trained to fill such positions as "Specialist leader" (*Sonderführer*). They receive the pay applicable to the position they are holding, but only by virtue of their appointment to the temporary position and without the disciplinary powers vested in the rank.

f. NONCOMMISSIONED OFFICERS (*Unteroffiziere*). Professional noncommissioned officers are under either a 12-year or a 4½-year service contract, except officer applicants, who are under contract for an indefinite period of service. Nonprofessionals are designated as reserve corporals, etc. (*Unteroffiziere,* etc., *d.R.*); the same applies if they are reserve officer candidates (*Fahnenjunker,* etc., *d.R.*).

g. WOMEN AUXILIARIES (*Helferinnen*). There are several women's auxiliary corps in the German Armed Forces, known as the corps of the headquarters auxiliaries (*Stabshelferinnen*); signal corps auxiliaries (*Nachrichtenhelferinnen*) of the Army, Air Force, *Waffen-SS,* and Navy; and antiaircraft auxiliaries (*Flakwaffenhelferinnen*) of the Air Force. All wear uniforms and are under military discipline, receiving free rations, quarters, and clothing. However, they are paid according to civil service rates and are not considered members of the Armed Forces. The ranks of their female leaders (*Führerinnen*) do not correspond to officer ranks. It is possible that they have been upgraded in status under recent total mobilization measures.

h. "CIVILIAN" SOLDIERS (*Volkssturm*). In October 1944, all German male civilians from 16 to 60 were made liable to emergency defense service under the Armed Forces in a national militia known as the "*Volkssturm*". They are distinguished by armbands and are stated to have military status. It is believed that they do not receive any service pay while in training but that they may be compensated when mobilized for combat away from their home area.

i. OTHER ARMED FORCES PERSONNEL (*Wehr-*

machtgefolge). A distinction must be made between members of the Armed Forces (*Wehrmachtangehörige*) who may be either soldiers or officials (*Beamte*), and persons employed by or attached to the Armed Forces (*Zugehörige zur Wehrmacht*), who are collectively referred to as Armed Forces auxiliaries (*Wehrmachtgefolge*). The women auxiliaries described above, as well as the numerous Party organizations when they operate with the Armed Forces, are in this general category.

8. Personal Documentation

a. SERVICE RECORD (*Wehrpass*). The basic personal record of the members of the Armed Forces is their service record. This is a book of passport size issued to them at the time of their first physical examination for military service. It contains a complete record of their pre-military service in the German Labor Service (*Reichsarbeitsdienst*), their military status at all times, and all their military activities until the expiration of their liability to military service. This book is in their personal possession only while they are in inactive status, and is retained at their company headquarters as long as they are on active service. In exchange for it, as soldiers, they carry on their person a pay and identification book issued to them at the time of their first induction.

b. PAYBOOK (*Soldbuch*). The paybook of the German soldier is his official means of identification and contains, in addition to personal data, a record of all units in which he has served and their replacement affiliations; his clothing and equipment record, inoculations, hospitalization; his promotions, pay rate group, payments received from units other than his own, decorations, furloughs, and other data pertaining to his person or his active service. The paybook contains both the soldier's military registration number (*Wehrnummer*), under which his service record was issued to him before his actual induction, and the inscription and number on his identification disc (*Beschriftung und Nummer der Erkennungsmarke*).

c. IDENTIFICATION DISC (*Erkennungsmarke*). The identification disc which the German soldier wears around his neck consists of two halves, both with identical inscriptions. It is issued to him by the unit (normally at company level) into which he is first inducted; both the name of that unit and the serial number under which the disc was issued to him are inscribed on it, as well as his blood type. Any unit, however, may issue a disc to a member who has lost his original one, with its own name and a new serial number.

d. UNIT ROSTER SHEET (*Kriegsstammrollenblatt*). Every Field Army unit and those units of the Replacement Army which are of Field Army or training type keep an individual roster sheet on every one of their members, containing the record of the individual's service in the unit. This sheet is to be closed upon the termination of that service and then forwarded direct to the soldier's home recruiting station (*Wehrersatzdienststelle*), where his basic military records are kept. There are two different forms: one for officers and officials of all ranks, the other for enlisted men.

e. BASIC MILITARY RECORDS. At the time of the first physical examination when the service record (*Wehrpass*) is issued to the soldier by his recruiting sub-area headquarters (*Wehrbezirkskommando*), the latter opens a corresponding basic military record book (*Wehrstammbuch*) for him, together with an accompanying health record book (*Gesundheitsbuch*) and a classification card (*Verwendungskartc*). His military registration card (*Wehrstammkarte*), which was made out by the police authorities as part of his miltary registration record (*Wehrstammblatt*), is pasted inside the front cover of the *Wehrstammbuch*. Actually, this card is an open envelope with the soldier's registration record on its face and containing a police report (*Polizeibericht*) on his conduct prior to registration.

f. MILITARY REGISTRATION NUMBER (*Wehrnummer*). This is determined at the time the *Wehrpass* is issued to the soldier; in other words, while he is still a civilian. He retains it permanently, regardless of whether he is in active service or not, as his identifying number with the authorities which administer the conscription laws. It normally consists of the following five elements (although there are some variations):

Name of the *Wehrbezirkskommando*.

Last two digits of the year of birth.

Number of military registration police precinct (in certain larger cities, number corresponding to first letter of family name).

Serial number of the conscription (or volunteer) roster sheet (*Wehrstammrollcnblatt*).

Number indicating registrant's place on that sheet (from 1 to 10).

g. UPKEEP OF MILITARY RECORDS. The basic military records accompany the soldier to his first induction unit, but upon his transfer from it are returned to and kept at his home recruiting station (*Wehrersatzdienststelle*), which normally is a recruiting sub-area headquarters (*Wehrbezirkskommando*) for officers or a subordinate military reporting office (*Wehrmeldeamt*) for enlisted men. The soldier's unit roster sheets, which are closed and forwarded to his home recruiting station upon his transfer from one unit to another, are filed in the inside rear cover pocket of his *Wehrstammbuch*. Since the autumn of 1944, the transfer into the *Wehrstammbuch* of entries from these or other documents that are received for filing in the pocket has been suspended until after the war; it is planned that the entries then be made from the *Wehrpass*, which is kept up at all times by the unit in which the soldier is serving.

The *Wehrersatzdienststelle* is the home recruiting station of all Germans who are subject to conscription and therefore is responsible for all members of the German Armed Forces, including volunteers, regardless of whether they serve in the Army, Air Force, Navy, or *Waffen-SS*. The *Wehrstammbuch* of naval personnel, however, is kept by their own home base replacement units. It does not contain any unit roster sheets (*Kriegsstammrollenblätter*), as these are replaced, in the Navy, by a conduct book (*Führungsbuch*) for enlisted men which follows them from unit to unit, as does their *Wehrpass*. The health record book (*Gesundheitsbuch*), which otherwise is kept at the *Wehrersatzdienststelle* together with the *Wehrstammbuch*, is in the personal possession of naval personnel as is, of course, their paybook.

Before 1944, the classification card (*Verwendungskarte*) was used for entering the soldier's training record and was forwarded to his first field unit for inspection, to be returned within 3 days to the home recruiting station. Since the autumn of 1944, the card has not been sent to the field; but the same purpose is served by the detailed training record sheet (*Ausbildungsnachweis*), introduced in 1943, which the soldier, upon his transfer to the field, carries in the pocket of his paybook; it is supposed to be destroyed by the field unit, but this is not always done.

Records peculiar to the *Waffen-SS* are the *SS* basic record card (*SS-Stammkarte*), which follows the soldier from unit to unit as does his *Wehrpass*, and the *SS* control card (*SS-Überwachungskarte*), which is kept by his *SS* replacement unit and never follows him into the field.

h. OFFICER RECORDS. Officers, in addition to the basic records described above have a personal record folder *(Personalnachweis)*. In the Navy, which has no unit roster sheets for either officers or enlisted men, the officer's *Personalnachweis* takes the place of the enlisted men's *Führungs-buch*. Otherwise, the officer's *Personalnachweis* normally is kept in several copies, which may be found at the replacement unit of his peacetime unit; at the corps area headquarters *(Wehrkreis-kommando)*; at the Army Personnel Office *(Heerespersonalamt)*; or in the case of reserve officers at their recruiting sub-area headquarters *(Wehrbezirkskommando)*.

In case of discharge or death, one copy is in all cases forwarded to the Armed Forces Welfare and Pension Office *(Wehrmachtfürsorge-und Versorgungsamt)* accompanied by the officer's medical record papers *(Krankenpapiere)*.

i. PUNISHMENT RECORDS. An individual excerpt from the unit punishment book *(Auszug aus dem Strafbuch)* is forwarded upon the transfer of an enlisted man, together with his *Wehrpass*, whereas the punishment record of an officer appears in his character and efficiency report *(Beur-teilungsnotiz)*. In the event of a disciplinary reduction in rank, the soldier's *Soldbuch, Wehrpass,* and *Kriegsstammrollenblatt* are closed by his unit and forwarded, for filing in the *Wehrstammbuch* pocket, to his home recruiting station, which issues a new *Wehrpass*. The unit itself issues a new *Soldbuch* at once, and a new *Kriegsstammrollen-blatt* is opened which, in the case of a former officer, must be of the enlisted man type. The reduction is entered only on the closed *Kriegs-stammrollenblatt*. The records of a degraded regular Air Force officer must be requested from the Air Force Personnel Office. In the Navy, the *Personalnachweis* of a degraded officer is closed, the reduction having been entered on it, is sent to his home recruiting station, and is replaced by an enlisted man's *Führungsbuch;* whereas the *Führungsbuch* of a degraded noncommissioned officer is continued after the reduction has been entered. In no case is the reduction entered in either the old or the new *Soldbuch* or *Wehrpass*.

j. TERMINATION OF SERVICE. The *Wehrpass* is given to the soldier upon his honorable discharge from active service, even when such a discharge is temporary (e.g. for occupational reasons). In the latter case, his *Soldbuch* is returned to him in exchange for the *Wehrpass* when he is recalled to active duty. Otherwise, the *Soldbuch* and all other basic military records remain on file at his home recruiting station. Discharged soldiers are given a discharge certificate *(Entlassungsschein)*.

In case of death, all basic military records of the soldier are filed by the home recruiting station except his *Wehrpass,* which is given to the next of kin. A report on his death and burial, together with the broken-off lower half of his identification disc and a description of the grave, is sent to the Armed Forces Information Bureau for War Casualties and Prisoners of War, which is the only agency authorized to handle inquiries. However, the *Waffen-SS* had its own information bureau.

Section III. THE HIGH COMMAND

I. Introduction

The basic principle under the German military system is unity of command. This principle is exemplified in the highest as well as the lower echelons. Under this system the Army, Navy, and Air Force are regarded as branches of a single service (*Die Wehrmacht*), headed by the Armed Forces High Command (*Oberkommando der Wehrmacht* or *OKW*)(1)*. The *OKW* controls all matters of inter-service policy in both peace and war. It is responsible for all preparation for national defense in time of peace, and for the conduct of operations in time of war. The head of the *OKW* is a cabinet member and represents the joint interest of the three branches with respect to other departments of the Government.

In effect, therefore, the German High Command is divided into four parts, as follows: Armed Forces High Command—*Oberkommando der Wehrmacht (OKW)*(2); Army High Command—*Oberkommando des Heeres (OKH)*(3); Navy High Command — *Oberkommando der Kriegsmarine (OKM)*(3); Air Force High Command—*Oberkommando der Luftwaffe (OKL)*(4).

Under this system it is not unusual in a task force for units of one branch of the Armed Forces to come under the immediate command of another branch. All personnel may be transferred from one branch to another in the same or equivalent rank. This, in fact, has been done on a very considerable scale in 1943 and 1944, with a transfer of thousands of members of the Air Force and Navy to the Army.

The *OKW* is supreme and responsible for the coordination of the active war effort by the three subordinate branches, while the *OKH* is responsible for all purely Army matters, just as each of the other two High Commands is responsible for the application of general policies within its own sphere.

In wartime, each High Command has a forward echelon (*1. Staffel*)(5) and a rear echelon (*2. Staffel*). The forward echelon moves to a location appropriate to the theater of main operations, while the rear echelon remains in Berlin. (Almost all elements of the rear echelon were evacuated from Berlin beginning in October

---

* See Section 4 for an explanation of the use of these numbers.

1943.) The object of this division is to insure that all purely routine and administrative matters will be handled in the rear and not obtrude themselves into the actual conduct of operations by the forward headquarters.

There is a fairly standardized method of indicating the relative size and importance of the various subdivisions within a high command. In descending order, these units with the accepted translations used in this book are:

> *Amt*—Office(6)
> *Amtsgruppe*—Group(**7**)
> *Abteilung*—Branch(8)
> *Gruppe*—Section(9)
> *Referat*—Desk(10)

In general (with some exceptions) an *Amt* or *Amtsgruppe* is headed by a general officer and an *Abteilung* by a field officer.

However, these subdivisions are not necessarily subordinate to one another schematically; i.e., the channel downward from an *Amt* may skip *Amtsgruppe* and go direct to *Abteilung* or even to *Referat*.

The following description gives the nomenclature and function of only the more important subdivisions of the Armed Forces High Command (*OKW*) and the Army High Command (*OKH*). All the German abbreviations used are explained in a glossary at the end of the section. It should be noted that this is the organization existing at the beginning of 1945, and that under present circumstances the High Command, like all other aspects of the German Armed Forces, is subject to rapid and unforeseen changes.

2. The *OKW* (11)

Hitler himself is the Supreme Commander of the Armed Forces (*Oberster Befehlshaber der Wehrmacht*)(12). Under him, Keitel is the Chief of the Armed Forces High Command (*Chef des OKW*)(13) and as such serves as Hitler's chief executive officer in the administration of the Armed Forces and the application of his policies and plans.

The operational part of the *OKW* is the Armed Forces Operations Staff (*Wehrmachtführungsstab*), which constitutes the main advisory body to Hitler on strategy and planning. It is located at the field headquarters of the *OKW*, which is known as the *Führerhauptquartier*(14). The other subdivisions of the *OKW* are mostly

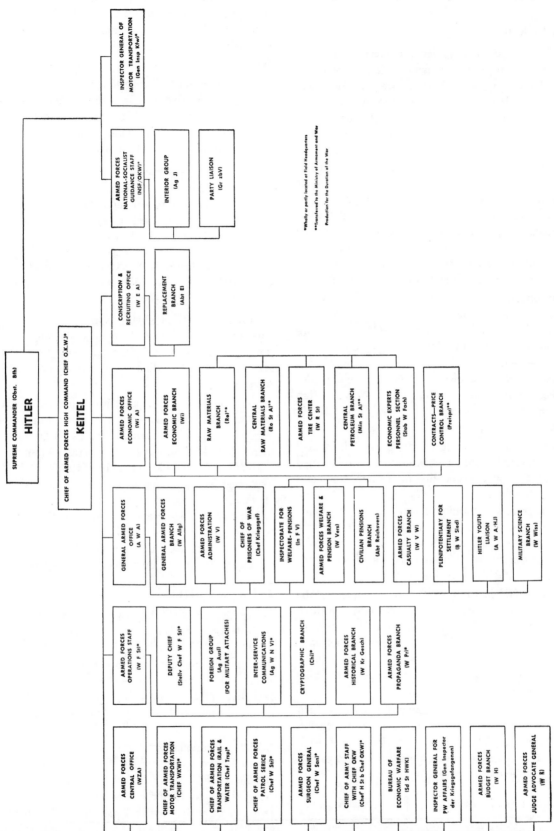

Figure 4.—Armed Forces High Command.

with the rear echelon and deal with numerous administrative matters of joint interest to the three branches of the Armed Forces.

The accompanying chart (*Figure 4*) shows the principal branches of the *OKW* and their subordination. Their functions are discussed in the following paragraphs.

a. ARMED FORCES CENTRAL OFFICE (*Wehrmachtzentralamt—WZA*) (15). The officer in charge of this agency is responsible for central organizational matters, such as increasing or reducing the personnel of branches of the High Command. The office also includes the Armed Forces Central Group (*Ag WZ*)(16).

b. CHIEF OF ARMED FORCES MOTOR TRANSPORTATION (*Chef des Wehrmachtkraftfahrwesens —Chef WKW*)(17). This officer is administrative head of all matters concerning motor transportation. At the same time he holds the position of Chief Motor Transport Officer in the Army General Staff (*Gen St d H/Gen Qu/Gen d Kfw*) and controls the Inspectorate of Motor Transport in the General Army Office (*AHA/Gen d Kfw/Jn 12*). His activities are subject to the close supervision of Hitler's personal appointee, the Inspector General of Motor Transport (*Gen Insp Kfw*).

c. CHIEF OF ARMED FORCES TRANSPORTATION (RAIL AND WATER) (*Chef des Transportwesens der Wehrmacht—Chef Trspw d W*)(18). This officer is administrative head of all rail and water transportation and also is believed to be the Chief Army Transportation Officer in the Army General Staff (*Gen St d H/Chef d Trspw*). Subordinate to him are the Field Transportation Branch (*F Abt*)(19), the Central Armed Forces Transportation Command (*W Trsp Ltg Mitte*)(20), and the Traffic Branch (*Verk Abt*)(21).

d. CHIEF OF THE ARMED FORCES PATROL SERVICE (*Chef des Wehrmachtstreifendienstes— Chef W Str D*)(22). This officer, appointed in March 1944, is head of all Armed Forces patrols and all welfare matters concerning troops away from their field units. The welfare function concerning troops in transit was formerly the responsibility of the General for Special Employment IV (*Gen.z.b.V. IV*)(23) in the *OKH*, an office which apparently was superseded by that of the Chief of the Armed Forces Patrol Service.

e. ARMED FORCES SURGEON GENERAL (*Chef des Wehrmachtsanitätswesens—Chef W San*)

(24). Subordinate to the Chief of the *OKW* and, in medical matters, to the Commissioner General of Medicine and Sanitation (*General-Kommissar des Führers für das Sanitäts- und Gesundheitswesen*). The Armed Forces Surgeon General formerly also held the positions of Chief Army Medical Inspector (*H San Insp*) and Army Surgeon (*H Arzt*). In August 1944, the personal union was dissolved, but the latter two positions, as well as the equivalent positions in the Navy and Air Force, are all subject to the supervision and control of the Armed Forces Surgeon General in medical matters.

f. CHIEF OF ARMY STAFF WITH CHIEF *OKW* (*Chef des Heeresstabes beim Chef OKW— Chef H St b Chef OKW*)(25). Chief Liaison Officer of the Army at Keitel's field headquarters.

g. BUREAU OF ECONOMIC WARFARE (*Sonderstab für Handelskrieg und wirtschaftliche Kampfmassnahmen—Sd St HWK*)(26). This is a small agency to represent the interests of the Armed Forces with other government agencies concerned with economic warfare and to coordinate global economic policies with Japan.

h. INSPECTOR GENERAL FOR PRISONER OF WAR AFFAIRS (*Generalinspekteur für das Kriegsgefangenenwesen der Wehrmacht—Gen Insp Kriegsgef*)(27). This personal appointee of Hitler is responsible for insuring the security of prisoner of war installations in Germany and the most effective employment of prisoner-of-war labor. He may issue orders to other *OKW* and *OKH* agencies concerned with prisoners of war.

i. ARMED FORCES BUDGET BRANCH (*Wehrmachthaushaltsabteilung—WH*) (28). This is concerned only with the budget of the *OKW* and not with those of the other high commands.

j. ARMED FORCES JUDGE ADVOCATE GENERAL (*Wehrmachtrechtsabteilung—WR*)(29).

k. ARMED FORCES OPERATIONS STAFF (*Wehrmachtführungsstab — WFSt*)(30). This is a joint general staff containing officers from all three branches. It is responsible for over-all planning and strategy and advises and assists Hitler in the planning and execution of military operations. It includes:

(1) *Deputy Chief of the Armed Forces Operations Staff* (*Stellvertretender Chef des Wehrmachtführungsstabes—Stellv Chef WFSt*) (31). This officer controls the staff proper, which consists of sections concerned with operations, organization, intelligence, and supply. Each

17

of these sections includes officers representing all three branches of the Armed Forces. (The intelligence section now embodies elements of the former counterintelligence branch and other operational portions of the old Foreign and Counterintelligence Office of the *OKW,* the bulk of which was taken over by the *SS* in the middle of 1944.)

(2) *Foreign Group (Amtsgruppe Ausland—Ag Ausl)* (32). This includes the Branch for Military Attaches of the *OKH (Att Abt d OKH)* (33). It also is concerned with acquisition of foreign newspapers, rules on travel to foreign countries, and relations of German military personnel with foreigners.

(3) *Armed Forces Signal Communications Group (Amtsgruppe Wehrmachtnachrichtenverbindungen—Ag WNV)* (34). This group maintains the trunk communications between the high commands and is the nerve center of the top command echelons. It has at least two signal regiments of the Army at its disposal to maintain a special network of land cables and radio channels linking the *OKW, OKH, OKL,* and *OKM* and the principal subordinate headquarters. It contains a radio communications branch *(Ag WNV/Fu)* (35) and a wire communications branch *(Ag WNV/KF)* (36).

(4) *Cryptographic Branch (Chiffrier-Abteilung—Chi)* (37).

(5) *Armed Forces Historical Branch (Kriegsgeschichtliche Abteilung der Wehrmacht—W Kr Gesch)* (38). Headed by the Führer's Official Military Historian (*Der Beauftr d Führers für die mil Geschichtsschr.* This officer also heads the Army Historical Branch (*Kr Gesch Heer*) and other historical agencies in the *OKH.* This branch records all military history which concerns the three branches of the Armed Forces as a whole.

(6) *Armed Forces Propaganda Branch (Abteilung für Wehrmachtpropaganda—W Pr)* (39). Headed by the Chief of the Propaganda Troops (*Chef Pr Tr*) (40), this branch is responsible for all types of military propaganda except that which is fed to the troops by the National-Socialist Guidance Staffs (*NSFSt*) of the various high commands. It includes sections for the administration of the propaganda troops, propaganda to the home front, military censorship, propaganda to foreign countries, and counterpropaganda.

l. GENERAL ARMED FORCES OFFICE (*Allgemeines Wehrmachtamt—AWA*) (41). This office is composed of independent branches in the *OKW,* grouped together for administrative purposes. It contains:

(1) *General Armed Forces Branch (Allgemeine Abteilung—W Allg)* (42).

(2) *Armed Forces Administration Group (Amtsgruppe Wehrmachtverwaltung—Ag WV)* (43). Responsible for the administration of all *OKW* agencies and *OKW* personnel and for certain fiscal matters.

(3) *Chief of Prisoners of War (Chef des Kriegsgefangenenwesens—Chef Kriegsgef)* (44). The administrative head of all matters relating both to German and to Allied prisoners of war, he also performs the function of inspector of prisoner-of-war installations. In this latter capacity he acts under the directives of the Inspector General for Prisoner-of-War Affairs (*Gen Insp Kriegsgef*), who comes directly under the Chief of the *OKW.* The agency is divided into a General Branch (*Kriegsgef Allg.*) (45) which deals with treatment, exchange, and release of prisoners; administrative and punitive matters; and relations with the protective powers and with the International Red Cross; and an Organization Branch (*Kriegsgef. Org.*) (46), which deals with the employment and living conditions of prisoners of war in German hands.

(4) *Inspectorate for Welfare and Pensions Agencies (Inspektion der Fürsorge und Versorgungsdienststellen im OKW—Jn FV)* (47). Welfare and pension matters for all branches of the Armed Forces are controlled by this agency. Subordinate to it are the Armed Forces Welfare and Pensions Branch (*W Vers*) (48), the Civilian Pensions Branch (*Abt. Reichsvers.*) (49), and the Armed Forces Education Branch (*WU*) (50). Until 1944 the Armed Forces Education Branch was a separate branch of the *AWA.*

(5) *Armed Forces Casualty Branch (Abteilung Wehrmachtverlustwesen—WVW)* (51).

(6) *Armed Forces Plenipotentiary For Settlement (Bevollmächtigter des OKW für Siedlungsfragen—BW Sied)* (52). Arranges for resettlement of Germans in annexed territory.

(7) *Hitler Youth Liaison (Vertreter der Wehrmacht beim Jugendführer des Deutschen Reichs—AWA/HJ)* (53). Represents the interests of the Armed Forces in the Hitler Youth organization.

(8) *Military Science Branch (Abteilung Wissenschaft—W Wiss)* (54). Studies develop-

ments of the physical sciences which affect the military.

m. ARMED FORCES ECONOMIC OFFICE (*Wehrwirtschaftsamt—Wi A*) (55). This office is responsible for long-range military-economic planning, the economic exploitation of occupied areas, and representing the interests of the Armed Forces with other government departments concerned with production, raw materials, labor, agriculture, and foreign trade. It contains:

(1) *Armed Forces Economic Branch* (*Wehrwirtschaftliche Abteilung—Wi*) (56). Concerned with general planning matters and control of the subordinate regional agencies of the office.

(2) *Raw Materials Branch* (*Rohstoffabteilung —Ro*) (57). This agency has been transferred to the control of the Ministry of Armament and War Production for the duration of the war. It included or cooperated with the Central Raw Materials Branch (*Ro St A*) (58), the Armed Forces Tire Center (*W R St*) (59) (still under the Armed Forces Economic Office), the Central Petroleum Branch (*Min St A*) (60), and the Economic Experts Personnel Section (*Stab W Fach*) (61) (still under the Armed Forces Economic Office).

(3) *Contracts and Price Control Branch* (*Vertrags- und Preisprüfwesen—Preispr*) (62). The fixing of prices for Armed Forces Contracts is supervised by this branch. It is now under the Ministry of Armament and War Production.

n. CONSCRIPTION AND RECRUITING OFFICE (*Wehrersatzamt—WEA*) (63). This office was created in the summer of 1943, when the function of controlling recruiting and conscription for the three branches of the Armed Forces was transferred from the Army High Command to the *OKW*. It controls the Replacement Branch (*Abt. E*) (64), which was formerly part of the Group for Replacement and General Troop Matters (*Ag E Tr*) in the *OKH*.

o. NATIONAL-SOCIALIST GUIDANCE STAFF OF THE *OKW* (*Nationalsozialistischer Führungsstab des OKW—NSF/OKW*) (65). Established in December 1943, this agency is to ensure uniform political indoctrination in the Armed Forces, in cooperation with the Party chancellery. It includes:

(1) *Interior Group* (*Amtsgruppe Inland— Ag J*) (66). Formerly a branch (*Abt.*) of the General Armed Forces Office (*AWA*), this was upgraded to a group (*Ag.*) and transferred to the National-Socialist Guidance Staff of the *OKW* during February 1944. It maintains liaison between the *OKW* and civilian agencies in Germany. It contains a domestic security branch (*Ag J/1*) (67), and an ideological guidance branch (*Ag J/2*) (68).

(2) *Party Liaison* (*Gruppe z.b.V.—Gr.z.b. V.*) (69). Formerly part of the General Armed Forces Office (*AWA*), this section was transferred to the control of the National-Socialist Guidance Staff of the *OKW* in 1944. It is believed to maintain the liaison with the National-Socialist Party and to control such matters as collections for charitable or Party purposes within the Armed Forces.

p. INSPECTOR GENERAL OF MOTOR TRANSPORT (*Generalinspekteur für das Kraftfahrwesen— Gen Insp Kfw*) (70). He is immediately subordinate to Hitler and coordinates all matters regarding motor transport. He may issue orders to other *OKW* and *OKH* offices concerned with motor transport.

3. The Army High Command (*OKH*)

a. GENERAL. Since the Army is by far the largest and most important of the three branches of the German Armed Forces, it was, from the outbreak of the war, the branch which Hitler was most anxious to control directly. Its headquarters in the field always has been located in the immediate vicinity of the *Führerhauptquartier*. In December 1941, after the failure of the Moscow offensive, Hitler removed Brauchitsch as Commander-in-Chief of the Army (*Oberbefehlshaber des Heeres* (70a)) and took over personal command himself. He has exercised this command ever since, and the result has been a partial merging or overlapping of the functions of the *OKW* and of the *OKH*. Keitel, while still Chief of the *OKW*, nevertheless also acts as Hitler's executive officer in matters pertaining to the Army alone. Similarly, it is often difficult to draw the line between the *de facto* authority and functions of the Army General Staff and those of the Armed Forces Operations Staff.

The accompanying chart (*Figure 5*) shows the principal branches of the *OKH* and their subordination. Their functions are discussed in the following paragraphs.

b. ARMY GENERAL STAFF (*Generalstab des Heeres—Gen St d H*) (71). This organization, which is a functional part of the Army High Command, must not be confused with the General Staff Corps. The latter, called in German

19

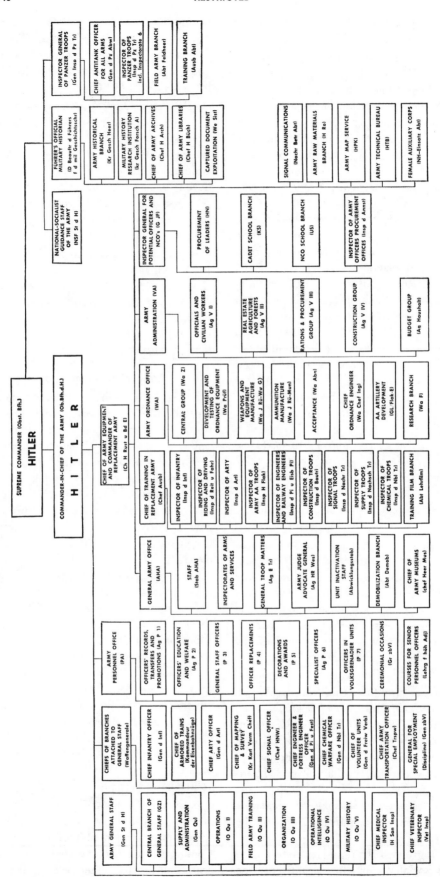

Figure 5.—Army High Command.

simply *Generalstab,* is a category of specially selected and carefully trained officers who fill almost all the important command as well as staff positions throughout the Army. The Army General Staff, on the other hand, occupies a position analogous to that of the War Department General Staff; it is the main advisory body to the Commander-in-Chief on operations, intelligence, organization, supply, and general matters of Army policy.

Both the Army General Staff and the General Staff Corps are headed by the Chief of the Army General Staff (*Chef des Generalstabs des Heeres* (72), also referred to simply as *Chef des Generalstabs*).

In time of war the Army General Staff is stationed at field headquarters, leaving only a small rear echelon in Berlin.

The Army General Staff basically consists of 12 branches which cover all the proper staff and planning functions and which are grouped under five senior officers known as *Oberquartiermeister I—V* (73). In wartime, a number of additional high-ranking officers are appointed as chief advisers on the employment of the various arms and services in the field and on certain other technical matters; some of these officers and the sections which they control are absorbed organically into the Army General Staff for the duration of the war, while others are regarded as attached to it. By far the most important of them is the Chief Supply and Administration Officer (*Generalquartiermeister*) (74), who is responsible for the whole supply and administrative structure of the Field Army. Since he and the other wartime appointees perform the functions of some of the regular branches of the General Staff, it is believed that the separate functioning of these particular branches is largely suspended in wartime. Moreover, with the partial merging of the field headquarters of the *OKW* and the *OKH* under Hitler's personal command at the end of 1941, some of the other normal functions of branches of the Army General Staff have been wholly or partly taken over by the Armed Forces Operations Staff (*WFSt*). Thus the grouping under *Oberquartiermeister* seems to have become largely meaningless, and it is even doubtful whether these positions are actually filled at the present time. Since, however, they are a part of the permanent organization of the Army General Staff, they are given here and on the accompanying chart with their appropriate functions and subordinate branches. It is indicated in each case below wherever the functions of a particular branch are believed to have been largely or wholly suspended or transferred to some other agency:

Central Branch (*Zentralabteilung—GZ*) (75). This branch is concerned principally with central administrative matters pertaining to the General Staff Corps rather than with the functions of the Army General Staff. Until 1943 it made all appointments and promotions of General Staff Corps officers at all echelons; this responsibility then was transferred to Branch 3 of the Army Personnel Office (*PA/P 3*).

FIRST SENIOR GENERAL STAFF OFFICER (*Oberquartiermeister I—O Qu I*) (76). This office which deals with operations and related matters is reported to have been vacant for some time, its function being performed largely by the operations sections of the Armed Forces Operations Staff (*WFSt*). The grouping *O Qu I* includes:

Branch 1 (*1. Abteilung* or *Op Abt*) (77). This branch, concerned with operations, develops and disseminates basic tactical rules and methods of conducting warfare. Its function of advising the Chief of Staff and Commander-in-Chief on actual operations and strategy has largely lapsed.

Branch 5 (*5. Abteilung*) (78). The function of this branch which deals with transport, has been handled since the beginning of the war by the Chief Transportation Officer attached to the General Staff (*Gen St d H/Chef Trspw*).

Branch 6 (*6. Abteilung*) (79). Functions of this branch which is concerned with rear echelons have been handled since the beginning of the war by the Chief Supply and Administration Officer (*Gen St d H/Gen Qu*).

Branch 9 (*9. Abteilung*) (80). Topography, specific responsibility of this branch, has been handled since 1941 by the Chief of Mapping and Survey in the General Staff (*Gen St d H/Kr Kart Verm Chef*).

Branch 10 (*10. Abteilung*) (81). Maneuvers and operational planning, now for the most part are divided among a number of other agencies of the *OKW* and *OKH,* both at field headquarters and at the rear echelon.

SECOND SENIOR GENERAL STAFF OFFICER (*Oberquartiermeister II—O Qu II*) (82). The training functions of this grouping largely are taken over in wartime by the Home Command; it includes:

Branch 4 (*4. Abteilung* or *Ausb. Abt.*) (83). This branch is responsible in wartime only for training within the Theater of Operations; all training in the Zone of the Interior is under the Chief of Training in the Replacement Army (*Chef Ausb*).

Branch 11 (*11. Abteilung*) (84). Military schools and officer training which are the functions of this branch are now entirely under the Home Command, especially the Inspector General for Potential Officers NCOs (*GJF*).

THIRD SENIOR GENERAL STAFF OFFICER (*Oberquartiermeister III—O Qu III*) (85). This grouping, responsible for organization includes:

Branch 2 (*2. Abteilung* or *Org. Abt.*) (86). This branch is responsible for laying down rules relating to various aspects of organization in the field and, in conjunction with the chiefs of arms and services attached to the General Staff, recommending to the General Army Office (*AHA*) the issuance of changes in the existing Tables of Organization.

Branch 8 (*8. Abteilung*) (87). The function of this branch which was concerned with technical services is now probably handled by other agencies such as the Chief of Technical Troops under the Chief Supply and Administration Officer (*Gen Qu/Gen d Techn Tr*).

FOURTH SENIOR GENERAL STAFF OFFICER (*Oberquartiermeister IV—O Qu IV*) (88). The intelligence branch is probably the only one of the five major groupings in the Army General Staff which is still fully operative. Its two geographical branches are subdivided into various geographical sections which collect and evaluate information and disseminate intelligence regarding the armies of the various countries in the form of printed manuals and periodic reports. The grouping includes:

Branch 3, Eastern Armies (*3. Abteilung, Frd Heere Ost*) (89). Deals with the armies of the Soviet Union, Scandinavia, the lower Balkans, Africa, and the Far East.

Branch 12, Western Armies (*12. Abteilung, Frd Heere West*) (90). Deals with the armies of Western Europe (Section II), Great Britain (Section III), the upper Balkans (Section IV), and the Western Hemisphere (Section V). The Western Hemisphere section was transferred from the Eastern Armies Branch to Western Armies Branch after Pearl Harbor.

FIFTH SENIOR GENERAL STAFF OFFICER (*Oberquartiermeister V—O Qu V*) (91). Deals with military history. This group formerly included special sections for historical research, Army libraries, and Army archives, all of which were transferred in 1942 to the Führer's Official Military Historian (*D. Beauftr d Führers für die mil Geschichtsschr*) (92). It still nominally includes Branch 7, Military Science Branch (*7. Abteilung* or *Kr Wiss Abt*) (93), but the functions of this branch are also believed to have been largely taken over by the new Army Historical Branch (*Kr Gesch Heer*) under the Führer's Official Military Historian.

CHIEF SUPPLY AND ADMINISTRATION OFFICER (*Generalquartiermeister—Gen Qu*) (94). This officer does not belong to the basic organization of the Army General Staff in peacetime but was appointed at the beginning of the war, in accordance with previous plans, to take charge of the whole supply and administrative structure of the Field Army. He was given an elaborate organization, described below, including a number of attached officers as chiefs of the various services for the Field Army; these officers bear the same relationship to the General Staff as the chiefs of arms except that they come under the Chief Supply and Administration Officer instead of being attached directly to the Chief of General Staff.

The organization given below is basically that which applied in the early stages of the war and takes into account only the more important of the temporary modifications which have occurred since. It should be noted that the first three sections, called supply sections (*Quartiermeister-Gruppen 1, 2, 3*) (95) are concerned with the planning, organization, and general operation of the services in the field; they are each headed by a General Staff Corps officer and may be regarded as constituting the G-4 division of the Army General Staff. All the other sections, which are numbered according to the standard German staff organization, deal with the actual functioning of the various services and are headed by the chiefs of these services for the Field Army.

Section Qu 1 (*Gruppe Qu 1*) (96). General planning and organization of supply in the field, establishment of communication lines and rear boundaries of the Theater of Operations, transport questions in conjunction with the Chief Army Transportation Officer (*Chef Trspw*), and control of those service troops not sub-allotted to army groups and armies.

Section Qu 2 (*Gruppe Qu 2*) (97). Civil affairs policies in the communications zone, especially the exploitation of the country for military purposes; evacuation, booty, and prisoners of war.

Section Qu 3 (*Gruppe Qu 3*) (98). Action on supply requisitions from army groups and armies for ordnance, fuel, and engineer equipment. These requisitions are adjusted in accordance with over-all plans and policies and are then forwarded to the authorities in the Zone of the Interior.

Section II a (*Gruppe II a, Adjutantur*) (99). Personnel and security matters within the staff of the Chief Supply and Administration Officer.

Section III, Field Legal Administration (*Gruppe III, Feldjustizverwaltung*) (100). Headed by the chief of the Judge Advocate General's Department in the field, responsible for questions of military law and jurisprudence. This section was upgraded to a branch and transferred to the control of the General for Special Employment (*Gen z b V*) sometime after the beginning of the Russian campaign.

Section IV a, Chief Army Administrative Officer (*Gruppe IVa, Heeresintendant*) (101). Responsible for the general control of administrative matters and the personnel who deal with them throughout the Field Army. These matters include pay, clothing, personal equipment, rations, billeting, and fiscal matters.

Section IV b, Army Surgeon (*Gruppe IV b, Heeresarzt—H Arzt*) (102). Controls all medical matters and medical personnel throughout the Field Army, subject to the direction of the Chief Army Medical Inspector (*H San Insp*). (At present these two positions are believed to be united in one person.)

Section IV c, Army Veterinarian (*Gruppe IV c, Heeresveterinär—H Vet*) (103). Controls all veterinary matters and veterinary personnel in the Field Army, subject to the direction of the Chief Veterinary Inspector (*Vet Insp*).

Section V, Chief Motor Transport Officer (*Gruppe V, General des Kraftfahrwesens—Gen d Kfw*) (104). Controls the motor maintenance troops in the Field Army and is responsible for general questions of availability and utilization of motor transport. He is simultaneously in charge of a group in the General Army Office (*AHA*) responsible for the same matters in the Zone of the Interior, and holds concurrently the office of Chief of Armed Forces Motor Transportation (*Chef WKW*) under the *OKW*.

Section Z, Civil Commissioner (*Gruppe Z, Zivilbeauftragter*) (105). Responsible for non-military matters in the civil administration of occupied areas in the Theater of Operations, including relations with the civil authorities and the discipline of the population; cooperates with Sections Qu 2 and III above. This section is believed to have been renamed Qu 5.

Chief of Supply Troops (*General der Nachschubtruppen*) (106). Controls all General Headquarters supply troops, working in cooperation with Section Qu 3 on questions of their employment. Known as *Heeresnachschubführer* until October 1942.

Section F. P., Army Postmaster (*Gruppe F. P., Heeresfeldpostmeister*) (107). Responsible for all questions relating to the Army Postal Service in the Field Army.

Chief of Technical Troops (*General der Technischen Truppen—Gen d Techn Tr*) (108). Chief adviser on the organization and employment of the technical troops. These troops, while classified as a combat arm, perform a number of highly technical services requiring specialized equipment for the armies in the field.

Senior Military Police Officer (*Höherer Feldgendarmerie-Offizier—Höh Feldgen Offz*) (109). Responsible for all matters concerning the organization and employment of the military police in the Field Army.

c. CHIEFS OF BRANCHES ATTACHED TO THE GENERAL STAFF. The Commander-in-Chief of the Army and the Chief of the Army General Staff have at their disposal in wartime a group of general officers representing the various combat arms who serve as the principal advisers on the organization, training, equipment, and tactical employment of their respective arms in the field. They usually have no actual command authority but may issue instructions and suggestions to the troops based on the evaluation of experience in the field. For the publication of technical manuals and the like they collaborate with the inspectorates of their branches in the General Army Office. They may also recommend changes in the organization or equipment of the troops to the Organization Branch of the General Staff (*Gen St d H/Org Abt*) for forwarding to the inspectorates.

Three officers in this category, whose titles begin with *Chef* instead of *General*, are regarded as organically absorbed into the General Staff for the duration of the war instead of being attached to it like the others.

The chiefs of those branches of the German

Army which are classified as service troops are likewise attached to the General Staff in wartime but, as has been shown above, are placed under the Chief Supply and Administration Officer. (The Chief of Technical Troops, which are officially classified as a combat arm, is nevertheless under the Chief Supply and Administration Officer since these troops actually have the function of service troops.)

The absence of a representative of the *Panzer* troops from this group of senior officers is explained by the creation in 1943 of the Inspector General of *Panzer* Troops (*Gen Insp d Pz Tr*) to supersede the previous Chief of Mobile Troops, who had been attached to the General Staff like the other chiefs of branches. The Inspector General of *Panzer* Troops is represented in the General Staff by his Chief Antitank Officer for All Arms (*Gen d Pz Abw aller Waffen*).

(1) *Chief Infantry Officer* (*General der Infanterie—Gen d Inf*)(110). Responsible for regular infantry, light infantry, mountain infantry, cavalry, and reconnaissance matters.

(2) *Chief of Armored Trains* (*Kommandeur der Eisenbahn-Panzerzüge—Kdr d Eisb Pz Züge*) (111).

(3) *Chief Artillery Officer* (*General der Artillerie—Gen d Art*)(112). Controls the Chief Coast and Fortress Artillery Officer (*Gen d H Küst u Fest Art*)(113), the Chief Army Antiaircraft Artillery Officer (*Gen d H Flak Tr*) (114), and the Chief Armored Artillery Officer (*Höh Offz Pz Art*)(115).

(4) *Chief of Mapping and Survey* (*Chef des Kriegskarten- und Vermessungswesens—Kr Kart Verm Chef*)(116). This officer is a part of the rear echelon of the General Staff (*Gen St d H/2. Staffel*) and is represented at field headquarters by the Commander of Mapping and Survey Troops (*Kdr d Kart u Verm Tr*)(117), who is his direct subordinate.

(5) *Chief Signal Officer* (*Chef des Heeresnachrichtenwesens—Chef HNW*)(118). Part of the General Staff in wartime, with offices at the rear echelon as well as at field headquarters.

(6) *Chief Engineer and Fortifications Officer* (*General der Pioniere und Festungen—Gen d Pi u Fest*)(119). Controls the Inspector of Fortifications (*Insp Fest*)(120) and shares with the General Army Office control of the Chief of Amphibious Engineers (*Höh Ldgs Pi Fü*)(121).

(7) *Chief Chemical Warfare Officer* (*General der Nebeltruppen—Gen d Nbl Tr*)(122).

(8) *Chief of Volunteer Units* (*General der Freiwilligenverbände—Gen d Freiw Verb*)(123). This post was created in January 1944 to replace that of the former General of Eastern Troops (*Gen d Ost Tr*)(124). It deals with the organization, equipment, training, and employment of units formed from impressed Soviet prisoners of war. The Chief of Volunteer Units is subordinate to the Chief of the Army General Staff in matters concerning the Field Army and to the Chief of Army Equipment and Commander of the Replacement Army (*Chef H Rüst u. BdE*) in matters affecting the Zone of the Interior. His permanent representative in the Replacement Army is the Commander of Volunteer Units (*Kdr d Freiw Verb*)(125).

(9) *Chief Army Transportation Officer* (*Chef des Transportwesens—Chef Trspw*)(126). Also believed to hold the post of Chief of Armed Forces Transportation (*Chef Trspw d W*). Part of the Army General Staff, responsible for rail and water transportation. He controls the Chief of Railway Troops (*Gen d Eisb Tr*)(127).

(10) *General for Special Employment* (*Discipline*) (*General zu besonderer Verwendung—Gen z b V*)(128). Responsible for the maintenance of discipline, counter-espionage, and legal matters in the Field Army. Controls the Branch for Army Matters (*Heer Wes Abt*), which is concerned with the maintenance of discipline; the Penal Section (*Gr Str*); and the Army Field Legal Branch (*H Feld Just Abt*), which was formerly the Field Legal Administration Section under the Chief Supply and Administration Officer.

d. MEDICAL AND VETERINARY INSPECTORS. The following chief inspectors are in charge of all medical and veterinary matters throughout the German Army and are directly under the Commander-in-Chief:

(1) *Chief Army Medical Inspector* (*Heeres-Sanitätsinspekteur—H San Insp*)(129). Instructs the Army Surgeon (*H Arzt*) on medical matters in the Field Army and controls medical matters in the Replacement Army, in the same manner as the inspectors of branches, through the Medical Inspectorate (*S Jn*) in the General Army Office. His activities are subject to the supervision and control of the Armed Forces Surgeon General (*Chef W San*). (At present the Chief Army Medical Inspector is believed to hold concurrently the office of Army Surgeon.)

(2) *Chief Veterinary Inspector* (*Veterinärin-*

spekteur—Vet Insp)(130). Instructs the Army Veterinary (*H Vet*) on veterinary matters in the Field Army and controls veterinary matters in the Replacement Army, in the same manner as the inspectors of branches, through the Veterinary Inspectorate (*V Jn*) in the General Army Office.

e. ARMY PERSONNEL OFFICE (*Heerespersonalamt—PA*)(131). This office is independent of both the General Staff and the Home Command and comes under the direct control of the Commander-in-Chief of the Army. It is responsible for all appointments, transfers, promotions, and other matters concerning all types of officers in the German Army. It therefore has been a powerful instrument in exercising control over the officer corps.

The order for the promotion of an officer to the rank of colonel or above is issued by Hitler himself on the recommendation of the Personnel Office. In lower ranks it makes the promotions on its own responsibility.

The authority to transfer various types of specialist officers (medical, veterinary, ordnance, motor maintenance, and Special Troop Service) is delegated by the Personnel Office, so far as the lower ranks are concerned, to the technical branches which deal with these services; for the upper ranks, the Personnel Office orders the transfers on the recommendation of the technical branches.

The Personnel Office does not concern itself with Armed Forces officials, who are dealt with exclusively by the Army Administration Office (*VA*); it should be noted, however, that two important former categories of these officials are now classified as officers in the new Special Troop Service and are therefore handled by the Personnel Office.

The Personnel Office includes seven main subdivisions designated as P 1, P 2, etc. Three of these are now groups (*Amtsgruppen*) with several subordinate branches each, while the others are independent branches (*Abteilungen*). Group P 6 is a recent offshoot of the basic Group P 1, and for this reason its subordinate branches are numbered consecutively with those of P 1.

While the bulk of the Personnel Office is normally stationed in wartime with the rear echelon of the High Command, each of its branches also has a forward echelon at field headquarters, where the major decisions in personnel matters are made.

(1) *Group P 1* (*Amtsgruppe P 1—Ag P 1*) (132). Responsible for all officers' records, appointments, transfers, and promotions as well as for basic directives regarding the handling of officer personnel matters. Its various branches deal with officers according to categories or branches of service. It includes:

(a) *Branch 1, Central Branch* (*1. Zentral-Abteilung*)(133). Handles basic policies and directives, including such general matters as the transfer of large groups of officers from other branches of the Armed Forces to the Army.

(b) *Branch 2* (*2. Abteilung*)(134). Infantry and cavalry officers.

(c) *Branch 3* (*3. Abteilung*)(135). Officers of the *Panzer* troops and of the supply troops.

(d) *Branch 4* (*4. Abteilung*)(136). Artillery and chemical warfare officers.

(e) *Branch 5* (*5. Abteilung*)(137). Engineer and signal officers.

(f) *Branch 6* (*6. Abteilung*)(138). Reserve officers and officers in recalled status (*Offiziere z. V.*).

Branch 7, which deals with specialist officers (medical, veterinary, ordnance, motor maintenance), is believed to have formed the nucleus for the new Group P 6 formed in May 1944 (see below).

(2) *Group P 2* (*Amtsgruppe P 2—Ag P 2*) (139). Responsible for officer education and welfare. It was expanded from a branch in August 1942 when "ideological training" for the officer corps was added to its functions. It includes:

(a) *Policy Section, formerly Branch 1* (*Chefgruppe, formerly 1. Abteilung*)(140). Education, questions of honor among officers, political matters, special cases involving general officers and high staff officers.

(b) *Branch 2* (*2. Abteilung*)(141). Final decisions in all individual cases involving honor, court-martial, and officer behavior.

(c) *Branch 3* (*3. Abteilung*)(142). Complaints, questions of Aryan ancestry, marriage, welfare measures, and personal assistance for officers and their dependents.

(3) *Branch P 3* (*Heeres-Personalabteilung 3—P 3*)(143). Responsible for all General Staff Corps officers, including their selection and training as well as their transfer and promotion. It took over full responsibility for these functions from the Central Branch of the Army General Staff (*Gen St d H/GZ*) in March 1943.

(4) *Branch P 4* (*Heeres-Personalabteilung 4—P 4*)(144). Responsible for officer replacements. Lays down general directives for the In-

spectot General for Potential Officers and Non-commissioned officers (*GJF*).

(5) *Branch P 5 (Heeres-Personalabteilung 5 —P 5)* (145). Responsible for decorations and awards. Divided into several sections, each dealing with a different type of decoration or award.

(6) *Group P 6 (Amtsgruppe P 6—Ag P 6)* (146). Responsible for personnel matters of officers in the specialist careers (*Sonderlaufbahnen*) and of specialist leaders (*Sonderführer*). It was formed in May 1944 as an offshoot of Group P 1 as a result of the creation of the Special Troop Service (*TSD*), comprising the administrative officers (*Intendanten*) and the judge advocates (*Wehrmachtrichter*), who were formerly classified as Armed Forces officials and dealt with by the Army Administration Office. The numbers of the branches in this group follow those of Group P 1. It includes:

(a) *Branch 7 (7. Abteilung)* (147). Medical, veterinary, ordnance, and motor maintenance officers. In the lower ranks the authority to transfer these officers is delegated to the Chief Army Medical Inspector (*H San Insp*), the Chief Veterinary Inspector (*Vet Insp*), the Ordnance Inspectorate (*Fz Jn*), and the Chief Motor Transport Officer (*Gen d Kfw*); in the upper ranks, transfers are made on the recommendation of these agencies.

(b) *Branch 8, General Branch (8. Allg.) Abteilung)* (148). Handles basic policies and issues general directives regarding officers controlled by the group.

(c) *Branch 9 (9. Abteilung)* (149). Probably handles the officers in the Special Troop Service (*TSD*).

(d) *Branch 10 (10. Abteilung (Sdf.))* (150). Responsible for personnel matters of specialist leaders (*Sdf*) (such as interpreters). They were formerly taken care of by Branch 7 when it was still part of Group 1.

(7) *Branch P 7 (Heeres-Personalabteilung 7 —P 7)* (151). Responsible for personnel matters of all officers belonging to Field Army units under the control of Himmler, primarily *Volks Grenadier* divisions (*VD*). This branch was formed in October 1944.

(8) *Special Section (Gruppe z b V)* (152). This section contains the officers who are charged with the handling out of decorations and medals and the performance of other ceremonial functions. It was formerly called Section for Representation and Honors (*Gruppe Rep/E*).

(9) *Courses for Senior Personnel Officers* (*Lehrgänge für höhere Adjutanten—Lehrg f höhere Adj*) (153). This section deals with the administration of special six to eight-week courses given by the Army Personnel Office for Senior Personnel Officers. These consist mainly of lectures on the functioning and policies of the Army Personnel Office and affiliated agencies.

f. CHIEF OF ARMY EQUIPMENT AND COMMANDER OF THE REPLACEMENT ARMY (*Chef der Heeresrüstung und Befehlshaber des Ersatzheeres —Chef H Rüst u BdE*) (154). This officer is the wartime deputy of the Commander-in-Chief of the Army charged with all the functions of the Zone of the Interior. These are primarily the conscription, training, aand replacement of personnel; the procurement, storage, and issue of equipment; and territorial administration. He controls all the principal offices of the High Command which are left behind as the rear echelon on mobilization, with the exception of the Personnel Office. These are discussed in the following six lettered paragraphs.

g. GENERAL ARMY OFFICE (*Allgemeines Heeresamt—AHA*) (155). Similar in function to the General Armed Forces Office in the *OKW* (*AWA*), this office is composed of a number of important, but partly unrelated, branches in the *OKH,* grouped together for administrative purposes. Its chief is believed to act as the deputy to the Chief of Army Equipment and Commander of the Replacement Army. It is used by various agencies both in the Home Command and in the Field Army and does most of the paper work for the *OKH*. It contains:

(1) *Staff (Stab AHA)* (156). The staff of the General Army Office is a central agency which approves the publications written by subordinate units and issues tables of organization, tables of equipment, manuals, and other publications. It includes the Army Regulations Administration (*Heeres-Druckvorschriftenverwaltung — HDvV*) (157), a section which issues all directives on clothing and uniforms (*Stab/Bkl*) (158), and a section concerned with technical developments in weapons and equipment (*Sonderstab A*) (159).

(2) *Inspectorates of Arms and Services.* There are approximately 15 of these inspectorates, grouped under the General Army Office, which are the principal agencies for handling the paper work for their respective arms and services. They have no command functions themselves but keep records and publish orders, directives, training manuals, and other material on behalf of the two

types of chiefs of arms and services: the inspectors (*Waffeninspekteure*) in the Replacement Army and the chiefs of branches (*Waffengenerale*) attached to the General Staff in the Field Army. They are referred to either as inspectorates (*Inspektionen—Jn*) or as branches (*Waffenabteilungen*). Most of them have numbers, ranging between 2 and 13, but several have been upgraded to the status of a group (*Amtsgruppe*) and control two numbered branches. *Jn 1,* the Inspectorate of Cadet Schools (*Inspektion der Kriegsschulen*), was in peacetime directly subordinate to the Commander-in-Chief of the Army; its function has now been taken over by the Inspector General for Potential Officers and Noncommissioned officers (*GJF*). The present inspectorates of arms and services are as follows:

(a) *Infantry Branch — Inspectorate 2 (Infanterieabteilung—Jn 2)* (160). Attached to the Infantry Branch is the Senior Infantry Officer for Land Fortifications (*Höh Inf Offz für die Landesbef*) (161), who is directly subordinate to the Chief of the General Army Office. He assists the Chief Engineer and Fortifications Officer (Inspector of Fortifications) (*Insp Fest*) at the Army General Staff in fortification matters concerning the infantry. He is also responsible for the uniform training of officers charged with the defense of fortifications.

(b) *Riding and Driving Branch—Inspectorate 3 (Abteilung Reit- und Fahrwesen—Jn 3)* (162). Concerned with the training of men who handle horses as riders or drivers.

(c) *Artillery Group (Amtsgruppe Artillerie—Ag Art)* (163). Formed in July 1944 to control the following two inspectorates:

Artillery Branch—Inspectorate 4 (*Artillerieabteilung—Jn 4*) (164).

Army Antiaircraft Artillery Branch—Inspectorate 13 (*Heeres-Flakartillerieabtetilung—Jn 13*) (165).

(d) *Engineer Branch — Inspectorate 5 (Pionierabteilung—Jn 5)* (166).

(e) *Inspectorate of Fortifications (Inspektion der Festungen—Jn Fest)* (167). Concerned with the training of fortress engineers.

(f) *Panzer Troop Branch — Inspectorate 6 (Abteilung Panzertruppe—Jn 6)* (168). Believed transferred to the control of the Inspector General of *Panzer* Troops (*Gen Insp d Pz Tr*) when that office was created in 1943.

(g) *Signal Group (Amtsgruppe Nachrichtenwesen)* (169). Formed in December 1943 with the expansion of Inspectorate 7. May be controlled by the Chief of Training (*Chef Ausb*) as well as the General Army Office. It includes:

Signal Branch—Inspectorate 7 (*Nachrichtentruppen-Abteilung—Jn 7*)(170).

Signal Equipment Branch (*Nachrichtengerät-Abteilung—N. Ger. Abt*)(171).

Army Communications Branch (*Heeresnachrichtenverbindungs-Abteilung — HNV*). Similar in function to the Armed Forces Communications Group in the *OKW (Ag WNV)* (172).

(h) *Supply Branch — Inspectorate 8 (Abteilung Nachschubtruppen—Jn 8)*(173). Attached to this branch is the Senior Officer of Administrative Troops (*Höh Off d Verw Tr*) (174), responsible for the uniform training of the administrative troops in the Replacement Army under the directives of the Chief of Training.

(i) *Chemical Warfare and Air Raid Protection Branch—Inspectorate 9 (Abteilung Nebeltruppe, Gasabwehr und Luftschutz—Jn 9)* (175).

(j) *Railway Engineer Branch — Inspectorate 10 (Eisenbahnpionier-Abteilung—Jn 10)* (176).

(k) *Branch for Technical Troops—Inspectorate 11 (Abteilung Technische Truppen—Jn 11)* (177).

(1) *Group of the Chief Motor Transport Officer (General des Kraftfahrwesens—Gen d Kfw)* (178). Formerly called Chief of Motorization (*Gen d Mot*) (179). The Chief Motor Transport Officer, in addition to being responsible for all motor transport in the field, also controls the following agencies in the General Army Office:

Motor Transport Branch—Inspectorate 12 (*Abteilung Kraftfahrwesen—Jn 12*) (180).

Chief of Motor Repair (*Chef des Instandsetzungswesen—Chef Inst*) (181).

Senior Motor Maintenance Troop Officer (*Höherer Offizier der Kraftfahrparktruppe—Höh Offz d Kf Pk Tr*) (182). He supervises the training of motor maintenance troops in the Replacement Army and his position is equivalent to that of an inspector.

(m) *Medical Inspectorate (Heeres-Sanitätsinspektion—S Jn)* (183). This inspectorate also contains the staff of the Chief Army Medical Inspector (*HSan Insp*) and is equivalent to a group. It includes:

Personnel Branch (*Personalabteilung—S Jn/Pers*) (184).

Organization Branch (*Organisationsabteilung —S Jn/Org*) (185).

Branch for Medical Science and Hygiene (*Abteilung für Wissenschaft und Gesundheitsführung—S Jn/Wi G*) (186).

(n) *Veterinary Inspectorate* (*Veterinärinspektion—V Jn*) (187). This inspectorate also contains the staff of the Chief Veterinary Inspector (*Vet Insp*).

(o) *Ordnance Inspectorate* (*Feldzeuginspektion—Fz Jn*) (188). The head of the inspectorate also holds the position of Chief Army Ordnance Officer (*Heeresfeldzeugmeister*) (189). As such he controls the entire system of ordnance depots in Germany.

(3) *Group for Replacement and General Troop Matters* (*Amtsgruppe Ersatzwesen und Allgemeine Truppenangelegenheiten — Ag E Tr*) (190). This group has generally the same responsibilities toward enlisted personnel as the Army Personnel Office (*PA*) has toward officers, except that it does not concern itself with individuals. It establishes policies and issues directives on all types of personnel matters. Until the summer of 1943 it included the Replacement Branch (*Abt E*), which has since been incorporated into the Conscription and Recruiting Office (*WEA*) in the *OKW*. It is believed that nevertheless the name of the group has thus far remained unchanged. It contains:

(a) *Branch for General Troop Matters* (*Abteilung für Allgemeine Truppenangelegenheiten—Tr Abt*) (191). This is the most important branch in the group, and probably of larger size than its name implies. It issues all types of orders to the troops, such as transfer regulations, promotion policies, and regulations regarding welfare and personal affairs. It includes a penal section, a section for noncommissioned officer affairs, and a section for German prisoners of war in Allied hands.

(b) *Chaplains Section* (*Gruppe Seelsorge—Gr S*) (192).

(c) *Branch for Billets and Maneuver Areas* (*Abteilung Unterkunft und Truppenübungsplätze —Abt U*) (193). Arranges for the requisition of premises needed for military purposes.

(4) *Army Judge Advocate General's Group* (*Amtsgruppe Heeresrechtswesen—Ag HR Wes*) (194). Contains a Judge Advocate's branch (HR) (195) and a legal section (*Just*).

(5) *Unit Inactivation Staff* (*Abwicklungsstab —Abw St*) (196). After Stalingrad an inactivation staff was set up to liquidate the affairs of units which were destroyed in the Sixth Army. It later was expanded to deal with those destroyed in Army Group Africa. In the summer of 1944 this staff was made a permanent part of the High Command structure, with the mission of inactivating all units destroyed on any front. It takes charge of any remaining funds which were the property of such units.

(6) *Demobilization Branch* (*Abteilung Demobilmachung—Abt Demob*) (197). Issues rules and directives for future demobilization.

(7) *Chief of Army Museums* (*Chef der Heeresmuseen—Chef Heer Mus*) (198).

h. CHIEF OF TRAINING IN THE REPLACEMENT ARMY (*Chef des Ausbildungswesens im Ersatzheer—Chef Ausb*) (199). Appointed in October 1942, this officer is immediately subordinate to the Chief of Army Equipment and Commander of the Replacement Army. He controls all training conducted within the Replacement Army, using as his representatives the inspectors of arms and services (*Waffeninspekteure*) (200) listed below. Through these inspectors he utilizes the facilities of the inspectorates of the corresponding arms and services in the General Army Office for working out the details of training programs and methods, the issuance of directives and manuals, and other paper work. The Chief of Training is not responsible for the specialized training of the medical, veterinary, ordnance, and motor maintenance troops, as this is handled by the inspectorates of these branches in the General Army Office operating under the direct control of their own independent inspectors.

The following are subordinate to the Chief of Training:

(1) Inspector of Infantry (*Inspekteur der Infanterie—Insp d Inf*) (201).

(2) Inspector of Riding and Driving (*Inspekteur des Reit- und Fahrwesens*) (202).

(3) Inspector of Artillery (*Inspekteur der Artillerie—Insp d Art*) (203).

(4) Inspector of Army Antiaircraft Troops (*Inspekteur der Heeresflaktruppen—Insp H Flak*) (204).

(5) Inspector of Engineers and Railway Engineers (*Inspekteur der Pioniere und Eisenbahnpioniere—Insp d Pi u Eisb Pi*) (205).

(6) Inspector of Construction Troops (*Inspekteur der Bautruppen—Insp d Bau Tr*) (206).

(7) Inspector of Signal Troops (*Inspekteur*

der Nachrichtentruppen—Insp d Nachr Tr) (207).

(8) Inspector of Supply Troops (*Inspekteur der Nachschubtruppen—Insp d Nachsch Tr)* (208).

(9) Inspector of Chemical Troops (*Inspekteur der Nebeltruppen—Insp d Nbl Tr)* (209).

(10) Training Film Branch (*Abteilung Lehrfilm)* (210). Controls the archives of the Army, the production and proper distribution of training films, and the training of film operators.

i. ARMY ORDNANCE OFFICE (*Heereswaffenamt*—Wa A) (211). This office is responsible for the design, testing, development, and acceptance of all ordnance equipment. It works in very close collaboration with the Ministry of Armament and War Production (*Reichsministerium für Bewaffnung und Kriegsproduktion*) some of whose branches are even located at the Army Ordnance Office. It is organized as follows:

(1) *Central Group (Zentral-Amtsgruppe des Heereswaffenamts— Wa Z)* (212). This group has no special ordnance functions but is only an administrative agency. It includes:

(a) *Organization Branch (Organisationsabteilung—Wa Z 1)* (213). Issues general directives on organization to subordinate ordnance agencies.

(b) *Administrative Section (Gruppe für Allgemeine Verwaltungsangelegenheiten—Wa Z 2)* (214). Responsible for general administrative matters.

(c) *Branch for Plant Efficiency (Betriebswirtschaftliche Abteilung—Wa Z 3)* (215).

(d) *Regulations Branch (Vorschriftenabteilung—Wa Z 4)* (216). Publishes all orders, manuals and directives originating in the Army Ordnance Office.

(e) *Branch for Housing, Construction, and Guard Matters (Allgemeine Unterbringungs-, Bau- und Überwachungsangelegenheiten—Wa Z 6)* (217). Responsible for the acquisition of premises and the construction and patrolling of Army Ordnance Office buildings.

(2) *Development and Testing Group (Amtsgruppe für Entwicklung und Prüfung—Wa Prüf)* (218). This group is responsible for the development and testing of ordnance equipment for all arms and services. Besides certain subdivisions which have special fields, there are those dealing with ordnance equipment of each combat arm; the numbers assigned to these branches

correspond mostly to those of the inspectorates of the same arm in the General Army Office. This group is composed of:

(a) *Ballistic and Ammunition Branch (Ballistische und Munitionsabteilung—Wa Prüf 1)* (219). Responsible for the development and testing of all types of ammunition. Divided into various sections dealing with ammunition of the different arms, special types of ammunition, firing tables, explosives, and other special technical matters connected with projectiles.

(b) *Infantry Branch (Infanterieabteilung— Wa Prüf 2)* (220).

(c) *Artillery Branch (Artillerieabteilung—Wa Prüf 4)* (221).

(d) *Engineer and Railway Engineer Branch (Pionier- und Eisenbahnpionier-Abteilung—Wa Prüf 5)* (222). Composed of sections dealing with engineer combat equipment, bridging and other river-crossing materials, engineering machines, water supply equipment, work tools, engineer transport vehicles, special construction equipment, and equipment for railway and waterway operation.

(e) *Fortress Engineer Branch (Festungspionierabteilung—Prüf Fest)* (223).

(f) *Panzer and Motorized Equipment Branch (Panzer- und Motorisierungsabteilung—Wa Prüf 6)* (224). Divided into a separate section for the development and testing of tanks and motorized equipment.

(g) *Signal Branch (Nachrichtenabteilung— Wa Prüf 7)* (225).

(h) *Branch for Optical, Survey, Meteorological, Artillery Fire Control, and Map-Printing Equipment (Abteilung für Optik, Messwesen, Heereswetterdienst, Feuerleitung und Kartendruck—Wa Prüf 8)* (226).

(i) *Gas Protection Branch (Gasschutzabteilung —Wa Prüf 9)*. Controls the Army Gas Protection laboratories at Spandau (*Heeres-Gasschutzlaboratorien Spandau)* (227).

(j) *Special Equipment Branch (Abteilung für Sondergerät—Wa Prüf 11)* (228). Possibly the branch responsible for the development of some of the V weapons.

(k) *Branch for Proving Grounds (Abteilung für Versuchsplätze—Wa Prüf 12)* (229). Controls the experimental stations which are located at most maneuver areas (*Truppenübungsplätze)*.

(3) *Group for Weapons and Equipment Manufacture (Amtsgruppe für Industrielle Rüstung—Waffen und Gerät—Wa J Rü—W u G)*

(230). This group is responsible for the procurement of all ordnance materiel except ammunition. Its main function is the placing of orders with industry. Here too the numbers of the branches mostly correspond to those of inspectorates of the same branch of service in the General Army Office. It includes:

(a) *Branch for General Army Equipment (Allgemeines Heeresgerät—Wa J Rü—W u G 1)* (231). Handles all types of equipment, including medical and veterinary.

(b) *Weapons Branch (Waffenabteilung—Wa J Rü—W u G 2)* (232). Divided into sections responsible for weapons of the various arms.

(c) *Engineer, Railway Engineer, and Fortress Equipment Branch (Pionier-, Eisenbahnpionier-, und Festungs-Geräteabteilung—Wa J Rü—W u G 5)* (233).

(d) *Tanks and Tractors Branch (Panzerkampfwagen- und Zugkraftwagen-Abteilung — Wa J Rü—W u G 6)* (234)

(e) *Signal Equipment Branch (Nachrichtengerätabteilung—Wa J Rü—W u G 7)* (235).

(f) *Optical and Precision Instruments Branch (Abteilung für optisches und feinmechanisches Gerät—Wa J Rü—W u G 8/ZO)* (236). Composed of various sections responsible for general optical instruments for all three services, special army optical instruments, precision antiaircraft artillery parts, artillery fire control parts, and the like.

(g) *Motor Vehicle Equipment Branch (Kraftwagengerätabteilung—Wa J Rü—W u G 12)* (237).

(4) *Group for Ammunition Manufacture (Amtsgruppe für Industrielle Rüstung (Munition)—Wa J Rü Mun)* (238). This group is responsible for all ordnance equipment. It includes:

(a) Ammunition Branch 1 *(Munitionsabteilung 1—Wa J Rü Mun 1)* (239).

(b) Ammunition Branch 2 *(Munitionsabteilung 2—Wa J Rü Mun 2)* (240).

(c) Ammunition Branch 3 *(Munitionsabteilung 3—Wa J Rü Mun 3 uzbV)* (241). Probably manufactures special types of munitions.

(d) Ammunition Branch 4 *(Munitionsabteilung 4—Wa J Rü Mun 4)* (242).

(e) Ammunition Branch 5 *(Munitionsabteilung 5—Wa J Rü Mun 5)* (243).

(5) *Acceptance Group (Amstgruppe für Abnahme—Wa Abn)* (244). This group is respon-

sible for seeing that all ordnance materiel is manufactured according to specifications and for accepting it on behalf of the Army. It controls the Acceptance Inspectors *(Abnahmeinspizienten)* (245) located in each *Wehrkreis*. It is composed of a Central Branch and Branches 1 and 2.

(6) *Chief Ordnance Engineer Group (Amtsgruppe Chefingenieur—Wa Chef Ing)* (246). This group contains various technical branches which design and supervise the manufacture of certain ordnance parts. It includes:

(a) The Chief Designer's Branch *(Chefkonstrukteur—Wa Chef Ing 1)* (247) contains a section which maintains liaison with the Reich Patent Office *(Reichspatentamt)*.

(b) Pig Iron Branch *(Halbzeugstelle—Wa Chef Ing 3/Hz)* (248).

(c) The Manufacture Branch *(Fabrikationsabteilung—Wa Chef Ing 4)* (249) contains various sections for studying methods of manufacture of weapons, vehicles, and other equipment.

(d) The Machine Recording Branch *(Maschinelles Berichtwesen—Wa Chef Ing 5 M B)* (250) is responsible for punch-card machines and other mechanical office aids.

(e) Section for the Manufacture of Machine Tools, Gauges, and Tools *(Fabrikationsgruppe Werkzeugmaschinen, Lehren und Werkzeuge—Wa Chef Ing 6)* (251).

(f) Section for the Manufacture of Ammunition *(Fabrikationsgruppe Munition—Wa Chef Ing 7)* (252).

(7) *Group for Antiaircraft Artillery Development (Amtsgruppe für Flakentwicklung—GL/Flak-E)* (253). Includes:

(a) Branch for Ballistics and Development of Antiaircraft Ammunition *(Abteilung für Ballistik und Entwicklung der Flakmunition—GL/Flak-E/1)* (254).

(b) Branch for the Development of Antiaircraft Equipment *(Abteilung für Gerätentwicklung—GL/Flak-E/2)* (255).

(c) Branch for Technical and General Matters *(Abteilung für technische und allgemeine Angelegenheiten—GL/Flak-E/3)* (256).

(d) Branch for Weapons Development *(Abteilung für Waffenentwicklung—GL/Flak-E/4)* (257).

(e) Antiaircraft Armament Branch *(Abteilung Flakrüstung—GL/Flak-Rü)* (258).

(8) *Ordnance Research Branch (Forschungs-abteilung—Wa F).*

j. ARMY ADMINISTRATION OFFICE *(Heeresver-waltungsamt—VA)* (259). This office is responsible for what is defined by the Germans as Army Administration *(Heeresverwaltung)*. Its responsibilities include mainly the procurement of rations, billets, pay, and clothing for the Army. Until May 1944 the personnel connected with Army Administration normally were Armed Forces officials *(Wehrmachtbeamte)*, divided into a large number of technical and non-technical "careers" *(Laufbahnen)*. At that time those in the important careers of the Administrative Service *(Verwaltungsdienst)* and of the Judge Advocates *(Wehrmachtrichter)* were made into a new category of officers in the Special Troop Service *(Truppensonderdienst—TSD)* (260). Their activities still are controlled by the Army Administration Office, but their promotions and transfers are now the responsibility of the Army Personnel Office *(PA)*.

The Administration Office includes:

(1) *Group for Officials and Civilian Workers (Amtsgruppe Allgemeine Heeresbeamten-, Angestellten-, Arbeiter- und Kassenangelegenheiten—Ag V 1)* (261). Responsible for personnel administration and pay for Armed Forces officials, salaried workers *(Angestellte)*, and wage earners *(Arbeiter)*. Consists of:

(a) Branch for Army Officials *(Heeresbeamtenabteilung—V 1)* (262).

(b) Branch for Civilian Workers *(Abteilung für Gefolgschaftsangelegenheiten des Heeres—V 8)* (263).

(c) Branch for Army Accounts and Pay of Officials *(Heereskassen- und Beamtenbesoldungsabteilung—V 9)* (264).

(d) Cashier of the *OKH (Amtskasse des Oberkommandos des Heeres—AK (OKH))* (265) is responsible for paying personnel of the *OKH*.

(e) Pay and Allowance Department of the *OKH (Gebührnisstelle des Oberkommandos des Heeres—G St OKH)* (266) handles pay and allowances of military personnel and Armed Forces officials in the *OKH*.

(f) Wage and Salary Office *(Lohnstelle des Oberkommandos des Heeres—Lohnst OKH)* (267) has sections concerned with salaried employees, wage earners, and various types of pay deductions.

(g) Accounting Offices of the Chief of Army Equipment and Commander of the Replacement Army *(Zahlmeistereien des Ch H Rüst u. B d E)* (268) have four accounting offices carrying the Roman numerals I to IV.

(2) *Group for Real Estate, Agriculture, and Forests (Amtsgruppe Liegenschaften, Land- und Forstwirtschaft—Ag V II)* (269). Includes:

(a) Branch for Real Estate of Garrisons and Procurement of Quarters *(Abteilung für Liegenschaften der Standorte und Wohnungsfürsorge—V 2)* (270).

(b) Branch for the Administration of Maneuver Areas *(Abteilung für Verwaltung von Übungsplätzen—V 6)* (271).

(c) Army Forestry Branch *(Heeresforstabteilung—V 10)* (272).

(3) *Rations and Procurement Group (Amtsgruppe Heeresverpflegungs- und -Beschaffungswesen—Ag V III)* (273). Responsible for the procurement and administration of rations. Includes:

(a) Army Rations Branch *(Heeresverpflegungsabteilung—V 3)* (274).

(b) Army Procurements Branch *(Heeresbeschaffungsabteilung—V 5)* (275).

(c) Rations Inspector in the *OKH (Verpflegungsinspekteur im OKH—Verpfl Insp OKH)* (276) is responsible for over-all planning of rations supplies in the whole Theater of War.

(4) *Construction Group (Amtsgruppe Bau—Ag V IV)* (277). Responsible for all army construction. Includes:

(a) Branch for Administration of Army Construction *(Heeresbauverwaltungsabteilung—V 4)* (278).

(b) Branch for Army Construction Activities *(Heeresbauwirtschaftsabteilung—V 7)* (279).

(5) *Budget Group (Amstgruppe Haushalts- und Besoldungswesen—Ag Haushalt)* (280). This group was formed in February 1944 by an amalgamation of four independent branches connected with budget and finance matters. Up to August 1944 it was immediately under the Chief of Army Equipment and Commander of the Replacement Army; it was placed under the control of the Chief of the Army Administration Office. It includes:

(a) Army Budget Branch *(Heeres-Haushaltsabteilung—H Haush)* (281).

(b) Central Branch in the *OKH (Zentralabteilung im OKH (Chef H Rüst u. BdE)—Z)* (282).

(c) Army Pay Branch (*Heeresbesoldungs-abteilung—H Bes Abt*)(283).

(d) Army Finance Branch (*Heeres-Finanzierungsabteilung*) (284).

k. INSPECTOR GENERAL FOR POTENTIAL OFFICERS AND NONCOMMISSIONED OFFICERS (*Generalinspekteur für den Führernachwuchs des Heeres—GJF*) (285). Formerly the Inspector of Army (Training and Education (*In EB*) (286); renamed and broadened in scope and authority in March 1944. Subordinate to the Chief of Army Equipment and Commander of the Replacement Army (*Chef H Rüst u BdE*). He is responsible for the uniform recruiting, National-Socialist instruction and guidance, and uniform training of all potential officers and noncommissioned officers (*Führernachwuchs*). He is in charge of all officer candidate and noncommissioned officer schools and determines the subject-matter and methods of instruction, particularly the political aspects. He controls:

(1) *Branch for the Procurement of Leaders* (*Abteilung Heeresnachwuchs—Abt. HN*)(287). This branch was independent up to 1944 but became subordinate to the Inspector General for Potential Officers and Noncommissioned Officers when he was appointed. This branch represents the Army in dealing with other services and agencies in all questions concerning the procurement of leaders.

(2) *Cadet School Branch* (*Abteilung Kriegsschulen—KS*)(288). Previously called Inspectorate 1 (*In 1*) and directly under the Chief of Army Equipment and Commander of the Replacement Army. Administers all officer candidate schools.

(3) *Noncommissioned Officer School Branch* (*Abteilung Unteroffizier-Vorschulen u. -Schulen —US*) (289).

(4) *Inspector of Army Officer Procurement Offices* (*Inspekteur der Annahmestellen für Offizierbewerber des Heeres—Insp d Annst*)(290). Set up in 1943 as an independent agency in the Army Personnel Office; transferred to the control of the Inspector General for Potential Officer and noncommissioned officers in 1944. Controls the officer candidate acceptance centers located in each *Wehrkreis*.

l. MISCELLANEOUS AGENCIES. The following are independent agencies, all immediately subordinate to the Chief of Army Equipment and Commander of the Replacement Army (*Chef H Rüst u. BdE*):

(1) *Signal Communications Branch of the Chief of Army Equipment and Commander of the Replacement Army* (*Nachrichten-Betriebs-Abteilung des Ch H Rüst u. BdE*) (291). Contains a telephone operating company, a telegraph company, a signal exploitation company, and a radio transmission center.

(2) *Army Raw Materials Branch* (*Heeres-Rohstoffabteilung—H Ro*)(292). Charged with the procurement of raw materials for the *OKH*. Formerly a subordinate unit of the Army Ordnance Office (*Rohstoffstelle OKH—Wa Chef Ing 2/Wa Ro*)(293), it was made an independent branch in 1942.

(3) *Army Map Service* (*Heeresplankammer—HPK*)(294). Contains a foreign maps branch, and a map production branch.

(4) *Army Technical Bureau* (*Heerestechnisches Büro* (*HTB*) (295). Believed to be a staff of engineers at the disposal of the *OKH*.

(5) *Women's Auxiliary Corps* (*Nachrichtenhelferinnen-Einsatzabteilung—NH-Einsatzabteilung*) (296). The women's auxiliary corps is believed to be subordinate to the Chief of Army Equipment and Commander of the Replacement Army. It is formed into special battalions (*Einsatzabteilungen*) and used throughout the Field and Replacement Armies for signal communications and office work at higher headquarters.

m. NATIONAL-SOCIALIST GUIDANCE STAFF OF THE ARMY (*Nationalsozialistischer Führungsstab des Heeres—NSF St d H*) (297). Established in March 1944 to control the uniform National-Socialist indoctrination and guidance in the Army. Directly subordinate to Hitler but attached to the Army High Command. Issues directives to the National-Socialist Guidance Officers (*NSFO*) in the field.

n. THE FÜHRER'S OFFICIAL MILITARY HISTORIAN (*Der Beauftragte des Führers für die militärische Geschichtsschreibung—D Beauftr d Führers für die mil Geschichtsschr*) (298). Appointed in 1942 to take charge of the writing of military history of World War II. Directly subordinate to Hitler but attached to the Army High Command. Upon his appointment, the agencies connected with military history in the Army were transferred from the jurisdiction of the Fifth Senior General Staff Officer (*O Qu V*) to his control but remained subordinate to the *OKH*. In addition, historical branches were set up at both the *OKW* and the *OKH* to record the war for the Armed Forces and for the Army respectively. This obviated the need for the Military Science Branch still under the *O Qu V*, and it is believed that its existence is only nominal. The Führer's Official Military Histórian controls within the *OKH*:

(1) *Army Historical Branch (Kriegsgeschichtliche Abteilung des Heeres—Kr Gesch Heer)* (299). Established in 1942. Probably took over all the functions of the Military Science Branch (*Kr Wiss Abt.*) in the Army General Staff. It includes the editorial staff of the magazine "Military Science Review" (*Militärwissenschaftliche Rundschau*).

(2) *Military History Research Institute (Kriegswissenschaftliche Forschungs-Anstalt)* (300). Originally under the control of the Army General Staff but believed to have been transferred to the control of the Führer's Official Military Historian, sometime after 1942.

(3) *Chief of Army Archives (Chef der Heeresarchive—Chef H Arch)* (301). Transferred from the Army General Staff in 1942. Army archives have been kept in Potsdam, with a branch office at Liegnitz.

(4) *Chief of Army Libraries (Chef der Heeresbüchereien—Chef H Büch)* (302). This position was created in 1942, first under the control of the Army General Staff and then transferred to Führer's Official Military Historian. Responsible for the administration of all military literature.

(5) *Captured Documents Exploitation Center (Wehrmacht-Sichtungsstelle—We Sist)* (303). Exploits captured documents (*Beuteakten*) for the whole of the Armed Forces.

o. INSPECTOR GENERAL OF *Panzer* TROOPS (*Generalinspekteur der Panzertruppen—Gen Insp d Pz Tr*) (304). Appointed in 1943 as a successor to the Chief of Mobile Troops (*General der Schnellen Truppen*) (305) who had been attached to the Army General Staff. Directly subordinate to Hitler but attached to the Army High Command. Controls the whole *Panzer* arm; responsible for its organization, training, and replacement system. His prerogative extend to the Air Force and *Waffen-SS Panzer* units. He controls:

(1) *Chief Antitank Officer for All Arms (General der Panzerabwehr aller Waffen)* (306). Appointed in November 1944 to coordinate antitank tactics throughout the Armed Forces. He also acts as liaison officer for the *Panzer* troops at the Army General Staff replacing the former *Panzer* Officer at the Army General Staff (*Pz Offz b Gen St d H*) (307).

(2) *Inspector of Panzer Troops (Inspekteur der Panzertruppen—Insp d Pz Tr)* (308). Has a function similar to that of the other inspectors in the *OKH* except that he is not controlled by the Chief of Training in the Replacement Army (*Chef Ausb*). He controls the *Panzer* Troop Branch, Inspectorate 6 (*Jn 6*) (309), although the latter may still be administratively under the General Army Office.

(3) *Field Army Branch (Abteilung Feldheer)* (310). This branch maintains liaison between the Inspector General of *Panzer* Troops and the Field Army. It is responsible for the proper evaluation and use of all combat experience and makes suggestions on the organization, training, and development of the *Panzer* arm.

(4) *Training Branch (Ausbildungs-Abteilung —Ausb Abt* (311). Formed in 1944, this branch took over the administration of the training of *Panzer* troops from Inspectorate 6. It issues a regular monthly periodical dealing with the experience of *Panzer* troops in the field.

4. Glossary and Index of German Terms and Abbreviations

This glossary consists of German designations for all the principal agencies of the Armed Forces and Army High Commands, together with their usual abbreviations and approximate translations. The glossary is designed to assist the reader in finding an explanation of the function of each agency. The numbers following the terms serve as a cross-reference to paragraph 3, where the explanations are numbered serially.

AK (OKH)—Amtskasse des Oberkommandos des Heeres (Cashier of the OKH) 205

Allgemeine Abteilung (General Armed Forces Branch) 42

Allgemeines Heeresamt (General Army Office) 155

Amt (Office) 6

Amtsgruppe—see Ag

Amtskasse des Oberkommandos des Herres (Cashier of the OKH) 265

Artillerieabteilung—Jn 4 (Artillery Branch, Inspectorate 4) 164

Att Abt d OKH—Attachéabteilung des OKH (Branch for Military Attachés of the OKH) 33

Ausb. Abt—Ausbildungs-Abteilung (Training Branch) 83, 311

AWA—Allgemeines Wehrmachtamt (General Armed Forces Office) 41

AWA/HJ—Vertreter der Wehrmacht beim Jugendführer des Deutschen Reichs (Hilter Youth Liaison) 53

BW Sied—Bevollmächtigter des OKW für Siedlungsfragen (Armed Forces Plenipotentiary for Settlement) 52

Chef Ausb—Chef des Ausbildungswesen im Ersatzheer (Chief of Training in the Replacement Army) 199

Chef der Heeresarchive (Chief of Army Archives) 301

Chef der Heeresbüchereien (Chief of Army Libraries) 302

Chef der Heeresmuseen (Chief of Army Museums) 198

Chef der Propagandatruppen (Chief of the Propaganda Troops) 40

Wa J Rü—WuG 12—Kraftwagengerätabteilung (Motor Vehicle Equipment Branch) 237

Chef des Ausbildungswesens im Ersatzheer (Chief of Training in the Replacement Army) 199

Chef Gen St d H—Chef des Generalstabs des Heeres (Chief of General Staff) 72

Chef des Heeresstabes beim Chef OKW (Chief of Army Staff with Chief OKW) 25

Chef HNV—Chef des Heeresnachrichtenwesens (Chief Signal Officer) 118

Chef des Instandsetzungswesens (Chief of Motor Repair) 181

Chef des Kriegsgefangenenwesens (Chief of Prisoners of War) 44

Chef des Kriegskarten- und Vermessungswesens (Chief of Mapping and Survey) 116

Chef des OKW (Chief of the Armed Forces High Command) 13

Chef des Transportwesens (Chief Army Transportation Officer) 126

Chef des Wehrmachtkraftfahrwesens (Chief of Armed Forces Motor Transportation) 17

Chef des Transportwesens der Wehrmacht (Chief of Armed Forces Transportation (Rail and Water) 18

Chef des Wehrmachtsanitätswesens - (Armed Forces Surgeon General) 24

Chef des Wehrmachtstreifendienstes (Chief of the Armed Forces Patrol Service) 22

Chefgruppe (Policy Section) 140

Chef H Arch—Chef der Heeresarchive (Chief of Army Archives) 301

Chef H Büch—Chef der Heeresbüchereien (Chief of Army Libraries) 302

Ch H Rüst u. BdE—Chef der Heeresrüstung und Befehlshaber des Ersatzheeres (Chief of Army Equipment and Commander of the Replacement Army) 154

Chef H St b Chef OKW—Chef des Heeresstabes beim Chef OKW (Chief of Army Staff with Chief OKW) 25

Chef Inst—Chef des Instandsetzungswesens (Chief of Motor Repair) 181

Chef Kriegsgef—Chef des Kriegsgefangenenwesens (Chief of Prisoners of War) 44

Chef Pr Tr—Chef der Propagandatruppen (Chief of the Propaganda Troops) 40

Chef Trspw—Chef des Transportwesens (Chief Army Transport Officer) 126

Chef Trspw d W—Chef des Transportwesens der Wehrmacht (Chief of Armed Forces Transportation (Rail and Water)) 18

Chef WKW—Chef des Wehrmachtkraftfahrwesens (Chief of Armed Forces Motor Transportation) 17

Chef W San—Chef des Wehrmachtsanitätswesens (Armed Forces Surgeon General) 24

Chef W Str D (Chief of the Armed Forces Patrol Service) 22

Chi—Chiffrier-Abteilung (Crytographic Branch) 37

Der Beauftr d Führers für die mil Geschichtsschr—Der Beauftragte des Führers für die militärische Geschichtsschreibung (Führer's official military historian) 38, 92, 298

Eisenbahnpionierabteilung—Jn 10 (Railway Engineer Branch, Inspectorate 10) 176

F Abt—Feldtransportabteilung (Field Transportation Branch) 19

Feldzeuginspektion—Fz Jn (Ordnance Inspectorate) 188

Forschungsabteilung (Ordnance Research Branch) 258

Frd Heere Ost—Fremde Heere Ost (Eastern Armies Branch) 89

Frd Heere West—Fremde Heere West (Western Armies Branch) 90

Führerhauptquartier (Field Headquarters of the OKW) 14

Fz Jn—Feldzeuginspektion (Ordnance Inspectorate) 188

Gen—See General

General der Artillerie (Chief Artillery Officer) 112

General der Eisenbahntruppen (Chief of Railway Troops) 127

General der Freiwilligenverbände (Chief of Volunteer Units) 123

General der Heeres-Flaktruppen (Chief Army Anti-Aircraft Artillery Officer) 114

General der Heeresküsten- und Festungsartillerie (Chief Coast and Fortress Artillery Officer) 113

General der Motorisierung (changed to Gen d Kfw) 179

General der Nachschubtruppen (Chief of Supply Troops) 106

General der Nebeltruppen (Chief Chemical Warfare Officer) 122

General der Osttruppen (changed to Gen d Freiw Verb) 124

General der Pioniere und Festungen (Chief Engineer and Fortifications Officer) 120

General der Panzerabwehr aller Waffen (Chief Antitank Officer for All Arms) 306

General der Schnellen Truppen (changed to Gen Insp d Pz Tr) 10

General des Kraftfahrwesens (Chief Motor Transport Officer) 104

General des Kraftfahrwesens/AHA (Group of the Chief Motor Transport Officer in the General Army Office) 178

General zu besonderer Verwendung (General for Special Employment (Discipline)) 128

Generalinspekteur der Panzertruppen (Inspector General of Panzer Troops) 304

Generalinspekteur des Kraftfahrwesens (Inspector General of Motor Transport) 70

Generalinspekteur für das Kriegsgefangenwesen der Wehrmacht (Inspector General for Prisoner of War Affairs) 27

Generalinspekteur für den Führernachwuchs des Heeres (Inspector General for Potential Officers and NCOs) 285

Generalquartiermeister (Chief Supply and Administration Officer) 74, 94

Generalstab des Heeres (Army General Staff) 71

General z b V IV (General for Special Employment IV—now Chef W Str D) 23

Gen Insp d Pz Tr—Generalinspekteur der Panzertruppen (Inspector General of Panzer Troops) 304

Gen Insp Kfw—Generalinspekteur für das Kraftfahrwesen (Inspector General of Motor Transport) 70

Gen Insp Kriegsgef—Generalinspekteur für das Kriegsgefangenenwesen der Wehrmacht (Inspector General for Prisoner of War Affairs) 27

Gen Qu—Generalquartiermeister (Chief Supply and Administration Officer) 74, 94

Gen St d H—Generalstab des Heeres (Army General Staff) 71

GJF—Generalinspekteur für den Führernachwuchs des Heeres (Inspector General for Potential Officers and NCOs) 285

GL/Flak-E—Amtsgruppe für Flakentwicklung (Group for Antiaircraft Artillery Development) 253

GL/Flak-E/1—Abteilung für Ballistik und Entwicklung der Flakmunition (Branch for Ballistics and Development of Antiaircraft Equipment) 254

GL/Flak-E/2—Abteilung für Gerätentwicklung (Branch for the Development of Antiaircraft Equipment) 255

GL/Flak-E/3—Abteilung für technische und allgemeine Angelegenheiten (Branch for Technical and General Matters)

GL/Flak-E/4—Abteilung für Waffenentwicklung (Branch for the Development of AA Weapons) 257

GL/Flak-Rü—Abteilung Flakrüstung (Antiaircraft Armament Branch) 258

G St OKH—Gebührnisstelle des OKH (Pay and Allowance Department of the OKH) 266

Gr—See Gruppe

Gr S—Gruppe Seelsorge (Chaplains' Section) 192

Gruppe (Section) 9

Gruppe IIa—Adjutantur (Personnel Section) 99

Gruppe III—Feldjustizverwaltung (Field Legal Administration Section) 100

Gruppe IVa—Heeres-Intendant (Chief Army Administration Officer) 101

Gruppe IVb—Heeresarzt (Army Surgeon) 102

Gruppe IVc—Heeresveterinär (Army Veterinarian) 103

Gruppe V—General des Kraftfahrwesens (Chief Motor Transport Officer) 104

Gruppe Z—Zivilbeauftragter (Civil Commissioner) 105

Gruppe FP—Heeresfeldpostmeister (Army Postmaster) 107

Gruppe z b V—Gruppe zur besonderen Verwendung (Party Liaison) 69

Gruppe z b V—Gruppe zur besonderen Verwendung (Ceremonial occasions) 152

G St OKH—Gebührnisstelle des OKH (Pay and Allowance Department of the OKH) 266

GZ—Zentralabteilung (Central Branch of Army General Staff) 75

H Arzt—Heeresarzt (Army Surgeon) 102

H Bes Abt—Heeresbesoldungsabteilung (Army Pay Branch) 283

Heeresbesoldungsabteilung (Army Pay Branch) 283

Heeresdruckvorschriftenverwaltung (Army Regulations administration) 157

Heeresfeldzeugmeister (Chief Army Ordnance Officer) 189

Heeres-Finanzierungstabteilung (Army Finance Branch) 284

Heeres-Flakartillerieabteilung—Jn 13 (Army Antiaircraft Artillery Branch, Inspectorate 13) 165

Heeres-Haushaltsabteilung (Army Budget Branch) 281

Heeres-Intendant (Chief Army Administrative Officer) 101

Heeres - Nachrichtenverbindungs - Abteilung (Army Communication Branch) 172

Heeres-Personalabteilung 3—P 3 (Branch P 3 General Staff Officers) 143

Heeres-Personalabteilung 4—P 4 (Branch P 4, Officer Replacements) 144

Heeres-Personalabteilung 5—P 5 (Branch P 5, Decorations and Medals) 145

Heeres-Personalabteilung 7—P 7 (Branch P 7, Officers in Volksgrenadier Units) 151

Heerespersonalamt (Army Personnel Office) 131

Heeresplankammer (Army Map Service) 294

Heeres-Rohstoffabteilung (Army Raw Materials Branch) 292

Heeres-Sanitätsinspekteur (Chief Army Medical Inspector) 129

Section IV. ORGANIZATION OF THE ARMY FOR WAR

1. Territorial Basis

In peacetime the organization and administration of the German Army were based on the division of the national territory into fifteen corps areas *(Wehrkreise)*. Each one of these contained the headquarters and component divisions of a corps and was as the same time the main territorial echelon for conscription, the administration of army property, local defense, and nearly all other military matters. The commander of the corps area was simultaneously the commanding general of the corps, which he was destined to lead into the field on the outbreak of war.

The corps areas as well as the corps were numbered with Roman numerals from I to XIII plus XVII and XVIII in Austria. Thus the I Corps was located in Corps Area I, and so on. The missing numbers—XIV, XV, and XVI— were used for three non-territorial corps set up to control the motorized, light, and *Panzer* divisions respectively. After the annexation of Austria, another non-territorial corps, XIX, was set up to control Austrian *Panzer* and light divisions.

By 1939 the German Army had been expanded from the seven divisions of the old *Reichswehr* to a total of 51 divisions plus corps troops. These consisted of 36 infantry and motorized divisions, numbered from 1 to 36, in Germany proper; three infantry divisions in Austria and the Sudeten areas; five *Panzer* divisions; four light divisions; and three mountain divisions. They were organized as follows:

Corps

(corps area)	Headquarters	Divisions		
I	Königsberg	1	11	21
II	Stettin	12	32	
III	Berlin	3	23	
IV	Dresden	4	14	24
V	Stuttgart	5	25	35
VI	Münster	6	16	26
VII	München	7	27	1 Mt
VIII	Breslau	8	18	28
IX	Kassel	9	15	
X	Hamburg	22	30	
XI	Hannover	19	31	
XII	Wiesbaden	33	34	36
XIII	Nürnberg	10	17	46
XVII	Wien	44	45	
XVIII	Salzburg	2 Mt	3 Mt	

Non-territorial Corps

XIV	Magdeburg	2 Mtz	13 Mtz	
		20 Mtz	29 Mtz	
XV	Jena	1 L	2 L	3 L
XVI	Berlin	1 Pz	3 Pz	
		4 Pz	5 Pz	
XIX	Wien	2 Pz	4 L	

After the Polish campaign in 1939, two new corps areas, XX and XXI, were created in annexed territory in the east; subsequently Corps Areas *Böhmen und Mähren* and *Generalgouvernement* were added.

2. Mobilization Plan

The German mobilization for the present war was a gradual process lasting several months. The High Command was determined to avoid the mistakes of 1914, when millions of men were drawn into the Army almost overnight to form second-rate reserve and *Landwehr* divisions with serious disruption of the economic life of the country. This time the reservists were called up individually and deliberately were mixed with the personnel of regular divisions so that most of the new units formed during the summer of 1939 were fully as efficient and well organized as the original ones. Most of the regular regiments added one or more supplementary battalions, composed of men of the older age classes who had had only 8 or 12 weeks of training; these battalions exchanged personnel with the regular battalions and were then organized into new divisions just before the attack on Poland.

3. Creation of the Field Army

On 27 August 1939, in accordance with carefully laid plans which had been developing since the latter part of June, the entire German Army was split from top to bottom into two mutually exclusive parts, which were to perform two distinct functions for the duration of the war. One part was to be concerned only with military operations and was known as the Field Army *(Feldheer)*; the other part was devoted to training, procurement, and administration in the Zone of the Interior and was called the Replacement Army *(Ersatzheer)*. The operational parts of the High Command, including the Commander-in-Chief and the bulk of the General Staff, established a field headquarters away from Berlin to control the Field Army. The rest of the High Command was placed under a deputy of

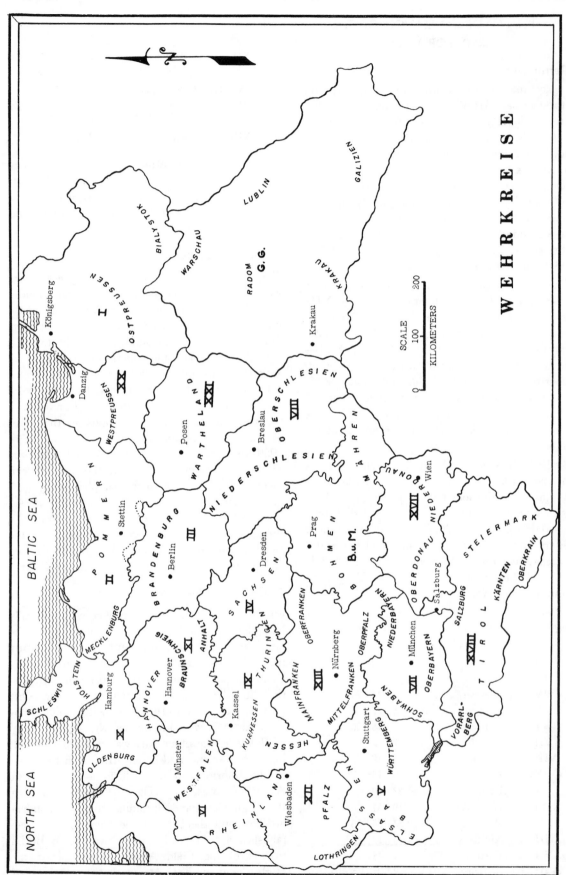

Figure 6.—German corps areas.

the Commander-in-Chief to be known as the Chief of Army Equipment and Commander of the Replacement Army *(Chef der Heeresrüstung und Befehlshaber des Ersatzheeres)*, responsible for maintaining the Field Army by the dispatch of replacements, the formation of new units, and the supply of materiel, as well as continuing the normal military functions at home.

At the same time each of the active corps took the field under its commanding general, and the corps areas were placed under deputy commands to control the Replacement Army, the permanent installations, and the conscription and training system. The new commander in each corps area was to be known by the dual title of Deputy Commanding General and Commander of the Corps Area *(Stellvertretender Kommandierender General und Befehlshaber im Wehrkreis)*. In his capacity as Deputy Commanding General he was to be responsible for all matters having to do with troop units of the Army, particularly the operation of the replacement system; as Commander of the Corps Area he was to exercise all territorial functions, such as conscription, control of permanent installations, and local defense, on behalf of the entire Armed Forces.

The corps of the new Field Army were organized into armies *(Armeen)*—an administrative and tactical echelon which had not existed in peacetime. These, in turn, were placed under the tactical control of army groups *(Heeresgruppen)*, which were directly responsible to field headquarters for the conduct of operations.

At the lower levels, each unit which took the field in 1939 left behind at its home station a rear echelon which was known as its replacement training unit *(Ersatzeinheit)*. An infantry regiment, for example, left behind an infantry replacement training battalion, bearing the same number, which was thenceforth to induct and train recruits, dispatch them to the field regiment as needed, and receive personnel back from the field unit if they were to be discharged or when they came out of general hospitals.

4. Functions of the Home Command

The functions of the wartime command for the Zone of the Interior may be described as threefold:

a. PERSONNEL. Conscription, training and replacement of personnel include control of mobilization policies and the actual call-up and induction of men; all types of military training, including the selection and schooling of officers and noncommissioned officers; the dispatch of personnel replacements to field units in response to their requisitions; and the organization of new units.

b. EQUIPMENT. Design, procurement, acceptance, and storage of equipment of all kinds, and its dispatch to the Field Army, involve: assessment of the future needs of the field; planning of production; obtaining the necessary raw materials and labor; development and testing of new weapons; fiscal matters; maintenance of suitable storage and transport facilities, and of headquarters to control them; and organization of the channels for supply requisitions and deliveries.

c. ADMINISTRATION. Administration of the permanent military installations in the Zone of the Interior and emergency defense of the home territory also are responsibilities of the Home Command. The latter function (which would become operative, for example, in case of a surprise airborne invasion of the heart of Germany) would be exercised by the Home Command only until an adequate Field Army force could be assembled to take charge of the operations.

The above functions of the Home Command are discussed in detail in Sections V and VI, of this chapter and in Chapter VI below.

5. Organization of the Theater of War

On the outbreak of war, all the parts of Europe and its adjacent waters which might be the scene of operations became, from the German point of view, the Theater of War *(Kriegsgebiet)*. Within this area the Germans distinguish between the Theater of Operations *(Operationsgebiet)* and the Zone of the Interior *(Heimatkriegsgebiet)*. Since, in the German concept, wars should be conducted as far as possible beyond their own frontiers, the military nomenclature also provides for an intermediate area known as the Zone of Military Administration *(Gebeit der Kreigsverwaltung)* or Occupied Territory *(Besetztes Gebiet)*; in fact, much of Europe was in this category during the years when the German armies were fighting in the distant steppes of Russia and in Africa.

The Theater of Operations itself is divided into the Combat Zone *(Gefechtsgebiet)* and the Communications Zone *(Rückwärtiges Gebiet)*. The latter may be entirely taken up by the Army Rear Areas *(Rückwärtige Armeegebiete)* or, if the line of communications is long, its rearward part may be the Army Group Rear Area (*Rückwärtiges Heeresgebiet*).

Each of the above subdivisions of the Theater of War is subject to a different type of administration by the military, mixed military and civil, or only the civil authorities. The arrangement is shown schematically in Figure 7.

The Zone of the Interior was extended in 1941 and 1942 to include Denmark, Alsace, Lorraine, Luxemburg, and those parts of Poland incorporated in the so-called Government General; it already included Bohemia and Moravia. By contrast, much of Germany itself was within the Theater of Operations and even within the Combat Zone by the end of 1944.

The Zone of the Interior is in general the area under the command of the Chief of Army Equipment and Commander of the Replacement Army. Special regulations provide for the division of authority whenever units or installations of the Replacement Army are stationed within the Theater of Operations, as has happened with the pushing back of the front lines into Germany. In such cases the field commander has no authority over the units or installations in ques-

tion; he may not conscript German males found in the area or make requisitions of horses or motor vehicles, for example, since this would upset the long-range and nation-wide programs of the Home Command for the utilization of personnel and equipment. Only under absolute military necessity may a field commander assume control of units or installations of the Replacement Army, and he must then immediately notify the Commander of the Replacement Army. The latter, on the other hand, must consult the field commander on any matter of fundamental importance affecting the area of joint interest. This arrangement well illustrates the careful distinction which the Germans make between the functions and authority of the Field Army and those of the Home Command.

Within the Communications Zone, the Army Group Rear Area (when it exists) is placed under the authority of a Commander of Army Group Rear Area (*Befehlshaber des rückwärtigen Heeresgebiets*), who has the status of a corps commander and is responsible to the Commander of the Army Group. His main tasks are to provide for the military administration of the area and to protect the security of the lines of com-

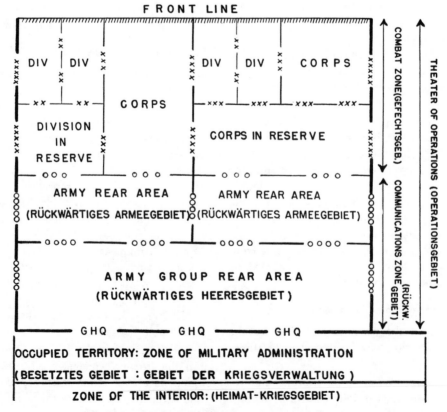

Figure 7.—Organization of the Theater of War.

munication so that the army group commander can devote himself entirely to combat operations. Similarly, the Army Rear Area is controlled by a Commander of Army Rear Area (*Kommandant des rückwärtigen Armeegebiets*) with the status of a division commander. The rear area commanders have at their disposal security (*Sicherungs*) units and police troops and set up various types of administrative headquarters.

6. Administration of Occupied Territory

In occupied territory, or the Zone of Military Administration (which in some cases has been the "friendly" territory of nations allied to Germany), the administrative structure is distinct from the operational control of any German combat units stationed in it. In France before the Allied landing in 1944, for example, the Military Administration under General von Stülpnagel was responsible for local security and for dealing with the French authorities and the population, but had no direct connection with von Rundstedt's army group which was stationed there for operational purposes. Distinct from both these commands were the training units in reserve divisions stationed in France, which came under the control of the Commander of the Replacement Army in Berlin for training and replacement purposes.

Typical of the flexibility of the German system was the great variety shown in the forms of military administration in the different occupied countries. In each case the form of German military control was adapted to the strategic needs as well as to the political, economic, and psychological factors. In Denmark there was officially no control at all, since the country was regarded as "protected" and not occupied; the German troops stationed there came under a Commander of German Troops in Denmark, while the administration of the country was left to the constitutional Danish government, subject only (until 1944) to German diplomatic pressure. At the opposite extreme was Poland, where no remnant of the previous native administration remained and the Germans had to have tight military control and even do most of the local policing. In France and some other countries the Germans worked largely through the native authorities but also set up their own administrative area headquarters (*Oberfeldkommandanturen*) and sub-area headquarters (*Feldkommandanturen*) as the local garrison commands.

Section V. FUNCTIONS OF THE CORPS AREA

I. Introduction

As has been shown, the Home Command in wartime is responsible for the replacement of personnel, the procurement of equipment, and territorial administration and defense. Most of these functions are exercised through the regional corps areas, which are the permanent basis for the organization and administration of the German Army. It is these functions which are discussed in this section.

A few functions of the Home Command are performed on a basis other than the territorial one of corps areas and are not included here. By far the most important of these is the procurement, acceptance, storage, and issue of ordnance materiel, which is handled by the Army Ordnance Office and the Ordnance Inspectorate operating through their own regional organization; this function is discussed in detail in Chapter VI below. Other types of supplies, with the exception of gasoline and lubricants, are administered by the corps areas after procurement policies have been established by the High Command.

2. Corps Area Responsibilities

The functions of the corps area headquarters in wartime may be divided into those which it performs as a territorial command and those which accrue to it as the deputy headquarters of a peacetime army corps which is now in the field. As a territorial command it is responsible to the Armed Forces High Command and has responsibilities affecting all three branches of the Armed Forces; in this capacity it is officially referred to as Corps Area Headquarters . . . (*Wehrkreiskommando* . . .). In its other capacity it is under the Army High Command alone and is referred to as Deputy Headquarters of the . . . Army Corps (*Stellvertretendes Generalkommando . . . Armeekorps*); as such it is responsible for the replacement training system for all the field units which are affiliated with it.

The following are the principal responsibilities of this combined headquarters:

Conscription of manpower, carried out through a system of conscription offices. (See Section VI of this chapter below.)

Training, conducted in training units which come under controlling staffs of regimental and division status and in military schools. (See Section VI.)

Replacement of personnel for the affiliated field units and formation of new units. (See Section VI.)

Local defense is provided for, in the first instance, by static units of various types, particularly the local defense battalions (*Landesschützen-Bataillone*), local construction units (*Landesbau-pioniere*), and river guard units (*Landespioniere*). Such units are controlled by a special administrative division staff (*Divisions-Kommando z.b.V.*), of which one was set up in each corps area early in the war. They provide guards for vital installations and for prisoner of war camps and furnish personnel for local garrison battalions (*Standortbataillone*) and companies. In case of emergency the corps area commander has extraordinary powers over civilian agencies as well as the military units and installations in his territory; he may then, for example, issue orders to the provincial and local authorities, commandeer transport and supplies, and take any other steps necessary until outside help arrives.

Any General Headquarters units of the Field Army which are temporarily stationed in the corps area are controlled by the corps area headquarters through its special administrative division staff (*Div. Kdo. z.b.V.*) or other appropriate command channel.

Auditing of the accounts of all field units affiliated with the corps area is another responsibility.

All military personnel, regardless of their own unit affiliation, are subject to the curfews and other disciplinary regulations issued by the local garrison commander within the corps area. These regulations are enforced by a patrol service maintained by the corps area headquarters as well as by the garrison headquarters. In all territorial matters the corps area commander has a large degree of autonomy. He allots units to garrisons and determines the areas controlled by the garrison commanders. He also controls the Corps Area Administration (*Wehrkreisverwaltung*) and its subordinate administrative offices so far as their activity concerns the troops stationed in the corps area.

3. Corps Area Headquarters Organization

The various responsibilities of the corps area commander and the corps area headquarters are reflected in the composition and functions of his regular staff and attached special command staffs.

In principle, the staff is organized like any normal corps staff. The differences result from the fact that it has, not an operational, but a replacement mission; furthermore it is not a mobile, but a static organization. Thus, for example, Section I b, which in a field unit handles supply of equipment and ammunition, is in this case also responsible for the supply of manpower and for sending replacements to the Field Army; Section I c, normally intelligence, is not primarily concerned with obtaining information about the enemy but with counterintelligence and security; and Sections II, personnel, and IV a, administration, are expanded, Section II serving also as the depository for personnel records while Section IV a is incorporated into the large and semi-autonomous organization of the Corps Area Administration (*Wehrkreisverwaltung*).

The staff is headed by a Chief of Staff (*Chef des Stabes*) and includes the following sections:

Section I is responsible for such matters as training, quarters, air raid protection, gas defense, transportation, training films, surveying and mapping, engineer units, and technical supervision of utilities in military installations.

Signal matters are handled in the I a Section by the Commander of Signal Troops (*Kommandeur der Nachrichtentruppen*). He in turn has a staff of his own concerned with training, activation, and replacement of signal units, supervision of radio traffic, static telephone installations, signal equipment, and female auxiliaries.

Section I b handles the supply of ordnance equipment and ammunition for units stationed in the corps area. As an echelon in the control of manpower, this section supervises the conscription offices (*Wehrersatzdienststellen*) and is responsible for issuing the orders for the transfer of replacements to units of the Field Army in response to their requisitions.

Section I c handles counterintelligence and security to the limited extent that the corps area headquarters participates in these activities. It also is concerned with Armed Forces propaganda and press relations, as well as the training and employment of interpreters. Formerly this section also handled troop welfare, morale building, and recreational activities; later, these became the responsibility of the National-Socialist Guidance Officer (*Nationalsozialistischer Führungsoffizier*) who is an independent staff officer in charge of a newly created section of the staff.

Section II, the personnel section, is divided into

Subsections II a, dealing with officer personnel, and II b, concerned with enlisted personnel. Subsection II a keeps individual records for all professional officers regardless of where they are employed and handles the recruiting of officer candidates and awards of decorations. Subsection II b deals with transfers and detachment of individual enlisted men to schools or for other duty. It does not keep individual records for enlisted personnel, as these are kept by the conscription offices. It also handles the recruiting of potential officer and noncommissioned officer candidates (*Annahmestellen für den Führernachwuchs*), deferment of essential workers, and furloughs and discharges.

Section III is headed by the corps judge (*Korpsrichter*); however the corps area headquarters is not an important echelon for legal matters.

Section IV a, administration, is headed by the *Korpsintendant* who at the same time has charge of the Corps Area Administration (*Wehrkreisverwaltung*).

Section IV b is headed by the Deputy Corps Surgeon (*Stellvertretender Korpsarzt,* also called *Wehrkreisarzt*), who advises the commander on medical questions and has a staff of his own. Under him special medical officers (*Truppenärzte*) supervise discharges for medical reasons which are handled through army discharge bureaus (*Heeresentlassungsstellen*).

Section IV c is the Deputy Corps Veterinarian (*Stellvertretender Korpsveterinär,* also called *Wehrkreisveterinär*), who has his own separate staff.

Section IV d comprises the Protestant and Catholic corps area chaplains (*Wehrkreispfarrer*).

Motor transport (*Heeres-Motorisierung*) is handled by a separate staff section, sometimes called Section V or referred to as the Corps Area Motor Transport Officer (*Wehrkreiskraftfahroffizier*). It deals with the issue of licenses for military drivers and vehicles; allocation and distribution of military vehicles, tires, equipment, gasoline, and oil; traffic control; and the supply of vehicles.

Independently of this section there exists a Commander of Motor Maintenance Troops (*Kommandeur der Kraftfahrparktruppe*), who controls motor maintenance training units, motor maintenance and repair parks, and parks for spare parts and tires. This commander is sometimes, if not always, the same man as the Corps Area Motor Transport Officer.

On the staff of each corps area headquarters a Section F, Welfare (*Fürsorge*), controls the activities of welfare officers (*Fürsorge-Offiziere*) who give advice and assistance to professional soldiers who are discharged or about to be discharged. All discharged non-professional soldiers are taken care of by the Ministry of Labor.

This section represents that part of the German Welfare and Pensions (*Fürsorge und Versorgung*) organization which is administered by the corps area commander. The other part, Pensions (*Versorgung*), is handled on a different level, the chain of command going from the Armed Forces High Command to one of three regional Welfare Groups (*Versorgungsgruppen*) which are located at Berlin, Breslau, and Munich. These control the Welfare and Pension Offices (*Fürsorge- und Versorgungsämter*), of which there is one in each corps area. These offices, which do not form part of the corps area organization, grant pensions for discharged professional soldiers and their dependents. The reason for the separation of these offices from the control of the corps area commander is the desire to achieve uniformity in the administration of pensions throughout the entire Reich.

Attached to the staff of each corps area headquarters is a Commander of Prisoners of War (*Kommandeur der Kriegsgefangenen im Wehrkreis . . .*), who is in charge of all prisoner of war camps in the corps area. He controls camps for officers (*Offizierslager* or *Oflag*) and camps for enlisted personnel (*Mannschafts-Stammlager* or *Stalag*), both types being designated by the Roman numeral of the corps area and distinguished by letters, as XII A, B, etc.

The Commander of Military Police Patrols (*Kommandeur des Streifendienstes*) is the superior of all road and railway patrols. He is directly subordinate to the corps area commander and works in close liaison with the garrison commanders.

The Officer for Military Economic Affairs (*Wehrwirtschaftsoffizier*) handles, for the corps area commander, all questions of military economics having a territorial bearing; he is at the same time a direct representative of the Armed Forces Economic Office in the Armed Forces High Command and liaison officer to the regional armament inspectorates (*Rüstungsinspektionen*) of the Ministry for Armaments and War Production (*Ministerium für Rüstung und Kriegsproduktion*).

4. Garrison Headquarters

The local territorial responsibilities of the corps area commander are exercised through Armed Forces Senior Garrison Officers (*Wehrmacht-Standortälteste*). In garrisons with permanent headquarters (*Kommandanturen*), or on maneuver areas (*Truppenübungsplätze*), the commander (*Kommandant*) is automatically the senior garrison officer.

If the majority of the units or installations in a garrison belong to the Navy or Air Force, the senior garrison officer may be taken from these branches of the Armed Forces instead of from the Army, but he remains subordinate to the corps area commander.

The area of the garrison town and its immediate vicinity is designated as the garrison district (*Standortbezirk*), its boundaries fixed by the senior garrison officer with the approval of the corps area commander. Within this district the senior garrison officer is fully responsible for discipline, local defense, and related matters on behalf of the entire Armed Forces; enlisted personnel, for example, require a pass to leave the garrison district.

All parts of the corps area which are not included in garrison districts are allotted by the corps area commander to so-called garrison areas (*Standortbereiche*), which are placed under the control of existing senior garrison officers for the exercise of the same functions as within the districts.

If there is an airport (*Fliegerhorst*) within the garrison district, it is treated as an autonomous district and placed under the command of a German Air Force officer.

The senior garrison officer is authorized to commandeer soldiers and horse-drawn vehicles in his area to do work for the general purposes of the garrison. In case of emergency he may mobilize special detachments.

The senior garrison officer issues regulations for garrison guards and patrols and cooperates with units of the Armed Forces Patrol Service (*Wehrmacht-Streifendienst*). He is responsible for local defense measures, especially for the air raid protection of all installations belonging to the Armed Forces, and for the efficiency of the air raid protection services.

The senior garrison officer is responsible for the maintenance of military discipline among all members of the Armed Forces within his territory; all military personnel on leave have to report at the garrison headquarters within 48 hours, and the senior garrison officer may declare certain restaurants or streets off limits.

5. Corps Area Administration

a. GENERAL. All administrative matters in the German Army are controlled at the top by the Army Administration Office (*Heeresverwaltungsamt*) in the Army High Command. Under this office the administrative agencies within Germany are organized on a territorial basis, with the Corps Area Administration (*Wehrkreisverwaltung*) as the next lower echelon. Below this, these matters are handled by the local garrison administrations (*Heeres-Standortverwaltungen*) and other specialized types of local administrative agencies. This entire system operates independently of the tactical chain of command. The word "administration" (*Verwaltung*) in the German Army covers primarily pay, rations, clothing, and billeting.

b. DUAL POSITION OF THE CORPS AREA ADMINISTRATION. The degree of independent authority of the Corps Area Administration in carrying out its duties depends on the nature of the subject matter, which is divided into two basic categories: those in which the Corps Area Administration acts independently of the Corps Area Headquarters and is responsible only to the Army Administration Office, and those in which it acts on the orders of the corps area commander. In the latter type of subject, the Corps Area Administration functions as the IV a, or administrative section, of the corps area staff, and these subjects are usually referred to as "IV a matters". They are mostly matters connected with the administration of the corps area headquarters itself or of the units directly subordinate to it.

The matters in which the Corps Area Administration acts independently are those which derive from its status as a responsible echelon in the territorial administrative structure. In these matters it has its own direct administrative channels, upwards to the Army Administration Office and downwards to the local garrison administrations. They include the following categories:

Pay, accounting, social insurance, and allowances.

Procurement, storage, and issue of utensils and general equipment.

Supervision of the handling of food in processing plants and in the ration depots.

Billeting, so far as it is not determined by the military decision of the corps area commander.

Building and civilian contracts.

Personnel matters of all administrative officers in the Corps Area Administration, its subordinate agencies, and Field Army units maintained by the corps area.

Training of administrative officers. In principle this separation into "IV a matters" and independently handled administrative matters is carried down to the lowest administrative echelons, although the scope of their independent authority is less comprehensive than that of the Corps Area Administration. This basic division of the administrative authority is characteristic of the dual functions and responsibilities of the administrative service of the German Army.

The head of the Corps Area Administration is an administrative officer in the Special Troop Service (*Truppensonderdienst*) with the title *Korpsintendant* who is at the same time the head of Section IV a of the staff of the corps area commander. As head of the Corps Area Administration the *Korpsintendant* is directly subordinate to the Army Administration Office; as a staff officer he is subordinate to the commanding general.

c. FUNCTIONS OF THE CORPS AREA ADMINIS-

TRATION. The principal function of the Corps Area Administration consists in supervising the various local offices in the corps area which constitute the executive organs of administration. The local administrative offices are:

Army garrison administrations (*Heeres-Standortverwaltungen*).

Army ration main depots (*Heeres-Verpflegungshauptämter*) and army ration depots (*Heeres-Verpflegungsämter*).

Hospital administrations (*Lazarettverwaltungen*).

Clothing offices (*Bekleidungsämter*).

Construction offices (*Heeresbauämter*).

Administrative offices of units of battalion or higher status located in the corps area (*Zahlmeistereien*).

An additional function of the Corps Area Administration is auditing the accounts of the battalion administrative officers (*Truppenzahlmeister*) of Field Army units affiliated with the corps area, wherever they are located. It may issue instructions to these officers, but they are technically subordinate not to it but to the Field

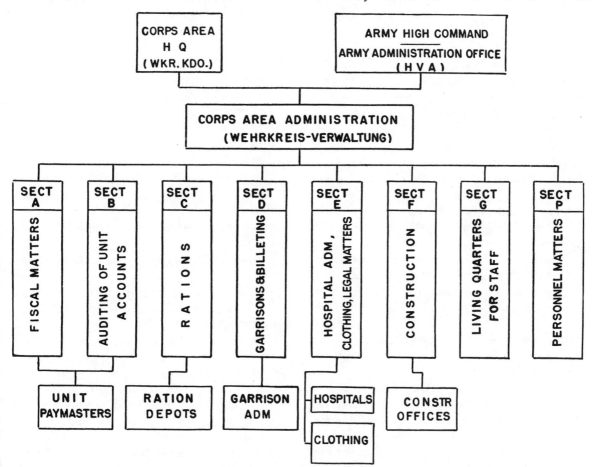

Figure 8.—Corps Area Administration.

Army administrative headquarters at higher echelons.

The Corps Area Administration is also responsible for personnel matters of administrative officers in units affiliated with the corps area and serves as their replacement unit. It also trains such officers.

d. ORGANIZATION OF THE CORPS AREA ADMINISTRATION. Corresponding to its responsibilities the Corps Area Administration is subdivided into the following sections (*Sachgebiete*):

Section A: Fiscal matters; interpretation of pay regulations; travel, moving, and transportation allowances; welfare and pensions; vocational schools of the Army; office equipment; libraries; general rules for cashiers, bookkeepers, and auditors; office regulations for paymasters.

Section B: For the duration of the war this section is known as the auditing office (*Abrechnungsintendantur*). It audits the accounts of unit paymasters in the field and of ordnance installations in the corps area.

Section C: Rations; procurement, administration, and issue of rations through the ration depots; procurement of forage for the remount depots; bakeries; troop-kitchens; ration supply for the troops while on maneuvers; auditing of the accounts of the ration depots and of those garrison administrations with a "rations" department; auditing of the accounts of the remount depots.

Section D: Supervision of the garrison administrations; auditing of their accounts; billeting; administration of real estate.

Section E: Administration of hospitals; auditing of their accounts; questions concerning civilian workers; legal matters so far as not dealt with in any of the other sections; clothing; supervision of clothing depots and auditing of their accounts.

Section F: Construction matters; supervision of the construction offices; civilian contracts.

Section G: Procurement of living quarters for members of the staff of the Corps Area Administration.

Section P: (P I) Personnel matters of the administrative officers. (P II) Personnel matters of civilian workers.

e. SPECIAL ADMINISTRATIVE HEADQUARTERS. Comparable with the Corps Area Administrations, but in a special position, is the Administration for Central Army Tasks (*Verwaltung für Zentralaufgaben des Heeres*). This office is organized in the same way as the Corps Area Administrations and carries out the administration for *OKH*-controlled establishments in Corps Area III such as demonstration units, army specialist schools, academies, and other institutions.

f. SUBORDINATE ADMINISTRATIVE AGENCIES. Of the various local administrative agencies subordinate to the Corps Area Administration, those which deal with rations and clothing form part of the organization of supply and are therefore dealt with in detail in Chapter VI below.

The most important of the remaining local offices are the garrison administrations (*Heeres-Standortverwaltungen*).

As a rule there is a garrison administration in every garrison and on every maneuver area; it is always designated by the name of the garrison town. Large cities may have more than one garrison administration.

The head of the garrison administration is an administrative officer who is appointed by the Army High Command and who is directly subordinate to the *Korpsintendant*. The head of the garrison administration is not on the staff of the garrison commander, and there is no subordination of the garrison administration to the garrison commander. The two are expected to cooperate closely, but in practice this dual authority leads at times to difficulties which have to be adjusted by agreement between the Corps Area Administration and the corps area commander.

The garrison administration normally consists of the following departments:

Real estate management (*Grundstücksverwaltung*).

Garrison finance office (*Heeresstandortkasse*).

Pay records for civilian workers (*Standortlohnstelle*).

Pay records for soldiers (*Standortgebührnisstelle*).

Utensils and general equipment depot (*Gerätelager*).

The real estate department handles the main task of the garrison administration, which is the management and utilization of the real estate including training area, and the erection, maintenance, and administration of the buildings and other installations owned or rented by the Army. Excluded from these are the garrison hospitals (*Standortlazarette*) and the installations of the remount depots, which are taken care of by these organizations themselves.

The garrison finance office has the task of making payments and keeping books and accounts for the garrison administration and the construction offices (*Heeresbauämter*). It also keeps the surplus cash for other local offices of the Army. Affiliated with a garrison finance office are all small unit pay offices (*Zahlstellen*) and branch pay offices (*Nebenzahlstellen*), which are only allowed to make cash payments and which therefore use the garrison finance office for other types of payment.

The pay office for civilian workers keeps the pay records for these groups and instructs the garrison finance office to make the corresponding payments.

The department handling pay records of soldiers in the field determines the regular service pay (*Wehrmachtbesoldung* for professional soldiers and *Kriegsbesoldung* for all other soldiers) and makes the corresponding payments through the garrison finance office to their accounts or dependents.

The utensils and general equipment depots store tools, utensils, and office equipment used in barracks and other installations. Such utensils and general equipment are procured by the Corps Area Administration, which orders one or several of the larger garrison administrations to effect the purchases for the entire area and store the goods.

Another type of local administrative agency is the hospital administration (*Lazarettverwaltung*). This is subordinate to the Corps Area Administration as well as to the medical officer in charge of the hospital. It deals independently, under the supervision of the Corps Area Administration, with payments, bookkeeping, and accounting for the hospital. In its concern for the medical personnel, officials, and hospitalized soldiers in matters of pay, rations, and clothing it occupies the same position as the administrative office (*Zahlmeister*) of a unit staff. With regard to the administration of the real estate and buildings belonging to the hospital it has the same responsibilities as the garrison administration has for other property.

Army construction offices (*Heeresbauämter* and *Heeresneubauämter*) are established by the Army High Command, which also appoints the head of the office and determines the size of his staff. The work of the construction offices is supervised by the Director of Construction (Section F) in the Corps Area Administration. Within their district Army construction offices deal with the technical side of the construction,

repair, and maintenance of buildings owned or rented by the Army and give advice to the other administrative agencies.

6. Medical Service and Installations

a. MEDICAL SERVICE. Within the Armed Forces the administration of the medical services and the use of the medical installations and facilities in Germany have been centralized to a high degree. In considering the medical organization of the Replacement Army it should be borne in mind that these facilities, to a varying degree, are also at the disposal of the other branches of the Armed Forces and of the *Waffen-SS*.

The Chief Army Medical Inspector (*Heeressanitätsinspekteur*), whose activities are supervised by the Armed Forces Surgeon General (*Chef des Wehrmachtsanitätswesens*), is stationed at the headquarters of the Commander of the Replacement Army but does not form part of his staff. He works through his own staff, the Army Medical Inspectorate (*Heeressanitätsinspektion*), which is part of the General Army Office (*Allgemeines Heeresamt*). He is the head of the medical services of the Field Army as well as of the Replacement Army. The Chief Army Medical Inspector is the superior of the medical personnel of the Army in disciplinary matters and questions concerning medical work. He decides on the assignment and promotion of medical officers.

Within the limits of the directives issued by the Armed Forces Surgeon General he has the following responsibilities:

Training of medical personnel.

Direction of the medical service including hygienic and sanitary measures in the Army.

Evacuation and hospitalization of casualties and the administration of all military hospitals.

Supply of drugs and medical equipment for the Army.

The permanent medical installations in Germany comprise medical units, hospitals, and supply installations which are all organized on a strictly territorial basis.

b. CORPS AREA SURGEONS. In the Replacement Army the channels of command go through the chief medical officers of the corps areas. These officers have a dual title. They are called deputy corps surgeon (*Stellvertretender Korpsarzt*) for orders which concern the troops and emanate from the deputy corps headquarters (*Stellvertretendes Generalkommando*), and corps area surgeon (*Wehrkreisarzt*) in all territorial matters which are handled under the authority of the corps area headquarters (*Wehrkreiskommando*). In this dual capacity they are on the staff of the corps area commander and head the IV b (medical) section of this staff. They are therefore subordinate to the commander of the corps area as well as to the Chief Army Medical Inspector. Within their territory the chief medical officers of the corps areas have the same functions and responsibilities as the Chief Army Medical Inspector.

c. MEDICAL UNITS. The corps area surgeons control the medical replacement battalions (*Sanitäts-Ersatzabteilungen*), one in each corps area, which train medical replacements for the Field Army. They also control the medical battalions (*Sanitäts-Abteilungen*), which during the war comprise all the medical personnel other than those in training, serving in the Replacement Army with units or in general hospitals. Each corps area usually has two or three medical battalions, which are designated by their headquarters town.

The medical battalions are composed of medical sections (*Heeres-Sanitätsstaffeln*) of varying size. The medical sections are the local sub-units of the medical battalions and generally can be found in every permanent garrison and every maneuver area. They are designated by the name of the garrison town.

The commander of the medical section is the local representative of the corps area surgeon and also serves as the garrison surgeon (*Standortarzt*) and head of the IV b section on the staff of the senior garrison officer. The garrison surgeon is therefore subordinate to the senior garrison officer as well as to the corps area surgeon. The garrison surgeon also controls the military hospitals in his area.

d. HOSPITALS. In peacetime all the larger garrisons had permanent garrison hospitals (*Sandort-Lazarette*). In addition there existed several Army tuberculosis hospitals (*Lazarette für Lungenkranke des Heeres*) and Army sanatoriums (*Kurlazarette des Heeres*).

In wartime all these hospitals are designated general hospitals (*Reservelazarette*). Thus the garrison hospitals became *Reservelazarette,* the tuberculosis hospitals *Reserve-Lazarette für Lungenkranke,* and the sanatoriums *Reserve-Kurlazarette.* In addition Army convalescents' homes (*Heeres-Genesungsheime*), general hospitals for

prisoners of war (*Reservelazarette für Kriegsgefangene*), and other types were created.

Since the peacetime facilities were entirely inadequate for the wartime needs, a large number of civilian institutions and suitable buildings such as civilian hospitals, hotels, and schools were taken over and converted into general hospitals. The general hospitals are designated by the name of the town, and Roman numerals if there is more than one general hospital in the town—for example *Reservelazarett Kassel III.* If a general hospital controls wards in separate buildings these usually are called part-hospitals (*Teillazarette*). The capacity of a general hospital may vary anywhere from 100 to 1,000 or more beds.

The medical personnel of a general hospital belong to the medical section (*Heeressanitätsstaffel*) which is stationed in that particular town or district. They therefore are affiliated permanently with one of the medical battalions (*Sanitätsabteilungen*) of the corps area.

For the purposes of medical supervision, general hospitals, with an aggregate of about 5,000 beds in a given area of the *Wehrkreis,* are grouped together into general hospital districts (*Reservelazarett-Bezirke*) which are under the supervision of senior medical officers.

The majority of the general hospitals are equipped and staffed to deal with a fairly wide range of casualties and diseases, but a few of them specialize, such as general hospitals for blind soldiers or for soldiers with brain injuries. In the military medical organization, the main types of casualties and diseases are indicated by a system of code numbers, running from 1 to 21, in order to facilitate the distribution of casualties to those hospitals which are best fitted for their treatment.

For the purposes of evacuation and distribution of casualties each general hospital in a given area is subordinate to a transportation headquarters (*Transport-Kommandantur*), where a medical liaison officer handles all these questions. The distribution itself is based on daily reports from the general hospitals to their local distributing centers (*Kranken-Verteilungs-Stelle*) giving the number of unoccupied beds.

All general hospitals form part of the Replacement Army and therefore, as a rule, all soldiers sent to a general hospital automatically are transferred from the Field Army to the Replacement Army. At times, when the Theater of Operations has extended into Germany proper, this rule has been modified, so that soldiers who are sent to general hospitals in the corps areas near the combat zone are transferred to the Replacement Army only after having stayed in the general hospital for 8 weeks; this is the same period that applies to field hospitals.

7. Veterinary Service

a. CONTROL. At the head of the veterinary services of the Armed Forces is the Veterinary Inspector (*Veterinärinspekteur*), who is stationed at the heaquarters of the Commander of the Replacement Army. Although subordinate to the latter, he receives his instructions regarding questions concerning both the Field Army and the Replacement Army direct from the Commander-in-Chief of the Army.

The staff of the Veterinary Inspector is the Veterinary Inspectorate in the General Army Office (*Allgemeines Heeresamt*).

The Veterinary Inspector is the superior of all veterinary and horse-shoeing personnel in all matters concerning their professional or vocational activity. He makes suggestions to the Army Personnel Office for the appointment of the higher ranking veterinary officers of the Army and makes these appointments himself for the lower ranks.

He instructs the Army Veterinarian (*Heeres-Veterinär*) with regard to the veterinary service in the Field Army, the evacuation of horses, and the replacement of horses and veterinary equipment.

In the Replacement Army the Veterinary Inspector directs the veterinary service in accordance with instructions given by the Commander of the Replacement Army. He is responsible for the training of veterinary and horse-shoeing personnel and the replacement of veterinary equipment. He gives the instructions for the distribution of horses evacuated from the field and their allocation to home horse hospitals (*Heimat-Pferde-Lazarette*).

In the Zone of the Interior the authority of the Veterinary Inspector is exercised through the deputy corps veterinarian (*Stellvertretender Korpsveterinär*), who is on the staff of the deputy corps commander as his IVc. He holds the alternative title of Corps Area Veterinarian (*Wehrkreisveterinär*) for his territorial functions.

Under the deputy corps veterinarian are the veterinary personnel and the veterinary installations located in his territory.

b. VETERINARY INSTALLATIONS. Each corps area has home horse hospitals (*Heimat-Pferde-lazarette*), to which are evacuated the horses which cannot be treated at the installations of the Field Army, and sick horses from the Replacement Army. The home horse hospitals are numbered with the Arabic number of the corps area, and if there is more than one horse hospital in a corps area they will be distinguished by adding 100, 200, etc., to the number.

Horses that have been cured go from the home horse hospital to a home horse park (*Heimat-pferdepark*). Each corps area has one home horse park. The Corps Veterinarian orders which horses from the home horse park are to go to the Field Army and which to the Replacement Army.

8. Other Installations

a. REMOUNTS. Army remount purchasing commissions (*Heeres-Remontierungskommissionen*) procure young horses for the Army. These commissions are outside the corps area structure and directly subordinate to the Army High Command.

The young horses purchased for the Army are stabled and maintained by Army remount depots (*Heeres-Remonteämter*) until they have reached the age for training in corps area riding and driving schools or delivery to troop units. The remount depots are independent of the remount purchasing commissions. They are subordinate to the corps area commander, but in certain respects they are under direct control of the Inspector of Riding and Driving at the Army High Command (*Inspekteur des Reit- und Fahrwesens*) so as to assure uniformity throughout all corps areas.

b. FORESTRY. The Army Forest and Fisheries Control Offices (*Heeres-Forstaufsichtsämter*) supervise the administration and utilization of forests and fisheries connected with properties belonging to the Army, such as maneuver areas. In Germany proper there are two of these control offices, at Berlin and Wiesbaden, controlling the local offices in the Corps Areas I-XIII.

These local offices are called Army Forest Offices (*Heeres-Forstämter*); they in turn supervise forestry offices (*Heeres-Oberförstereien* and *Heeres-Revierförstereien*).

The Army forest and fisheries control offices act in conjunction with the respective corps area headquarters on matters concerning the troops and with the corps area administrations in fiscal and bookkeeping questions.

c. MILITARY PRISONS. Military prisons are inter-service institutions. They are not organized on a territorial basis but generally have several corps areas allotted to them.

There are various kinds of military prisons, each kind receiving prisoners of a different category. These prisoners originate from the Replacement Army as well as from the Field Army.

Wehrmacht-Gefängnisse, which are responsible directly to the Armed Forces High Command, receive soldiers who are condemned to terms for more than 3 months. They are also used for prisoners of war who are sentenced to terms of imprisonment.

Wehrmacht-Untersuchungsgefängnisse accept prisoners with sentences of up to 3 months.

Wehrmacht-Haftanstalten are subordinate to garrison headquarters and take prisoners with sentences of up to 6 weeks.

There is one *Wehrmacht-Festungshaftanstalt,* which takes soldiers whose sentences specify that they are to be confined to a fortress, i.e., that their offense is not a dishonorable one.

d. ARMED FORCES SIGNAL HEADQUARTERS (*Wehrmacht-Nachrichtenkommandanturen*) are designated by the towns in which they are located. They are regional liaison offices between the Armed Forces and the German Postal Service (*Deutsche Reichspost*). In addition to their liaison functions they collect data on installations for long-distance communications which are of military importance.

Section VI. CONSCRIPTION, REPLACEMENT, AND TRAINING

I. Introduction

This section deals with the entire system of personnel replacement for the Field Army. The units of the Field Army do not procure their own replacements independently. Replacements for the field units are obtained only through the specified units of the Replacement Army, and those for the units of the Replacement Army in turn come only through the home recruiting stations. Thus, the following main divisions of the replacement system are obvious:

Conscription—the function of the home recruiting stations (*Wehrersatzdienststellen*) under the Armed Forces High Command (*OKW*).

Replacement and Training—the primary function of the Replacement Army (*Ersatzheer*).

The following pages describe the machinery for the registration and supervision of those liable to service, their induction and training in one of the numerous replacement and training units and schools of the Replacement Army, their dispatch to a field unit, and their return to a replacement unit. The principle of affiliation between field and replacement units, the fact that developments in the Field Army are often preceded by corresponding developments in the Replacement Army, and the presence of units of the Replacement Army on the fighting fronts show that, although the German Army was divided into two parts in 1939, the Field Army and Replacement Army are closely interlinked and cannot be fully understood except as complementary parts of a whole.

2. Conscription System

a. HISTORICAL DEVELOPMENT. Systematic universal military training in modern times is an invention of the Germans and has been developed to its highest degree of refinement by them. It grew out of the mass armies which were necessary to overthrow Napoleon and was introduced by a Prussian law of 3 September 1814 as a part of the far-reaching army reforms initiated by Scharnhorst and his colleagues to cope with the new forms of warfare. Ever since then universal compulsory military service has existed in Germany, with the exception of the period from 1918 to 1935, when it was forbidden by the Treaty of Versailles.

b. BASIC LAWS. On 16 March 1935 the universal service system (*allegemeine Wehrpflicht*) was reintroduced by the Law Regarding the Structure of the Armed Forces (*Gesetz über den Aufbau der Wehrmacht*). This law stated in three short sentences that military service was to be based on the principle of universal liability, and that the Army was to be expanded (initially) to a strength of 36 divisions. This was followed on 21 May 1935 by the Military Service Law (*Wehrgesetz*), which established the purpose and scope of universal service, administrative control of civilian manpower, categories of manpower according to age and training status, rights and duties of military personnel, and methods of callup and discharge. This law, and the decrees issued under it, still govern the German conscription system after 5 years of war.

c. CONTROLLING AGENCIES. The execution of the system for exercising military supervision of men liable to military service and for examining and conscripting them from civilian life into the Armed Forces is a joint responsibility of the German civilian and military authorities.

(1) *Civilian.* The Minister of the Interior, controlling all police authorities and the ordinary local registration of the civilian population, is responsible for the registration of men liable for military service. This occurs through the local and district police authorities.

(2) *Civilian and military.* The Minister of the Interior and the Minister of War jointly issued and jointly apply the Decree regarding Military Examination and Drafting *(Verordnung über die Musterung und Aushebung),* which involves collaboration of the civilian and military authorities during the phase between first registration and induction. They were also jointly responsible for dividing each corps area into suitable recruiting areas and sub-areas in such a way as both to meet the military needs and to fit, so far as possible, the existing civilian administrative subdivisions of the country.

(3) *Military.* The Armed Forces High Command controls the machinery for the call-up, induction, and discharge of personnel. This includes the recruiting area and sub-area headquarters which examine and draft recruits and represent the military interests in the administrative control of civilian manpower before and after service.

(4) *Chain of military command.* This being a ma r which concerns all three branches of the Arme es, it is supervised by the Replacement Branch *(Abteilung Ersatzwesen)* of the Conscription and Recruiting Office *(Wehrersatzamt)* in the Armed Forces High Command *(OKW).* Emanating from this agency, orders are issued through the various *Wehrkreis* headquarters *(Wehrkreiskommandos, Wkr.Kdo.)* to the recruiting area inspectorates *(Wehrersatzinspektionen, W.E.I.)* and from there to the recruiting sub-area headquarters *(Wehrbezirkskommandos, W.B.K.).* These control the Military Reporting Offices *(Wehrmeldeämter, W.M.A.)* and set up from time to time in their districts the examining boards *(Musterungsstäbe, Must. Stb.).* Most *Wehrkreise* contain two or three recruiting areas, but *Wehrkeis VI,* comprising the populous Ruhr and Rhineland region, has four, while *Wehrkreise VII, XX, XXI, Böhmen und Mähren,* and *Generalgouvernement* consist of only one such area each. The number of recruiting sub-areas in each area varies between four and a dozen according to local needs. Each recruiting area is controlled by an Inspector of Recruiting Area *(Wehrersatzinspekteur),* who is

a general officer with the status and disciplinary authority of a division commander. (In some cases he may be a naval or air officer, since the recruiting system operates jointly for all three branches.) Recruiting sub-areas are commanded by lieutenant colonels or colonels selected from the class of officers whose suitability for active service in the field has ceased. They have the status of regimental commanders.

There are two recruiting sub-area headquarters which do not come under any *Wehrkreis* headquarters but directly under the Armed Forces High Command. The Recruiting Sub-Area Headquarters "Ausland" *(Wehrbezirkskommando Ausland in Berlin)* deals with the registration, control, deferment, and call-up of German citizens in foreign countries (occupied or neutral). During the war it has established branches abroad in occupied countries; in neutral countries it is assisted in its mission by the German consulates. The Maritime Recruiting Sub-Area Headquarters *(Wehrbezirkskommando See),* with its seat at Hamburg, has the supervision of manpower of all Germans in the merchant marine.

d. CLASSIFICATION OF MANPOWER. (1) *Basic concept.* "Military service is honorary service to the German people. Every German is liable to military service. In time of war, in addition to liability to military service, every German man and every German women is liable to service to the Fatherland." These are the opening clauses of the Military Service Law of 21 May 1935.

(2) *Extent of liability.* In time of peace all German males were liable to military service from their 18th birthday until the 31 March following their 45th birthday. (31 March is the end of the German fiscal year.) In East Prussia (separated from the rest of Germany by the Polish corridor), liability was extended until the 31 March following the 55th birthday. The Minister of War was empowered to extend liability in either direction in time of war, and it now extends from 17 (the class born in 1928) to 61 (the 1884 class).

(3) *Reserve status.* All men not doing their active military service are classified into the following categories:

Reserve I: Those under 35 who have completed their regular period of active service and been discharged. There are only very few fit men in this group today.

Reserve II: Those under 35 who have been

through a period of short-term training. This applied before the war to some of the older classes.

Ersatzreserve I: Fit men under 35 who have not been trained.

Ersatzreserve II: Unfit and limited-service men under 35 who have not been trained.

Landwehr I: Trained men between 35 and 45 (actually from 31 March of the year in which the 35th birthday occurs until the 31 March following the 45th birthday).

Landwehr II: Untrained men between 35 and 45.

Landsturm I: Trained men between 45 and 55 (actually from the 31 March following the 45th birthday until the 31 March following the 55th birthday).

Landsturm II: Untrained men between 45 and 55. (The two categories of *Landsturm* applied in peacetime only to East Prussia; they now include men up to 61.)

(4) *Exclusion.* The following categories of men are described as "unworthy to bear arms" and therefore "excluded from military service":

Those sentenced to penal servitude (*Zuchthaus*).

Those who do not possess the honorary civil rights.

Those subjected to "security and improvement" measures (concentration camp for supposed habitual criminals).

Those deprived of their "worthiness to bear arms" by a court martial.

Those sentenced for activities inimical to the state.

Jews also are excluded from military service, but in wartime are required to do other types of service.

(5) *Exemption.* Completely unfit men are released from liability to military service. Roman Catholics who have taken holy orders (*Subdiakonatsweihe*) were not conscripted in time of peace. No other category of person is exempt.

(6) *Deferment.* No German can be deferred for military service in peace or war for purely personal reasons or by reason of his dependency status except in cases of extreme hardship. Deferment of indispensable employees in essential industries may be applied for by the employer, but it is granted only according to a very rigid quota system. No general class of men is deferred, and each case is judged on its merits. Application for deferment must be repeated at frequent intervals.

e. CONSCRIPTION PROCEDURE. (1) *Registration.* Usually in the spring of each year in peacetime, under directives issued by the High Command, the incoming class (normally those who were turning 20 during the year) was summoned by the district police authorities (*Kreispolizeibehörde*) by means of public notices to appear at the local police stations for military registration (*polizeiliche Erfassung*). It should be noted that under the German administration system the local police always have a complete roster of all residents of their precincts, based on the required registration of residents.

After the outbreak of the war the older classes who had not been covered by this system were registered in a similar manner, and by the end of 1940 all the classes back to those born in 1900 had been registered. The upper age limit was later extended to the 1897 class, then to 1894, and finally in 1944 to the 1884 class. The incoming classes have been registered systematically, each class being summoned at a slightly earlier age than the previous one.

(2) *First examination.* Shortly after the registration the recruiting sub-area headquarters (*Wehrbezirkskommando*) issues orders for the holding of the first examination (*Musterung*) of the registrants. This is carried out according to local registration districts by an examining board (*Musterungsstab*) which included representatives of the military authorities, the district and local police, the civilian administrative authorities (municipalities or rural district), and the German Labor Service, as well as medical officers. On this occasion the registrants are classified according to their physical fitness. Since December 1943 the categories used have been: fit for regular service (*Kriegsverwendungsfähig—Kv.*); fit for limited service in the field (*bedingt kriegsverwendungsfähig*); fit only for labor service (*arbeitsverwendungsfähig — av.*); totally unfit (*wehruntauglich—wu.*); and temporarily unfit (*zeitlich untauglich*). Medical standards have been lowered progressively since 1942.

Following their medical classification the registrants are placed in a reserve category (normally *Ersatzreserve I*).

(3) *Drafting.* In peacetime final action on the question of whether or not each individual was to be called up for regular service was taken at a second examination or drafting (*Aushebung*). This was conducted by the same authorities as the first examination and resulted

either in a deferment or in definite assignment to a branch of service. The registrant then was told to go home and await orders. In wartime the procedure has been accelerated, and the drafting is now combined with the call-up.

(4) *Call-up.* The actual call-up *(Einberufung)* is issued by mail by the recruiting sub-area headquarters in the form of an induction order *(Gestellungsbefehl)* directing the registrant to report at a specified time at the headquarters of a unit (in wartime a replacement unit).

(5) *Induction.* Recruits reporting at a battalion headquarters are first subjected to roll-call and then distributed to the subordinate companies, where the final medical examination and actual induction *(Einstellung)* takes place. Induction is followed by a mental and physical test to determine the most suitable employment of each man and the administration of the oath of allegiance.

(6) *Volunteers.* Volunteer applicants for the officer and noncommissioned officer careers apply at reception centers for potential officers and noncommissioned officers *(Annahmestellen für den Führernachwuchs),* which come under the Inspector General for Potential Officers and noncommissioned officers *(GJF).* Within limits, the volunteers are given the privilege of selecting their arm or branch of service.

In January 1945 these reception centers were combined with the recruiting centers for the *Waffen-SS* to form new "Combined Recruiting Centers of the Army and *Waffen-SS*" *(Ergänzungsstellen des Heeres und der Waffen-SS).* Under Himmler's orders, one of these was established in each *Wehrkreis,* with branch offices in all major cities. They also deal with volunteers to the ranks for *Volks Grenadier* divisions and thus facilitate the distribution of manpower under *SS* control.

Volunteers to the ranks have been numerous during the war, though much less so than in 1914-1918. At the beginning of the war the lower age limit was 17 (instead of 18 for conscripts); it later was lowered to 16½ and then (in 1944) to 16. In the past 2 years a large proportion of the youngest age class has been induced by various kinds of pressure to volunteer, largely for the *Waffen-SS.*

(7) *Discharge.* Discharge before completion of the normal period of service was possible in peacetime if a man became "unworthy to bear arms" (by reason of conviction for a major criminal offense) or totally unfit, or if it was discovered that he had been inducted by error. Both this type of discharge and the normal discharge after two years of service were carried out by the unit itself. In wartime this has been modified. In order to be discharged from active service members of the Field Army first must be transferred to the Replacement Army, either by their own unit or by a hospital. In order to relieve these units, however, and to reduce the distance which the infirm soldier must travel to his place of discharge, army discharge centers *(Heeres-Entlassungs-Stellen)* have been established to handle medical discharge cases. The *Waffen-SS* has its own corresponding medical discharge center. In the German Air Force, the physical examinations for reception and discharge are given in both combined reception and discharge centers *(Annahme- und Entlassungsstellen),* which handle either procedure all the way through.

(8) *Foreigners.* Foreigners and stateless persons, in case they are classified as "racial" Germans, may volunteer for service in the German Army. If they live within Germany, applications are handled by the competent recruiting sub-area headquarters; if they live in foreign countries, they are dealt with by the Recruiting Sub-area Headquarters *Ausland* in Berlin. Volunteers from the Nordic countries (Norway, Sweden, Denmark, Netherlands, Belgium) may be inducted without the acquisition of German citizenship. Applications are handled by the Recruiting Sub-area Headquarters *Ausland* in Berlin.

Since about 1943 virtually all "racial" Germans living in Balkan countries under German domination have been required to "volunteer". The concept of "racial" Germans *(Volksdeutsche)* has been interpreted very widely by the High Command with the growing stringency of the manpower situation. Especially in the annexed areas of Poland, people who knew scarcely a word of German were classified as belonging to Section 3 of the German Racial List *(Abteilung 3 der Deutschen Volksliste);* this meant that they were vested with German citizenship for a probationary period of 10 years and were liable to military service but could not rise above the rank of private first class.

Many thousands of genuine foreigners from other occupied countries have been persuaded to join the German Army, often through political or economic pressure. The procedure for their enlistment has varied widely for different nationalities and at different times.

f. HANDLING OF CONSCRIPTS. The three branches of the Armed Forces submit to the Armed Forces High Command, their personnel requirements on the 15th of each month for the second month, following. According to the demands and the general replacement situation the various *Wehrkreis* headquarters then receive orders specifying how many men are to be inducted for each branch of the Armed Forces.

The Armed Forces High Command determines which age groups are to be drawn upon according to the type of service for which they are required. The *Wehrkreis* headquarters are bound by these arrangements but may accept volunteers of all age groups.

If men of a certain type are not available within the *Wehrkreis* where they are required, the Armed Forces High Command may order the transfer of recruits from one *Wehrkreis* to another.

Within the *Wehrkreis,* the *Wehrkreis* headquarters is responsible for distributing the replacement requisitions among the recruiting area and sub-area headquarters as rapidly as possible and with due regard to the varying characteristics of the population in different districts. City areas provide the best material for motorized units, country areas for cavalry and horse-drawn units. A mixing of rural and urban elements is to be aimed at in the interests of regional and national solidarity.

The Navy accepts volunteers from all parts of the *Reich.* For its seagoing personnel it has a priority on recruits who, by reason of their place of residence or previous experience, are classified as belonging to the "seafaring population" *(seemännische Bevölkerung); ;* to man its shore installations it takes conscripts from the Maritime *Wehrkreise—I, II, X,* and *XX.* The Air Force has a similar priority on conscripts (classified as part of the "aeronautical population" *(fliegerische Bevölkerung),* which includes those who have belonged to gliding clubs or who joined the aviation branch of the Hitler Youth.

The Army aims at assigning every individual conscript to the type of unit for which his physical condition, his civilian background, and his special abilities best fit him. With this in view, certain standing regulations have been introduced. Thus mountaineers called up in *Wehrkreise* that maintain no mountain units automatically are

transferred to *Wehrkreise* which do—from *Wehrkreise VI, XII,* and *XX* to *Wehrkreis VII* and from *Wehrkreise II, III, IV, VIII, IX, X, XI, XXI,* and *Böhmen und Mähren* to *Wehrkreis XVIII.*

In general, transfers from one *Wehrkreis* to another are not made unless there is a cogent reason for them, and they were not frequent until growing man-power difficulties began to make it impossible for some *Wehrkreise* to meet their obligations from their own resources. In principle, a conscript trains and fights in the company of men from his own province. One significant deviation from this policy was in the treatment of conscripts from the annexed areas of Poland, France, and Yugoslavia. Alsatians generally were sent for training to northeastern Germany *(Wehrkreis II)* and Poles to the Berlin area *(Wehrkreis III)* or to the southwest *(Wehrkreis V).*

3. Replacement Training System

a. BASIC PRINCIPLE. Every unit in the Field Army is affiliated for personnel replacement purposes with a specific unit of the Replacement Training Army, located in its own original *Wehrkreis* and known as an *Ersatz* unit. The function of the latter is to induct recruits, to provide for their training, and to see that they are held in readiness to be sent off to the field unit in batches or individually as required.

The normal location of the *Ersatz* unit is the home station of the affiliated field unit, to which the soldiers expect ultimately to return for their discharge or for reassignment. For example, a soldier who is wounded and goes to a reserve hospital in the Zone of the Interior will be sent, on leaving the hospital, to his affiliated *Ersatz* unit before being returned to the field.

Whenever feasible, trained replacements are sent by an *Ersatz* unit to a field unit with which it is affiliated. If, however, a man for any reason is diverted to a different field unit, or if he subsequently is transferred from one field unit to another, the affiliated *Ersatz* unit of his new field unit must be entered on Page 4 of his paybook under the heading "present competent *Ersatz* unit" *(jetzt zuständiger Ersatztruppenteil).*

In order to understand the intricacies of the present *Ersatz* system it is well to trace the successive stages of its development.

b. ORIGINAL OPERATION OF THE SYSTEM. Each infantry regiment which took to the field at

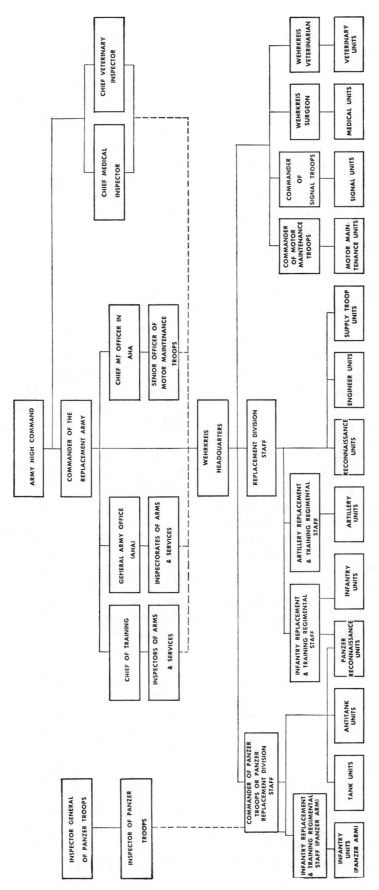

Figure 9.—Control of replacement and training units.

the beginning of the war left behind at its home station a battalion cadre bearing its own number and known as its *Ersatz* battalion. The primary purpose of this battalion was to receive recruits, train them, and dispatch them as replacements to the field regiment. At any given time it included one or more of each of the following types of companies:

Reception companies (*Stammkompanien*), consisting of new recruits and cadre personnel.

Training companies (*Ausbildungskompanien*), also known as *Rekruteneinheiten*. These companies provided for the training of the inducted untrained volunteers. After the training was finished the recruits joined the transfer company, if they were not transferred to the Field Army immediately.

Transfer companies (*Marschkompanien*) which were pools of trained replacements ready to depart for the field unit.

Convalescent companies (*Genesendenkompanien*), consisting of men released from reserve hospitals who were being prepared for return to the field. All other replacement training units are organized in a corresponding manner.

c. ORIGINAL AFFILIATION SYSTEM. The three replacement training battalions corresponding to the three infantry regiments of a field division were controlled by an infantry replacement training regimental staff (*Grenadier-Ersatz-Regiment—Gr.Ers.Rgt.*) bearing the number of the division. Thus, the 2d, 23d, and 44th Infantry Regiments, belonging to the 11th Infantry Division, were represented by the 2d, 23d, and 44th Infantry Replacement Training Battalions controlled by the 11th Infantry Replacement Training Regimental Staff at Allenstein in *Wehrkreis I*, the home station of the division. Replacement training regimental staffs usually were commanded by colonels.

The replacement training regimental staff also controlled from three to five infantry specialist replacement training companies which provided the personnel for the infantry howitzer companies, antitank companies, signal sub-units, engineer platoons, and mounted platoons of the three infantry field regiments.

The other components of the field division—the artillery regiment, reconnaissance battalion, antitank battalion, engineer battalion, and signal battalion, were affiliated in a similar way with replacement training units of their respective arms back in the *Wehrkreis* from which they came.

All the artillery replacement training battalions

in any *Wehrkreis* were controlled by two or more artillery replacement training regimental staffs bearing the numbers of artillery field regiments originally raised in that *Wehrkreis*. The replacement training battalions for the smaller divisional components likewise bore the numbers of some of the corresponding field units from the *Wehrkreis*, but usually one such replacement training battalion would provide replacements for the corresponding field battalions of several divisions. Altogether over 50 types of regular replacement training units existed.

d. CHAIN OF COMMAND IN THE REPLACEMENT ARMY. The replacement training units are subordinate to the *Wehrkreis* Headquarters (*Wehrkreiskommandos*) in their capacity as Deputy Corps Headquarters (*Stellvertretende Generalkommandos, Stv.Gen.Kdo.*) through the following intermediate staffs:

One or more Replacement Division Staffs (*Division Nummer ...., Div. Nr. ....*) controlling the replacement training units either directly, as in the case of independent units of the supporting arms and services (reconnaissance, engineer, supply troop replacement training battalions) or through several infantry and artillery replacement training regimental staffs (*Grenadier-Ersatz-Regiment, Gr.Ers.Rgt.* and *Artillerie-Ersatz-Regiment, Art.Ers.Rgt.*).

Possibly one *Panzer* Replacement Division Staff (*Panzer-Division Nummer ...., Pz.Div.Nr. ....*) or a Commander of *Panzer* Troops (*Kommandeur der Panzertruppen, Kdr.d.Pz.Tr.*) of either brigade or regimental status, controlling the replacement training units either directly, as in the case of the independent battalions (tank, antitank, and *Panzer* reconnaissance replacement training battalions) or through one or two motorized infantry or *Panzer Grenadier* replacement training regimental staffs.

The Commander of Motor Maintenance Units (*Kommandeur der Kraftfahrparktruppe, Kdr.d. Kf.Pk.Tr.*), controlling motor maintenance replacement training units.

The Commander of Signal Troops (*Kommandeur der Nachrichtentruppe, Kdr.d.Nachr.Tr.*), controlling signal replacement training battalions.

Wehrkreis Surgeon (*Wehrkreisarzt* in his capacity as *Stellvertretender Korpsarzt*), controlling medical replacement training units.

Wehrkreis Veterinarian (*Wehrkreisveterinär* in his capacity as *Stellvertretender Korpsveterinär*).

The Deputy Corps Commanders, who are not

only the commanders of the replacement training units but also commanders in the *Wehrkreis,* are subordinate to the Commander of the Replacement Army (*Befehlshaber des Ersatzheeres*). They have the right to shift the location of units of the Replacement Army within their areas but must notify the Commander of the Replacement Army.

The responsibility of the Commander of the Replacement Army and of his subordinate headquarters and offices for maintaining the Field Army on a wartime footing remains in effect when parts of the Replacement Army are located in the Theater of Operations.

The number of replacement division staffs in each *Wehrkreis* is regulated by the Army High Command. They are responsible for the uniformity of training in their subordinate replacement training units. They are to be kept free from all administrative duties. Regarding correspondence they are to participate only in what concerns the training, arming and equipment of replacement training units, as well as the maintenance of discipline (including proceedings of law) and the personal matters of their subordinate officers and officials. Should there be several replacement division staffs in one *Wehrkreis,* the deputy corps headquarters orders which replacement training units are subordinated to either one.

e. REQUISITIONING OF REPLACEMENTS. The field unit may request replacements if there is a deficiency of more than 10 per cent of their table of organization strength. Replacements for specialists, such as communication personnel or technicians, are to be requested as soon as their absence would hamper the efficiency of the field unit. Every independent field unit (regiment, independent battalion) sends its requests for replacements through channels to the division headquarters. The division forwards them direct to the competent deputy corps headquarters.

The deputy corps headquarters thereupon issues orders to the appropriate replacement units. The replacement division staffs usually are consulted only with regard to the state of training of the replacements before the deputy corps commander disposes of them. The commanders of the replacement training regimental staffs participate fully in this matter. If the records which every deputy corps headquarters has to keep show that the competent replacement training unit cannot provide all or any of the replacements, the deputy corps headquarters passes this order to another

replacement training unit. If an adjustment is not possible within the competent area, the Commander of the Replacement Army is notified and orders another *Wehrkreis* to provide the replacements. The replacement training units have to notify the deputy corps headquarters at once on what date the replacements will be ready to leave.

Although the requisitions are strictly channelized, direct relations between the field unit and the competent training unit at home always were considered desirable, in order to strengthen the feeling of comradeship. This was achieved not only through the personal connections but also through circular letters and newspapers.

f. LATER MODIFICATIONS OF THE REPLACEMENT TRAINING SYSTEM, 1939–AUTUMN 1942. (1) *Early change in the affiliation system.* The system of numerical affiliation between replacement training units and field units, applying particularly to the infantry units, was valid in general for the four initial waves of divisions sent to the field by each *Wehrkreis* in the summer and autumn of 1939. These were the "active", or peacetime, divisions, numbered from 1 to 36, 44, 45 and 46; those raised from reservists, numbered 52 to 98; those raised from *Landwehr* personnel, from 205 to 246; and those formed from so-called *Ergänzungs* units (special "supplementary" peacetime units for short-term training of men in the intermediate classes 1901 to 1913), from 251 to 269.

The component units of divisions formed subsequent to the initial mobilization period, on the other hand, usually were not given new replacement training units of their own, but were assigned, through the corresponding Deputy Corps Headquarters, an affiliation with existing replacement training units of their respective arms. Thus each infantry replacement training battalion eventually had to feed replacements to several field regiments, only one of which bore its own number. Similarly, when the infantry component in the *Panzer* divisions was increased from one regiment to two in 1940, the second regiment usually was affiliated with the existing replacement training battalion of the original regiment. Some replacement training units were converted outright into field units; on the other hand some field units were later dissolved. These changes tended to upset the principle of numerical affiliation, which underwent further changes in the following years.

It was the practice from the very beginning to collect groups of trained replacements of the various arms in the *Wehrkreis* and assemble them into loosely organized special personnel transfer battalions known later as *Marschbataillone* for the purpose of conducting them to the combat zone. Originally each such transfer unit normally was destined for a particular division, and often carried the number of that division, preceded by the Roman numeral of the *Wehrkreis* and followed by a serial number. Such battalions usually were attached to the rear echelon of the division in the field, and from there the personnel was filtered into the various divisional components as needed, or they filled up field replacement pools.

After the start of the Russian campaign, it was found expedient, in view of the long distances involved, to draw on these field replacement pools in some cases without regard to their *Wehrkreis* of origin or the division for which they originally were intended. Thus a division which had suffered particularly heavy losses might receive a large portion of the personnel which had been trained and dispatched to the field for a different division in an adjacent and less active sector. In other cases, all the divisions under a given corps or in a particular area would share a single field replacement battalion. In the African theater, for a time at least, there was only one field replacement battalion for all the divisions of the Africa Corps, although they came from different *Wehrkreise*. In the middle of 1941, moreover, all units in Africa were assigned affiliations with replacement training units in *Wehrkreise III* and *XII,* regardless of the location of their previous replacement training units; this was done in order to concentrate the specialized training which the men required for operations in the desert.

All such measures resulted in a further breaking down of the system of numerical affiliation and in some cases even a departure from the rule that the great majority of men in a given unit should come from the same *Wehrkreis*. It must be borne in mind, however, that all these, as well as all subsequent modifications up to the beginning of 1945 in the detailed operations of the replacement training systems, never have violated its basic principle : namely, that every field unit at all times must be affiliated with a specified replacement training unit to which all men leaving the Field Army are automatically sent.

(2) *Early movements of replacement training units.* Despite the fact that the original replacement training units were intended to remain at the home stations of their corresponding field units, acting more or less as the rear echelon of the latter, there have been numerous shifts of units in the Replacement Army from one part of Germany to another and from Germany into occupied countries and back again for varying reasons. From 1939 to 1941, when Germany still had neighbors to be attacked, the replacement training units were withdrawn from the border regions several months before an offensive was to commence in order to free the barrack space and other military facilities for the assembling of field forces. After the area was no longer being used for this purpose, the replacement training units generally returned to their home stations.

Replacement training units, with their controlling replacement division staffs temporarily thus transferred to another *Wehrkreis,* are subordinate to the deputy corps headquarters of this *Wehrkreis* for administrative purposes as well as for the general supervision of their training ; the replacement division staffs, however, are the direct recipients of requisitions of replacements from the field units in this case, and at the same time the contact with the home *Wehrkreis* was not completely broken off. New conscripts, normally given orders by their local recruiting sub-area headquarters to report to a replacement training unit not far from their home town, were sent in these cases either individually, or in small groups, on long train journeys before induction or were assembled in special collecting points known as *Wehrkreis-Ersatz-Depots*. The latter were also used for receiving men who returned from the field as convalescents or for any other reason. After the units returned to the *Wehrkreis* these depots were dissolved.

All these moves and a number of others, concurrent with or subsequent to them, served the additional purpose of garrisoning the annexed or conquered areas adjacent to Germany proper and thus relieved the field forces of this responsibility. At the same time barracks and training grounds in Germany were freed for the formation of new units for the constantly expanding German Army, and the recruits were given training away from home and under conditions more like those in the field. All these moves prior to the autumn of 1942 (except those whose primary motive was the evacuation of assembly areas) were by units in border *Wehrkreise* into adjacent occupied or annexed territory immediately across the border. The movements thus amounted to a slight extension of the German Zone of the Interior in all directions.

g. REORGANIZATION OF THE REPLACEMENT ARMY IN THE AUTUMN OF 1942. (1) *Principle.* The most far reaching change in the replacement training system took place on or about 1 October 1942 when all basic replacement training units were broken up into their two elements—one to handle induction and replacement and the other to handle training. The induction and replacement unit retained the designation *Ersatz.* But henceforth it was concerned only with receipt of recruits from the conscription offices; issue of their personal equipment and their paybooks; short military indoctrination of recruits; forwarding of recruits as speedily as possible to its sister training unit; receipt of convalescents and sending them back to a field unit; and with the processing of men from its affiliated field units who for any reason were to be discharged. The newly created training unit (*Ausbildungseinheit*) bore the same number as the *Ersatz* unit and was to receive the men from the *Ersatz* unit, give them their training, and then dispatch them to an affiliated field unit.

(2) *Movements following the reorganization.* The purpose of this measure apparently was to facilitate a shift of most training activities farther into the occupied countries, particularly in the west, without seriously affecting the efficiency of the induction and replacement procedure back in the *Wehrkreise.*

The disadvantages of the earlier removal of the replacement training units from their home stations, from the administrative point of view, were almost sufficient to outweigh the advantages. For this reason, none of the earlier moves except those dictated by military necessity were very far from home, and the practice of garrisoning more distant occupied territories with replacement training units never was resorted to under the old system. It was probably these considerations, as much as it was the growing shortage of man-power, which caused the German authorities, in September 1942, to divide all the basic replacement training units into their two parts, even though in some cases they were reunited under a new name. This made it possible for the replacement units to occupy their home stations, and for the training units to enjoy complete freedom of movement. The latter henceforth were used in large numbers to occupy different parts of France, the Low Countries, Denmark, Poland, Lithuania, the Soviet Union, and northern Italy in the form of reserve divisions. Combined training thus could be carried on under more realistic conditions, and numerous fully organized field divisions were released for service on active fighting fronts. In most cases the units from a given *Wehrkreis* went to the country nearest them. In the case of the basic infantry training units, approximately two-thirds moved out in this way, and only one-third remained within greater Germany.

(3) *Changes at battalion level.* Under the original system each infantry replacement training battalion, as already indicated, normally contained a reception company, four training companies, and one or more convalescent and transfer companies. At the time of the reorganization the training companies were withdrawn under the battalion staff, and a new replacement battalion staff was created to control the remaining components having purely replacement functions. In some cases, apparently, the new training battalion established a transfer company of its own as a pool for trained men awaiting transfer to the Field Army, while in other cases it seemed to send them to the transfer company of the replacement battalion.

In practice, the change took place in either one or the other of the following ways: In the case of replacement training units which were already in newly acquired or occupied territories in the autumn of 1942, the replacement elements in some cases returned to their home stations to resume their normal induction and replacement functions and retained the name *Grenadier-Ersatz-Bataillon,* etc. The training elements then usually were incorporated into reserve divisions and moved farther afield, receiving the name reserve battalion (*Reserve-Bataillon*), etc.; if they remained in Greater Germany they were called training battalions (*Ausbildungs-Bataillone*), etc. In other cases (both in Germany and in adjacent occupied or annexed territory) both elements remained in the same area and took the form of combined replacement and training battalions (*Ersatz- und Ausbildungsbataillone*).

The above remarks apply to the various other arms as well as to the infantry. Most of the service troops remained at their home stations as combined replacement and training battalions.

(4) *Changes at regimental level.* Many of their replacement training regimental staffs became staffs of reserve regiments (*Reserve-Regiment*) in occupied territory. The only regimental

staffs remaining in the *Wehrkreise* after the reorganization were combined replacement and training regimental staffs (*Ersatz- und Ausbildungs-Regimenter*). These controlled combined replacement and training battalions and specialists companies remaining in the *Wehrkreise*. In addition, new infantry replacement regimental staffs (*Grenadier-Ersatz-Regimenter*) were created to control replacement battalions and specialist replacement companies whose training elements had become reserve units. These new regimental staffs received new numbers mostly in the 500 series, and had no affiliation with a field division bearing the same number. However, some of the companies controlled by these new staffs retained their original numbers. Thus the original numerical affiliation system had almost disappeared at regimental level.

In the artillery the original regimental staffs that remained in the *Wehrkreis* took over the functions of those which went out to reserve divisions.

(5) *Changes at division level.* For occupational and defensive purposes, as well as for the conduct of combined training exercises, the reserve units in occupied territory were organized into a new type of training division known as a reserve division (*Reservedivision*) which still remained part of the Replacement Army. This was done in all cases except one by the conversion of one of the former replacement division staffs in the *Wehrkreise*. If not enough staffs remained in a *Wehrkreis* to supervise the induction and replacement activities of replacement units as well as the training of combined replacement and training units, a new staff was created, sometimes taking a number 300 higher than that of the departed reserve division. Other new replacement division staffs were created by conversions of special administrative division staffs (*Divisionskommando z.b.V., Div. Kdo. z.b.V.*) As a result the number of the replacement division staffs was only slightly diminished from 34 in September, 1942 to 29 in 1943. Each reserve division controlled a group of reserve regiments and supporting units from its own *Wehrkreis,* but the allotment of battalions within the regiment no longer followed the original pattern based on the subordination of infantry regiments to the field division of the same number. Sometimes the battalions took the numbers I, II, and III, and the regimental number, with or without addition of their own original numbers. In other respects,

also, the reserve divisions took on the character of defensive field divisions. For instance, some of them received divisional rear service units, numbered 900 plus the reserve division number. These services were part of the Field Army. This system of reserve divisions was developed steadily throughout 1943. After the summer of 1943 new reserve divisions also were formed from *Panzer* and motorized training units (*Reserve-Panzer-Divisionen*) which until then had been stationed in the Zone of the Interior.

(6) *Reserve corps.* To control the replacement functions of reserve divisions (i.e., the dispatch of trained replacements to the Field Army) a number of reserve corps (*Reservekorps*) and one or more reserve *Panzer* corps (*Reserve-Panzerkorps*) were formed. Orders issued to deputy corps headquarters relating to these functions were now also addressed to the reserve corps, indicating that they acted as channels for replacement requisitions in the same manner as deputy corps headquarters. However, at least some reserve corps controlled one or more defensive infantry divisions of the Field Army as well as their reserve divisions.

h. THE ULTIMATE FATE OF THE RESERVE DIVISIONS. Altogether, the training units of the different *Wehrkreise* formed 26 reserve divisions in 1942 and 1943, four of which were reserve *Panzer* divisions. Thirteen were in the West, seven in the East, three in Denmark, two in Croatia, and one in Italy. From this large number it is evident that field divisions were relieved from defensive and occupational duties to an appreciable extent. In 1943, even before the last reserve divisions were formed, a number of them were converted into divisions of the Field Army. Two of them in the East became field training divisions (*Feldausbildungsdivisionen, Feld-Ausb. Div.*), which, although retaining training functions in addition to their line of communication duties, no longer formed part of the replacement and training structure of their *Wehrkreise*. A third reserve division in Croatia was converted into a light (*Jäger*) division, and three other reserve divisions received the designation static (*bodenständige*) divisions.

Thus by the end of 1943, 23 reserve divisions were in existence including the three static divisions. During 1943 several of these divisions were engaged against partisans while others became firmly established along the Channel coast.

During 1944 the reserve divisions rapidly disintegrated. Of the five reserve divisions in the East, two were destroyed or disbanded, and three went into combat. The remaining reserve division in Croatia apparently was disbanded early in the year. All the 13 reserve divisions in the West disappeared. Three reserve *Panzer* divisions were merged with remnants of *Panzer* or *Panzer Grenadier* field divisions and lost their identity. Three reserve divisions on the Channel coast were converted to field divisions in February, 1944. Two others were disbanded in July and August, after giving up most of their personnel to divisions that had suffered heavy losses in the Invasion. The five reserve divisions in southern France and on the Biscay coast were engaged against the Allied landing in southern France and upgraded to field divisions. The reserve mountain division in Italy also may have been upgraded to a field division during the year. Of the three reserve divisions in Denmark, two appear to have remained intact during 1944, while the third was in the process of being converted. Thus by the end of 1944, a maximum of six to seven reserve divisions remained, of which perhaps only two were able to fulfill the functions for which they were originally created.

The reserve divisions had definite disadvantages as well as advantages. They were good for training and garrison functions during the winter of 1942-43 and for the greater part of 1943. But when they received definite defense assignments, especially on the Channel coast, they no longer could concern themselves with training. Neither could they afford to send trained replacements to field divisions and to replace them with untrained recruits and thereby imperil their combat effectiveness.

The seriousness of the situation was intensified by the fact that during 1942-43 two-thirds of the "training" had been moved out of Germany to take place in these reserve divisions. As a result, at a critical period the continuity of training had to be interrupted, and a new start made in the *Wehrkreise* within Germany.

i. RESUMPTION OF TRAINING WITHIN GERMANY. New training facilities had to be provided as one reserve division after another ceased its training functions. For a time, some of the reserve divisions had training battalions (*Ausbildungs-Bataillone*) which could train personnel without interfering with the new defense responsibilities of the reserve divisions. But following the Invasion in June 1944, recruits no longer were sent to the reserve divisions in the West.

Training gradually was resumed within Germany. At first some *Wehrkreise* dispatched recruits to existing training or combined replacement and training units of their own *Wehrkreise* within Greater Germany, and in one case even to the training units of a neighboring *Wehrkreis*. Subsequently first one and then other training companies were added within the different *Wehrkreise,* and replacement units were expanded into combined replacement and training units. By the late summer of 1944, virtually all replacement units in some *Wehrkreise* had regained their training functions and had become combined replacement and training units. This was especially the case with the replacement units of the former reserve *Panzer* divisions in the West. Other *Wehrkreise* did not start expanding their training facilities until late in 1944. In some cases the reforming of artillery training units preceded the reforming of infantry training units. In some instances, to help control combined replacement and training battalions in the infantry and facilitate their possible employment in the field, the old ratio of three replacement and training battalions to one staff was restored through a new wave of combined replacement and training regimental staffs.

The resumption of training was aided by the fact that pure replacement battalions had always maintained a skeleton force of instructors and cadre personnel to provide a minimum of training in the reception, transfer, and convalescent companies. Also many reserve divisions returned their instructors and cadres to their *Wehrkreis* when they were converted or disbanded.

j. DEVELOPMENTS DURING THE SUMMER AND AUTUMN OF 1944. In the summer of 1944, when the *Reichsführer-SS* took over the command of the Replacement Army, a number of trends became emphasized. Training hours were lengthened, and the training period was reduced to an average of 6 weeks. Air Force and Navy personnel were retained for the Army, and the *Volkssturm* was created. Paper work was simplified, and *Wehrkreis* borders were adjusted. Economy and simplification were achieved through:

(1) *Changes in the affiliation system.* A basic change of the affiliation system for infantry regiments occurred. A single infantry replacement battalion became the competent replacement unit

for all the infantry regiments of one infantry division or two static or security divisions. As a result, infantry regiments no longer had a replacement battalion carrying their own number, and the traditional relationship that originally existed between the old units of the Replacement Army and the Field Army thereby practically was abolished.

(2) *Economy measures.* Several infantry specialist replacement and training companies were combined, as were also some infantry specialist replacement and training battalions. A number of replacement and training battalions for service troops, especially for veterinary units, were disbanded.

(3) *New methods of transferring replacements to the Field Army.* New methods for requesting and transferring men from the Replacement Army to the Field Army were established in the first half of 1944. The manpower problem did not permit an even distribution of replacements (with the exception of specialists), but demanded a concentrated supply of men to units with the highest priority. To achieve this purpose army groups and independent army headquarters were charged with the allocation of replacements. The transfer of men from the units of the Replacement Army no longer took place by means of loosely organized groups but in one of the following principal ways: In combat transfer battalions (*Kampfmarschbataillone*) having a strength of about 900 men with better armament and larger cadre personnel than before; in transfer battalions of 700 to 1000 men; or in transfer companies of 100 to 250 men. The combat transfer battalion was newly created, whereas the transfer battalion for infantry and *Panzer* troops received the table of organization of the field replacement battalion. Convalescents were returned to the field in convalescent transfer companies (*Genesenen-Marschkompanien*) of 100 to 250 men. In general, however, the importance of the transfer battalion was diminished, in part because of the rapidly changing situation in the west. The name "combat transfer battalion" indicates that the battalion as such is considered a fighting unit.

k. REPLACEMENT ARMY UNITS IN COMBAT. In the first years of the war, replacement and training units as such took part in combat only in isolated instances. Yet during the Allied advance through France and Belgium in August 1944, and at the time of the Allied airborne landing in Holland, five or more replacement division

Wehrkreis	Inf Repl Bns (Inf arm)	Inf Repl Bns (Panzer arm)	Tk Repl Bns	AT Repl Bns	Arty Repl Bns	C W Repl Bns	Engr Repl Bns	Sig Repl Bns	Total of Repl Bns for Combat Troops	Affiliated Fld Divs (Inf arm)	Affiliated Fld Divs (Panzer arm)
I	25	2	1	1	7	—	3	1	40	11	1
II	16	1	—	1	8	—	3	1	30	16	1
III	23	10	1	2	6	—	8	1	51	15	8
IV	24	2	1	1	6	—	5	1	40	11	1
V	20	4	1	1	5	—	5	1	37	12	2
VI	29	5	2	1	8	—	6	2	53	20	4
VII	18	2	—	1	6	—	5	1	33	13	1
VIII	24	5	1	1	7	—	5	1	44	15	3
IX	18	7	2	1	5	—	4	4	41	17	4
X	18	2	—	1	6	6	3	2	38	16	1
XI	16	2	—	1	6	1	3	2	31	17	2
XII	25	2	1	1	7	—	6	1	43	13	1
XIII	21	3	1	1	7	—	3	1	37	11	2
XVII	19	2	2	1	6	—	4	1	35	11	2
XVIII	9	—	—	1	4	—	3	1	18	7	—
Total:	305	49	13	16	94	7	66	21	571	205	33

Figure 10.—Distribution of combined replacement and training battalions for combat troops and affiliated field divisions by Wehrkreise at the end of 1944.

staffs from the four western *Wehrkreise* were transferred to the Western Front with the combat elements of their subordinate units.

The untrained recruits, unfit convalescents, and cadre personnel necessary for maintaining the replacement and training schedule remained behind. In some instances, a "reserve" staff probably stayed at the home station to control replacement elements and rebuild the training structure. These hastily collected divisions received a variety of names, of which "combat divisions" (*Kampfdivision*, also *Div. Nr. .... (K)*) seems to have been the most common. Five such divisions were actually in line, and a sixth was in charge of fortification work. The subordinate units originally kept the numbers they had in the Replacement Army, but later were renumbered as organic field units. Four of the former replacement division staffs were upgraded to field divisions, and a fifth was dissolved. In addition, the border *Wehrkreis* furnished numerous independent battle groups, block units (*Sperrverbände*), and other units, which eventually were absorbed by various field units at the front. Local defense duties of the replacement and training units are fulfilled by alarm units (*Alarmeinheiten*).

1. STRENGTH AND DISTRIBUTION OF THE REPLACEMENT ARMY AT THE END OF 1944. The accompanying table (*Figure 10*) shows by *Wehrkreise* the distribution of replacement battalions for combat troops and affiliated field divisions at the end of 1944.

Each of the 15 *Wehrkreise* existing at the outbreak of the war has, in addition to the replacement battalions for combat troops, one to three replacement division staffs, and two to five infantry replacement regimental staffs. Most of the latter control three to four infantry specialist replacement companies. Each of these *Wehrkreise* (except *I* and *XVIII*) also has one to two *Panzer Grenadier* or motorized replacement regimental staffs, containing two or three specialist replacement companies and one to two artillery replacement regimental staffs. The infantry replacement battalions of both these arms contain reconnaissance battalions. In addition, there are two chemical warfare replacement regimental staffs in *Wehrkreis X*. The many other replacement units—mostly of service troops, such as supply troops, motor maintenance troops, and medical troops—are not represented in the table since there is generally only one in each *Wehrkreis*.

Also not represented are the four important replacement and training brigades for the *Grossdeutschland, Feldherrnhalle,* Croatian, and "999" units, which are outside the regular series of replacement units.

Wehrkreis XVIII has mostly mountain troops. *Wehrkreis XX, XXI, Böhmen und Mähren,* and *Generalgouvernement* are omitted, since they control only a very few units. Since units in *Wehrkreise XX* and *XXI* are connected with *Wehrkreis II,* and units in *Wehrkreis Böhmen und Mähren* properly belong to *Wehrkreise XIII* and *XVII,* they are listed under *Wehrkreise II, XIII,* and *XVII, respectively.* In general, units are listed under the *Wehrkreis* that controls them, and not necesarily under the *Wehrkreis* in which they are located. Although the units in the table have been designated simply as replacement units most of them are actually combined replacement and training units.

The strength of battalions will fluctuate greatly, depending upon whether they have just received new recruits or convalescents or depleted their organization by sending replacements to the field. Thus some battalions in the table may have a strength of 500 men and others over 1500.

Affiliated field divisions are given to permit a comparison between the replacement units and "their" field units. General Headquarters troops and disbanded or destroyed field divisions are not included, and converted field divisions could not be attributed to a specific *Wehrkreis.* The present affiliation is the controlling one, even though the division was mobilized in another *Wehrkreis.*

Demonstration regiments and battalions and the many military schools contain additional reserves of manpower. With the latter, however, attached *"kommandiert"* personnel is carried by the old unit and not by the school.

At the end of 1943 there were possibly 2,000,000 men in the Replacement Army; at the end of 1944 there were probably considerably less. On the whole, units of the Replacement Army were remarkably stable during the 5 years of war, with regard to type, number, and in some cases also with regard to the location of the replacement elements.

However, major changes did occur in the replacement division staffs, regimental staffs, and specialist companies in the years 1942 to 1944. Most of the units dissolved were in the artillery battalion series. Additional units or new types

Headquarters Infantry Division
Headquarters Infantry Division ....Infantry Replacement and Training Battalion
   Division Map Section...........................3d Battalion Motorized Artillery Demonstration Regiment
   Military Police Squad...........................Military Police Replacement Regiment
Infantry Regiment
   (2d and 3d Regiments like the 1st Regiment)
Headquarters Company......................Infantry Replacement and Training Battalion
   Cyclist Platoon............................Reconnaissance Replacement and Training Battalion
   Engineer Platoon ....Infantry Engineer Replacement and Training Company
   Communication Platoon ....Infantry Signal Replacement and Training Company
Infantry Battalion ....Infantry Replacement and Training Battalion
   (2d Battalion like the 1st Battalion)
Infantry Howitzer Company.........................Infantry Howitzer Replacement and Training Company
Antitank Company ....Infantry Antitank Replacement and Training Company
Division Füsilier Company ....Reconnaissance Replacement and Training Battalion
Antitank Battalion
Motorized Antitank Company.......................Antitank Replacement and Training Battalion
Armored Tank Destroyer Company....................Antitank Replacement and Training Battalion
Antiaircraft Machine-gun Company....................Antiaircraft Machine-gun Replacement and Training Battalion

Artillery Regiment
Headquarters Battery ....Light Artillery Replacement and Training Battalion
1st Antitank Artillery Battalion.......................Light Motorized Artillery and Training Battalion
2d and 3d Artillery Battalions..........................Light Artillery Replacement and Training Battalion
4th Artillery Battalion.............................Medium Artillery Replacement and Training Battalion
Engineer Battalion ....Engineer Replacement and Training Battalion
Signal Battalion ....Signal Replacement and Training Battalion
Field Replacement Battalion
Cadre Personnel ....Infantry Replacement and Training Battalion
Supply Regiment
Headquarters Troop ....Motor Transport Supply Troop Replacement and Training Battalion
   Motor Transport Supply Company.................Motor Transport Supply Troop Replacement and Training Battalion
   Supply Troop (Horse-Drawn) ....Supply Troop Replacement and Training Battalion
   Supply Platoon ....Supply Troop Replacement and Training Battalion (Horse-Drawn)
Ordnance Company ....Local Defense Replacement and Training Battalion
Workshop Company ....Motor Maintenance Replacement and Training Battalion
Administrative Company
   Bakers and Butchers............................Administrative Training Replacement and Training Battalion
   Drivers ....Motor Transport Training Replacement and Training Battalion
   Other Personnel ....Local Defense Replacement and Training Battalion
Medical Company ....Medical Replacement and Training Battalion
   Ambulance Platoon ....Medical Replacement and Training Battalion
Veterinary Company ....Veterinary Replacement and Training Battalion
Field Post Office...............................Field Post Replacement and Training Battalion

Figure 11.—Replacement affiliation of a division, late 1944.

---

of units were created whenever necessary, often preceding developments in the Field Army, as witnessed by the formation of assault gun, and *Panzer* howitzer replacement and training battalions, mortar training companies, and replacement and training battalions for troops with stomach and ear ailments.

m. EXAMPLE OF AFFILIATION BETWEEN A FIELD DIVISION AND ITS REPLACEMENT AND TRAINING UNITS. The table above shows how the replacement training system, although greatly

modified, is worked out to the smallest detail. The table was valid for a *Volks Grenadier* division as late as November 1944. The replacement units shown are mostly of the combined replacement and training type, even though they are designated as replacement units.

n. RECENT DEVELOPMENTS. After the Allied advance through France in August 1944, most of the replacement and training units from the outlying areas of the western *Wehrkreise* were withdrawn farther east within the *Wehrkreise*. Evidently efforts were being made to preserve the replacement and training structure within the *Wehrkreise,* even though they were part of the Theater of Operations. A similar attempt was made in *Wehrkreis I* on the Eastern Front. In some instances, replacement units were moved to another *Wehrkreis,* but then only to locations just across the boundary.

Late in 1944, *Wehrkreis XII,* the middle one of the western *Wehrkreise,* moved some of its replacements far inland into the central *Wehrkreise.* These units, however, still remain at the disposal of *Wehrkreis XII.*

Early in 1945 affiliation between replacement units and field units was still valid as affiliation from the field unit to the replacement unit, but generally not in the other direction.

4. Training

a. INTRODUCTION. (1) *Types of training establishments.* The general military training of the German soldier takes place principally in the training units of the Replacement Army, although a certain amount of training also is given in its replacement units. Training units also are prepared to conduct special courses in order to provide some types of specialized personnel, as required by the Field Army, and to secure a pool of personnel trained with particular care as potential officers and noncommissioned officers. In addition to these general training units, numerous schools and courses have been established with the specific purpose of training potential officers and noncommissioned officers. Other schools, designated as special-service schools (*Waffenschulen*), have the function of providing specialized training for officers and enlisted men of their particular branch of service, developing its arms, equipment, and tactics with the help of their demonstration units, and furnishing instructors for the Army. In addition, specialist training schools are established to provide instruction for ordnance officers, technical officials, and particularly noncommissioned officer-technicians, or for officers and noncommissioned officers of all arms and services as specialists in certain particular functions, such as air raid and gas protection.

(2) *Chain of command.* The training in most types of replacement and training units, which are under the command of the *Wehrkreis* headquarters exercised through intermediate staffs, is coordinated by the Chief of Training in the Replacement Army. He exercises his authority through the Inspectors of Arms and Services, who issue directives regarding the particular training in their arms to the *Wehrkreis* headquarters. These directives are based on tactical doctrines worked out in detail by the Inspectorates of Arms and Services in the General Army Office, which, in turn, follow instructions from the Chief of Training and his Inspectors.

The directives for the training of *Panzer* troops are issued by the Inspector General of *Panzer* Troops, who is directly subordinate to Hitler. The training of medical troops is directed by the Chief Army Medical Inspector, who is directly subordinate to the Army High Command, and that of veterinary troops by the Chief Veterinary Inspector, immediately under the Armed Forces High Command.

The training of potential officers and noncommissioned officers wherever it occurs, takes place either under the command or under the supervision of the Inspector General for Potential Officers and noncommissioned officers. His authority is restricted to supervision when this type of training takes place in establishments under the command of the Chief of Training, the Inspector General of *Panzer* Troops, or any *Wehrkreis* headquarters. Special-service schools and specialist training schools are under the command of the Chief of Training with the exception of the Schools for *Panzer* Troops, which are commanded by the Inspector General of *Panzer* Troops.

(3) *Supplementary training.* The paragraphs below describe how the various types of training units and schools discharge their functions. It should be kept in mind that these functions are supplemented in many ways. A considerable part of the military training in Germany is given in the form of pre-Army training by other military and auxiliary organizations. Special abilities found in various civilian occupations are put to use by the Army, and only personnel with a certain professional background are trained for a number of technical employments within the Army. Civilian establishments sometimes are used for the training of Army personnel; for example, technical courses often are conducted in factories producing special types of equipment.

b. GENERAL TRAINING. (1) *Organization of training units.* In principle, the training unit is a true image of the field unit which it supplies with trained replacements. Thus, the infantry

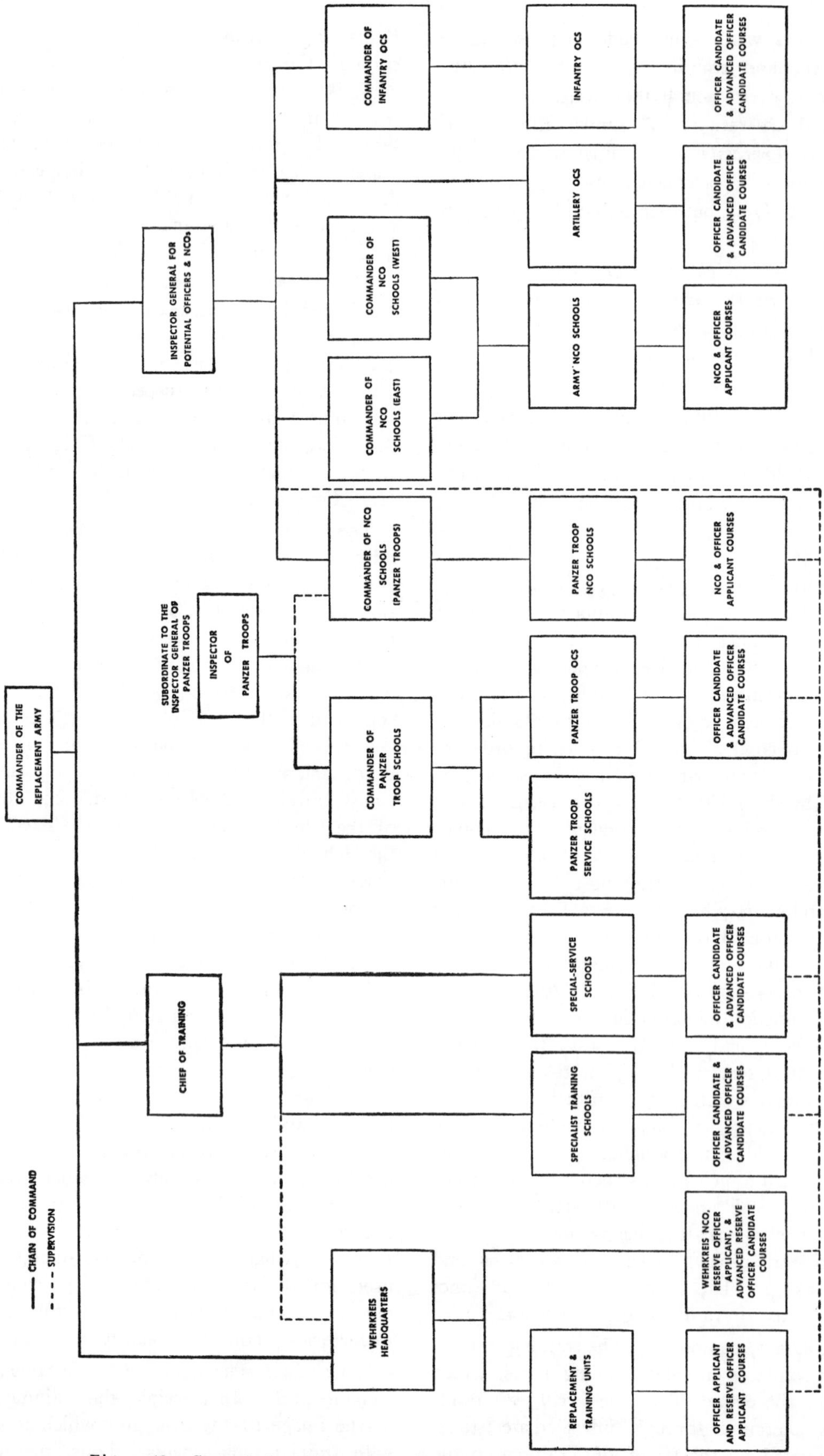

Figure 12.—Control of training of potential officers and noncommissioned officers.

training battalion, just like any battalion of an infantry regiment, consists of the 1st, 2d, and 3d rifle training companies, and the 4th machine-gun training company. This principle has been somewhat modified, however, in order to take advantage of specialized training personnel and to expedite the training; thus, drivers of horse-drawn vehicles, for example, usually are not trained within each training company but combined into a special detachment within the battalion. The infantry training regimental staff, in accordance with the normal (pre-1944) composition of a regular infantry regiment, usually controls three infantry training battalions, a 13th infantry-howitzer training company, and a 14th infantry anti-tank training company; in addition, however, it often has controlled a 15th infantry signal training company, and every second or third staff a 16th infantry engineer training company to furnish trained personnel for the signal platoons in battalion headquarters and the signal and engineers platoons in the regimental headquarters company. Recently, a 17th mortar training company has been added to train crews for the heavy mortars, introduced into the 4th and 8th companies of the infantry regiments of regular infantry divisions. Only one training company for infantry mounted platoons in each *Wehrkreis* trained replacements for the mounted platoons of all the infantry regiments under its responsibility.

Recent developments, including the introduction of new weapons and the growing scarcity of training personnel in conjunction with the increasing pressure of time, have accentuated the tendency of concentration and specialization of training, and continuous reorganizations of the field divisions have made the similarity between field and training units less and less evident.

(2) *Program in training units.* The main responsibility for the training of recruits rests with the commander of the training unit of company size (company, battery, troop). The detailed training schedule is prepared within the framework of the company. The battalion commander supervises the progress of the training in the companies of his battalion and inspects the recruits at the end of their basic training. The commanders of higher echelons coordinate the training in the units under their command and supervise it. They are also responsible for the education and training of officers and potential officers and noncommissioned officers within these units. The latter are often placed in special companies within the training battalions and regiments.

The basic training (*Grundausbildung*) in infantry training units normally is planned for 16 weeks; actually this period now is reduced to 8 weeks in most cases. This period may be followed by an indefinite period of advanced training (*Erweiterungsausbildung*), lasting up to the time of transfer of the recruits to a field unit. The basic training usually is divided into three parts, the first of which is devoted to individual training, the second to the training of the individual recruit within the framework of the squad, and the third to the training of the squad within the framework of the platoon. During the advanced training period, the scope of training is amplified to include exercises on reinforced company or, in artillery and chemical warfare troops, even battalion level. The basic training components, listed in order of the importace attributed to them, are: combat training, firing, lectures, drilling, sports. The drill for the modern German soldier is far from what is generally believed; drilling of the famous goose-step is not permitted, and "present arms" is not taught.

(3) *Training in replacement units.* Although according to their organization basically not equipped for training purposes, the replacement units nevertheless perform training functions on a reduced scale. This is done in three ways:

After their induction into a replacement unit which is not stationed in the same location as its corresponding training unit, the recruits immediately are combined into training groups to undergo a one to three-week period of preparatory training (*Vor-Ausbildung*) until they can be sent to a training unit.

Regular training functions are performed in the convalescent components of replacement units. Their purpose is to restore the health and physique of convalescents until they regain full fitness for field duty, and also to select and train instructors for the training units. For the latter purpose special courses are conducted by the convalescent units.

After regaining their fitness for field duty, the convalescents are sent to the transfer components (*Marschkompanien*, etc.) of their replacement units, where they are given advanced training until the time of their transfer to a field unit.

c. NONCOMMISSIONED OFFICER TRAINING. (1) *General categories.* The two basic categories of noncommissioned officers are the ones enlisting for either 12 or 4½ years, called active or professional noncommissioned officers, and the conscripts promoted to noncommissioned officer's rank, called reserve noncommissioned officers. The active noncommissioned officers may either serve in ordinary noncommissioned officers' functions in the various arms and services or they may receive specialized training as technicians. Typical training establishments for ordinary noncommissioned officers are the Army noncommissioned officers' schools (*Heeres-Unteroffizier-Schulen*), for technicians the specialist training schools and the special-service schools (*Waffen-Schulen*) of chemical warfare troops, engineers, and signal troops. In peacetime, noncommissioned officers serving 12 years were, at the end of their service, trained for civilian occupations in Army vocational schools (*Heeresfachschulen*) and Armed Forces vocational schools (*Wehrmachtfachschulen*); in wartime, this vocational training is restricted to the rehabilitation of men no longer fit for service. The reserve noncommissioned officers receive special training in noncommissioned officer courses (*Unterführer-Lehrgänge*), which may be conducted in the Field Army as well as in the Replacement Army at various echelons.

(2) *Ordinary noncommissioned officers. (a) Selection.* In peacetime and to an even larger degree, in wartime, the German High Command considers the possession of a highly qualified noncommissioned officer corps as of vital importance for the effectiveness of the Army and endeavors by all means of propaganda to fill its ranks. For the professional noncommissioned officer corps two sources are open:

Volunteers for the noncommissioned officer career may apply at the age of 16½ years and, if accepted by a selection center for potential Army officers and noncommissioned officers, enter the Army at the age of 17 as noncommissioned officer applicants (*Unteroffizier-Bewerber,* usually abbreviated *U.B.*). Some of these may have had pre-Army training for this career as junior cadets (*Jungschützen*) in Army noncommissioned officer preparatory schools (*Heeres-Unteroffizier-Vorschulen*).

Conscripts already in service who wish to enlist for either 12 or 4½ years must have a good record as leaders in combat, instructors, and disciplinarians. They can enlist only after one year's service and are finally accepted only after 2 years' service. Only those are accepted for a 12-year term

who will be not over 38 years of age at the end of their service period; the age limit for men enlisting for 4½ years is 28 years. If acceptable, these men are appointed noncommissioned officer applicants by their battalion commanders.

(b) *Training of noncommissioned officer applicants.* The noncommissioned officer applicants belonging to units of the Replacement Army are normally educated and trained at the Army noncommissioned officer schools. Up to February 1944, the training period of a noncommissioned officer applicant volunteer at an Army noncommissioned officer school was 10 months. The first 4 months were devoted to basic training, and during the remaining 6 months the applicant received training as a squad leader in his particular branch of service. In February 1944, the basic training was removed entirely from the Army noncommissioned officer schools, and the applicant volunteers thenceforth were to be sent to training units of their appropriate arms for basic training, together with the other recruits inducted at the same time. The advanced training period, for applicant volunteers and appointed applicants alike, was reduced to 5 months for branches having Army noncommissioned officer schools of their own, and to 3 months for some specialized branches, whose applicants are trained at schools of related branches. These periods may be supplemented by an additional period of 1 or 3 months, respectively, spent in training units, making a total advanced training period of 6 months before the applicants graduate from the Army noncommissioned officer school and are promoted to privates first class (*Gefreite*). They then are transferred to a field unit.

At present, there are about 22 Army noncommissioned officer schools for infantry, one for mountain infantry, seven for *Panzer* troops, two for artillery, two for engineers, and one for signal troops. These schools are usually organized like a battalion of their respective arms; the Army noncommissioned officer schools for *Panzer* troops are specialized in one of the main branches of this arm (*Panzer Grenadiers,* tank crews, antitank personnel, *Panzer* reconnaissance personnel).

Men enlisting for long-term service while serving in the Field Army (*Kapitulanten des Feldheeres*) may take part either in a noncommissioned officer applicant course conducted by a field headquarters, especially in a divisional combat school, or in a course at a field noncommissioned officer school (*Feld-Unteroffizier-Schule*). In their training, these schools approach field conditions to a much larger degree than the Army noncommissioned officer schools; their training periods last only about 2½ months. There is one field noncommissioned officer school for each of the three most important arms: infantry, *Panzer* troops, and artillery. They originally were located in occupied territories, but now apparently have been removed to Germany proper. They are believed to be organized like a regiment of their respective arms, including some or all of its more important special branches.

(3) *Noncommissioned officer technicians. (a) Selection.* A number of careers as technicians (*Sonderlaufbahnen*) are open for active noncommissioned officers who, as a rule, must have enlisted for 12 years; exceptions are the medical technicians, blacksmith technicians, and musicians, who will also be accepted if they enlist for the 4½-year period. For most of these careers, qualified professional backgrounds are required. Upon

terminating their enlistment period, most of these technicians have the opportunity, after taking additional courses at the appropriate specialist training schools, to become advanced technical or administrative officials.

(b) Training. In addition to an apprenticeship in Army units or headquarters required for most of the technician careers, courses of varying length are conducted for the various types of technicians at the specialist training schools and some special-service schools. In many cases, short or wartime courses have been established to supply sufficient personnel for the wartime Army; the men participating in these courses, however, usually will not become full-fledged technicians upon graduating from these courses but only after taking additional courses at a later opportunity. These men are not necessarily active soldiers; if they did not enlist for long-term service, they are designated as reserve noncommissioned officer technicians.

NCO Technician	German Designation	Training School	Length of Course Peace	War (where known)
Supply Technician (H-Dr T)	Schirrmeister (F)	Army Riding and Driving School	12 months	
Supply Technician (MT)	Schirrmeister (K)	School for Army Motorization	4 months	
Supply Technician (Engr)	Schirrmeister (P)	Engineer School 2	3 months	
Supply Technician (Tech Engr)	Schirrmeister (PT)			
Supply Technician (Ry Engr)	Schirrmeister (EP)	Railway Engineer School		
Supply Technician (CW)	Schirrmeister (Ch)	School for Chemical Warfare Troops	7 months	4½ months
Supply Technician (SL)	Schirrmeister (Sch)	Spandau Army Equipment Depot	6 months	
Supply Technician (Ord)	Schirrmeister (Fz)			
Ordnance Technician	Feuerwerker	Army Ordnance Technician Schools I and II	18 months	6 months
Weapon Technician	Waffen-Unteroffizier	Army Weapon Technician Schools I and II	12 months	3-5 months
Signal Supply Technician	Funkmeister	Army Signal School II	9 months	3 months
Pigeoneer	Brieftaubenmeister	School for Dog and Pigeon Service	7 months	
Fortress-Engineer Technician	Festungspionier-Unteroffizier	Fortress Engineer School	3 years	
Fortress Maintenance Technician	Wall-Unteroffizier	Fortress Maintenance School	12 months	
Medical Technician	Sanitäts-Unteroffizier	Medical schools	9 months	
Blacksmith Technician	Beschlagschmied-Unteroffizier	Army Blacksmith schools	4 months	2 months
Musician Technician	Musiker			

The table on page 73 shows the various types of technicians, the duration of their courses, and the schools conducting these courses.

(4) *Training of reserve noncommissioned officer applicants.* Conscripts who are acceptable as future noncommissioned officers and are considered for promotion, but who are not enlisting for a definite service period, are appointed reserve noncommissioned officer applicants (*Reserve-Unteroffizier-Bewerber* usually abbreviated *R.U. B.*) by their battalion commanders. The training of the reserve officer applicants normally takes place at *Wehrkreis* noncommissioned officer courses (*Wehrkreis-Unterführer-Lehrgänge*), although reserve officer applicants recently have also been trained at Army noncommissioned officer schools. Each of the original *Wehrkreise* has one *Wehrkreis* noncommissioned course, usually located at a maneuver area within the *Wehrkreis* itself or in a neighboring *Wehrkreis*. These courses are more or less organized like infantry regiments, but often include, in addition to regular infantry components, other types of specialist sub-units, such as a reconnaissance troop, a mortar training company, or a field howitzer battery. In some *Wehrkreise*, sub-units of the *Wehrkreis* noncommissioned officer course for arms other than infantry may be established with existing training units or Army noncommissioned officer schools of these arms. In *Wehrkreis IX,* in addition to its regular *Wehrkreis* noncommissioned officer course, such a course for *Panzer* troops has been identified.

(5) *Training of noncommissioned officers for special functions.* A number of noncommissioned officers are employed in functions requiring special training without being technicians. These may be trained within their own or other units or headquarters by practical experience and apprenticeship, or in special courses conducted by units or headquarters (in the field usually by the division combat schools, in the Replacement Army by the *Wehrkreise*), or at specialist training schools.

(a) *Training by practical experience.* First sergeants (*Hauptfeldwebel*), clothing supply sergeants (*Bekleidungs-Unteroffiziere*), and similar types of special function noncommissioned officers usually are trained in this manner.

(b) *Training in special courses conducted by units and headquarters.* This type of training usually applies to company clerks (*Rechnungs-führer*) and to supply sergeants for weapons and equipment (*Gerät-Unteroffiziere*).

(c) *Training at specialist training schools.* Gas protection noncommissioned officers (*Gasschutz-Unteroffiziere*) take courses at Army Gas Protection Schools 1 and 2, or at the *Wehrkreis* gas protection courses. Other noncommissioned officers receive special training in fire fighting at the Army Air Raid Protection School or at the *Wehrkreis* air raid protection courses. Field cook noncommissioned officers (*Feldkoch-Unteroffiziere*), mess sergeants (*Küchen-Unteroffiziere*), and mess clerks (*Küchenbuchführer*) are trained at *Wehrkreis* cook schools or by field cook instruction staffs.

(6) *Training of intelligence personnel.* Linguists who may be employed as interpreters (*Dolmetscher*) in all branches of the Army, but particularly as intelligence personnel, usually hold the position of specialist leaders (*Sonderführer*) regardless of their actual noncommissioned officer or officer rank. They receive linguistic and intelligence training in the interpreter companies, of which there is one in each *Wehrkreis,* and in the Interpreter Demonstration Battalion. In addition, a Signal Interpreter Replacement and Training Battalion trains signal intelligence personnel.

d. THE TRAINING OF POTENTIAL OFFICERS. (1) *General.* The system for training German officer replacements in wartime normally extends over a period of between 16 and 20 months (including prescribed service in the field) and is divided into three main phases. These phases differ slightly for active and reserve officer replacements, but the duration and standard of training are identical. The only difference between active and reserve officers is that the former enroll for an unlimited period of service and have to meet slightly higher physical requirements. For both categories, the training during the three main phases takes place in schools and courses devoted to this particular purpose. In the first phase, these are either officer applicant courses or reserve officer applicant courses; in the second phase officer candidate schools or courses; and in the third phase advanced officer candidate courses.

In certain cases selected enlisted men who are over 30 years old and have served in the field in combat units may become officers without attending officer candidate schools or courses but merely after a very few months of additional service in the field as officer candidates.

The following paragraphs outline the normal procedure for selecting and training active and reserve officer replacements.

(2) *Potential active officers (aktiver Offizier-Nachwuchs).* (a) *Selection.* Future active officers are selected in the following three ways:

Untrained volunteers, usually at the age of 16 or 17, after a preliminary selection by a selection center for future Army officers and noncommissioned officers (*Annahmestelle für den Führernachwuchs des Heeres*), enroll for an unlimited period and enter the Army as officer applicants (*Offizier-Bewerber,* usually abbreviated *O.B.*).

Conscripts already serving who are under 28 and decide to apply for the active officer career first are appointed reserve officer applicants (*Reserve-Offizier-Bewerber,* usually abbreviated *R.O.B.*), or if they have already attained noncommissioned officer grade, reserve officer candidates (*Fahnenjunker der Reserve,* usually abbreviated *Fhj.d.R.*), by their regimental (or independent battalion) commanders. A note is added to the record indicating that they intend to adopt the active officer career. They are accepted for this career upon graduating from the officer candidate course, but they must first attend a reserve officer applicant course if they have not already attained noncommissioned officer grade.

Professional noncommissioned officers may, after at least 2 months of service in the field, be appointed officer candidates (*Fahnenjunker,* usually abbreviated *Fhj.*) and be sent to an officer candidate course.

(b) *Officer applicant training.* This first phase of the training of future officers lasts 10 months and is designed for the untrained volunteer officer applicants. It is divided into the following two periods:

Four months of basic training in a training unit.

Six months of noncommissioned officer training in an officer applicant course (*O.B.-Lehrgang*). These courses usually take place at Army noncommissioned officer schools, some of which are reserved exclusively to this type of courses. In some special branches, officer applicant courses are held at the special-service schools or at training units. Upon graduation from the course, in which they are especially trained as squad leaders, the applicants are usually promoted to noncommissioned officers.

(c) *Officer candidate training.* After completion of their training in the Replacement Army, the officer applicants are transferred to a field unit for a period of not longer than 3 months in order to demonstrate their leadership abilities in the field. The latest tendency has been to reduce this period as much as possible, even down to a very few days, in order to preserve the potential officers who, after completion of 10 months of training in the Replacement Army, represent a valuable investment of the Army. As soon as they have proved themselves in the field they are appointed officer candidates (*Fahnenjunker*) and sent to an officer candidate course (*Fhj.-Lehrgang*) of 3 to 4 months' duration. These courses are usually conducted at the special-service schools; the infantry, *Panzer* troops, and artillery, however, have separate officer candidate schools and courses. It should be noted that these courses are not only attended by personnel who have passed through the officer applicant training period but also by conscript and professional noncommissioned officers who have been appointed reserve officer candidates by their regimental (or independent battalion) commanders. Toward the middle of the course, the candidates are promoted to officer candidate-staff sergeants (*Fahnenjunker-Feldwebel,* usually abbreviated *Fhj. Fw.*); upon graduation they are promoted to advanced officer candiates (*Oberfähnriche,* usually abbreviated *Obfähnr.*).

(d) *Advanced officer candidate training.* After completing the officer candidate course, the candidates attend an advanced officer candidate course (*Oberfähnr.Lehrgang*) lasting 3 months. These courses usually are conducted at the special-service schools. For advanced officer candidates of the infantry they may be conducted at especially designated infantry officer candidate schools, and for those of the *Panzer* troops at the *Panzer* troop advanced officer candidate schools. Upon graduation from these courses, the candidates are promoted to second lieutenants (*Leutnant,* usually abbreviated *Lt.*) (The word "promote"—*befördern* is always used; German officers are not commissioned).

(3) *Potential reserve officers (Reserve-Offizier-Nachwuchs).* (a) *Selection.* Potential reserve officers are selected in the following ways:

Untrained volunteers may be accepted by the selection centers for potential Army officers and noncommissioned officers as aspirants for the reserve officer career (*Anwärter für die Reserve-*

Offizier-Laufbahn). They are appointed reserve officer applicants by the regimental (or independent battalion) commander of their responsible replacement unit after 4 months' service.

During the conscription procedure suitable men may be selected by the commanders of recruiting sub-area headquarters. They have a similar career to that of the untrained volunteers described above.

Conscripts in basic training may be appointed reserve officer applicants by the regimental (or independent battalion) commander of their replacement or training unit.

Conscripts already serving for some time may be appointed reserve officer applicants, or, if they have already attained noncommissioned officer grade and, within 1 year previous to the date of their appointment, have proved themselves in a field unit, may be appointed reserve officer candidates, by the regimental (or independent battalion) commander of their field or replacement unit.

(b) *Reserve officer applicant training.* Untrained potential reserve officers first undergo 4 months of basic training, after which they are appointed reserve officer applicants. Reserve officer applicants who have had their basic training spend 6 months in a reserve officer applicant course (*R.O.B.-Lehrgang*). These courses usually are conducted by the headquarters of replacement and training units, and some infantry and artillery replacement regiments have special officer replacement companies and batteries (*Offizier-Nachwuchs-Kompanien-Batterien*) for this purpose. Recently, however, the ones for infantry officer applicants have been more and more concentrated on *Wehrkreis* level; the *Wehrkreis* headquarters may designate a particular infantry replacement battalion as an officer replacement battalion (*Offizier-Nachwuchs-Bataillon*), or conduct a special *Wehrkreis* reserve officer applicant course (*Wkr. R.O.B.-Lehrgang*). Upon conclusion of this course, in which they are primarily trained as squad leaders, the applicants are usually promoted to noncommissioned officers.

(c) *Reserve officer candidate training.* After completion of their training in the Replacement Army, the reserve officer applicants, just like the active officer applicants, are transferred to a field unit to prove themselves worthy, and then are appointed reserve officer candidates. Subsequently, they attend the same officer candidate schools or courses as the active officer candidates. During these courses, they are promoted to reserve officer candidate-staff sergeants (*Fhj.Fw.d.R.*), and upon their termination to advanced reserve officer candidates (*Oberfähnrich der Reserve,* usually abbreviated *Oberfähnr.d.R.*).

(d) *Advanced reserve officer candidate training.* The courses for advanced reserve officer candidates usually are conducted by the *Wehrkreis* headquarters. Upon graduation from these courses, the candidates are promoted to reserve second lieutenants (*Leutnant der Reserve,* usually abbreviated *Lt.d.R.*).

(4) *Potential officer specialists.* Slightly different rules apply for the training of potential officers in specialist careers who, in addition to their military education, require a certain type of professional training. These are the careers of medical officer, veterinary officer, ordnance officer, and officer of the motor maintenance troops. In addition, the administrative officer and judge advocate careers in the Special Troop Service require special rules regarding the replacement of their officers.

(a) *Potential medical officers (Sanitäts-Offizier-Nachwuchs).* Active medical officer applicants are selected from secondary school graduate volunteers by the *Wehrkreis* surgeon in connection with the recruiting sub-area commander. They take part in the officer applicant training conducted for potential infantry officers, and after its conclusion and a short assignment to a field unit are appointed officer candidates. At that time, they are assigned to the Medical Officer Academy and begin taking medical courses at the university. After a certain period of time they are promoted to medical technical sergeant (*Feldunterarzt*). Upon passing their medical examination, they become officers. Soldiers of the Field and Replacement Army may be accepted for this career if they fulfill the requirements. Doctors and medical students may become reserve medical officers. While taking medical courses at universities, the reserve medical officer candidates are assigned to medical officer feeder battalions (*Sanitätsoffizier-Ergänzungs-Abteilungen*).

(b) *Potential veterinary officers (Veterinär-Offizier-Nachwuchs).* Like the medical officer applicants, the active veterinary officer applicants are selected from young civilian volunteers and from soldiers of the Field and Replacement Armies. Their officer applicant training takes place in a mounted replacement and training unit. After their promotion to officer candidates they are assigned to the Army Veterinary Academy. They become active officers upon passing their veterinarian examinations. Veterinarians and veterinary students may become reserve veterinary officers.

(c) *Potential ordnance officers (Offizier (W)-Nachwuchs).* Active ordnance officers are recruited from active ordnance technicians; reserve ordnance officers from ordnance technicians with wartime training who did not enlist for the 12-year period. They are selected by their regimental (or independent battalion) commander and sent to an ordnance officer candidate course (*Fahnenjunker (W)-Lehrgang*) at Army Ordnance School I. During this course, which lasts 3 months for active ordnance technicians, and 9 months for reserve ordnance technicians, they are appointed ordnance officer candidates (*Fahnenjunker (W)*) by the commander of the Army Ordnance School. Upon graduating from these courses, they are promoted to ordnance lieutenants (*Leutnant (W)*).

(d) *Potential officers of the motor maintenance troops (Offizier-Nachwuchs der Kraftfahrparktruppe).* Active motor maintenance officers are recruited from supply technicians (MT) who are appointed officer candidates by their regimental (or independent battalion) commander and sent to officer candidate courses at the Motor Maintenance Troop School. In addition, active or reserve advanced officer candidates of other arms may be taken over into the motor maintenance troops to receive 2 to 3 months of special training at the Motor Maintenance Troop School, provided they have the required technical background. Soldiers in motor maintenance units who are over 38 years old, after at least 18 months of service, may be sent to the officer candidate courses at the Motor Maintenance Troop School; younger men may be transferred to a tank or *Panzer Grenadier* regiment and sent to a *Panzer* troop officer candidate course, to become reserve motor maintenance officers.

(e) *Potential officers of the Special Troop Service (Offizier-Nachwuchs des Truppensonderdienstes).* The Special Troop Service includes the administrative career (*Laufbahn des Verwaltungsdienstes*) and the judge advocate career (*Laufbahn der Wehrmachtrichter*). The officers of the administrative career are recruited from soldiers acceptable as officers of the fighting troops. Officer candidates of this career in the lower brackets are trained at the Army Administration School; active officer candidates in the higher brackets are believed to be assigned to the Administrative Academy while taking law courses at the University of Berlin. The officers of the judge advocate career are recruited from soldiers who are acceptable as officers of the fighting troops and, at the same time, have the professional qualifications to become judge advocates.

(5) *The training of officers for special functions.* Officers employed in specialized functions within the scope of their particular branch of service are trained for these functions at the special-service schools of their arm. The most important ones of these are: Infantry School, Mountain Infantry School, Reconnaissance and Cavalry School, Bergen and Krampnitz Schools for *Panzer* Troops, Artillery Schools I and II, School for Chemical Warfare Troops, Engineer Schools 1 and 2, Army Signal Schools I and II, Army Supply Troop School, Motor Maintenance Troop School, Army Administration School.

Officers who are employed in special functions not in connection with their branch of service are trained in schools or courses established for this purpose which are described below.

General Staff Corps Officers (*Generalstabs-Offiziere*) belong to the General Staff Corps (*Generalstab*), and usually are appointed either to the Army General Staff (*Generalstab des Heeres*) or to one of the General Staff assignments (*Generalstabsstellen*) on lower staffs. These latter are believed to be the assignments as chief of staff, assistant chief of staff for operations—G-3 (*I-a*), assistant chief of staff for supply—G-4 (*Quartiermeister, I-b*), assistant chief of staff for intelligence —G-2 (*I-c*) of headquarters down to corps, and as G-3 in divisions. Active officers, usually with the rank of captain, who are not over 28 years old, have exceptional personalities, are qualified for a leading position, and have shown exceptional performance in at least 6 months of service at the front may be recommended for General Staff Corps training by their commanding officers. If accepted, they are, according to the regular training schedule, assigned to the War Academy for a period of 1 year, The first month of this period is spent at a special-service school and the next 6 months at the War Academy itself. The aspirants then are attached to the General Staff Corps (*Generalstab*) for 5 months and are taken into it permanently if accepted.

(6) *Senior personnel officers* (*Höhere Adjutanten*). Courses for senior personnel officers are conducted by the Army Personnel Office. They are usually held at leading Army schools, such as the War Academy or a special-service school.

(7) *Battalion c o m m a n d e r s* (*Btl.-(Abt.-) Führer*). Special courses for battalion commanders are conducted at an Army School for Battalion Commanders.

(8) *Company commanders* (*Kompanieführer*). Schools for company commanders may be estab-lished by armies or army groups in their rear areas.

(9) *National-Socialist guidance officers* (*NS-Führungsoffiziere*), usually abbreviated (*NSFO*). National-Socialist guidance officers for divisions and higher headquarters take part in courses con-ducted by an Instruction Staff for NS Indoc-trination.

(10) *Gas protection officers* (*Gasabwehr-Offiziere*) usually abbreviated *Gabo*). Courses for gas protection officers are conducted at Army Gas Protection Schools 1 and 2.

CHAPTER II

ORGANIZATION OF THE
FIELD FORCES

Section I. OVER-ALL FIELD ORGANIZATION

The High Command frameworks below the Army High Command are the Army Groups (*Heeresgruppenkommandos*) that are formed for particular campaigns to control two to four Armies in a single Theater of Operations, or in an important and more or less self-contained sector under such a theater. Since 1941 the total number of army groups has been between four and twelve.

The chart on page 3 shows the variations in the number of Armies (*Armeeoberkommandos*) per army group, of corps per army and of divisions per corps.

Section II. HIGH COMMAND IN THE FIELD

Under the German military system the basic principle is unity of command at all levels. Thus the Army, Navy, and Air Force are considered branches of a single service, the Armed Forces (*Wehrmacht*). This joint High Command is responsible for the whole preparation of defense in time of peace and for the general conduct of war; it appoints commands for the joint task forces in the field and sees to it that the efforts of the three branches of the armed forces are thoroughly coordinated.

In time of war the Armed Forces High Command, as well as the High Command of each of the three branches establishes a field headquarters away from Berlin for the conduct of operations. Its location at any given time depends on the theater to which the main attention is being directed. In the case of the Navy, it is usually at one of the naval bases while the headquarters of the Army, the Air Force and the Armed Forces have been in close proximity to each other

at various points since the spring of 1941. The Commander-in-Chief and the bulk of the General Staff of each High Command are stationed at field headquarters, while the non-operational branches back in the Zone of the Interior continue to handle all basic administrative matters, procurement, mobilization, training and replacement of personnel, and equipment.

Hitler is the Supreme Commander of the Armed Forces (*Oberster Befehlshaber der Wehrmacht*). His Deputy as such is General Field Marshall Wilhelm Keitel, Chief of the Armed Forces High Command (*Chef des Oberkommando der Wehrmacht*).

Under the Armed Forces High Command the functions of the joint general staff are performed by what is known as the Armed Forces Operations Staff (*Wehrmachtführungsstaf-W.F.St*).

The field headquarters of the Armed Forces High Command which includes the principal sections of the Armed Forces Operations Staff is known as the *Führerhauptquartier*. During the Polish campaign it was stationed between Berlin and the Polish Frontier, moving to the Rhineland for the Western campaign in 1940, back to the East in 1941, and again to the West in 1944. Hitler's headquarters (*Führerhauptquartier*) is believed to have moved recently to southern Germany where it is probably located in the vicinity of Berchtesgaden.

The personnel of the Armed Forces High Command is drawn from all three branches, but the Army naturally has the largest representation.

The name of a command, organization, or unit deriving from the Armed Forces High Command is often prefixed by *Wehrmacht-* or *Führungs* in order to distinguish it from a similar command, organization, or unit in one of the three branches.

Since December 1941, when von Brauchitsch was dismissed as Commander-in-Chief of the Army (*Oberbefehlshaber des Heeres*), and Hitler took direct control of the Army, the field head-

U.S. Designations:	A H Comd (O K H)	A Gps (Heeresgruppen-kommandos)	As (Armeeoberkommandos)	Corps (Korps)	Divs (Divisionen)
C G	Oberbefehlshaber des Heeres	Oberbefehlshaber der Heeresgruppe	Befehlshaber des Armeeoberkommandos	Kommandierender General	Divisionskommandeur
C of S	Chef des Generalstabes des Heeres	Chef des Generalstabes	Chef des Generalstabes	Chef des Generalstabes	(I-a)
G-1 Offs	Heerespersonalamt	II-a, 1. Adjutant	II-a, 1. Adjutant	II-a, 1. Adjutant	II-a, 1. Adjutant
G-1 EM	Allgemeines Heeresamt. Truppenabteilung	II-c, 2. Adjutant	II-c, 2. Adjutant	II-c, 2. Adjutant	II-c, 2. Adjutant
G-2	Oberquartiermeister IV	I-c, 3. General-stabsoffizier	I-c, 3. General-stabsoffizier	I-c, 3. General-stabsoffizier	I-c, 3. General-stabsoffizier
G-3 Opns	Oberquartiermeister I	I-a, 1. General-stabsoffizier	I-a, 1. General-stabsoffizier	I-a, 1. General-stabsoffizier	I-a, 1. General-stabsoffizier
G-3 Tng	Oberquartiermeister II	I-d, 4. General-stabsoffizier	I-d, 4. General-stabsoffizier		
G-4	Generalquartiermeister (Gen. Qu.)	I-c, 2. General-stabsoffizier	Oberquartiermeister (O. Qu.)	Quartiermeister (Q. Qu.)	I-c, 2. General-stabsoffizier
C Arty O	General der Artillerie	Stabsoffizier der Artillerie (Stoart)	Höherer Artillerie-kommandeur (Harko)	Artillerie-kommandeur (Arko)	Artillerie-führer (Arfü)
C Engr O	General der Pioniere und Festungen	General der Pioniere (Gen. d. Pi.)	Armeepionierführer (A. Pi. Fü.)	Stabsoffizier der Pioniere (Stopi)	Kommandeur des Pionierbataillons
C Sig O	Chef des Heeres-nachrichtenwesens	Heeresgruppennah-richtenführer (H. Gr. Nachr. Fü.)	Armeenachrichten-führer (A. Nachr. Fü.)	Korpsnachrich-tenführer	Kommandeur der Nachrichtenabteilung
C Clm O	General der Nebeltruppen	Höherer Kommandeur der Nebeltruppen?	Stabsoffizier für Gasabwehr	Gasabwehroffizier (Gabo)	Gasabwehroffizier or Gasschutzoffizier (Gabo)
C AT O	General für Panzerabwehr	Stabsoffizier für Panzerbekämpfung?	Stabsoffizier für Panzerbekämpfung (Stopak)	Stabsoffizier für Panzerbekämpfung	Kommandeur der Panzerjägerabteilung

Figure 1.—German designations of Stf Offs and Secs in the higher echelons.

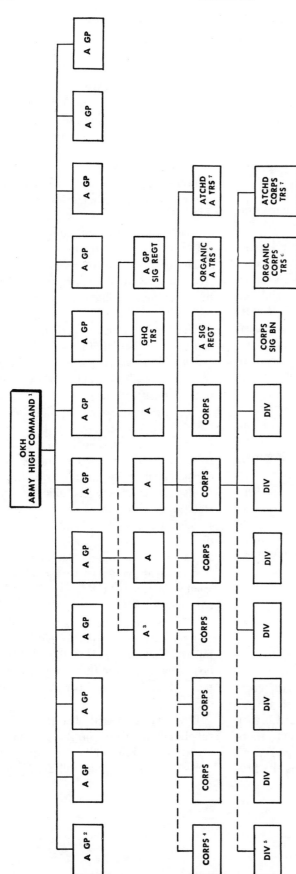

1. The highest echelon of the High Command framework now consists of 12 army groups.

2. Each army group has two to four armies. There are three types of armies: ordinary armies, *Panzer* armies, and one parachute army.

3. Each army has two to seven corps. There are six types of corps: Infantry; Mountain, *Panzer*; Parachute; Corps Commands, and Reserve.

4. Each corps has two to seven divisions.

5. For the different type of divisions see charts, Section V.

6. Organic army group troops are—besides the army group signal regiment—various staffs and units dealing with administrative and operational matters within its territory, including the rear area. Organic army troops are—besides the army signal regiment—various police units, supply staffs, a field post office and a propaganda company. Organic corps troops are—besides the corps signal battalion—a police detachment, a supply staff, a bridge column, a map-printing unit, a medical company, a veterinary company, a field post office and various other services.

7. Attached troops vary according to mission. (For the types of GHQ units see Sections VI and VII.)

Figure 2.—Over-all field organization.

quarters of the Army High Command virtually has been merged with that of the Armed Forces High Command. The functions of the two, however, have remained distinct, and there has been no personal union except at the top. Keitel acts as Hitler's deputy in the latter's capacity as Commander-in-Chief of the Army as well as in his capacity as Supreme Commander of the Armed Forces.

For the organization of the Armed Forces High Command see Figure 4, Chapter 1.

For the organization of the Army High Command see Figure 5, Chapter 1.

The *Führerhauptquartier* is frequently located in special trains. It is at all times well protected against air or land attacks by crack *SS* units. In addition to those the following two units of the elite army motorized division, the *Grossdeutschland Panzer Grenadier* Division, have been temporarily charged with that protection and were therefore awarded the honor of including "The *Führer*" in their unit designation. These units are:

The *Führer* Escort Brigade, which consists of three infantry battalions, one artillery battalion, one tank regiment (including one battalion of *Pz. Kpfw.IV* and one battalion of assault guns), and one engineer company;

The *Führer Grenadier* Brigade which consists of:

Two infantry battalions (one motorized and one armored); one battalion of self-propelled artillery; one assault gun company; one Panther tank battalion.

Section III. ORGANIZATION OF HIGHER HEADQUARTERS

The headquarters of all German divisions, corps, armies, and army groups consist of command staffs (*Kommandobehörden*) which are organized in a uniform manner. Corps and higher staffs are known as senior command staffs (*höhere Kommandobehörden*). They are headed by a chief of staff, whereas in divisions the first

General Staff officer in charge of operations is simultaneously head of the staff.

The sections of these staffs are numbered with Roman numerals and letters. Similar to the custom in the U. S. Army, the numbers represent the sections as well as the men in charge of them. Originally the positions of I-a, I-b, I-c and I-d were all reserved for officers of the German General Staff Corps, but in 1944 the I-c at division and I-d at army and army group were frequently identified as not being General Staff officers. Figure 3 shows in numerical order the designations of the staff officers and sections, and Figure 4 shows the same staff officers and sections as they function operationally.

The headquarters of an army group is organized similarly to that of an army, but the ranks of the officers holding corresponding positions are higher.

The headquarters of a corps also is organized similarly to that of an army; however, the specialist officers more frequently take command in the field of all the units of their arm whether organic or attached.

The headquarters of divisions also are organized similarly with most of the specialist officers being simultaneously in command of the units of their arms, e.g. the commanding officer of the division artillery regiment (*Artillerieführer-Arfü*) is also the chief artillery officer on the specialist staff of the division commander. When General Headquarters artillery units are attached to the division this *Arfü* usually is subordinated to a special artillery commander known as *Artilleriekommandeur* whose small special staff is supplemented in action by the organic staff of the division artillery regiment.

While some of the designations of staff officers and sections remain unchanged in all echelons of higher headquarters (as the U. S. designations do) several of these titles vary in accordance with the rank and echelon in which they are functioning.

It should be noted that the main channel of supplies flows from the Zone of the Interior via army to division, while the army group and the corps are primarily tactical headquarters.

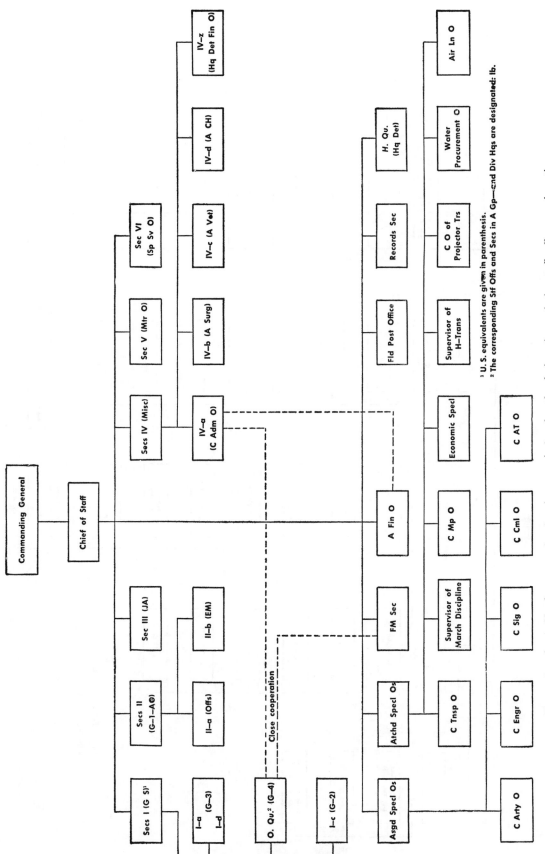

Figure 3.—Army Headquarters showing in numerical order the designations of the staff officers and sections.

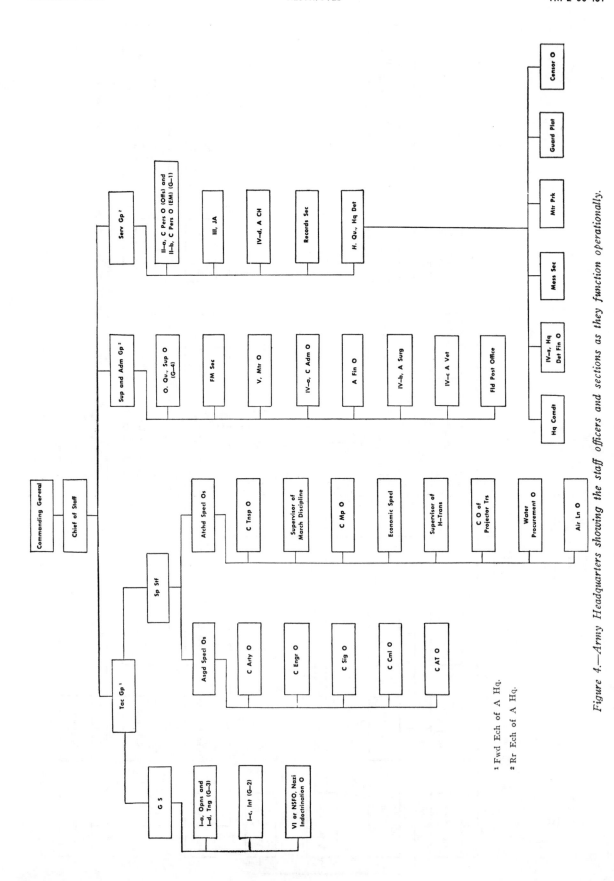

Figure 4.—Army Headquarters showing the staff officers and sections as they function operationally.

1 Fwd Ech of A Hq.

2 Rr Ech of A Hq.

Section IV. PRINCIPLES AND TRENDS IN UNIT ORGANIZATION AND EQUIPMENT

The German Army, like the U. S. Army, believes in uniform organization for standard units up to and including companies, troops, and batteries. These either are combined as components of battalions, regiments, and divisions, or temporarily grouped in varying combinations as components of task forces or combat groups. Each standard unit of company size has a table of organization and table of equipment number designating its particular type, and each smaller unit adds a letter to that number designating its place within that standard unit. The following figures showing the organization, strength, and equipment of various German units are based on these tables of organization and equipment, but in the field the strength of any unit will vary in accordance with its specific mission and local conditions. However, even in the greatest deviation from the tables of organization and equipment, the basic pattern still will be clearly recognizable.

As shown in Figure 2 in Section I, the German Army in the field is organized into army groups, armies, corps, and divisions. Divisions are the largest units in the German Army known to have a prescribed organization, and those divisions which function as tactical units are normally the smallest formations which include units of various arms and services resulting in operational self-sufficiency.

General Headquarters, army, and corps troops are being allotted temporarily to lower echelons in a flexible manner, in accordance with operational plans or local tactical necessities.

From the outbreak of the War until the summer of 1943, comparatively only minor changes occurred in the tables of organization of most types of German divisions. The average divisional table of organization strength for that period was about 15,000 to 17,000 and with the normally attached troops it usually reached about 20,000. From the summer of 1943 until now, however, several series of new tables of organization and equipment have been issued for almost all types of divisions showing revolutionary changes in their strength and equipment. In all these reorganizations the trend is clearly towards

an economizing of manpower and a simultaneous increase in firepower. This is being accomplished by a careful distribution of large numbers of automatic small arms, by lowering the number of mortars, antitank guns, and tanks, but at the same time increasing potentially their calibers and weights. These changes resulted in the lowering of the table of organization strength of the average German division to approximately 11,000 to 13,000 in January 1945 and further drastic action in that direction may be expected. The various types of German Army, *SS*, and Air Force divisions are shown in the following Section V, while their components and the general headquarters troops are listed in Sections VI and VII.

Section V. DIVISIONS

I. Comparative Charts

The main types of German divisions, their German designations, and strengths are listed in the first two columns of Figure 5. The remaining columns on the upper part of that chart show the main components for the first 13 types of divisions. Figure 6 shows the type distribution of weapons and equipment in the first 13 types of divisions mentioned above.

The following paragraphs of this section cover the more important types of German divisions and Sections VI and VII include the components of these divisions as well as General Headquarters troops listed together in accordance with their arm or service. These sections cover in great detail the three most numerous types of German divisions: the Infantry Division, 1944 Type; the *Volks Grenadier* Division; and the Armored Division, as well as the other types of divisions with their most important components only.

Most of this information is based on factual evidence, and wherever such was not available the best possible estimates have been made. This refers particularly to the strength figures of the division staffs controlling various units (lower part of Figure 5), as such staffs may be temporarily in charge of much smaller or much larger numbers of men in accordance with tactical and local conditions.

DIVISIONS

TYPES OF DIVISIONS	Personnel	COMPONENTS			
		Hq	Rcn	Sig	Inf
Infantry Division, Old Type............................ (*Infanteriedivision*) (3 Inf Regts of 3 Bns each)	17,000	Div Hq	Rcn Bn	Sig Bn	Inf Regt
Infantry Division, 1944 Type[1]......................... (*Infanteriedivision n.A*, later *Kriegsetat 44*) (3 Inf Regts of 2 Bns each)	12,500	Div Hq	*Füs.* Bn	Sig Bn	Inf Regt
Infantry Division, Two Regiment Type................. (*Infanteriedivision*) (2 Inf Regts of 3 Bns each)	10,000	Div Hq	*Füs.* Co	Sig Bn	Inf Regt
Volks Grenadier Division............................... (*Volksgrenadierdivision*) (3 Inf Regts of 2 Bns each)	10,000	Div Hq	*Füs.* Co	Sig Bn	Inf Regt
SS Infantry Division.................................. (*SS Grenadierdivision*) (3 *SS* Inf Regts of 2 Bns each)	14,000	Div Hq	*SS* Rcn Bn	*SS* Sig Bn	*SS* Inf Regt
Army Mountain Division................................ (*Gebirgsdivision*) (2 Mt Inf Regts of 3 Bns each)	13,000	Div Hq	Mt Rcn Bn	Mt Sig Bn	Mt Inf Regt
Army Light Division.................................... (*Jägerdivision*) (2 Light Inf Regts of 3 Bns each)	13,000	Div Hq	Bcl Bn	Sig Bn	Light Inf Regt
SS Mountain Division.................................. (*SS Gebirgsdivision*) (2 Mt Inf Regts of 4 Bns each)	16,000	Div Hq	*SS* Mt Rcn Bn	*SS* Mt Sig Bn	*SS* Mt Inf Regt
Army Motorized Division............................... (*Panzergrenadierdivision*) (2 Mt Inf Regts of 3 Bns each)	14,000	Div Hq	Armd Rcn Bn	Armd Sig Bn	Mtz Inf Regt
SS Motorized Division................................. (*SS Panzergrenadierdivision*) (2 *SS* Mtz Inf Regts of 3 Bns each)	15,000	Div Hq	*SS* Armd Rcn Bn	*SS* Sig Bn	*SS Pz. Gren.* Regt
Army Armored Division................................ (*2 Pz. Gren.* Regts of 2 Bns each)	14,000	Div Hq and Hq Co	Rcn Bn	Armd Sig Bn	*Pz. Gren.* Regt
SS Armored Division.................................. (*SS-Panzerdivision*) (2 *Pz. Gren.* Regts of 3 Bns each)	17,000	Div Hq and Hq Co	*SS* Armd Rcn Bn	*SS* Armd Sig Bn	*SS Pz. Gren.* Regt
Air Force Parachute Division........................... (*Fallschirmjägerdivision*) (3 Prcht R Regts of 3 Bns each)	16,000	Div Hq	Rcn Co	Prcht Sig Bn	Prcht Rifle Regt
Air Force Field Division................................ *Luftwaffenfelddivision*) (3 Inf Regts of 2 Bns each)	12,500	Absorbed by the Army. Organized similarly to the Infantry Division, 1944 Type.			
Cavalry Division....................................... (*Kavalleriedivision*) (4 Cav Regts of 2 Bns each)	16,000	Cossack and *SS* Cavalry Divisions consisting of two cavalry brigades, a weak artillery regiment and the usual supporting units.			
Line of Communication Division......................... (*Sicherungsdivision*)	10,000	Designed for mopping-up duties in the rear areas; may consist of two reinforced regiments or of a number of independent battalions.			
Coast Defense Division................................. (*Küstenverteidigungsdivision*)	10,000	Consists of a division staff controlling fortress battalions and coast artillery units in a coastal sector.			
Assault Division....................................... (*Sturmdivision*)	10,000	An honorary title for some divisions with reduced infantry personnel and a concentration of heavy fire power and automatic weapons.			
Frontier Guard Division................................ (*Grenzwachdivision*)	13,000	Consists of a division staff controlling certain frontier guard units.			
Special Administrative Division Staff.................... (*Divisionskommando z.b.v.*)	10,000	Consists of a division staff controlling *Landesschützen* Battalions and GHQ troops stationed in a corps area in Germany.			
Replacement Division Staff............................. (*Div.Nr.....*)	15,000	A division staff within a corps area in Germany to supervise the induction of personnel and replacements for field units.			
Reserve Division....................................... (*Reservedivision*)	16,000	Controls reserve units for training, occupational, and defensive duties.			
Field Training Division................................. (*Feldausbildungsdivision*)	16,000	Controls field training regiments in the rear of the Eastern Front.			
Non-Motorized Air Force Antiaircraft Division.......... (*Flakdivision*) (*verlegefähig*)	10,000	Consists of a division staff controlling antiaircraft and searchlight regiments having limited mobility.			
Motorized Air Force Antiaircraft Division............... (*Flakdivision*) (*motorisiert*)	19,000	Consists of a division staff controlling motorized antiaircraft and searchlight regiments.			

[1] This type of division is believed to have been superseded by the Infantry Division, Type 1945 (*Infanteriedivision 45*), in which the various components of the division have been reduced by approximately 10%, resulting in a total personnel of about 11,500.

Figure 5.

DIVISIONS

COMPONENTS

Inf	Inf	Arty	Armd	AA	Projectors	AT	Engr	Serv
Inf Regt	Inf Regt	Arty Regt	—	—	—	AT Bn	Engr Bn	Div Serv
Inf Regt	Inf Regt	Arty Regt	—	—	—	AT Bn	Engr Bn	Div Serv
Inf Regt	—	Arty Regt	—	AA Co	—	AT Co	Engr Bn	Div Serv
Inf Regt	Inf Regt	Arty Regt	—	—	—	AT Bn	Engr Bn	Sup Regt
SS Inf Regt	SS Inf Regt	SS Arty Regt	—	SS AA Bn	—	SS AT Bn	SS Engr Bn	Div Serv
Mt Inf Regt	—	Mt Arty Regt	—	—	—	AT Bn	Mt Engr Bn	Div Serv
Light Inf Regt	—	Arty Regt	—	—	—	AT Bn	Engr Bn	Div Serv
SS Mt Inf Regt	—	SS Mt Arty Regt	SS Tk or Assault Gun Co	SS AA Bn	—	SS AT Bn	SS Mt Engr Bn	Div Serv
Mtz Inf Regt	—	Armd Arty Regt	Tk or Assault Gun Bn	AA Bn	—	AT Bn	Armd Engr Bn	Div Serv
SS Pz. Gren. Regt	—	SS Armd Arty Regt	SS Tk Bn	SS AA Bn	—	SS AT Bn or Assault Gun Bn	SS Armd Engr Bn	Div Serv
Pz. Gren. Regt	—	Armd Arty Regt	Tk Regt	AA Bn	—	AT Bn	Armd Engr Bn	Div Serv
SS Pz. Gren. Regt	—	—	SS Tk Regt	SS AA Bn	SS Rkt Projector Bn	SS AT or Assault Gun Bn	SS Armd Engr Bn	Div Serv
Prcht Rifle Regt	Prcht Rifle Regt	Prcht Arty Regt	—	Prcht AA Bn	Prcht Hv Mort Bn	Prcht AT Bn	Prcht Engr Bn	Div Serv

Figure 5. (Continued)

DIVISIONS

Weapons and equipment (type distribution in the main types of divisions listed under paragraph 1.)

TYPES OF DIVISIONS	Rs or Cbns	Pistols	Sub-MGs	LMGs	Hv MGs	81-mm Morts	120-mm Morts	Bazookas or AT Rs	Flame Throwers	150- or 210-mm Rkt Projectors	20-mm AA Guns	20-mm AT or Tk Guns	28/20-mm AT Guns
Infantry Division, Old Type..........	15500	1100	700	527	116	58		90	20			11	
Infantry Division, 1944 Type.........	9069	1981	1503	566	90	48	28	108	20		12		
Infantry Division, Two Regiment Type..	—	—	—	497	52	42	24	—	16		12		
Volks Grenadier Division.............	6054	1536	2064	369	54	42	24	216	12				
Army Mountain Division............	—	—	—	485	84	48	24	72	20		12		
Army Motorized Division............	9455	3222	1441	1019	82	52	24	—	26		75	38	
Army Armored Division.............	9186	3317	1543	1157	64	46	16	—	68		74	38	3
SS Armored Division................	11513	4064	2050	1465	100	58	24	—	74	18	114	33	3
Air Force Parachute Division.........	9689	3810	3026	930	80	125	63	250	20		39		

SS Infantry Division—Organized and equipped similarly to the Infantry Division 1944 Type, however with an additional Antiaircraft Battalion and slightly stronger components.

Army Light Division—Organized and equipped similarly to the Army Mountain Division with slightly more motorization.

SS Mountain Division—Organized similarly to the Army Mountain Division, however with two more Mountain Infantry Battalions, one Antiaircraft Battalion and a Tank or Assault Gun Company.

SS Motorized Division—Organized similarly to the Army Motorized Division, however with additional Antiaircraft Companies and an Artillery Observation Battery.

Figure 6.

DIVISIONS

Weapons and equipment (type distribution in the main types of divisions listed under paragraph 1.)

37-mm AA/AT Guns	75-mm AT Guns (Mtr-Dr)	75-mm AT Guns (SP)	75-mm Tk Guns (Long)	75-mm Tk Guns (Superlong)	88-mm AA/AT Guns	75-mm Inf-Hows	75-mm Inf-Hows (SP)	150-mm Inf-Hows	150-mm Inf-Hows (SP)	75-mm Guns	105-mm Gun/Hows	105-mm Gun/Hows (SP)	150-mm Hows	150-mm Hows (SP)	Pz. Kpfw. IV's	Pz. Kpfw. V's	Mtr Vehicles	Mtrcls	H-Dr Vehicles	Hs
	75					20		6			36		12				942	452	1133	5375
	21	14				18		6			36		12				615	168	1466	4662
	20				12	12		4			24						543	218	726	2734
9	9	14				38				18	24		12				426	119	1142	3002
3	24					14		4		24	12		12				500	200	1000	5000
	30	44	48		8			12			12	12	12	6	48		2637	469		
8	12	47	52	51	8		12	12			12	12	12	6	52	51	2685	480		
8	12	69	64	62	12		24	12			12	12	12 and 12 Hv Guns	6	64	62	3329	530		
	21	14			12	20					24		12				2141	389		

Figure 6. (Continued)

2. Infantry Divisions

Despite the important role which has been played by specialized branches of the German Army, the infantry has been and remains today the foundation for most German operations.

a. INFANTRY DIVISION, OLD TYPE (*Infanteriedivision*) (THREE REGIMENTS OF THREE BATTALIONS EACH). Contrary to the American conception of a completely motorized infantry division, the German infantry divisions mostly have relied on horse-drawn vehicles for their transportation. In recent reorganizations the proportion of motorization in these types of divisions has decreased even more. Except for the reorganization of the infantry platoon from three to four squads after the Polish campaign in 1939, and the temporary increase in the number of horses in the divisions employed in Russia from 1941 to 1943, the German three-regiment, nine-battalion division remained unchanged for all practical purposes until the fall of 1943. This type of division probably will not be encountered any more; however, as it has been the basic type of German infantry division for a period of about 4 years, it is shown in Figures 7 and 8 and designated for explanatory purposes as the Infantry Division, Old Type.

b. INFANTRY DIVISION, 1944 TYPE (*Infanteriedivision n.A* later *Kriegestat 44*) (THREE-REGIMENTS OF TWO BATTALIONS EACH). In October 1943 the Germans reorganized radically their infantry divisions in reducing the infantry regiments from three to two battalions, and the other divisional components were revised accordingly. In the remaining six infantry battalions the number of squads per rifle platoon was reduced from four to three, but without having much effect on the fire power of the division since the caliber of the mortars and antitank guns has been increased, and the number of machine guns kept unchanged. This type of division was designated Infantry Division, New Type (*Infanteriedivision n.A.*). This type of infantry division will not be discussed further here, as it soon was designated the Infantry Division, 1944 Type (*Infanteriedivision Kriegestat 44*). This redesignation took place in May 1944 after the following additional economies were put into effect. The strength of the squad was reduced from ten to nine, the number of light machine guns per rifle company from 16 to 13, and the strength of the trains on all levels was reduced sharply. Figures 9 and 10 show the Infantry Division, 1944 Type, but newest regulations point towards a further reduction of the components of that type of division by approximately 10 per cent and the redesignation of the thus reorganized division as Infantry Division, Type 1945 (*Infanteriedivisions 45*). It has just been learned that all German infantry divisions are to be reorganized on the basis of the Infantry Division, Type 45, and that the organization and strength of that division are almost identical with those of the *Volks Grenadier* Division. (See subparagraph d below and Section VI, paragraph 2, subparagraph a (5).)

c. INFANTRY DIVISION, TWO REGIMENT TYPE (*Infanteriedivision*) (TWO REGIMENTS OF THREE BATTALIONS EACH). Independent of the various stages of organization of the three regiment infantry divisions, the Germans have formed, since the spring of 1941, a number of two-regiment, six-battalion, infantry divisions with weaker components and over-all reduced strength and fire power. The number of this type of divisions recently has been reduced by the reorganization of several into three-regiment divisions. We refer to this type of division as Infantry Division, Two-Regiment Type.

d. *Volks Grenadier* DIVISION (*Volksgrenadierdivision*) (THREE REGIMENTS OF TWO BATTALIONS EACH). In September 1944, after Heinrich Himmler, the Chief of the *SS*, the Police and the Minister of the Interior had become also the Chief of Army Equipment and Commander of the Replacement Training Army, a new type of infantry division, the "Peoples Infantry Division" (*Volks Grenadier* Division) was created. The political significance of this type of division lies in designating it: "the Peoples," and thus stressing the emergency of the Fatherland. As the members of the *Volks Grenadier* Division are reported to be interchangeable with the members of the *SS* divisions, it is believed that through their creation the influence of the *SS* on the Army has been strengthened. To increase the *Esprit de Corps* of its members, supporting General Headquarters units also have been designated *Volks* Artillery Corps, *Volks* Engineer Brigades, and *Volks* Rocket Projector Brigades, all of which will be discussed in Section VII.

From the organization point of view, the significance of the *Volks Grenadier* Division lies in its decrease of personnel and increase of small automatic weapons, particularly submachine guns.

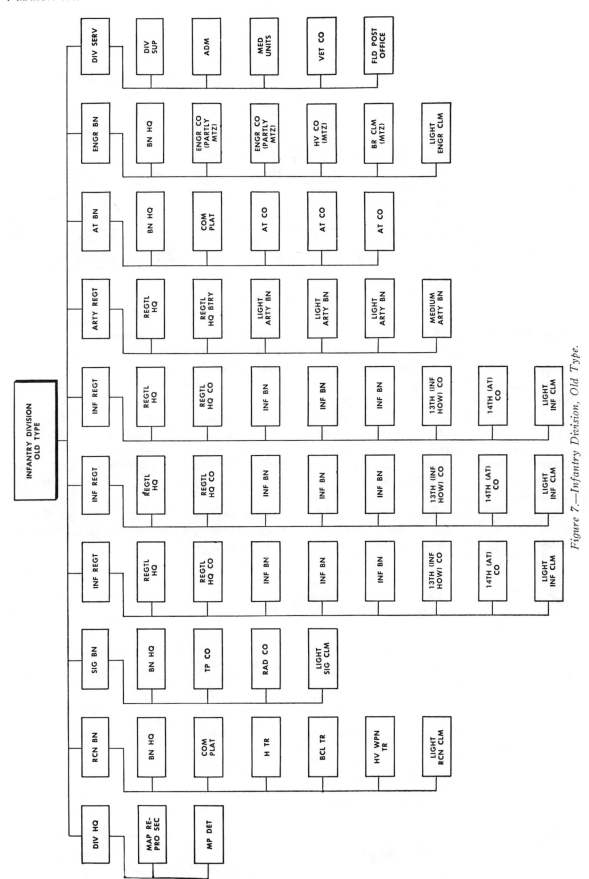

Figure 7.—Infantry Division, Old Type.

UNIT	Pers	LMGs	Hv MGs	7.92-mm AT Rs	75-mm AT Guns	20-mm AA/AT Guns	50-mm Morts	81-mm Morts	75-mm Inf Hows	150-mm Inf Hows	105-mm Gun/Hows	105-mm Guns	150-mm Hows	Flame Throwers	Armd C	Mtrcls	Mtr Vehicles	H-Dr Vehicles	Hs
Div Hq	158	2														17	31		
Rcn Bn	625	25	8		3	3	3	4	2						3	45	30	3	213
Sig Bn	474	17														32	103	7	52
Inf Regt	3,250	123	36	27	12		27	18	6	2						47	73	210	683
Inf Regt	3,250	123	36	27	12		27	18	6	2						47	73	210	683
Inf Regt	3,250	123	36	27	12		27	18	6	2						47	73	210	683
Arty Regt	2,500	32									36	4	8			40	105	229	2,274
AT Bn	550	18			36											45	114		
Engr Bn	843	34		9										20		44	87	19	52
Div Serv	2,300	30				8										88	253	245	735
Total[1]	17,200	527	116	90	75	11	84	58	20	6	36	4	8	20	3	452	942	1,133	5,375

[1] A Repl Bn may be added to any Inf Div.

Figure 8.—Infantry Division, Old Type, total strength 17,200.

Also company and battalion trains have been merged into battalion supply platoons, thus freeing the company commander from all duties other than operational and facilitating a more even distribution of all types of supplies with less personnel. Bazookas replace all antitank guns in the infantry regiments; the artillery regiment is organized in batteries of six guns instead of four, with one battalion of eighteen 75-mm guns replacing a normal battalion of twelve 105-mm gun/howitzers. An additional new feature is the formation of a divisional supply regiment which combines all the divisional services except the military police detachment which has been assigned to the division headquarters. This type of division is shown on the Figures 14 and 15 as *Volks Grenadier* Division.

e. SS INFANTRY DIVISION (*SS Grenadierdivisionen*) (THREE SS REGIMENTS OF TWO BATTALIONS EACH). The great majority of German infantry divisions are army infantry divisions. However, there are also several SS infantry divisions (*SS-Grenadierdivisionen*) which have been formed by the armed SS (*Waffen-SS*). This type of division is organized similarly to the Infantry Division, 1944 Type, but it has slightly stronger components and includes an organic antiaircraft battalion.

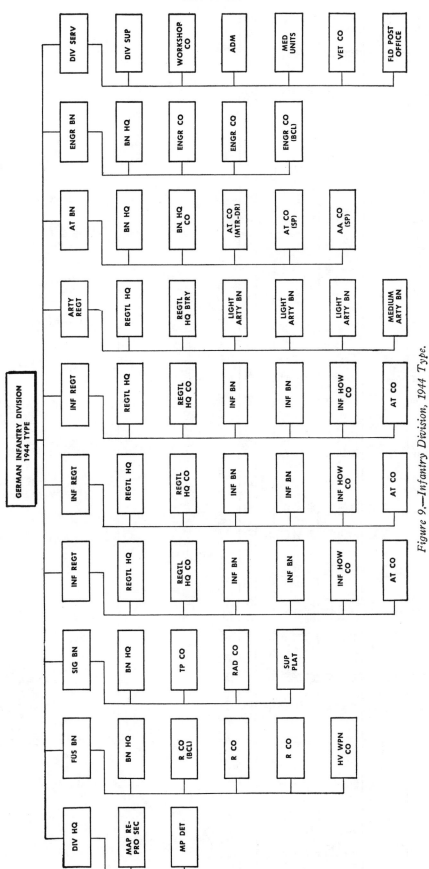

Figure 9.—Infantry Division, 1944 Type.

UNIT	Offs	NCOs	Pvts	Rs or Cbns	Pistols	Sub-MGs	LMGs	Hv MGs	81-mm Morts	120-mm Morts	Bazookas	Flame Throwers	20-mm AA Guns (SP)	75-mm AT Guns (Mtr-Dr)	75-mm AT Guns (SP)	75-mm Inf-Hows	150-mm Inf-Hows	105-mm Gun/Hows	150-mm Hows	Mtr Vehicles	Mtrcls	H.-Dr. Vehicles	Trs	Hs
Div Hq	34	87	106	121	92	12	5													32	21		1	
Füs Bn	15	113	580	477	122	127	43	12	6	4										8	5	102	57	165
Sig Bn	16	80	283	326	18	35	11													76	13	14	2	54
Inf Regt	48	316	1,644	1,373	350	332	107	24	12	8	36			3		6	2			45	20	242	130	495
Inf Regt	48	316	1,644	1,373	350	332	107	24	12	8	36			3		6	2			45	20	242	130	495
Inf Regt	48	316	1,644	1,373	350	332	107	24	12	8	36			3		6	2			45	20	242	130	495
Arty Regt[2]	85	460	1,906	2,065	307	164	69											36	12	30	7	441	34	2,318
AT Bn	17	123	344	318	123	81	29						12	12	14					113	20		17	
Engr Bn	18	92	510	432	136	71	31	6	6			20								17	19	52	25	97
Div. Serv.[1]	58	219	1,182	1,181	133	17	57													204	23	131	25	543
Total	387[3]	2,122	9,843	9,069	1,981	1,503	566	90	48	28	108	20	12	21	14	18	6	36	12	615	168	1,466	551	4,656

[1] A Fld Repl Bn with a C Sch may be added to any Inf Div.
[2] The Arty Regt may be reduced in some Divs by 39 NCOs, 399 Pvts, 545 Hs, three 105-mm Gun/Hows, three 150-mm Hows, and other equipment.
[3] Including 71 officials.

Figure 10.—Infantry Division, 1944 Type, total strength 12,352.

UNIT	Offs	NCOs	Pvts	Rs or Cbns	Pistols	Sub-MGs	LMGs	Mtr Vehicles	Mtrcls	Trs
Div Hq	33[1]	61	92	95	81	7	2	25	21	1
Map Repro Sec		1	7	7	1			2		
MP Det	1	25	7	19	10	5	3	5		
Total	34[1]	87	106	121	92	12	5	32	21	1

[1] Including 10 officials.

Figure 11.—Division Headquarters, Infantry Division, 1944 Type, total strength 227.

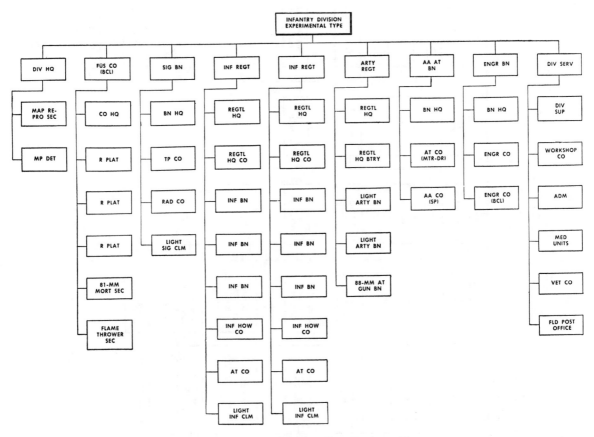

Figure 12.—Infantry Division, Two-Regiment Type.

UNIT	Pers	LMGs	Hv MGs	81-mm Morts	120-mm Morts	Flame Throwers	20-mm AA Guns	75-mm AT Guns	88-mm AT Guns	75-mm Inf Hows	150-mm Inf Hows	105-mm Gun/Hows	Mtr Vehicles	Mtrcls	H-Dr Vehicles	Hs
Div Hq	150	2											48	15		
Füs Co (Bcl)	120	16		2		2							5	3	5	20
Sig Bn ...:..........	402	11											86	20	6	25
Inf Regt	2,645	178	24	18	12			3		6	2		51	44	244	631
Inf Regt	2,645	178	24	18	12			3		6	2		51	44	244	631
Arty Regt	1,755	43							12			24	52	28	106	968
AA/AT Bn	350	17					12	14					88	24		
Engr Bn	397	22	4	4		14							3	7	35	68
Div Serv	1,395	30											159	33	86	391
Total	9,859	497	52	42	24	16	12	20	12	12	4	24	543	218	726	2,734

A Fld Repl Bn with a C Sch may be added to any Inf Div.

Figure 13.—Infantry Division, Two-Regiment Type, total strength 9,859.

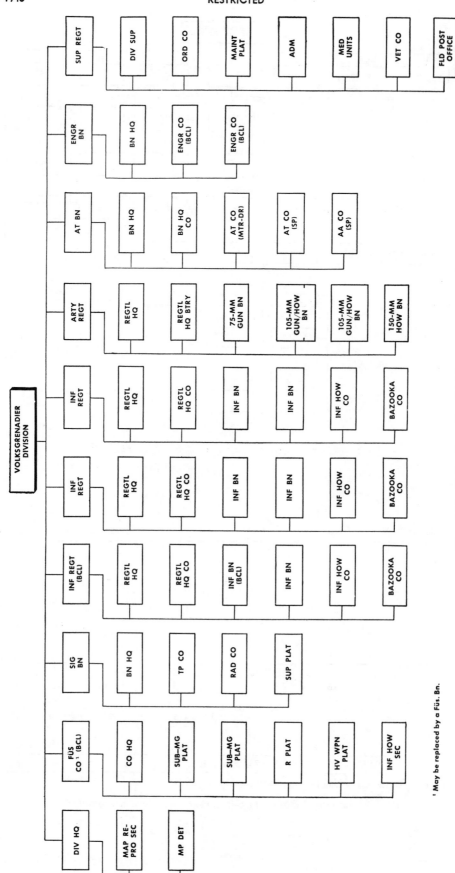

Figure 14.—*Volks Grenadier Division.*

¹ May be replaced by a Füs. Bn.

UNIT	Offs	NCOs	Pvts	Rs or Cbns	Pistols	Sub-MGs	LMGs	Hy MGs	81-mm Morts	120-mm Morts	Bazookas	Flame Throwers	37-mm AA Guns (SP)	75-mm AT Guns (Mtr-Dr)	75-mm AT Guns (SP)	75-mm Inf Hows	75-mm Guns	105-mm Gun/Hows	150-mm Hows	Mtr Vehicles	Mtrcls	H-Dr Vehicles	Trs	Hs	Bcls
Div Hq	34	87	106	121	92	12	5													32	21		1		5
Füs Co [2]	3	28	169	89	26	84	8	2	2							2					1	19	10	56	166
Sig Bn	14	57	234	266	34	5	11													44	10	12	2	44	4
Inf Regt (Bcl)	46	267	1,598	1,048	269	597	79	16	12	8	72					12				10	10	223	84	524	698
Inf Regt	46	267	1,541	991	269	597	79	16	12	8	72					12				9	10	219	84	430	100
Inf Regt [1]	46	267	1,541	991	269	597	79	16	12	8	72					12				9	10	219	84	430	100
Arty Regt	75	405	1,264	1,405	201	132	45										18	24	12	99	13	285	30	1,062	49
AT Bn	17	119	324	326	140	26	30						9	9	14					100	18		16		297
Engr Bn	15	66	361	316	115	11	18	4	4			12								12	14	35	17	68	103
Sup Regt	46	161	868	951	121	3	15													111	12	130	18	388	
Total	342 [3]	1,724	8,006	6,504	1,536	2,064	369	54	42	24	216	12	9	9	14	38	18	24	12	426	119	1,142	346	3,002	1,522

[1] A Fld Repl Bn with a C Sch may be added to any *Volks Gren. Div.*
[2] May be replaced by a **Füs. Bn.**
[3] Including 49 officials.

Figure 15.—Volks Grenadier Division, total strength 10,072.

UNIT	Pers	LMGs	Hv MGs	81-mm Morts	120-mm Morts	Bazookas	Flame Throwers	20-mm AA Guns (SP)	37-mm AT Guns	75-mm AT Guns	75-mm Mt Inf Hows	150-mm Mt Inf Hows	75-mm Mt Hows	105-mm Mt Hows	150-mm Hows
Div Hq	195	2													
Mt Rcn Bn	650	38	6	6					3		2				
Mt Sig Bn	453	11													
Mt Inf Regt	3,064	130	36	18	12	36				3	6	2			
Mt Inf Regt	3,064	130	36	18	12	36				3	6	2			
Mt Arty Regt	2,230	69											24	12	12
AT Bn	500	15						12		18					
Mt Engr Bn	900	31	6	6			20								
Div Serv	2,000	59													
Total	13,056	485	84	48	24	72	20	12	3	24	14	4	24	12	12

A Fld Repl Bn with a C Sch may be added to any Mt Div.

Figure 16.—Army Mountain Division, total strength 13,056.

3. Mountain and Light Divisions

a. Army Mountain Division (*Gebirgasdivision*) (Two Mountain Infantry Regiments of Three Battalions Each.). German Army Mountain divisions are organized and specially equipped for mountain warfare as well as for warfare in difficult terrain. Their means of transportation therefore will vary from a large number of pack horses and mules in higher mountains to a fair proportion of motorization in flat country. The principle of decentralizing heavy weapons is particularly adapted to the relatively independent mountain infantry battalions which are as administratively and tactically self-sufficient as possible. The German army mountain division consists of two mountain infantry regiments with a total of six battalions; and a mountain artillery regiment, with 75-mm mountain howitzers, 105-mm gun/howitzers, and 150-mm howitzers. Its reconnaissance battalion usually uses bicycles for transportation and is therefore highly mobile.

b. Army Light Division (*Jägerdivision*) (Two Light Infantry Regiments of Three Battalions Each). The Army Light Division is organized similarly to the Army Mountain Division but is believed to have more motorization and less mountain equipment.

c. SS Mountain Division (*SS Gebirgsdivision*) (Two SS Mountain Infantry Regiments of Four Battalions Each). The SS Mountain Division is organized similarly to the Army Mountain Division, but it has stronger components and includes an antiaircraft battalion. The SS Mountain Infantry Regiment may have in addition to three mountain infantry battalions a fourth mountain infantry battalion or several regimental companies.

4. Motorized Divisions

a. Army Motorized Division (*Panzergrenadierdivision*) (Two Motorized Infantry Regiments of Three Battalions Each). The Army Motorized Division has two motorized infantry regiments of three battalions each but otherwise is organized similarly to the Army Armored Division except that it has a tank or assault gun battalion instead of a tank regiment. The motorized infantry battalions originally were organized exactly as the normal infantry battalions, except they used trucks as means of transportation. During the year 1944, however, the components of the motorized infantry battalion have been reorganized along the lines of the *Panzer Grenadier* battalions in armored divisions. The two infantry regiments are usually designated (*Infanterieregiment-(mot)*), but in some divisions they officially adopted the designation of *Panzer Grenadier* regiment.

b. SS Motorized Division (*SS-Panzergrenadierdivision*) (Two SS Motorized Infantry Regiments of Three Battalions Each). The SS Motorized Division is organized similarly to the Army Motorized Division, except that its infantry regiments include additional regimental companies, and the tank batalion has a greater strength and a larger number of tanks. The SS motorized infantry regiments are designated SS *Panzer Grenadier* regiments.

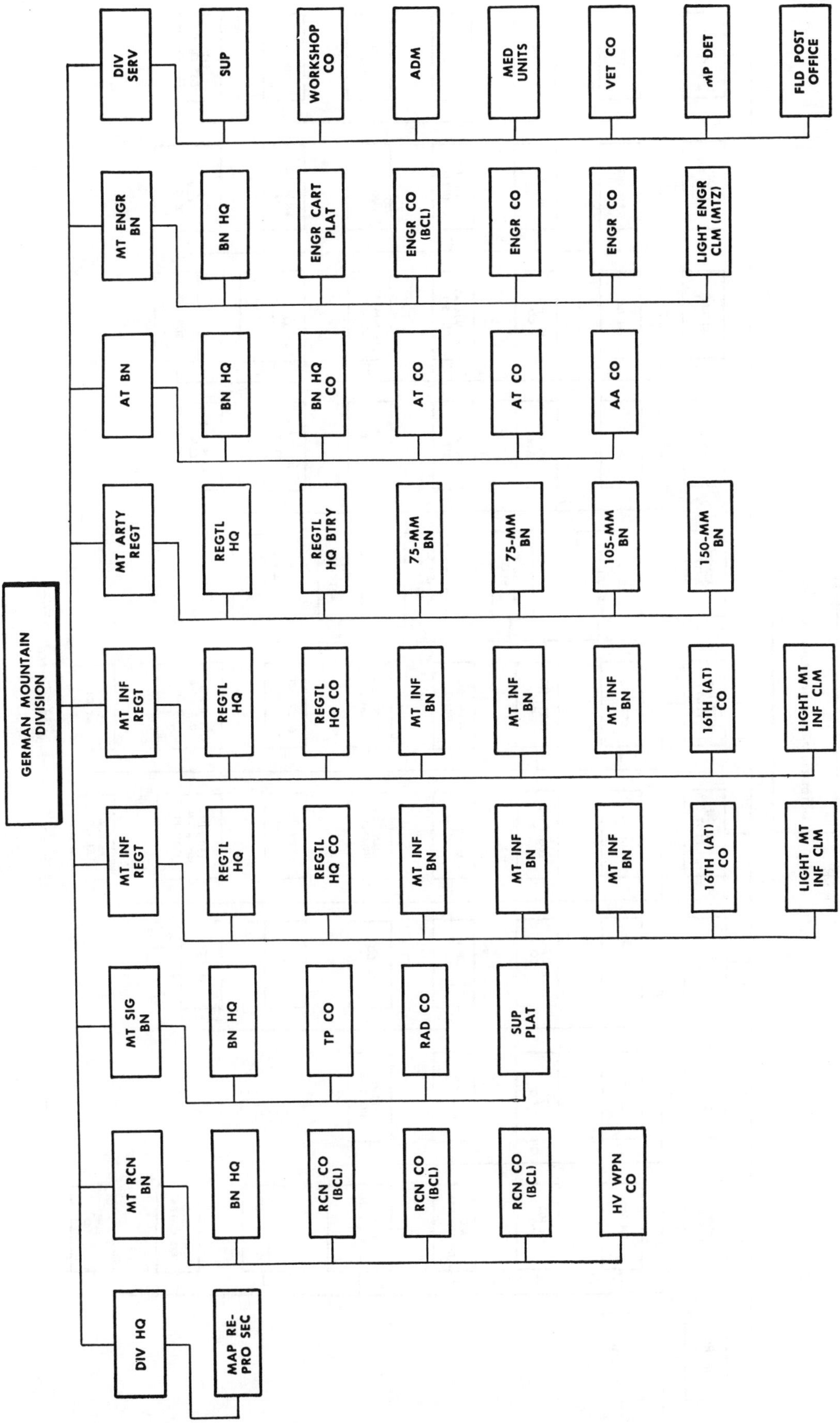

Figure 17.—Army Mountain Division.

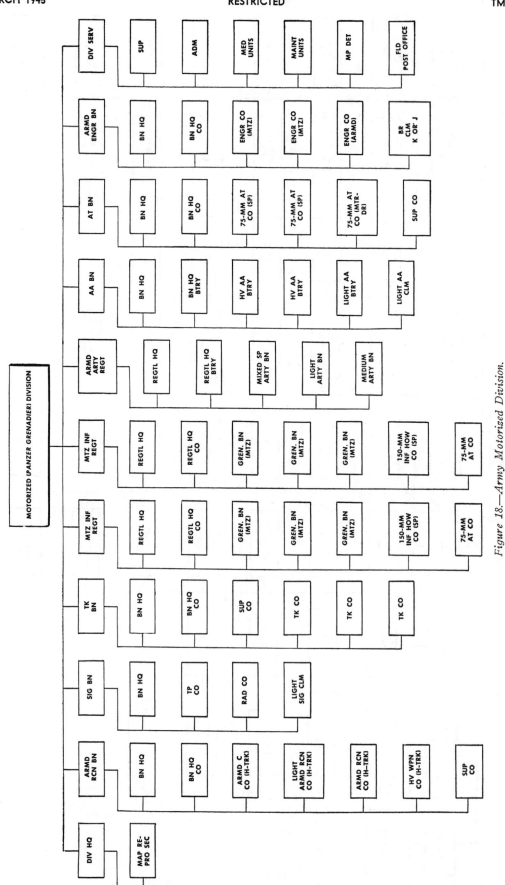

Figure 18.—Army Motorized Division.

UNIT	Offs	NCOs	Pvts	Rs or Cbns	Pistols	Sub-MGs	LMGs	Hv MGs	81-mm Morts	120-mm Morts	Flame Throwers	20-mm AA Guns	20-mm AA Guns Four-Barreled (SP)	20-mm AT Guns	75-mm AT Guns (Mtr-Dr)	75-mm AT Guns (SP)	75-mm Tk Guns (Long)	88-mm AA Guns	150-mm Inf Hows (SP)	105-mm Gun	105-mm Gun/Hows (Mtr-Dr)	105-mm Gun/Hows (SP)	150-mm Hows (Mtr-Dr)	150-mm Hows (SP)	Pz. Kpfw. IV's	Mtr Vehicles	Mtrcls
Div Hq	32	31	78	95	44	3	2																			32	8
Armd Rcn Bn	27	223	692	434	300	206	147	4	10		6			35		13										193	22
Sig Bn	13	83	360	400	50	40	17																			107	14
Tk Bn	27	212	328	229	286	95	112					3					48								48	94	18
Mtz Inf Regt	85	545	2,413	1,938	789	316	201	36	18	12		18			9				6							502	108
Mtz Inf Regt	85	545	2,413	1,938	789	316	201	36	18	12		18			9				6							502	108
Armd Arty Regt	69	365	1,215	1,217	343	203	92					9									12	12	12	6		407	31
AA Bn	22	142	600	673	69	47	18					18							8							171	16
AT Bn	20	166	327	271	142	100	47								12	31										135	17
Engr Bn	24	116	733	552	245	102	96	6	6		20			3												171	42
Div Serv	64	292	1,529	1,708	165	13	86																			323	85
Total	468[1]	2,720	10,688	9,455	3,222	1,441	1,019	82	52	24	26	63	3	38	30	44	48	8	12		12	12	12	6	48	2,637[2]	469

[1] Including 64 officials.
[2] Including 184 Armd vehicles.

Figure 19.—Army Motorized Division, total strength, 13,876.

5. Armored Divisions

a. ARMY ARMORED DIVISION *(Panzerdivision)* (Two *Panzer Grenadier* REGIMENTS OF TWO BATTALIONS EACH). Every German large-scale attack and counterattack in this war was spearheaded by armored *(Panzer)* divisions. These thrusting attacks account for the great importance the armored divisions play within the German armed forces and for the especially well trained personnel and newest types of weapons and equipment in the armored division. In order to keep the weapons and equipment in accordance with the newest development at all times, the reorganizations within that type of division have been continuous since the outbreak of the war and are still continuing.

In 1939 the German armored divisions which spearheaded the attack into Poland consisted of a tank brigade of two tank regiments, a *Panzer Grenadier* brigade of two regiments, and the supporting elements. The tank brigade consisted of about 400 light and medium tanks, about two-thirds of which were *Pz. Kpfw. I* and *II* and one-third were *Pz. Kpfw. III* and *IV*. During the winter of 1940 the Germans formed additional armored divisions and reduced the tank components of each to one regiment of approximately 200 tanks. When these divisions went into action in the French campaign, the bulk of the tanks were *Pz. Kpfw. III* and *IV*. In 1941 and 1942 the number of tanks per regiment was further reduced, the *Pz. Kpfw. I* were withdrawn, and the *Pz. Kpfw. II* were used mainly for reconnaissance purposes. In the fall of 1943 the German High Command issued a new table of organization for the armored division specifying a total number of about 200 tanks of the *Pz. Kpfw. IV* and *V* type exclusively. This planned strength, however, remained only a theory, as no armored division encountered had more than 150 tanks, and most of the divisions had approximately 100 only. Early in 1944 the German High Command issued an order that all companies and

battalion trains in the tank regiment, in the *Panzer Grenadier* regiments, and in the armored reconnaissance battalion should be reduced in strength and merged into supply companies on the battalion level, thus freeing the company commanders from all duties other than operational and facilitating a more even distribution of all types of supplies with curtailed personnel. The most important changes which occurred in the organization of other components of the armored division will be covered under the appropriate branches of arms or services in Sections VI and VII.

While the last known tables of organization of the army armored division still specify 17 tanks for each of the four companies in the tank battalion, current front reports indicate that a new set of tables of organization is being issued specifying the components as shown in Figures 20-22.

b. SS ARMORED DIVISION *(SS-Panzerdivision)* (Two *Panzer Grenadier* REGIMENTS OF THREE BATTALIONS EACH). The *SS* Armored Division is organized similarly to the Army Armored Division except that it has stronger components. The tank regiment has a larger number of tanks, each of the *Panzer Grenadier* regiments has a *Panzer Grenadier* battalion and an antiaircraft company, the armored artillery regiment has one more armored artillery battalion (170-mm guns or 210-mm howitzers), the armored engineer battalion usually has an additional bridge column, and the division includes a rocket projector battalion and an assault gun battalion. The divisional services are also proportionately stronger.

In accordance with the above, the *SS* Armored Division may be considered the strongest type of division in the German armed forces. Only the Air Force Parachute Armored Division, Herman Goering, and the Army Armored divisions, *Panzer Lehr* and *Grossdeutschland*, are believed to be of equal strength.

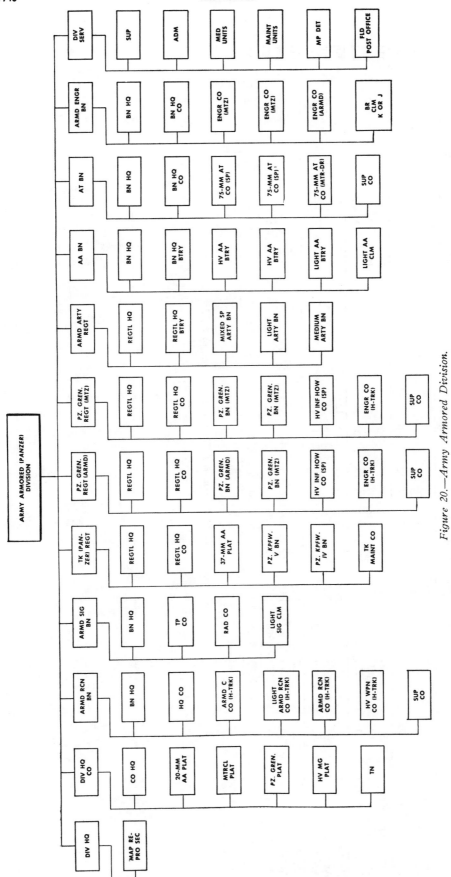

Figure 20.—Army Armored Division.

Figure 21.—Army Armored Division, total strength 13,725.

UNIT	Offs	NCOs	Pvts	Rs or Cbns	Pistols	Sub-MGs	LMGs	Hv MGs	81-mm Morts	120-mm Morts	Flame Throwers	20-mm AA Guns	20-mm AT Guns	28/20-mm AT Guns	37-mm AA Guns (SP)	75-mm AT Guns (Mtr-Dr)	75-mm AT Guns (SP)	75-mm Tk Guns (Long)	75-mm Tk Guns (Superlong)	88-mm AA Guns	75-mm Inf Hows (SP)	150-mm Inf Hows (SP)	105-mm Gun Hows (Mtr-Dr)	105-mm Hows (SP)	150-mm Hows (Mtr-Dr)	150-mm Hows (SP)	Pz. Kpfw. IV's	Pz. Kpfw. V's	Mtr Vehicles	Mtrcls
Div Hq	32[1]	31	78	95	44	3																								32	8
Div Hq Co	3	37	179	138	65	19	16	2	2									3												31	28
Armd Rcn Bn	27	223	692	434	300	206	147	4	10		6	4	35				13													199	22
Armd Sig Bn	16	103	396	444	69	51	35																							114	14
Tk (Pz) Regt.	69	553	1,039	822	704	228	252					6						52	51									52	51	313	53
Pz. Gren. Regt. (Armd)	64	436	1,794	1,373	595	336	224	26	14	8	24	25			8						12	6								406	81
Pz. Gren. Regt. (Mtz)	61	410	1,787	1,449	574	235	144	26	14	8	18	12																		380	83
Armd Arty Regt.	69	365	1,215	1,217	343	203	92					9										6	12	12	12	6				407	31
AA Bn	22	142	600	673	69	47	18					18								8										171	16
AT Bn	20	166	327	271	142	100	47									12	31													135	17
Armd Engr Bn	24	118	743	562	247	102	96	6	6		20		3	3																174	42
Div Serv	64	292	1,529	1,708	165	13	86																							323	85
Total	471[1]	2,876	10,379	9,186	3,317	1,543	1,157	64	46	16	68	74	38	3	8	12	47	52	51	8	12	12	12	12	12	6	52	51	2,685[2]	480

[1] Including 69 officials.
[2] Including 357 Armd vehicles.

Figure 22.—Division Headquarters, Army Armored Division, total strength 360.

UNIT	Offs	NCOs	Pvts	Rs or Cbns	Pistols	Sub-MGs	LMGs	Hv MGs	81-mm Morts	20-mm AA Guns (SP)	75-mm AT Guns	Mtr Vehicles	Mtrcls
Armd Div Hq	32[1]	30	71	86	43	3						30	8
Map Repro Sec		1	7	7	1							2	
Div Hq Co	3	37	179	138	65	19	16	2	2	4	3	31	28
Total	35[1]	68	257	231	109	22	16	2	2	4	3	63	36

[1] Including ten officials.

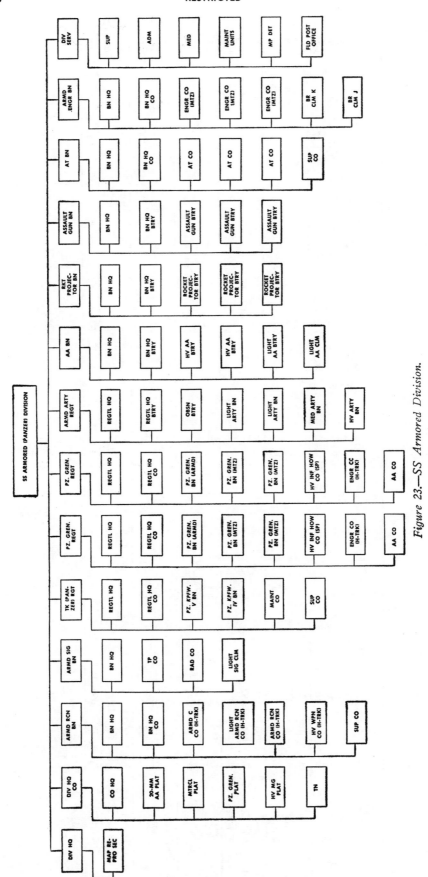

Figure 23.—SS Armored Division.

UNIT	Offs	NCOs	Pvts	Rs or Cbns	Pistols	Sub-MGs	LMGs	Hv MGs	81-mm Morts	120-mm Morts	Flame Throwers	150 or 210-mm Rkt Projectors	20-mm AA Guns	20-mm AT Guns	28/20-mm AT Guns	37-mm AA Guns (SP)	75-mm AT Guns (Mtr-Dr)	75-mm AT Guns (SP)	75-mm Tk Guns (Long)	75-mm Tk Guns (Superlong)	88-mm AA Guns	75-mm Inf Hows (SP)	150-mm Inf Hows (SP)	105-mm Gun Hows (Mtr-Dr)	105-mm Gun Hows (SP)	150-mm Hows (Mtr-Dr)	150-mm Hows (SP)	170-mm Guns	Pz. Kpfw. IV's	Pz. Kpfw. V's	Mtr Vehicles	Mtrcls
Div Hq	32	31	78	95	44	3																									32	8
Div Hq Co.	3	37	179	138	65	19	16	2	2				4																		31	28
Armd Rcn Bn	27	223	692	434	300	206	147	4	10		6			35				13													193	22
Armd Sig Bn.....	16	103	396	444	69	51	35																								114	14
Tk (*Pz.*) Regt...	70	614	1,087	816	719	245	296						6			8			64	62									64	62	313	53
Pz. Gren. Regt....	89	598	2,555	1,957	852	443	284	38	20	12	24		43									12	6								527	88
Pz. Gren. Regt....	89	598	2,555	1,957	852	443	284	38	20	12	24		43									12	6								527	88
Armd Arty Regt..	89	473	1,605	1,636	409	255	109	12																12	12	12	6	12			534	40
AA Bn	22	148	654	729	73	47	22						18								12										181	16
Bn Rkt Projector.	14	101	358	380	40	53	18					18																			107	8
Assault Gun Bn...	15	111	218	294	80	70	22											22													100	11
AT Bn	20	166	327	271	142	100	47										12	31													135	17
Armd Engr Bn ...	26	132	826	654	254	102	99	6	6		20			3	3																212	52
Div Serv	64	292	1,529	1,708	165	13	86																								323	85
Total	576[1]	3,627	13,059	11,513	4,064	2,050	1,465	100	58	24	74	18	114	38	3	8	12	69	64	62	12	24	12	12	12	12	6	12	64	62	3,329[2]	530

[1] Including 62 officials.
[2] Including 359 Armd vehicles.

Figure 24.—SS Armored Division, total strength 17,262.

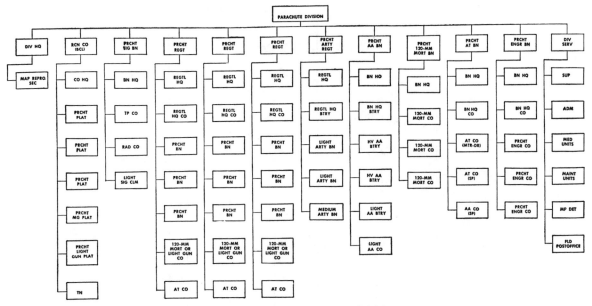

Figure 25.—Air Force Parachute Division.

6. Air Force Parachute Division (*Fallschirmjagerdivision*) (Three Parachute Rifle Regiments of Three Battalions Each)

As the abovementioned *SS* Armored Division may be considered the strongest type of division in the German armed forces, the German Air Force Parachute Division is believed to be the strongest type of the various infantry divisions. While in the course of this war small German parachute units have been employed successfully as airborne troops in various campaigns, in the West, in the Balkans, in Crete and Sicily, one generally may consider the present Air Force Parachute divisions as especially carefully selected, well trained, and equipped crack infantry divisions, with only a small percentage of their personnel having received training as parachutists in the American sense of the word. The significant organizational difference between the parachute division and the army infantry division is that each of the three parachute rifle regiments has three battalions and a larger allotment of machine guns than the corresponding army units. The parachute artillery regiment has only three battalions (two light and one medium), but the division includes a parachute antiaircraft battalion and a parachute 120-mm mortar battalion.

7. Air Force Field Division (*Luftwaffenfelddivision* (Three Infantry Regiments of Two Battalions Each)

The Air Force Field Divisions were formed in the later part of 1942 from surplus personnel of the antiaircraft artillery, the air signal troops, the ground crews of the flying troops, and administrative units, as well as a certain number of recruits and foreigners. Most of these divisions were sent to the Russian front in the winter of 1942-1943 but some also were encountered on the Italian front and in France. The organization of this type of division varied, but it is believed that the basic pattern was originally a two-regiment, three-battalion division, with normal supporting units and an additional antiaircraft battalion. In the fall of 1943 the Air Force Field divisions were absorbed by the Army. Many of them had suffered heavy losses and were disbanded in 1943 and 1944, and the remaining few were reorganized along the lines of the Infantry Division, 1944 Type.

8. Cavalry Division (*Kavallariedivision*) (Four Cavalry Regiments of Two Battalions Each)

The only army cavalry division identified is the Cossack Division which consists of Don, Kuban, and Terek Cossacks; some German officers and noncommissioned officers; and possibly elements of other nationalities.

The *Waffen-SS* is believed to have two cavalry divisions.

All three of these cavalry divisions are organized similarly and consist of two cavalry brigades of two regiments each, a weak artillery regiment, a reconnaissance battalion, a signal bat-

UNIT	Pers	Rs or Cbns	Pistols	Sub-MGs	LMGs	Hv MGs	81-mm Morts	120-mm Morts	Bazookas	Flame Throwers	20-mm AA Guns (Mtr-Dr)	20-mm AA Guns (SP)	75-mm AT Guns (Mtr-Dr)	75-mm AT Guns (SP)	88-mm AA Guns	75-mm Light Guns	105-mm Gun/Hows	150-mm Hows	Mtr Vehicles	Mtrcls
Div Hq	194	102	82	7	2	2			6										27	21
Rcn Co.	200	89	26	84	8		2		4							2			10	1
Prcht Sig Bn	379	326	18	35	11				6										83	13
Prcht R Regt	3,206	1,651	968	751	224	24	39	9	54				3			6			304	71
Prcht R Regt	3,206	1,651	968	751	224	24	39	9	54				3			6			304	71
Prcht R Regt	3,206	1,651	968	751	224	24	39	9	54				3			6			304	71
Prcht Arty Regt	1,571	1,250	218	168	53				12		9						24	12	396	30
Prcht AA Bn	824	729	73	47	22				12		18				12				181	16
Prcht 120-mm Mort Bn.	594	290	87	258	42			36	6										123	33
Prcht AT Bn	484	318	123	81	29	6			36			12	12	14					113	20
Prcht Engr Bn	620	432	136	71	31		6		6	20									43	19
Div Serv	1,492	1,200	143	22	60														253	23
Total	15,976	9,689	3,810	3,026	930	80	125	63	250	20	27	12	21	14	12	20	24	12	2,141	389

Figure 26.—Air Force Parachute Division, total strength 15,976.

talion, an engineer battalion, and the divisional services.

9. Line of Communication Division (*Sicherungsdivision*)

Designed for mopping-up duties in the rear areas, such a division may consist of two reinforced regiments or of a number of independent battalions.

10. Coast Defense Division (*Kustenverteidigungsdivision*)

This consists of a division staff controlling fortress battalions and coast artillery units in a coastal sector.

11. Assault Division (*Sturmdivision*)

This is an honorary title for some divisions with reduced infantry personnel and a concentration of heavy firepower and automatic weapons.

12. Frontier Guard Division (*Grenzwachdivision*)

This consists of a division staff controlling certain frontier guard units.

13. Special Administrative Division Staff (*Divisionskommando z.b.V.*)

This consists of a division staff controlling *Landesschützen* Battalions and General Headquarters troops stationed in a corps area in Germany.

14. Replacement Division Staff (*Div. Nr. . . . .*)

This is a division staff within a corps area in Germany to supervise the induction of personnel and replacements for field units.

15. Reserve Division (*Reservedivision*)

This controls reserve units for training, occupation, and defensive duties. This type of division is organized similarly to field infantry divisions; it has a preponderance of infantry, engineers, and static artillery, but the other elements are believed to be very much under strength. In spite of that, several reserve divisions have been redesignated combat divisions (*Kampfdivisionen*) and went into action on short notice.

16. Field Training Division (*Feldausbildungsdivision*)

This controls field training regiments in the rear of the Eastern Front. Is believed to be organized similarly to the Reserve Division and therefore may be encountered in the field.

17. Antiaircraft Division (*Flakdivision*)

Under the German system, antiaircraft defense is in the main the responsibility of the German Air Force, although the German Army also has a large number of antiaircraft units of its own. While the composition and equipment of antiaircraft batteries generally are standardized, the formation of these into battalions, regiments, divisions, or units of equivalent size, however, is subject to more variations than in any other of the German arms. The average non-motorized, air force, antiaircraft division, which is shown in the following figure, usually is located in the Zone of the Interior. It has a large number of trailers but very little motorization, and depends for mobility on separate transportation units. As pointed out above, many other combinations of the units shown as divisional components may be encountered frequently.

UNIT	Pers	LMGs	20-mm AA Guns	20-mm AA Guns (Four-Barreled)	37-mm AA Guns	88-mm AA Guns	105-mm AA Guns	60-cm SLs	105-cm SLs	200-cm SLs	Bar Blns	Mtr Vehicles	Tlrs	Mtrcls
Div Hq	200	2										30	1	20
Air Def Sig Bn	300	11										44	12	10
Hv SL Regt	2,043	29							90	18		94	255	52
AA Regt	2,448	38	52	9	12	24	16	16			72	109	238	55
AA Regt	2,448	38	52	9	12	24	16	16			72	109	238	55
AA Regt	2,448	38	52	9	12	24	16	16			72	109	238	55
Air Med Unit	250	2										37		2
Total	10,137	158	156	27	36	72	48	48	90	18	216	532	982	249

In motorized AA units the number of personnel is approximately twice as high.

Figure 27.—Antiaircraft Division in Zone of Interior, total strength 10,137.

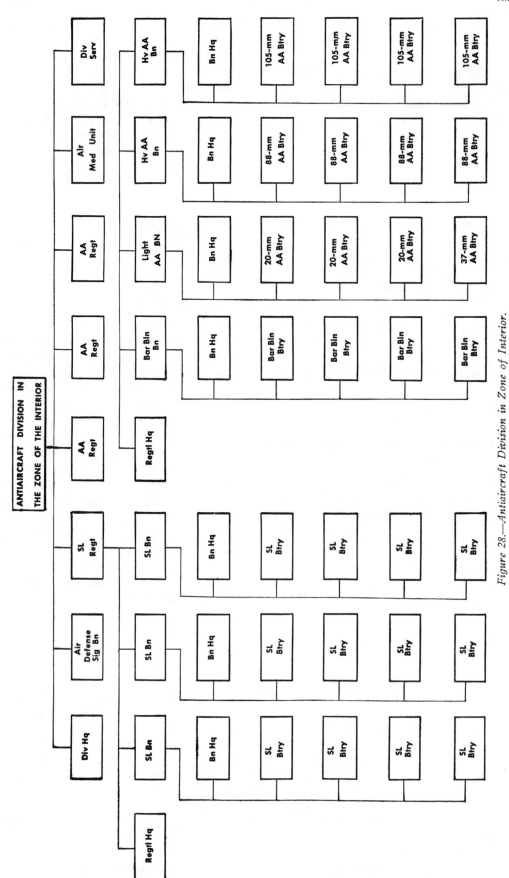

Figure 28.—Antiaircraft Division in Zone of Interior.

Section VI. COMBAT TROOPS
(FECHTENDE TRUPPEN)

I. General

This section consists of a list of the more important types of combat units in the German armed forces, of the status of regiments and below with particulars on their organization. They are arranged according to the arms and services (*Waffengattungen*), divided into organic units (integral parts of divisions) and General Headquarters units (*Heerestruppen*) (units held in the General Headquarters pool from which they are allotted to army groups, armies, and corps and sub-allotted temporarily to divisions for specific operations).

2. Organic Infantry Units

a. GENERAL. For the purpose of clarity we are including under this paragraph all units which are infantry units in accordance with the American conception. The Germans consider security troops (*Sicherungstruppen*) a separate category of units of the field army, but in reality they consist principally of infantry. Similarly, the Germans consider armored infantry (*Panzergrenadiere*) as belonging to the armored arm and not to the infantry.

On the other hand, the Germans include reconnaissance and other former cavalry units as a part of the infantry arm which are listed in this section under paragraph 19, Reconnaissance Units. The designation of the infantry regiment was changed to *Grenadierregiment* in 1942 by special order of Hitler to honor the infantry arm. The same applies to the infantry battalion now called *Grenadierbataillon* and to the infantry company *Grenadierkompanie*.

b. INFANTRY REGIMENT.

(1) *Old Type Regiment.* The infantry regiments of the Infantry Division, Old Type, may be considered the basic type of German infantry regiments, as their organization remained for all practical purposes unchanged from the beginning of 1940 until the end of 1943. Each of the three regiments of the Infantry Division, Old Type, consisted of three infantry battalions, a thirteenth infantry howitzer company, and a fourteenth anti-tank company. In spite of the fact that the Infantry Division, Old Type, will not be encountered any more, it is believed that this type of regiment has formed the basic pattern and tradi-

UNIT	Offs	NCOs	Pvts	Rs or Cbns	Pistols	Sub-MGs	LMGs	Hv MGs	81-mm Morts	120-mm Morts	Bazookas	75-mm AT Guns	75-mm Inf Hows	150-mm Inf Hows	Mtr Vehicles	Mtrcls	H-Dr Vehicles	Trlrs	Hs	Bcls
Regtl Hq	7	1	16	16	7	2									3	3			8	2
Regtl Hq Co	5	28	165	143	26	32	10								5	5	28	6	84	9
Inf Bn	15	113	580	477	122	127	43	12	6	4					8	5	92	57	165	17
Inf Bn	15	113	580	477	122	127	43	12	6	4					8	5	92	57	165	17
Inf How Co[1]	3	32	149	140	22	27	5						6	2	8	2	22	2	63	3
AT Co[2]	3	29	154	120	51	17	6				36	3			13		8	8	10	6
Total	48[3]	316	1,644	1,373	350	332	107	24	12	8	36	3	6	2	45	20	242	130	495	54

[1] Referred to by the traditional designation: "13" Co.
[2] Referred to by the traditional designation: "14" Co.
[3] Including six officials.

Figure 29.—Infantry Regiment, Infantry Division, 1944 Type, total strength 2,008.

tion for most of the infantry regiments now in the field.

(2) *1944 Type Regiment.* The above type of regiment has been superseded by the infantry regiment in the Infantry Division, 1944 Type, which consists also of three regiments, but each regiment has only two battalions in addition to the infantry howitzer and antitank companies. (See *Figures 29* to *39.*)

(3) *Three-Battalion Regiment.* In addition to the type of infantry regiment mentioned in subparagraph (2), another type may be encountered which is similar to the basic one mentioned in subparagraph (1). It is the three-battalion regiment of the infantry division, two-regiment type. However, it is believed that there is a trend toward reorganizing that type of division on a three-regiment, two-battalion basis. After such a reorganization, the regiment probably will be similar to the Infantry Regiment, 1944 Type.

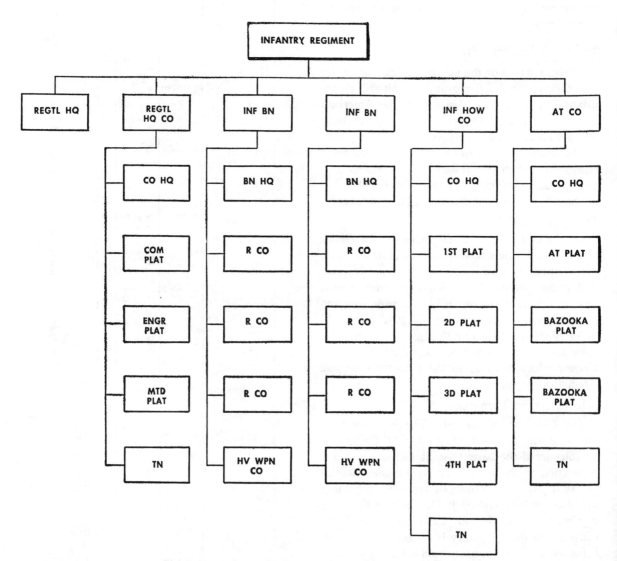

Figure 30.—Infantry Regiment, Infantry Division, 1944 Type.

UNIT	Offs	NCOs	Pvts	Rs or Cbns	Pistols	Sub-MGs	LMGs	Mtr Vehicles	H-Dr Vehicles	Tlrs	Hs	Bcls
Co Hq	1	5	2	3	5	1					1	3
1st (Com) Plat	1	2	29	23	1	9			6	6	7	
20 (Engr) Plat	1	7	65	53	8	13	6		6		13	2
30 (Mtd) Plat[1]		4	27	20	4	7	3		1		31	
Tn	2[2]	10	42	44	8	2	1	5	15		32	4
Total	5[2]	28	165	143	26	32	10	5	28	6	84	9

[1] The Mtd Plat may be replaced by a Bcl Plat with 29 Bcls and 2 Hs.
[2] Including two officials.

Figure 31.—Regimental Headquarters Company, Infantry Division, 1944 Type, total strength 198.

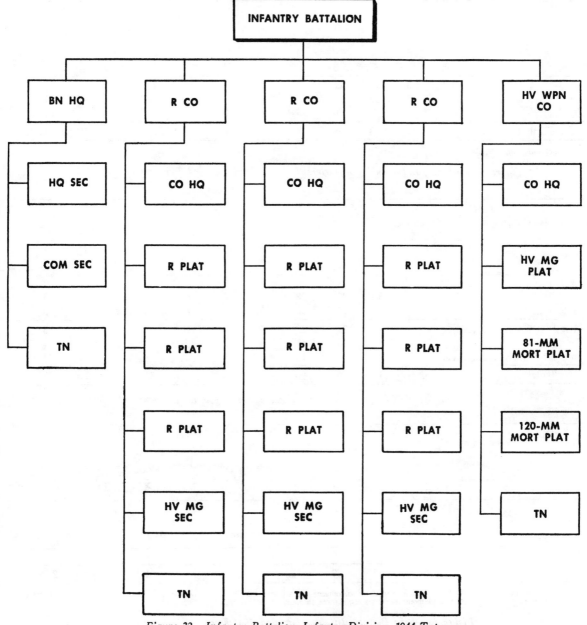

Figure 32.—Infantry Battalion, Infantry Division, 1944 Type.

UNIT	Offs	NCOs	Pvts	Rs Cbns	Pistols	Sub-MGs	LMGs	Hv MGs	81-mm Morts	120-mm Morts	Mtr Vehicles	Mtrcls	H-Dr Vehicles	Tlrs	Hs	Bcls
Bn Hq	6[1]	13	58	58	8	14	1				1	2	16	4	33	6
R Co	2	21	119	96	22	28	13	2					15	11	27	3
R Co	2	21	119	96	22	28	13	2					15	11	27	3
R Co	2	21	119	96	22	28	13	2					15	11	27	3
Hv Wpn Co	3	37	165	131	48	29	3	6	6	4	7	3	31	20	51	2
Total	15[1]	113	580	477	122	127	43	12	6	4	8	5	92	57	165	17

[1] Including two officials.

Figure 33.—Infantry Battalion, Infantry Division, 1944 Type, total strength 708.

UNIT	Offs	NCOs	Pvts	Rs or Cbns	Pistols	Sub-MGs	LMGs	Mtr Vehicles	Mtrcls	H-Dr Vehicles	Tlrs	Hs	Bcls
Hq Sec	4	3	10	11	5	4		1	2			4	3
Com Sec		3	22	17		8				4	4	4	
Tn	2[1]	7	26	30	3	2	1			12		25	3
Total	6[1]	13	58	58	8	14	1	1	2	16	4	33	6

[1] Including two officials.

Figure 34.—Infantry Battalion Headquarters, Infantry Division, 1944 Type, total strength 77.

UNIT	Offs	NCOs	Pvts	Rs or Cbns	Pistols	Sub-MGs	LMGs	Hv MGs	H-Dr Vehicles	Tlrs	Hs	Bcls
Co Hq	1	3	8	8	2	3			1	1	2	2
1st R Plat	1	3	29	22	5	7	4		2	2	3	
2d R Plat		4	29	22	5	7	4		2	2	3	
3d R Plat		4	29	22	5	7	4		2	2	3	
Hv MG Sec		3	15	11	4	3		2	3	2	4	
Tn		4	9	11	1	1	1		5	2	12	1
Total	2	21	119	96	22	28	13	2	15	11	27	3

Figure 35.—Rifle Company, Infantry Division, 1944 Type, total strength 142.

UNIT	Offs[1]	NCOs[1]	Pvts	Rs or Cbns	Pistols	Sub-MGs	LMGs	H-Dr Vehicles	Tlrs	Hs
Plat Hq	1		5	4	2	1	1	2	2	3
R Sqd		1	8	6	1	2	1			
R Sqd		1	8	6	1	2	1			
R Sqd		1	8	6	1	2	1			
Total	1	3	29	22	5	7	4	2	2	3

Only the 1st Plat of the R Co is commanded by an officer; the 2d and 3d Plats are commanded by NCOs, and consequently the number of NCOs in these two platoons increases from three to four.

Figure 36.—Rifle Platoon, Infantry Division, 1944 Type, total strength 33.

UNIT	Offs	NCOs	Pvts	Rs or Cbns	Pistols	Sub-MGs	LMGs	Hv MGs	81-mm Morts	120-mm Morts	Mtr Vehicles	Mtrcls	H-Dr Vehicles	Tlrs	Hs	Bcls
Co Hq	1	4	15	15	2	4						1	2	2	5	1
1st (HvMG) Plat	1	9	45	31	15	10		6					8	6	11	
20 (81-mm Mort) Plat (H-Dr)		10	56	37	23	6			6				15	12	19	
30 (120-mm Mort) Plat (Mtz)	1	7	39	36	5	7	2			4	7	2				
Tn		7	10	12	3	2	1						6		16	1
Total	3	37	165	131	48	29	3	6	6	4	7	3	31	20	51	2

Figure 37.—Heavy Weapons Company, Infantry Division, 1944 Type, total strength 205.

UNIT	Offs	NCOs	Pvts	Rs or Cbns	Pistols	Sub-MGs	LMGs	75-mm Inf Hows	150-mm Inf Hows	Mtr Vehicles	Mtrcls	H-Dr Vehicles	Tlrs	Hs	Bcls
Co Hq	1	4	13	14	3	2				1		2	2	5	2
1st (75-mm Inf How) Plat	1	5	30	27	4	6	1	2				5		15	
2d (75-mm Inf How) Plat		6	30	27	4	6	1	2				5		15	
3d (75-mm Inf How) Plat		6	30	27	4	6	1	2				5		15	
4th (150-mm Inf How) Plat	1	5	33	29	5	6	1		2	6	2				
Tn		6	13	16	2	1	1			1		5		13	1
Total	3	32	149	140	22	27	5	6	2	8	2	22	2	63	3

Referred to by the traditional designation: "13th" Co.

Figure 38.—Infantry Howitzer Company, Infantry Division, 1944 Type, total strength 184.

UNIT	Offs	NCOs	Pvts	Rs or Cbns	Pistols	Sub-MGs	LMGs	Bazookas	75-mm AT Guns	Mtr Vehicles	Mtrcls	H-Dr Vehicles	Tlrs	Hs	Bcls
Co Hq	1	10	26	29	6	3				1	4			2	6
1st (75-mm AT) Plat (Mtz).........	1	4	28	25	4	5	3		3	5	1				
2d (Bazooka) Plat (H-Dr)..........		5	43	25	19	4	1	18				4	4	4	
3d (Bazooka) Plat (H-Dr)	1	4	43	25	19	4	1	18				4	4	4	
Tn (Mtz)		6	14	16	3	1	1			7					
Total	3	29	154	120	51	17	6	36	3	13	5	8	8	10	6

Referred to by the traditional designation: "14th" Co.

Figure 39.—Antitank Company (partly mortorized), Infantry Division, 1944 Type, total sertngth 186.

(4) *Volks Grenadier Regiment*. The infantry regiment in the *Volks Grenadier* Division shows a completely new organization. The infantry company and battalion trains are merged to a supply platoon on a battalion level. The infantry company consists of two sub-machine gun platoons and a rifle platoon. The heavy-weapons company of the infantry battalion includes an infantry howitzer platoon. The regimental infantry howitzer company is equipped with 120-mm mortars and 75-mm infantry howitzers only, and the regimental antitank company has been replaced by a bazooka company equipped with 72 bazookas. (See *Figures 40* to *50*.)

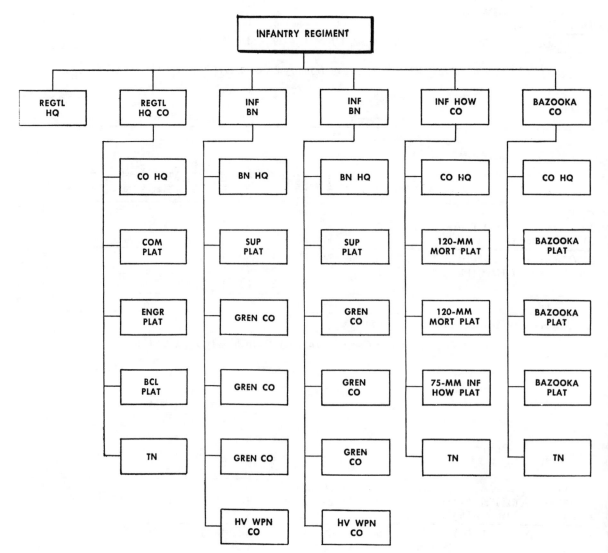

Figure 40.—Infantry Regiment, Volks Grenadier Division.

UNIT	Offs	NCOs	Pvts	Rs or Cbns	Pistols	Sub-MGs	LMGs	Hv MGs	81-mm Morts	120-mm Morts	Bazookas	75-mm Inf Hows	Mtr Vehicles	Mtrcls	H-Dr Vehicles	Tlrs	Hs	Bcls
Regtl Hq	6	1	12	4	3	14							2	3			8	2
Regtl Hq Co	5	25	157	133	22	32	10						1		27	6	53	38
Inf Bn	15	95	532	309	80	253	30	8	6			4	2	3	70	32	125	27
Inf Bn	15	95	532	309	80	253	30	8	6			4	2	3	70	32	125	27
Inf How Co[1]	3	32	162	145	21	31	5			8		4	1		33	2	89	4
Bazooka Co[2]	2	19	146	91	63	14	4				72		1	1	19	12	30	2
Total	46[3]	267	1,541	991	269	597	79	16	12	8	72	12	9	10	219	84	430	100

[1] Referred to by the traditional designation: "13th" Co.
[2] Referred to by the traditional designation: "14th" Co.
[3] Including four officials.

Figure 41.—Infantry Regiment, Volks Grenadier Division, total strength 1,854.

UNIT	Offs	NCOs	Pvts	Rs or Cbns	Pistols	Sub-MGs	LMGs	Mtr Vehicles	H-Dr Vehicles	Tlrs	Hs	Bcls
Co Hq	1	5	2	3	4	1					1	3
1st (Com) Plat	1	2	29	23		9			6	6	7	
2d (Engr) Plat	1	7	65	53	7	13	6		6		13	2
3d (Bcl) Plat		4	27	20	4	7	3		1		2	29
Tn	2[1]	7	34	34	7	2	1	1	14		30	4
Total	5[1]	25	157	133	22	32	10	1	27	6	53	38

[1] Including two officials.

Figure 42.—Regimental Headquarters Company, Volks Grenadier Division, total strength 187.

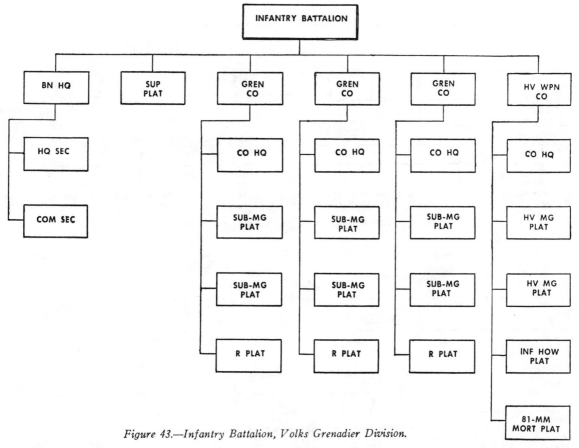

Figure 43.—Infantry Battalion, Volks Grenadier Division.

UNIT	Offs	NCOs	Pvts	Rs or Cbns	Pistols	Sub-MGs	LMGs	Hv MGs	81-mm Morts	75-mm Inf Hows	Mtr Vehicles	Mtrcls	H-Dr Vehicles	Tlrs	Hs	Bcls
Bn Hq	4	6	34	21	3	20	1				1	2	4	4	8	3
Sup Plat	2[1]	6	39	42	3	2	1				1		17		42	4
Gren. Co	2	16	101	46	9	64	9						7	4	10	5
Gren. Co	2	16	101	46	9	64	9						7	4	10	5
Gren. Co	2	16	101	46	9	64	9						7	4	10	5
Hv Wpn Co	3	35	156	108	47	39	1	8	6	4		1	28	16	45	5
Total	15[1]	95	532	309	80	253	30	8	6	4	2	3	70	32	125	27

[1] Including one official.

Figure 44.—Infantry Battalion, Volks Grenadier Division, total strength 642.

UNIT	Offs	NCOs	Pvts	Rs or Cbns	Pistols	Sub-MGs	LMGs	H-Dr Vehicles	Tlrs	Hs	Bcls
Co Hq	1	5	14	16	1	3		1	1	1	5
1st (Sub-MG) Plat	1	3	29	5	2	26	3	2	1	3	
2d (Sub-MG) Plat		4	29	5	2	26	3	2	1	3	
3d (R) Plat		4	29	20	4	9	3	2	1	3	
Total	2	16	101	46	9	64	9	7	4	10	5

Figure 45.—Infantry Company, Volks Grenadier Division, total strength 119.

UNIT	Offs[1]	NCOs[1]	Pvts	Rs or Cbns	Pistols	Sub-MGs	LMGs	H-Dr Vehicles	Tlrs	Hs
Plat Hq	1		5	2	1	3	2	2	1	3
Sub-MG Sqd		1	8			9				
Sub-MG Sqd		1	8			9				
R Sqd		1	8	3	1	5	1			
Total	1	3	29	5	2	26	3	2	1	3

Only the 1st Plat of the Gren Co is commanded by an officer; the 2d (Sub-MG) and 3d (R) Plats are commanded by NCOs and consequently the number of NCOs in these Plats increases by three to four.

Figure 46.—Submachine gun Platoon, Volks Grenadier Division, total strength 33.

UNIT	Offs	NCOs	Pvts	Rs or Cbns	Pistols	Sub-MGs	LMGs	H-Dr Vehicles	Tlrs	Hs
Plat Hq		1	5	2	1	3		2	1	3
R Sqd		1	8	6	1	2	1			
R Sqd		1	8	6	1	2	1			
R Sqd		1	8	6	1	2	1			
Total		4	29	20	4	9	3	2	1	3

Figure 47.—Rifle Platoon, Volks Grenadier Division, total strength 33.

UNIT	Offs	NCOs	Pvts	Rs or Cbns	Pistols	Sub-MGs	LMGs	Hv MGs	81-mm Mort	75-mm Inf Hows	Mtrcl	H-Dr Vehicles	Tlrs	Hs	Bcls
Co Hq	1	8	15	14	3	7					1	2	2	5	4
1st (MG) Plat	1	6	22	11	9	9		4				2	1	3	
2d (MG) Plat		7	22	11	9	9		4				2	1	3	
3d (Inf How) Plat	1	7	44	38	5	9	1			4		7		15	1
4th (Medium Mort) Plat		7	53	34	21	5			6			15	12	19	
Total	3	35	156	108	47	39	1	8	6	4	1	28	16	45	5

Figure 48.—Heavy weapons Company, Volks Grenadier Division, total strength 194.

UNIT	Offs	NCOs	Pvts	Rs or Cbns	Pistols	Sub-MGs	LMGs	120-mm Morts	75-mm Inf Hows	Mtr Vehicles	H-Dr Vehicles	Tlrs	Hs	Bcls
Co Hq	1	4	15	13	2	5					2	2	5	2
120-mm Mort Plat...........	1	7	44	38	6	8	2	4			9		27	
120-mm Mort Plat...........		8	44	38	6	8	2	4			9		27	
75-mm Inf How Plat........	1	7	44	38	5	9	1		4		8		17	1
Tns		6	15	18	2	1				1	5		13	1
Total	3	32	162	145	21	31	5	8	4	1	33	2	89	4

Referred to by the traditional designation: "13th" Co.

Figure 49.—Infantry Howitzer Company, Volks Grenadier Division, total strength 197.

UNIT	Offs	NCOs	Pvts	Rs or Cbns	Pistols	Sub-MGs	LMGs	Bazookas	Mtr Vehicles	Mtrcls	H-Dr Vehicles	Tlrs	Hs	Bcls
Co Hq	1		2	2	1	1			1					
Bazooka Plat	1	4	45	26	20	4	1	18			5	4	6	
Bazooka Plat		5	45	26	20	4	1	18			5	4	6	
Bazooka Plat		5	45	26	20	4	1	18			5	4	6	
Tn		5	9	11	2	1	1	18[2]		1	4		12	2
Total[1]	2	19	146	91	63	14	4	72	1	1	19	12	30	2

[1] Referred to by the traditional designation: "14th" Co.
[2] In reserve.

Figure 50.—Bazooka Company, Volks Grenadier Division, total strength 167.

(5) *Volks Grenadier Bicycle Regiment.* One of the three infantry regiments in the *Volks Grenadier* Division is an infantry regiment (bicycle). That regiment includes one infantry battalion (bicycle), and one normal infantry battalion, a regimental infantry howitzer company, and a regimental bazooka company as shown in sub-paragraph (4). This infantry regiment (bicycle) may be employed in the same way as the other two battalions of the *Volks Grenadier* Division or may be used as a mobile reserve. (See *Figures 51* to *54.*)

The newest type of standard German infantry regiment is the Infantry Regiment of the Division, Type 45, which is believed to have become the pattern for all German infantry regiments (see *Figures 55* and *56*).

UNIT	Offs	NCOs	Pvts	Rs or Cbns	Pistols	Sub-MGs	LMGs	Hv MGs	81-mm Morts	120-mm Morts	Bazookas	75-mm Inf Hows	Mtr Vehicles	Mtrcl	H-Dr Vehicles	Tlrs	Hs	Bcls
Regtl Hq	6	1	12	4	3	14							2	3			8	2
Regtl Hq Co	5	25	157	133	22	32	10						1		27	6	53	38
Inf Bn (Bcl)	15	95	589	366	80	253	30	8	6			4	3	3	74	32	219	625
Inf Bn	15	95	532	309	80	253	30	8	6			4	2	3	70	32	125	27
Inf How Co[1]	3	32	162	145	21	31	5			8		4	1		33	2	89	4
Bazooka Co[2]	2	19	146	91	63	14	4				72		1	1	19	12	30	2
Total	46[3]	267	1,598	1,048	269	597	79	16	12	8	72	12	10	10	223	84	524	698

[1] Referred to by the traditional designation: "13th" Co.
[2] Referred to by the traditional designation: "14th" Co.
[3] Including four officials.

Figure 51.—Infantry Regiment (bicycle), Volks Grenadier Division, total strength 1,911.

UNIT	Offs	NCOs	Pvts	Rs or Cbns	Pistols	Sub-MGs	LMGs	Hv MGs	81-mm Morts	75-mm Inf Hows	Mtr Vehicles	Mtrcls	H-Dr Vehicles	Tlrs	Hs	Bcls
Bn Hq	4	6	35	22	3	20	1				2	2	4	4	12	30
Sup Plat	2[1]	6	51	54	3	2	1				1		17		54	24
Gren. Co. (Bcl)	2	16	110	55	9	64	9						8	4	24	130
Gren. Co. (Bcl)	2	16	110	55	9	64	9						8	4	24	130
Gren. Co. (Bcl)	2	16	110	55	9	64	9						8	4	24	130
Hv Wpn Co (Bcl)	3	35	173	125	47	39	1	8	6	4		1	29	16	81	181
Total	15[1]	95	589	366	80	253	30	8	6	4	3	3	74	32	219	625

[1] Including one official.

Figure 52.—Infantry Battalion (bicycle), Volks Grenadier Division, total strength 699.

UNIT	Offs	NCOs	Pvts	Rs or Cbns	Pistols	Sub-MGs	LMGs	H-Dr Vehicles	Tlrs	Hs	Bcls
Co Hq	1	5	17	19	1	3		2	1	6	34
1st (Sub-MG) Plat	1	3	31	7	2	26	3	2	1	6	32
2d (Sub-MG) Plat		4	31	7	2	26	3	2	1	6	32
3d (R) Plat		4	31	22	4	9	3	2	1	6	32
Total	2	16	110	55	9	64	9	8	4	24	130

Figure 53.—Infantry Company (bicycle), Volks Grenadier Division, total strength 128.

UNIT	Offs	NCOs	Pvts	Rs or Cbns	Pistols	Sub-MGs	LMGs	Hv MGs	81-mm Morts	75-mm Inf Hows	Mtrcls	H-Dr Vehicles	Tlrs	Hs	Bcls
Co Hq	1	8	18	17	3	7					1	3	2	11	38
1st (MG) Plat	1	6	24	13	9	9		4				4	2	12	54
2d (MG) Plat		7	24	13	9	9		4				7		21	43
3d (Inf How) Plat	1	7	48	42	5	9	1			4		15	12	37	46
4th (Medium Mort) Plat		7	59	40	21	5			6						
Total	3	35	173	125	47	39	1	8	6	4	1	29	16	81	181

Figure 54.—Heavy Weapons Company (bicycle), Volks Grenadier Division, total strength 211.

UNIT	Offs	Officials	NCOs	Pvts	Incl Hiwis	Rs	Pistols	Sniper Rs	R Grenade Launchers	Sub-MGs	Assault Rs 44	LMGs	Hv MGs	81-mm Morts	120-mm Morts	Bazookas	75-mm Inf Hows	150-mm Inf Hows	Mtr Vehicles	Mtrcls	H-Dr Vehicles	Trrs	Hs	Bcls
Regtl Hq and Hq Co	12	1	30	165	18	126	26	10	9	46		10							3	3	27	6	61	40
Inf Bn	14	1	95	534	40	284	86	18	35	91	165	30	8	6			4		2	3	70	32	125	27
Inf Bn	14	1	95	534	40	284	86	18	35	91	165	30	8	6			4		2	3	70	32	125	27
Inf How Co	3		30	153	14	137	21		4	28		5			8			2	1	1	34	6	108	3
AT Co	2		19	146	6	91	62			14		4				72			1		19	12	30	2
Total	45	3	269	1,532	118	922	281	46	83	270	330	79	16	12	8	72	8	2	9	10	220	88	449	99

Figure 55.—Infantry Regiment of Infantry Division 45, total strength 1,849.

UNIT	Offs	Officials	NCOs	Pvts	Incl Hiwis[1]	Rs	Pistols	Sniper Rs	R Grenade Launchers	Sub-MGs	Assault Rs 44	LMGs	Hv MGs	81-mm Morts	75-mm Inf Hows	Mtr Vehicles	Mtrcls	H-Dr Vehicles	Trrs	Hs	Bcls
Bn Hq & Sup Plat	5	1	12	73	12	63	6		3	22		2				2	2	21	4	50	7
Gren Co	2		16	101	4	37	11	6	9	10	55	9						7	4	10	5
Gren Co	2		16	101	4	37	11	6	9	10	55	9						7	4	10	5
Gren Co	2		16	101	4	37	11	6	9	10	55	9						7	4	10	5
Hv Co	3		35	158	16	110	47		5	39		1	8	6	4		1	28	16	45	5
Total	14	1	95	534	40	284	86	18	35	91	165	30	8	6	4	2	3	70	32	125	27

¹ Hilfswilliger (Hiwi) is a Foreign Auxiliary, usually an Ex-pw.

Figure 56.—Infantry Battalion of Infantry Division 45, total strength 644.

(6) *SS Infantry Regiment.* In the SS Infantry Division the infantry regiment is similar to the Infantry Regiment, 1944 Type.

(7) *Mountain Infantry Regiment.* There are usually two regiments per mountain division organized especially for mountain warfare by making each of the three battalions self-sufficient. The normal infantry howitzer company is lacking, but mountain infantry howitzers are organic in each battalion. (See *Figures 57* to *59..*)

(8) *The Light Infantry Regiment.* Light divisions usually have two regiments organized similarly to the Army Mountain Division but have slightly more motorization.

(9) *The SS Mountain Infantry Regiment.* The two infantry regiments per *SS* Mountain Division are organized similarly to the Army Mountain Regiment; however, they have either a

fourth battalion or additional regimental companies.

(10) *The Motorized Infantry Regiment (Grenadierregiment (Mot)).* Normally there are two regiments to the Motorized Division, consisting of three motorized infantry battalions, heavy infantry howitzer company (self-propelled), and an antitank company. The motorized infantry battalions originally were organized similarly to normal infantry battalions; however, in 1944 they were reorganized along the lines of the armored infantry battalions (*Panzergrenadierbataillons*) of the Armored Division. (See *Figures 60* and *61.*)

(11) *The SS Motorized Infantry Regiment (SS-Panzer Grenadier Regiment).* Two regiments per *SS* Motorized Division are organized similarly to the army motorized regiment; however, it has an additional antiaircraft company.

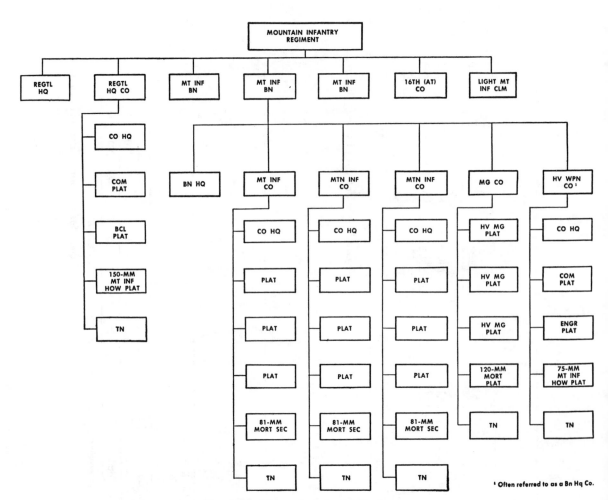

Figure 57.—Mountain Infantry Regiment.

UNIT	Pers	LMGs	Hv MGs	81-mm Morts	120-mm Morts	Bazookas	75-mm AT Guns	75-mm Mt Inf Hows	150-mm Mt Inf Hows
Regtl Hq	25								
Regtl Hq Co	182	4							2
Mt Inf Bn......................	877	40	12	6	4			2	
Mt Inf Bn......................	877	40	12	6	4			2	
Mt Inf Bn......................	877	40	12	6	4			2	
16th (AT) Co..................	190	6				36	3		
Light Mt Clm..................	36								
Total	3,064	130	36	18	12	36	3	6	2

Figure 58.—Mountain Infantry Regiment, total strength 3,064.

UNIT	Pers	LMGs	Hv MGs	81-mm Morts	120-mm Morts	75-mm Mt Inf Hows
Bn Hq	27					
Mt Inf Co........	147	12		2		
Mt Inf Co........	147	12		2		
Mt Inf Co........	147	12		2		
MG Co	208		12		4	
Hv Wpn Co[1]......	201	4				2
Total	877	40	12	6	4	2

[1] Often referred to as a Bn Hq Co.

Figure 59.—Mountain Infantry Battalion, total strength 877.

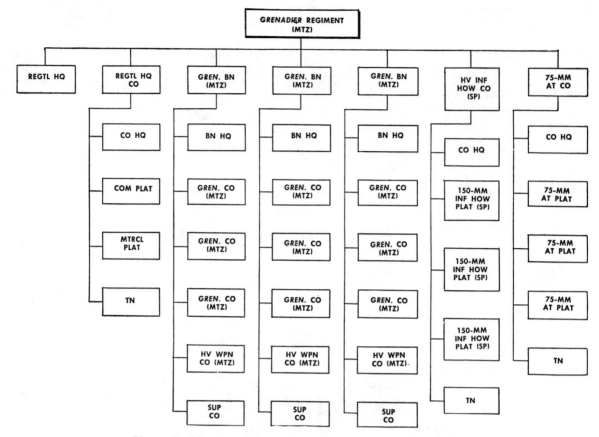

Figure 60.—Motorized Infantry Regiment, Panzer Grenadier Division.

UNIT	Offs	NCOs	Pvts	Rs or Cbns	Pistols	Sub-MGs	LMGs	Hv MGs	81-mm Morts	120-mm Morts	20-mm AA Guns	150-mm Inf Hows (SP)	75-mm AT Guns	Mtr Vehicles	Mtrcls
Regtl Hq	6	2	8	7	6	3								3	3
Regtl Hq Co	3	47	97	93	50	4	4							22	18
Gren. Bn (Mtz)	23	148	697	548	229	91	60	12	6	4	6			143	25
Gren. Bn (Mtz)	23	148	697	548	229	91	60	12	6	4	6			143	25
Gren. Bn (Mtz)	23	148	697	548	229	91	60	12	6	4	6			143	25
150-mm Inf How Co (SP)	3	31	108	92	28	22	8					6		25	5
75-mm AT Co	4	21	109	102	18	14	9						9	23	7
Total	85	545	2,413	1,938	789	316	201	36	18	12	18	6	9	502	108

Figure 61.—Motorized Infantry Regiment, Panzer Grenadier Division, total strength 3,043.

(12) *The Panzer Grenadier Regiment.* The two regiments of the Armored Division are composed of only two battalions, a heavy infantry howitzer company (self-propelled), and an engineer company. One of the four battalions in the division is designated armored (*Gepanzert* or *Gp.*), because it is equipped with armored personnel carriers with mounted arms enabling the crews to fight from their vehicles. The other three battalions of the division are motorized only. The regiment, of which the armored battalion is a component, also is designated armored. The other regiment which contains two motorized battalions

is designated motorized. (See *Figures 62* to *75.*)

(13) *The SS Armored Infantry Regiment (SS Panzer Grenadier Regiment).* There are two per *SS* Armored Division, each consisting of one armored and two motorized *Panzer Grenadier* battalions, a heavy infantry howitzer company (self-propelled), an engineer company (half-track), and an antiaircraft company. Components of the regiment are organized like those of the Army *Panzer Grenadier* Regiment. (For the *SS Panzer Grenadier* Regiment see *Figure 76*; for the breakdown of the components see *Figures 64* and *65.*)

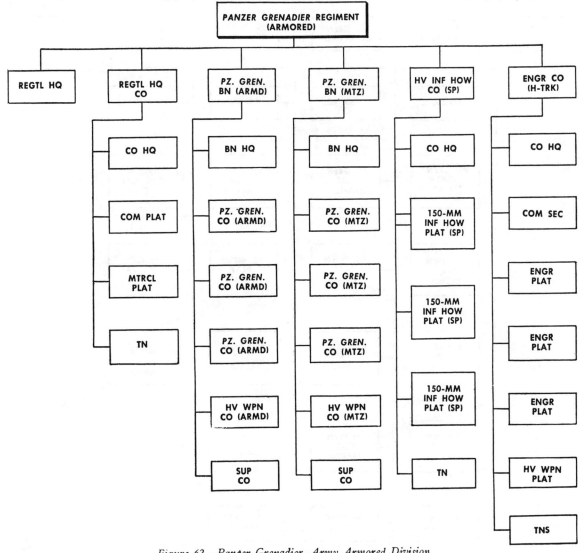

Figure 62.—Panzer Grenadier, Army Armored Division.

UNIT	Offs	NCOs	Pvts	Rs or Cbns	Pistols	Sub-MGs	LMGs	Hv MGs	81-mm Morts	120-mm Morts	Flame Throwers	20-mm AA Guns (Mtr-Dr)	75-mm Inf Hows (SP)	150-mm Inf Hows (SP)	Mtr Vehicles	Mtrcls
Regtl Hq	6	2	8	7	6	3									3	3
Regtl Hq Co (Armd)........	3	47	97	93	50	4	14								29	17
Pz.Gren. Bn (Armd)........	26	168	673	456	242	179	115	12	6	4		18	12		158²	24
Pz.Gren. Bn (Mtz)..........	23	148	697	548	229	91	60	12	6	4		6			143	25
Hv Inf How Co (SP).......	3	31	108	92	28	22	8							6	25	5
Engr Co (H-Trk)...........	3	40	211	177	40	37	27	2	2		24	1			48	7
Total	64¹	436	1,794	1,373	595	336	224	26	14	8	24	25	12	6	406	81

¹ Including eight officials.
² Including 125 Armd Pers carriers.

Figure 63.—Panzer Grenadier Regiment, Army Armored Division, total strength 2,294

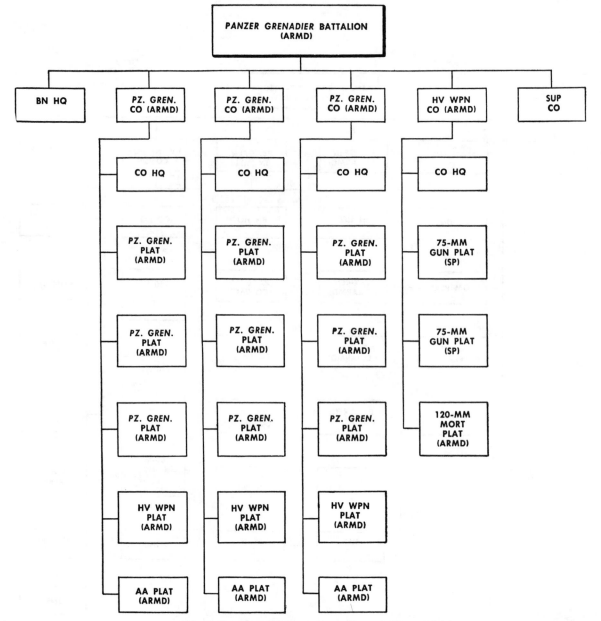

Figure 64.—Panzer Grenadier Battalion, Army Armored Division.

UNIT	Offs	NCOs	Pvts	Rs or Cbns	Pistols	Sub-MGs	LMGs	Hv MGs	81-mm Morts	120-mm Morts	20-mm AA Guns (Mtr-Dr)	75-mm Inf Hows (SP)	Mtr Vehicles	Mtrcls
Bn Hq	4	9	30	24	9	10	6						8	4
Pz. Gren. Co (Armd)	4	32	147	83	55	45	29	4	2		6	2	25	4
Pz. Gren. Co (Armd)	4	32	147	83	55	45	29	4	2		6	2	25	4
Pz. Gren. Co (Armd)	4	32	147	83	55	45	29	4	2		6	2	25	4
Hv Wpn Co (Armd)	3	23	74	46	31	32	17			4		6	21	6
Sup Co	7[1]	40	128	137	37	2	5						54	2
Total	26[1]	168	673	456	242	179	115	12	6	4	18	12	158[2]	24

[1] Including three officials.
[2] Including 87 Armd vehicles

Figure 65.—Panzer Grenadier Battalion, Army Armored Division, total strength 867.

UNIT	Offs	NCOs	Pvts	Rs or Cbns	Pistols	Sub-MGs	LMGs	Hv MGs	81-mm Morts	20-mm AA Guns	75-mm Inf Hows (SP)	Mtr Vehicles	Mtrcls
Co Hq	1	7	8	11	2	3	2					4	2
Pz. Gren. Plat (Armd)	1	3	26	12	10	8	9					4	
Pz. Gren. Plat (Armd)		4	26	12	10	8	9					4	
Pz. Gren. Plat (Armd)		4	26	12	10	8	9					4	
Hv Wpn Plat (Armd)	1	8	41	28	12	10		4	2		2	4	2
AA Plat (Armd)	1	6	20	8	11	8				6		5	
Total	4	32	147	83	55	45	29	4	2	6	2	25[1]	4

[1] Including 21 Armd pers carriers.

Figure 66.—Panzer Grenadier Company, Army Armored Division, total strength 183.

UNIT	Offs	NCOs	Pvts	Rs or Cbns	Pistols	Sub-MGs	LMGs	120-mm Morts	75-mm Inf Hows (SP)	Mtr Vehicles	Mtrcls
Co Hq	1	7	11	13	3	4	2			4	3
75-mm Inf How Plat (SP)	1	8	26	15	13	15	8		6	9	1
120-mm Mort Plat (Armd)	1	8	37	18	15	13	7	4		8	2
Total	3	23	74	46	31	32	17	4	6	21[1]	6

[1] Including 17 Armd vehicles.

Figure 67.—Heavy Weapons Company, Army Armored Division, total strength 100.

UNIT	Offs	NCOs	Pvts	Rs or Cbns	Pistols	Sub-MGs	LMGs	Hv MGs	81-mm Morts	Flame Throwers	20-mm AA Guns (Mtr-Dr)	Mtr Vehicles	Mtrcls
Co Hq	1	5	8	7	5	2	1				1	3	1
Engr Plat	1	7	50	41	7	10	8			8		10	2
Engr Plat	1	7	50	41	7	10	8			8		10	2
Engr Plat		8	50	41	7	10	8			8		10	2
Hv MG Sec		3	12	8	5	2		2				1	
81-mm Mort Sec		3	14	7	8	2	2		2			2	
Maint Sec		2	8	9	1							3	
Tns		5	19	23		1						9	
Total	3	40	211	177	40	37	27	2	2	24	1	48[1]	7

[1] Including 28 Armd vehicles.

Figure 68.—Engineer Company (half-tracked), Panzer Grenadier Regiment, total strength 254.

UNIT	Offs	NCOs	Pvts	Rs or Cbns	Pistols	Sub-MGs	LMGs	Hv MGs	81-mm Morts	120-mm Morts	Flame Throwers	20-mm AA Guns(Mtr-Dr)	150-mm Inf Hows (SP)	Mtr Vehicles	Mtrcls
Regtl Hq	6	2	8	7	6	3								3	3
Regtl Hq Co	3	47	97	93	50	4	4							22	18
Pz. Gren. Bn (Mtz)............	23	148	697	548	229	91	60	12	6	4		6		143	25
Pz. Gren. Bn (Mtz)............	23	148	697	548	229	91	60	12	6	4		6		143	25
150-mm Inf How Co (SP)......	3	31	108	92	28	22	8						6	34	5
Engr Co (Mtz)................	3	34	180	161	32	24	12	2	2		18			35	7
Total	61[1]	410	1,787	1,449	574	235	144	26	14	8	18	12	6	380	83

[1] Including eight officials.

Figure 69.—Panzer Grenadier Regiment (motorized), Army Armored Division, total strength 2,258.

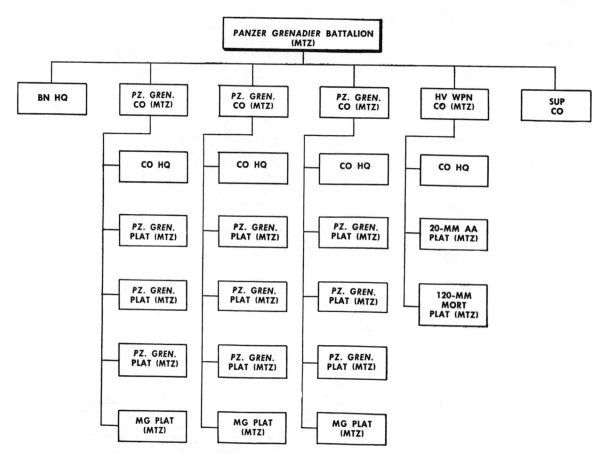

Figure 70.—Panzer Grenadier Battalion (motorized), Army Armored Division.

UNIT	Offs	NCOs	Pvts	Rs or Cbns	Pistols	Sub-MGs	LMGs	Hv MGs	81-mm Morts	120-mm Morts	20-mm AA Guns(M-Dr)	Mtr Vehicles	Mtrcls
Bn Hq	4	9	29	36	4	2						9	4
Pz. Gren. Co. (Mtz)	3	29	165	115	59	23	18	4	2			24	4
Pz. Gren. Co. (Mtz)	3	29	165	115	59	23	18	4	2			24	4
Pz. Gren. Co. (Mtz)	3	29	165	115	59	23	18	4	2			24	4
Hv Wpn Co (Mtz)	3	22	79	63	24	17	2			4	6	20	5
Sup Co	7[1]	30	94	104	24	3	4					42	4
Total	23[1]	148	697	548	229	91	60	12	6	4	6	143	25

[1] Including three officials.

Figure 71.—Panzer Grenadier Battalion (motorized), Army Armored Division, total strength 868.

UNIT	Offs	NCOs	Pvts	Rs or Cbns	Pistols	Sub-MGs	LMGs	Hv MGs	81-mm Morts	Mtr Vehicles	Mtrcls
Co Hq	1	7	9	10	3	4				3	4
Pz. Gren. Plat (Mtz)	1	4	38	26	13	4	6			5	
Pz. Gren. Plat (Mtz)		5	38	26	13	4	6			5	
Pz. Gren. Plat (Mtz)		5	38	26	13	4	6			5	
MG Plat (Mtz)	1	8	42	27	17	7		4	2	6	
Total	3	29	165	115	59	23	18	4	2	24	4

Figure 72.—Panzer Grenadier Company (motorized), Army Armored Division, total strength 197.

UNIT	Offs	NCOs	Pvts	Rs or Cbns	Pistols	Sub-MGs	LMGs	120-mm Morts	20-mm AA Guns (M-Dr)	Mtr Vehicles	Mtrcls
Co Hq	1	7	10	13	2	3				4	2
20-mm AA Plat	1	7	32	18	14	8			6	8	1
120-mm Mort Plat	1	8	37	32	8	6	2	4		8	2
Total	3	22	79	63	24	17	2	4	6	20	5

Figure 73.—Heavy Weapons Company (motorized), Army Armored Division, total strength 104.

UNIT	Offs	NCOs	Pvts	Rs or Cbns	Pistols	Sub-MGs	LMGs	150-mm Inf Hows (SP)	Mtr Vehicles	Mtrcls
Co Hq	1	5	13	8	7	4	2		3	2
150-mm Inf How Plat	1	5	23	18	6	5	2	2	6	1
150-mm Inf How Plat	1	5	23	18	6	5	2	2	6	1
150-mm Inf How Plat		6	23	18	6	5	2	2	6	1
Mun Sec		1	5	5		1			3	
Maint Sec		3	10	13					4	
Tns		6	11	12	3	2			6	
Total	3	31	108	92	28	22	8	6	34	5

Figure 74.—150-mm Infantry Howitzer Company (self-propelled), Army Armored Division, total strength 172.

UNIT	Offs	NCOs	Pvts	Rs or Cbns	Pistols	Sub-MGs	LMGs	Hv MGs	81-mm Morts	Flame Throwers	Mtr Vehicles	Mtrcls
Co Hq	1	3	5	5	1	3					1	3
Com Sec		2	8	10							3	
Engr Plat	1	5	41	36	5	6	4			6	6	1
Engr Plat	1	5	41	36	5	6	4			6	6	1
Engr Plat		6	41	36	5	6	4			6	6	1
81-mm Mort Sec		3	14	8	8	1			2		2	
Hv MG Sec		3	12	8	5	2		2			2	
Maint Sec		1	3	4							1	1
Tns		6	15	18	3						8	
Total	3	34	180	161	32	24	12	2	2	18	35	7

Figure 75.—Engineer Company (motorized), Army Armored Division, total strength 217.

UNIT	Offs	NCOs	Pvts	Rs or Cbns	Pistols	Sub-MGs	LMGs	Hv MGs	81-mm Morts	120-mm Morts	Flame Throwers	20-mm AA Guns(Mtr-Dr)	75-mm Inf Hows (SP)	150-mm Inf Hows (SP)	Mtr Vehicles	Mtrcls
Regtl Hq	6	2	8	7	6	3										
Regtl Hq Co	3	47	97	93	50	4	14									
Pz. Gren. Bn (Armd)	26	168	673	456	242	179	115	12	6	4		18	12		152	24
Pz. Gren. Bn (Mtz)	23	148	697	548	229	91	60	12	6	4		6			143	25
Pz. Gren. Bn (Mtz)	23	148	697	548	229	91	60	12	6	4		6			143	25
Hv Inf How Co (SP)	3	31	108	92	28	22	8							6	25	5
Engr Hq (H-Trk)	3	40	211	177	40	37	27	2	2		24	1			48	7
AA Co	2	14	64	36	28	16						12			16	2
Total	89[1]	598	2,555	1,957	852	443	284	38	20	12	24	43	12	6	527[2]	88

[1] Including 11 officials.
[2] Including 89 Armd vehicles.

Figure 76.—SS Panzer Grenadier Regiment, SS Armored Division, total strength 3,242.

(14) *The Parachute Rifle Regiment.* Three per Parachute Rifle Division, these consist of three parachute rifle battalions, a 120-mm mortar or a light gun company, and an antitank company. These regiments usually are employed as crack infantry. They include some men trained for airborne operations, but most of the so-called parachutists are well trained infantrymen only. The equipment includes a high proportion of small automatic weapons, bazookas, and antitank rocket pistols. (See *Figures 77* to *82.*)

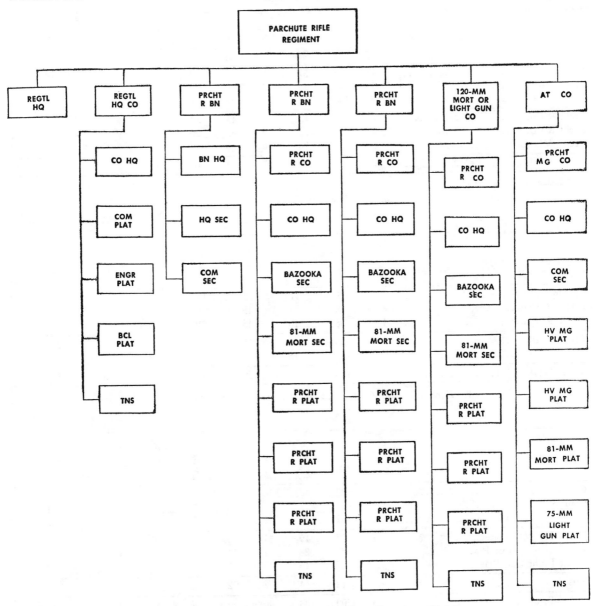

Figure 77.—Parachute Rifle Regiment, Air Force Parachute Division.

UNIT	Offs	EM	Rs or Cbns	Pistols	Sub-MGs	LMGs	Hv MGs	81-mm Morts	120-mm Morts	Bazookas	75-mm AT Guns	75-mm Light Guns	Mtr Vehicles	Mtrcls
Regtl Hq	7	60	36	17	10	3							13	4
Regtl Hq Co........................	6	225	182	89	37	11							12	1
Prcht R Bn.........................	25	828	410	257	214	66	8	13				2	81	19
Prcht R Bn.........................	25	828	410	257	214	66	8	13				2	81	19
Prcht R Bn.........................	25	828	410	257	214	66	8	13				2	81	19
120-mm Mort or Light Gun Co.........	5	158	83	40	45	6			9				19	4
AT Co	3	183	120	51	17	6				54	3		17	5
Total	96[1]	3,110	1,651	968	751	224	24	39	9	54	3	6	304	71

[1] Including 12 officials.

Figure 78.—Parachute Rifle Regiment, Air Force Parachute Division, total strength 3,206.

UNIT	Offs	EM	Rs or Cbns	Pistols	Sub-MGs	LMGs	Hv MGs	81-mm Morts	75-mm Light Guns	Mtr Vehicles	Mtrcls
Bn Hq	7[1]	89	57	21	20	2				12	5
Com Plat	1	41	29	13	9	2				6	1
Prcht R Co......................	4	166	72	59	43	20		3		15	3
Prcht R Co......................	4	166	72	59	43	20		3		15	3
Prcht R Co......................	4	166	72	59	43	20		3		15	3
Prcht MG Co.....................	5	200	108	46	56	2	8	4	2	18	4
Total	25[1]	828	410	257	214	66	8	13	2	81	19

[1] Including three officials.

Figure 79.—Parachute Rifle Battalion, Air Force Parachute Division, total strength 853.

UNIT	Offs	EM	Rs or Cbns	Pistols	Sub-MGs	LMGs	81-mm Morts	Mtr Vehicles	Mtrcls
Co Hq	1	35	11	12	14		3	3	3
Prcht R Plat....................	1	38	16	15	9	6		2	
Prcht R Plat....................	1	38	16	15	9	6		2	
Prcht R Plat....................	1	38	16	15	9	6		2	
Tns		17	13	2	2	2		6	
Total	4	166	72	59	43	20	3	15	3

Figure 80.—Parachute Rifle Company, Air Force Parachute Division, total strength 170.

UNIT	Offs	EM	Rs or Cbns	Pistols	Sub-MGs	LMGs	Hv MGs	81-mm Morts	Light Guns	Mtr Vehicles	Mtrcls
Co Hq	1	22	6	6	12					2	4
Com Sec		11	7		4					1	
Prcht Hv MG Plat.................	1	37	19	11	9		4			2	
Prcht Hv MG Plat.................	1	37	19	11	9		4			2	
Prcht 81-mm Mort Plat.............	1	48	28	11	11			4		3	
Prcht Light Gun Plat:.............	1	27	15	5	9				2	2	
Tns		18	14	2	2	2				6	
Total	5	200	108	46	56	2	8	4	2	18	4

Figure 81.—Parachute Machine-Gun Company, Air Force Parachute Division, total strength 205.

UNIT	Offs	EM	Rs or Cbns	Pistols	Sub-MGs	LMGs	120-mm Morts	Mtr Vehicles	Mtrcls
Co Hq	2	13	3	5	9	1		1	4
Com Sec		18	12		6			2	
Prcht 120-mm Mort Plat...........	1	33	15	11	9	1	3	3	
Prcht 120-mm Mort Plat...........	1	33	15	11	9	1	3	3	
Prcht 120-mm Mort Plat...........	1	33	15	11	9	1	3	3	
Mun Sec		11	10		1			2	
Tns		17	13	2	2	2		5	
Total	5	158	83	40	45	6	9	19	4

Note: Some Prcht Regts may have 75-mm or 105-mm Light (Recoilless) Guns instead of the 120-mm Morts.

Figure 82.—Parachute 120-mm Mortar or Light Gun Company, Air Force Parachute Division, total strength 163.

c. FIELD REPLACEMENT BATTALION (*Feldersatzbataillon*). Field replacement battalions consist of three to five companies containing replacement elements for the various arms and divisional combat school. They may be found in all types of divisions and are a training unit as well as a field reserve for the entire division. Their personnel may be drawn from other divisional units or may consist of fresh reserves from the rear areas. Figures 83 and 84 show the Field Replacement Battalions of the Infantry Division, 1944 Type, and of the Army Armored (*Panzer*) Division, but their organization in other types of divisions is very similar.

d. INFANTRY ANTIAIRCRAFT COMPANY (*Inf. Fla-Kp.*) The infantry antiaircraft company is organic in all types of infantry divisions and is usually self propelled. It is subordinated for administrative purposes to the divisional antitank battalion, but receives all tactical directives from the division. It is equipped with 20-mm and 37-mm antiaircraft guns. It may be employed for both antiaircraft and antitank defense. Similarly organized antiaircraft companies organic in the armored division are believed to belong to the armored arm while most of the non-organic light antiaircraft companies belong to the air force.

3. General Headquarters

a. FORTRESS BRIGADE (*Festungsbrigade*). Independent static infantry brigades.

b. FORTRESS REGIMENT (*Festungsregiment*). Regimental staffs controlling fortress battalions.

c. FORTRESS BATTALIONS (*Festungsbataillon*). Static infantry battalions employed in the defense of fixed fortifications. It consists largely of *Landesschützen* personnel. It often is attached for tactical purposes to divisions operating in the same combat area.

d. PERMANENT FORTRESS BATTALION (*Festungsstammabteilung*). Formed as a cadre personnel, it is attached to corps manning fortifications in coastal sectors and now is found in the Westwall defenses. The battalions carry the Roman numeral of the corps to which they are attached, but also have been identified with Arabic numbers in the 300 series. These units may occur as *Festungsstammregimenter* (permanent fortress regiments) or as *Festungsstammkompanie* (permanent fortress companies) depending on the size of the sector to which they are assigned.

UNIT	Ofrs	NCOs	Pvts	Rs or Cbns	Pistols	Sub-MGs	LMGs	Hv MGs	81-mm Morts	120-mm Morts	Flame Throwers	20-mm AA Guns	50-mm AT Guns	75-mm AT Guns	75-mm Inf Hows	105-mm Gun/Hows	Mtr Vehicles	Mtrcls	H-Dr Vehicles	Hs
Bn Hq	2		2	2	2	2											1	1		
C Sch	13	78	5	5	31	81	50	12	6	4	2	1	1	1	1	1	2	15		
Sup Co	3[3]	19	53	84	6	6												10	31	63
Repl Pool			750	750																
Total	18[1]	97	810	841[2]	39	89	50	12	6	4	2	1	1	1	1	1	3	26	31	63

[1] Including one official.
[2] Including 20 SARs.

Figure 83.—Field Replacement Battalion, Infantry Division 1944 type, total strength 925.

UNIT	Offs	NCOs	Pvts	Rs or Cbns	Pistols	Sub-MGs	LMGs	Hv MGs	81-mm Morts	120-mm Morts	Flame Throwers	20-mm AA Guns	75-mm AT Guns	75-mm Inf Hows	105-mm Gun/Hows	Mtr Vehicles	Mtrcls	H-Dr Vehicles	Hs
Bn Hq	2		2	2	2											1			
C Sch	13	78	5	5	31	86													
Sup Co	3¹	13	57	66	7		50	12	6	2	2	1	1	1	1	8²	3	24	48
Repl Pool.......			200	200															
Repl Pool.......			200	200															
Repl Pool.......			200	200															
Repl Pool.......			200	200															
Total	18¹	91	864	873	40	86	50	12	6	2	2	1	1	1	1	9²	3	24	48

¹ Including one official.
² Various types of armored vehicles may be attached for demonstration purposes.

Figure 84.—Field Replacement Battalion, Army Armored Division, total strength 973.

e. MACHINE-GUN BATTALION (*Maschinenge-wehrbataillon*). The independent machine-gun battalion consists of three companies equipped with heavy machine guns and bazookas and a heavy weapons company. It probably has been redesignated fortress machine-gun battalion.

f. FORTRESS MACHINE-GUN BATTALION (*Fes-tungs-Maschinengewehrbataillon*). These static machine-gun battalions are composed largely of *Landesschützen* personnel. Their organization is similar to a *Maschinengewehrbataillon* except for the mobility.

g. SUPER-HEAVY MACHINE-GUN BATTALION (*Überschweres Maschinengewehrbataillon*). Organization of this battalion is probably similar to that of the *Maschinengewehrbataillon*. It is equipped wth 20-mm and 37-mm antiaircraft guns and bazookas.

h. LIGHT ANTIAIRCRAFT BATTALION (*Flaba-taillon*). This consists of light antiaircraft companies organized similarly to those found organically in the infantry divisions. It is believed that many light antiaircraft battalions have been reformed and redesignated super-heavy machine-gun battalions and are being employed as mobile defense units of fortified zones.

i. TANK DESTRUCTION BATTALION (*Panzerver-störer Bataillon*). This battalion is equipped with bazookas and other infantry antitank weapons.

j. HEAVY MORTAR BATTALION (*Schweres Granatwerferbataillon*). This consists of three companies. Each company has twelve heavy mortars (120-mm).

k. ALPINE INFANTRY BATTALION (*Hochge-birgsbataillon*). The personnel of this battalion is especially trained for warfare in high terrain and mountain climbing.

1. LOCAL DEFENSE (*Landesschützen*) REGIMENT AND BATTALION. A local defense regiment controls a varying number of battalions which are composed of two to six companies. The average company strength is 150, and total battalion strength may vary between 400 and 900. These units originally were employed for guard duties at vital installations and as support for the military administration in occupied territories.

m. SECURITY REGIMENT AND BATTALION (*Sicherungsregiment*). Numerous *Landesschüt-zen* battalions have received additional transportation and equipment and been redesignated security battalions (*Sicherungsbataillone*). While the strength of these battalions varies, similarly to that of the local defense battalions, Figures 85 and 86 show an average security battalion as it may be encountered in the field.

Several such battalions may be controlled by a security regiment which usually is attached to commanders of army groups or army rear areas.

n. For a complete list of all infantry and security units see the "Order of Battle of the German Army", March 1945 edition.

UNIT	Offs	NCOs	Pvts	Rs or Cbns	Pistols	Sub-MGs	LMGs	Hv MGs	81-mm Morts	Mtr Vehicles	Mtrcls	H-Dr Vehicles	Hs
Bn Hq	4	3	11	12	5	4				1	2		6
Com Sec		4	14	14		4						2	2
Security Co	2	24	135	97	30	39	10	2	2	2		12	28
Security Co	2	24	135	97	30	39	10	2	2	2		12	28
Security Co	2	24	135	97	30	39	10	2	2	2		12	28
Tns	1[1]	8	18	20	5	2	1					10	21
Total[2]	11[1]	87	448	337	100	127	31	6	6	7	2	48	113

[1] Including one official.
[2] A reduced Bn has a T/O strength of 11-78-419 and accordingly less fire power and transportation.

Figure 85.—Security Battalion, total strength 508-546.

UNIT	Offs	NCOs	Pvts	Rs or Cbns	Pistols	Sub-MGs	LMGs	Hv MGs	81-mm Morts	Mtr Vehicles	H-Dr Vehicles	Hs
Co Hq	1	3	6	6	2	3				1		1
1st Plat	1	3	32	22	5	10	3				2	4
2nd Plat		4	32	22	5	10	3				2	4
3d Plat		4	32	22	5	10	3				2	4
4th (Hv Wpn) Plat......................		6	25	15	12	5		2	2		3	7
Tns		4	8	10	1	1	1			1	3	8
Total	2	24	135	97	30	39	10	2	2	2	12	28

Figure 86.—Security Company, Security Battalion, total strength 161.

4. Armored Organic Units

Armored troops (*Panzertruppen*), created as an arm in April 1943, include many units which, according to the American conception, belong to other arms. This refers specifically to the *Panzer Grenadier* units which the Germans include in the armored troops arm, while we consider them as belonging to the infantry; tank destroyer units; and armored reconnaissance units, each of which we consider as belonging to their appropriate arm while the Germans include them under armored troops.

a. THE ARMY TANK (*Panzer*) REGIMENT. This consists of two tank battalions of three companies each, but a fourth, an assault gun company, frequently may be encountered. It is believed

that the tables of organization specify 14 tanks for each of the companies, distributed as follows: two in company headquarters, and four in each of the three platoons. One battalion usually is equipped with *Pz. Kpfw. V* tanks, and the other with *Pz. Kpfw. IV* tanks. (See *Figures 87 to 96.*)

b. THE SS TANK (*Panzer*) REGIMENT. This regiment is organized similarly to the Army Tank (*Panzer*) Regiment except that the tank companies are believed to consist of 17 instead of 14 tanks. They are distributed as follows: two in company headquarters and five in each of the three platoons. The *SS* tank regiment has therefore more strength and fire power than the Army Tank Regiment. (See *Figures 97 to 101.*)

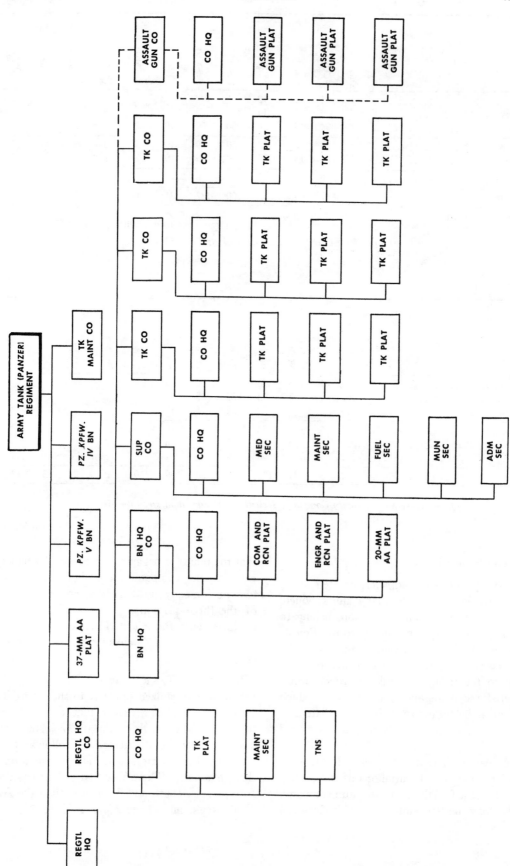

Figure 87.—Tank Regiment, Army Armored Division.

UNIT	Offs	NCOs	Pvts	Rs or Cbns	Pistols	Sub-MGs	LMGs	20-mm AA Guns Four-Barreled (SP)	37-mm AA Guns (SP)	75-mm Tk Guns (Long)	75-mm Tk Guns (Super-long)	Pz. Kpfw. IV's	Pz. Kpfw. V's	Mtr Vehicles	Mtrcls
Regtl Hq	4	3	7	9	3	2								2	4
Regtl Hq Co.........	4	51	54	37	71	8	14			4	3	4	3	15	5
37-mm AA Plat (SP)[1]	1	27	49	19	42	16	8		8					7	2
Pz. Kpfw. V Bn......	27	221	416	319	285	103	114	3			48		48	127	18
Pz. Kpfw. IV Bn......	27	212	328	229	286	95	112	3		48		48		94	18
Tk Maint Co.........	6	39	185	209	17	4	4							68	6
Total	69[2]	553	1,039	822	704	228	252	6	8	52	51	52	51	313[3]	53

[1] May be replaced by a flame-thrower Tk Plat with six flame-thrower *Pz. Kpfw. III's.*
[2] Including seven officials.
[3] Including ten Armd vehicles.

Figure 88.—Tank Regiment, Army Armored Division, total strength 1,661.

UNIT	Offs	NCOs	Pvts	Rs or Cbns	Pistols	Sub-MGs	l MGs	75-mm Tk Guns (Long)	75-mm Tk Guns (Super-long)	Pz. Kpfw. IV's	Pz. Kpfw. V's	Mtr Vehicles	Mtrcls
Co Hq	1		2	2		1						1	1
Com Plat		8	8	3	13	3	6		3		3	1	1
Tk Plat	1	11	8		20	4	8	4		4			
Maint Sec		3	11	11	3							3	1
Tns	2	29	25	21	35							10	2
Total	4	51	54	37	71	8	14	4	3	4	3	15	5

Figure 89.—Tank Regiment Headquarters Company, Army Armored Division, total strength 109.

UNIT	Offs	NCOs	Pvts	Rs or Cbns	Pistols	Sub-MGs	LMGs	20-mm AA Guns Four-Barreled (SP)	75-mm Tk Guns (Super-long)	Pz. Kpfw. V's	Mtr Vehicles	Mtrcls
Bn Hq	4	4	7	11	1	3	2				4	2
Bn Hq Co	4	32	99	61	53	22	24	3	6	6	19	8
Sup Co	7	59	211	226	21	30	4				98	2
Tk Co	4	42	33	7	70	16	28		14	14	2	2
Tk Co	4	42	33	7	70	16	28		14	14	2	2
Tk Co	4	42	33	7	70	16	28		14	14	2	2
Total	27[1]	221	416	319	285	103	114	3	48	48	127[2]	18

[1] Including two officials.
[2] Including five Armd vehicles.

Figure 90.—Pz. Kpfw. V (Panther) tank battalion, Army Armored Division, total strength 664.

137

UNIT	Offs	NCOs	Pvts	Rs or Cbns	Pistols	Sub-MGs	LMGs	20-mm AA Guns Four-Barreled (SP)	75-mm Tk Guns[1]	Pz. Kpfw. IV's or V's	Mtr Vehicles	Mtrcls
Co Hq	1	2	2	3	2						1	
Com and Rcn Plat	1	18	17	2	27	8	12		6	6	3	
Engr and Rcn Plat	1	8	45	32	12	10	11				11	7
20-mm AA Plat (SP)	1	4	35	24	12	4	1	3			4	1
Total	4	32	99	61	53	22	24	3	6	6	19[2]	8

[1] Long-barreled in *Pz. Kpfw. IV*; superlong-barreled in *Pz. Kpfw. V*.
[2] Including five Armd vehicles.

Figure 91.—Tank Battalion Headquarters Company, Army Armored Division, total strength 135.

UNIT	Offs	NCOs	Pvts	Rs or Cbns	Pistols	Sub-MGs	LMGs	Mtr Vehicles	Mtrcls
Co Hq	3	5	14	13	7	2		4	2
Med Serv	1	3	5	2	6	1		3	
Maint Serv (Mtr Vehicles and Wpns)	2	34	130	137	4	25		42	
Fuel Serv		4	22	23	2	1	2	21	
Mun Serv		3	15	16	1	1	1	14	
Adm Serv	1	10	25	35	1		1	14	
Total	7[1]	59	211	226	21	30	4	98	2

[1] Including two officials.

Figure 92.—Pz. Kpfw. V (Panther) Tank Battalion Supply Company, Army Armored Division, total strength 277.

UNIT	Offs	NCOs	Pvts	Rs or Cbns	Pistols	Sub-MGs	LMGs	75-mm Tk Guns[1]	Pz. Kpfw. IV's or V's	Mtr Vehicles	Mtrcls
Co Hq	1	9	9	7	10	4	4	2	2	2	2
Tk Plat	1	11	8		20	4	8	4	4		
Tk Plat	1	11	8		20	4	8	4	4		
Tk Plat	1	11	8		20	4	8	4	4		
Total	4	42	33	7	70	16	28	14	14	2	2

[1] Long-barreled in *Pz. Kpfw. IV*; superlong-barreled in *Pz. Kpfw. V*.

Figure 93.—Tank Company, Army Armored Division, total strength 79.

UNIT	Offs	NCOs	Pvts	Rs or Cbns	Pistols	Sub-MGs	LMGs	Mtr Vehicles	Mtrcls
Co Hq	3	5	14	13	7	2		4	2
Med Serv	1	2	5	2	6			3	
Maint Serv (Mtr Vehicles and Wpns)	2	28	59	65	4	20		27	
Fuel Serv		3	9	10	1	1	1	8	
Mun Serv		3	12	13	1	1	1	11	
Adm Serv	1	10	24	34	1		1	13	
Total	7[1]	51	123	137	20	24	3	66	2

[1] Including two officials.

Figure 94.—Pz. Kpfw. IV Tank Battalion Supply Company, Army Armored Division, total strength 181.

UNIT	Offs	NCOs	Pvts	Rs or Cbns	Pistols	Sub-MGs	LMGs	20-mm AT Guns Four-Barreled (SP)	75-mm Tk Guns (Long)	Pz. Kpfw. IV's	Mtr Vehicles	Mtrcls
Bn Hq	4	3	7	10	3	1	1				3	2
Bn Hq Co	4	32	99	61	53	22	24	3	6	6	19	8
Sup Co	7	51	123	137	20	24	3				66	2
Tk Co	4	42	33	7	70	16	28		14	14	2	2
Tk Co	4	42	33	7	70	16	28		14	14	2	2
Tk Co	4	42	33	7	70	16	28		14	14	2	2
Total	27[1]	212	328	229	286	95	112	3	48	48	94[2]	18

[1] Including two officials.
[2] Including five Armd vehicles.

Figure 95.—Pz. Kpfw. IV, Tank Battalion, Army Armored Division, total strength 567.

UNIT	Offs	NCOs	Pvts	Rs or Cbns	Pistols	Sub-MGs	LMGs	Mtr Vehicles	Mtrcls
Co Hq	3		8	8	2	1		4	2
Tk Maint Plat	1	9	50	59	1		1	14	1
Tk Maint Plat	1	9	50	59	1		1	14	1
Tk Salv Plat		7	39	37	6	3	2	15	1
Ord Sec	1	1	8	8	2			5	
Sig Equip Rep Sec		4	8	10	2			4	
Spare Parts Sec		2	6	8				4	
Tn		7	16	20	3			8	1
Total	6[1]	39	185	209	17	4	4	68	6

[1] Including three officials.

Figure 96.—Tank Maintenance Company, Army Armored Division, total strength 230.

UNIT	Offs	NCOs	Pvts	Rs or Cbns	Pistols	Sub-MGs	LMGs	20-mm AA Guns Four-Barreled (SP)	37-mm AA Guns (SP)	75-mm Tk Guns (Long)	75-mm Tk Guns (Super-long)	Pz. Kpfw. IV's	Pz. Kpfw. V's	Mtr Vehicles	Mtrcls
Regtl Hq	4	3	7	9	3	2								2	4
Regtl Hq Co	5	54	56	37	76	9	16			5	3	5	3	15	5
37-mm AA Co. (SP)[1]	1	27	49	19	42	16	8		8					7	2
Pz. Kpfw. V Bn	27	250	439	316	290	111	135	3			59		59	127	18
Pz. Kpfw. IV Bn	27	241	351	226	291	103	133	3		59		59		94	18
Tk Maint Co	6	39	185	209	17	4	4							68	6
Total	70[2]	614	1,087	816	719	245	296	6	8	64	62	64	62	313[3]	53

[1] May be replaced by a flame-thrower Tk Plat with six flame-thrower *Pz. Kpfw. III's.*
[2] Including seven officials.
[3] Including ten Armd vehicles.

Figure 97.—SS Tank Regiment, SS Armored Division, total strength 1,771.

c. THE TANK BATTALION. In the Army Motorized Division this battalion is organized similarly to the tank battalions in the Army Armored Division; it sometimes may be replaced by an assault gun battalion.

d. THE TANK BATTALION. In the *SS* Motorized Division it is organized similarly to the tank battalions in the *SS* Armored Division.

e. THE *SS* TANK COMPANY. In the *SS* Mountain Division this is organized similarly to the *SS* tank companies in the *SS* Armored Division; it may be replaced sometimes by an assault gun company.

f. FLAME-THROWER TANK PLATOONS. These consist of six flame-throwing *Pz. Kpfw. II* tanks, and are frequently organic in the tank regiment (Army and *SS*). They are either a part of the regimental headquarters company or are assigned directly to the regimental headquarters.

UNIT	Offs	NCOs	Pvts	Rs or Cbns	Pistols	Sub-MGs	LMGs	20-mm AA Guns Four-Barreled (SP)	75-mm Tk Guns (Super-long)	Pz. Kpfw. V's	Mtr Vehicles	Mtrcls
Bn Hq	4	4	7	11	1	3	2				4	2
Bn Hq Co...................	4	37	104	61	61	24	27	3	8	8	19	8
Sup Co	7	59	211	226	21	30	4				98	2
Tk Co	4	50	39	6	69	18	34		17	17	2	2
Tk Co	4	50	39	6	69	18	34		17	17	2	2
Tk Co	4	50	39	6	69	18	34		17	17	2	2
Total	27[1]	250	439	316	290	111	135	3	59	59	127[2]	18

[1] Including two officials.
[2] Including five Armd vehicles.

Figure 98.—Pz. Kpfw. V, Tank Battalion, SS Armored Division, total strength 716.

UNIT	Offs	NCOs	Pvts	Rs or Cbns	Pistols	Sub-MGs	LMGs	20-mm AT Guns Four-Barreled (SP)	75-mm Tk Guns[1]	Pz. Kpfw. IV's or V's	Mtr Vehicles	Mtrcls
Co Hq	1	2	2	3	2						1	
Com and Rcn Plat..........	1	23	22	2	35	10	16		8	8	3	
Engr and Rcn Plat..........	1	8	45	32	12	10	11				11	7
AA Plat	1	4	35	24	12	4		3			4	1
Total	4	37	104	61	61	24	27	3	8	8	19[2]	8

[1] Long-barreled guns in *Pz. Kpfw. IV*, superlong in *Pz. Kpfw. V*.
[2] Including five Armd vehicles.

Figure 99.—SS Tank Battalion Headquarters Company, SS Armored Division, total strength 145.

UNIT	Offs	NCOs	Pvts	Rs or Cbns	Pistols	Sub-MGs	LMGs	75-mm Tk Guns[1]	Pz. Kpfw. IV's or V's	Mtr Vehicles	Mtrcls
Co Hq	1	8	9	6	9	3	4	2	2	2	2
Tk Plat	1	14	10		20	5	10	5	5		
Tk Plat	1	14	10		20	5	10	5	5		
Tk Plat	1	14	10		20	5	10	5	5		
Total	4	50	39	6	69	18	34	17	17	2	2

[1] Long-barreled guns in *Pz. Kpfw. IV*, superlong in *Pz. Kpfw. V*.

Figure 100.—SS Tank Company, SS Armored Division, total strength 93.

UNIT	Offs	NCOs	Pvts	Rs or Cbns	Pistols	Sub-MGs	LMGs	20-mm AA Guns Four-Barreled (SP)	75-mm Tk Guns (Long)	Pz. Kpfw. IV's	Mtr Vehicles	Mtrcls
Bn Hq	4	3	7	10	3	1	1				3	2
Bn Hq Co	4	37	104	61	61	24	27	3	8	8	19	8
Sup Co	7	51	123	137	20	24	3				66	2
Tk Co	4	50	39	6	69	18	34		17	17	2	2
Tk Co	4	50	39	6	69	18	34		17	17	2	2
Tk Co	4	50	39	6	69	18	34		17	17	2	2
Total	27[1]	241	351	226	291	103	133	3	59	59	94[2]	18

[1] Including two officials.
[2] Including five Armd vehicles.

Figure 101.—Pz. Kpfw. IV, SS Tank Battalion, SS Armored Division, total strength 619.

5. Armored General Headquarters Units

a. THE GENERAL HEADQUARTERS *Pz. Kpfw.* VI (Tiger) BATTALION. This type of tank battalion frequently allotted to corps is the heaviest tank battalion in the German Armed forces. (See *Figures 102 to 103*.)

b. THE GENERAL HEADQUARTERS *Pz. Kpfw.* V (Panther) BATTALION. This is organized similarly to the *Pz. Kpfw. VI* (Tiger) battalion except that some may have 17 tanks per company instead of 14.

c. THE TANK FLAME-THROWER BATTALION. This is an independent battalion, normally found employed under armored corps. It consists of

three companies of flame-thrower tanks, either *Pz. Kpfw. II*, which has two flame throwers, or with *Pz. Kpfw. III*, which has only one flame thrower, but of greater range. *Pz. Kpfw. II* tank platoons originally were organic in the flame-thrower tank battalion, but it is believed that they have been withdrawn because of their light weight and armament.

d. THE HEAVY TANK COMPANY (Tiger) (*FKL*) (REMOTE CONTROL TANK) This company is usually found allotted from General Headquarters but may also be found organic in crack armored divisions. It has 14 Tiger tanks and 36 remote controlled B-IV tanks. (See *Figure 104*.)

UNIT	Offs	NCO's	Pvts	Rs or Cbns	Pistols	Sub-MGs	LMGs	20-mm AA Guns Four-Barreled (SP)	88-mm Tk Guns	Pz. Kpfw. VI	Mtr Vehicles	Mtrcls
Bn Hq	4	4	7	11	1	3	2				4	2
Bn Hq Co	4	27	89	51	48	22	18	3	3	3	19	8
Sup Co	7	59	211	226	21	30	4				98	2
Tk Co	4	42	33	7	70	16	28		14	14	2	2
Tk Co	4	42	33	7	70	16	28		14	14	2	2
Tk Co	4	42	33	7	70	16	28		14	14	2	2
Total	27[1]	216	406	309	280	103	108	3	45	45	127[2]	18

[1] Including two officials.
[2] Including eight Armd vehicles.

Figure 102.—GHQ Pz. Kpfw. VI, (Tiger) Battalion, total strength 649.

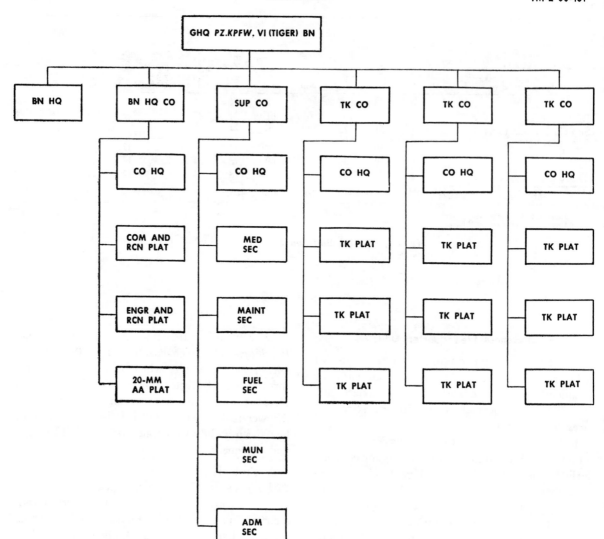

Figure 103.—Heavy Tank Company (Tiger) (FKL) (Remote Control), total strenght 188.

UNIT	Offs	NCOs	Pvts	Rs or Cbns	Pistols	Sub-MGs	LMGs	88-mm Tk Guns	Pz. Kpfw. VI	Remote Control Tks	Mtr Vehicles	Mtrcls
Co Hq	2	8	9	5	14	2	4	2	2		2	3
Plat	1	13	18	2	30	5	9	4	4	9		
Plat	1	13	18	2	30	5	9	4	4	9		
Plat		14	18	2	30	5	9	4	4	9		
Maint Sec		6	30	26	10	4	1				10	
Tns		7	30	22	15	2	1			9	10	1
Total	4	61	123	59	129	23	33	14	14	36	22	4

Figure 104.—Heavy Tank Company (Tiger) (FKL) (Remote Control), total strength 188.

6. Organic Artillery Units

In the German Army much of the field artillery and all the Army coast artillery and railway artillery belong to the General Headquarters pool. The coastal artillery is in peace time exclusively the responsibility of the Navy, but in war time the Army also has formed coast artillery units principally for the protection of coasts in occupied areas. Coast artillery, Naval or Army, normally is assigned to the sector command in which it is located. Units are allotted from this pool to army groups or armies according to operational needs. They then may be sub-allotted to corps or divisions, in which case they usually are placed under the control of special artillery commanders and staffs. Divisional artillery is frequently reinforced by General Headquarters artillery, army antiaircraft artillery, and projector units. Figures 105-121.

a. ARTILLERY REGIMENT *(Artillerieregiment).* One to a division, this regiment varies in composition according to the type of the division. Several types exist.

(1) *In Infantry Division, Type 1944.* Four battalions (I, II, and III equipped with 105-mm gun-howitzers and IV with 150-mm howitzers.

(2) *In Volks Grenadier Division.* Four battalions (I equipped with 75-mm AT guns, II and III with 105-mm gun/howitzers, and IV with 150-mm howitzers).

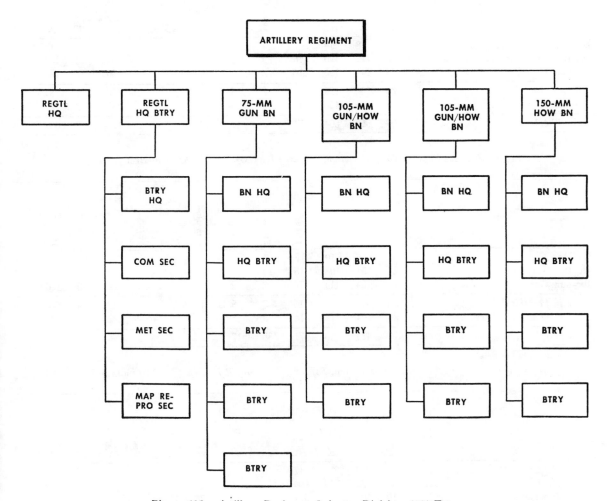

Figure 105.—Artillery Regiment, Infantry Division, 1944 Type.

UNIT	Offs	NCOs	Pvts	Rs or Cbns	Pistols	Sub-MGs	LMGs	105-mm Gun/Hows	150-mm Hows	Mtr Vehicles	Mtrcls	H-Dr Vehicles	Tlrs	Hs	Bcls
Regtl Hq	5	2	18	17	6	7				3	2			8	1
Regtl Hq Btry........	4	22	59	64	17	6	1			2	1	29	2	65	3
1st (Light) Bn........	19	109	424	460	71	38	17	12		7	1	96	8	516	13
2d (Light) Bn........	19	109	424	460	71	38	17	12		7	1	96	8	516	13
3d (Light) Bn........	19	109	424	460	71	38	17	12		7	1	96	8	516	13
4th (Medium) Bn.....	19	109	557	604	71	37	17		12	4	1	124	8	697	13
Total	85[1]	460	1,906	2,065	307	164	69	36	12	30	7	441	34	2,318	56

[1] Including ten officials.

Figure 106.—Artillery Regiment, Infantry Division, 1944 Type, total strength 2,451.

UNIT	Offs	NCOs	Pvts	Rs or Cbns	Pistols	Sub-MGs	LMGs	150-mm Hows	Mtr Vehicles	Mtrcls	H-Dr Vehicles	Tlrs	Hs	Bcls
Bn Hq	6	3	8	10	7	4			2	1			12	1
Hq Btry Incl Tns.............	4[1]	22	111	126	16	9	2		2		34	2	142	3
150-mm How Btry...........	3	28	146	156	16	8	5	4			30	2	181	3
150-mm How Btry...........	3	28	146	156	16	8	5	4			30	2	181	3
150-mm How Btry...........	3	28	146	156	16	8	5	4			30	2	181	3
Total	19[1]	109	557	604	71	37	17	12	4	1	124	8	697	13

[1] Including two officials.

Figure 107.—Medium Artillery Battalion, Infantry Division, 1944 Type, total strength 685.

UNIT	Offs	NCOs	Pvts	Rs or Cbns	Pistols	Sub-MGs	LMGs	105-mm Gun/Hows	Mtr Vehicles	Mtrcls	H-Dr Vehicles	Tlrs	Hs	Bcls
Bn Hq	6	3	8	10	7	4			2	1			12	1
Hq Btry Incl Tns.............	4[1]	22	104	108	16	10	2		5		30	2	126	3
105-mm Gun/How Btry.......	3	28	104	114	16	8	5	4			22	2	126	3
105-mm Gun/How Btry.......	3	28	104	114	16	8	5	4			22	2	126	3
105-mm Gun/How Btry.......	3	28	104	114	16	8	5	4			22	2	126	3
Total	19[1]	109	424	460	71	38	17	12	7	1	96	8	516	13

[1] Including two officials.

Figure 108.—Light Artillery Battalion, Infantry Division, 1944 Type, total strength 552.

UNIT	Offs	NCOs	Pvts	Rs or Cbns	Pistols	Sub-MGs	LMGs	105-mm Gun/Hows	150-mm Hows	Mtr Vehicles	Mtrcls	H-Dr Vehicles	Hs
Regtl Hq	5	2	18	17	6	7				3	2		8
Regtl Hq Btry..................	4	22	59	64	17	6	1			2	1	29	65
1st (Light) Bn.................	19	100	344	371	74	37	17	11		7	1	70	406
2d (Light) Bn.................	19	100	344	371	74	37	17	11		7	1	70	406
3d (Light) Bn.................	19	100	344	371	74	37	17	11		7	1	70	406
4th (Medium) Bn...............	19	97	398	422	74	67	17		9	4	1	90	476
Total	85[1]	421	1,507	1,616	319	191	69	33	9	30	7	329	1,767

[1] Including ten officials.

Figure 109.—Artillery Regiment (Reduced Strength and Fire Power), Infantry Division, 1944 Type, total strength 2,013.

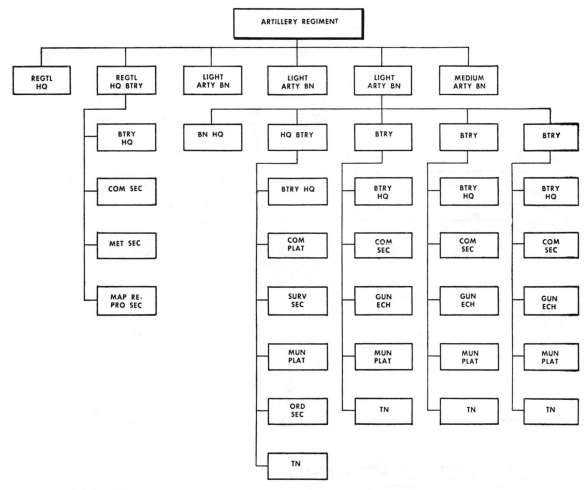

Figure 110.—Artillery Regiment, Volks Grenadier Division.

UNIT	Offs	NCOs	Pvts	Rs or Cbns	Pistols	Sub-MGs	LMGs	75-mm Guns	105-mm Gun/Hows	150-mm Hows	Mtr Vehicles	Mtrcls	H-Dr Vehicles	Tlrs	Hs	Bcls
Regtl Hq	5	3	7	7	3	5									4	
Regtl Hq Btry............	4	23	68	74	14	7	1				7	2	15	4	42	4
75-mm Gun Bn...........	18	123	372	416	55	36	14	18			30	1	71	8	267	12
105-mm Gun/How Bn......	16	85	270	300	43	28	10		12		22	1	56	6	211	10
105-mm Gun/How Bn......	16	85	270	300	43	28	10		12		22	1	56	6	211	10
150-mm How Bn.........	16	86	277	308	43	28	10			12	18	8	87	6	327	13
Total	75[1]	405	1,264	1,405	201	132	45	18	24	12	99	13	285	30	1,062	49

[1] Including ten officials.

Figure 111.—Artillery Regiment, Volks Grenadier Division, total strength 1,744.

145

UNIT	Offs	NCOs	Pvts	Rs or Cbns	Pistols	Sub-MGs	LMGs	75-mm Guns	Mtr Vehicles	Mtrcls	H-Dr Vehicles	Tlrs	Hs	Bcls
Bn Hq	5	3	7	9	3	3			3	1			9	1
Hq Btry	4	24	101	107	13	9	2		3		26	2	90	5
75-mm Gun Btry	3	30	88	100	13	8	4	6	8		15	2	56	2
75-mm Gun Btry	3	33	88	100	13	8	4	6	8		15	2	56	2
75-mm Gun Btry	3	33	88	100	13	8	4	6	8		15	2	56	2
Total	18[1]	123	372	416	55	36	14	18	30	1	71	8	267	12

[1] Including two officials.

Figure 112.—Artillery Regiment, Volks Grenadier Division, total strength 513.

UNIT	Offs	NCOs	Pvts	Rs or Cbns	Pistols	Sub-MGs	LMGs	105-mm Gun/Hows	Mtr Vehicles	Mtrcls	H-Dr Vehicles	Tlrs	Hs	Bcls
Bn Hq	6	3	8	10	3	4			3	1			9	1
Hq Btry	4	22	88	92	14	8	2		3		26	2	90	5
105-mm Gun/How Btry	3	30	87	99	13	8	4	6	8		15	2	56	2
105-mm Gun/How Btry	3	30	87	99	13	8	4	6	8		15	2	56	2
Total	16[1]	85	270	300	43	28	10	12	22	1	56	6	211	10

[1] Including two officials.

Figure 113.—105-mm Gun-Howitzer Battalion, Volks Grenadier Division, total strength 371.

UNIT	Offs	NCOs	Pvts	Rs or Cbns	Pistols	Sub-MGs	LMGs	150-mm Hows	Mtr Vehicles	Mtrcls	H-Dr Vehicles	Tlrs	Hs	Bcls
Bn Hq	6	3	8	10	3	4				1			9	1
Bn Hq Btry	4	23	95	100	14	8	2		6	5	29	2	100	
150-mm How Btry	3	30	87	99	13	8	4	6	6	1	29	2	109	6
150-mm How Btry	3	30	87	99	13	8	4	6	6	1	29	2	109	6
Total	16[1]	86	277	308	43	28	10	12	18	8	87	6	327	13

[1] Including two officials.

Figure 114.—150-mm Howitzer Battalion, Volks Grenadier Division, total strength 379.

(3) *In Armored and Motorized Divisions.* Three battalions (I normally equipped with two batteries of 105-mm gun/howitzers and one battery of 150-mm howitzers all self-propelled, II equipped with 105-mm gun howitzers, and III with 150-mm howitzers). *Panzer* and *Panzer Grenadier* divisions also have a separate Army antiaircraft artillery battalion as an organic divisional component. In *SS Panzer* divisions a heavy artillery battalion, usually equipped with 170-mm guns, is added as the fourth battalion in the artillery regiment.

(4) *In Light and Mountain Divisions.* It has four battalions—I and II equipped with 75-mm mountain howitzers and III with 105-mm gun-howitzers. The organization of IV may vary but it normally is equipped with 150-mm howitzers.

All the types of artillery battalions organic in divisions may be found with some variations in the General Headquarters pool.

b. THE ARMY ANTIAIRCRAFT ARTILLERY BATTALION (*Heeresflakartillerieabteilung*). One to a *Panzer* and a motorized division, consisting of two 88-mm antiaircraft batteries and one 20-mm antiaircraft battery.

c. THE ASSAULT-GUN BATTALION (*Sturmgeschützabteilung*). This sometimes replaces the antitank battalion in *Panzer Grenadier* divisions. Those in company strength, but designated battalions organic in infantry, light, and mountain divisions, were renamed *Panzerjägerkompanie* in the fall of 1944. Most of those in the General Headquarters pool were renamed Assault Gun Brigades, however, a few General Headquarters assault gun battalions are believed to have kept their designation.

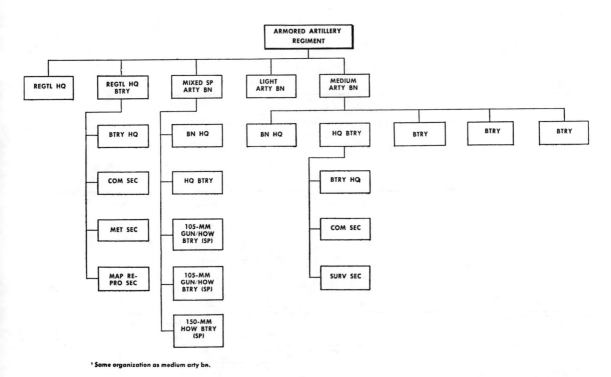

' *Same organization as medium arty bn.*

Figure 115.—Armored Artillery Regiment, Army Armored Division.

UNIT	Offs	NCOs	Pvts	Rs or Cbns	Pistols	Sub-MGs	LMGs	20-mm AA Guns	105-mm Gun/Hows	105-mm Guns Hows (SP)	150-mm Hows	150-mm Hows (SP)	Mtr Vehicles	Mtrcls
Regtl Hq	6	4	10	11	9	6							7	1
Regtl Hq Btry	3	18	52	58	11	6	2						18	2
Mixed SP Arty Bn........	20	127	411	348	191	87	56	3		12		6	133²	10
Light Arty Bn.............	20	108	352	381	66	52	17	3	12				122	9
Medium Arty Bn.........	20	108	390	419	66	52	17	3			12		127	9
Total	69¹	365	1 215	1,217	343	203	92	9	12	12	12	6	407²	31

¹ Including eleven officials.
² Including 27 Armd vehicles.

Figure 116.—Armored Artillery Regiment, Army Armored Division, total strength 1,649.

UNIT	Offs	NCOs	Pvts	Rs or Cbns	Pistols	Sub-MGs	LMGs	Mtr Vehicles	Mtrcls
Btry Hq	1	1	1	2	1	1		1	1
Com Plat		7	27	30	2	2		6	
Ord Maint Sec	2¹	4	7	8	5	1		2	
Mtr Vehicle Maint Sec		1	3	3			1	2	
Tns		5	14	15	3	1	2	7	1
Total	3¹	18	52	58	11	6	2	18	2

¹ Including two officials.

Figure 117.—Artillery Regiment Headquarters Battery, Armored Division, total strength 73.

UNIT	Offs	NCOs	Pvts	Rs or Cbns	Pistols	Sub-MGs	LMGs	20-mm AA Guns	105-mm Guns/How (SP)	150-mm Hows (SP)	Mtr Vehicles	Mtrcls
Bn Hq	6	3	4	6	7	5					3	1
Bn Hq Btry	5¹	31	128	120	40	16	5	3			46²	3
105-mm Gun/How Btry (SP)..........	3	31	91	72	48	22	17		6		28	2
105-mm Gun/How Btry (SP)..........	3	31	91	72	48	22	17		6		28	2
150-mm How Btry (SP)...............	3	31	97	78	48	22	17			6	28	2
Total	20¹	127	411	348	191	87	56	3	12	6	133²	10

¹ Including three officials.
² Including 27 Armd vehicles.

Figure 118.—Mixed Self-Propelled Battalion, Army Armored Division, total strength 558.

UNIT	Offs	NCOs	Pvts	Rs or Cbns	Pistols	Sub-MGs	LMGs	20-mm AA Guns	105-mm Gun/Hows	Mtr Vehicles	Mtrcls
Bn Hq	6	3	6	8	7	5				5	1
Bn Hq Btry	5[1]	27	100	109	17	11	2	3		36	2
105-mm Gun/How Btry....	3	26	82	88	14	12	5		4	27	2
105-mm Gun/How Btry....	3	26	82	88	14	12	5		4	27	2
105-mm Gun/How Btry....	3	26	82	88	14	12	5		4	27	2
Total	20[1]	108	352	381	66	52	17	3	12	122	9

[1] Including three officials.

Figure 119.—Light Artillery Battalion, Army Armored Division, total strength 480.

UNIT	Offs	NCOs	Pvts	Rs or Cbns	Pistols	Sub-MGs	LMGs	20-mm AA Guns	150-mm Hows	Mtr Vehicles	Mtrcls
Bn Hq	6	3	6	8	7	5				5	1
Bn Hq Btry	5[1]	27	102	111	17	11	2	3		41	2
150-mm How Btry.........	3	26	94	100	14	12	5		4	27	2
150-mm How Btry.........	3	26	94	100	14	12	5		4	27	2
150-mm How Btry.........	3	26	94	100	14	12	5		4	27	2
Total	20[1]	108	390	419	66	52	17	3	12	127	9

[1] Including three officials.

Figure 120.—Medium Artillery Battalion, Army Armored Division, total strength 518.

UNIT	Offs	NCOs	Pvts	Rs or Cbns	Pistols	Sub-MGs	LMGs	20-mm AA Guns	88-mm AA Guns	Light SLs	Mtr Vehicles	Mtrcls
Bn Hq	5	3	5	5	5	3					3	3
Bn Hq Btry	7[1]	27	122	136	19	11	2				42	2
Hv AA Btry	3	34	130	149	12	10	4	3	4		31	2
Hv AA Btry	3	34	130	149	12	10	4	3	4		31	2
Light AA Btry	3	38	146	164	18	12	6	12[2]		4	41	5
Light AA Clm	1	6	67	70	3	1	2				23	2
Total	22[1]	142	600	673	69	47	18	18[2]	8	4	171	16

[1] Including four officials.
[2] The twelve 20-mm AA guns may be sometimes replaced by nine 37-mm AA guns.

Figure 121.—Antiaircraft Battalion, Army Armored Division, total strength 764.

7. General Headquarters Artillery Units

a. THE ARTILLERY DIVISION. This consists of a divisional staff controlling several artillery regiments. Such divisions were encountered on the Eastern Front in the beginning of 1944 but it is believed that such a concentration of fire power may also occur in other theaters. (See *Figure 122.*)

UNIT	150-mm Rkt Projectors	105-mm Gun/Hows	105-mm Guns	122-mm Hows	155-mm Hows
Rkt Projector Bn.........	18				
105-mm Arty Regt.......		24	12		
105-mm Arty Regt.......		24	12		
Mixed Arty Regt........				24	12
Total	18	48	24	24	12

Figure 122.—Artillery Division.

b. ARTILLERY BRIGADE (*Artilleriebrigade*). This is an independent artillery brigade consisting of a varying number of artillery batteries. All or most artillery brigades have been converted to *Volksartilleriekorps*.

c. THE ASSAULT GUN BRIGADE (*Sturmgeschützbrigade*). This is a redesignated General Headquarters assault gun brigade. The strength and fire power of the Assault Gun Battalions, which were greater than those of ordinary battalions may have warranted this differentiation in nomenclature from organic assault gun battalions which were actually only of battalion strength, but the redesignation also may have been motivated by the aim to raise the morale. The guns of assault gun brigades are sometimes referred to as *Sturmartillerie*.

d. THE VOLKS ARTILLERY CORPS (*Volksartilleriekorps*). This corps is an independent General Headquarters unit which has been converted from artillery brigades. The corps is probably composed of six battalions which may be equipped with 75-mm antitank guns, 105-mm howitzers, and 150-mm and 170-mm howitzers.

e. THE FORTRESS ARTILLERY REGIMENT (*Festungsartillerieregiment*). This controls several fortress artillery battalions.

f. THE FORTRESS ARTILLERY BATTALION. (*Festungsartillerieabteilung*). These are static artillery battalions organized in the summer of 1944, equipped with German and captured guns.

g. THE ARMY COAST ARTILLERY REGIMENT (*Heeresküstenartillerieregiment*). This normally controls two or three army coast artillery battalions and possibly any number of independent batteries.

h. THE ARMY COAST ARTILLERY BATTALION (*Heeresküstenartillerieabteilung*). This battalion varies in composition. It may be organized as a regular battalion with three batteries or as battalion staff controlling a larger number of independent batteries.

i. THE NAVAL COAST ARTILLERY BATTALION (*Marineartillerieabteilung*). This battalion, which varies in composition, belongs to the German Navy but may come under the Army coast command in which it is located.

j. ARTILLERY ANTITANK GUN BATTALION (*Artillerie-Pak-Abteilung*). Equipped with 75 or 88-mm antitank guns.

k. MAPPING AND SURVEYING UNITS (*Karten- und Vermessungseinheiten*). Mapping and surveying units belong to the artillery although German orders have at times referred to them as a separate arm.

(1) *The Artillery Observation Battalion* (*Beobachtungsabteilung*). Normally allotted to corps, but often attached to divisional artillery regiments, it contains a sound-ranging battery, light-ranging battery, and meteorological platoon.

(2) *Light-ranging battery* (*Lichtessbatterie*). Normally one to an observation battalion.

(3) *Sound-ranging battery* (*Schallmessbatterie*). Normally one to an observation battalion.

(4) *Army or Corps Map Reproduction Center* (*Armee or Korpskartenstelle*). Previously known as *Armee-or Korpskartenlager*.

(5) *Printing and Survey Battalion* (*Druck- und Vermessungsabteilung*). Probably similar to a *Vermessungs-und Kartenabteilung*.

(6) *Map Printing Battalion* (*Karten-Druckereiabteilung*).

(7) *Survey and Mapping Battalion* (*Vermessungs-und Kartenabteilung*). In General Headquarters, to be allotted to army groups or armies, obtains topographical information and prints maps and photos which are used for operational purposes.

(8) *Astronomical Survey Platoon* (*Astronomischer Messzug*).

(9) *Observation Battalion Battery* (*Ballonbatterie*).

(10) *Magnet Survey Battery* (*Magnet-Messbatterie*).

(11) *Velocity Measurement Platoon* (*Velozitätsmesszug*).

(12) *Metcorological Platoon* (*Wetterpeilzug*). Makes air analyses for artillery units but does not engage in weather forecasting.

8. Antitank Units *(Panzeriager)*

Most of the antitank units are considered by the Germans as part of the armored (*Panzer*) arm. It should be noted, however, that the personnel of the antitank companies in infantry regiments and the personnel in the antiaircraft companies in the antitank battalions belong to the infantry arm.

Almost all German divisions include antitank battalions in their organic components. These battalions usually consist of three companies, of which two are always antitank companies, while the third is either an antitank or an antiaircraft company. (See *Figures 123 to 125.*)

It should be noted that the majority of all heavy antiaircraft guns are dual-purpose guns, and units equipped with them therefore may be employed for the support of the antitank units.

Similarly, artillery units, particularly those equipped with artillery antitank guns or light cannons, at any time may be employed as antitank units. In addition, there is a clear trend to equip almost every unit in the German Armed Forces with a generous allotment of bazookas and rocket antitank pistols. The allotment of these small antitank weapons, however, has been so irregular that they had to be omitted in many of the tables of organization listed herein.

9. General Headquarters Antitank Units

Numerous types of motor-drawn and self-propelled antitank gun units may be allotted from the General Headquarters pool to corps or divisions in accordance with tactical needs. Self-propelled General Headquarters units sometimes have been referred to as assault gun battalions or brigades. The strongest type of General Headquarters antitank battalions is the Tiger-P antitank battalion. It consists of three companies of fourteen 88-mm antitank guns mounted on the Tiger-P chassis. (See *Figures 126 to 129.*)

The Fortress Antitank Gun Battalion (*Festungs-Pak-Bataillon*) is similar to ordinary antitank battalions except that it has very limited transport facilities.

The Fortress Antitank Gun Command (*Festungs-Pak-Verband*) is a staff controlling several independent fortress antitank gun companies in a given sector.

The Fortress Antitank Gun Company (*Festungs-Pak Kompanie*) is an independent static antitank gun company attached for administrative purposes to a fortress antitank gun command and for tactical purposes to the field unit which mans the sector. It is equipped with 76.2 (Russian) and 88-mm antitank guns.

UNIT	Offs	NCOs	Pvts	Rs. or Cbns	Pistols	Sub-MGs	LMGs	20-mm AA Guns (SP)	75-mm AT Guns (Mtr-Dr)	75-mm AT Guns (SP)	Mtr Vehicles	Mtrcls	Tlrs
Bn Hq	5	1	6	7	5						2	3	
Bn Hq Co	4[1]	20	49	58	13	2	1				23	2	4
1st (75-mm) AT Co (Mtr-Dr)....	3	24	104	99	50	16	12		12		36	5	
2d (75-mm) AT Co (SP)........	3	44	72	59	29	31	14			14	28	4	7
3d (20-mm) AA Co (SP)........	2	34	113	95	26	32	2	12			24	6	6
Total	17[1]	123	344	318	123	81	29	12	12	14	113	20	17

[1] Including three officials.

Figure 123.—Antitank Battalion, Infantry Division, 1944 Type, total strength 484.

UNIT	Offs	NCOs	Pvts	Rs or Cbns	Pistols	Sub-MGs	LMGs	37-mm AA Guns (SP)	75-mm AT Guns (Mtr-Dr)	75-mm AT Guns (SP)	Mtr Vehicles	Mtrcls	Tlrs
Bn Hq	5	1	6	7	5						2	3	
Bn Hq Co	4[1]	20	49	58	13	2	1				23	2	4
1st (75-mm) AT Co (M-Dr)......	3	20	84	87	44	4	9		9		28	4	
2d (75-mm) AT Co (SP)........	3	44	72	69	40	10	16			14	28	4	7
3d (37-mm) AA Co (SP)........	2	34	113	105	38	10	4	9			19	5	5
Total	17[1]	119	324	326	140	26	30	9	9	14	100	18	16

[1] Including three officials.

Figure 124.—Antitank Battalion, Volks Grenadier Division, total strength 460.

UNIT	Offs	NCOs	Pvts	Rs or Cbns	Pistols	Sub-MGs	LMGs	75-mm AT Guns (Mtr-Dr)	75-mm AT Guns (SP)	Mtr Vehicles	Mtrcls
Bn Hq	4	1	6	7	4					2	2
Bn Hq Co	1	20	27	29	10	9	4		3	15	1
75-mm AT Co (SP)[1]......	3	40	30	11	33	29	14		14	19	4
75-mm AT Co (SP)[1]......	3	40	30	11	33	29	14		14	19	4
75-mm AT Co (Mtr-Dr)...	3	20	94	59	41	17	12	12		17	4
Sup Co	6[2]	45	140	154	21	16	3			63	2
Total	20[3]	166	327	271	142	100	47	12	31	135	17

[1] Frequently referred to as Assault **Gun Co.**
[2] Including three officials.

Figure 125.—Antitank Battalion, Army Armored Division, total strength 513.

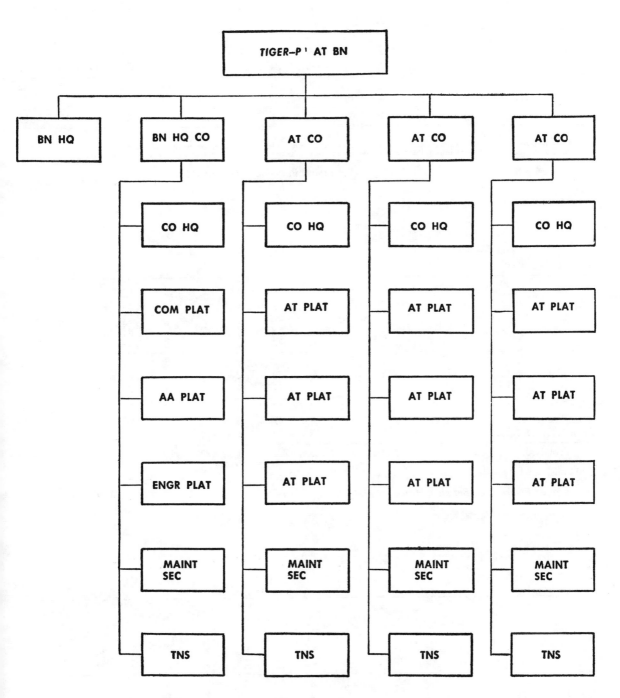

[1] The *Pz. Jag. Tiger–P* (Porsche) also known as the *Ferdinand* or *Elephant*, consists of the 8.8-cm *Stu. K. 43/1* on the *Tiger–P* Chassis.

Figure 126.—The Tiger-P Antitank Battalion.

UNIT	Offs	NCOs	Pvts	Rs or Cbns	Pistols	Sub-MGs	LMGs	20-mm AA Guns Four-Barreled (SP)	88-mm AT Guns on Tk chassis	Mtr Vehicles	Mtrcls
Bn Hq	4	4	7	11	1	3	2			4	2
Bn Hq Co	7	55	235	222	71	22	10	3	3	83	13
AT Co	4	67	130	84	117	34	16		14	35	12
AT Co	4	67	130	84	117	34	16		14	35	12
AT Co	4	67	130	84	117	34	16		14	35	12
Total	23[1]	260	632[2]	485	423	127	60	3	45	192	51

[1] Including three officials.
[2] It is believed that various changes in the T/O recently have been made to economize on manpower. These include the merging of the Co Tns and Maint Secs into a Bn Sup Co and result in a reduction of the total strength of the Bn to about 700.

Figure 127.—Tiger-P Antitank Battalion, total strength 915.

UNIT	Offs	NCOs	Pvts	Rs or Cbns	Pistols	Sub-MGs	LMGs	20-mm AA Guns Four-Barreled (SP)	88-mm AT Guns on the chassis	Mtr Vehicles	Mtrcls
Co Hq	2	11	9	3	19	6	3		3	1	2
Com Plat	1	8	23	30	2					10	1
AA Plat		5	41	27	19	4	1	3		7	3
Engr Plat	1	3	23	17	6	4	3			4	4
Maint Sec	1	9	41	47	4	4				16	
Trains	2	19	98	98	21	4	3			45	3
Total	7[1]	55	235	222	71	22	10	3	3	83	13

[1] Including three officials.

Figure 128.—Battalion Headquarters Company, Tiger-P Antitank Battalion, total strength 297.

UNIT	Offs	NCOs	Pvts	Rs or Cbns	Pistols	Sub-MGs	LMGs	88-mm AT Guns on Tk chassis	Mtr Vehicles	Mtrcls
Co Hq	2	8	13	10	13	4	2	2	2	4
1st Plat	1	14	20	9	26	9	4	4	4	2
2d Plat	1	14	20	9	26	9	4	4	4	2
3d Plat		15	20	9	26	9	4	4	4	2
Maint Sec		3	23	21	5	3			8	
Tns		13	34	26	21		2		13	2
Total	4	67	130	84	117	34	16	14	35	12

Figure 129.—Antitank Company, Tiger-P Antitank Battalion, total strength 201.

10. Chemical Warfare Units *(Nebeltruppen)*

Chemical warfare battalions are organic in *SS* Armored Divisions, and possibly in some correspondingly strong Army or Air Force divisions. Usually, however, they are allotted from General Headquarters to armies, corps, and divisions. The standard tactical units of the chemical warfare troops are:

a. ROCKET PROJECTOR BATTALION (MOTORIZED) *(Werferabteilung (mot.))*.

b. HEAVY ROCKET PROJECTOR BATTALION (MOTORIZED *(Schwere Werferabteilung (mot.))*.

c. MOUNTAIN ROCKET PROJECTOR BATTALION *(Gebirgswerferabteilung)*.

The first two types of battalions are usually components of rocket-projector regiments, normally three battalions per regiment. A rocket-projector battalion is designated heavy when it has more than one heavy-projector battalion (210, 300 or 280/320-mm). Two rocket-projector regiments usually compose a rocket-projector brigade. one of which has been identified as *Volkswerferbrigade* with all its components adding the prefix *"Volks"* to their unit designation. Rocket-projector units until now have been employed in firing high explosive, incendiary, and smoke rockets, but all of them also are equipped and trained for gas warfare. All rocket-projector battalions also are equipped and their personnel trained for street and road contamination as well as decontamination.

d. In addition to the above listed projector battalions, there is also an independent armored projector company *(Panzerwerferbatterie)* which is an independent unit of two platoons, each equipped with four 150-mm armored rocket projectors. This is a 10-barrelled projector mounted on a medium armored carrier. The company may be employed either attached to a projector battalion or as an independent company. (For details on rocket projector regiment (motorized) see *Figures 130 to 132*.)

The following two units are not included by the Germans in the chemical warfare arm but are considered parts of the medical services.

e. TROOP DECONTAMINATION COMPANY *(Truppenentgiftungskompanie)*. This unit is composed of medical personnel attached to the General Headquarters pool. It is motorized and is sent wherever high gas casualties occur. The company is capable of decontaminating personnel, clothing, and equipment. It carries supplies of replacement clothing, and is said to be able to decontaminate and reclothe 150 men per hour.

f. TROOP DECONTAMINATION PLATOON *(Truppenentgiftungszug)*. It is reported that one or two of this type of unit may be found in any type of division. They are medical troops, equipped with gas protective clothing and responsible for the establishment of decontamination centers and, presumably, for the care of gas casualties.

g. HORSE DECONTAMINATION UNIT *(Pferdentgiftungstrupp)*. This is a veterinary unit, formed within veterinary companies and veterinary hospitals from the personnel and with the equipment already within these units. It is motorized and can be sent wherever needed. The capacity of this unit is stated to be 10 to 20 horses per hour.

h. AIR DEFENSE BATTALION *(Luftschutzabteilung)*. This is an Air Force unit, used to clear up the results of enemy air attacks on important installations. It is equipped for decontamination of terrain, streets, clothing, and equipment.

i. GAS PROTECTION WITHIN THE ARMED FORCES. Each headquarters down to battalion level has a gas officer, and each company has a gas noncommissioned officer. They are charged with instructing their units in proper gas protective measures and with periodic inspection of all gas protective equipment.

Found at all levels and in all units of a division are the Gas Detection Squads *(Gasspürtrupps)* and the Decontamination Squads *(Entgiftungstrupps)*. They are fighting troops with additional gas training. Gas Detection Squads consist of one noncommissioned officer and three privates. The duties of the squad are simple gas detection and, upon occasion, minor decontamination. The squad is equipped with light protective clothing, gas detectors, and gas warning devices. Decontamination Squads consist of one noncommissioned officer and six privates. They are equipped for decontamination of personnel, terrain, weapons, and equipment.

11. Organic Engineer Units

This arm includes the regular combat engineers, as well as fortress engineers, construction engineers, and regional engineers. On the other hand, the engineer arm does not include railway engineers and railway operating troops, and these therefore are listed separately. (See paragraph 13, below.)

It should be noted that the personnel of engineer platoons in organic divisional units (other than the organic engineer battalion) belong to the arm of the unit which they are serving and not to the engineer arm, although they are trained to perform minor engineer functions.

Engineer units often form small detachments within their unit for special missions (such as flame-thrower detachments and mine-detection detachments).

An engineer battalion (*Pionierbataillon*) is organic in every German division, varying in strength and composition according to the type of division. (See *Figures 133* to *135*.)

The engineer battalion in the Two-Regiment Infantry Division is similar to that in the *Volks Grenadier* Division except that its components are slightly weaker.

The armored engineer battalion in the Motorized Division is very similar to the armored battalion in the Army Armored Division.

The armored engineer battalion in the *SS* Armored Division is similar to the armored engineer battalion in the Army Armored Division. It has, however, two bridge columns instead of only one.

A mountain engineer battalion is approximately equal in strength to an armored engineer battalion; however, it includes mountain climbing devices and trestle bridge equipment.

The parachute engineer battalion is believed to be organized similarly to the engineer battalion in the Infantry Division, 1944 Type.

Bridge columns were, until 1943, an organic component of the engineer battalions in all types of divisions. At the time of the major reorganization of German divisions the bridge columns were withdrawn to corps from all but the armored divisions. The different types of bridge columns are designated by various capital letters, i.e., "B," "J," "K," and "T," each of which represents the type of bridge-building equipment used. Of these, the bridge column "B" has sufficient equipment for building longer bridges than does column "K." However, bridges built by column "B" are of wood, while those built by column "K" are steel.

Armored engineer platoons, Goliath, about 35 men strong, may be included in any type of engineer battalion. These platoons specifically are equipped for the handling of the cable-controlled, small, armored demolition-charge carrier, the Goliath (not to be confused with the large radio controlled demolition carrier, B-IV, which is employed by the Tiger (*FKL*) Company and the crew of which belongs to the armored arm, while the Goliath crew belongs to engineers).

12. General Headquarters Engineers

As the reorganizations of German divisions of 1943 and 1944 have greatly reduced the strength of most types of organic engineer battalions, the General Headquarters engineer units have gained considerably in their importance.

Engineer bridging battalions consisting of four bridging companies and an engineer park company, with a total strength of about 900, may be allotted from the General Headquarters pool.

Various types of bridge columns listed under paragraph 11, sub-paragraph g, are usually allotted to corps.

Various types of engineer battalions, sometimes controlled by regimental staffs, may be employed in the support of the division engineers according to tactical requirements.

The construction engineers belonged formerly to a separate arm of inferior status known as construction troops (*Bautruppen*). They were reclassified as engineers in the fall of 1943, and included in the designation of their regiments and various types of battalions their new arm: engineers (*Pioniere*).

For a complete list of identified engineer units see "Order of Battle of the German Army," March, 1945, edition,

13. Railway Engineers

Railway Engineers (*Eisenbahnpioniere* or *Eisenbahntruppen*) constitute a separate arm. All railway engineer units are alloted by the General Headquarters pool.

The railway engineer regiments (*Eisenbahnpionierregiment*) consist of two battalions of four companies each. The companies operate independently, and frequently make use of prisoner-of-war labor. Their main work is the maintenance and repair of tracks and the building of railway bridges.

Railway Construction Companies (*Eisenbahnpionierbaukompanien*) are specialist companies engaged in various types of railway construction work.

14. Railway Operating Troops

Railway Operating Troops (*Eisenbahnbetriebstruppen*) (formerly part of the railway engineers)

were created as a separate arm in November, 1943, and include all railway operating units.

They are responsible for the operation of military traffic; for providing engineers, guards, and antiaircraft protection for military trains, and for supervising the repair of bomb damage to railroads.

15. Organic Signal Troops *(Nachrichtentruppen)*

It should be noted that the personnel of signal platoons and organic divisional units other than the organic signal battalion belong to the arm of the units in which they serve, although they are trained to perform minor signal tasks. The propaganda troops, which formerly belonged to the signal troops, are now a separate arm. (See paragraph 17 below.)

A Signal Battalion *(Nachrichtenbataillon)* is organic in every German division, varying in strength and composition according to the type of division. (See *Figures 136* to *138.*)

The signal battalions in all German divisions are composed of a telephone company, a radio company, and a light signal column or a battalion supply platoon. Their equipment and strength, however, vary considerably in accordance with their type of employment.

16. General Headquarters Signal Units

These are allotted to all echelons of the German Armed Forces, from the Armed Forces High Command itself down to corps and divisions.

The Armed Forces Signal Regiment *(Führungsnachrichtenregiment)* is under direct control of the Armed Forces High Command. Its primary mission is to maintain signal communications between Hitler's headquarters *(Führerhauptquartier)*, army groups, and army headquarters, as well as among the three branches of the armed forces.

The Armed Forces Signal Command *(Wehrmachtnachrichtenkommandantur)* is an interservice signal headquarters which supervises operations of permanent signal installations.

The Army Group or Army Signal Regiment *(Heeres-* or *Armeenachrichtenregiment)* is found with either an army group or an army.

The Field Signal Command *(Feldnachrichtenkommandantur)* is found in each army. It is a static signal headquarters responsible for the permanent signal installations in the army area.

The Corps Signal Battalion *(Korpsnachrichtenabteilung)* is found with each corps.

The Railway Signal Regiment *(Eisenbahnnachrichtenregiment)* controls a varying number of railway signal battalions.

The Women's Auxiliary Signal Battalion *(Nachrichtenhelferinnenabteilung)* is engaged in signal work, such as radio, telephone, and telegraph operation.

Independent specialist companies are engaged in various types of signal work. Their function usually is shown by their title. For a complete list of identified signal units see "Order of Battle of the German Army", March, 1945 edition.

17. Propaganda Troops *(Propagandatruppen)*

Formerly belonging to the signal troops, these became a separate arm in the beginning of 1943. They consist mainly of news reporters, photographers, film camera men, and radio commentators. Their main function is front line reporting, but they also conduct propaganda addressed to the enemy as well as to German troops. The basic unit is the propaganda company. (See *Figure 139.*)

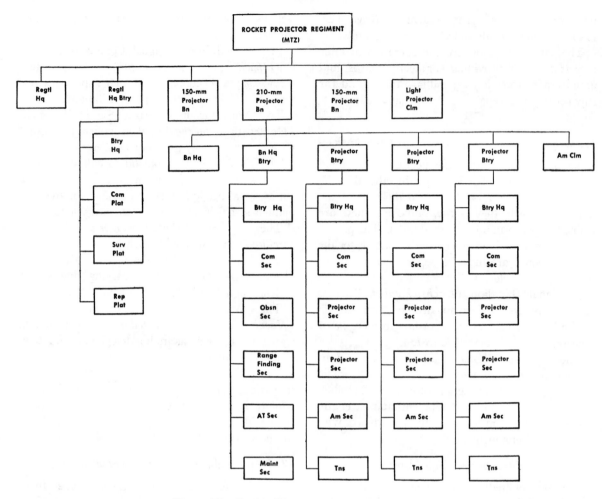

Figure 130.—Rocket Projector Regiment (motorized).

UNIT	Pers	LMGs	75-mm AT Guns	Rkt Projectors	Mtr Vehicles	Mtrcls
Regtl Hq	31				7	3
Regtl Hq Btry	110	2			20	2
Projector Bn	555	20	4	18	109	9
Projector Bn	555	20	4	18	109	9
Projector Bn	555	20	4	18	109	9
Light Projector Clm..........................	70				20	5
Total	1,876	62	12	54	374	37

A Rkt projector Regt (Mtz) consists of either two 150-mm projector Bns plus one Hv projector Bn (210 or 280/320-mm), or three 150-mm projector Bns. A Hv projector Regt (Mtz) consists of two Hv projector Bns (210 or 280/320-mm), plus one 150-mm projector Bns.

Figure 131.—Rocket Projector Regiment (motorized), total strength 1,876.

UNIT	Offs	NCOs	Pvts	Rs or Cbns	Pistols	Sub-MGs	LMGs	75-mm AT Guns	Rkt Projectors	Mtr Vehicles	Mtrcls
Bn Hq	2	3	10	10	3	2				3	1
Bn Hq Btry	3	12	70	70	9	6	2	1		13	2
Projector Btry	3	27	105	113	10	12	6	1	6	31	2
Projector Btry	3	27	105	113	10	12	6	1	6	31	2
Projector Btry	3	27	105	113	10	12	6	1	6	31	2
Am Clm		5	45	45	2	3					
Total	14	101	440	464	44	47	20	4	18	109	9

Figure 132.—Rocket Projector Battalion (motorized), total strength 555.

UNIT	Offs	NCOs	Pvts	Rs or Cbns	Pistols	Sub-MGs	LMGs	Hv MGs	81-mm Morts	Flame Throwers	Mtr Vehicles	Mtrcls	H-Dr Vehicles	Tlrs	IIs
Bn Hq	9[1]	14	60	65	18	7	4			2	14	10	4	1	10
Engr Co	3	26	150	122	40	21	9	2	2	6	1	3	16	8	29
Engr Co	3	26	150	122	40	21	9	2	2	6	1	3	16	8	29
Engr Co (Bcl)........	3	26	150	123	38	22	9	2	2	6	1	3	16	8	29
Total	18[1]	92	510	432	136	71	31	6	6	20	17	19	52	25	97

[1] Including three officials.

Figure 133.—Engineer Battalion, Infantry Division, 1944 Type, total strength 620.

UNIT	Offs	NCOs	Pvts	Rs or Cbns	Pistols	Sub-MGs	LMGs	Hv MGs	81-mm Morts	Flame Throwers	Mtr Vehicles	Mtrcls	H-Dr Vehicles	Tlrs	Hs	Bcls
Bn Hq	9[1]	14	61	60	17	7					10	8	3	1	10	37
Engr Co (Bcl).................	3	26	150	128	49	2	9	2	2	6	1	3	16	8	29	130
Engr Co (Bcl).................	3	26	150	128	49	2	9	2	2	6	1	3	16	8	29	130
Total	15[1]	66	361	316	115	11	18	4	4	12	12	14	35	17	68	297

[1] Including three officials.

Figure 134.—Engineer Battalion, Volks Grenadier Division, total strength 442.

UNIT	Offs	NCOs	Pvts	Rs or Cbns	Pistols	Sub-MGs	LMGs	Hv MGs	81-mm Morts	Flame Throwers	20-mm AT Guns	28/20-mm AT Guns	Mtr Vehicles	Mtrcls
Bn Hq	3	3	13	9	6	4	3						4	2
Bn Hq Co	9[2]	22	128	136	27	12	11			2			48	10
Engr Co (Mtz)	3	25	167	128	41	21	18	2	2	6			24	7
Engr Co (Mtz)	3	25	167	128	41	21	18	2	2	6			24	7
Engr Co (Armd)	4	29	185	69	125	44	43	2	2	6	3	3	36	6
Br Clm K (Mtz)[1]	2	14	83	92	7		3						38	10
Total	24[2]	118	743	562	247	102	96	6	6	20	3	3	174[3]	42

[1] May be replaced by a similar Br Clm, Type J.
[2] Including five officials.
[3] Including 31 Armd vehicles.

Figure 135.—Armored Engineer Battalion, Army Armored Division, total strength 885.

UNIT	Offs	NCOs	Pvts	Rs or Cbns	Pistols	Sub-MGs	LMGs	Mtr Vehicles	Mtrcls	H-Dr Vehicles	Tlrs	Hs
Bn Hq	6[1]	6	8	9	8	3		4	3			
1st (Tp) Co	4	37	132	154	4	15	5	35	4	7	2	42
2d (Rad) Co (Mtz)	4	27	105	122	3	11	4	30	4			
Sup Plat	2	10	38	41	3	6	2	7	2	7		12
Total	16[1]	80	283	326	18	35	11	76	13	14	2	54

[1] Including three officials.

Figure 136.—Signal Battalion, Infantry Division, 1944 Type, total strength 379.

UNIT	Offs	NCOs	Pvts	Rs or Cbns	Pistols	Sub-MGs	LMGs	Mtr Vehicles	Mtrcls	H-Dr Vehicles	Tlrs	Hs	Bcls
Bn Hq	6	6	8	9	8	3		4	3				4
Tp Co	3	27	112	131	10	1	5	19	3	6	2	34	
Rad Co	3	17	85	94	10	1	4	16	3				
Sup Plat	2	7	29	32	6		2	5	1	6		10	
Total	14[1]	57	234	266	34	5	11	44	10	12	2	44	4

[1] Including three officials.

Figure 137.—Signal Battalion, Volks Grenadier Division, total strength 305.

UNIT	Offs	NCOs	Pvts	Rs or Cbns	Pistols	Sub-MGs	LMGs	Mtr Vehicles	Mtrcls
Bn Hq	7[1]	9	26	28	13	3		11	2
Armd Tp Co	4	39	150	175	17	21	14	44	6
Armd Rad Co	4	50	200	216	37	25	20	50	6
Light Sig Clm	1	5	20	25	2	2	1	9	
Total	16[1]	103	396	444	69	51	35	114[2]	14

[1] Including three officials.
[2] Including 20 Armd vehicles.

Figure 138.—Armored Signal Battalion, Army Armored Division, total strength 515.

UNIT	Offs	NCOs	Pvts	Mtr Vehicles	Mtrcls
Co Hq	11[1]	3	17	6	4
Light War Reporters Plat	9	5	8	7	3
Light War Reporters Plat	9	5	8	7	3
Hv War Reporters Plat.............................	9	5	14	9	2
Propaganda Plat	8	23	26	15	6
Working Det	2	8	22	8	5
Tns		8	10	4	3
Total	48 [1]	57	105	56	26

[1] Including eight officials.

Figure 139.—Propaganda Company, total strength 210.

18. Organic Reconnaissance Units

Most types of German field divisions include an organic reconnaissance battalion, and the remainder have strong reconnaissance companies. The following are the basic types of the divisional reconnaissance units:

The reconnaissance battalion of the Infantry Division, Old Type, consisted of a horse cavalry troop, a bicycle troop, and a heavy weapons troop. For many years it was the basic reconnaissance unit of the German Army. Since the end 1943, however, it has been replaced by the *Füsilier* battalion.

The *Füsilier* battalion of the Infantry Division, 1944 Type, consists of three rifle companies and a heavy weapons company. This battalion may be employed either on reconnaissance missions or as a crack divisional reserve unit. (See *Figure 140.*)

When, at the end of 1944, the tables of organization for the newly formed *Volks Grenadier* divisions were issued, the reconnaissance unit for that type of division was specified to be a strong *Füsilier* company, highly mobile through a large allotment of bicycles. (See *Figure 141.*)

Front reports indicate, however, that there is a trend toward increasing the strength of the *Füsilier* battalion again.

The armored reconnaissance battalion, after many reorganizations in recent years, became a very strong and highly mobile standard type of reconnaissance unit in most types of German armored and motorized divisions. (See *Figures 142* and *143.*)

The Mountain Battalion (*Aufklärungsabteilung*) is organic in army and *SS* mountain divisions and in light divisions. It consists of three bicycle companies and a heavy weapons company.

One of the bicycle companies, however, sometimes may be replaced by a motorcycle company. For the strength and equipment of the mountain reconnaissance battalion, see Section V, Paragraph 3.

The Mobile Battalion (*Schnelle Abteilung*) was formed in 1943 by merging the reconnaissance and antitank battalions. A considerable number of infantry divisions adopted that type of a reconnaissance unit. Early in 1944, however, the mobile battalions started to revert to their former status of a separate antitank battalion and a separate reconnaissance battalion. At that time the latter was reformed and redesignated *Füsilier* battalion.

19. General Headquarters Reconnaissance Units

The Mobile Battalion (*Schnelle Abteilung*) is a component of the Mobile Brigade (*Schnelle Brigade*). It normally is composed of a mounted troop, two bicycle troops, and a heavy weapons troop. It also may contain organic antitank units.

The Mounted Regiment (*Reiterregiment*) recently has been identified. A new table of organization for cavalry regiments exists, however, and new units may be formed.

The Motorcycle Company (*Kradschützenkompanie*) still may be found in organic reconnaissance units in mountain and light infantry divisions and also a component of a General Headquarters motorcycle battalion.

In addition to reconnaissance units mentioned in this paragraph, there are also numerous regimental and battalion reconnaissance platoons and squads, but the personnel in these units belongs to the arm of the regiment in which they are serving.

RESTRICTED

UNIT	Offs	NCOs	Pvts	Rs or Cbns	Pistols	Sub-MGs	LMGs	Hv MGs	81-mm Morts	120-mm Morts	Mtr Vehicles	Mtrcls	H-Dr Vehicles	Tlrs	Hs
Bn Hq	6[1]	13	58	58	8	14	1				1	2	16	4	33
R Co (Bcl)	2	21	119	96	22	28	13	2					15	11	27
R Co	2	21	119	96	22	28	13	2					15	11	27
R Co	2	21	119	96	22	28	13	2					15	11	27
Hv Wpn Co..........	3	37	165	131	48	29	3	6	6	4	7	3	41	20	51
Total	15[1]	113	580	477	122	127	43	12	6	4	8	5	102	57	165

[1] Including two officials.

Figure 140.—Füsilier Battalion, Infantry Division, 1944 Type, total strength 708.

UNIT	Offs	NCOs	Pvts	Rs or Cbns	Pistols	Sub-MGs	LMGs	Hv MGs	81-mm Morts	75-mm Inf Hows	Mtrcls	H-Dr Vehicles	Tlrs	Hs	Bcls
Co. Hq	1	8	18	17	3	7					1	3	2	11	18
Sub-MG Plat (Bcl)......	1	3	31	7	2	26	2					2	1	6	32
Sub-MG Plat (Bcl)......		4	31	7	2	26	2					2	1	6	32
R Plat (Bcl)		4	31	22	4	9	3					2	1	6	32
Hv Wpn Plat	1	5	34	17	12	11		2	2			6	5	16	29
Inf How Sec		4	24	19	3	5	1			2		4		11	23
Total	3	28	169	89	26	84	8	2	2	2	1	19	10	56	166

[1] May be replaced by a Füs Bn similar to the Inf Bn (Bcl).

Figure 141.—Füsilier Company, Volks Grenadier Division, total strength 200.

UNIT	Offs	NCOs	Pvts	Rs or Cbns	Pistols	Sub-MGs	LMGs	Hv MGs	81-mm Morts	Flame Throwers	20-mm Guns (Mtd)	75-mm Guns (SP)	Mtr Vehicles	Mtrcls
Bn Hq	4	6	12	13	4	5	3						4	4
Bn Hq Co	3	33	80	27	61	28	23				13	3	23	2
Armd Car Co	3	29	53	7	45	33	25				16		27	2
Armd Rcn Co	3	36	144	83	55	45	29	4	2		6	2	21	4
Light Armd Rcn Co	3	39	125	65	51	51	44		2			2	30	3
Hv Wpn Co	4	32	122	67	53	38	19		6	6			27	4
Sup Co	7[1]	48	156	172	31	6	4						67	3
Total	27[1]	223	692	434	300	206	147	4	10	6	35	13	199[2]	22

[1] Including three officials.
[2] Including 124 Armd vehicles.

Figure 142.—Armored Reconnaissance Battalion, Army Armored Division, total strength 942.

UNIT	Offs	NCOs	Pvts	Rs or Cbns	Pistols	Sub-MGs	LMGs	81-mm Morts	Flame Throwers	75-mm Guns	Mtr Vehicles	Mtrcls
Co Hq	1	8	10	12	3	4	2				4	3
75-mm Gun Plat	1	7	24	4	17	11	2			6	8	
81-mm Mort Plat	1	12	43	24	20	12	2	6			8	
Engr Plat	1	5	45	27	13	11	13		6		7	1
Total	4	32	122	67	53	38	19	6	6	6	27[1]	4

[1] Including 25 Armd vehicles.

Figure 143.—Heavy Weapons Company, Armored Reconnaissance Battalion, total strength 158.

UNIT	Offs	NCOs	Pvts	LMGs	150-cm SLs	200-cm SLs	Mtr Vehicles	Tlrs	Mtrcls
Regtl Hq	5	5	29	2			4		3
Com Sec		2	13				3		1
Hv SL Bn...........................	16	97	550	9	30	6	29	85	16
Hv SL Bn...........................	16	97	550	9	30	6	29	85	16
Hv SL Bn...........................	16	97	550	9	30	6	29	85	16
Total	53[1]	298	1,692	29	90	18	94	255	52

[1] Including ten officials.

Figure 144.—Heavy Searchlight Regiment (non-motorized), total strength 2,043.

20. Air Force Antiaircraft Field Units and Air Force Antiaircraft Units in the Zone of the Interior

a. MOBILE UNITS. The composition of antiaircraft units larger than batteries varies greatly in accordance with local conditions, as already indicated in Section V, paragraph 17. Normally an antiaircraft battalion consists of three to five batteries, with a maximum of eight. An antiaircraft regiment normally consists of from three to four battalions, with a maximum of six. Divisions have three or four regiments.

Motorized antiaircraft units have a smaller number of components than do non-motorized units. In accordance with their type of motorization they are designated:

Motor-drawn (*mot.* or *mot. Z*); mounted on half-tracks (*mot. G1*); self-propelled (*mot. s.*).

Non-motorized units are designated:

Mobile (*v* for *verlegefähig*); or Static (*o* for *ortsfest*).

The personnel strength of motorized units is usually approximately double that of non-motorized ones.

Mobile antiaircraft units have large numbers of trailers but very little motorization and depend for mobility on separate transportation units, as already stated in Section V, paragraph 17. Static units usually are employed for the protection of specific targets.

For the difference in German designations of antiaircraft units and antiaircraft units in the Zone of the Interior, see *Figure 145.*

The main components of the non-motorized antiaircraft division described in Section V, paragraph 17, are one heavy searchlight regiment and three antiaircraft regiments (see *Figures 144 to 150*). Any of the above units may also be encountered as motorized antiaircraft with corresponding higher strength. However, the basic tactical motorized antiaircraft units are the mixed antiaircraft battalion, the light antiaircraft battalion, and the heavy searchlight battalion. Any combination of these units totaling three or four battalions may be components of a motorized antiaircraft regiment, but most frequently regiments of three mixed antiaircraft battalions probably will be encountered. (See *Figures 151 to 154.*)

The Germans designate antiaircraft units equipped with 20-mm or 37-mm guns as light;

163

antiaircraft units equipped with 88-mm, 105-mm, 128-mm, or 150-mm as heavy (or, in the case of the latter, possibly super-heavy) ; and antiaircraft units including both these types of equipment as mixed. Similarly, they designate units with 60-cm searchlights as light, and with 150-cm or 200-cm searchlights as heavy. The following types of antiaircraft battalions frequently may be encountered:

Motorized Battalions

Mixed antiaircraft battalions (three heavy and two or three light batteries).

Light antiaircraft battalion (three or four-light batteries).

Searchlight antiaircraft battalion (three or four heavy searchlight batteries).

Non-motorized and Static Battalions

Mixed antiaircraft battalion (four heavy and two light batteries).

Light antiaircraft battalion (three light batteries).

Heavy antiaircraft battalion (four heavy batteries).

Searchlight antiaircraft battalion (four heavy searchlight batteries).

Barrage balloon battalion (four to six barrage balloon batteries).

The German Air Force has the main responsibility for antiaircraft defense of the Zone of the Interior and of the Field Army. For the employment of antiaircraft units with the latter, see *Figure 145.*

b. RAILWAY ANTIAIRCRAFT (*Eisenbahnflak*). Railway antiaircraft regiments consist of three heavy or two heavy and one light antiaircraft battalions. Each railway antiaircraft battalion consists of three to four batteries which are the tactical units in the employment of the railway antiaircraft guns. Railway batteries usually consist of single- or four-barrelled 20-mm, 37-mm, 88-mm, 105-mm, or 128-mm guns mounted on railway cars.

c. TOWER MOUNTED ANTIAIRCRAFT BATTALIONS (*Turmflakabteilung*). Tower mounted antiaircraft battalions are equipped with 20-mm (single-barrelled, and four-barrelled) and 105-mm and 128-mm double-barrelled antiaircraft guns. The guns are mounted on one or two platforms of concrete antiaircraft towers constructed in the vicinity of vital installations and of large cities.

d. ARMY ANTIAIRCRAFT BATTALION (*Heeresflak*). Army antiaircraft battalions are found organically in all armored, motorized, and parachute divisions, as well as in all types of *SS* divisions. They are discussed in paragraph 6, as they belong to the artillery arm.

e. LIGHT ARMY ANTIAIRCRAFT BATTALION (*Fla Bataillon*). Light army antiaircraft battalions are found in General Headquarters. They are discussed in paragraph 3, as they belong in the infantry arm.

f. LIGHT ARMY ANTIAIRCRAFT COMPANY (*Fla Kompanie*). Light army antiaircraft companies are found with most types of ground personnel, mostly antiaircraft personnel. The strength of the regiment is about 3,000 men, and it is believed to have three or four battalions of three or four batteries each. Each battery of about 150 men probably operates three launching sites, so that the battalion may operate between nine and twelve and the regiment between 27 and 48 launching sites.

g. NAVAL ANTIAIRCRAFT UNITS (*Marine Flak*). The following are the three types of naval antiaircraft units:

Antiaircraft guns mounted on board of ships and manned by the ship's crew.

Antiaircraft units manning guns for the protection of shore installations (usually static batteries).

Antiaircraft batteries mounted on barges for the protection of approaches to vital naval installations.

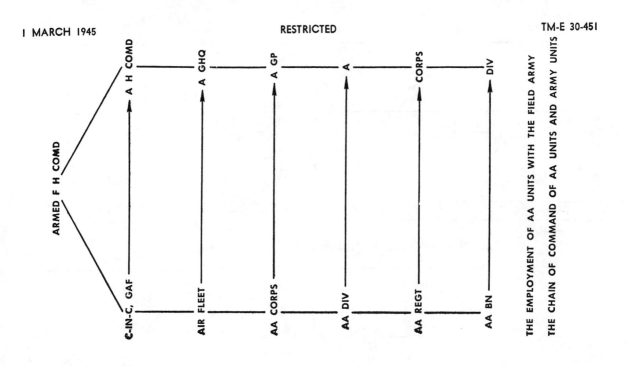

THE EMPLOYMENT OF AA UNITS WITH THE FIELD ARMY

THE CHAIN OF COMMAND OF AA UNITS AND ARMY UNITS

Figure 145.

THE CORRESPONDING GERMAN DESIGNATIONS FOR AA FIELD UNITS
AND AA UNITS IN THE ZONE OF THE INTERIOR.

UNIT	Offs	NCOs	Pvts	LMGs	150-cm SLs	200-cm SLs	Mtr Vehicles	Tlrs	Mtrcls
Bn Hq	8[1]	14	44	1			13	5	3
Com Sec		3	16				4		1
SL Btry	2	20	125	2	7	2	3	20	3
SL Btry	2	20	125	2	7	2	3	20	3
SL Btry	2	20	120	2	8	1	3	20	3
SL Btry	2	20	120	2	8	1	3	20	3
Total	16[1]	97	550	9	30	6	29	85	16

[1] Including two officials.

Figure 146.—Heavy Searchlight Battalion (non-motorized), total strength 662.

UNIT	Offs	NCOs	Pvts	LMGs	20-mm AA Guns	20-mm AA Guns (Four-Barreled)	37-mm AA Guns	88-mm AA Guns	105-mm AA Guns	60-cm SLs	Bar Blns	Mtr Vehicles	Tlrs	Mtrcls
Regtl Hq	7	7	42	2								7		4
Bar Bln Bn	16	97	580	9							72	29	85	16
Light AA Bn	19	134	524	9	36	9	12			16		19	67	11
Hv AA Bn	16	104	391	9	8			24				27	43	12
Hv AA Bn	16	104	391	9	8				16			27	43	12
Total	74[1]	446	1,928	38	52	9	12	24	16	16	72	109	238	55

[1] Including ten officials.

Figure 147.—Antiaircraft Regiment (non-motorized), total strength 2,448.

UNIT	Offs	NCOs	Pvts	LMGs	Bar Blns	Mtr Vehicles	Tlrs	Mtrcls
Bn Hq	8[1]	14	44	1		13	5	3
Com Sec		3	16			4		1
Bar Bln Btry	2	20	130	2	18	3	20	3
Bar Bln Btry	2	20	130	2	18	3	20	3
Bar Bln Btry	2	20	130	2	18	3	20	3
Bar Bln Btry	2	20	130	2	18	3	20	3
Total	16[1]	97	580	9	72	29	85	16

[1] Including two officials.

Figure 148.—Barrage Balloon Battalion, total strength 693.

UNIT	Offs	NCOs	Pvts	LMGs	20-mm AA Guns	20-mm AA Guns (Four-Barreled)	37-mm AA Guns	60-cm SLs	Mtr Vehicles	Tlrs	Mtrcls
Bn Hq	7[1]	13	36	1					9	3	3
Com Sec		1	8						2		
20-mm AA Btry	3	30	120	2	12	3		4	2	16	2
20-mm AA Btry	3	30	120	2	12	3		4	2	16	2
20-mm AA Btry	3	30	120	2	12	3		4	2	16	2
37-mm AA Btry	3	30	120	2			12	4	2	16	2
Total	19[1]	134	524	9	36	9	12	16	19	67	11

[1] Including two officials.

Figure 149.—Light Antiaircraft Battalion (non-motorized), total strength 677.

UNIT	Offs	NCOs	Pvts	LMGs	20-mm AA Guns	88-mm AA Guns	Mtr Vehicles	Tlrs	Mtrcls
Bn Hq	8[1]	17	51	1			15	7	3
Com Sec		3	16				4		1
88-mm Btry	2	21	81	2	2	6	2	9	2
88-mm Btry	2	21	81	2	2	6	2	9	2
88-mm Btry	2	21	81	2	2	6	2	9	2
88-mm Btry	2	21	81	2	2	6	2	9	2
Total	16[1]	104	391	9	8	24[2]	27	43	12

[1] Including two officials.
[2] Some Hv AA Bns may consist of four 105-mm Btries with a total of 16 guns.

Figure 150.—Heavy Antiaircraft Battalion (non-motorized), total strength 511.

UNIT	Offs	NCOs	Pvts	Rs or Cbns	Pistols	Sub-MGs	LMGs	20-mm AA Guns	20-mm AA Guns (Four-Barreled)	88-mm AA Guns	Mtr Vehicles	Mtrcls	60-cm SLs
Regtl Hq	9[1]	34	123	140	20	10	2				25	5	
Mixed AA Bn	39	403	908	1,051	241	93	17	30	18	12	339	38	12
Mixed AA Bn	39	403	908	1,051	241	93	17	30	18	12	339	38	12
Mixed AA Bn	39	403	908	1,051	241	93	17	30	18	12	339	38	12
Total	126[1]	1,243	2,847	3,293	743	289	53	90	54	36	1,042	119	36

[1] Including ten officials.

Figure 151.—Antiaircraft Regiment (motorized), total strength 4,216.

UNIT	Offs	NCOs	Pvts	Rs or Cbns	Pistols	Sub-MGs	LMGs	20-mm AA Guns	20-mm AA Guns (Four-Barreled)	88-mm AA Guns	Mtr Vehicles	Mtrcls	60-cm SLs
Bn Hq and Com Plat	6[2]	31	93	74	41	19	1				28	11	
88-mm Btry	4	53	110	149	12	10	2	4		4	36	3	
88-mm Btry	4	53	110	149	12	10	2	4		4	36	3	
88-mm Btry	4	53	110	149	12	10	2	4		4	36	3	
20-mm Btry[1]	6	65	139	151	51	14	2	9	3		58	5	4
20-mm Btry	6	65	139	151	51	14	2	9	3		58	5	4
20-mm Btry (Four-Barreled)	7	73	151	163	59	15	4		12		59	6	4
Hv AA Clm	2	10	56	65	3	1	2				28	2	
Total	39[2]	403	908	1,051	241	93	17	30	18	12	339	38	12

[1] In some Bns replaced by a 37-mm Btry with nine guns.
[2] Including two officials.

Figure 152.—Mixed Antiaircraft Battalion, Antiaircraft Regiment (motorized), total strength 1,350.

UNIT	Offs	NCOs	Pvts	Rs or Cbns	Pistols	Sub-MGs	LMGs	20-mm AA Guns	20-mm AA Guns (Four-Barreled)	60-cm SLs	Mtr. Vehicles	Mtrcls
Bn Hq and Com Plat	5[1]	26	81	62	36	18	1				23	8
20-mm Btry	6	65	139	151	51	14	2	9	3	4	58	5
20-mm Btry	6	65	139	151	51	14	2	9	3	4	58	5
20-mm Btry	6	65	139	151	51	14	2	9	3	4	58	5
Light AA Clm	1	6	51	56	2	1					23	2
Total	24[1]	227	549	571	191	61	7	27	9	12	220	25

[1] Including two officials.
Some light AA Bns may have four Btries and about 1,000 men.

Figure 153.—Light Antiaircraft Battalion (motorized), total strength 800.

UNIT	Offs	NCOs	Pvts	LMGs	150-cm SLs	200-cm SLs	Mtr. Vehicles	Tlrs	Mtrcls
Bn Hq and Com Plat	6[1]	20	90	1			25	5	6
Hv SL Btry	3	25	180	2	8	1	50	20	5
Hv SL Btry	3	25	180	2	8	1	50	20	5
Hv SL Btry	3	25	180	2	8	1	50	20	5
Total	15[1]	95	630	7	24	3	175	65	21

[1] Including two officials.
Some Hv SL Bns may have four Btries and about 950 men.

Figure 154.—Heavy Searchlight Battalion (motorized), total strength 740.

21. Miscellaneous Combat Units

a. FORMATION OF TASK FORCES. It is the purpose of this section to explain briefly how the various elements of the German Armed Forces are combined to form effective combat teams. Figures 1-4 should be consulted in conjunction with this text.

The Navy, the Air Force, and the Armed *SS* (*Waffen-SS*), like the Army, are composed of many different types of units. The Navy includes battalions of coast artillery, naval antiaircraft artillery, naval aviation units, and the various types of combat fleet units. In addition to its regular aviation units the German Air Force has different types of antiaircraft units; aircraft warn-

ing service organizations; and communications, engineer, balloon barrage, and administrative units.

All types of units in the German Army, Navy, Air Force, and Armed *SS* may be considered as groups or pools. Unit organizations are withdrawn from these pools to form task forces, which then function as teams for specific missions.

Normally the commander is selected from the service which predominates in the task force or whose interests are paramount.

Since missions and circumstances vary, each task force is likely to be composed differently from any other. German organizations above the division should be regarded as basic command frameworks, with a minimum of organically assigned combat and administrative units; task forces are formed around these frameworks.

An effort always is made to retain a maximum number of combat units in the various types of General Headquarters pools. Consequently, when a large German unit, such as a corps or a division, is engaged in combat it almost always will be reinforced by units from the General Headquarters pools. When the amount of reinforcement is large, additional commanders and staffs also will be attached. The great influence which General Headquarters reinforcements can have on the combat power of a standard organization, such as a division, should not be overlooked.

The German system as thus outlined is both rigid and flexible. It is rigid in the sense that all the units in any single pool are as nearly alike as possible; it is flexible because the principle of combining units from the various pools is utilized to obtain any sort of combat organization which may be required for a given purpose.

Every German task force assigned to a mission is tactically and administratively an independent and self-contained organization. Coordination with other units is arranged in advance. The force never is required to depend on other units to carry out its mission.

The German system of organization for combat is both economical and effective. It enables the commanders to concentrate combat power at the most vulnerable points without changing basic dispositions. The method also is deceptive to the enemy, as it prevents an easy estimate of German strength in any particular situation.

The administrative organization for supply and evacuation is arranged in a manner similar to that of the combat organization and is employed in conformity with the principle that the administrative plan must support the tactical or strategical plan. Like the tactical organization, the German administrative organizations differ with the situation.

One of the outstanding characteristics of the German military system is unity of command. All units engaged on a single mission are under one commander, who is charged by one authority with responsibility for the success of the mission. As a corollary, two or more German commands never are assigned the same mission simultaneously. Units from the Air Force, the Navy, the Army, and the Armed *SS* all serve together under a commander chosen from any of the four branches. Likewise, in basic training great emphasis is placed on cooperation among the services and among different branches of the same service.

To sum up, it always should be borne in mind when confronting any situation involving German forces that the predominating note in all German military thought is the combination of all arms and services necessary for any specific mission into a task force (or combat team) under a single commander.

This holds true for all German task forces from the highest echelons down to the reinforced regiments, battalions, and companies. (See *Figures 155 to 163.*)

b. THE ARMORED BRIGADES (*Panzerbrigaden*). These were formed in the summer of 1943 with the following components:

> Brigade headquarters.
> Brigade headquarters company.
> Tank battalion.
> *Panzer Grenadier* Division (armored).
> Armored engineer company.
> Sixty-ton column.
> Medium maintenance platoon.

Several armored brigades, however, were encountered in the field with two *Panzer Grenadier* battalions and two tank battalions. Almost all armored brigades located on the Western Front have been incorporated into armored divisions, which were badly in need of replacements.

c. ARMORED TRAINS (*Eisenbahnpanzerzüge*). Armored trains have been employed by the Germans successfully since the outbreak of the war with the objective of surprising the enemy by the sudden occupation of a strategically located railroad station or to protect vital lines of communication against partisan and guerrilla attacks. Armored train, Type EP-42, consists of six armored, infantry, artillery, and antiaircraft railway cars. The train is armed with two 105-mm gunhowitzers mounted on special cars; two antiaircraft cars, each with one four-barreled, 20-mm antiaircraft gun, one 76.2-mm Russian gun; and two infantry railway cars with two 81-mm mortars, one heavy machine gun, and 22 light machine guns. The total strength of that armored train is about 113.

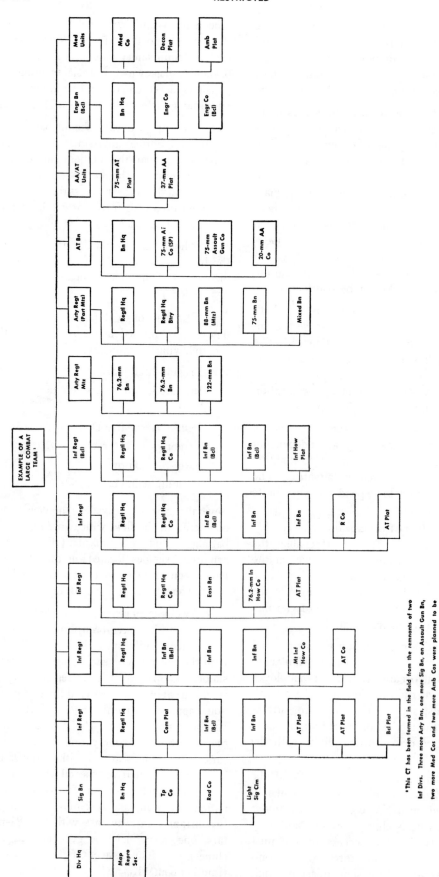

Figure 155.—Example of a Large Combat Team.

¹ This CT has been formed in the field from the remnants of two Inf Divs. Three more Arty Bns, one more Sig Bn, an Assault Gun Bn, two more Med Cos and two more Amb Cos were planned to be included into this CT, but only the listed units were the actual components at the time of the report.

UNIT	Offs	NCOs	Pvts	LMGs	Hv MGs	81-mm Morts	120-mm Morts	Bazookas	Flame Throwers	20-mm AA/AT Guns (Mtr-Dr)	20-mm AA Guns (SP)	37-mm AA Guns	45-mm AA Guns	50-mm AT Guns	75-mm Guns (Mtr-Dr)	75-mm Guns (SP)	75-mm MT Hows	75-mm Inf-Hows	76.2-mm Guns	88-mm Guns	122-mm Hows	122-mm Guns
Div Hq	14	55	86	2																		
Sig Bn	9	58	184	12																		
Inf Regt	20	124	693	53	4	5																
Inf Regt	17	115	838	56	3	5		3						2	1		4		1			
Inf Regt (East)	12	32	375	21	5	1	4						2		4				5			
Inf Regt	31	140	799	75	5	5									2							
Inf Regt (Bcl)	16	111	642	50	5	5												2				
Arty Regt (Mtz)	25	164	710	33						9									24		8	4
Arty Regt (Partly Mtz)	30	239	1,460	32											3		2		7	6	4	
AT Bn	10	94	315	25						8	4					13						
AA/AT Units	3	23	118	2								2			2							
Engr Bn (Bcl)	8	47	305	18	6	6			20													
Med Units	5	35	157	4																		
Total	200	1,237	6,682	383	28	27	4	3	20	17	4	2	2	2	15	13	6	2	37	6	12	4

Figure 156.—Example of a Large Combat Team, total strength 8,119.

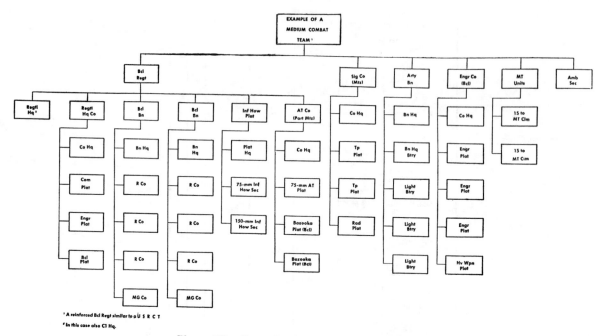

Figure 157.—Example of a Medium Combat Team.

UNIT	Offs	NCOs	Pvts	LMGs	Hv MGs	81-mm Morts	Bazookas	Flame Throwers	75-mm AT Guns	75-mm Inf Hows	150-mm Inf Hows	105-mm Gun/Hows
Bcl Regt	46	278	1,510	91	12	19	34		3	2	1	
Sig Co (Mtz)...............	1	5	50									
Arty Bn	15	100	400	9								12
Engr Co (Bcl)...............	3	20	120	3	1	1		2				
MT Units		3	12	2								
Amb Sec		1	4									
Total	65	407	2,096	105	13	20	34	2	3	2	1	12

Figure 158.—Example of a Medium Combat Team, total strength 2,568.

UNIT	Offs	NCOs	Pvts	LMGs	Hv MGs	81-mm Morts	Bazookas	75-mm AT Guns	75-mm Inf Hows	150-mm Inf Hows
Regtl Hq	7	1	16							
Regtl Hq Co............................	5	28	165	9						
Bcl Bn	15	100	550	37	6	9				
Bcl Bn	15	110	570	38	6	10				
Inf How Plat	1	10	55	4					2	1
AT Co (Part Mtz).......................	3	29	154	3			34	3		
Total	46	278	1,510	91	12	19	34	3	2	1

Figure 159.—Bicycle Regiment, Medium Combat Team, total strength 1,834.

UNIT	Offs	NCOs	Pvts	Rs or Cbns	Pistols	Sub-MGs	LMGs	Hv MGs	Rkt Pistols	81-mm Morts	Bazookas	20-mm AA Guns	75-mm AT Guns	Mtr Vehicles	Mtrcls	H-Dr Vehicles	Bcls
CT Hq	1			3	1									1			1
Hv Wpn Co	2	4	50	43	8	3	2			2	—	4		5			1
R Co	1	11	75	65	14	9	9	2	6								
AT Co	2	5	38	38	3	4					9		2	5	1	6	3
Total	6	20	163	149	26	16	11	2	6	2	9	4	2	11	1	6	5

Figure 160.—Example of a Small Combat Team, total strength 189.

UNIT	Offs	NCOs	Pvts	Rs or Cbns	Pistols	Sub-MGs	LMGs	81-mm Morts	Bazookas	20-mm AA Guns	Mtr Vehicles	Bcls
20-mm AA Plat	1	4	37	34	6	3	2		—	4	4	1
81-mm Mort Plat	1		13	9	2			2			1	
Total	2	4	50	43	8	3	2	2	—	4	5	1

Figure 161.—Heavy Weapons Company, Small Combat Team, total strength 56.

UNIT	Offs	NCOs	Pvts	Rs or Cbns	Pistols	Sub-MGs	LMGs	Hv MGs	Rkt Pistols
Co Hq	1	1	5	6		1			
R Sqd		1	7	6	1	1	1		
R Sqd		1	7	4	2	1	1		
R Sqd		2	8	7	2	1	2		
R Sqd		1	8	6	2	1	2		
Hv MG Sec		2	6	6	4			2	
Engr Counter Attack Sec		2	28	24	3	3	3		
Engr AT Plat		1	6	6		1			6
Total	1	11	75	65	14	9	9	2	6

Figure 162.—Rifle Company, Small Combat Team, total strength 87.

UNIT	Offs	NCOs	Pvts	Rs or Cbns	Pistols	Sub-MGs	Bazookas	75-mm AA Guns	Mtr Vehicles	Mtrcls	H-Dr Vehicles	Bcls
Co Hq	1	1	4	4	1	1				1		1
Mun Sec		1	2	1	2				2			
Bazooka Sqd		1	9	9		1	9				6	
AT Gun Plat	1	2	23	24		2		2	3			2
Total	2	5	38	38	3	4	9	2	5	1	6	3

Figure 163.—Antitank Company, Small Combat Team, total strength 45.

d. MILITIA (*Volkssturm*) UNITS. In October, 1944 a decree was issued by Hitler calling up all able-bodied German men between the ages of 16 and 60 for the defense of the Fatherland. That decree calls for the creation of a people's militia (*Volkssturm*) under the leadership of Himmler in his function as Commander-in-Chief of the Replacement Training Army.

It is believed that the Party in general, and the Storm Troop Organization (*SA*) and the National Socialist Motor Corps (*NSKK*) in particular, have been charged with the part time training of these men who are to remain on their jobs until a direct threat endangers their area. In such an emergency they will be called to the ranks, come under the command of the army, and be issued weapons, brassards with the inscription *"Deutscher Volkssturm Wehrmacht"* and

identification papers as members of the German Armed Forces. Their employment probably is limited to defensive fighting in trenches, woods, and streets, since their units are equipped with small automatic weapons, machine guns, and bazookas only, but it is possible that light and medium mortars will be added later.

It is difficult to determine definitely the tables of organization for militia units as these will vary greatly in accordance with local conditions and the manpower and weapons available, but indications from the front lines point toward the following average tables of organization for the basic militia unit, the Militia Battalion. (See *Figures 164 to 167.*)

In some cases several militia battalions may be combined in a militia regiment.

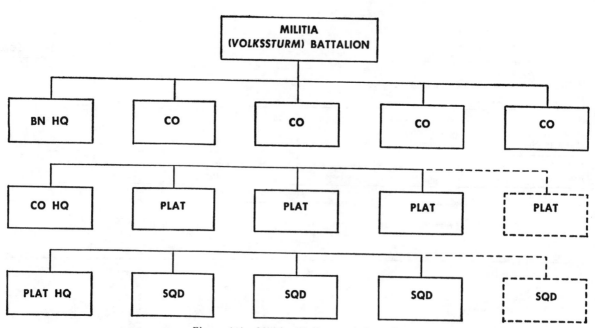

Figure 164.—Militia (Volkssturm) Battalion.

UNIT	Bn Comdr	Co Leader	Plat Leader	Sqd Leader	Pvts	Rs or Cbns	Pistols	Sub-MGs	LMGs	Bazookas	Rkt Pistols
Bn Hq	1	2	1	2	2	2	2	4			
Co		1	4	14	83	38	13	33	9	9	9
Co		1	4	14	83	38	13	33	9	9	9
Co		1	4	14	83	38	13	33	9	9	9
Co		1	4	14	83	38	13	33	9	9	9
Total[1]	1	6	17	58	334	154	54	136	36	36	36

[1] With companies of maximum strength the Bn total may increase to 1-6-21-90-570 or 688 men and the firepower accordingly.

Figure 165.—Militia (Volkssturm) Battalion, total strength 416-688.

UNIT	Co Leader	Plat Leader	Sqd Leader	Pvts	Rs or Cbns	Pistols	Sub-MGs	LMGs	Bazookas	Rkt Pistols
Co Hq	1	1	2	2	2	1	3			
Plat		1	4	27	12	4	10	3	3	3
Plat		1	4	27	12	4	10	3	3	3
Plat		1	4	27	12	4	10	3	3	3
Total[1]	1	4	14	83	38	13	33	9	9	9

[1] With four Plats of four Sqds each the Co strength may increase to 1-5-22-142 and the fire power accordingly.

Figure 166.—Militia (Volkssturm) Company, total strength 102-170.

UNIT	Plat Leader	Sqd Leader	Pvts	Rs or Cbns	Pistols	Sub-MGs	LMGs	Bazookas	Rkt Pistols
Plat Hq	1	1	3	3	1	1			
Sqd		1	8	3	1	3	1	1	1
Sqd		1	8	3	1	3	1	1	1
Sqd		1	8	3	1	3	1	1	1
Total[1]	1	4	27	12	4	10	3	3	3

[1] With four Sqds per Plat the Plat strength may increase to 1-5-35 and the fire power accordingly.

Figure 167.—Militia (Volkssturm) Platoon, total strength 32-41.

Section VII. SERVICE TROOPS

I. General

Every German division includes in its organic components the divisional services which vary in strength in accordance with the size and type of the division. The divisional services of all types of divisions, however, are organized on the basis of the same standard pattern and include the following components:

Divisional Supply Troops (*Nachschubtruppen*).

Administrative Troops (*Verwaltungstruppen*).

Medical Troops (*Sanitätstruppen*).

A Field Post Office (*Feldpostamt*).

Motor Maintenance Troops (*Kraftfahrparktruppen*), varying in size in accordance with the degree of motorization of the division.

Veterinary Troops (*Veterinärtruppen*). Only in divisions with horse transport.

A Military Police Detachment (*Feldgendarmerietrupp*) which in some divisions is withdrawn from the divisional services and assigned to the divisional headquarters.

There is a trend in the German Armed Forces to centralize all types of service units. It began early in 1944 in the armored division when service companies were set up for each battalion of tank and *Panzer Grenadier* regiments and for the armored reconnaissance battalion. Late in 1944 *Volks Grenadier* divisions were formed with infantry battalions having supply platoons instead of the traditional battalion and company trains, and with divisional services combined into a divisional supply regiment. This was done as a part of the policy to facilitate a more even distribution of all types of supply with less personnel and to free company commanders from any other than operational duties.

For a compilation of the divisional services of the three most numerous types of divisions see *Figures 168* to *170*.

2. Supply Troops

The supply and motor maintenance units of the German Army, originally combined under transport troops, were divided later into two separate arms. The motor maintenance units were grouped under the motor maintenance troops (see paragraph below), while the transport and supply units were classified as supply troops. Railway operating troops are an independent arm although they work in conjunction with the supply troops.

The commander of the division rear services (*Kommandeur der Divisionsnachschubtruppen-Kodina*), formerly known as *Divisionsnachschubführer-Dinafu*), commands the divisional service troops.

The light column (*Leichte Kolonne*), found in most types of infantry regiments, consists of 39 wagons carrying all types of supplies except rations. It serves as a supply reserve for the subordinate battalions.

The trains (*Trosse*) are battalion and company supply units. They consist of a combat train, a rations train (a second rations train in the battalion), and a baggage train. The company baggage train and the second battalion rations train are usually motorized. The second battalion rations train consists of one truck hauling supplies from the division distribution point.

The repair company (*Instandestzungskompanie*) repairs equipment and weapons except motor vehicles. Several units of this type may be found in a division.

3. Administrative Troops

Administrative troops usually include a number of civilian specialists (*Beamte*) in various positions. These are listed in the preceding tables of organization as officers, but designated in footnotes, as officials.

The rations supply office (*Verpflegungsamt*) supervises the requisitioning and supply of rations for troop units. It erects rations supply distributing points which are refilled regularly by the bakery and slaughter units and from which the troop units obtain their rations.

The slaughter platoon, found in all divisions, slaughters cattle which it preferably procures locally. Existing installations are used whenever possible.

The bakery company found in all divisions, uses wherever possible, existing local installations.

4. Medical Troops

One or two medical companies, and one to three motorized ambulance platoons are organic components of all divisions. Until 1943 most types of divisions included also a field hospital, but these have been withdrawn to higher echelons and

UNIT	Offs	NCOs	Pvts	Rs or Cbns	Pistols	Sub-MGs	LMGs	Mtr Vehicles	Mtrcls	H-Dr Vehicles	Tlrs	Hs
Div Sup	14	62	366	294	36	5	26	60	13	103		392
Workshop Co	6	21	110	113	24		4	21	1		6	
Adm	10	34	193	216	14	3	8	37	3		15	
Med Units	21	76	372	413	32	7	12	74	4	17	3	46
Vet Co	4	19	133	130	24	2	6	8	2	11	1	105
Fld Post Office	3	7	8	15	3		1	4				
Total	58[1]	219	1,182	1,181	133	17	57	204	23	131	25	543

[1] Including 22 officials.

Figure 168.—Division Services, German Infantry Division, 1944 Type, total strength 1,459.

UNIT	Offs	NCOs	Pvts	Rs or Cbns	Pistols	Sub-MGs	LMGs	Mtr Vehicles	Mtrcls
Div Sup	15	95	640	695	50	5	46	122	35
Adm	10	34	193	220	14	3	12	37	25
Med Units	23	83	402	450	58		11	95	10
Maint Units	12	48	279	309	30		14	60	10
MP Det	1	25	7	19	10	5	2	5	5
Fld Post Office	3	7	8	15	3		1	4	
Total	64[1]	292	1,529	1,708	165	13	86	323	85

[1] Including 18 officials.

Figure 169.—Division Services, Army Armored Division, total strength 1,885.

UNIT	Offs	NCOs	Pvts	Rs or Cbns	Pistols	Sub-MGs	LMGs	Mtr Vehicles	Mtrcls	H-Dr Vehicles	Tlrs	Hs	Bcls
Regtl Hq	8	6	12	18	5	3	1	6	3				40
120 Ton Clm (Mtz)	2	17	95	112	2		2	19	1				
30 Ton Clm	2	12	80	92	2		1			42		100	5
30 Ton Clm	2	12	80	92	2		1			42		100	5
Sup Plat	1	3	60	65	1		1			19		48	3
Ord Co	3	18	67	83	3		1	5	1				10
Maint Plat	2	8	50	58	2		1	6	1		4		5
Adm Co	8	22	134	156	8		3	28	1		11		5
Med Co	10	34	150	167	27		2	16	2	17	2	46	20
Amb Plat	1	5	34		40			21	2				
Vet Co	4	15	100	102	17		2	7	1	10	1	94	10
Fld Post Office	3	9	6	6	12			3					
Total	46[1]	161	868	951	121	3	15	111	12	130	18	388	103

[1] Including eight officials.

Figure 170.—Supply Regiment, Volks Grenadier Division, total strength 1,075.

are being allotted to divisions in accordance with the tactical requirements. For the procedure of evacuation of wounded and the definition of medical units see Section V, paragraph 3.

5. Field Post Office

There is a field post office in every German division acting as a branch post office of an army of which the division is a part.

6. Motor Maintenance Troops

The supply and motor maintenance units of the German Army, which originally combined all transport troops (*Fahrtruppen*), were divided into two separate arms in the fall of 1942. The transportation and supply units now are classified as supply troops (see paragraph 2 above), while the motor maintenance units are grouped under the motor maintenance troops. Their great efficiency has been proved when servicing numerous makes of motor vehicles taken from all occupied countries. Workshops are designated usually as workshop companies (*Werkstattkompanien*), or as mobile repair shops (*Kraftwagenwerkstätte*).

7. Veterinary Troops

The great majority of German divisions use horses as means of transportation and have a veterinary company which consists of a horse collecting platoon, a horse hospital, and a fodder platoon. Because of the importance which horses still play within the German Army, there is an elaborate system of veterinary units and horse hospitals in the field as well as in the Zone of the Interior.

8. Military Police

The military police duties are divided between the military police (*Feldgendarmerie*), whose main task is the maintenance of traffic discipline, and guard troops (*Wachtruppen*), primarily concerned with the guarding of vital military installations in the field. The latter also take charge of prisoners of war and escort them to the rear areas. Patrol duties and the maintenance of military discipline are carried out both by army and *SS* patrols and the military police.

The guard battalion is an independent battalion assigned to army groups and armies.

A military police battalion is found with each army and consists of three or four military police companies.

Military police detachments are organic in every German division. They were originally a part of the divisional services, but may be found now frequently within the division headquarters.

9. Miscellaneous Units

For a list of all identified units of the service troops arm, see "Order of Battle of the German Army," March 1945 edition.

10. Abbreviations

All abbreviations are according to TM 20-205 and/or FM 21-30. It should be noted that there are no official abbreviations for:

Bazooka	Pistol
Corps	Pool
Flame thrower	Post Office
Gun	Vehicle
Light	Workshop
Medium	

The abbreviation Sub-MG has been adopted instead of SMG to avoid confusion with *Schweres Machinen Gewehr* which means "Heavy Machine Gun."

The following list of abbreviations is used in connection with the organization charts.

A	Army
AA	Antiaircraft
AA/AT	Antiaircraft-Antitank
Adm	Administration
Amb	Ambulance
Armd C	Armored Car
Arty	Artillery
Asgd	Assigned
AT	Antitank
Atchd	Attached
Bar Bln	Barrage Balloon
Bcl	Bicycle
Bn	Battalion
Br	Bridge
Btry	Battery
C	Combat
C of S	Chief of Staff
Cbn	Carbine
CG	Commanding General
CH	Chaplain
Clm	Column
Cml	Chemical
Co	Company

Com	Command	Mtz	Motorized
Comdt	Commandant	Mun	Munitions
C Sch	Combat School	NCO	Noncommissioned Officer
Ct	Combat team	Offs	Officers
Decon	Decontamination	Ord	Ordnance
Det	Detachment	Pers	Personnel
Div	Division	Plat	Platoon
Ech	Echelon	Prcht	Parachute
Engr	Engineer	Pvts	Privates
Fin	Finance	*Pz.*	*Panzer*
Fld	Field	*Pz. Gren.*	*Panzer Grenadier*
Füs	Füselier	*Pz. Kpfw.*	*Panzer Kampfwagen* (Tank)
Fwd Ech	Forward Echelon	R	Rifle
GHQ	General Headquarters	Rad	Radio
Gp	Group	Rcn	Reconnaissance
Gren	*Grenadier*	Regt	Regiment
GS	General Staff	Regtl	Regimental
Gun/How	Gun-Howitzer	Repl	Replacement
H	Horse	Repro	Reproduction
H-Dr	Horse-drawn	Rkt	Rocket
H-Trk	Half-track	Rr Ech	Rear echelon
How	Howitzer	SAR	Semiautomatic Rifle
Hq	Headquarters	Sch	School
Hv MG	Heavy Machine Gun	Sec	Section
Hv Wpn Co	Heavy Weapons Company	Serv	Service
Incl	Including	Sig	Signal
Inf	Infantry	SL	Searchlight
Int	Intelligence	Sp	Self-propelled
JA	Judge Advocate	Spcl	Specialist
LMG	Light Machine Gun	Sp Stf	Special Staff
Ln O	Liaison Officer	Sq	Squad
Med	Medical	Sub-MG	Sub-Machine Gun
Met	Meteorological	Sup	Supply
MG	Machine Gun	Surg	Surgeon
Mort	Mortar	Surv	Survey
MP	Military police	Tac	Tactical
MT	Motor Transport	Tlr	Trailer
Mt	Mountain	Tn	Train
Mtd	Mounted	Tng	Training
Mtr	Motor	Tp	Telephone
Mtrcls	Motorcycles	Tr	Troop
Mtr-Dr	Motor-drawn	Vet	Veterinary

CHAPTER III

OTHER MILITARY AND AUXILIARY ORGANIZATIONS

Section I. *SS* AND POLICE

1. Introduction

Any description of organization, mission, and structure of the SS cannot be understood unless one tries to conceive it inwardly with one's blood and heart. It cannot be explained why we contain so much strength though we number so few.

　　　　　　　　　　　　　Heinrich Himmler.

The *SS*, or *Schutzstaffel*, is the Protective Guard of the National-Socialist Party (*NSDAP*). Officially an independent *Gliederung* (Branch) of the Party, led by Heinrich Himmler, it actually has a status and importance far exceeding those of the other branches and even those of the Party itself. From its original function of guarding the person of Party leaders and speakers, the *SS* developed even before the war, into a far-flung organization to protect the entire Nazi movement against all internal enemies. More recently, it has extended its influence and power into every conceivable aspect of German national life and has finally acquired a large measure of control over the Army itself. It is more than a state within a state; it is superior to both the Party and the government.

The rise of the *SS* has been gradual but unceasing. Because of its origin and its own experience as an underground organization, it has always understood how to combat systematically and unrelentingly any subversive activities in the Reich and in all occupied areas. It was by extension of its responsibility for internal political security that the *SS* first acquired control of the Secret State Police and later (in 1936) of the entire police forces of Germany. Quite naturally therefore, it was given the policing powers in most of the countries occupied by Germany during the war. It was also logical that the *SS*, as the elite corps of the Party, should take part in the march into Austria and Czechoslovakia along with the troops of the Army, and that it should furnish small contingents of trained men to fight in the

Polish campaign in 1939. This led to the building up of the *Waffen-SS*, at first consisting of the equivalent of two or three divisions and finally growing to a substantial and favored branch of the armed forces of the nation. In 1943 the *SS* gained control of the powerful Ministry of the Interior, in which it had already constituted the most important group in the form of the police. During 1943 and 1944 the *SS* gained more and more influence in the Army itself, taking over successively control of political indoctrination, of the intelligence services, and of the whole replacement, training, and material procurement system.

Apart from these obvious acquisitions of power and authority, the *SS* has steadily extended its influence into many branches of German life which would seem, on the surface, to have little or nothing to do with its original or derived mission. High-ranking officers of the *SS* now occupy controlling positions in most of the central departments of the government, in regional and local administration, in heavy industry, finance, and commerce, and in cultural and charitable activities. Directly or indirectly the *SS* controls the training of youth in the Hitler Youth organization, the storm troops (*SA*), and most of the other Party organizations and activities.

The character and purposes of the *SS* would not be clear without reference to its mystical worship of the German "race". This is exemplified not only by the physical requirements for becoming an *SS* man, but also by a vast program of procreation propaganda, resettlement of populations, eradication of elements considered racially undesirable, genealogical research, and welfare. Typical of the *SS* is its insistence that the abbreviation of its title always be printed or typed as the runic symbol of victory and arbitrariness:

ᛋᛋ

The development of *SS power* is intimately

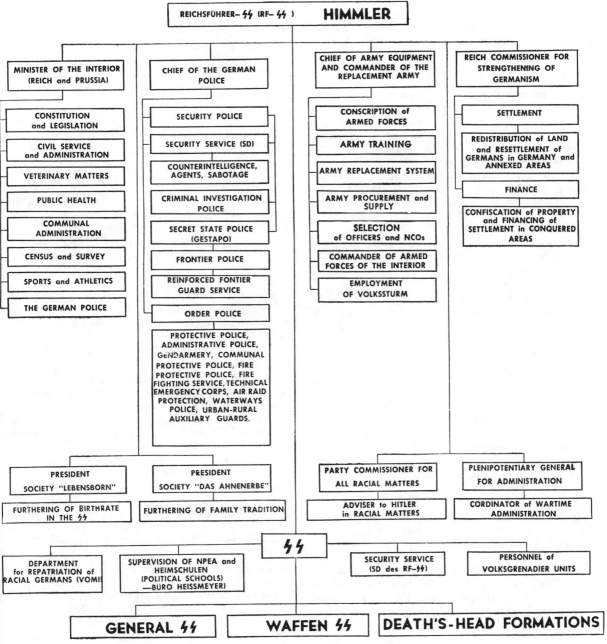

| REICHSFÜHRER-SS (RF-SS) | HIMMLER |

| MINISTER OF THE INTERIOR (REICH and PRUSSIA) | CHIEF OF THE GERMAN POLICE | CHIEF OF ARMY EQUIPMENT AND COMMANDER OF THE REPLACEMENT ARMY | REICH COMMISSIONER FOR STRENGTHENING OF GERMANISM |

Figure 1.—Functions of the Reichsführer—SS.

linked to the career of Heinrich Himmler. This seemingly unassuming and quiet-mannered man has obtained one important post after another until today more power is concentrated in his person than in any other man except Hitler. Indeed, his power is much more absolute than that of Hitler, since the latter's actions and decisions are necessarily influenced by various pressure groups within the Party, by consideration of public opinion, and by other outside forces.

Wherever Himmler has secured a position, he has taken the *SS* with him. His plurality of offices represents not merely a personal union of powers but the acquisition of successive fields for the extension and infiltration of *SS* influence. It is significant in this connection that in all his various capacities Himmler always uses his original title of *Reichsführer-SS* (abbreviated *RF-SS*). The *SS* is at once the basis and the instrument of Himmler's strength.

For this reason a description of the functions of the *RF-SS* is the most effective way of indicating the present position of the *SS* in Germany.

2. External Functions of the *RF-SS*

As shown in the accompanying chart (*Figure 1*), the *RF-SS* holds eight separate offices besides those resulting directly from his position as commander of the *SS* proper. They are:

a. REICH AND PRUSSIAN MINISTER OF THE INTERIOR (*Reichs- und Preussischer Minister des Innern*). In this capacity, which he acquired in August 1943, Himmler controls a department for constitutional and legislative matters, the administration of the German civil service (*Beamentum*), veterinary matters, and public health, the federalized communal administration, census and survey, and the administration of sports and athletics. This ministry also controls the federalized German police, of which Himmler was the chief long before he became the Minister of the Interior.

b. CHIEF OF THE GERMAN POLICE (*Chef der Deutschen Polizei—ChdDtP*). In this office, which he has held since June 1936, the *RF-SS* has succeeded in creating a closely knit national police force fully in accord with the purposes of the *SS*. The principal measures by which this was accomplished were the federalizing of the former state and local police organizations, the institution of a personnel policy controlled by the *SS*, the extension of the scope and authority of the police as a whole to new fields, and the interweaving of the administration and functions of the Party Security Service (*Sicherheitsdienst des Reichsführers-SS—SD des RF-SS*) with those of the Security Police (*Sicherheitspolizei—Sipo*). The two last-named organizations were combined under the Central Security Department (*Reichssicherheitshauptamt—RSHA*).

The German police organization, as such, is divided into two categories, the Security Police and the Order Police (*Ordnungspolizei—Orpo*).

(1) The Security Police has two branches: The Criminal Investigation Police (*Kriminalpolizei—Kripo*) and the Secret State Police (*Geheime Staatspolizei—Gestapo*). Under the control of the *RF-SS* the functions of the Criminal Investigation Police have undergone many changes, and it now constitutes a valuable ally of the Secret State Police. The latter, as the political branch of the police, has always led the fight against subversive elements in Germany and served as the executive arm in the process of ridding Germany of "undesirable" elements. An adjunct of the Gestapo is the Frontier Police (*Grenzpolizei*), which was greatly strengthened in 1944 by attaching to it the Reinforced Frontier Guard Service (*Verstärkte Grenzaufsichtsdienst*). The latter is properly a branch of the Reich Ministry of Finance and now serves the combined purposes of this ministry and of the political police. Together, these organizations have the new and important mission of preventing the desertion of military personnel, as well as the escape of foreign civilian workers across the borders of the Reich.

(2) The Order Police includes the regular uniformed police and has acquired control of a number of auxiliary organizations which are not always concerned with strictly police functions.

Components of the Order Police are:

Protective Police (*Schutzpolizei—Schupo*), a regular police force operating in towns and cities with more than about 5,000 inhabitants.

Communal Protective Police (*Schutzpolizei der Gemeinden*), a regular police force for towns too small to have the urban Protective Police mentioned above.

Gendarmery (*Gendarmerie*), a regular police force for rural communities.

Administrative Police (*Verwaltungspolizei*), for such routine functions as registration of residents, inspection of buildings, and the keeping of police records.

Fire Protection Police (*Feuerschutzpolizei*), a federalized communal fire-fighting organization with police status.

Fire-Fighting Services (*Feuerwehren*), a federalized organization of voluntary fire fighters, replacing former private societies and associations.

Air Raid Protection Police (*Luftschutzpolizei*), responsible for aid and clearance measures during air raids.

Urban and Rural Auxiliary Guards (*Stadt- und Landwacht*), auxiliary police organizations of part-time volunteers in urban and rural areas.

Technical Emergency Corps (*Technische Nothilfe—TN*), which provides technically trained personnel for emergency work of all kinds, especially in case of a breakdown of public services.

c. CHIEF OF ARMY EQUIPMENT AND COMMANDER OF THE REPLACEMENT ARMY (*Chef der Heeresrüstung und Befehlshaber des Ersatzheeres—Ch H Rüst u.BdE*). In this function, which he acquired in July 1944, the *RF-SS* controls the conscription of the Armed Forces, the Army training and replacement system, and Army procurement and supply. He is responsible for the selection and training of future officers and noncommissioned officers and, in his capacity as commander of all forces in the Zone of the Interior, he controls the *Volkssturm* and orders its employment.

d. REICH COMMISSIONER FOR THE STRENGTHENING OF GERMANISM (*Reichskommissar für die Festigung des Deutschen Volkstums—RKV*). Since October 1939, when he received this appointment, the *RF-SS* has been the highest authority on all matters concerning the settling of Germans in annexed areas. A vast organization was created to deal with the redistribution of property which fell to the Germans as spoils of war.

e. PRESIDENT OF THE SOCIETY "FOUNTAIN OF LIFE" (*Verein "Lebensborn e.V."*). Through this organization, which he founded in September 1936, the *RF-SS* takes active control of the numerous measures which the *SS* has devised in order to insure the "victory of births of good blood".

f. PRESIDENT OF THE SOCIETY "THE ANCESTRAL HERITAGE" (*Verein "Das Ahnenerbe"*). This group deals with racial and genealogical matters and fosters interest in family tradition and racial purity.

g. PARTY COMMISSIONER FOR ALL RACIAL MATTERS (*Beauftragter der NSDAP für alle Volkstumsfragen*). In this function, which is his only official one within the Party proper, the *RF-SS* acts as the chief adviser to the *Führer* on racial matters, and as the coordinator between the Party and his own function as Reich Commissioner for the Strengthening of Germanism.

h. PLENIPOTENTIARY GENERAL FOR ADMINISTRATION (*Generalbevollmächtigter für die Verwaltung*). This appointment went with that of Minister of the Interior, the previous incumbent (Frick) having received it at the beginning of the war, to coordinate all wartime national administration problems.

3. Internal Special Functions of the *RF-SS*

In his capacity as commander of the *SS* proper, Himmler has four special functions not directly connected with the organization and administration of the *SS*. They are:

a. The Department for the Repatriation of Racial Germans (*Volksdeutsche Mittelstelle—Vomi*) is a bureau which is characterized as a Main Department (*Hauptamt*) because it comes directly under the *RF-SS*. Since October 1939 this department has carried out the far-flung resettlement plans for "racial" Germans from the western borderlands of Russia. Hundreds of thousands of such persons have been transferred to the annexed areas of Poland.

b. The Bureau Main Department *SS-Obergruppenführer Heissmeyer* (*Dienststelle Hauptamt SS-Obergruppenführer Heissmeyer*) has as its chief mission the control of the National Political Educational Institutes (*Nationalpolitische Erziehungsanstalten—NPEA*) and Boarding Schools (*Heimschulen*). The former are schools for selected pupils from all over Germany who are supposed to attain a high scholastic record while subjected to most severe indoctrination in Party ideology. *Heimschulen* are designed for the children of soldiers or of civil service officials who cannot maintain a permanent residence. These schools, in which political indoctrination is especially accentuated, have grown rapidly in number to accommodate large numbers of children rendered homeless by air raids.

c. The Security Service (*Sicherheitsdienst des RF-SS —SD or SD des RF-SS*) is nominally a branch of the General *SS* but is controlled, under Himmler, by the Central Security Office (*Reichssicherheitshauptamt*) along with the Security Police. It is officially the intelligence service of the Party against internal enemies, while the Security Police (including the Gestapo) is the executive agent for combatting them. From its original mission the *SD* has constantly grown in scope and in 1944 absorbed the bulk of the *Abwehr*, the intelligence organization of the Armed Forces. Many of its members were until recently engaged in occupied areas, but their number inside Germany has greatly increased with the shrinking of the areas still occupied. At the same time their importance in Germany has developed steadily and their preparations for the eventuality of defeat can be expected to be the most efficient and far reaching.

d. With the formation of *Volks Grenadier* units in the latter part of 1944 the *RF-SS* became responsible for the personnel of these units, acting through a new special branch of the Army Personnel Office (*PA/P 7*). It is believed that such personnel are more or less interchangeable with the members of the *Waffen-SS*.

4. SS Control of Public Life

As impressive as the list of the functions of the *RF-SS* must appear, it is by no means more than an indication of the power of the *SS*, which has enlarged its position and range of influence steadily by an unobtrusive but thorough policy of infiltration. Dominating almost every branch of official and semi-official German life, the *SS* has become a super-government composed of a racially conscious "order" of men (and women) bound by a rigid set of rules, the foremost of these being unswerving loyalty to one's immediate chief and unquestioning obedience. This strict discipline ensures the complete subservience to the *SS*, even of those members who joined originally merely as an expedient to be entitled to wear the black uniform and to climb the ladder of political, economic, or even artistic success.

A few statistics may serve to show to what extent this most powerful body has permeated the Third Reich:

Hitler's personal entourage includes at least six *SS* men.

The Party Reich Directors (*Reichsleiter*) include ten *SS* men out of a total of 16. Most of the six non-*SS* members have suffered a loss of power and prestige in the past two years. Ten of the 26 posts in the Reich Cabinet are held by *SS* men. Thirty-nine *SS* men with the rank of colonel or above hold other important posts in the Reich Ministries.

Most of the *Reichsstatthalter*, provincial presidents, state ministers, and secretaries and vice-presidents of state governments are men whose high *SS* rank is not always the most publicized feature of their careers. In municipal affairs numerous mayors are identified with the *SS*.

The permeation of all branches and levels of government in Germany by officers of the *SS* is matched on a nearly equal scale in industry, finance, commerce, cultural activities, and charitable organizations.

5. Organization of the SS

a. FUNCTIONAL ORGANIZATION. **The *SS*** proper is divided functionally into three main groups:

(1) *The General SS* (*Allgemeine SS*), composed of the ordinary part-time members of General *SS* regiments (*SS-Standarten*), the full-time members (normally with the rank of major or above) of General *SS* units and headquarters, and non-active members attached to units and headquarters of the General *SS*. The General *SS* is not maintained by the state; its expenditures are borne by the Party and ultimately controlled by the Party Treasurer, who himself holds the rank of a full general of the *SS*.

In certain occupied countries (e.g. Norway, Holland) organizations have been set up which are modeled on the General *SS*. These are known as Germanic *SS* (*Germanische SS*) and have their own central organization, ultimately subordinate to the *RF-SS* in Germany.

(2) *The Armed SS* (*Waffen-SS*). This category comprises the full-time military organization

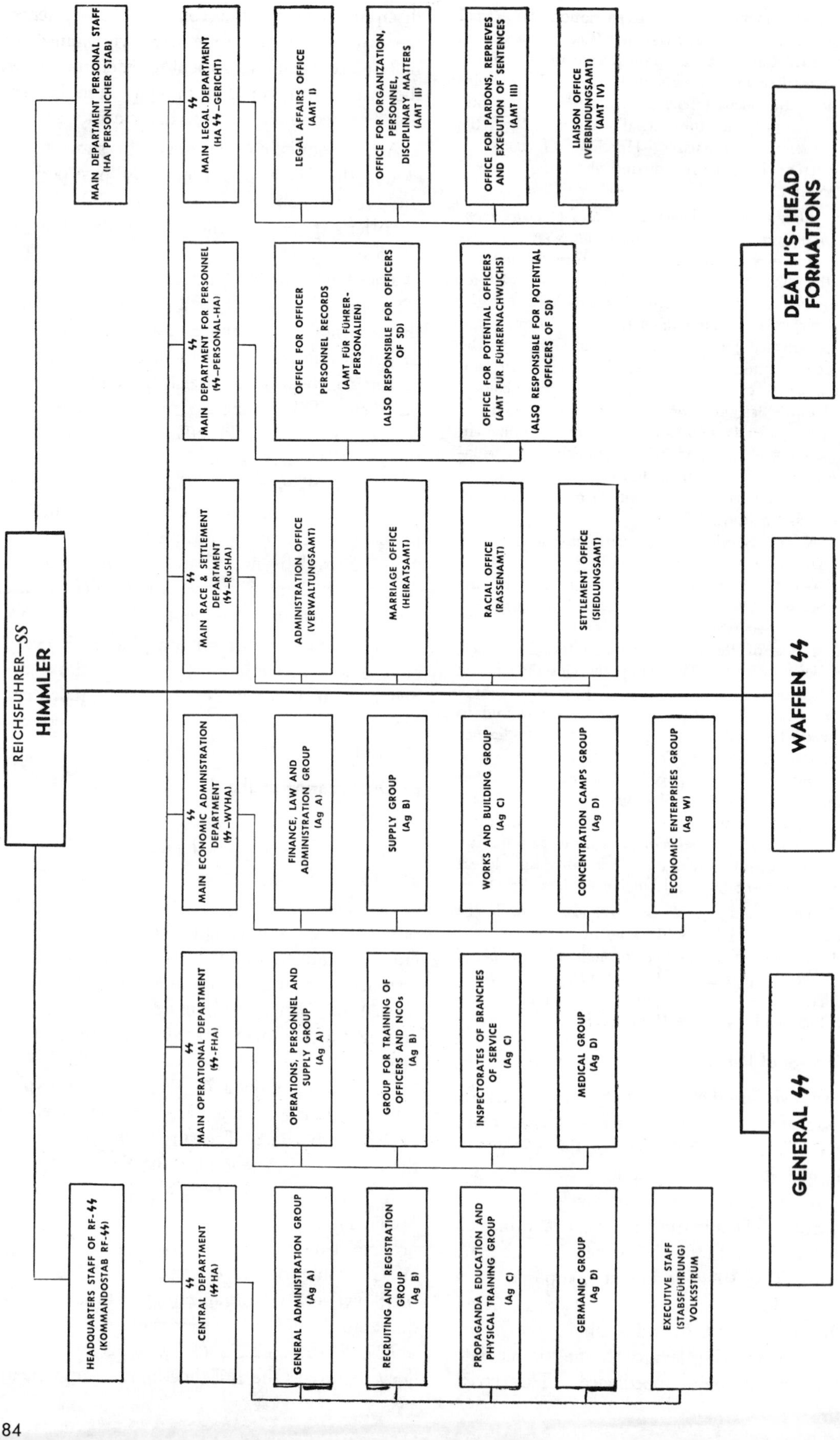

Figure 2.—SS High Command.

of the *SS* together with their training and replacement units, schools, and installations. It is a specially regulated public instrument of the Reich on the model of the Army and is now considered a component part of the Armed Forces. Its expenses are borne by the State.

(3) *The Death's-Head Formations (SS-Totenkopfverbände)*. These consist mainly of the guard units of concentration camps. Their development from the General *SS* is closely identified with the work of the Gestapo. Their expenses are a responsibility of the State.

b. HIGH COMMAND ORGANIZATION. The *SS* High Command is known as the *Reichsführung-SS* and consists of the *RF-SS*, his staffs, and the chiefs of the Main Departments *(Hauptämter)* described below. These Main Departments administer the internal affairs of the three functional subdivisions of the *SS*.

(1) The Headquarters Staff of the *RF-SS (Kommandostab RF-SS)* is located at the Field Command Post of the *RF-SS (Feldkommandostelle RF-SS)* which is usually near Hitler's headquarters in the field *(Führerhauptquartier)*.

(2) The Main Department Personal Staff *(Hauptamt Persönlicher Stab—HA Pers. Stab)* is a permanent installation at Himmler's rear headquarters to assist him in the execution of his manifold tasks.

(3) The *SS* Central Department *(SS-Hauptamt—SS-HA)* is responsible for miscellaneous over-all administrative and personnel matters. It is divided into the following five groups *(Amtsgruppen—Ag)*:

Group A handles general administration matter.
Group B takes care of recruiting and registration of all categories of *SS* personnel.
Group C is responsible for propaganda, education, and physical training.
Group D controls the Germanic *SS (Germanische SS)* including recruitment in cooperation with Group B.
The Executive Staff of the German *Volkssturm (Stabsführung des Deutschen Volkssturms)* has been identified in the *SS* Central Department and presumably handles the responsibilities of the *RF-SS* connected with this national militia.

(4) The *SS* Main Operational Department *(SS-Führungshauptamt—SS-FHA)* concerns itself largely with the *Waffen-SS*. It grew out of the former Operational Office in the *SS* Central Department in 1940. Its long-time chief, Hans Jüttner, is now the deputy of the *RF-SS* in his capacity as Chief of Army Equipment and Commander of the Replacement Army. This Main Department contains the following four groups:

Group A controls operations, personnel, and supply. It includes the Headquarters Offices *(Kommandoämter)* of the General *SS* and of the *Waffen-SS*.
Group B is responsible for the selection and training of officers and noncommissioned officers.
Group C consists of the inspectorates of the various branches of service.
Group D is in charge of medical matters for the entire *SS*.

(5) The *SS* Main Economic Administrative Department *(SS-Wirtschaftsverwaltungshauptamt—SS-WVHA)* is responsible for fiscal matters, administration of *SS* property and concentration camps, and control of supply installations. It is divided into five groups as follows:

Group A includes finance, law, and certain general administration matters.
Group B is responsible for supply installations and procurement and delivery of certain types of supplies for *SS* units and headquarters.
Group C administers the works and buildings of the *SS*, including the construction of buildings.
Group D administers all concentration camps.
Group W manages the economic enterprises of the *SS*.

(6) The *SS* Main Race and Settlement Department *(SS-Rasse- und -Siedlungshauptamt—SS-RuSHA)* contains the following four offices *Ämter)*:

Administration Office *(Verwaltungsamt)*.
Marriage Office *(Heiratsamt)* which rigidly controls the selection of suitable wives by *SS* men.
Racial Office *(Rassenamt)*, which selects future *SS* men and handles the tasks of racial selection connected with the function of the *RF-SS* as Reich Commissioner for the Strengthening of Germanism.
Settlement Office *(Siedlungsamt)*, which deals with the settlement of discharged *SS* men, especially in the annexed eastern areas.

The above offices of the Main Race and Settlement Department are further divided into Main Branches *(Hauptabteilungen)*. One of these is the Main Welfare Branch, which handles the problems of welfare and pensions in close cooperation with the *SS* Main Welfare and Pension Department *(SS-Hauptfürsorge- und- Versorgungsamt)* in the Reich Ministry of the Interior.

(7) The *SS* Main Department for Personnel *(SS-Personalhauptamt—SS-Pers.HA)* is the central recording office for all *SS* officers and potential officers, including those of the Security Service *(SD)*. It is not itself responsible for promotions and appointments. It is divided into two offices *(Ämter)*:

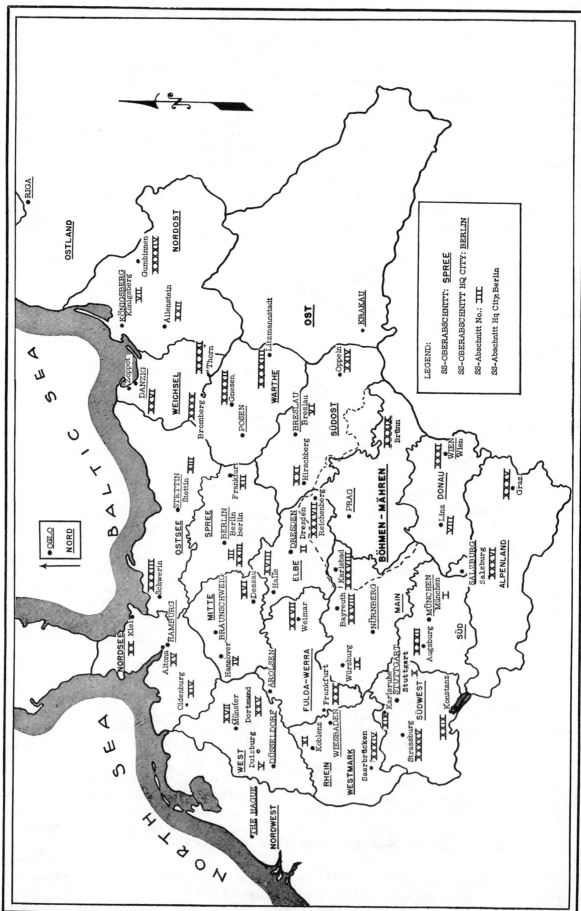

Figure 3.—SS regional organization.

The Office of Officer Personnel Records (*Amt für Führerpersonalien*).

The Office for Potential Officers (*Amt für Führernachwuchs*).

(8) The *SS* Main Legal Department (*Hauptamt SS-Gericht—HA SS-Gericht*) is concerned with the special jurisprudence which operates within the *SS* and police organization. It is divided into four offices (*Ämter*):

Office I is the Legal Affairs Office.

Office II is the Office for Organization, Personnel, and Disciplinary Matters.

Office III is the Office for Pardons, Reprieves, and the Execution of Sentences.

Office IV is a Liaison Office (*Verbindungsamt*).

c. REGIONAL ORGANIZATION. (1) *General.* The basis of the regional organization of the *SS* is the district (*Oberabschnitt—Oa.*). There are seventeen of these districts in Germany proper and each coincides exactly with a *Wehrkreis* (Army corps area). The *SS* districts are known by geographical names, but it has become a convenient and growing custom to add to the name the Roman numeral of the corresponding *Wehrkreis*. With two exceptions, the headquarters of the district is in the same city as that of the *Wehrkreis*. In addition six districts have been organized in occupied countries and are known by names according to their geographical location. One of these, named "Ukraine" was dissolved early in 1944.

The control of a district is entrusted to a Higher *SS* and Police Commander (*Höherer SS und Polizeiführer—HSSPf*), who normally commands both the *SS* and police units and installations in the district.

Occupied areas which have not been organized into *SS* districts are also commanded by an *HSSPf*, whose functions are analogous to those of the *HSSPf* of a district.

In certain areas a regional organization of the *Waffen-SS* exists side by side with the general regional organization of the *SS* and police. These areas are controlled, for special purposes of the *Waffen-SS* only, by territorial Commanders of the *Waffen-SS* (*Befehlshaber der Waffen-SS—Bfh.d.W-SS*).

(2) *Authority of the HSSPf.* (a) *General functions.* The *HSSPf* is the representative of the *RF-SS* at any given military territorial headquarters, or, where they exist, at the headquarters of the Reich commissioners (*Reichskommissare*) for occupied areas. As such he is the official adviser in all *SS* and police matters to the regional representatives of the Reich government administering any part of such an area.

He is the commander of the *SS* district if the area under his jurisdiction is constituted as such.

The *HSSPf* commands the *SS* and police units and installations in his area except those which have been subordinated to the *OKH* for operations and those which are commanded by a territorial commander of the *Waffen-SS*.

Operational commands have been assigned to an *HSSPf* under different circumstances and in varying degrees. Such commands have consisted of special staffs for combating partisans (*SS und Polizei-Führungsstab für Bandenbekämpfung*) and battle groups which were formed hastily from the forces normally commanded by the *HSSPf* when his area was invaded or threatened. A number of personalities have in this way graduated from assignment as *HSSPf* to that of the commander of an *SS* corps.

Various special offices are sometimes combined with that of the *HSSPf* in certain areas. For example, the *HSSPf* in Prague holds the position of Minister of State for Bohemia and Moravia (*Staatsminister für Böhmen und Mähren*) and acts as the deputy to the Reich Protector of this area. The *HSSPf* in the Government General holds the position of State Secretary for Security Matters (*Staatssekretär des Sicherheitswesens*).

With the increasing danger to Germany proper new responsibilities have been thrust upon the *HSSPf*, especially in the border areas. In some cases he has assumed active command of all units of the auxiliary organizations of the Reich and of the Party, except those of the Todt Organization (*OT*), so far as they have been organized for defensive combat tasks. In case of an invasion of his area he has been ordered to attach himself and all the units under him, including those of the *SS* and police, to the commander of the *Wehrkreis* and to act as his deputy for the latter if necessary.

The full title of an *HSSPf* may indicate the *Wehrkreis* (e.g. *HSSPf Wehrkreis X*), the geographical name of the *Oberabschnitt* (*HSSPf Nordsee*), or its headquarters city (*HSSPf Hamburg*). In occupied or annexed areas the title varies. The following examples are given as illustrations: *HSSPf beim Reichskommissar für die besetzten niederländischen Gebiets* is also encountered as *HSSPf Nordwest* or as *HSSPf den Haag*. The *HSSPf* in Greece was normally designated *HSSPf Griechenland*.

Each *HSSPf* is assisted by a Chief of Staff (*Stabsführer*) in the execution of all his duties. The latter is also the Chief of Staff of the *SS* district in those areas where the *HSSPf* is also the commander of such a district.

(b) *Organization of SS districts.* In Greater Germany (excluding Bohemia-Moravia and the Government General), the *HSSPf* has two separate staffs for his two main functions. One staff assists him in the command and administration of the *SS*, another in that of the police.

The staff of the *SS* within the *SS* district consists of the following officers under the Chief of Staff:

Administrative Officer.
Chief Medical Officer.
Director of Training.
Chief Personnel Officer.
Chief Signal Officer.

The Administrative Officer heads the Administrative Office (*Verwaltungsamt*), which operates under the control of the *SS* Main Economic Administrative Department and handles all matters of finance and supply within the district.

Each district is divided into two or more sub-districts (*Abschnitte*), each having its own headquarters. These sub-districts are distinguished by Roman numerals. Their commanders are known as *Führer des SS-Abschnitts*. The headquarters of the *SS* sub-districts are organized on the same general lines as those of the district; both are closely parallel to the standard German staff organization for any military unit or headquarters, including the numbers and letters used for the sections and sub-sections.

Each of the districts inside Germany has a *Waffen-SS* recruiting center (*Ergänzungsstelle*) administered directly by the *SS* Central Department. It also has a section for racial and settlement matters (*Rasse- und Siedlungswesen*), which is under the supervision of the *SS* Main Race and Settlement Department.

The staff of the *HSSPf* for the command and administration of the police includes the following two leading police officers under the Chief of Staff:

Inspector of the Security Police and of the Security Service (*Inspekteur der Sicherheitspolizei und des Sicherheitsdienstes—IdSuSD*, sometimes also given as *IdS*).

Inspector of the Order Police (*Inspekteur der Ordnungspolizei—IdO*). This officer controls the commander of the Barrack Police (those elements of the Protective Police who live in barracks), who has the title of Commander of the Protective Police (*Kommandeur der Schutzpolizei*).

These inspectors have complete administrative departments covering all aspects of police activities which are assigned to their respective branches.

Certain areas adjacent to Germany, particularly Alsace, Lorraine, and Luxemburg, have been incorporated into *Wehrkreise* while their civil administration has remained separate. For these areas a dual nomenclature exists for the leading members of the police staff of the *HSSPf*. They are referred to as Inspectors in the old part of the district and as Senior Commanders (*Befehlshaber*) of their respective branches for the annexed areas. The latter nomenclature coincides with that of the corresponding officers in areas outside the Reich proper as described below.

The organization of *SS* districts outside Greater Germany (namely *Ost, Nordwest, Nord, Ostland,* and formerly *Ukraine*) is identical to that inside Germany with the following exceptions:

There is an economic section directly subordinate to the *HSSPf*. This is headed by an officer known as *SS-Wirtschafter* and replaces the administrative office in the *SS* district.

The sub-districts of *SS* districts do not exist. Instead, one or more *SS* and Police Commanders (*SS und Polizeiführer—SSPf*) may exist. These are representatives of the *HSSPf* in all his functions for the sub-area which is assigned to them.

A *Waffen-SS* Recruiting Inspectorate (*Ersatzinspektion der Waffen-SS*) replaces the *Waffen-SS* Recruiting Center.

The leading officers on the staff of the *HSSPf* for the command and administration of the police have the following titles and functions:

Senior Commander of the Security Police and of the Security Service (*Befehlshaber der Sicherheitspolizei und des Sicherheitsdienstes—BdSuSD* or *BdS*). He may control subordinate area commanders (*Kommandeure—KdSuSD* or *KdS*).

Senior Commander of the Order Police (*Befehlshaber der Ordnungspolizei—BdO*). He may control subordinate Commanders (*KdO*).

These Senior Commanders have complete administrative departments covering all aspects of police activities which are assigned to their respective branches.

The above deviations in the organization of

the police, but not those relating to the *SS,* also apply to the district *Böhmen-Mähren.*

(c) *Organization of areas which are not SS districts.* In occupied areas which are not constituted as *SS* districts, the *HSSPf* retains his dual function as commander of all *SS* and police forces. There is considerably less emphasis on *SS* matters and normally no special staff for the latter exists. The police functions take on added significance because the *HSSPf* not only concerns himself with the German police forces but also controls, in varying degrees, the native police in the area. The nomenclature of the police officers coincides with that in *SS* districts outside Greater Germany.

In Italy several *HSSPf's* have been installed. They are subordinated to one Supreme *SS* and Police Commander *(Höchster SS und Polizeiführer—Höchst. SSPf).* It is believed that the general organization of the areas controlled by these officers differs little from that of the *HSSPf* and subordinate *SSPf's* in other occupied areas.

(3) *Territorial commanders of the Waffen-SS.* In certain selected areas the *SS* High Command has installed territorial commanders of the *Waffen-SS (Befehlshaber der Waffen-SS—Bfh. d.W-SS).* These represent the regional echelon of the *SS* High Command for the *Waffen-SS* only. They execute its directives and are in complete command of all units of the *Waffen-SS* in their areas. The commander of the *Waffen-SS* shares with the *HSSPf* control of the static installations of the *Waffen-SS,* but is otherwise completetly independent of him. Such commanders have been identified in the Netherlands, in Bohemia and Moravia, in the area of the *SS* district *"Ostland",* and in Hungary.

The commander of the *Waffen-SS* may take on operational assignments under the command of the *OKH.*

The staff organization of these commanders is comparable to that of a corps. The various members of his staff represent the different offices of the High Command and the Inspectorates of the branches of service.

(4) *List of SS districts.* The following is a list of the *SS* districts together with their headquarters and the corresponding *Wehrkreise.*

Oa.	Headquarters	Wehrkreis
Nordost	Königsberg	I
Ostsee	Stettin	II
Spree	Berlin	III
Elbe	Dresden	IV
Südwest	Stuttgart	V
West	Düsseldorf	VI
Süd	München	VII
Südost	Breslau	VIII
Fulda-Werra	Arolsen	IX
Nordsee	Hamburg	X
Mitte	Braunschweig	XI
Rhein-West-mark	Wiesbaden	XII
Main	Nürnberg	XIII
Donau	Wein	XVII
Alpenland	Salzburg	XVIII
Weichsel	Danzig	XX
Warthe	Posen	XXI
Nordwest	Den Haag	(Netherlands)
Nord	Oslo	(Norway)
Ost	Krakau	Generalgouvernement
Böhmen-Mähren	Prague	Böhmen und Mähren
Ostland	Riga	(Ostland)

(5) *List of SS sub-districts.* Each district comprises an average of two or three sub-districts *(Abschnitte)* distinguished by Roman numerals. The sub-districts are also colloquially referred to by the names of the regions which they comprise or by the location of their headquarters.

Number	Oa.	Headquarters
I	Süd	München
II	Elbe	Dresden
III	Spree	Berlin
IV	Mitte	Hannover
V	West	Duisburg
VI	Südost	Breslau
VII	Nordost	Königsberg
VIII	Donau	Linz
IX	Main	Würzburg
X	Südwest	Stuttgart
XI	Rhein-West-mark	Koblenz
XII	Spree	Frankfurt/Oder
XIII	Ostsee	Stettin
XIV	Nordsee	Oldenburg
XV	Nordsee	Hamburg-Altona
XVI	Mitte	Dessau
XVII	West	Münster
XVIII	Elbe	Halle/Saale
XIX	Südwest	Karlsruhe
XX	Nordsee	Kiel
XXI	Südost	Hirschberg
XXII	Nordost	Allenstein

XXIII	Spree	Berlin
XXIV	Südost	Oppeln
XXV	West	Dortmund
XXVI	Weichsel	Zoppot
XXVII	Fulda-Werra	Weimar
XXVIII	Main	Bayreuth
XXIX	Südwest	Konstanz
XXX	Rhein-West-mark	Frankfurt/Main
XXXI	Donau	Wien
XXXII	Süd	Augsburg
XXXIII	Ostsee	Schwerin
XXXIV	Rhein-West-mark	Saarbrücken
XXXV	Alpenland	Graz
XXXVI	Alpenland	Salzburg
XXXVII	Böhmen-Mähren	Reichenberg
XXXVIII	Böhmen-Mähren	Karlsbad
XXXIX	Böhmen-Mähren	Brünn
XXXX	Weichsel	Bromberg
XXXXI	Weichsel	Thorn
XXXXII	Warthe	Gnesen
XXXXIII	Warthe	Litzmannstadt
XXXXIV	Nordost	Gumbinnen
XXXXV	Südwest	Strassburg

(6) *SS regiments.* The organization of the SS in the echelons below the sub-districts is on a unit rather than a territorial basis, although each unit controls a definite territory. Each sub-district headquarters controls two to four SS infantry regiments (*SS-Fuss-Standarten*). After 5 years of war these regiments are now no more than skeleton cadres carrying on the tradition and, to a limited extent, the functions of the organization until their members in the Armed Forces and *Waffen-SS* are demobilized. Regiments are numbered consecutively from 1 to 125.

Each regiment is normally composed of three active battalions (*Sturmbanne*) and one reserve battalion (*Reserve-Sturmbann*). The active battalions bear Roman numerals.

Each active battalion consists of four companies (*Stürme*) and a medical detachment (*Sanitätsstaffel*). One of the four companies may serve locally as a guard company (*Wachkompanie*) and one as an emergency company (*Alarm-Kompanie*), while the remaining two are assigned to general duties.

A reserve battalion has two reserve companies and a reserve medical detachment.

Recruiting battalions (*Ergänzungs-Sturmbanne*) are reserve battalions which undergo 3 months drilling prior to summary transfer to the *Waffen-SS*.

Each company is divided into three or four platoons (*Trupps*), each composed of three sections (*Scharen*). The file (*Rotte*) is the smallest unit of the SS.

There are a number of specialist and technical units (*Sondereinheiten*) in the SS. Among them are: cavalry regiments (*SS-Reiterstandarten (R)*); signal battalions (*SS-Nachrichten-Sturmbanne (N)*); engineer battalions (*SS-Pionier-Sturmbanne (Pi)*); medical companies (*SS-Sanitäts-Stürme (San. St.)*); motor transport companies (*SS-Kraftfahr-Stürme (K)*); motor-cycle companies (*SS-Kradstürme*).

Within each district there is also a supplementary reserve formation (*Stammabteilung*), which is organized into territorial sub-units (*Bezirke*).

6. The *Waffen-SS*

a. ORIGIN AND GROWTH. Ever since 1933 a portion of the SS has been armed and trained along military lines and served on a full-time basis, living in special barracks. These troops were originally known as the *SS-Verfügungstruppen (SS-VT)*, the name indicating that they were held at the disposition of Hitler for any purpose whatever. By 1939 four regiments (*Standarten*) of these troops had been organized.

The *Verfügungstruppen* took part in the occupation of Austria and Czechoslovakia side by side with the troops of the Army. During the months preceding the outbreak of the war they were given intensive military training and were formed into regular military units which then took an active part in the Polish campaign. Elements of the Death's Head Formations (*Totenkopfverbände*) also took the field as military units.

During the following winter and spring the regiments which had fought in Poland were expanded into brigades and later into full divisions. This purely military branch of the SS was at first known as the *Bewaffnete SS* (literally "Armed SS") and later as the *Waffen-SS*. The *Leibstandarte SS "Adolf Hitler"* became the SS division of the same name; the *Standarte "Deutschland"*, together with the Austrian *Standarte "Der Führer"*, formed the *Verfügungs Division*, to which a third regiment "Langemarck" was presently added to form the division "Das Reich"; and the *Totenkopf* units were formed into the *"Totenkopf"* Division. These three divisions were to be the nucleus of the *Waffen-SS* in its rapid expansion which followed.

The *Waffen-SS* is based on the tradition of the General *SS*. It retained the strict racial selection and the emphasis on political indoctrination of the *SS*. The reasons for its formation were as much political as they were a welcome opportunity to acquire for the *SS* the officer material which was to prove so valuable later on.

With the intensification of the war the *Waffen-SS* became the proponent of the recruiting of "Nordic" peoples for military service in the interest of Germany. In 1940 the *Standarten "Nordland"* and *"Westland"* were created in order to incorporate such "Germanic" volunteers into the *Waffen-SS*. They were combined with the existing *Standarte "Germania"* to form the *"Wiking"* Division.

In the subsequent years the *Waffen-SS* proceeded to form native "Legions" in most occupied areas. These, in turn, were later converted into *Waffen-SS* brigades and divisions.

A slackening in the principles of racial selection occurred only after the war took on much less favorable aspects. During 1943 and 1944 the *SS* turned more and more toward frantic recruiting of all available manpower in occupied areas. While its major effort was directed toward the incorporation of the "racial" Germans (*Volksdeutsche*), a method was devised which permitted the recruiting of foreigners of all nationalities on a grand scale, while retaining at least some semblance of the original principles of "Nordic" superiority. Spreading foreigners thinly throughout trustworthy established units soon proved insufficient to digest the mass of recruits. Consequently divisions of foreigners were formed which received a sprinkling of regular *Waffen-SS* cadres. Finally the necessity arose to complement the officer corps of the *Waffen-SS* with foreigners.

Still very much concerned with the racial aspects of its units, the *Waffen-SS* developed a system of nomenclature which dubs the unit as foreign by an addition to its name.

Units containing a high percentage of "racial" Germans and "Germanic" volunteers (i.e. Scandinavians, Dutch, Flemings, Walloons, and Frenchmen), carry the designation *"Freiwilligen-"* as part of their names, e.g. *11. SS-Freiwilligen-Panzergrenadier-Division "Nordland"*. Units containing a preponderance of "non-Germanic" personnel, especially members of the Slavic and Baltic peoples, carry the designation *"Waffen-"*

as part of their names, e.g. *15. Waffen-Grenadier-Division-SS* (*Lett. Nr. 1*). Officers of "non-Germanic" origin cannot become full-fledged members of the *SS* officer corps. They are designated as *Waffen-Führer der SS*, and the individual rank is always given in the same manner, e.g. *Waffen-Untersturmführer*.

There is no doubt that this rapid expansion has somewhat modified the character of the *Waffen-SS* as a political elite formation. Nevertheless, the crack divisions of this organization may still be expected to fight to the very end, especially since the individual soldier and especially the individual officer have been made to feel personally involved in the endless series of war crimes, and strong propaganda has convinced most that their treatment, either in captivity or after defeat, will compare very unfavorably with that accorded other members of the armed forces.

The *Waffen-SS* at present consists of at least 31 divisions and three brigades, as well as a number of independent smaller units. Of the divisions seven are *Panzer* divisions. They form the strongest and politically most reliable portion of the *Waffen-SS*. The balance consists of five *Panzer Grenadier* divisions, five mountain divisions (of which at least one is believed to have been disbanded), seven infantry divisions, and two cavalry divisions. Three other divisions have been identified, but their type is not certain. About a third of the divisions are classified as "non-Germanic". Of the brigades at least one is of the *Panzer Grenadier* type and its strength is little less than that of a division.

Of the 13 identified *SS* Corps five are *Panzer* corps, two mountain corps, four infantry corps and two of uncertain type. At least one *SS Panzer* Army exists. It played a prominent part in the Ardennes counteroffensive in December 1944.

Among the divisions of the *Waffen-SS* one is designated as the *SS-Polizei Division*. This is the only unit made up of members of the police which has been fully incorporated into the *Waffen-SS*. It is not to be confused with the *SS-Polizei-Regimenter*, which have remained part of the police and are described in a separate section below.

b. RECRUITING, TRAINING, AND REPLACEMENT IN THE *Waffen-SS*. (1) *Recruiting*. (a) *General*. In principle, no new members were accepted for the *SS* after 1933 except from selected graduates of the Hitler Youth. The creation of

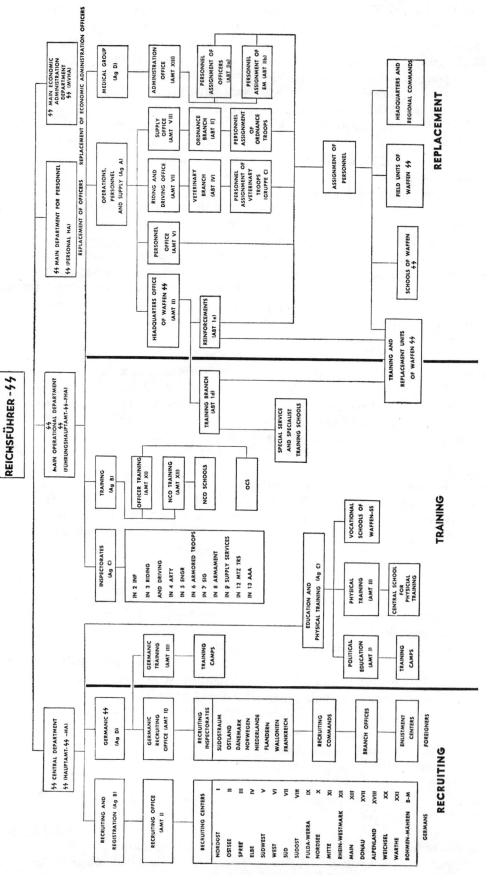

Figure 4.—Control of SS recruiting, training, and replacement.

the *Waffen-SS* and its rapid growth have caused the partial suspension of this rule, although service in the *Waffen-SS* does not necessarily entail membership in the General *SS*.

(b) *Pre-war recruitment.* Suitable *SS* candidates were singled out while still in the Hitler Youth. In particular boys who had proved themselves, often under *SS* leadership, in the HJ patrol service (*HJ-Streifendienst*) were welcomed as future *SS* men. If the candidate satisfied *SS* requirements with respect to political reliability, racial purity, and physique, he was accepted at the age of 18 as a candidate (*Bewerber*). On the occasion of the annual Party Congress (*Reichsparteitag*) in September of the same year, he was accepted as an aspirant (*Anwärter*), received an *SS* certificate (*SS-Ausweis*), and was enrolled in the ranks of the *SS*.

(c) *Wartime recruitment.* Recruitment and enrollment of new members for the *SS* have become of particular importance in view of the great expansion of the *Waffen-SS* during the war. The *SS* Central Department (*SS-Hauptamt*) is responsible for recruiting and registration of Germans and of "Germanic" and "non-Germanic" foreigners for the *Waffen-SS*. It exercises such functions for German and "Germanic" personnel through the Recruiting and Registration Group (*Amtsgruppe B*), and for "non-Germanic" foreigners through Group D—Germanic SS (*Amtsgruppe D*).

The *SS Main Operational Department* (*SS-Führungshauptamt—SS-FHA*), which is responsible for the operational control of the *Waffen-SS,* lays down the general policy on recruiting and notifies its special requirements from time to time. The *SS* Central Department, however, remains responsible for the whole recruiting system of both the General *SS* and the *Waffen-SS*. Recruiting for the General *SS*, now almost at a standstill as a result of the war, is carried out through its own local units.

Service in the *Waffen-SS* is, at least officially, voluntary. The *Waffen-SS* claims priority over all other branches of the Armed Forces in the selection of recruits. To meet the high rate of casualties and the expansion of *Waffen-SS* field divisions, service in the *Waffen-SS* was made compulsory for all members of the General *SS* and voluntary transfer of personnel after being inducted into any of the other branches of the Armed Forces was permitted. Since 1943 a great amount of pressure has been exerted on mem-

bers of the Hitler Youth to "volunteer" for the *Waffen-SS*. Still more recently, complete Army, Navy, and Air Force units were taken over by the *Waffen-SS*, given *SS* training, and incorporated into its field units.

(d) *Recruitment machinery within Germany.* The enlistment drives of the *Waffen-SS* within Germany, at first occurring at irregular intervals, are now practically continuous, indicating the great need for replacements. *The SS-Standarte "Kurt Eggers",* through its various agencies is the most successful propaganda machinery for the *Waffen-SS*. Through its war reporter battalion (*Kriegsberichter Abteilung*) it publicizes the important role of the *Waffen-SS* in the German press. Recruitment for the *Waffen-SS* is regionally organized and controlled by the recruiting office (*Ergänzungsamt—Amt I*), which is subordinate to the Recruiting and Registration Group. The regional organization consists of recruiting centers (*Ergänzungsstellen*), which are named in accordance with the *SS* districts (*SS-Oberabschnitte*) in which they are located. They also carry the Roman numeral of the *Wehrkreis* and are always located at the *Wehrkreis* headquarters city, except in *SS* district *"Mitte"*, where the recruiting center is at Braunschweig instead of Hannover, and *SS* district *"Weichsel"*, where it is at Gotenhafen instead of Danzig. Some of these recruiting centers also maintain branch offices outside Germany for the recruitment of racial Germans (*Volksdeutsche*). The recruiting centers, in cooperation with various State and military authorities effect the release of the examined and accepted applicants by the Reich Labor Service and by the recruiting sub-area headquarters (*Wehrbezirkskommando*). The recruits are then sent to a specific training and replacement unit or maneuver area of the *Waffen-SS*.

In January 1945, the recruiting centers for the *Waffen-SS* were combined with those of the Army for its volunteers for the officer and non-commissioned officer careers and for *Volks Grenadier* divisions. Under Himmler's orders "combined recruiting centers of the Army and *Waffen-SS*" (*Ergänzungsstellen des Heeres und der Waffen-SS*) were set up in each *Wehrkreis*, with branch offices in all major cities.

(e) *Recruitment machinery outside Germany.* The original decision to enlist "Germanic" and "non-Germanic" foreigners to serve with the *Waffen-SS* was based on the propaganda rather than on the fighting value of these volunteers. No doubt for this reason the men were mostly organized in small independent national legions.

In Scandinavia and the occupied countries of the West, the recruiting was undertaken largely by the local Nazi and Quisling parties; in the Baltic states by the German controlled governments; and in the Balkans by the German authorities in agreement with the governments concerned. With the growing need for reinforcements, a large element of compulsion entered into the recruiting campaigns. At the same time the small uneconomic legions were reorganized into regiments and battalions, either to be incorporated into existing *Waffen-SS* divisions or to form the basis for new divisions and brigades. Early in 1943 the German government, in exchange for promises to deliver certain quantities of war equipment, obtained from the governments of Rumania, Hungary, and Slovakia their consent to an all-out recruiting drive for the *Waffen-SS* among the "racial" Germans domiciled in those countries. In effect, all able-bodied men who could be considered to be of German origin, including some who could scarcely speak the language, were induced by various forms of social and economic pressure to volunteer, and many men already serving in the Armies of these three countries were transferred to the Germans. Well over 100,000 men were obtained in this manner and were distributed among all the divisions of the *Waffen-SS*.

The whole of this foreign recruiting organization is controlled by the Germanic recruiting office (*Germanisches Ergänzungsamt—Amt II*) in the Germanic *SS* group (*Amtsgruppe D—Ag D*). Orginally this recruiting organization consisted of a number of recruiting commands (*Ersatzkommandos*) established in the principal cities of the occupied countries. Subsequently these were reorganized as *SS* recruiting inspectorates (*SS-Ersatzinspektionen*) responsible for recruiting over a wide area, e.g. *SS* recruiting inspectorate *Südostraum* at Vienna for the whole of the Balkans. Such inspectorates control a number of recruiting commands covering smaller areas, which again are subdivided into branch offices (*Nebenstellen*); finally, there are various enlistment centers (*Werbestellen*) under each branch office.

(2) *Training*. (a) *General*. Propaganda on behalf of the *SS*, political education, physical training, pre-military and technical training, as well as training within the *SS*, are the responsibility of the *SS* Central Department. However, the responsibility for the military training of *Waffen-SS* units devolves entirely on the *SS* Main Operational Department.

Before the war the *SS* aspirant in his first year of service trained for the *SA* Defense Training Badge (*SA-Wehrabzeichen*) and the Reich Sports Badge in bronze (*bronzenes Reichssportabzeichen*). He was then called up first for six months of service in the Reich Labor Service, and then for his term of duty in the German Army. After two and a half years, he returned to the *SS* to receive further intensive training and indoctrination. Finally, on the ninth of November following his return to civil life, he was inducted into the *SS* as a full *SS* man. The outbreak of the war and the creation of the *Waffen-SS* interrupted this training schedule.

(b) *Propaganda and political education*. The Office for Political Education (*Amt Weltanschauliche Erziehung—Amt I*) in the Education and Physical Training Group (*Amtsgruppe C—Ag C*) is responsible for propaganda and the political education of German personnel. This is carried out mainly in two ways. In the first place this office supervises the issuance of a number of propaganda publications, such as the *Waffen-SS* recruiting handbook *"Dich ruft die Waffen-SS"*, the series of *SS* educational booklets (*SS-Schulungshefte*), a news magazine for *SS* and Police (*SS-Informationsdienst*), and an illustrated magazine with stories and articles for more general consumption (*SS-Leitheft*). Secondly, this office holds political education courses for *SS* officers and enlisted personnel in *SS* training camps (*SS-Ausbildungslager*) and in addition is responsible for the appointment of education officers (*Schulungsoffiziere*) to the staffs of the *SS* training schools. Political and propaganda directives for the *Waffen-SS* also emanate from this office.

The foreign recruits often require special indoctrination before they can be handed over to the *Waffen-SS* as fit for its military training. To meet this need special training camps (*Ausbildungslager*) were established. Such camps and the whole political education of foreign volunteers are under the control and supervision of the Office for Germanic Training (*Germanische Erziehung—Amt III*) in the Germanic *SS* group. This office issues a number of propaganda publications for foreign volunteers, including a magazine for each nationality in its own language and also a number of newspapers.

(c) *Physical and preliminary training.* The Office for Physical Training (*Amt für Leibeserziehung—Amt II*) in the Education and Physical Training Group is charged with the responsibility for physical training of all branches of the SS. The SS instructors in athletics and physical culture are trained at the SS Central School for Physical Training (*SS-Reichsschule für Leibesübungen*), and special SS manuals on the subject are issued. In addition the Office for Physical Training has set up special physical training camps for the Germanic SS outside the Reich. The SS has for some time taken a very active interest in the premilitary training programs of the Hitler Youth and other Party organizations.

(d) *Technical training.* As part of the general program of training and preparation for the *Waffen-SS,* special SS Higher Vocational Schools (*SS-Berufsoberschulen*) have been set up under the control and direction of the Education and Physical Training Group for giving higher technical training to candidates for the *Waffen-SS.* All German boys who are apprentices or students in business, trade, or agriculture, and are attending a trade or technical school may apply for entry into such a school as officer applicants of the *Waffen-SS.* The wartime course is limited to 1½ years and is free to the selected candidates.

The Vocational Schools of the *Waffen-SS* (*Berufsschulen der Waffen-SS*) give similar training, though of a lower standard.

(e) *Military training.* The military training of the *Waffen-SS* is controlled entirely by the SS Main Operational Department, which exercises this function through three main agencies:

The Training Branch (*Abt 1 d*) in the Headquarters Office of the *Waffen-SS* (*Kommandoamt der Waffen-SS—Amt II*) supervises and coordinates the whole sphere of training in the *Waffen-SS.* This branch is divided into a number of sections, each of which is responsible for a certain type of training. Its mission includes close cooperation with all other offices and inspectorates concerned with military training, liaison with the training agencies of the German Army, and issuance and control of all instructional material. It also registers and controls the training of future SS staff officers, providing courses for supply officers (*1 b-Lehrgänge*) and for intelligence officers (*1 c-Lehrgänge*).

The SS inspectorates (*SS-Inspektionen*), which are combined into an inspectorate group (*Amtsgruppe C—Ag C*), are responsible for the technical and unit training within the various branches of service. There are ten such inspectorates, numbered in a broken series from one to 13. Each one is headed by an Inspector (*Inspekteur*), who is directly responsible to the Chief of the SS Main Operational Department. It may control experimental and demonstration units and staffs, and it usually works in close liaison with the corresponding inspectorate in the *OKH.*

The Training Group (*Amtsgruppe B—Ag B*) is responsible for individual officer and noncommissioned officer training. It exercises these functions through the Office for Officer Training (*Amt Führerausbildung—Amt XI*), which controls all officer candidate schools (*SS-Junkerschulen*) and courses, and the Office for Noncommissioned Officer Training (*Amt Unterführerausbildung*), which controls all noncommissioned officer schools and courses.

(f) *Schools and courses.* During 1943 and 1944 the *Waffen-SS* established schools and courses for almost all branches of military affairs needed by a complete and well balanced military organization. As a result, it is now thoroughly equipped with schooling facilities of its own, although certain highly specialized types of personnel are still trained in special SS courses at regular Army schools.

The SS schools may be divided into four categories: special service schools, officer candidate schools, noncommissioned officer schools, and specialist training establishments.

Almost all the schools of the *Waffen-SS* have certain basic elements of organization in common, which are analogous to those of Army schools. They are headed by a commander who is assisted by a headquarters staff (*Kommandostab*). Under this they have instruction groups (*Lehrgruppen*) of battalion status and inspectorates (*Inspektionen*) of company status.

Special-service schools (*Waffenschulen*) have the function of providing specialized and advanced training for officers and enlisted personnel in their particular branch of service (*Waffengattung*). The *Waffen-SS* has special-service schools for mountain infantry, cavalry, *Panzer Grenadiers,* and *Panzer* troops, but not for ordinary infantry; this is explained by the fact that all *Waffen-SS* field divisions except some of those which are composed principally of non-

German personnel are either *Panzer, Panzer Grenadier,* cavalry, or mountain divisions.

The courses at the special-service schools may be divided into three main categories: reserve officer candidate courses (*Reserve-Junker-Lehrgänge—RJL*); preparatory courses (*Vorbereitungs-Lehrgänge*) for officer applicants (*Führer-Bewerber—FB*) and reserve officer applicants (*Reserve-Führer-Bewerber—RFB*); and courses for technicians, which are found mainly at the special-service schools of the signal troops and artillery and which use special technical equipment peculiar to their respective arms.

Most of the *Waffen-SS* special-service schools have demonstration regiments (*Lehrregimenter*) attached to them for demonstrating and instructing and also for experimenting with new weapons and tactics.

Officer candidate schools are discussed in the separate section on the officer corps below.

The two basic types of establishments for the training of noncommissioned officers for the *Waffen-SS* are the noncommissioned officer schools and separate noncommissioned officer courses. The former are for professional noncommissioned officers and the latter for reserve noncommissioned officers.

The *SS* noncommissioned officer schools (*SS-Unterführer-Schulen*), which train German and "Germanic" personnel, and the *SS* and foreign personnel noncommissioned officer schools (*SS-und Waffen-Unterführer-Schulen*), which train German and "non-Germanic" personnel, are organized into either one or two battalions, a battalion consisting of a headquarters and four companies. Each company usually trains noncommissioned officers for a different branch of service. On completing the course an *SS* noncommissioned officer applicant (*SS-Unterführer-Bewerber*) is appointed *SS* noncommissioned officer candidate (*SS-Unterführer-Anwärter*); he may become a sergeant (*SS-Unterscharführer*) only after demonstrating his abilities in a troop unit.

Besides the courses for professional noncommissioned officers held at the noncommissioned officer schools, the *Waffen-SS* conducts short-term noncommissioned officer courses (*Unterführer-Lehrgänge*) for reserve noncommissioned officers. These are usually held in the field divisions during quiet periods.

Specialist training establishments have the mission of training of officer technicians (*Technische Führer der Sonderlaufbahnen*) and particularly noncommissioned officer technicians (*Unterführer der Sonderlaufbahnen*). Specialist training establishments include the Motor Technical School of the *Waffen-SS* (*Kraftfahrtechnische Lehranstalt der Waffen-SS* at Vienna, the Ordnance Technical School of the *Waffen-SS* (*Waffentechnische Lehranstalt der Waffen-SS*) at Dachau, riding and driving schools, motor transport supply-troop schools, and a number of other types.

(3) *Replacement.* Unlike the Army, the *Waffen-SS* does not decentralize the control of its replacement system to its regional headquarters in Germany. The entire replacement system of the *Waffen-SS* is administered centrally by the *SS* Main Operational Department. Replacement requisitions from field units for ordinary personnel are sent through this department direct to the replacement units concerned. Those for officers go to the *SS* Main Department for Personnel (*SS-Personnel Hauptamt*), except that for all officers in the economic administrative service the *SS* Main Economic Administrative Department (*SS-Wirtschaft-Verwaltungs-Hauptamt*) is the responsible replacement agency.

The entire system of transferring and assigning *Waffen-SS* personnel to training and replacement units, field units, schools, and headquarters is controlled by the reinforcement branch (*Abt I e*) in the Headquarters Office of the *Waffen-SS* (*Kommandoamt der Waffen-SS—Amt II*). This branch works in close cooperation with various other agencies regarding the transfer and assignment of specialist personnel. For example, the veterinary troops of the *Waffen-SS* are supervised by the Veterinary Branch (*Abt IV*) in the Riding and Driving Office (*Amt Reit- und -Fahrwesen—Amt VI*), which also conducts their training and courses, while all ordnance troops are controlled by the Ordnance Branch (*Abt II*) in the office for supply (*Nachschubamt—Amt VII*). Both these branches maintain personnel assignment sections for their respective specialist personnel. Medical personnel comes under the control of the Administration Office (*Amt XIII*) in the Medical Group (*Sanitätswesen der Waffen-SS-Amtsgruppe D—Ag D*).

c. OFFICER CORPS OF THE *Waffen-SS.* (1) *General.* The *SS* Main Department for Personnel (*SS-Personal - Hauptamt — SS - Pers HA*) keeps a central card file on all officers of the *SS.* The original officer corps of the *SS* comprised a number of different categories, mainly dependent upon the nature of their employment. The creation of the *Waffen-SS* and its employment as a powerful military force necessitated the formation of a separate officer corps for the *Waffen-SS*. An officer may, and often does, have different ranks in the two corps.

(2) *Selection of prospective officers.* The selection, registration, and training of prospective officers for the *Waffen-SS* is the responsibility of the *SS* Main Operational Department, which exercises this function through the Office for Officer Training (*Amt Führerausbildung—Amt XI*) in the Training Group (*Amtsgruppe B*). At the time of induction the recruiting center reports officer material to this office. Every volunteer has the opportunity to enter the officer career of the *Waffen-SS*, depending upon three qualifications, namely, his character as a German, his performance as a National Socialist and a member of the *SS*, and his qualifications as a soldier and leader.

Men selected as prospective officer candidates proceed to a training and replacement unit or training camp of the *Waffen-SS*. The unit commander concerned decides whether a candidate is fit or unfit for the officer career of the *Waffen-SS* after he has completed his basic training. The branch of service to which an approved candidate is to be allotted is then determined by the Office for Officer Training in consultation with the various offices and inspectorates of the *SS* Main Operational Department.

The officer corps of the *Waffen-SS* comprises three categories:

(a) *Active officers of the Waffen-SS* (*Aktive Führer der Waffen-SS*), those who adopt the career of *SS* officer. The elite of this category includes all pre-war graduates of the *SS* officer candidate schools.

(b) *Reserve officers of the Waffen-SS* (*Reserve-Führer der Waffen-SS*).

(c) *Foreign officers of the SS* (*Waffen-Führer der SS*). This category includes all active and reserve officers of "non-Germanic" nationalities. Those eligible include men who previously held a commission in their own armies and those who show leadership qualifications in the ranks of the *Waffen-SS*. This category, however, does not include officers coming from "Germanic" countries, who may become full-fledged officers (*SS-Führer*) of either the active or reserve category

(3) *Officer candidate schools. Waffen-SS* schools designed to train and provide officer ma-

terial are of two basic types: *SS* officer candidate schools (*SS-Junkerschulen*), which train German and "Germanic" officers; and *SS* and foreign personnel officer candidate schools (*SS- und Waffen-Junkerschulen*), which train both German personnel and "non-Germanic" foreigners. The courses last about 6 months and are differentiated as either war-officer-candidate courses (*Kriegsjunker-Lehrgänge*) or war-officer-candidate courses for foreign personnel (*Kriegs-Waffenjunker-Lehrgänge*).

(a) *Active officers.* The active officer candidates of the *Waffen-SS* attend the war-officer-candidate courses (*Kriegjunker-Lehrgänge*) held at the officer candidate schools. These candidates must have previously completed a preparatory course (*Vorbereitungs-Lehrgäng*) held either at a special-service school or at a training and replacement unit of the *Waffen-SS*. They start this course as active officer applicants (*Führer-Bewerber—FB*) and subsequently receive the title of *SS-Junker* and the equivalent rank of the lowest grade of sergeant (*Unterscharführer*). After the mid-term examinations at the officer candidate school they become *Standartenjunker* with the equivalent rank of *Scharführer,* and after the final examination *Standardtenoberjunker* (equivalent to *Hauptscharführer*). Candidates then return to their units and, after a minimum of two months, are appointed 2d Lieutenant (*Untersturmführer*) by the *RF-SS* upon the recommendation of their regimental commanders.

(b) *Reserve officers.* Reserve officer candidates of the *Waffen-SS*, after taking a preparatory course as *Reserve-Führer-Bewerber—RFB*, become *SS-Junker der Reserve* and then attend a reserve officer candidate course (*Reserve-Junker-Lehrgang*), held at a special-service school of the *Waffen-SS* and lasting about 4 months. After the mid-term examinations they become *Standartenjunker der Reserve,* and after the final examinations *Standartenoberjunker der Reserve.* Foreign officers of the reserve (*Waffen-Führer der Reserve*) also attend the reserve officer candidate courses.

Like active officer candidates, the graduates become officers only after at least 2 months of service with a unit.

(c) *Foreign officers of the SS.* "Non-Germanic" officer candidates attend a war officer candidate course for foreign personnel (*Kriegs-Waffenjunker-Lehrgang*) held at the *SS* and foreign personnel officer-candidate schools (*SS- und*

Waffenjunker-Schulen). After its completion they return to their units and after a period of 2 months are appointed *Waffen-Untersturmführer* by the *RF-SS* upon the recommendation of their regimental commander.

(4) *Officer candidate courses.* Apart from the regular courses at the officer-candidate schools described above, the *Waffen-SS* conducts the following special officer-candidate courses:

Courses for partly disabled *SS* officer candidates (*Lehrgänge für versehrte SS-Junker*) held at the officer-candidate schools.

Special course for Panzer officer candidates (*Panzer-Junker-Sonderlehrgang*).

(5) *Other officer training establishments.* The *Waffen-SS* maintains medical and economic administrative officer training establishments with the function of providing for and supervising the military education of prospective active medical and economic administrative officers of the *Waffen-SS* during the period of their studies at universities and other institutions.

(6) *Specialist careers.* All officer candidates choosing a specialist career (*Sonderlaufbahn*) must have certain basic qualifications. They must have spent half a year with a field unit and successfully graduated from an officer candidate school of the *Waffen-SS*.

The following are the various specialist careers of the *Waffen-SS*:

(a) *Medical career.* This includes:

Physician (*SS-Führer und Arzt*)

Medical technician (*SS-Führer im Sanitätstechn. Dienst*)

Dentist (*SS-Führer und Zahnarzt*)

Pharmacist (*SS-Führer und Apotheker*)

The Medical Academy of the *Waffen-SS* provides for the training of all officers in the medical career. Besides their formal training students attend lectures and practical demonstrations at various universities.

(b) *Veterinary career.* This includes:

Veterinary (*SS-Führer und Veterinär*)

Veterinary technician (*SS-Führer im Veterinärtechn. Dienst*)

Officers in the veterinary career receive their specialist training in the Blacksmith School as well as in the veterinary training and replacement unit of the *Waffen-SS*.

(c) *Administrative career.* The Officer School of the Economic Administrative Service of the *SS* gives lectures and provides practical application for officers in the administrative career. Be-

sides lectures at universities, the training includes practical experience and instruction at an administrative office of the *Waffen-SS*.

(d) *Ordnance technician career.* This includes:

Ordnance supply officer (*SS-Führer im Waffen- und Munitionsdienst*)

Ordnance officer technician (*Techn.SS-Führer W*)

Engineering officer (*Techn.SS-Führer W Ing.*)

The Ordnance Technical School and the engineering schools of the *Waffen-SS* provide for the specialized training of these officers. They also attend lectures and receive practical application at technical institutions.

(e) *Motor technical career.* This includes:

Motor officers (*Technische SS-Führer (K) I*)

Motor officers (*Technische SS-Führer (K) II*)

The Motor Technical School of the *Waffen-SS* provides for and supervises the training of these officers.

(f) *Other specialist careers of the Waffen-SS* include:

Officer technician (sig) (*Technische SS-Führer (N)*)

Judge advocate (*SS-Führer und Richter*)

Notary (*SS-Führer und Beurkundungsführer*)

Water supply officer (*SS-Führer und Wehrgeologe*)

Bandmaster (*SS-Führer und Musikführer*)

The officers in these specialist careers, besides their instruction at technical schools and other establishments of the *Waffen-SS*, receive specialized training at the special-service schools or specialist training schools of the *Waffen-SS*.

d. SUPPLY SYSTEM OF THE *Waffen-SS*. (1) *General.* Units of the *Waffen-SS* operating under the tactical control of the Army utilize the regular Army supply channels for supplies of rations, fuel, heavy equipment, and ammunition. In addition, however, the *SS* maintains its own system of supply distinct from that of the Armed Forces and not subject to control or supervision by the latter. For this purpose a large network of depots and stores has been built up in Germany and in occupied territory.

(2) *Control.* Operationally these depots and stores come under the control of the *SS* Main Operational Department, which is responsible for the equipment and supply of *SS* units and establishments when not under the tactical control of

the Army. The *SS* Main Economic Administrative Department, on the other hand, is responsible for the detailed administration of these depots, or for the general supervision of administration where there is decentralization of its authority, e.g. to the economic official (*SS-Wirtschafter*) with a Higher *SS* and police commander in occupied territory. The actual responsibility for supply is divided between the *SS* Main Operational Department, which is responsible for initial equipment and the supply and maintenance of arms, ammunition, technical equipment, and transport vehicles, and the *SS* Main Economic Administrative Department, which is responsible for rations, clothing, personal equipment, coal, wood, and fodder.

For certain types of heavy equipment which are obtainable only from Army depots, agreement is reached between the *OKH* and the *SS* Main Operational Department, which becomes responsible for the general supervision of stocks, maintenance, and repair once such equipment has been handed over to an *SS* unit.

Although the *SS* and Police supply and administration system in wartime operates primarily for the *Waffen-SS* and *SS* police units, its organization and installations are also at the disposal of the General *SS* and the *SS* Death's-Head Formations.

(3) *Regional organization of supply.* The *SS* Main Economic Administrative Department controls all regional supply depots. There is a marked tendency for *SS* depots and administrative services to be grouped around concentration camps, notably Dachau and Oranienburg. This arrangement centralized administrative matters, as the concentration camps come under the control of the *SS* Main Economic Administrative Department, and the inmates of such camps provide a cheap source of labor.

At each *SS* district headquarters in Germany proper there is an administrative office (*Verwaltungsamt*) which controls and supervises all supply depots and installations within its area. Similarly at the *SS* sub-district headquarters there is an administrative branch (*Verwaltungsabteilung*) with the same functions. At the headquarters of an *SS* garrison command (*SS-Standortbereich*) there is an *SS* garrison administration headquarters (*SS-Standortverwaltung*) dealing with supply and finance in its area and directly subordinate to the respective *SS* district and sub-district.

In occupied territory, there is an economic section controlled by an official (*SS-Wirtschafter*) on the staff of an *HSSPf*. He is responsible for the administration of all depots and supplies in his region. Where field units of the *Waffen-SS* are likely to operate in a particular area for a considerable period, special supply bases (*Stützpunkte*) are usually established at convenient points. These are small and temporary in character.

(4) *Channels of supply.* All *Waffen-SS* units requisition their supplies from the *SS* Main Operational Department, which either makes the issue itself or instructs the *SS* Main Economic Administrative Department to do so. The latter then either dispatches the material direct to the unit from one of the central depots or from the factory, or arranges for it to be made available to the unit at the nearest convenient sub-depot.

The main stocks of supply are held in central *SS* depots. These are of two kinds:

Main supply depots (*SS-Hauptwirtschaftslager—HWL*), containing miscellaneous types of supplies.

Special depots, including *SS* ordnance depots, motor transport supply depots and parks, signal equipment depots, medical equipment depots, and clothing depots.

From these central depots, outlying sub-depots are supplied. These may be either *SS* supply depots (*SS-Nachschublager*), mainly found near the borders of Germany and in occupied territory, or *SS* troop supply depots (*SS-Truppenwirtschaftslager—TWL*), which hold stocks of clothing, light equipment, fuel, and other goods.

At the time, when the supply lines on the Eastern Front were too far extended, *SS* supply service headquarters (*SS-Nachschubkommandanturen*) were established. Each of these was in itself an important group of depots and administrative offices. Although subordinate for administrative purposes to the *SS* economic official with the local *HSSPf*, it was the primary link between the *SS* main departments and main depots in Germany and the *SS* units and sub-depots in its own area. It served both as a distribution center and a supply base, and in its depots were held arms, ammunition, motor transport equipment, captured material, clothing, fuel, coal, wood, building material, and other goods. It was also empowered, subject to the approval of the *SS* economic official with the *HSSPF*, to make contracts with or purchases from private firms in its area.

(5) *Veterinary supply service.* The *Waffen-*

SS maintains its own channel of supply for its cavalry and non-motorized units. Horses for the *Waffen-SS* are procured through *SS* remount depots (*SS-Remonteämter*), which were mainly found until recently in occupied territory. These depots forward the horses to the *SS* riding and driving schools (*SS-Reit-und-Fahrschulen*), from where they either go to a unit direct or to an *SS* base veterinary depot (*SS-Heimatpferdepark*), which in turn forwards them to an *SS* veterinary depot (*SS-Pferdepark*) in a forward area, usually attached to an *SS* corps. These corps will then make distribution among their divisions which have veterinary companies. Wounded horses, after treatment in the field, go to an *SS* veterinary hospital (*SS-Pferdelazarett*) in a forward area and then to an *SS* base veterinary hospital (*SS-Heimatpferdelazarett*) in Germany. Veterinary equipment for *Waffen-SS* units can be obtained from the *SS* Central Veterinary Park (*SS-Hauptveterinärpark*) by way of one of the veterinary parks in forward areas.

(6) *Movement of supplies.* The transportation of *SS* supplies is coordinated by the transportation officer (*Transportoffizier—TO*) in the *SS* Main Operational Department. He maintains liaison both with other *SS* main departments where necessary and also with the German railway authorities and the transportation authorities of the German Army. Subordinate to him are a number of regional transportation officers, found mainly in those districts close to the German border. Other transportation officers are stationed at principal railway stations in Germany and in occupied territory. At railway junctions particularly important for *SS* movement, *SS* reloading stations (*SS-Umschlagstellen*) are established.

(7) *Repair and maintenance of vehicles and equipment.* In forward areas, besides the repair and recovery sections at divisions, independent sections may operate at supply depots or at supply service headquarters. In Germany facilities for repair exist at the appropriate *SS* central depots and also at the *SS* Ordnance Testing Workshop (*SS-Waffenamt-Prüfungswerkstätte*) and the *SS* Ordnance Works (*SS-Ausrüstungswerke*). Extensive use is also made of Army repair facilities.

(8) *Medical services.* General supervision over the medical services of the *SS* is exercised by two officers, the Chief *SS* and Police Medical Officer (*Reichsarzt SS und Polizei*), who is attached to the Personal Staff *RF-SS* (*Persönlicher Stab RF-SS*), and the Head of the *SS* Medical Group, who acts as Inspector General of *SS* Medical Services.

Actual administration is carried out by the Medical Group (*Sanitätswesen der Waffen-SS—Amtsgruppe D*) in the *SS* Main Operational Department, which controls *SS* hospitals and medical services in Germany and in occupied territory as well as the medical units attached to *SS* units in the field. It does not, however, automatically follow that all *SS* casualties are evacuated through *SS* medical channels. Local circumstances may make it difficult or inexpedient to use *SS* medical facilities, and it frequently happens that *SS* wounded are evacuated as far as base hospitals in Germany entirely through regular Army medical channels.

A great number of *SS* medical institutions, *SS* hospitals (*SS-Lazarette*), and *SS* convalescent homes (*SS-Genesungsheime*) have been identified both in Germany and in occupied areas.

e. EMPLOYMENT OF THE *Waffen-SS* IN THE FIELD.

Hitler is nominally the Supreme Commander of the *Waffen-SS*. This command is exercised only through the *RF-SS*, and it has become very doubtful of late whether Hitler has retained any power to direct Himmler in this or any other capacity.

The field headquarters of the *RF-SS* (*Feldkommandostelle RF-SS*) represents nominally the highest echelon in the direction of the employment of the *Waffen-SS*. Since Himmler is not always present at this headquarters, proper allowance should be made for the fact that the *RF-SS* will decide in person about such employment, regardless of his whereabouts at the time. No unit of the *Waffen-SS* may be dissolved, under any circumstances, by anybody but the *RF-SS*.

For military operations, units of the *Waffen-SS* are placed under command of the *OKH*. In the beginning individual units were assigned to army groups and armies as needed, although an effort was made to give them independent tasks wherever possible. Special emphasis was placed on the propaganda value of their employment, and many spectacular missions were assigned to them, although their military importance and difficulty were often exaggerated. With the progress of the Russian campaign these units became involved in tougher combat assignments. Due to the strict selection of their personnel, not only from a political point of view but also from that of health, stamina, and stature, these units were in a position to take full advantage of the strong propaganda efforts which the *SS* made in their behalf. Gaining a reputation as an elite force, divisions of the *Waffen-SS* began to control regular Army units engaged in the immediate vicinity. The next step was the formation of *SS* corps which, under *OKH* command, controlled *SS* divisions and brigades. Soon certain *SS* corps held command over a small group of *SS* units and a much larger proportion of regular Army units. Eventually, certain *SS* corps commanded Army units only. For a brief period, in 1943, an *SS* Army existed which held mainly administrative functions in northern Italy. But in the autumn of 1944, when the Sixth *Panzer* Army was formed, a large unit of the German Army was for the first time designated as an *SS* unit. Previous to that event, *SS* generals had held Army commands under the *OKH* in a few instances during the defense of Normandy and the withdrawal from France.

The territorial commanders of the *Waffen-SS* (*Befehlshaber der Waffen-SS*), who have been installed in certain occupied and annexed areas, take charge of operations only in certain special cases. For example, a coast defense sector (*Küstenverteidigungsabschnitt*) in the Netherlands was commanded by such an officer under the Commanding General in the Netherlands (LXXXVIII Army Corps). His command included training and replacement units of the *Waffen-SS,* of the *SS* Police, and of the Air Force.

In theory, the influence of the *RF-SS* ceases with the subordination of *Waffen-SS* units to the Army. In effect, however, much evidence points to the fact that he retains the right to pass on the type of employment which the Army may prescribe.

The temporary relief of Rundstedt as commander of the Western Front in 1944 is attributed, at least in part, to a conflict between him and the *RF-SS* resulting from discrepancies of opinion as to the employment of the *Waffen-SS* in that theater.

Units of the *Waffen-SS* have been employed in all theatres of the war, except in North Africa and in the original campaign in Norway. From the small beginning of regimental units participating in the Polish campaign, active employment of *Waffen-SS* units grew to at least two divisions in the Western and Balkan drives of 1940 and 1941. One division was engaged in Finland from the beginning of the Russian campaign. In Rus-

sia itself the number of *Waffen-SS* units engaged grew from five divisions in 1942 to at least four corps and 13 divisions for the better part of 1944. An *SS* brigade participated in the defense of Corsica and was later committed as a division in the Italian theater, while another appeared there to assist in the internal tasks resulting from the Italian collapse. To this were added a new division and a new brigade in 1944. Two corps and at least seven divisions fought at various times against the partisans in Yugoslavia, and one division formed an important component of the occupation forces in Greece. Two *Waffen-SS* corps and six divisions were employed in Normandy and participated in the withdrawal from France. On the Western Front one Army, at least six corps, and a minimum of nine divisions were opposing Allied forces at the beginning of 1945. Two or three corps, nine divisions, and two brigades formed the strength of the *Waffen-SS* in Hungary at that time.

Corps units of the *Waffen-SS*, such as *Panzer,* heavy artillery, observation, projector, signal, reconnaissance, and antiaircraft battalions and smaller units of the same and other types, may be used as tactical support for both *Waffen-SS* and Army units.

Ever since the *SS* increased its power over the Army so suddenly in July 1944, rumors have persisted that individual members of the *Waffen-SS* became attached to regular Army units, especially in the low echelons, in order to increase the reliability of these troops. The fact that units of the *Waffen-SS* were used to prevent mass desertions or withdrawals contrary to orders **is** established. *Waffen-SS* personnel forms the nucleus of the *Volks Grenadier* and probably also the *Volkssturm* units. To some extent personnel of the *Waffen-SS* was exchanged with Army personnel, while whole contingents of Air Corps and Navy personnel were repeatedly pressed into the service of the *Waffen-SS* when it became urgently necessary to reform badly mauled *Waffen-SS* units.

Another recent trend is the assumption of command functions in the *Waffen-SS* by high-ranking Army officers. They appear with *SS* ranks equivalent to their former Army ranks. Although this procedure may be caused merely by military expediency, it is not likely that a high-ranking German officer would assume an *SS* rank without coming under the special disciplinary rules of the *SS* and without having reconciled himself to its program, ideals, and plans for the future.

7. SS Police Units

a. INTRODUCTION. Parts of the German Order Police (*Ordnungspolizei—Orpo*) have maintained a strict military organization patterned after that of the regular Army. Known as the Barrack Police (*Kasernierte Polizei*), a branch of the Protective Police (*Schutzpolizei—Schupo*), they are quartered in large towns in Germany, usually in company strength. These units are commanded in each locality by a Commander of the Protective Police (*Kommandeur der Schutzpolizei*), who receives his orders from the Inspector of the Order Police (*Inspekteur der Ordnungspolizei*), a member of the staff of the *HSSPf* in each district. Their function is to act as a mobile reserve for the ordinary municipal police. They may be described as the lineal descendants of the old "green" police (*Landespolizei*), a quasi-military body of men permitted to Germany by the Treaty of Versailles.

For service abroad during the war these Barrack Police have been formed into *SS* police regiments (*SS-Polizei-Regimenter*) and *SS*-Police Battalions (*SS-Polizei-Bataillone*), most of them motorized, which are organized and equipped on a military basis but usually lack heavy weapons.

The development of these units started with the formation of centuries (*Hundertschaften*) in 1939, which soon developed into independent battalions. A battalion consists of about 550 men, organized into a headquarters and four companies, and equipped with rifles, machine guns, antitank guns, and armored cars. Battalions were originally numbered in the series 1 to 325. Most of them were reorganized into regiments in 1943 and numbered in one consecutive series running up to about 37. Most of these regiments appear simply as *SS-Polizei-regiment* (followed by its number), but at least one regiment is an *SS-Polizei-Gebirgsjäger-Regiment* (SS Police Mountain Infantry Regiment).

The ideology and general bearing of these units are similar to those of the *Waffen-SS*. They have gained a very similar reputation for their conduct, especially as occupation troops. These units are not part of the *Waffen-SS,* and they should not be confused with the *SS-Polizei-Division,* a *Waffen-SS* division composed of police personnel.

b. RECRUITING, TRAINING, AND REPLACEMENT. (1) *Recruiting.* Before the war candidates for the Protective Police had to meet very high standards of health and physique, to be members of the *SS* or some other Party organization, and to pass a special aptitude test. The expansion of the *SS* police units during the war made it necessary to relax these requirements. At the same time an effort was made to recruit men who had been discharged from the regular Armed Forces for one reason or another, and special privileges were offered them in the form of advanced noncommissioned officer ratings depending on the number of years of previous service.

Later on the recruiting authorities for the *SS* police units, just like those for the *Waffen-SS,* resorted more and more to the manpower of occupied countries, especially in Eastern and Southeastern Europe. These men were first used in separate units known as *Schutzmannschaften* or militia, chiefly for guard duties and small-scale counter-partisan activities; such units were then incorporated into the *SS* police organization, sometimes forming entire regiments which were called police volunteer regiments (*Polizei-Freiwilligen-Regimenter*).

(2) *Training.* The police organization maintains its own school system but frequently has to use the school facilities of either the Army or the *Waffen-SS.* All training activities are controlled and supervised by the Headquarters Office (*Kommandant*) of the Order Police in the Main Department of the Order Police (*Hauptamt Ordnungspolizei*). Personnel after induction receive basic training in the special-service schools of the police (*Polizei-Waffenschulen*) and specialized training either at the specialist training establishments of the police or the specialist training schools of the Army or *Waffen-SS.*

Noncommissioned officer and officer candidate schools of the Police provide for the training of noncommissioned officer and officer material. In addition special noncommissioned officer and officer candidate courses are held at the special-service schools of the police.

(3) *Replacement.* The replacement system of the police is likewise the responsibility of the Headquarters Office in the Main Department of the Order Police. This office includes a personnel office, a reinforcement branch, and an administration and law office which performs the functions of replacement and assignment of personnel in a manner very similar to that of the corresponding offices of the *SS* High Command.

The actual replacement units of the *SS* police regiments are the special-service schools, which were formerly called instruction battalions (*Lehr-Bataillione*). These units receive their personnel from the recruit assembly centers (*Erfassungsdienststellen*) of the Protective Police. For officers and specialist personnel, the responsible replacement units are the officer candidate schools and specialist training schools.

c. OFFICER CORPS. All officers of the Protective Police are recruited in wartime from graduates of the *SS* officer candidate schools (*SS-Junkerschulen*). They are then given special police training at police officer schools. All officers now have dual rank in the *SS* and the Protective Police.

d. SUPPLY. The *SS* police regiments have their own supply depots and their own channels of supply. They receive such supplies from the Main Ordnance Depot of the Order Police (*Hauptzeugamt der Ordnungspolizei*) and from the police procurement depots (*Polizei-Beschaffungsämter*) as well as from the clothing distribution centers of the police (*Bekleidungslieferstellen der Polizei*). For certain types of supply, however, they depend upon the supply depots and installations of the *Waffen-SS* or those of the Army.

e. EMPLOYMENT OF *SS* POLICE UNITS IN THE FIELD. The employment of police units for military purposes dates back to 1939, when a *Räumungshundertschaft der Polizei* was engaged in directing refugees who were evacuated from the western border areas. Their main mission was to keep the roads clear for the columns of the Armed Forces. The expansion into battalions was brought about in order to cope with the type of guerrilla warfare which originated in Russia behind the lines of the swiftly advancing German forces. Numerous units employed here gained valuable experience which they put to good use in their later missions in Yugoslavia, Greece, Italy, and France. *SS* police units were also stationed wherever large-scale construction of defense works was in progress, e.g. at the Atlantic Wall and in the Mediterranean defense zone. At times *SS* police units joined with combat troops in the front lines, especially where defensive operations became urgent. In most cases only elements of *SS* police regiments have been identified in one place. Battalions of the same regiment have been found in different sectors and even on different fronts.

Normally these units come under the regional command of the *HSSPf* represented by the commander of the Order Police. In certain areas special headquarters have been formed under the *HSSPf* to carry out such tasks as the combating of partisans. Sometimes *SS* police units have been placed under Army command for military operations, or they may be directly subordinate to a commander of the *Waffen-SS* who in turn comes under the Army.

Section II. AUXILIARY ORGANIZATIONS

1. Introduction

Certain militarized organizations have developed from independent or Party formations to full-fledged partners of the Armed Forces. In the field, when they operate directly for the Armed Forces, they are described as attached to them (*Wehrmachtgefolge*); but they also perform many supply, construction, policing, and training tasks of military importance when not actually associated with military units.

2. Labor Service

The German Labor Service (*Reichsarbeitsdienst —RAD*) arose from a Party organization set up in 1931 and known as the *NS-Arbeitsdienst* for the purpose of easing unemployment. It grew in importance with the rearmament of Germany, and a law in 1935 made service in the *RAD,* now separated from the Party and made into a State organization, compulsory for all young Germans. The strength of the *RAD* in 1939 is estimated at 360,000 men; it is now considerably less. The *RAD* is a Supreme Reich Authority with the same status as the Ministries. It has nevertheless maintained its strong ties to the Party, documented by the position of its chief, the *Reichsarbeitsführer,* as a member of the High Command (*Reichsleitung*) of the Party.

The mission of the *RAD* in peacetime consisted in the creation of jobs, the performance of public works, the revival of interest in the dignity of manual labor, and above all the physical hardening, disciplining, and political indoctrination of its members.

The *RAD* has its own regional organization based on 40 *Arbeitsgaue* which contain numerous groups (*Gruppen*) and detachments (*Abteilungen*). A detachment normally consists of about 200 men.

Army	SS	Police	TN (and other auxiliary police)	RAD	OT	NSKK	Party-Officials#	SA and NSFK	HJ
Gren.	SS-Mann	Anwärter	Anwärter	Arbeitsmann	Arbeiter	Sturmmann	Helfer	Sturmmann##	Hitlerjunge
Ob. Gren.	Sturmmann			Vormann	Vormann	Obersturmmann	Oberhelfer	Obersturmmann##	Rottenführer
Gefr.	Rottenführer	Unterwachtmeister	Unterwachtmeister	Obervormann	Meister	Rottenführer	Arbeitsleiter	Rottenführer	Oberrottenführer
Ob. Gefr.		Rottwachtmeister	Rottwachtmeister	Hauptvormann	Obermeister		Oberarbeitsleiter		
Stabsgefr.				Untertruppführer			Hauptarbeitsleiter		
Unt. Offz.	Unterscharführer	Wachtmeister	Wachtmeister	Truppführer	Truppführer	Scharführer		Scharführer	Kameradschaftsführer
Unt. Feldw.	Scharführer	Oberwachtmeister	Oberwachtmeister			Oberscharführer		Oberscharführer	Oberkameradschaftsführer
Feldw.	Oberscharführer	Zugwachtmeister	Zugwachtmeister	Obertruppführer	Obertruppführer	Truppführer	Bereitschaftsleiter	Truppführer	Scharführer
Ob. Feldw.	Hauptscharführer	Hauptwachtmeister	Hauptwachtmeister		Haupttruppführer	Obertruppführer	Oberbereitschaftsleiter	Obertruppführer	Oberscharführer
Stabsfeldw.	Sturmscharführer		Bereitschaftswachtmeister			Haupttruppführer	Hauptbereitschaftsleiter	Haupttruppführer	
		Meister	Meister	Unterfeldmeister					
		Obermeister							
Lt.	Untersturmführer	Leutnan	Zugführer	Feldmeister	Frontführer	Sturmführer	Einsatzleiter	Sturmführer	Gefolgschaftsführer
Ob. Lt.	Obersturmführer	Oberleutnant	Oberzugführer	Oberfeldmeister	Oberfrontführer	Obersturmführer	Obereinsatzleiter	Obersturmführer	Obergefolgschaftsführer
Hauptmann	Hauptsturmführer	Hauptmann	Bereitschaftsführer	Oberstfeldmeister	Hauptfrontführer	Hauptsturmführer	Haupteinsatzleiter	Hauptsturmführer	Hauptgefolgschaftsführer
Major	Sturmbannführer	Major	Abteilungsführer	Arbeitsführer	Stabsfrontführer	Staffelführer	Gemeinschaftsleiter	Sturmbannführer	Stammführer
Obst. Lt.	Obersturmbannführer	Oberstleutnant	Oberabteilungsführer	Oberarbeitsführer	Oberstabsfrontführer	Oberstaffelführer	Hauptgemeinschaftsleiter	Obersturmbannführer	Oberstammführer
Oberst	Standartenführer	Oberst	Landesführer	Oberstarbeitsführer	Oberstfrontführer	Standartenführer	Hauptabschnittsführer	Standartenführer	Bannführer
	Oberführer					Oberführer	Hauptbereichsleiter	Oberführer	Hauptbannführer
Gen. Maj.	Brigadeführer	Generalmajor		Generalarbeitsführer	Einsatzleiter	Brigadeführer	Hauptdienstleiter	Brigadeführer	Gebietsführer
Gen. Lt.	Gruppenführer	Generalleutnant	(Chef der TN)	Obergeneralarbeitsführer	Einsatzgruppenleiter II	Gruppenführer	Hauptbefehlsleiter	Gruppenführer	Obergebietsführer
General	Obergruppenführer	General			Einsatzgruppenleiter I	Obergruppenführer	Gauleiter	Obergruppenführer	Stabsführer
Gen. Obst.	Oberstgruppenführer	Generaloberst		Reichsarbeitsführer	Chef der OT	Korpsführer	Reichsleiter	Stabschef der SA	Reichsjugendführer
Gen. Feldm.	Reichsführer-SS								

\# This is only a selection of the many Party ranks.

\#\# SA-Sturmmann equals NSFK-Mann.
SA-Obersturmmann equals NSFK-Sturmmann.

Figure 5.—Table of equivalent ranks.

The work done by the *RAD* was of substantial military value even in peacetime. It helped to build fortifications and formed the nucleus of the construction battalions of the Army and Air Force at the outbreak of war. Such battalions, which were originally formed by the outright conversion of *RAD* groups, had an average strength of 2,000 men and consisted of four construction companies and three construction columns. These units prepared the way for the work of the engineers and did the pick and shovel work under them. During the Polish campaign the work consisted of road and railway repair work and of construction of airfields. In addition they brought up supplies, collected and sorted captured equipment, and helped with the harvest. In December 1939 the *RAD* reverted to its original form and continued to carry out its wartime duties under its own commanders and under *RAD* rules and administration. By 1943 the *RAD* men were completely militarized. In addition to the shovel work, they were employed to lay minefields and man fortifications and were taught antitank and antiaircraft defense. In 1944 such employment became more general while conditions inside Germany necessitated the use of the *RAD* to operate antiaircraft batteries, fight fires, clear bomb damage, and build temporary quarters for the bombed-out.

Units remaining in the field or finding themselves in German areas which became parts of the fighting front were often incorporated into the *Wehrmacht* without further ado.

3. Todt Organization

The *Organisation Todt (OT)* was first formed by the late Dr. Todt in 1938 to build the western defenses known in Germany as the Westwall. In wartime its *Einsatzgruppen* (Work Groups) were employed as construction units in almost all defensive construction works, especially those in France, Italy, and the Lowlands. The *OT* cooperates closely with private firms in its missions for the *Wehrmacht* and employs increasing numbers of foreign laborers. Its liaison with the Army is maintained through the fortress engineer staffs (*Festungspionierstäbe*). The transport system of the *OT* is maintained by the *NSKK* (see below). The German personnel of the *OT* is armed in order to be prepared for any surprise attack while working on the building site. Most of the men belong to age groups which are expected to have received military training during the last war. Refresher courses are held.

4. Nazi Party Motor Transport Corps

The *Nationalsozialistisches Kraftfahrkorps (NSKK)* was organized under its present title in 1931 to increase the mobility of the *SA* (Brownshirts). After 1933 the *NSKK* turned to the training of drivers for the eventual use of the Armed Forces.

As a branch (*Gliederung*) of the Party, the NSKK has its own regional organization which is divided into *Motorobergruppen* and further into *Motorgruppen*. Membership is on a voluntary basis.

Since the outbreak of war the *NSKK* has fulfilled three important functions. It has organized pre-military training in the motorized branch of the Hitler Youth, it has provided an auxiliary transportation service in the communications zone in support of the Armed Forces, and it has trained tank crews for the Army. For the transport function *NSKK* units were organized as four separate brigades (*Brigaden*).

With the forming of the *Volkssturm* in October 1944 the *NSKK* became responsible for its automotive training.

5. Technical Emergency Corps

The *Technische Nothilfe (TN)*, often referred to as the *Teno,* is a branch of the Order Police (*Ordnungspolizei*). It is a corps of engineers, technicians, and skilled and semi-skilled specialists in construction work, public utilities operation, communications, metal salvage, and other related fields.

Most of its members are men over military age. General requirements are those of the *SS* and Police.

Founded in 1919 as a strike-breaking organization the *TN* was retained after 1933 as a force of the state to cope with emergencies and dangers to the public. Incorporated into the police in 1937, the *TN* continued to perform its original mission in wartime. In addition, units of the *TN* were employed in construction and repair work and in many other technical tasks with the Armed Forces. Portions of these units have been incorporated into the Army as technical troops (*Technische Truppen*), which have since lost their identity as *TN* units entirely. *TN* units are known to have performed engineer functions for *SS-Polizei* units which were employed in defensive tasks in forward echelons.

6. Volkssturm

Founded by Hitler in October 1944, this national militia organization represents an ultimate effort to mobilize all available manpower for employment in total war. It includes all German men between the ages of sixteen and sixty who are not in the Armed Forces and who are able to bear arms. The members of the *Volkssturm* are described as soldiers for the duration of their employment, which is to take place locally wherever a given area is threatened. The *Volkssturm* has the mission of reinforcing the active strength of the Armed Forces and defending German soil to the last. It is recruited under the auspices of the Party, whose formations join in providing its cadres and officers. The leadership in the Party regions is assigned to the *Gauleiter,* the rifle training to the *SA,* and the automotive training to the *NSKK.* Beyond that all installations and institutions of the Party serve to form and train the new units. Himmler, as Commander of the Replacement Army, is responsible for the organization of the *Volkssturm* and for ordering its mobilization and employment in any particular area.

Section III.　OTHER PARTY ORGANIZATIONS

Certain uniformed organizations of the Party in addition to those described above may also be regarded as potential auxiliary units to the German military forces. They have been encountered performing important functions of a quasi-military nature in the occupied countries and will all, without exception, be called upon for either combat or supporting duties in the defense of any part of Germany proper under immediate military threat.

The National-Socialist Party itself (*Nationalsozialistische Deutsche Arbeiterpartei—NSDAP*) has an elaborate hierarchy of central, regional, and local headquarters with departments for all its manifold interests at all levels. Through this apparatus it is able to keep a close watch on all aspects of German life and all the activities of the citizens. Its High Command (*Reichsleitung*) at Munich includes bureaus (*Ämter*) which more or less parallel the Ministries of the national government in Berlin. The heads of the principal activities are called *Reichsleiter,* of whom some 16 now exist. These, together with the *Gauleiter* who head the 43 Party regions (*Gaue*), constitute the top leadership of the Party. Under them are vast numbers of Party functionaries known as political leaders (*Politische Leiter*), who have their own complicated system of ranks and uniforms and are well suited to organizing and guiding resistance within Germany.

To train the corps of political leaders in Nazi ideology and methods the Party has established a system of special schools, including four "castles of the order" (*Ordensburgen*) for highly select students and a large number of regional and district training "castles" (*Gau-* and *Kreis-Schulungsburgen*).

When the *Volkssturm* was created in October 1944, responsibility for recruiting and organizing it locally was vested in the *Gauleiter.* This is the first occasion on which the Party authorities as such have been entrusted with a function which is primarily military in nature.

Besides its regular regional and functional subdivisions the Party includes four special branches (*Gliederungen*)—the *SA, SS, NSKK,* and *HJ*—and a number of affiliated formations (*angeschlossene Verbände*), each of which is a self-contained organization with its own particular mission, regional structure, ranks, uniforms, and significance to the war effort of the nation. Since these have not been discussed in the previous sections they are dealt with briefly below.

1. Storm Troops (*Sturmabteilungen SA*)

These are organized on a pattern similar to that of the *SS.* The highest regional subdivision is the *Gruppe,* which is divided into *Standarten,* or regiments. As the oldest semi-military organization of the Party, the *SA* is designed as the Party's instrument for the training and indoctrination of its members and for supporting its domestic political aims in public. Membership in the *SA* is voluntary. Leading *SA* personalities for a time entertained hopes of an eventual merging of their organization with the Armed Forces, so as to create a "Brown Army" under their personal leadership. At the same time these leaders hoped to demand stronger revolutionary action by the Party in keeping with the anti-capitalistic tendencies inherent in the *SA,* which has always drawn its members chiefly from the lower middle-class and the lower bureaucracy. These tendencies were forcibly destroyed in the purge of 1934, in which Himmler played a leading part. From then on the *SS,* previously an organization within the *SA,* grew steadily in power and the *SA* sank into relative political unimportance. Since 1943 a rejuvenation of the *SA* has taken place, largely under the auspices of the *SS.*

Since 1939 the *SA* has made a substantial contribution to the German war effort through its assigned responsibility for military training preceding or following the period of regular military service. It also trains those who were rejected by the Armed Forces for physical reasons. In 1944 the *SA* was entrusted with the task of teaching every German marksmanship, and with the forming of the *Volkssturm* in October 1944 the *SA* became responsible for its rifle training.

The bulk of the pre-war members of the *SA* were drawn into the Army, whose 60th *Panzer Grenadier* Division is composed mainly of *SA* men and carries the name *"Feldherrnhalle"* in honor of the most elite peacetime regiment of the *SA*.

2. National-Socialist Aviation Corps *(National-sozialistisches Fliegerkorps—NSFK)*

This organization incorporated the existing associations for aviation into one Party-controlled organization in April 1937. The mission of the *NSFK* consists in pre-military training of prospective members of the Air Force, post-military training of its reservists, and general furthering of air-mindedness among the German people. Particularly outstanding have been its efforts in the development of the use of gliders. Its regional organization, like that of the *SA,* is based on *Gruppen* and *Standarten.* Membership is voluntary and excludes simultaneous membership in the *SS, SA,* or *NSKK.*

3. Hitler Youth *(Hitler-Jugend—HJ)*

All German youths between the ages of 10 and 18 belong to this organization of the Party, which is charged with their thorough pre-military training and political indoctrination. Pre-military training has been greatly expanded in the course of this war. For this purpose about 300 *Wehrertüchtigungslager* (military fitness camps) were installed, beginning in 1943. Participants in these training courses were subsequently incorporated into the Armed Forces and especially into the *Waffen-SS,* whose 12th *Panzer* Division bears the name *"Hitler-Jugend".* Graduates of the *HJ* become eligible for Party membership. They may either choose a career as Party functionaries *(Politische Leiter)* or may join the *SS, SA, NSKK,* or *NSFK.*

Girls belong to a branch of the *HJ* known as the League of German Girls *(Bund Deutscher Mädel—BDM)* and join the Party Women's Organization *(NS-Frauenschaft)* upon reaching the age of 21.

The *HJ* for boys is divided into the *Hitler-Jugend* proper (for boys from 14 to 18) and the *Deutsches Jungvolk—DJ,* for boys from 10 to 14. Its regional organization is based on *Gebiete,* which are further divided into *Banne, Stämme, Gefolgschaften, Scharen,* and *Kameradschaften.*

Units of the *HJ* have been committed to "war employment" *(Kriegseinsatz),* discharging such duties as fire fighting and air raid protection. They have also been widely employed to help with the harvest and as conductors, mail clerks, postmen, and street cleaners as well as for salvage activities and collections for war charities. Since 1943 most members of the *HJ* have had to serve as antiaircraft auxiliaries *(HJ-Luftwaffenhelfer* and *HJ-Marinehelfer),* performing many functions in the antiaircraft batteries, which relieve older men for combat duty.

Bazooka battalions *(Panzerschreckabteilungen)* have recently been formed from *HJ* personnel. Close liaison between the *HJ* and both the Armed Forces and the *Waffen-SS* is maintained by means of specially appointed liaison officers. The elite of the *HJ* is used in its special Patrol Service *(Streifendienst),* which combines all the tasks of a junior *SS* and police force. The members of this group are most unscrupulous and are used as raiding squads and informers. In Poland they formed pursuit detachments *(Rollkommandos)* serving under officers of the *SS* Death's-Head Formations.

Section IV. EMERGENCY DEFENSE OF GERMAN SOIL

Detailed plans exist for the rapid mobilization of all the auxiliary organizations described in the above paragraphs in case of the actual invasion of, or immediate military threat to, any part of Germany proper. Elaborate administrative preparations have been made for their operational control and chain of command in such an emergency.

The commander of each corps area *(Wehrkreis)* has always been responsible for organizing the emergency defense of his territory. Since, however, he normally controls only the static military forces and installations of the Armed Forces proper, the Higher *SS* and Police Commander *(HSSPf)* has been designated to join him in case of invasion and to take control of all the other available manpower in the area which is organized in a form suitable to aid in its defense. He is not to be subordinated to the *Wehrkreis* commander but must cooperate with him and will deputize for him if necessary. The only exception to this is the Todt Organization, whose units and installations pass directly to the control of the *Wehrkreis* commander in such an emergency.

Under the *HSSPf* the *Wehrkreis* is divided, for emergency defense, into security zones (*Sicherungsbereiche*), each headed by a commander of the Protective Police (*Schupo*). In case of invasion each such commander joins the Armed Forces commander (*Wehrmachtkommandant*) in the major garrison area which most nearly coincides with the security zone. The Armed Forces commander then acts, in collaboration with the security zone commander, as "combat commander" (*Kampfkommandant*) of the area, a concept introduced in 1944 for commanders who take full charge of areas which are expected to become cut off and which must be defended to the "last cartridge". The commander of the security zone will take the place of the combat commander in case he should become a casualty, unless there is another officer senior to him in the area.

The organizations which come under the control of the Higher *SS* and Police Commander in emergency include the *Waffen-SS,* Security Police, Protective Police, Rural Police, special employment units of the General *SS* (*SS-z.b.V.*), special employment units of the *SA* (*SA-z.b.V.*), Urban and Rural Auxiliary Guards, Fire-fighting Police and Fire-fighting Services, Technical Emergency Corps, German Labor Service, Postal and Railway Security Forces, Industrial Emergency Units (*Industrie-Alarmeinheiten*), Plant Protection Service (*Werkschutz*), the German Red Cross, and the *Volkssturm*.

This arrangement for the emergency defense of German soil is in sharp contrast to the established prerogatives of the Army in military matters in that responsibility as well as actual control of the defending forces is to be shared between the proper territorial military authority and the representative of its principal rival, the *SS*.

CHAPTER IV

TACTICS

Section I. GENERAL TACTICAL DOCTRINES

I. Basic Doctrines

An outstanding characteristic of the German nation is its fondness for everything connected with militarism. This is based not only on traditional sentiment but also on long-range and intense education that glorifies the military spirit. This gives the German military leaders the essential foundation for aggressive military operations.

The Germans believe that only the offensive can achieve success on the field, particularly when combined with the element of surprise. German military literature, for the past century, has emphasized the need for aggressiveness in all military operations.

The Germans have been thoroughly aware of the psychological component in warfare and have developed systematic terrorization to a high degree.

At the same time they have placed considerable reliance on novel and sensational weapons such as the mass use of armor, the robot bomb, and the super-heavy tank. Their principal weaknesses in this regard have been their failure to integrate these new techniques with established arms and tactics—German field artillery, for example, did not maintain pace with German armor—and their devotion to automatic weapons at the expense of accuracy.

A highly trained officer corps and a thoroughly disciplined army are the necessary elements to implement this aggressive philosophy. German tactical doctrines stress the responsibility and the initiative of subordinates. The belief of former years that the German Army was inflexible and lacking in initiative has been completely destroyed in this war, in which aggressive and daring leadership has been responsible for many bold decisions. Yet, while the Germans have many excellent tacticians, they tend to repeat the same type of maneuvers, a fact which has been fully exploited by Allied commanders.

The German specialization in particular types of warfare such as mountain, desert, winter, or the attack on fortified positions, showed thorough preparation and ingenuity. At the same time the Germans had been quite willing to learn from their opponents and on numerous occasions have copied Allied tactics and weapons.

2. Recent Tactical Trends

From the time when the German Army was forced on the defensive by the Allied armies, German tactical doctrines have undergone modifications such as renunciation (except in unstated instances) of air support, and the substitution of linear defense for elastic offensive defense.

The primary goal of Germany today is to gain time and to achieve victory in a political sense, since the Germans are no longer capable of a military victory. Of necessity their military operations now supplement this effort and have become a large-scale delaying action.

3. Exercise of Command

The U. S. and German doctrines applied in exercise of the command are virtually identical. The Germans stress the necessity of the staff in assisting the commander to evaluate the situation and in preparing and disseminating orders to the lower units. They emphasize that the commander should be well forward with his units not only for the purpose of facilitating communication, but also because his presence has a salutary effect on the troops.

Section II. RECONNAISSANCE

I. General

a. PURPOSE. The purpose of reconnaissance and the types of units employed to obtain information are similar in the U. S. and the German Armies. German tactical principles of reconnaissance, however, diverge somewhat from those of the U. S. The Germans stress aggressiveness, attempt to obtain superiority in the area to be reconnoitered, and strive for continuous observation of the enemy. They believe in employing reconnaissance units in force as a rule. They expect and are prepared to fight to obtain the desired information. Often they assign supplementary tasks to their reconnaissance units, such as sabotage behind enemy lines, harassment, or counter-reconnaissance.

b. TECHNIQUE. Only enough reconnaissance troops are sent on a mission to assure superiority in the area to be reconnoitered. Reserves are kept on hand to be committed when the reconnaissance must be intensified, when the original force meets strong enemy opposition, or when the direction and area to be reconnoitered are changed. The Germans encourage aggressive action against enemy security forces. When their reconnaissance units meet superior enemy forces, they fight a delaying action while other units attempt to flank the enemy.

c. CLASSIFICATION. Reconnaissance is classified by the Germans as operational, tactical, and battle reconnaissance—corresponding to the U. S. distant, close, and battle reconnaissance.

2. Operational Reconnaissance (Operative Aufklarung)

Operational reconnaissance, penetrating over a large area in great depth, provides the basis for strategic planning and action. This type of reconnaissance is intended to determine the location and activities of enemy forces, particularly localities of rail concentrations, forward or rearward displacements of personnel, loading or unloading areas of army elements, the construction of field or permanent fortifications, and hostile air force concentrations. Identification of large enemy motorized elements, especially on an open flank, is important. Operational reconnaissance is carried out by the Air Force and by motorized units. Aerial photography units operate at altitudes of 16,500 to 26,500 feet. Since missions assigned to operational air reconnaissance units are gener-

ally limited to the observation of important roads and railroads, reconnaissance sectors and areas normally are not assigned. The motorized units employed for operational reconnaissance have only directions and objectives assigned.

3. Tactical Reconnaissance (Taktische Aufklarung)

a. PURPOSE. Tactical reconnaissance, carried out in the area behind the operational reconnaissance, provides the basis for the commitment of troops. Its mission embraces identification of the enemy's organization, disposition, strength, and antiaircraft defense; determination of the enemy's reinforcement capabilities; and terrain reconnaissance of advanced sectors. Air Force reconnaissance units and motorized and mounted reconnaissance battalions are employed for tactical reconnaissance. Their direction and radius of employment are based upon the results of the operational reconnaissance.

b. AIR RECONNAISSANCE. Tactical air reconnaissance is normally made from altitudes of 6,500 to 16,000 feet. As a rule, air reconnaissance units are assigned specific reconnaissance areas, the boundaries of which normally do not coincide with sectors assigned to ground units. Reconnaissance planes generally are employed singly.

c. GROUND RECONNAISSANCE. Sectors of responsibility are assigned to ground tactical reconnaissance battalions. In order to make them independent or to facilitate their change of direction, battalions may be assigned only reconnaissance objectives. In such instances, boundary lines separate adjacent units. The Germans avoid using main roads as boundary lines, defining the sectors in such a way that main roads fall within the reconnaissance sectors. The width of a sector is determined by the situation, the type and strength of the reconnaissance battalion, the road net, and the terrain. In general, the width of a sector assigned to a motorized reconnaissance battalion does not exceed 30 miles.

d. ORDERS FOR TACTICAL RECONNAISSANCE. Orders issued to a reconnaissance battalion or its patrols normally contain, in addition to the mission, the following:

(1) Line of departure.

(2) Information concerning adjacent reconnaissance units.

(3) Sector boundaries or direction of operation.

(4) Objectives.

(5) Phase lines.

(6) Instructions for transmission of reports.

(7) Location of immediate objectives whose attainment is to be reported.

(8) Instructions regarding air-ground liaison.

(9) Time of departure, route, and objective of the main force.

e. TACTICAL RECONNAISSANCE PROCEDURES. When a motorized reconnaissance column expects contact with the enemy, it advances by bounds. The length of bounds depends on the cover the terrain offers as well as on the road net. As the distance from the enemy decreases, the bounds are shortened. The Germans utilize roads as long as possible and usually use different routes for the advance and the return.

The reconnaissance battalion commander normally sends out patrols which advance by bounds. Their distance in front of the battalion depends on the situation, the terrain, and the range of the signal equipment, but as a rule they are not more than an hour's traveling distance (about 25 miles) ahead of the battalion. The battalion serves as the reserve for the patrols and as an advance message center (*Meldekopf*), collecting the messages and relaying them to the rear. Armored reconnaissance cars, armored half-tracks, or motorcycles compose the motorized reconnaissance patrols, whose exact composition depends on their mission and on the situation. Motorcycles are used to fill in gaps and intervals, thereby thickening the reconnaissance net.

When the proximity of the enemy does not permit profitable employment of the motorized reconnaissance battalion, it is withdrawn and the motorized elements of the divisional reconnaissance battalion take over.

Divisional reconnaissance battalions seldom operate more than one day's march (18 miles) in front of the division, covering an area approximately 6 miles wide.

4. Battle Reconnaissance *(Gefechtsaufklarung)*

a. GENERAL. Battle reconnaissance as a rule is begun when the opposing forces begin to deploy. All troops participating in battle carry out battle reconnaissance through patrols, artillery observation posts, observation battalions, and air reconnaissance units. The information obtained on the organization and strength of the enemy provides the basis for the conduct of the battle.

b. ARMORED CAR PATROLS. The *Panzer* division dispatches armored reconnaissance units equipped with armored vehicles and numerous automatic weapons. The armored reconnaissance unit is fast and has a wide radius of action.

Armored car patrols normally are composed of three armored reconnaissance cars, one of which is equipped with radio. An artillery observer often accompanies the patrol so that in an emergency fire can be brought down quickly. This type of patrol usually is organized for missions lasting one to two days. Tasks are defined clearly, and nothing is allowed to interfere with the patrol's main objective. If enemy forces are met, action is avoided unless the force is so weak that it can be destroyed without diverting the patrol from its main task. If enemy action is anticipated, the patrol is reinforced with self-propelled guns and occasionally with tanks. Engineers and motorcyclists are often attached to the patrol to deal with road blocks and demolitions.

While scouting a woods, a favorite German ruse is to drive the leading car toward its edge, halt briefly to observe, and then drive off rapidly, hoping to draw fire that will disclose the enemy positions.

At road blocks, the leading car opens fire. If fire is not returned, men dismount and go forward to attach tow ropes to the road block. If necessary, the patrol dismounts and proceeds with machine guns to reconnoiter on foot.

A patrol is never split up, but in open country distances between cars may be as much as 200 to 300 yards.

c. OBSERVATION BATTALION AND AIR RECONNAISSANCE. The German observation battalion locates enemy artillery and heavy weapons positions by sound and flash ranging and evaluated aerial photographs. The Air Force assists in battle reconnaissance by observing the distribution of the enemy's forces, his artillery, bivouac and movements, reserves, tank assemblies, and any other special occurrences behind the front. In general, air battle reconnaissance is executed under 6,000 feet.

d. BATTLE RECONNAISSANCE PATROLS *(Spähtruppen)*. The Germans send out reconnaissance patrols, consisting of a noncommissioned officer and three or four men, to get such information as the location of enemy positions and minefields. They generally avoid contact and retreat when fired on.

e. COMBAT PATROLS *(Gefechtsspähtruppen* or *Stosstruppen)*. These consist of at least one noncommissioned officer and eight men, but are usually much stronger. As a rule the combat patrol is commanded by a sergeant who has under him 15 to 20 men, organized in two equal sections, each commanded by a section leader. These are raiding patrols, and their mission often includes bringing back prisoners of war. Since Allied air supremacy has neutralized German air reconnaisance to a great extent, the Germans have placed increased importance on prisoners of war, especially officers, as a source of information on enemy strength, dispositions, and intentions.

Combat or other types of patrols are often sent out to test the strength of enemy outposts. If an outpost proves to be weakly held, the patrol attacks, occupies the position, and remains there until relieved by troops from the rear. If the patrol is strongly garrisoned, the patrol attempts to return with a prisoner of war.

f. SPECIAL PATROLS (*Spähtruppen mit besonderen Aufgaben*). These vary in strength in accordance with their special mission. Special patrols are sent out to carry out such tasks as demolitions, engaging of enemy patrols that have penetrated German positions, and ambushing enemy supply columns.

g. MISCELLANEOUS PATROLS. Engineer patrols are employed to reconnoiter approaches to fortified areas, defiles, or rivers. Artillery patrols, usually consisting of an officer and a few mounted men, reconnoiter routes of approach, observation posts, and firing positions.

h. TERRAIN RECONNAISSANCE (*Geländeerkundung*). The Germans place great emphasis on terrain reconnaissance, realizing the influence terrain has upon the conduct of operations. Most of their usual reconnaissance missions include terrain reconnaissance tasks. Terrain may be so important at times as to require reconnaissance by special units. Ground and air reconnaissance units give special attention to the road net—its density, condition, road blocks, mines, and demolitions—as well as to the terrain itself, particularly tank country.

i. EQUIPMENT AND SUPPORT. The Germans equip their ground battle-reconnaissance patrols with machine pistols and one or two light machine guns that are used to cover the patrol's approach or withdrawal. Engineers often are attached to guide a patrol through German minefields and to clear a way through enemy wire or mines. Artillery support is given in the form of harassing fire put down just before the patrol reaches its objective. Sometimes the artillery fires into adjacent sectors to mislead the enemy as to the

actual area to be reconnoitered. In other instances, artillery and mortars that have registered during the previous day shell during the night the area to be reconnoitered. As soon as the barrage is lifted, the patrol advances under cover of machine-gun fire from flanking positions.

Section III. MARCHES

I. General

The formations and the organizations of the march column in day or night advances are the same in the German Army as in the U. S. Army and are governed by the same principles. For a smooth functioning of the march the Germans stress: systematic training and practice; attention to physical welfare; care of vehicles and equipment; previous reconnaissance of routes; warning orders; and the issue of detailed march orders.

2. Organization and Control of the March Column

In order to secure the march column against enemy attacks, the Germans divide the column in the same manner as U. S. doctrine prescribes, namely into Advance Guard (*Vorhut*), Main Body (*Gros*), and Rear Guard (*Nachhut*). German equivalents for the U. S. terms are:

Advance Guard

Spitze	Point
Spitzenkompanie	Advance party
Vortrupp	Support
Haupttrupp	Reserve

Rear Guard

Nachspitze	Rear point
Nachspitzenkompanie	Rear party
Nachtrupp	Support
Haupttrupp	Reserve

The issue of orders for march and traffic control is the responsibility of the higher command. Movement by road of formations from battalion strength upwards is carried out in the Zone of the Interior at the orders of the Army High Command (*OKH*) or a headquarters acting on the orders of the Army High Command. In the Theater of War such movements are controlled by Army Headquarters, which issues orders in accordance with instructions from Army High Command or the Army Group. Movements in the areas of military commanders of line-of-communication areas are controlled by orders of the commanders of such areas.

Orders for movement are issued to the formations of fighting troops by the operations group of headquarters; those to supply services and units in the line-of-communication area emanate from the supply and administrative group.

The Germans set up a well organized traffic control service which is under the orders of the operations group. All traffic control services usually wear orange-red brassards, while the members of the military police are distinguished by metal gorgets.

The Germans allot to each front-line division its own road or sector of advance, usually marked by advance parties. General Headquarters or any other troops directed simultaneously on the same roads, are subordinated to the division for the duration of the move. All-weather roads usually are allotted to motorized or armored divisions, while subsidiary roads are assigned to infantry divisions.

3. Conduct of the March

When a German infantry division advances along several routes, an infantry element normally forms the head of each main body. The commander of the main body usually marches at or near the head of the main body. The motorized elements of the division, unless employed on reconnaissance or security missions, are organized into one or more motor echelons which follow the march column by bounds, or move in a column along a separate road. Before the march begins, the division signal battalion lays a trunk telephone line as far forward as the situation permits and extends this line while the march proceeds. The leading signal unit usually marches with the support of the advance guard and establishes telephone stations at important points. In a march along several roads the trunk line normally is laid along the route of the division commander and his staff. In addition to the construction of the trunk line, the Germans stress radio communications to the rear and flanks, as well as the use of messengers mounted on horses, bicycles, or motorcycles.

4. Security of March Columns

As a rule the Germans allot motorized units for the protection of the flanks and rear of march columns. However, a smaller unit, such as a battalion, may advance without flank security detachments.

The Germans are very much concerned about antiaircraft protective measures and often march in open columns (*Fliegermarschtiefe*); an advance in deployed formation (*Fliegermarschbreite*) is seldom practical. Antiaircraft defense is concentrated at important terrain features, such as bridges, crossroads, and defiles. Because of Allied air supremacy the Germans now instruct their troops to conduct movements and the transport of supplies only at night, and without lights. They also order their troops to leave burned out vehicles standing on the road to attract fresh attacks by enemy aircraft.

Section IV. OFFENSIVE

I. General

The fundamental principle of German offensive doctrine is to encircle and destroy the enemy. The objective of the combined arms in attack is to bring the armored forces and the infantry into decisive action against the enemy with sufficient fire power and shock. Superiority in force and fire power, the employment of armored forces, as well as the surprise element, play a great part in the offensive.

Coordination between the combined arms under a strong unified command is, the Germans emphasize, an absolute requisite to the success of these shock tactics. This has become more and more true as the Allies have developed effective antitank weapons and have adopted deeper defenses, limiting the self-sufficiency of German tanks. To counter these measures, the Germans have increased the mobility and armor protection of their motor-borne infantry, and have mounted a large proportion of both their direct and indirect heavy support weapons on self-propelled carriages.

In attempting thoroughly to paralyze the defender up to the moment of the tank-infantry assault, the Germans realize that even the most formidable forces are never sufficient for overwhelming superiority on the entire front. They therefore select a point of main effort (*Schwerpunkt*) for a breakthrough, allotting narrow sectors of attack (*Gefechtsstreifen*) to the troops committed at the decisive locality. There they also mass the bulk of their heavy weapons and reserves. The other sectors of the front are engaged by weaker, diversionary forces. In selecting the point of main effort, the Germans consider weaknesses in the enemy's defensive position; suitability of the terrain, especially for tanks and for cooperation of all arms; approach routes; and possibilities for supporting fire, especially artillery. Although the Germans select a point of main effort in all attacks, they usually also make plans for shifting their main effort if they meet unexpected success elsewhere. To allow such shifts, sufficient reserves and a strong, unified command are organized.

An attack on a narrow front, according to German doctrine, must have sufficient forces at its disposal to widen the penetration while maintaining its impetus, and to protect the flanks of the penetration. Once the attack is launched, it must drive straight to its objective, regardless of opposition.

2. Types of Attack

a. FLANK ATTACK (*Flankenangriff*). The Germans consider that the most effective attack is against the enemy's flank. The flank attack develops either from the approach march—sometimes through a turning movement—or from flank marches. It attempts to surprise the enemy and permit him no time for countermeasures. Since mobility and the deception of the enemy at other positions are required, the flank attack is most successfully mounted from a distance; the troop movements necessary for the maneuver can be executed in close proximity to the enemy only with unusually favorable terrain or at night. Attacks are launched on both flanks only when the Germans consider their forces clearly superior.

b. ENVELOPMENT (*Umfassungsangriff*). The envelopment is a combination flank-and-frontal attack especially favored by the Germans. The envelopment may be directed on either or both the enemy's flanks, and is accompanied by a simultaneous frontal attack to fix the enemy's forces. The deeper the envelopment goes into the enemy's flanks, the greater becomes the danger of being enveloped oneself. The Germans therefore emphasize the necessity of strong reserves and organization of the enveloping forces in depth. Success of the envelopment depends on the extent to which the enemy is able to dispose his forces in the threatened direction.

c. ENCIRCLEMENT (*Einkreisung*). An encirclement, the Germans think, is a particularly decisive form of attack, but usually more difficult to execute than a flank attack or an envelopment. In an encirclement, the enemy is not attacked at

all in front, or is attacked in front only by light forces, while the main attacking force passes entirely around him, with the objective of maneuvering him out of position. This requires extreme mobility and deception.

d. FRONTAL ATTACK (*Frontalangriff*). The Germans consider the frontal attack the most difficult of execution. It strikes the enemy at his strongest point, and therefore requires superiority of men and materiel. A frontal attack should be made only at a point where the infantry can break through into favorable terrain in the depth of the enemy position. The frontage of the attack should be wider than the actual area (*Schwerpunkt*) chosen for penetration, in order to tie down the enemy on the flanks of the breakthrough. Adequate reserves must be held ready to counter the employment of the enemy's reserves.

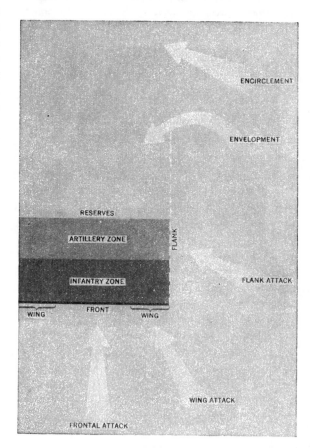

Figure 1.—Forms of attack.

e. WING ATTACK (*Flügelangriff*). An attack directed at one or both of the enemy's wings has, the Germans teach, a better chance of success than a central frontal attack, since only a part of the enemy's weapons are faced, and only one flank of the attacking force or forces is exposed to enemy fire. Bending back one wing may give an opportunity for a flank attack, or for a single or double envelopment.

f. PENETRATION (*Einbruch*) AND BREAK-THROUGH (*Durchbruch*). These are not separate forms of attack, but rather the exploitation of a successful attack on the enemy's front, wing, or flank. The penetration destroys the continuity of the hostile front. The broader the penetration, the deeper can the penetration wedge be driven. Strong reserves throw back enemy counterattacks against the flanks of the penetration. German units are trained to exploit a penetration to the maximum so that it may develop into a complete breakthrough before hostile countermeasures can be launched on an effective scale. The deeper the attacker penetrates, the more effectively can he envelop and frustrate the attempts of the enemy to close his front again by withdrawal to the rear. The attacking forces attempt to reduce individual enemy positions by encircling and isolating them. The Germans do not consider a breakthrough successful until they overcome the enemy's artillery positions, which usually is the special task of tanks. Reserve units roll up the enemy's front from the newly created flanks.

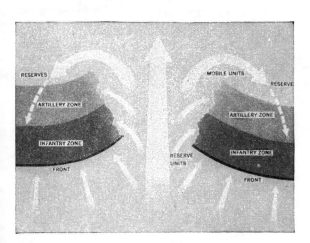

Figure 2.—Breakthrough.

The Germans often refer to this maneuver as "*Keil und Kessel*".

3. Organization of the Attack

a. ATTACK ORDER. The attack order (*Angriffsbefehl*) generally contains the objective of the attack, the disposition of the infantry, unit sectors and boundaries, disposition and support

missions of the artillery, location of reserves, and the time of attack. The order is not drawn up in accordance with any stereotyped form, but as a rule follows this pattern:

(1) Estimate of the situation (disposition of hostile and friendly troops).

(2) Mission.

(3) Assembly areas for the forward companies; objective; sector boundaries; orders for the continuation of combat reconnaissance.

(4) Instructions for the preparation of the heavy-weapons fire support, especially for massed fire.

(5) Orders to the artillery for fire preparation and coordination.

(6) Assembly areas for the reserves.

(7) Time of attack.

(8) Instructions for rear services (medical service and supplies).

(9) Location of command posts.

(10) Miscellaneous.

b. SECTORS OF ATTACK. The width of a sector assigned to an infantry unit in the attack depends on the unit's mission and battle strength, on terrain conditions, on the available fire support of all arms, and on the probable strength of enemy resistance. Normally the sector assigned to a platoon is between 165 and 220 yards. A company attack sector is about 330 to 550 yards. A battalion sector is 440 to 1,100 yards, while a division sector may be 4,400 to 5,500 yards. These sectors also provide the boundaries for the other arms, especially for the artillery in support of the infantry, although the artillery may utilize favorable observation positions in neighboring sectors. This also applies to the heavy infantry weapons.

For large units the sectors are determined from the map; for smaller units, from the terrain. These sectors extend as deep into enemy territory as the plan of battle may require. As the situation develops, changes are frequently made. Important points always lie within units' sectors, unless they are to be attacked by several units. The Germans do not consider it necessary to occupy the whole width of the sector with troops. Open flanks ordinarily are not bounded.

c. FIRE PLAN. Fire superiority is achieved through coordination of the infantry and artillery weapons. The basis for the fire plan (*Feuer-*

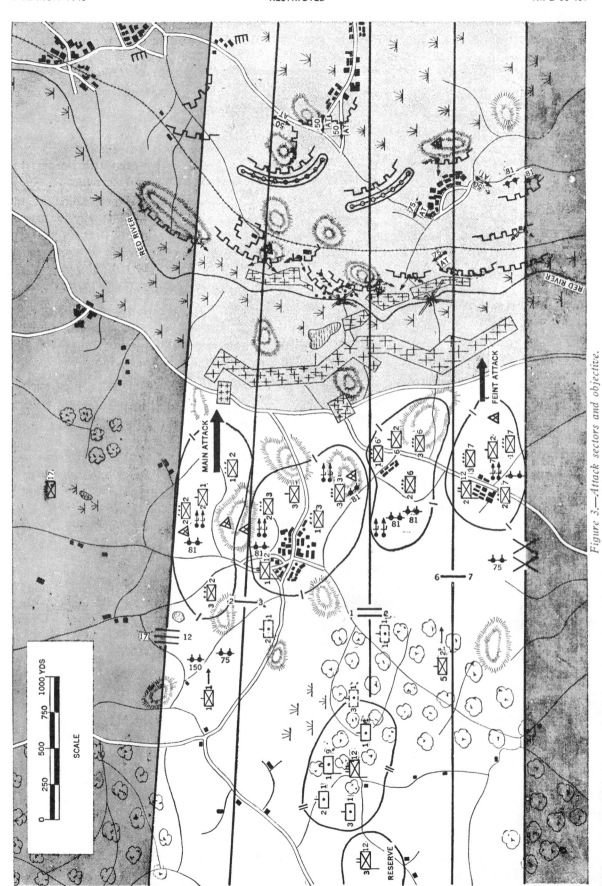

Figure 3.—Attack sectors and objective.

plan) is the regulation of the commitment of all weapons.

The fire plan includes the following:

(1) Assignment of combat missions.

(2) Distribution of observation sectors and fields of fire for the infantry and the artillery.

(3) An estimate of capabilities of the artillery for effective execution of the combat mission.

(4) Orders for the commencement of fire and fire schedules.

(5) Orders for the preparation for massed fire.

(6) Instructions for ammunition supply.

The Germans stress the coordination of flat and high trajectory weapons so that all dead spaces are covered by fire. Lack of signal equipment, however, often hinders the application of this principle.

4. Conduct of the Attack

a. GENERAL. Most of the German successes in the present war have been achieved with armored formations. Years of secret training and equipping were devoted to the development of the *Panzer* division. The original German *Blitzkrieg* tactics were based on the belief in the irresistible power of tank formations operating independently with the support of dive-bombers. Considerable modifications have taken place in this theory over the past few years. At the present time, the offensive tactics of the Germans are less spectacularly bold than they were in 1939, but the fundamental theory behind them has changed remarkably little, though in their armored tactics they stress more tank-infantry coordination since unlimited air support is no longer at their command.

The main weight of all major German attacks since 1939 was borne by the *Panzer* division. Where infantry divisions have been employed, they were limited to local attacks on a comparatively minor scale or to mopping up in rear of the *Panzer* divisions. The Germans never envisaged a full-scale attack by infantry formations on fixed defenses. German tactics have been to outflank or encircle the main area of the enemy defenses with tank formations and to have the infantry roll up the defenses from the rear, or to break frontally through the enemy defenses with massed tanks and develop the famous *"Keil und Kessel"* maneuver.

The Germans learned at heavy cost the futility of charging a hostile antitank defense with tank concentrations and of engaging in tank-versus-tank combat without having superiority in range and armament. They have learned that large formations of tanks cannot achieve a breakthrough, opposed by an effective screen of antitank guns, without the assistance of other arms. Therefore attention has to be given to the combined tactics of tanks and *Panzer Grenadiers,* the mechanized or motorized infantry who accompany the tanks.

Great emphasis in German offensive theory is laid on the role of the artillery, but in practice the artillery-support role has devolved to an ever-increasing degree on the tanks and assault guns. Nevertheless, the principle that the supporting fire should be concentrated on a narrow frontage where the tanks and infantry are most likely to achieve a breakthrough has been retained.

The fact that a part of the enemy resistance is likely to remain undisclosed until the attack has already begun has caused the Germans permanently to decentralize a portion of the field artillery. This tendency has led to the emergence and continual development of the assault guns, whose main function is the close support of infantry and tanks in the attack. Their armor and mobility allow them to operate much farther forward than the field artillery.

The tendency to detach field artillery battalions from their field artillery regiment remains strong. In fact, this tendency is so prevalent that a concentration of massed artillery preceding an attack seldom is achieved, necessitating, as it does, a great degree of centralized control. The Germans, however, replace the massed artillery fire to a large extent with the fire of multi-barreled mortars and rocket projectors, though these latter have not the accuracy of the former.

The Germans make a clear distinction between an attack made from movement and an attack from a prepared position, which is the more common of the two.

b. ATTACK BY MECHANIZED AND MOTORIZED FORCES. (1) *The attack.* In armored-force operations, the Germans stress the need for the concentrated employment, at the decisive place and time, of the entire combined command of tanks and other arms, less necessary reserves. The tanks constitute the striking force of such a command and normally advance as the first echelon of the attack. Their primary mission is to break through and attack the enemy artillery, rather than to seek out and destroy enemy tanks, which can be more effectively engaged by antitank units. The mission of the other arms is to assist the

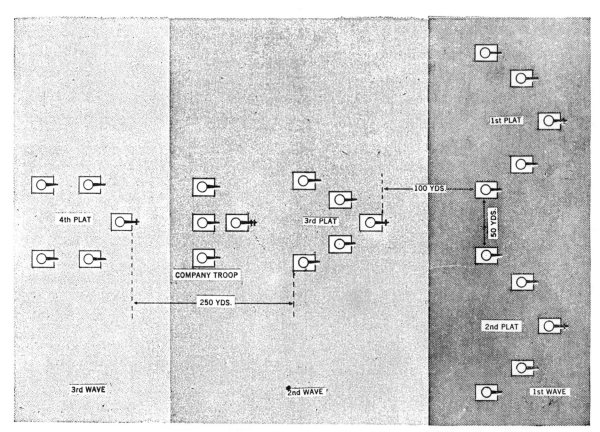

Figure 4.—German tank formation, battalion in "Blunt Wedge".

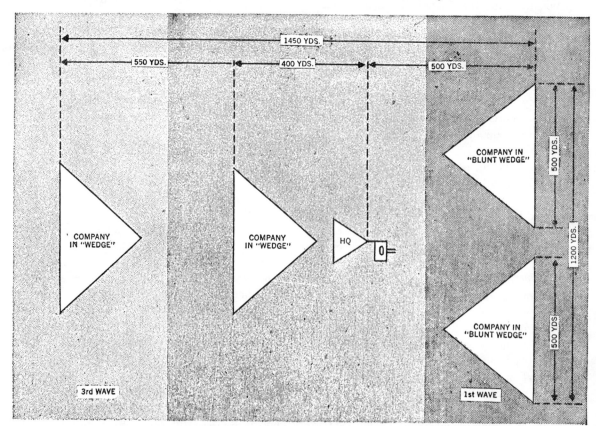

Figure 5.—German tank formation, company in "Blunt Wedge".

tanks in their advance, and particularly to eliminate antitank weapons. The smallest combat unit in such a force of combined arms is the company.

The basic formation for the tank platoon, company, and battalion are file, double file, wedge, and blunt wedge. The type of formation used for a specific task depends to a large extent on terrain conditions and the strength of enemy opposition. A German tank platoon normally consists of one command tank and two tank squads of two tanks each.

The tank regiment normally attacks in waves, in either of the following manners:

The tank regiment is echeloned in depth, one tank battalion following the other. The regimental commander's location is between the two battalions. This formation has the advantages of a sufficiently wide front (about 1,100 yards), and close contact by the commander of his units in the conduct of the attack. The normal depth of such a formation is about 3,000 yards. This is the usual form of the tank attack. When two tank battalions are attacking, one behind the other, it takes them about half an hour to pass their own infantry.

When the two-battalions-abreast formation is employed, it is almost essential that another tank regiment form the following wave. This formation usually has the disadvantage of being too wide. The regimental commander cannot observe his units, and he has no units of his own behind him which he can commit in a decisive moment. The attack normally proceeds in three waves.

The first wave thrusts to the enemy's antitank defense and artillery positions.

The second wave provides covering fire for the first wave, and then attacks the enemy's infantry positions, preceded, accompanied, or followed by part of the *Panzer Grenadiers,* who dismount as close as possible to the point where they must engage the enemy. The objectives of the second wave are the remaining antitank positions, positions of heavy infantry-support weapons, and machine-gun emplacements which hold up the advance of the infantry.

The third wave, accompanied by the remainder of the *Panzer Grenadiers,* mops up.

These three waves now often are telescoped into two, the first wave speeding through the enemy's position as far as his gun positions, the second crushing the enemy's forward positions in detail and mopping up the opposition not dealt with by the first wave or which has revived since the first wave passed through.

A typical attack formation of this type might be divided up among the *Panzer* division's units as follows: the first wave, on a frontage of about 2,000 to 3,000 yards, might consist of one tank battalion, two companies forward, supported on the flanks by elements of the assault gun battalion. Close to the rear of the first wave usually follow one or two *Panzer Grenadier* companies in armored half-tracks. About 150 yards to the rear of the first wave moves the second wave, formed of the second tank battalion in the same formation, closely followed by the remainder of the armored *Panzer Grenadiers,* who are in turn followed at some distance by the motorized *Panzer Grenadiers.* The flanks are protected by antitank guns which normally operate by platoons, moving by bounds. The artillery forward observer travels in his armored vehicles with the first wave, while the artillery commander of the supporting artillery units usually travels with the tank commander. Assault guns normally also accompany the second wave.

The tanks help each other forward by fire and movement, medium or heavy tanks taking up hull-down firing positions and giving covering fire while the faster tanks advance to the next commanding feature. Then the latter give covering fire to the former moving forward to their next bound.

Once the first wave has reached the rear of the enemy's forward defenses, it pushes straight on to attack the enemy's artillery. As soon as these positions have been neutralized, the tanks reform beyond the artillery positions and either prepare to exploit the attack or form an all-round defensive position on suitable ground.

The tank unit commander, as the leader of the strongest unit, is in most cases in command of the combat team, and all the other participating arms (*Panzer Grenadiers,* artillery, engineers, and antitank units) are placed under him. The Germans realize that a strong and unified command is an essential feature of any military operation. For certain missions, however, tank units are attached to another arm, in which case the tank commander is consulted before the final plans for the operations are made.

(2) *Infantry-tank cooperation.* When the enemy has well prepared positions with natural or constructed tank obstacles, the German infantry attacks before the tanks and clears the way. The

objective of the infantry is to penetrate into the enemy position and destroy enemy antitank weapons to the limit of its strength and the fire power of its own support weapons, augmented by additional support and covering fire from the tanks and self-propelled weapons sited in their rear.

Only after the destruction of the enemy antitank defense can the tanks be employed on the battle line to the fullest advantage.

When the tank obstacles in front of the enemy position already are destroyed, and no additional tank obstacles are expected in the depth of the enemy's main defensive position, the infantry breaks through simultaneously with the tank unit. The infantry attack is conducted in the same manner as it would be without the cooperation of tanks. Heavy infantry weapons are kept in readiness to fire at possible newly discovered antitank positions. Of particular importance is protection of the open flanks by echeloning the flank units and employing heavy weapons at the flanks.

In most cases, the infantry follows the tanks closely, taking advantage of the fire power and paralyzing effect of the tanks upon the enemy's defense. The Germans normally transport the infantry to the line of departure on tanks or troop-carrying vehicles in order to protect the infantry and to increase its speed. The infantry leaves the vehicles at the last possible moment, and goes into action mainly with light automatic weapons.

The tanks advance by bounds from cover to cover, reconnoitering the terrain ahead and providing protective fire for the dismounted *Panzer Grenadiers*. The tanks do not slow their advance to enable the infantry to keep continuous pace with them, but advance alone and wait under cover until the infantry catches up with the advance. Terrain that does not offer sufficient cover is crossed with the greatest possible speed.

The infantry attacks in small formations also by bounds under the fire cover of its own heavy weapons and of the tanks, staying away from individual tanks because they draw the strongest enemy fire.

When a tank company attacks with infantry, there are normally two platoons on the line, one platoon back, and the fourth platoon in reserve. The interval between tanks is usually 100 to 120 yards. The tank's machine guns usually engage

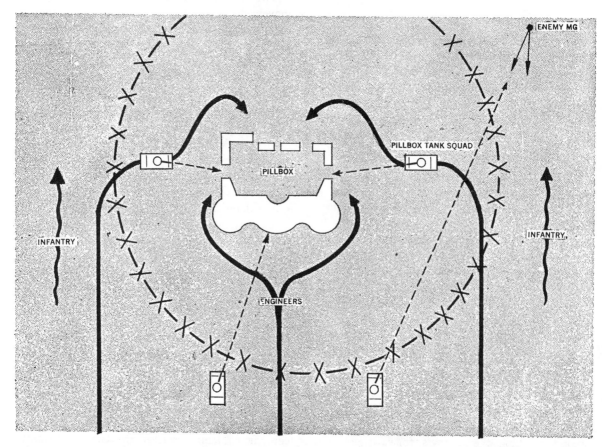

Figure 6.—Attack against an enemy pillbox.

infantry targets at about 1,000 yards range and under, while the tank guns engage targets at 2,000 to 2,500 yards.

The coordination between tanks and *Panzer Grenadiers* moving into combat on armored half-tracks is similar to the technique employed in a purely armored formation, since the armored half-tracks are not only troop-carrying vehicles but also combat vehicles. When the terrain is favorable for tank warfare, the *Panzer Grenadiers* in their armored half-tracks follow immediately with the second wave, after the first tank wave has overrun the opponent's position. A deep and narrow formation is employed. After the penetration, the main mission of the *Panzer Grenadiers* is to overcome the enemy positions which survived the first wave.

In attacking enemy pillboxes the Germans use combat groups consisting of tanks, infantry, and engineers, assisted by artillery. The normal composition of a combat group attacking one bunker is one platoon of tanks and one platoon of infantry reinforced by one squad of engineers. Before the combat group is committed against the enemy pillbox, artillery fires high explosives and smoke shells at the neighboring pillboxes to isolate them, shells the terrain between pillboxes, and conducts counterbattery fire. Under the protection of this fire, the combat group advances close to the pillbox while other infantry units attack the enemy in the terrain between the pillboxes.

One tank squad covers the advances of the other tank squads and the infantry platoon by direct fire against the pillbox, particularly against the observation and weapons' openings. The first tank squad halts under cover whenever possible and covers the advance of the second tank squad.

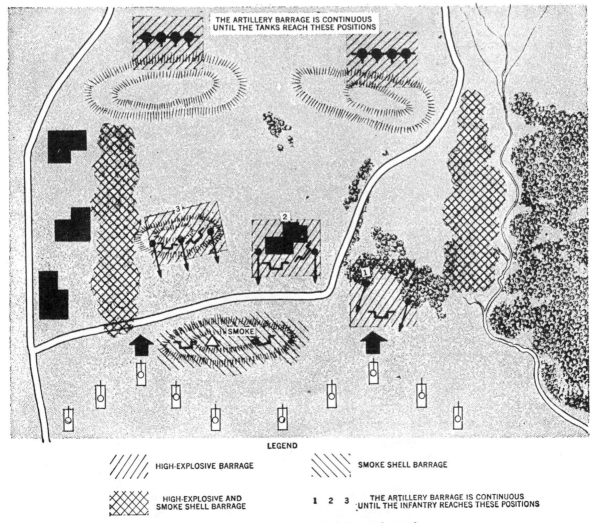

LEGEND

////// HIGH-EXPLOSIVE BARRAGE   \\\\\\ SMOKE SHELL BARRAGE

XXXXX HIGH-EXPLOSIVE AND
XXXXX SMOKE SHELL BARRAGE   1 2 3   THE ARTILLERY BARRAGE IS CONTINUOUS
                                                     UNTIL THE INFANTRY REACHES THESE POSITIONS

Figure 7.—Artillery support during a tank attack.

When the combat group reaches a barbed wire obstacle surrounding the pillbox, the two tank squads have different missions. One tank squad remains in front of the pillbox, and its tanks are driven into a position from which they can overlook the terrain, and watch out for antitank guns and machine gun emplacements, while the other tank squad (the pillbox tank squad) rolls across the obstacle to enable the infantry and engineers to get close to the pillbox. The pillbox tank squad then fires on the pillbox at close range. The infantry squad meanwhile takes the surrounding terrain and covers the engineers who blast the entrance of the pillbox with TNT.

(3) *Artillery-tank coordination.* Artillery support is of decisive importance for the preparation and the successful conduct of a tank attack. A unified command for the entire artillery controls the artillery fire as long as the infantry and tank units are fighting on the same line. When the tanks break through the enemy forward defense lines, the self-propelled artillery or any other artillery battalion designated for the support of the tank unit is placed under the command of the tank unit commander.

The Germans believe that the artillery fire must not check the momentum of the attack. Consequently the heaviest fire must fall well ahead of the tanks or outside their sector.

The mission of the artillery preparation before the attack is to destroy, or at least to neutralize, the opponent's antitank defense in the area between the line of contact and the regimental reserve line. Continuous counterbattery fire prevents the enemy from shelling the tank assembly area and from breaking up the preparation of the tank attack.

The artillery has the following missions before the tank attack:

Counterbattery fire on enemy artillery located in positions which command the ground over which the tank attack is to be made.

Concentrations on enemy tanks in assembly areas.

Harassing fire on all areas in which the antitank units are located or suspected. Fire is heaviest on areas in which tanks cannot operate but from which they can be engaged effectively.

Adjusting fire with high explosives on probable enemy observation posts commanding the sector to be attacked. These observation posts are blinded with smoke as soon as the attack begins.

Experience has taught the Germans that the flanks of a tank attack are vulnerable. Therefore they assign to the artillery and the rocket projector units the task of protecting flanks by barrages using high explosives and smoke shells.

The artillery has the following missions during the tank attack:

Counterbattery fire.

Blinding enemy observation posts.

As the attack progresses, engaging successive lines of antitank defense, especially areas to the rear and flanks of the sector attacked.

Screening the flanks of the attack with smoke and neutralizing the enemy's infantry and rear areas.

Delaying the movement and deployment of enemy reserves, particularly tanks.

The Germans stress that this wide variety of tasks must not lead to the wholesale dispersal of effort. The main task of the artillery is at all times the destruction of the enemy's antitank weapons, tanks, and artillery.

Liaison between artillery and tanks during the attack is established by the commanding officers and the artillery liaison group, which normally moves with the first wave. Artillery forward observers, if possible in armored observation posts, ride with the most forward elements. A German field expedient is for the tank unit to take along a forward observer in one of its tanks. It often happens that the tankman himself has to take over the observation for the artillery. He himself can request artillery fire and shift concentrations when the situation requires such changes. Figure 10 represents a map with superimposed coordinate system and artillery reference points used by tank commanders to help them in this task.

c. The Infantry Division in the Attack. (1) *General principles for employment.* German teaching envisages infantry divisions being employed to make a penetration in the enemy defensive positions through which armored and mechanized formations can pass. During the course of this war, however, no major attack has been carried out by infantry divisions without the support of *Panzer* divisions. In fact, more major attacks have been carried out by *Panzer* divisions, with only a minimum of ordinary infantry elements. Infantry divisions have been employed almost entirely in a role of consolidation, following up the armored and mechanized formations, systematically eliminating centers of resistance by-passed by the latter, or exploiting the latter's

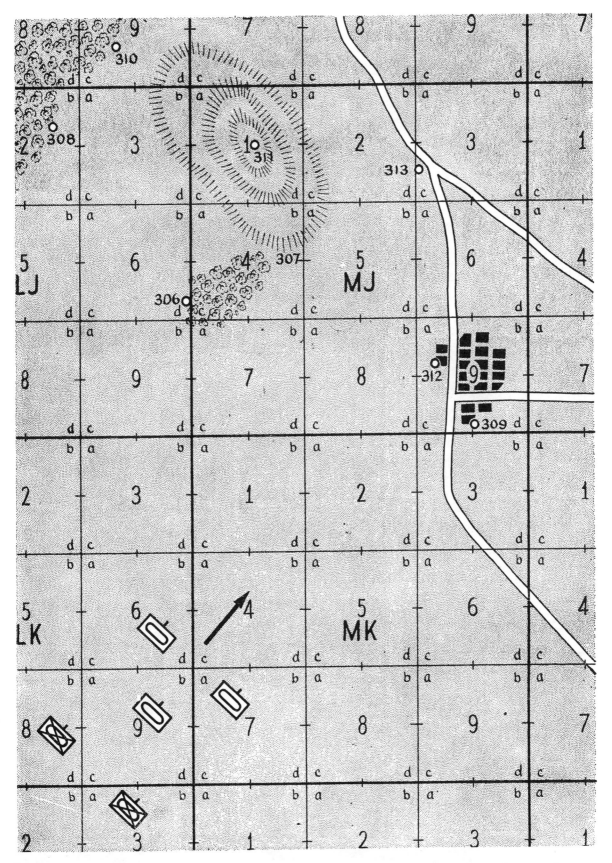

Figure 8.—Map with superimposed coordinate system and artillery reference points used by tank commanders.

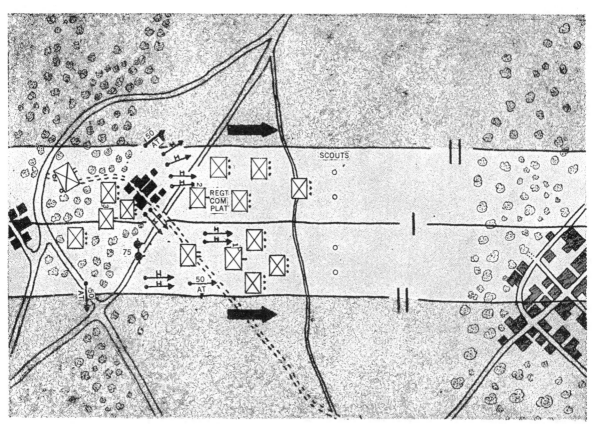

Figure 9.—Deployment of a German infantry battalion (1st stage).

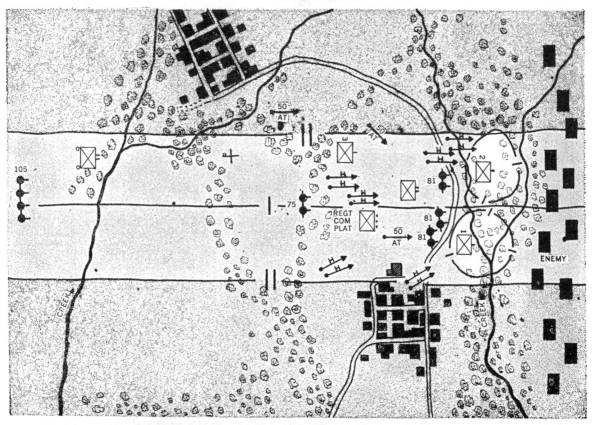

Figure 10.—Deployment of a German infantry battalion (2nd stage).

success by mopping up demoralized enemy defenses to the flanks of the armored breakthrough—in short, consolidating and holding the ground won by the mechanized formations.

In view of the unspectacular role allotted to the infantry division it is difficult to give information about other than minor infantry tactics, such as attacks on a small scale.

(2) *Preparation for the attack.* The method of forming up for an infantry assault on a prepared position is similar to that employed by the *Panzer* division. While the infantry is in assembly positions, the artillery makes all preparations for the support of the attack. It draws out hostile artillery fire and executes counterbattery fire against known enemy batteries. Large troop concentrations and especially important targets are taken under fire at great ranges. In order not to betray their full strength and intentions, the Germans withhold a portion of their batteries from these missions. They also try to deceive the enemy as to their intentions by covering other sectors simultaneously with fire. When possible, preparation for an attack is avoided during the day in order to prevent Allied observation. Occasionally, to obtain a success by surprise, the Germans launch attacks without artillery preparation. Surprise attacks also are launched under cover of darkness or fog.

The Germans normally occupy their line of departure by means of infiltration in order to avoid losses. Their orders direct what actions have to be taken when companies run into enemy defenses; when enemy fire is opened from the flank; when an enemy counterattack is launched; when objectives are reached; when companies appear to be getting dispersed; when part of a company pushes too far ahead of neighboring units or is held up.

The heavy machine guns of the rearward company and some of the mortars and heavy mortars are assigned to deal with enemy flanking fire.

The commander of the heavy company is normally at the battalion headquarters, from which he can control the fire of the infantry heavy support weapons.

(3) *Deployment.* (a) *First stage.* The Germans carry out deployment in two stages. They call the first stage *Entfaltung* or "shaking out", which is equivalent to the development of a march column according to U. S. procedure. In the first stage (*Figure 9*), an infantry regiment normally deploys down to battalions, although the

procedure may go down to companies if a high state of preparedness is necessary. Features of the first stage of deployment are as follows:

Companies retain their combat vehicles until their weapons and equipment arrive at the off-carrier position, which is located as far forward as the situation permits.

The Germans often place only one company forward, the main strength of the battalion being kept under control of the battalion commander as long as possible so that he may employ it in the most advantageous direction for attack.

If the condition of the terrain and enemy fire cause a change of intervals between units, the normal intervals are resumed as soon as possible.

Support weapons are used to cover the "shaking out" phase of deployment and the subsequent advance, the weapons being kept within the march column between the companies or behind the battalion.

After the first stage of deployment has been carried out, the leading elements of the battalion may be ordered to seize important tactical features.

When deploying by night or in woods, a careful reconnaissance is made, routes are marked, and strong protection is placed forward. Intervals between units are shorter.

After the first stage of deployment has been completed, the battalion commander marches with the leading elements and normally will send reconnaissance patrols ahead or reconnoiter the enemy position himself. The commanders of support weapons accompany him, reconnoitering for firing positions.

(b) *Second stage.* The second stage (*Figure 10*), called *Entwicklung* (development), is deployment in detail, which is the final action of the company extending itself down to platoons and squads. Features of the second stage of deployment are as follows:

The companies deploy in depth as soon as they come within range of artillery fire. An advance in columns of files is considered desirable because it affords a small target and the company is easier to control, but before adopting this formation the danger of enfilade fire is weighed.

If enemy fire and difficult terrain necessitate further deployment, the companies disperse in depth by sections. Reserves and support weapons also adopt open formations, but they remain far enough behind to avoid coming under the fire directed at the leading elements.

When the rifle companies are deployed, they exploit all possible cover as they advance, employing column-of-file formations with irregular distances. The leading elements are not extended until they are to engage in a fire fight. The elements that follow continue advancing in file.

In determining when to deploy, the Germans take into consideration additional physical strain placed on men when they march cross-country.

(4) *Technique of attack.* The infantry attack on prepared positions is made in the same sequence as that of the *Panzer* division, namely penetration, breakthrough, exploitation by the reserves. In the infantry attack, however, the first phase is a series of local attacks by so-called assault detachments (*Stosstrupps*) with the aim of overcoming key points in the enemy defenses, so that wedges into the enemy's forward positions can be established from which the attack can be driven forward into the depth of the enemy position, or rolling up the positions on either flank of the wedge.

Assault detachments normally are composed of infantry with engineers attached. A typical assault detachment consists of the following: one officer; obstacle clearing party, consisting of two to six men for each lane to be cleared, equipped with small arms, wire-cutters, and bangalore torpedoes and other explosives; embrasure-blasting party consisting of three or four men equipped with grenades and demolition or pole charges. This party may also include, though it may work independently, a flame-thrower party, consisting normally of two men; covering parties, normally two or three parties of varying size from three men with one light machine gun to full platoons; smoke party consisting of two or three men equipped with smoke candles or grenades; supply party, carrying reserves of equipment and ammunition, their strength depending on the size of the assault detachment.

Attacks most often are made at dawn, and are preceded normally by heavy artillery preparation, one purpose of which is to make shell holes which afford cover for the advancing assault detachments as they move forward. When the latter reach the wire obstacles surrounding the enemy position, Very signals are fired, calling for available artillery fire to be brought on the position to seal it off from flanking positions. If, by reason of proximity of the assault detachment to the artillery's danger zone, the former cannot be protected by covering fire, the smoke party may lay a smoke screen. The obstacle-clearing party then cuts one or more lanes through the wire, using wire cutters or bangalore torpedoes. The embrasure-blasting party passes through and attacks the embrasures. Flame throwers, if employed, are not intended by themselves to cause the surrender of the position, but to cover the advance of the embrasure-blasting party with its explosive charges which are considered the decisive weapon.

Antitank guns may be used to give close support to the embrasure-blasting party, being manhandled from cover to cover. They will attack the embrasure with armor-piercing ammunition and also give protection against possible tank-supported counterattacks.

It is probable that several such operations will be in progress on any one sector at any one time before an attack, in the first place to probe for weak spots, and in the second place to keep the enemy in uncertainty as to the final point of main effort of the attack. German feint attacks have often been delivered in such strength or with such violence as to be indistinguishable from the main attack.

Once a wedge has been firmly established in the enemy positions, the second phase of the attack begins. Troops so far held in their assembly area, or slowly making headway under cover of the artillery fire supporting the first phase of the attack, advance to cut the enemy position in two and to roll up the positions flanking the wedge.

Because the Germans anticipate enemy defenses organized in depth, and because these are unlikely to be fully disclosed until after the beginning of the attack, they do not make detailed plans for close-support covering fire, which would be hard to work out in advance, but tend to decentralize their support weapons and artillery for the second phase of the assault, in which reinforced battalions, companies, or platoons fight their own way forward, independently of their flanking units, until they have gained their final objective.

Attack on lightly defended positions is more similar to the conduct of the attack by the *Panzer* division. The first phase is likely to be a deployed attack on a two-regiment front, the third regiment in reserve.

The Germans believe that in the advance extended formation of units is advantageous because it forces the enemy to scatter his fire.

To counteract the overwhelming Allied superiority in artillery and planes which frequently knock out the attack before it is under way, the Germans have been known to use the following method. Small groups of less than platoon size infiltrate mainly at night over a period of three to four days into the hostile battle position or at least well behind the advanced positions. During the day the infiltrated groups conceal themselves, but if caught pass themselves off as ordinary patrols to avoid raising suspicion. When the actual attack is launched these units try to give the impression that the defender is surrounded and often cause great confusion.

When the Germans go over from the attack to the defense, even if only temporarily, they concentrate the supporting weapons around the commander of the unit that is to be supported, so that he can control the fire plan.

(5) *Infantry-assault gun coordination.* The assault guns are organized in assault gun battalions and are under the control of the division commander.

The Germans regard their self-propelled assault guns as decisive weapons to be employed particularly at the point of main effort. In cooperation with infantry they facilitate the penetration and breakthrough. These weapons, the Germans believe, complement artillery fire by their ability to follow the infantry right up to an objective. Their use for small actions before an attack is forbidden so as not to betray their presence. Surprise is sought by bringing them into position by night and camouflaging their assembly area. Used primarily to neutralize enemy support weapons at short ranges over open sights, assault guns are preferably employed in concentrations; to employ them singly or in comparatively small number is frowned upon by the Germans.

German assault guns advance with or just behind the infantry; they never go ahead of the infantry. When an objective is reached, the assault guns do not remain with the infantry while the position is being consolidated but retire about 1,000 yards to await further assignment.

In close combat the assault guns are rather helpless and therefore it is the task of the infantry to keep the enemy away from the assault guns. Newly-organized assault-gun escort batteries have the same task.

(6) *Artillery.* The Germans employ their field

artillery in general support (*Allgemeine Unterstützung*) or in direct support (*Unmittelbare Unterstützung*), in the same manner as the U. S. Army. The Germans consider the battalion as the firing unit. Splitting up an artillery battalion into batteries and placing batteries under an infantry battalion is the exception justified only when the infantry battalion has an independent mission (for example, flank protection) or when the terrain does not permit unified fire control by artillery battalion commanders. Single commitment of guns is against German tactical doctrine. Various recent reports, however, describe deviations from the prescribed practice. Normally the Germans do not employ single field artillery pieces for direct fire, as, for instance, the Russians do. But much use is made of roving guns (*Arbeitsgeschütz*), and of guns firing from alternate positions to make identification more difficult. Standing German orders call for the preparation of alternate firing positions, which, however, are used now only in cases of very heavy counterbattery fire, as the gasoline shortage keeps all movements to a minimum. The Germans often designate the number two piece as the roving gun, and, unlike the other pieces, it normally is not dug in. It frequently changes its position, which is about 250 to 300 yards from the rest of the battery.

The German artillery often engages a target from a lateral position. This deception, particularly identified with longer range weapons, is extended by employing another gun, often of lighter caliber, in a carefully coordinated attack on the same target. Flash simulators also increase the difficulty of visual location of active guns.

The first step to obtain infantry-artillery coordination is taken in the attack order and is assured by direct contact between the commanders, artillery liaison units (*Artillerieverbindungskommando*), and direct contact between artillery observers and infantry units.

The Germans also employ forward observers (*Vorgeschobene Beobachter*), who have the same task as their U. S. counterpart.

The signal equipment necessary for communication between units, liaison units, and observers is only partly organic. The Germans keep most of the signal equipment centralized in the division signal battalion, which allots equipment as needed to the various units.

In the attack the greater part of the artillery

supports the main effort. The remainder of the artillery is assigned the mission of flank protection against possible enemy counterattacks.

5. Meeting Engagement *(Begegnungsgefecht)*

In the meeting engagement the Germans believe that the advantage lies with the side which succeeds first in making effective preparation for the attack and thereby deprives the enemy of his freedom of action. When both adversaries attack immediately from march columns, the decisive factors are the initiative of the junior officers and the efficiency of the troops. The senior commander quickly coordinates the functions of the various officers, while the advance guard secures for him freedom of action and the opportunity for a speedy deployment of his troops.

6. Pursuit

U. S. and German tactical doctrines on pursuit are very much alike. Pursuit begins when the enemy is no longer able to maintain his position and abandons the combat area with the bulk of his forces. The object of the pursuit is the complete annihilation of the retreating or routed enemy. Effective pursuit requires great initiative from commanders of all echelons of command, who must not hesitate to start pursuit immediately, even when their troops are exhausted. The enemy must be given no time to pause to reorganize his forces and reconstitute his defense.

The pursuit is conducted on a broad front by means of fire and movement. When making for distant objectives every effort is made to get around the enemy's flanks and effect a surprise attack in his rear. However, care must be taken that enemy attack on one's own flank does not cause deflection from the original direction.

Fast-moving troops are used in the pursuit. These troops often are organized into pursuit or advance sections. The infantry scatters the enemy and by-passes resisting enemy strongpoints, leaving their destruction to units following in the rear. Part of the artillery places concentrations at the avenues of retreat, while the remainder displaces forward in echelon, providing continuous support for the units in front. The Germans emphasize that a pursuit without the necessary artillery support may lead to disaster. Assault guns travel well forward with the rapidly advancing infantry, their comparatively heavy armament enabling them to crush quickly and decisively any enemy forces attempting to make

a stand. Combat aviation bombs routes of retreat and strafes the hostile forces in direct support of the ground attack. Combat engineers repair damaged roads, facilitating the continuous flow of supply and troops.

Pursuit, after a successful breakthrough, is regarded by the Germans as an ideal mission for the *Panzer* division. *Panzer Grenadiers* in armored half-tracks or in unarmored vehicles and tanks supplement each other in pursuing the enemy. During the advance on roads, the tanks form the point. However, through wooded areas or larger villages the *Panzer Grenadiers* take over the point. Tanks and *Panzer Grenadiers* stay close together so that either, according to the situation, can be committed as soon as enemy resistance is encountered. Tanks are normally not used in units of less than company strength.

Section V. DEFENSIVE

I. General

In German doctrine the object of the defense (*Verteidigung*, or *Abwehr*) is to halt the hostile attack, or to gain time pending development of a more favorable situation for resumption of the offensive. Thus German and U. S. doctrine are essentially the same: only the offensive leads to decisive successes.

In the last two years German defensive operations have become increasingly passive in nature. The Germans formerly placed the greatest stress on immediate and violent counterattacks as effective means of destroying the attacking enemy. This required great mobility and large reserves. At present more emphasis is placed on the construction of defensive positions, and counterattacks are frequently local in character. It is most likely that this passive type of defense is only an expedient due to German shortages of mobile equipment and manpower.

2. Organization for Defense

a. GENERAL. The Germans attempt to break a hostile attack in front of the main line of resistance (*Hauptkampflinie*), at the forward limit of the battle position (*Hauptkampffeld*), or to force the enemy to abandon his attack.

As in U. S. practice, the commander usually determines from the map the main battlefield and assigns a general line as guide for the location of the main line of resistance, to ensure continuity of the defensive position. Lower echelon commanders fix the main line of resistance on the ground, since only on the terrain, after thorough reconnaissance, can the details of the defense be decided. A recent official German directive states, however, that reconnaissance must not delay the construction of defensive positions.

Organization of the defensive position follows a conventional pattern and includes an advanced position (*Vorgeschobene Stellung*), and an outpost position (*Gefechtsvorposten*), both of which usually are under immediate command of the area commander. A reserve position may also be provided.

The width and depth of a German defense area depend upon the terrain and the proportional strength of friendly and hostile forces. In general, however, the width of a defensive sector assigned to a unit is approximately twice the width of the sector when the same unit attacks. Normal sectors are: platoon, 220 to 550 yards; company, 440 to 1,100 yards; battalion, 880 to 2,200 yards; regiment, 2,200 to 3,300 yards; division, 6,600 to 11,000 yards.

b. ADVANCED POSITION. The Germans organize the advanced position 5,000 to 7,000 yards in front of the main line of resistance, within the range of their medium artillery. A position is selected which will prevent seizure by the enemy of important terrain features, provide good observation points for friendly artillery, and, if possible, deceive the enemy as to the location of the main line of resistance. Troops manning these positions attempt to make the enemy deploy his forces prematurely and, if possible, in the wrong direction.

The forces in the advanced position are usually reconnaissance detachments, which include machine-gun, armored-car, and antitank-gun units, the fire power and mobility of which make them suitable for this type of employment. In general they occupy important features, such as railroads, river crossings, cross-roads, and commanding ground. Forces in advanced positions are not expected to hold at all cost; in the face of superior enemy fire they retire along predetermined routes under over of their medium artillery.

c. OUTPOST POSITIONS. Outpost positions normally are established 2,000 to 5,000 yards in front of the main line of resistance. When the fronts are stabilized, the outpost position is the only position forward of the main line of resistance. The

location, which depends upon the terrain, is always within range of friendly light artillery.

German outpost positions are occupied in strength varying from platoons to companies, depending upon the mission, terrain, width of the sector, and the number of troops available. Often they are only weakly occupied as long as the advanced positions are in front of them. Ordinarily outposts are established by infantry units drawn from the main battle position, supported by the fire of close-support weapons, such as mortars and infantry guns. Antitank guns often are attached to these outpost units to repel hostile armored reconnaissance units. The main weapon, however, is the light machine gun which opens fire at ranges of about 1,300 yards, while riflemen commence fire at about 850 yards.

Firing positions are selected by the Germans to facilitate unobserved withdrawal of the outposts to the main battle position when hostile pressure becomes too strong. Several alternate positions are prepared for each weapon, and shifts are made by day and night to make it difficult for the opponent to detect and dislodge the outpost troops. Positions normally are selected at the edges of woods, villages, hedgerows, or hills. A good field of fire is considered mandatory, and the organization of firing positions is simple. Numerous dummy positions are constructed, including knee-deep trenches filled with leaves to simulate depth and occupancy. During the day, positions are manned by guards; at night, advanced listening posts, particularly alert at dusk and dawn, warn the troops of the enemy's approach. Small, prepared attacks with limited objectives under the protection of the outposts are utilized to interfere with the hostile preparations and secure information.

Withdrawal of the outposts is conducted so as not to hinder the fire of the main battle position. After the outposts are abandoned, they are likely to be covered by carefully registered fire of heavy weapons in order to prevent their occupation by the enemy.

d. MAIN LINE OF RESISTANCE. The Germans organize their battle position in depth, with individual strongpoints connected to form an uninterrupted belt. The strongpoints, constructed for all-around defense, and surrounded by barbed-wire obstacles and mine belts, contain one or more heavy weapons supplemented by machine guns, mortars, and riflemen. The smallest strongpoint is occupied by a reinforced squad. Squad

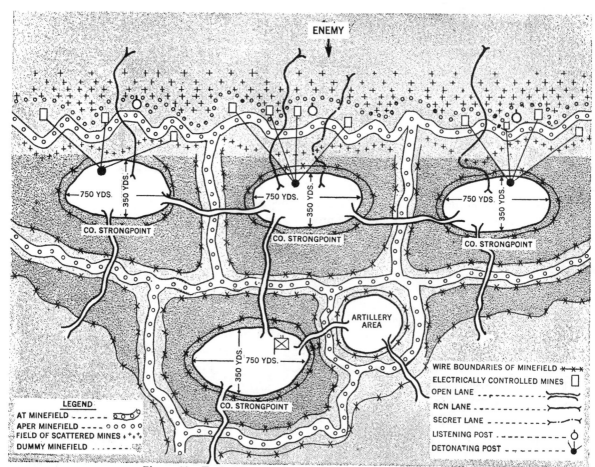

Figure 11.—Typical layout of a reinforced battalion strongpoint.

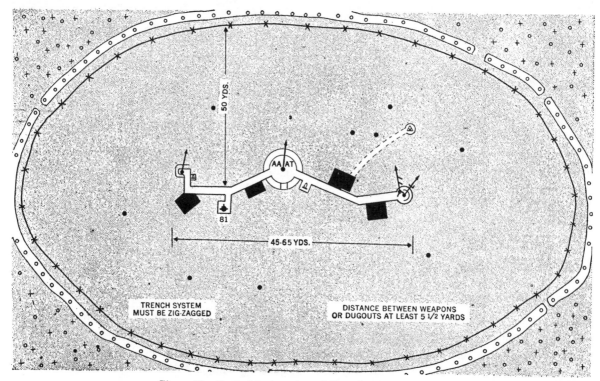

Figure 12.—Typical layout of a reinforced squad strongpoint.

strongpoints normally are incorporated into platoon strongpoints, and the latter into company strongpoints, etc.

The Germans make the maximum use of reverse slopes in their defensive positions. Forward-slope positions are usually avoided as they are detected too early by the enemy and are likely to be destroyed by massed fire. Since organization of a position in woods requires much time and labor, and strong occupation is requisite to compensate for poor observation, the Germans also avoid woods when time is short and labor scarce. Battle positions are laid out so that woods are neither in, nor directly in front or in rear of, defense installations. The Germans believe, however, that when it is possible to establish a well prepared position in a woods, a position so located offers the same advantages as a reverse slope.

When the Germans decide to construct defensive positions on terrain divided by a stream, they organize bridgeheads on the bank on the hostile side where the terrain facilitates crossings. Where the river forms a re-entrant bend into enemy-held terrain, a second position is constructed at the base of the bend. On narrow rivers and creeks, the entire German main line of resistance is on the hostile side of the river, and the stream becomes the tank obstacle of the position. (See antimechanized defense.) When the friendly side of the river consists of swampland, it is used as an obstacle, and the hostile bank is not included in the defense system.

The Germans endeavor to provide all parts of their position with strong support from artillery and heavy infantry weapons. A detailed fire plan is prepared in advance by the infantry and coordinated with the artillery plan. Provision is made for fire in front of the forward limit of the battle position, which is partly protected by minefields and other obstacles. Alternate positions are dug so that support weapons may be shifted and fired rapidly. The mass of the artillery lays concentrated fire both close to and well in front of the main line of resistance, and is sited to cover the spaces between the effective fire zones of front-line units.

The Germans in general adhere to the principle of "effect before cover" in determining priorities for constructing the various installations in a defense position. First they build combat trenches; erect infantry obstacles such as barbed-wire fences; and construct machine-gun positions, dugouts, foxholes, and antitank positions. They clear fields of fire by careful cutting of underbrush but try to avoid cutting down trees in order to preserve concealment of the position. The underbrush is left in front of the position as far as 1 to 3 yards. They organize observation posts for artillery and heavy infantry weapons, increase the depth of the battle position, dig communication trenches and emplacements for the heavy infantry weapons, and build command posts. Finally, they construct emplacements for the artillery, dig antitank ditches within the battle position, and build dummy positions.

The Germans insist on thorough camouflage. Whenever practicable, trenches and wire obstacles are placed along natural terrain lines such as rows of brush or edges of fields. Trenches are dug zig-zag at obtuse angles, 330 to 660 yards long, depending on the terrain. Machine-guns are emplaced in trenches 1 to 3 yards in length. To avoid silhouettes, the Germans heap more earth behind the trenches than in front. Dugouts for riflemen and for machine-gun positions normally provide sufficient protection against enemy artillery and mortar fire. Whenever possible, three layers of logs and earth are used as cover.

e. RESERVE POSITION. Occasionally a reserve position is organized and troops in the main battle position retire to it, but only under heavy pressure. This reserve position is constructed far enough to the rear to compel hostile artillery to displace forward in order to bring it under fire. Motorized reserve units normally are kept there for counterattacks which are planned in advance.

f. ANTIMECHANIZED DEFENSE. In constructing a defensive position the Germans stress construction of obstacles and antitank defenses. If possible they select tank-proof terrain, and natural tank obstacles, such as steep slopes, are improved. Very steep forward slopes are made at least 8 yards deep, while uphill slopes are made 2 to 3 yards high. Originally the Germans constructed antitank ditches well forward of the main line of resistance, but experience taught them that such ditches offered favorable jumping-off positions for hostile infantry and also revealed the location of the main line of resistance. At the present time, therefore, antitank ditches normally are dug in the area between the main line of resistance and the artillery positions. They are built in an uninterrupted line to avoid leaving passages that can be exploited by the enemy. All crossings essential to assure the maneuver-

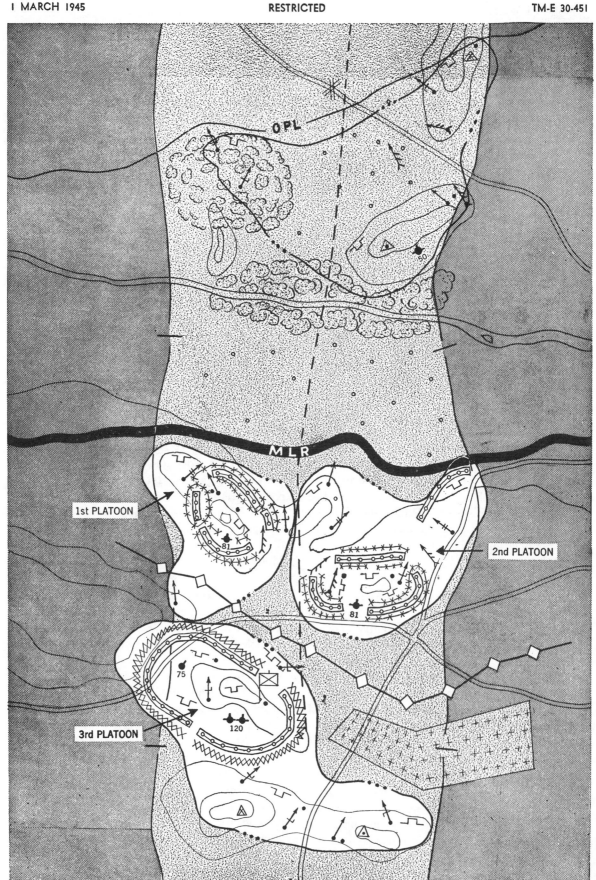

Figure 13.—German company in a defensive position.

ability of friendly troops are built so that they can be blown up on the shortest notice.

The Germans are aware that obstacles of any kind are effective only when covered by fire from various weapons. Consequently, there usually are trenches behind the antitank ditches from which machine-gun and antitank-gun fire can cover the entire length of the tank obstacle.

The Germans learned that dense minefields in front of their positions were an inadequate tank obstacle, because the enemy usually neutralized them by massed artillery fire or by concentrated air bombardment before launching a large-scale attack. Now German minefields normally are laid within the main battle position, and only single mines are dispersed in pattern at wide intervals in front of the main line of resistance. Particular stress is placed on the mining of roads. Routes of withdrawal which have to be left open are prepared for mining, and, if time does not permit placing of actual mines, dummy mines are installed.

The Germans employ many kinds of tank obstacles. They recently have used static flame throwers dug into the ground. Usually sited in pairs and in conjunction with other tank obstacles, they are fired by well concealed personnel as soon as hostile tanks come within range.

German antitank guns are disposed in depth, with some well forward. They often are dug in and carefully concealed to prevent the enemy from discovering the location and strength of the antitank defenses prior to attack. In emplacing antitank guns, the Germans prefer positions in enfilade or on reverse slopes. They normally employ two to three antitank guns in each position, protecting them from infantry attacks with light machine guns. Ranges at which the Germans open fire upon hostile tanks vary according to the caliber of the gun and its position. Although single antitank guns sometimes engage enemy tanks at ranges up to 1,000 yards, main antitank defenses usually hold their fire until the range is reduced to about 150 to 300 yards. The employment of close-combat antitank teams supplements the antitank defense. When the hostile tank attack is repulsed, the antitank guns move to alternate positions.

The Germans emphasize that the use of smoke can be of great assistance in defeating enemy tank attacks. Smoke shells are fired into the attacking formation about one-third the distance back from the leading echelon. Thus the Germans avoid blinding their own antitank gunners, and leading hostile tanks not only are left without adequate support but are silhouetted against the smoke. The Germans also rely on the smoke being sucked into the tanks and forcing the crews to dismount.

3. Conduct of the Defense

German defense of a position, whether hastily prepared or complete in all details, is conducted on the same principles. Unless they are compelled by manpower and materiel shortages to rely on the strength of their positions, the Germans prefer heavy concentrations of fire and powerful, coordinated counterattacks by mobile reserves of all arms. They apply the principle of selecting a point of main effort (*Schwerpunkt*) to the defense as well as to the attack. This principle necessarily is applied in reverse order in the defensive, the main effort being made opposite the point where the enemy is making his main attack.

German artillery attempts to disrupt a hostile attack before it reaches the defensive positions. The Germans state that it is invaluable to install observation posts simultaneously in the main line of resistance, in the advanced position, and in the immediate vicinity of the gun position. Thus they try to keep a hostile force constantly under observation and fire even when it achieves a penetration. The artillery regiment commander controls the fire as long as possible, although requests for artillery barrages may be made by unit commanders as low as platoon leaders. Capabilities of German heavy mortars, which like all other support weapons usually are sited on reverse slopes, are exploited, with a present trend toward mortar-fire concentration.

When a part of the battle position is lost, the area is taken under artillery fire to annihilate enemy forces which have penetrated it. The Germans normally organize reserve units, even when only relatively few troops are available. Immediate local counterthrusts by infantry elements and support weapons near the penetration endeavor to hurl back the enemy before he has an opportunity to establish himself. These small counterthrusts, which normally closely follow the artillery fire, preferably are directed at the flanks of the penetrations.

When the enemy succeeds in making a large penetration or breakthrough, the German higher echelon commander decides whether a general counterattack should be launched to restore the position or whether the main battle position should be reestablished farther to the rear. The counterattack is directed against the hostile flank, where possible, and is prepared thoroughly. Assembly area, time, objective, zone, artillery support, and employment of tanks, self-propelled artillery, assault guns, and air units are controlled by one commander.

German antiaircraft defense, which is unable to give adequate protection everywhere because of Allied air supremacy, is concentrated at important points. The main mission of the light and medium antiaircraft artillery is the protection of roads. Accuracy of Allied air reconnaissance compels the German antiaircraft artillery to change positions from day to day, the changeover being made during the night. The Germans also enforce a preliminary two-hour fire silence in the new position to try to trap enemy fighter-bombers. Searchlights often are placed parallel to a protected road to prevent enemy aircraft from illuminating the road by flares. This is particularly important since the Germans normally bring forward their relief troops, rations, and ammunition during the night.

4. Defense of Towns

The Germans regard towns and villages as excellent strongpoints, particularly if the buildings are of masonry. Towns also are regarded as excellent antitank positions because of the considerable infantry-artillery effort necessary to neutralize them.

In defending a town or village, the Germans locate their main line of resistance well within the built-up portion; the edges of the town, which provide easy targets for artillery fire, are believed to be too vulnerable. The main line of resistance is laid out irregularly in order to develop flanking fire, and every effort is made to conceal its location until the last possible moment. Minor strongpoints are maintained forward of the line in order to break up attacks and provide additional flanking fire. Cul-de-sacs are organized and attempts made to trap attacking forces in them for destruction by counterattacking mobile reserves. These reserves are kept in readiness within the town itself, but other reserve forces are held outside the town to prevent hostile flanking maneuvers.

Both occupied and unoccupied buildings are booby-trapped in organizing the defended positions. Entrances to buildings are blocked, and all windows opened so as not to disclose those from which fire is maintained. Rooms are darkened, and passages are cut in the walls between buildings. To avoid detection, the Germans fire from the middle of the rooms, and frequently change their positions, while communication is maintained through cellars and over roofs. Machine guns are sited low, usually in basements, to provide better grazing fire. Chimneys and cornices are used as cover for men on roofs; tiles may be removed to provide loopholes. Searchlights are mounted to illuminate fields of fire; in their absence vehicle headlights may be used as substitutes. When houses collapse, the defense is carried on from cellars, and rubble heaps of destroyed areas are organized into strongpoints.

Tanks are considered to be ineffective within a defended town, although the Germans have used them in static, dug-in positions at cross-roads and squares. As a result of their experiences on the Eastern Front, the Germans believe single tanks are too vulnerable to Molotov cocktails, magnetic mines, and explosive charges. When the Germans themselves use these antitank weapons, they employ them from foxholes dug outside the perimeter of the town. Efforts are made to destroy enemy tanks immobilized by antitank action, either within or outside the town, in order to prevent their recovery or use as artillery observation posts and machine-gun nests. Antipersonnel mines are interspersed in antitank minefields because the attacking infantry are considered the chief menace.

Assault guns may provide direct defensive support fire if attacking forces break through and disorganize the German position. To secure the added protection afforded by masonry walls, the Germans may locate assault guns or tanks within buildings and use them against hostile armored vehicles and infantry. Counterattacks, supported by assault guns or tanks, will not be withheld until the situation has become desperate; indeed, surprise counterattacks may be launched at any time.

For the defense of village strongpoints special battle commandants (*Kampfkommandanten*) are appointed. The battle commandant is usually the senior officer and the tactical commander of all military forces, emergency units, and civil organizations in his area. He has the disciplinary power of a regimental commander.

In the case of fairly small villages, consolidation of the place itself is usually deemed sufficient. For larger localities an outer defense

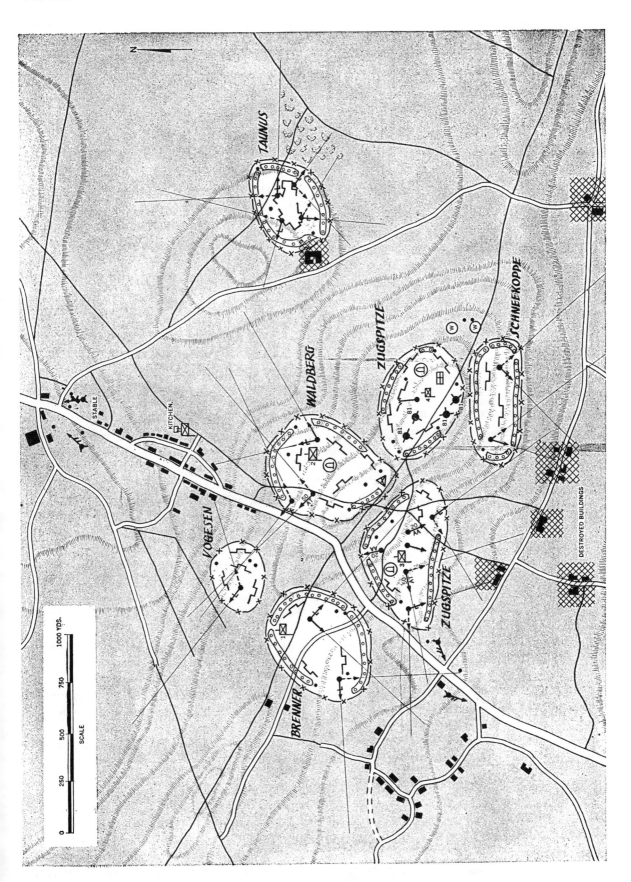

TAUNUS

SCHNEEKOPPE

ZUGSPITZE

WALDBERG

STABLE

KITCHEN.

VOGESEN

ZUGSPITZE

BRENNER

DESTROYED BUILDINGS

1000 YDS.

750

500

SCALE

250

0

system is constructed in addition to the inner defenses.

The inner defense system consists of a number of concentric positions which are broken down into perimeter positions, intermediate positions, and the inner ring position. The inner defense system is divided into sectors, each forming a strongpoint system in itself, with the strongpoints protected by all-around antitank and infantry obstacles and connected with each other by trenches.

The perimeter ring position is the most important part of the inner defenses and consists of one or more continuous trench systems, each with a deep main battle zone. The forward edge often is beyond the outskirts of the village, unless this creates unfavorable conditions for the antitank defense, in which case it is within the village itself. Artillery and heavy support weapons are employed as whole units in support of the perimeter ring position, although single guns may be detached for the defense of strongpoints and roads. The nearer the fighting approaches the inner ring, the more likely it will be that the Germans will split up the support weapons units for close co-operation with infantry assault groups.

The outer defense system likewise consists of a number of concentric positions, approximately 4 to 6 miles apart, so as to force the enemy artillery to displace to engage each one. For defense of larger towns the Germans organize the outside ring about 12½ to 18½ miles beyond the outskirts whenever feasible. Beyond this outside defense ring, about 2,200 yards forward, are the advanced positions, with covering units still further forward on main roads and railways.

Patrols of all types, including motorized and cyclist patrols, give early warning of the enemy's approach and keep him under continuous observation. Non-military outposts, such as police sentries, party officials, and local farmers also are used for these duties.

Sector boundaries for companies and battalions are defined from the outside defense ring to the center of the town or village. Usually they do not coincide with vital main roads, which always are defended by entire companies or battalions. Every strongpoint, defense block (combined adjacent buildings), and sector has local reserves; mobile reserves, consisting of combat groups comprised of infantry, tanks, assault and self-propelled guns, are employed for counterattacks of a larger scale.

In addition to regular military units the Ger-

mans employ emergency units, organized from personnel of Army, Navy, and Air Force in town defense. Besides these regularly organized emergency units, improvised emergency units are formed from stragglers, remnants of formations, and units in process of reorganization. Utilization of emergency units is only temporary. Their main tasks, of local nature, are protection of headquarters, supply points, airfields, etc., and garrison service in fortifications.

5. Doctrine of Westwall System

The Germans consider economy of force the fundamental principle in planning zones of permanent fortifications. They originally built the Westwall as a protective barrier along the French frontier to permit commitment of maximum forces offensively in the East. Thus, in 1939, they were able to hold in the West with approximately 20 divisions, while employing 40 to 50 divisions against Poland.

When Westwall construction ceased in 1940, German strategy in the West was offensive, envisioning an invasion of France by a wide envelopment, with the bulk of the German forces in the North, where the Westwall defenses were relatively weak. The pivot of maneuver was south of the Moselle River, where the Westwall defenses were strongest.

The Germans never have discarded the principle that offensive action is the best protection. When their armies were forced back to the Westwall in 1944, they used this defensive system as a base for offensive operations in selected areas, as in the Saar and the Eifel. Advantage also was taken of this protected zone for the free lateral movement of troops; shelters were utilized for the cover and concealment of reserve forces, weapons, and supplies.

German Westwall tactics are based on a stubborn defense of individual fortifications, local counterattacks against areas of penetration, and counterattack by general mobile reserves against areas of deep penetration. German troops are not permitted to develop a static-defense complex which might foster the idea that a position once surrounded is lost. Bunker garrisons are taught to continue resistance even though surrounded, because their perseverance impedes the attackers' advance and facilitates counterattacks. Troops are trained in the principle that the decision usually is achieved by the infantry in the open between bunkers. Organic heavy infantry weapons and artillery are the backbone of German defense

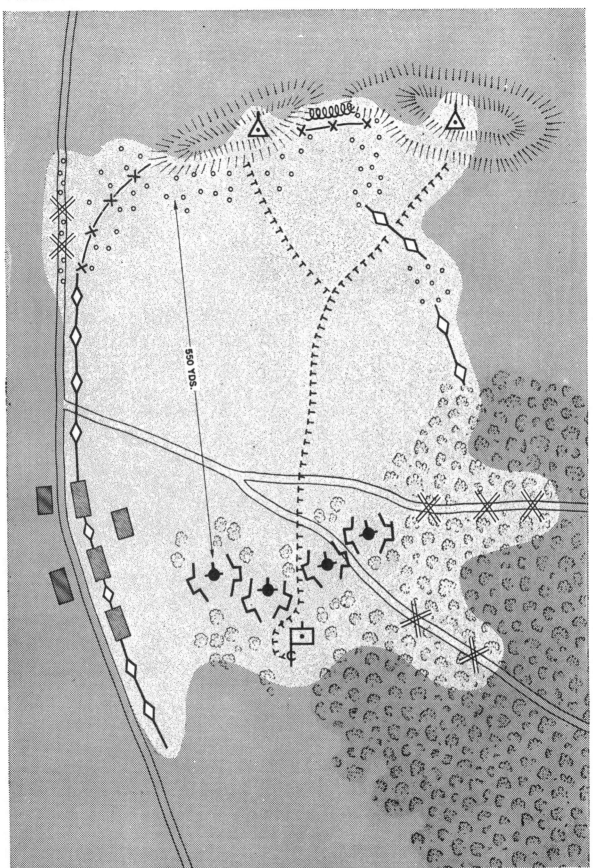

Figure 15.—Antitank defense of an artillery battery firing position.

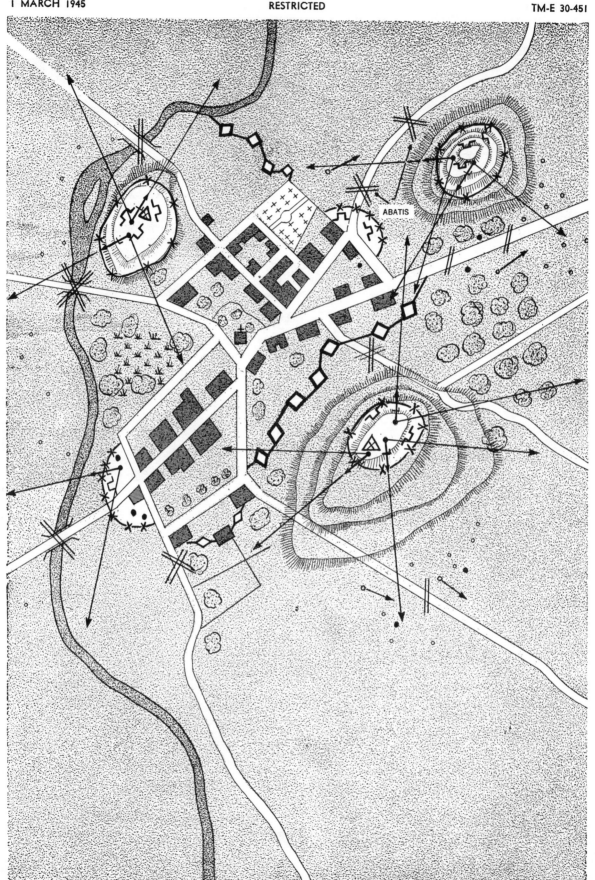

ABATIS

Figure 16.—Defense of a community.

in the Westwall, just as in mobile warfare. Reserves habitually are left under cover until the time for counterattack arrives.

Surprise is always attempted. For example, bunkers and heavy weapons frequently are sited on reverse slopes, not only for concealment and protection in defilade, but also to open fire suddenly upon the unwary attacker crossing the crest or moving around the nose of a hill. The attacker penetrating the Westwall defense system must be prepared to cope with unexpected resistance flaring up in his rear areas, surprise by accurate flanking and enfilade fire at short and medium ranges, sudden counterattacks by forces not known to be in the areas, and counterattacks in increasing strength as the penetration progresses.

German doctrine prescribes that the intact portion of the defenses must continue the battle, regardless of the situation at the penetrated area, until the appropriate command orders a readjustment of the line. Penetrations normally are dealt with as follows: by mobile reserves which seal them off frontally; by counterattack or counteroffensive from protected flanks to threaten the rear areas of the penetrating force; or by both, as in the Aachen area. At any rate, the Germans will attempt to destroy the penetration before the attacker has reorganized and consolidated his gains. Here again the principle of economy of force is generally followed. German troops may be taken from strongly protected and little threatened areas in order to concentrate on adequate counterattacking or counteroffensive force. Hence the attacker should have sufficient strength to ward off strong countermeasures and at the same time exploit the advantages gained by a penetration.

Section VI. RETROGRADE MOVEMENTS

I. Withdrawal from Action (Abbrechen des Gefechts)

a. GENERAL. The Germans break off an engagement for one or more of the following reasons: when it has served its purpose; when conditions require the employment of the troops, or part of them, on another front; when a continuation of the battle gives no promise of success; or when defeat is imminent.

When an attack exhausts itself without attaining its objective, the Germans assume the defensive as the first step in withdrawing from action. If the defense must be continued in a rearward position, the breaking of contact, the retirement, and the resumption of the defense are carefully planned beforehand. Positions in the rear are prepared for the reception of the troops, particularly if they have been engaged in heavy fighting. The retirement is made in conjunction with that of adjacent units, and stress is placed on maintaining the cohesiveness of the retiring forces.

By maintaining the usual fire of all arms, the Germans try to deceive their enemy as long as possible as to the continued occupation in force of their original position.

In view of the severe losses inflicted by Allied planes and armored forces on German troops during daylight disengagements, the Germans try to await darkness before withdrawing from action. At night they break off combat on a wide front and move back along routes as nearly perpendicular as possible to terrain features suitable for fighting delaying actions. When the situation forces them to withdraw during daylight, they do so by unit sectors, coordinating the movements of adjacent units.

b. ORDERS. The German company commander follows this outline in drafting his orders for breaking off an engagement:

General instructions. Rearward movement of supplies, ammunition-carrying vehicles, and equipment.

Reconnaissance and marking of routes of withdrawal.

Detailed instructions. Combat orders for the covering forces (reconnaissance units, heavy support weapons, medical personnel, infantry combat wagons, and infantry engineers).

Type, time, and march order for the withdrawal of the rifle platoons and heavy weapons.

Assembly areas.

Location of the company commander.

2. Retreat (Ruckzug)

a. GENERAL. Retreat is a forced retirement which is ordered by the Germans only when all possibilities for success are exhausted. The objective is to place enough distance between friendly and hostile forces to enable the former to conduct an orderly withdrawal and to occupy new positions to the rear.

b. COVERING FORCES. The German usually organize covering forces from troops in closest contact with the enemy—either whole tactical units or elements from several. These forces attempt to make the enemy believe that the position is still fully occupied. Engineers prepare additional obstacles, minefields, and booby traps forward of and within the positions to be held. A portion of the artillery and heavy infantry weapons support the covering forces. They maintain as long as possible their former fire activity to deceive the enemy, even when fulfilment of their mission means the loss of individual guns. The sector assigned to a covering force is usually too wide to be under effective control of a single commander, but the actions of the various commanders are closely coordinated. Orders specify whether the covering forces are to remain in contact with the hostile forces until they begin to advance, or to follow the main body after a specified interval.

c. REAR GUARD (*Nachhut*). (1) As the distance from the enemy increases, the retiring troops form march columns. Where possible, a division's retirement takes place along two parallel routes. The freshest troops available are used as rear guards. Since the rear guard cannot expect support from the retreating main body, it must be relatively strong. It is composed of infantry units. Generally the divisional field artillery retires with the main body, none being assigned to the rear guard. Self-propelled and heavy infantry-support guns, and even howitzers, are frequently attached to the rear guard. Tanks also may be assigned. A typical rear guard for each route in a division retirement is one infantry battalion to which are attached elements of the reconnaissance unit, to protect the flanks, and of the engineer unit, to prepare demolitions.

(2) The rear guard infantry battalion normally employs only one of its rifle companies on active rear guard tasks. The three rifle companies perform this function in turn as long as their strength remains approximately even. If the terrain demands it, two companies are employed at a time. Two or more antitank guns and half of the self-propelled or heavy infantry guns allotted to the full rear guard support the rearmost rifle company or companies. When pressure becomes too strong, the single rifle company is withdrawn through the two remaining rifle companies which are supported by the remainder of the attached weapons. Variations of this leapfrogging progress are repeated until darkness, when a general disengagement takes place and the original formation is resumed.

(3) Rear guards withdraw by bounds to selected but not prepared positions. The extent to which positions eventually can be prepared depends on the proximity of the pursuing forces,

the length of time each particular position is likely to be held, and the decision of the individual company and platoon commanders. During each stage of the retreat, the commander of the rear company can order a withdrawal to the main rear guard position, but withdrawal from each main rear guard position is ordered by the commander of the main body. Frequently the speed of withdrawal is based on a time-distance schedule. During the withdrawal from a certain town, rear guards were instructed to retire not more than 3,000 yards a day.

(4) Experience has shown that in certain types of country a reinforced rear guard company generally can hold up very superior forces on a front as wide as three miles. In one instance of a withdrawal from a defensive position along a river line, a German *Panzer* division, which had one *Panzer Grenadier* battalion and attached elements as its rear guard, was covered by one rifle company reinforced by a company of tanks, four infantry guns (including two self-propelled), and a battery of medium howitzers. The tanks were mainly used to cover the withdrawal of the rifle elements. On another occasion a similar rear party had a number of heavy mortars attached. These covered the infantry withdrawal with the help of four tanks, which also carried the mortars back to the next bound.

(5) Particularly suited for rear guard tasks, because of its armor and high fire power, is the armored reconnaissance battalion of the *Panzer* division. When employing the armored reconnaissance battalion in terrain that affords cover, the Germans site well camouflaged, armored half-tracks in wooded areas, flat reverse slopes, or high grain fields, and open fire with all weapons at very close range. The armored half-tracks then penetrate into the confused enemy and, after repulsing him, retreat to previously organized alternate positions.

3. Delaying Action

a. BASIC PRINCIPLES. The Germans make a distinction between "delaying engagements" (*Hinhaltendes Gefecht*) and "delaying action" (*Hinhaltender Widerstand*). A delaying engagement is primarily the general plan of the higher commander for holding back the enemy. Delaying actions are the measures taken by lower units to carry out the higher commander's plan.

The purpose of delaying actions is to enable the main German force to disengage itself from battle, retire in order, and establish a new defensive position. Delaying actions therefore seek to deceive the enemy as to German strength, dispositions, and intentions; to prevent the enemy from committing the main German forces; and to prevent close pursuit of the main forces by the enemy. These measures are accomplished by rear guards, special battle groups, and strongpoints, all of which are characterized by high automatic fire power, mobility, and economy in numerical strength.

Delaying actions are organized not in a main defensive belt, but on lines of resistance (*Widerstandslinien*). The distance between such lines is great enough to prevent the enemy from engaging two of them from the same artillery position. He is compelled to displace and move up his artillery to engage each line. These lines of resistance are normally established along forward slopes to facilitate disengagement and withdrawal under cover. The delaying actions are fought forward of the lines of resistance with mobile forces. Furthermore, battle outposts are organized forward of each line.

The main delaying weapons are machine guns, mortars, and self-propelled weapons. Tanks are used in small groups.

Maintenance of contact is a most conspicuous principle in the Germans' conduct of a withdrawal and delaying action. The size, composition, direction, and intention of the attacking enemy force are observed at all times.

b. CONDUCT OF THE DELAYING ACTION. During a delaying action, wide sectors are covered by artillery units widely deployed—guns are sited by sections if necessary—and by widely distributed infantry-support weapons. The defense is then further organized by establishing strongpoints manned by small groups.

The positions from which delaying actions are fought are characterized by very slight depth. As a general rule, a unit is responsible for double the front normally allocated in defensive fighting. A company sector is 650 to 1,300 yards; a battalion sector 1,750 to 4,400 yards; a regimental sector 4,400 to 6,600 yards; and a division sector 13,000 to 22,000 yards.

In leaving a line of resistance, German covering forces attempt to disengage by night. If that is not possible, their actions are governed by the following principle: the enemy is not allowed to come closer to them than they are from their next line of resistance. The troops must be able to reach the new position before the enemy reaches the old one, or their losses will be excessive.

The troops therefore do not retire in the face of enemy patrols—every effort is made to destroy such patrols—but only when the enemy mounts an attack. If it can be ascertained that the enemy is preparing for a massed attack, the Germans make a timely withdrawal to avoid exposing the troops to enemy artillery concentrations. Advance elements employ smoke to enable them to make a getaway in a critical situation. Riflemen cover the disengagement of heavy weapons, which move back by bounds. Every opportunity is taken to make limited counterattacks in order to inflict casualties on an enemy who advances recklessly.

Fire is opened at extreme ranges on an enemy advancing for a major attack. Enemy reconnaissance forces are allowed to approach, however, and then an effort is made to destroy them.

Counterattacks on a large scale are avoided, except when the enemy threatens to penetrate the line of resistance. When that occurs, the Germans counterattack with the main forces of the rear guard and seek to restore the situation in order that the program of staged withdrawal may be continued. Local counterattacks are made for the protection or retention of some feature essential to the safe conduct of the main withdrawal, or to gain time for the preparation of the line of resistance or phase line.

The area between the lines of resistance is called the intermediate area (*Zwischenfeld*). Explicit orders are given as to whether the intermediate area is to be covered in one bound or is to be fought over. The latter necessity arises especially when the next line of resistance has not been fully prepared and time must be gained. Detachments must reach the line of resistance early enough to insure that all the main positions are occupied in time.

The supply of ammunition is carefully organized. A great deal of ammunition is required for delaying actions because a few weapons on a broad front must do as much as or even more than the normal number of guns in a defensive position. When ammunition is scarce, the Germans specify, down to sections if necessary, the quantity of ammunition that may be used at each position. Every commander maintains a supply of ammunition for emergencies.

The Germans stress the importance of deceiving the enemy by every means. Artillery and heavy weapons are moved continually to give an impression of greater strength. Dummy positions and camouflage are also widely used.

So that isolated groups may be adequately directed, signal communication receives special attention.

In delaying actions in mountainous terrain, the Germans make greater use of their reconnaisance and engineer units than of any other component. Reconnaisance units are almost continuously in contact with advance and flanking enemy elements, and participate in most rear-guard and battle-group engagements.

c. STRONGPOINTS IN DELAYING ACTION. The Germans cover the rear guard's resistance or phase lines by a system of strongpoints or defended localities. Just as it is a function of the rear guards to prevent a pursuing force from making contact with the main body while it is on the move, so it is the function of strongpoints to prevent the penetration of resistance or phase lines until the main body has withdrawn to its next position.

In manning strongpoints, the Germans show the same economy of force they show in forming rear guards. Typical fire power of a strongpoint in close country is one or two self-propelled guns, two heavy mortars, and up to six machine guns. In open country, one self-propelled gun is normally employed, supplemented by three tanks and a small party of infantry with mortars and machine guns in armored half-tracks.

Strongpoints generally are organized on the hedgehog principle. Provision is made for all-around fire, but the strongpoints are not necessarily mutually self-supporting. They are normally located on commanding features, and sometimes on the forward edges of villages or hamlets if these dominate road or terrain bottlenecks. In flat country, however, villages usually are not occupied except by snipers, but positions are occupied in the rear of the villages to engage enemy vanguards debouching from them. Weapons are not dug in, and positions are frequently changed. Counterbattery fire thereby is rendered very difficult as there are no prepared positions to be spotted from the air. The Germans thus force their enemy to launch a full-scale attack supported by artillery to dislodge the garrison of the strongpoint, which normally withdraws just before the attack can materialize. Approaches to strongpoints which cannot be covered by fire are frequently mined. Extensive minefields are fre-

quently laid at the heads of re-entrants in hilly terrain.

d. BATTLE GROUPS IN DELAYING ACTION. Battle groups normally are organized for the execution of some specific task in the withdrawal, such as a local counterattack or the defense of some particular feature whose retention is necessary for the security of the main withdrawal.

Battle groups, which the Germans employ for offensive and defensive as well as delaying missions, vary in size from a company or two, with attached close support weapons, to a regiment or several battalions reinforced with tanks, artillery, antiaircraft, engineer, and reconnaissance elements. In all cases the Germans seek to make them as self-sufficient as possible in combat. In actual practice, however, the composition of German battle groups appears often to have been dictated less by the theory of what units should be put together to form a self-sufficient combat force, than by the demands of an emergency situation which commanders have been forced to meet with the insufficient and normally disassociated units at their disposal.

German battle groups may be organized for short, long, or changing missions. They are usually known by the name of their commander.

e. DEMOLITIONS AND OBSTACLES. To prevent the pursuing enemy columns from approaching close enough to engage even their rear guard elements, the Germans continually employ demolitions and obstacles of all kinds. The thoroughness with which engineer operations have been carried out has increased steadily throughout the war. Culverts and bridges are completely destroyed. Roads and all natural detours are mined, cratered, or blocked by felled trees; in streets and villages, streets are blocked by the wreckage of buildings. Vertical rail obstacles are placed to obstruct main routes; mines often are laid for 30 yards around the edge of the obstacle. Wooden box mines are used to a large extent as demolition charges, and aerial bombs and artillery shells are sometimes similarly employed.

Frequently rear parties are committed to a delaying engagement in order to cover the preparation of demolitions immediately behind them. During static periods in the general withdrawal, when the Germans occupy their line of resistance or phase line, engineer units prepare demolitions in the rear. After the withdrawal, these demolitions are covered by sniper fire, machine guns, and self-propelled weapons as long as possible.

Section VII.   MINEFIELDS

I. General

The Germans make extensive use of mines which they consider a most effective defensive weapon. Minefields are utilized chiefly to cover defensive actions and retreats, although limited use is made of them in offensive actions for flank protection. In a static situation the Germans regard minefields as an element of the front-line position, laid out according to an over-all mine plan developed in close conjunction with that for the fields of fire of all weapons. Within recent months, standard German doctrine for minefield location has been modified. Instead of laying dense minefields in front of the main line of resistance, dispersed mines are laid there, while the minefields proper are sited within the main battle position.

2. Surveying of Minefields

The Germans consider it necessary to survey the location of minefields and individual mines within the minefields. German engineers are instructed to choose reference points (*Festpunkte or FP*) for minefields which easily can be identified. At a grade crossing, at the intersection of two improved roads, at the edge of a village, or some such favorable location, this can be done without any difficulty. In some instances, however, the Germans are forced to use "guide wire" and auxiliary fixed points (*Vermessungspunkte or VP*). A type of auxiliary fixed point that has proved practicable is the center of an equilateral triangle with sides 15 to 25 feet long. The corner points and the fixed point itself may be stakes, rails, or concrete or steel girders about 3 feet in length connected with barbed wire. Such a fixed point can be reestablished easily because even heavy shelling will rarely destroy more than one or two stakes.

A minefield is limited by the four corner points A_1, A_2, A_3, and A_4. The corner points are marked clockwise, A_1 and A_2 forming the base line on the German side. The survey of the field refers to one or both points of the base line. Auxiliary fixed points, called "mine stakes" (*Minenpfähle*), are used if necessary. Fixed points may be reference points found on the map or auxiliary fixed points established by the troops. Distances are measured in meters; azimuth readings are taken on the German issue compass—divided into 6,400 mils like the U. S. compass but read counterclockwise, and marked with the letters *KZ* (*Kompasszahl*). The new-type compass called

"march compass" has clockwise graduation and is indicated with the letters *MKZ*. The Germans use the magnetic azimuth and always proceed in their survey from the friendly toward the enemy side.

The Germans believe that it is advantageous to lay a continuous chain of reference points 600 to 900 feet apart, through a division sector. This chain can be used to determine the location of ditches, trenches, obstacles, and pillboxes, as well as minefields. Individual points are designated with Roman numerals, starting on the right flank of the division sector.

3. Laying of Minefields

a. PATTERNS. To assure the greatest possible effect, minefields normally are laid out in definite patterns. The Germans make an exception to this practice, however, in sectors where they do not intend to undertake offensive actions. There they disperse the mines irregularly in the areas between defensive positions.

The main belts of a major antitank minefield laid in uniform pattern normally consist of antitank mines with a sprinkling of antipersonnel mines in the forward edge of the field. Both types may be fitted with anti-lifting devices, and some of the antipersonnel mines have trip wires attached. In some instances, these mines are placed in the intervals between the diagonal wires of a double-apron fence, with trip wires fastened to the diagonals.

A number of antitank mines are laid in the forward edge of antipersonnel minefields to prevent armored vehicles from detonating the main belt of antipersonnel mines. The forward edges of minefields of all types often are sown with explosive charges placed in wooden boxes fitted with pressure fuzes. These act as both antitank and antipersonnel mines, and discourage the use of detectors to locate the mines.

Forward of most regular fields, and particularly in front of lanes, mines may be found widely spaced or scattered at random in unmarked groups. Mines also are laid in spaces running out at right angles from the forward edge of the minefield to damage vehicles moving along the field in search of lanes.

All pressure-type antitank and antipersonnel mines are laid in lines. For measuring distances and spaces, the troops use a mine-measuring wire (*Minenmessdraht*) which they themselves make

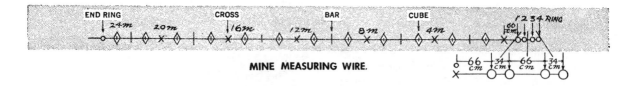

MINE MEASURING WIRE.

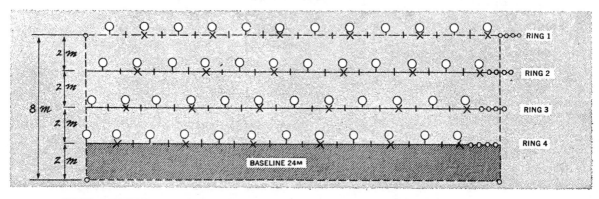

BURIED T-MINES (T-MINE 42 OR T-MINE 43), WITH 2-METER SPACING BOTH LATERALLY AND IN DEPTH.

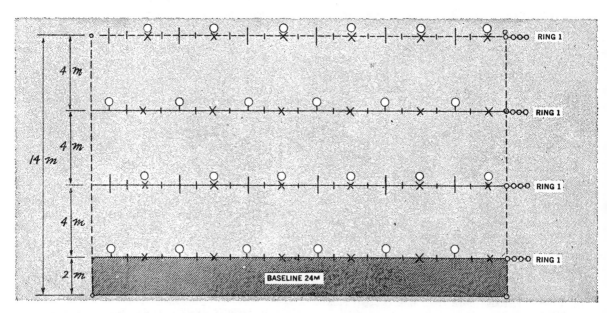

T-MINES (T-MINE 42 OR T-MINE 43) LAID ON SURFACE, WITH 4-METER SPACING BOTH LATERALLY AND IN DEPTH.

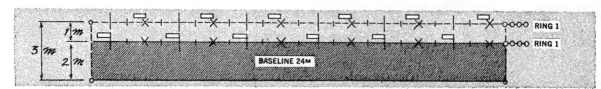

RIEGEL-MINES 43, BURIED OR LAID ON SURFACE.

AS A RULE TWO ROWS OF MINES ARE USED, BUT FOR EXTRA PROTECTION IN SPECIAL SECTORS FOUR ROWS ARE LAID, WITH THE THIRD AND FOURTH ROWS MOVED TWO "RINGS" TO THE LEFT WITH REFERENCE TO THE FIRST AND SECOND LINES.

Figure 17.—Mine Measuring Wire and Minefield Patterns.

from old telephone wire. (See *Figure 15.*) The mine-measuring wire is 24 meters (about 25 yards) long, and every meter (3 feet 3 inches) is marked with a piece of wood. The rings on the ends are about 5 inches in diameter. The measuring wire, in addition to measuring the distance between fixed points, serves to lay out right angles by staking out a triangle with sides of 6, 8, and 10 meters respectively. Spaces between mines are determined by reference to the marks on wire; the four rings on one end are used to offset the rows.

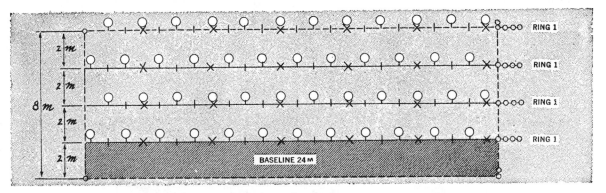

S-MINES WITH 2-METER SPACING BOTH LATERALLY AND IN DEPTH.

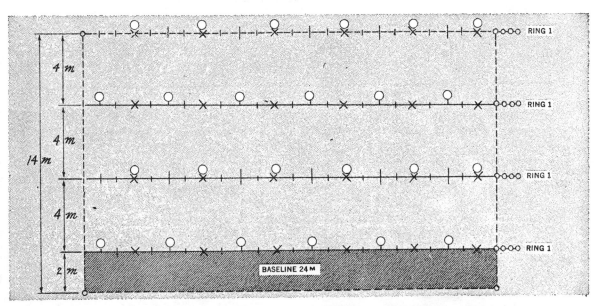

S-MINES WITH 4-METER SPACING BOTH LATERALLY AND IN DEPTH.

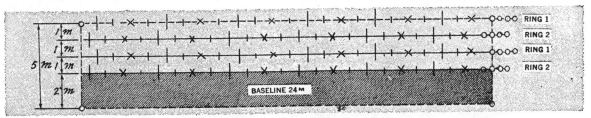

SCHU-MINES 42, SPACED ½-METER LATERALLY AND 1-METER IN DEPTH. THE MINES ARE PLACED AT ½-METER INTERVALS ALONG THE MEASURING WIRE.

Figure 18.—Minefield Patterns.

Type of Mine	How Laid	Interval between Mines	Number of Rows	Density per 1 Meter of Front
T-Mine 35	Buried	4 m (4.4 yds)	8	2
			12	3
			16	4
T-Mine 42 T-Mine 43	Laid on surface	4 m (4.4 yds)	8	2
			12	3
			16	4
	Buried	2 m (2.2 yds)	4	2
			6	3
			8	4
R-Mine 43	Buried or laid on surface	about 4 m (4.4 yds)	2	½
			4	1
S-Mine 35	Buried	4 m (4.4 yds)	4	1
			8	2
			12	3
	Buried	2 m (2.2 yds)	2	1
			4	2
			6	3
Schü-Mine 42	Buried	1 m (1.1 yds)	1	1
			2	2
			3	3
		½ m (0.55 yd)	1	2
			2	4

The density of a minefield depends upon the interval between mines and the number of rows. The table above represents the density.

Mine lanes are left open for patrols, and passage lanes for assault troops. For permanent patrols new lanes are made from time to time, and the old ones closed. A mine-free safety strip is provided on the Germans' side.

The Germans normally lay mine belts in individual sections 80 by 105 feet. The sections usually are staggered, and, for extensive mine belts, they are combined in units of three or four to form forward or reverse arrowheads, or echelons. Minefields arranged in echelon are surveyed by using corner posts on the hostile side of intermediate minefields as survey points.

The Germans emphasize that minefields must be covered by fire, although during a hasty withdrawal they often do not follow this principle. It is common for a regular minefield to have a listening post with two men at the rearward edge; about 70 or 80 yards farther to the rear there usually is a covering party of four or five men armed with one or two light machine guns.

When the Germans are in hasty withdrawal, they usually lay a large number of small nuisance minefields. These fields contain many different types of mines, which often are unmarked and show every evidence of hurried laying. The consequent lack of pattern uniformity makes their detection and clearance a laborious and dangerous task. Though no consistency is noted in layout and types of mines used in such fields, the Germans show certain preferences in their choice of sites for them.

b. LOCATION. In general, mines are laid either close to, or on, roads; on airfields and railways; and along telegraph routes. Surfaced portions of roads usually are avoided by the hasty mine layer, but khaki-painted T-Mines sometimes are placed on the surface at dips in the road, in the hope that drivers will be unable to check their vehicles in time to avoid them. The Germans also place mines along the shoulders of the road opposite narrow places where drivers have to detour to pass, and at the entrances to defiles where they have to pull off the road to wait for vehicles moving in the opposite direction. Other places usually sown with antitank mines are turnouts, sharp bends, the unsurfaced islands sometimes found at crossroads, berms, and well worn wheel ruts.

c. CONCEALMENT. The Germans, with great ingenuity, attempt to make their mines difficult to detect. They bury them as much as 24 inches below the surface where they explode only after passage of a number of vehicles has compacted the earth cover sufficiently to operate the fuze. They put explosives in wooden boxes to prevent the effective operation of ordinary mine detectors, and mark tire prints in the earth on top of the mine by drawing a detached axle and wheels over it.

The Germans also show considerable ingenuity in siting random antipersonnel mines on the line of the hostile advance. Road demolitions are plentifully sown with S-Mines, and kilometer posts at points where vehicular drivers have to dismount to read directions are similarly treated. S-Mines also are placed in ditches, often close to the trip-wire peg of another mine.

Nuisance fields on lines of communication generally are closely spaced, occasionally so closely as to cause sympathetic detonation. This is particularly possible when mines are laid with their pressure plates almost flush with the surface of the ground and only lightly covered with earth.

German dummy minefields take various forms. In some cases a trip wire is laid to give the appearance of a minefield perimeter wire, with the usual lanes, and the ground is disturbed at regular intervals. Scrap metal, often dispersed with

real mines, is placed in shallow holes to cause a reaction in the mine detector. Dummy mines often are wired in and connected with booby traps.

4. Marking of Minefields

The Germans stress the marking of minefields and attempt to mark them in such a manner that they cannot be recognized by the enemy but can easily be found by their own troops. Their methods of marking minefields are not uniform. The front edge of a field often is unmarked and unwired; the rear edge seldom so. Some fields have been found unmarked, but because of many accidents caused by their own minefields, the Germans issued orders within recent months making proper marking obligatory.

The following are typical examples of markings by the Germans, the type used depending on the situation and terrain: corner-post marking stakes; double-apron fence on the enemy side and a single trip wire on the friendly side, or the reverse; single knee-high wires; cattle fencing; empty mine crates; and signs.

The length of marking stakes varies with the terrain. They are flattened on one side for a length of about 8 inches. The flat surface is painted red, with the letter *M* (*Minen*) in black.

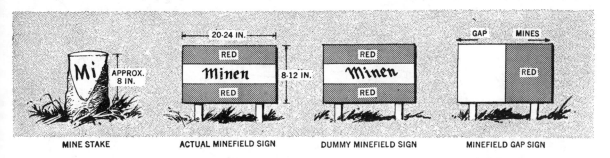

MINE STAKE   ACTUAL MINEFIELD SIGN   DUMMY MINEFIELD SIGN   MINEFIELD GAP SIGN

OTHER TYPES OF SIGNS AT ACTUAL MINEFIELDS   OTHER TYPES OF MINEFIELD GAP SIGNS

Figure 19.—Minefield signs.

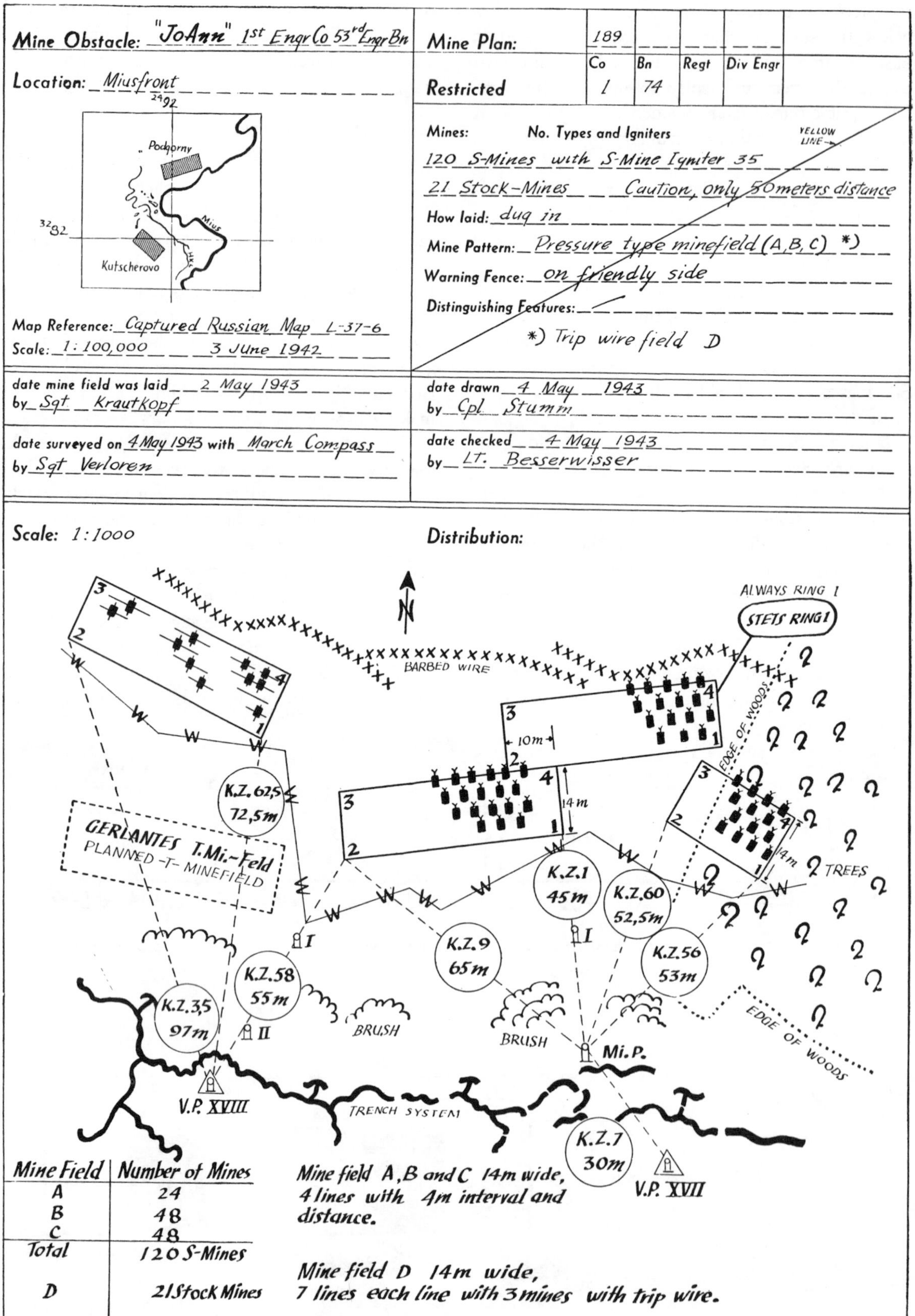

Mine Obstacle: "JoAnn" 1st Engr Co 53rd Engr Bn

Location: Miusfront

Map Reference: Captured Russian Map L-37-6
Scale: 1:100,000　　　 3 June 1942

Mine Plan:	189			
	Co	Bn	Regt	Div Engr
Restricted	1	74		

Mines:　　No. Types and Igniters　　　　YELLOW LINE →
120 S-Mines with S-Mine Igniter 35
21 Stock-Mines　　　 Caution, only 50 meters distance
How laid: dug in
Mine Pattern: Pressure type minefield (A, B, C) *)
Warning Fence: on friendly side
Distinguishing Features:

*) Trip wire field D

date mine field was laid　 2 May 1943
by Sgt Krautkopf

date drawn 4 May 1943
by Cpl Stumm

date surveyed on 4 May 1943 with March Compass
by Sgt Verloren

date checked　 4 May 1943
by LT. Besserwisser

Scale: 1:1000　　　　　　　　　　Distribution:

Mine Field	Number of Mines
A	24
B	48
C	48
Total	120 S-Mines
D	21 Stock Mines

Mine field A, B and C 14m wide,
4 lines with 4m interval and
distance.

Mine field D 14m wide,
7 lines each line with 3 mines with trip wire.

Figure 20.—German mine plan.

Mine Obstacle: _"Pauline"_

Location: _South of Ladoga Lake_

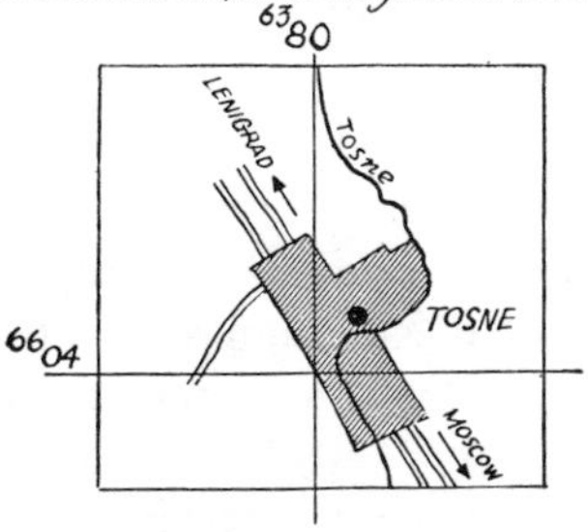

Map Reference: _Russia_ _O-36-34_
Scale: _1:100,000_ _July 1941_

Mine Plan:	578			
	Co	Bn	Regt	Div Engr
Restricted	3	122		

Mines: No. Types and Igniters   YELLOW LINE →

17 concealed charges with 17 clockwork
long delay igniters

How laid: ____

Mine Pattern: ____

Warning Fence: ____

Distinguishing Features: ____

date mine field was laid _26 and 27 August 43_ by _Capt. Wurst_	date drawn _27 Aug 43_ by _Cpl Schlegel_
date surveyed on _26 Aug 43_ with ____ by _Capt. Wurst_	date checked _28 Aug 43_ by _Maj. Knopf, Bn Co._

Scale: approx 1:5000   Distribution:

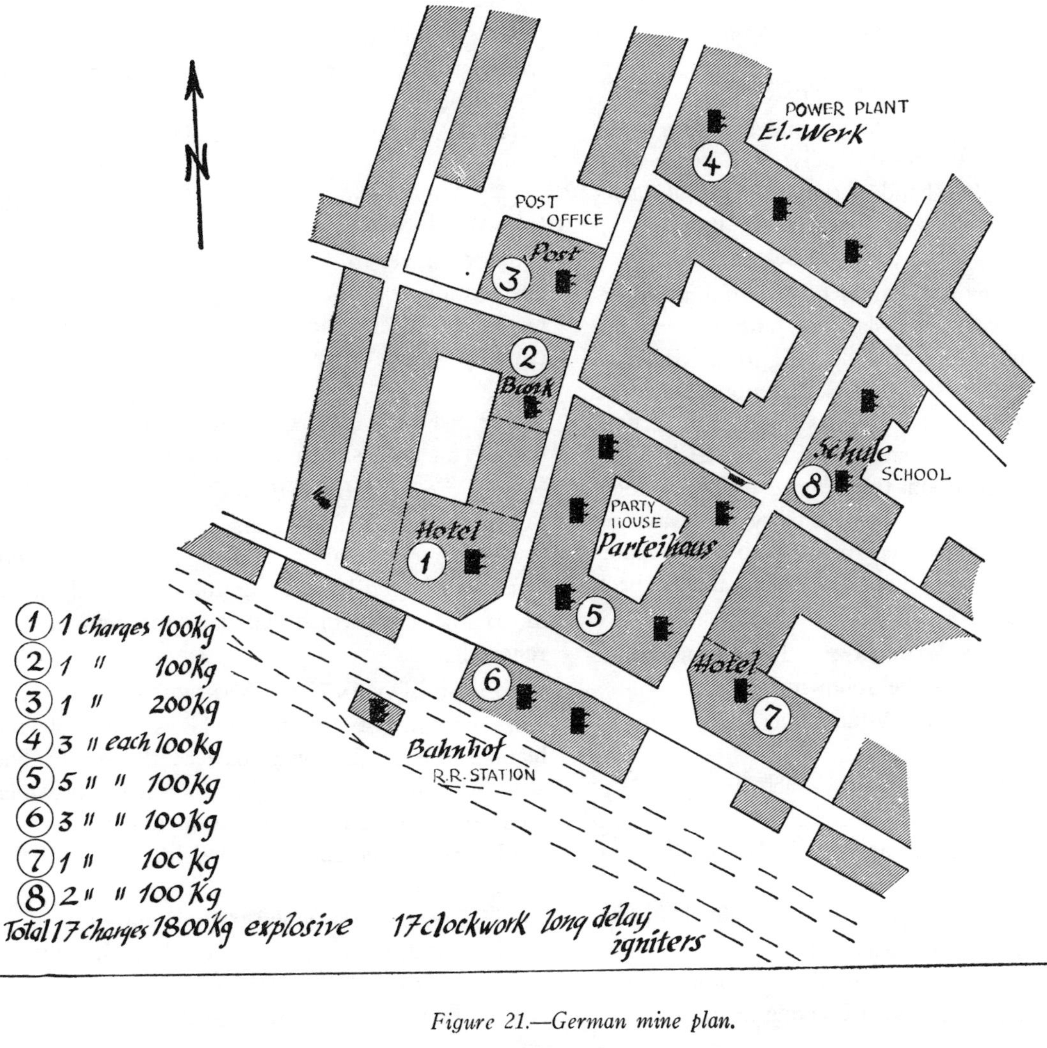

1. 1 charges 100kg
2. 1 " 100kg
3. 1 " 200kg
4. 3 " each 100kg
5. 5 " " 100kg
6. 3 " " 100kg
7. 1 " 100 kg
8. 2 " " 100 kg

Total 17 charges 1800kg explosive   17 clockwork long delay igniters

Figure 21.—German mine plan.

Such stakes are used only on the friendly edges of minefields.

Signs are painted in red and white on boards or pieces of sheet metal, and fastened to two stakes. The edges of minefields are marked with signs showing horizontal stripes. Edges of lanes through the fields are shown by vertically divided signs with the white portion on the side of the lane, and the red portion on the side of the mine-field (danger). The reverse side of the signs (the side toward the enemy) is painted olive drab. If red paint is not available, the Germans substitute black-and-white signs. They are painted with the following words:

> *Minen*—for mines
>
> *Gasse* or *Gassen*—for mine lanes
>
> *Entimint*—for an area cleared of mines.

Minefields are marked with vertical lettering, dummy minefields with slanting letters. This distinction, however, is supposed to be made known only to the German engineer troops because other troops may divulge the location of dummy mine-fields by crossing them.

5. Mine Plans, Sketches, and Reports

A German mine plan shows one or more fields in all necessary technical details. A German mine map, on the other hand, shows all mine obstacles within one front sector and their tactical significance, but without technical details.

The Germans use a number of different forms for their reports and sketches, although all are based on the same principle. Figure 17 shows a very commonly used form. The upper third of the mine map form provides space for written specifications and a small situation sketch. The drawing is made on the blank space provided. It is the engineers' responsibility to draw up mine maps, and to keep them up to date. Additional remarks sometimes are placed on the back of the sheet.

a. DETAILS OF MINE MAP. The German mine map usually shows the following details:

(1) Name of the obstacle and designation of the unit which laid it.

(2) Name of the area in which the obstacle is located.

(3) Grid reference and particulars of the map sheet referred to.

(4) Obstacle shown in the little sketch in red.

(5) Date minefield was laid.

(6) Name and rank of officer or noncommissioned officer in charge of laying field.

(7) Day of survey and instrument used (old or new compass—German issue).

(8) Name and rank of officer or noncommissioned officer in charge of survey.

b. MINE DATA IN MAP. The following data are given on the mines:

(1) Number, type and igniter. (Example: 72 T-Mine with *T-Mi.Z. 42,* booby-trapped.)

(2) Whether or not the mines are dug in.

(3) Number of rows, and number of mines per row.

(4) Fence (Example: warning fence on friendly side.)

(5) Special features (Example: destroyed enemy tank in center, on enemy side.)

c. MINEFIELD-TYPE IDENTIFICATION IN MAP. Colored lines drawn diagonally across the upper right-hand field of the mine map identify the type of the minefield as follows:

(1) A red diagonal line designates fields which cannot be cleared because some or all mines are booby-trapped.

(2) A yellow diagonal line designates fields which can be cleared by using data from mine document.

(3) A green diagonal line designates dummy minefields.

(4) Mines taken up or exploded are marked in red.

The number of the minefield plan and unit designation appears on the upper right-hand corner of the sheet. Battalion, regiment, and division engineers make their notes in the space provided for them.

For S-Mines laid 50 meters (55 yards) from the German lines, a note is made in red letters: *VORSICHT, NUR 50 METER ABSTAND!* (Caution, only 50 meters distance!)

In case electrical ignition is provided, a note is made showing how the igniters will be disposed of, if the unit which has laid the minefield is relieved.

d. INFORMATION IN MINEFIELD DRAWING. The drawing of the minefield is made in the blank space on the lower part of the sheet. The scale is from 1:500 to 1:2,000 whenever possible. The following information is included:

(1) Shape and size of minefield.

(2) Pattern.

(3) Location of booby-trapped mines.

(4) Location of survey points with azimuth and distances.

(5) Type and location of warning fence.

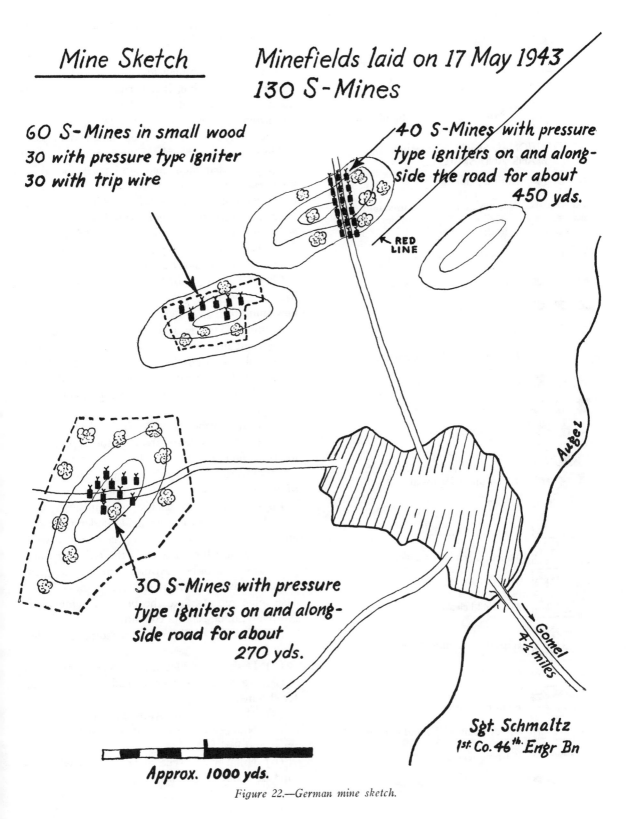

Mine Sketch   Minefields laid on 17 May 1943
130 S-Mines

60 S-Mines in small wood
30 with pressure type igniter
30 with trip wire

40 S-Mines with pressure
type igniters on and alongside the road for about
450 yds.

RED LINE

30 S-Mines with pressure
type igniters on and alongside road for about
270 yds.

Augel

Gomel
4½ miles

Sgt. Schmaltz
1st Co. 46th Engr Bn

Approx. 1000 yds.

Figure 22.—German mine sketch.

CONVENTIONAL SIGNS FOR MINE MAPS

 Terrain impassable for tanks

 Antitank ditch or obstacle

Antitank mine field

Antipersonnel mine field

3)
4) Mines per meter width of front

CONVENTIONAL SIGNS FOR MINE PLANS AND SKETCHES

● ● ● Antitank mines

 Index number to be used only if different types of mines are laid in the same field.

o o o Improvised antitank mines

S-Mines

Stock Mines

Schu-Mines 42

☐ ☐ ☐ Improvised antipersonnel mines

 Small hidden charges

 Large hidden charges

 Observation mines

 Booby-trapped mines

 Taken-up or destroyed

 Scattered mines

 Deliberate mine field

 Mines lying on the surface

 Mines below the surface

 Mine field cleared or destroyed

 Gaps through mine fields

 Dummy mine fields

 Built-in hidden charges

Survey points (VP) and Fix points (**FP)**

-W—W—W- Warning fences

➡ Direction of enemy attack

(6) Location of the front lines and fortifications.

(7) Neighboring minefields, mine lanes, terrain features, special features.

The Germans believe that it is not necessary to mark on the minefield drawing the location of every single mine, if a partial drawing is sufficient. The German mine plans contain the detail symbols shown in Figure 18, while simple tactical signs are sufficient for minefield maps.

The Germans complete their mine plans at company or battalion command posts, based on sketches and data compiled while the field is being laid out. They make five copies of all mine plans and distribute them as follows: One for engineer company which is in charge of the minefield; two for division; one for army; one for central file in *Dessau-Rosslau.*

Changes in the minefield are recorded on the back of the mine plan. After three changes a new mine plan is drawn.

A mine sketch is a simplified mine plan used to transmit information on a minefield as rapidly as possible. It is not drawn to scale, and is drawn whenever the tactical situation, bad weather, or other circumstances prevent the preparation of mine plans.

Front-line troops receive from the engineers instructions or sketches showing the approximate location and extent of the minefield. These sketches, as a rule, do not contain details on types of mines or igniters, pattern, and survey points.

Engineer units in charge of minefields keep records of changes in minefields under their care and keep these records with their units, while mine plans are turned over to the relieving units.

e. MINE REPORTS. Armies generally designate certain areas for fields of scattered mines. In this case mine reports take the place of mine plans. Normally, mine reports contain:

(1) Number of the order authorizing scattering of mines.

(2) Designation of units scattering the mines.

(3) Name and number of field containing scattered mines.

(4) Map location of scattered minefield.

(5) Number of mines scattered, subdivided by types and igniters.

(6) Number and type of booby-trapped mines, kind of booby trap.

Section VIII. SPECIAL OPERATIONS

1. Town and Street Fighting

In attacking a town or village, the Germans employ flanking and encircling tactics. They attempt to cut off water, electricity, gas, and other utilities. While carrying out the flanking maneuver, they pin down the defenders with heavy artillery fire and aerial bombardment. When it is necessary to make a direct assault, the Germans concentrate all available heavy weapons, including artillery and air units, on one target. They favor as targets for their massed fire the forward edges of the community, especially detached groups of buildings and isolated houses. During the fire concentration the infantry assembles and attacks the objective immediately upon termination of artillery fire. Tanks and assault guns accompany the infantry, and with their fire immobilize any new enemy forces which may appear. They also support the infantry in sweeping away barricades, blasting passages through walls, and crushing wire obstacles. Guns and mortars are used against concealed positions, and antitank guns cover side streets against possible flanking operations. Machine guns engage snipers on roofs.

The immediate objective of the Germans is to divide the area occupied by the enemy. These areas then are isolated into as many smaller areas as possible, in order to deny the enemy freedom of movement.

Another form of attack employed by the Germans is to drive through a community and establish good positions beyond the town to block the retreat of the defender. Then they try to annihilate the enemy within the community.

The assaulting troops are divided into a number of columns and make a series of coordinated parallel attacks. Attacks from opposite directions and conflicting angles are avoided, since they lead to confusion and to firing on friendly troops. The columns are sub-divided into assault and mop-up groups. Assault detachments of engineers, equipped with demolition equipment, flame throwers, and grenades, accompany the infantry. Where possible, the Germans blast holes through the walls of rows of buildings along the route of advance in order to provide the infantry with covered approaches. These passages afford protection for bringing up supplies and evacuating casualties. Houses are cleared of defenders by small-arms fire. Streets are avoided as much as possible by the Germans who infiltrate simultaneously through back yards and over roofs. They attempt to further the advance by seizing high buildings which offer dominating positions and wide fields of fire.

When compelled to advance through streets, the Germans move in two files, one on each side of the thoroughfare. The left side is preferred as it is more advantageous for firing right-handed from doorways. Consideration is given to the problem of fighting against defenders organized not only in depth but in height. Consequently the men receive specific assignments to watch the rooms, the various floors of buildings, and cellar windows. Side streets are immediately blocked, and at night searchlights are kept ready to illuminate roofs.

As soon as a building is occupied, the Germans organize it into a strongpoint. Windows and other openings are converted into loopholes and embrasures. Cellars and attics are occupied first in organizing for defense.

Even buildings which have been completely destroyed are kept under constant observation to prevent their reoccupation by the enemy. From occupied buildings the Germans deliver continuous machine-gun and rifle fire with the object of denying the enemy the opportunity to occupy alternate positions.

Underground corridors and sewers, which provide excellent cover for defenders, are attacked with determination. When immediate clearance or smoking-out is not possible, the entrances are barricaded, blasted, or guarded.

Aware that their tanks and assault guns are vulnerable to attacks by tank-hunting units, the Germans assign infantry to protect them. Barricades and obstacles are cleared by infantry and engineers. All able-bodied civilians, regardless of danger, are summoned to clear the streets of debris.

When a section of a town is occupied, the Germans close up all side streets leading from the occupied area, block all exits of houses, and then begin a house-to-house search with details assigned to special tasks, such as mopping up roofs, attics, basements, courtyards, and staircases.

2. Attack on Fortified Positions

The Germans realize the difficulty of attacking a strongly fortified enemy position and prepare such an attack well in advance of the actual operation. Before attacking a large and intricately fortified position covering a large area—a classical example was the assault on the Belgian Fortress Eben Emael—the Germans attempt to secure, in addition to information obtained through normal reconnaissance, its exact plan by the employment of agents and fifth columnists. When time permits, they construct a duplicate of the fortification on similar terrain well in the interior of Germany, as they did with Eben Emael. In building such installations for intensive rehearsal training of specially-organized combat teams, the Germans spare neither labor nor expense. These special combat teams usually consist of combat engineers, reinforced by infantry, antitank, and chemical warfare units.

The attack on the fortress usually is preceded by an intensive dive-bomber bombardment and long-range heavy-artillery fire. The purpose of these bombardments is to destroy obstacles and minefields, and to create bomb craters which not only provide cover for assaulting troops but also may be converted into firing positions. Often paratroopers land in close proximity to the fortification just prior to the assault, immediately establishing radio communication with the combat-team headquarters.

The climactic phase of the operation is the assault. Its primary objective is to get the engineers forward to certain selected works. During the approach, and until the engineers reach the fortifications, the artillery delivers fire of maximum intensity. Antitank guns lay direct fire against the embrasures, and chemical-warfare units employ smoke to blind forts and adjacent supporting works. The infantry covers the embrasures with rifle and machine-gun fire and remains in readiness to move forward and consolidate any success the engineers may gain. Engineers crawl forward, utilizing shell holes for cover. They are equipped with hand grenades, blocks of TNT, and submachine guns. Some groups use bangalore torpedoes, some pole-charges, while still others are armed with heavy flame throwers. With TNT and pole charges, they attempt to demolish systematically the weaker works, such as embrasures, ports, turrets, joints, and doors.

3. Combat in Woods

When attacking in woods, the Germans usually divide the area into company sectors. The Germans stress constant reconnaissance to discover the most weakly manned enemy position. This reconnaissance is carried out, even though company strength becomes temporarily reduced. Reconnaissance patrols usually move clockwise from their original position. The company commander reviews the reconnaissance reports in detail with his platoon and section leaders.

The company usually deploys in wedge formation when advancing. In order to achieve surprise, the Germans often leave the roads and advance cross-country.

As soon as the point of the wedge of the company is in sight of the enemy, the Germans creep forward to close-combat range, always keeping contact with adjacent and supporting units. The company then storms the enemy's position, using the greatest possible number of hand grenades, pole charges, and close-combat weapons. The advance elements attempt to break into the hostile position as deeply as possible, the body of the wedge widening the peneration on both sides. The company commander then decides whether to roll up the enemy position on the more important flank or to hold the ground until reinforcements arrive before continuing the attack.

Each platoon details at least one observer, armed with an automatic weapon, to neutralize enemy treetop snipers. The Germans believe that bursts of fire, rather than single shots, are necessary to deal effectively with such snipers.

The Germans consider fighting in wooded areas as the primary task of riflemen and machine gunners, since the employment of heavy-support weapons often is impossible. The Germans occasionally dismount heavy machine guns and use them as light machine guns. Antitank guns of small caliber and light infantry howitzers sometimes are brought forward manually, and when indirect fire is not possible they engage targets directly. Light mortars are employed individually. From Finnish troops, the Germans learned a successful method of using mortars in woods. The mortar observers, accompanied by a telephone operator, move with the advanced element. The line back to the mortar crew is exactly 200 yards long. One man is detailed to see that the line does not get hung on the way and as far as possible runs in a straight line. When the advanced element contacts the enemy, the observer judges the distance from himself to the target and adds the 200 yards to the mortar range. Bracketing of fire for adjustment is considered too dangerous because of the close proximity of friend and foe.

When the Germans leave a woods or have to cross a large clearing within the wooded area, the troops work themselves close to the edge of the woods. Then all the men leave the woods simultaneously, rushing at least 100 yards before seeking cover.

4. Combat in Mountains

a. GENERAL. The German principles of combat in mountain areas correspond in general to those employed on level terrain. The peculiarities of mountain terrain, such as limited routes, extreme weather conditions, and difficult communications, necessitate additional considerations in the tactics employed. The greatest differences occur in the higher mountains, where the Germans utilize specially trained mountain troops, which include the renowned Tyrolean and Bavarian mountaineers.

The Germans emphasize that all operations will be of longer duration in mountainous country than in lowlands, and therefore make proper allowance for the factors of time and space. For every 330 yards ascent or 550 yards descent they add 1 hour to the time estimate for covering a given distance on the map. Movements, command, and supply in mountain areas represent sources of difficulty, according to the Germans.

b. TACTICAL CHARACTERISTICS OF MOUNTAIN WARFARE. The Germans divide their units into numerous marching groups, which normally consist of a reinforced infantry company, an artillery battery, and an engineer platoon. In this manner the Germans counteract the danger of ambush, since each group is able to fight independently. The Germans locate their engineer units well forward with the advance guard so that they may assist in road repairs. The Germans realize that small enemy forces can retard the advance of a whole column and therefore they have single guns sited well forward. They also organize stationary and mobile patrols for flank protection.

The skill and leadership of junior commanders are severely tested in mountain warfare, as forces generally are split into small groups, the efficient command of which requires a high standard of training and discipline. Columns often are separated by large areas and impassable country, and since lateral communication is often very difficult, command of deployed units becomes much more complicated than over level terrain.

Normally supplies are organized in two echelons, the mountain and valley echelon.

The Germans make extensive use of high-trajectory weapons in mountain fighting, although antitank guns and heavy machine guns are used for covering road blocks. The effectiveness of the mountain artillery depends on carefully selected observation posts which are in communication with the single gun positions.

Radio is the primary means of communication, since the laying of telephone wire is not considered feasible.

c. MOUNTAIN TACTICS. Attacks across mountains are made to protect the flanks of the main attack, to work around the enemy rear, or to provide flanking fire for the main attack. The Germans attempt to seize commanding heights and mountain passes.

The Germans select their assembly areas as close to the enemy as possible to make possible a short assault. Supporting weapons are attached to companies, and where feasible, to platoons.

In defense, the Germans organize their advance positions on the forward slope, while the main battle position with heavy-support weapons is located on the reverse slope. The greater part of a unit often is held in reserve. This necessitates the organization of relatively narrow sectors, which, however, results in an organization of ground favorable for counterattacks.

5. Winter Warfare

Many of the techniques of German winter warfare were developed from those of the mountain troops, which were adapted easily to conditions of extreme cold.

Ski patrols are the chief means of reconnaissance in snow-covered terrain. As a rule, the strength of the patrol is a squad, reinforced by infantry soldiers trained as engineers, artillery observers, and a communication detachment. In addition to normal reconnaissance missions, patrols obtain information as to the depth of the snow, load capacity of ice surfaces, and danger of avalanches. These ski patrols normally blaze trails by marking trees or rocks and by erecting poles or flags. Stakes are used to indicate the extremities of roads.

Under winter conditions, German units keep support weapons and artillery well forward while on the march. Their antitank weapons are distributed throughout the entire column. Ski

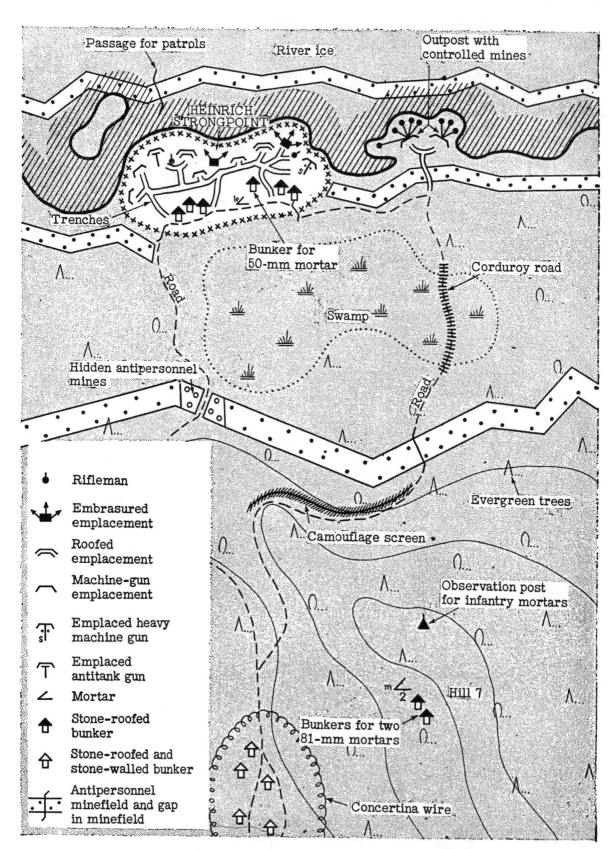

Figure 23.—Typical German winter position along a river in Karelia.

Passage for patrols
River ice
Outpost with controlled mines
HEINRICH STRONGPOINT
Trenches
Bunker for 50-mm mortar
Corduroy road
Swamp
Hidden antipersonnel mines
Road
Road
Evergreen trees
Camouflage screen
Observation post for infantry mortars
Hill 7
Bunkers for two 81-mm mortars
Concertina wire

- Rifleman
- Embrasured emplacement
- Roofed emplacement
- Machine-gun emplacement
- Emplaced heavy machine gun
- Emplaced antitank gun
- Mortar
- Stone-roofed bunker
- Stone-roofed and stone-walled bunker
- Antipersonnel minefield and gap in minefield

troops are organized to guard the flanks. Sleighs are added for the transport of weapons and supplies.

The Germans assign to trail units the task of cutting tracks for the formations that follow. The strength of the trail unit of a company is one or two squads; that of a battalion up to two platoons. In difficult terrain their strength may be doubled. Trail units are divided into a number of trail detachments consisting of six to ten men, echeloned behind the first of the trail units. The march formation of ski troops is generally single file; usually parallel trails are used to reduce the length of the column.

In winter warfare, attacks with limited objectives are the rule. The Germans attempt wherever possible to combine frontal and flank attacks under conditions of extreme cold and snow. They employ support weapons as far forward as practicable. Attacks often are made by ski troops; because of the difficulty of transporting artillery, ski troops frequently have to dispense with artillery support. For this reason the Germans consider it all the more necessary to concentrate heavy and light infantry weapons at points of main effort and to coordinate high and flat trajectory weapons. When pack howitzers are available, they can be dismantled and brought forward on sledges. Assault guns can effectively support ski troops in snow under 16 inches deep. They either accompany the attack as far as road conditions allow or move into positions at effective range, not exceeding 3,500 yards, on specially cleared paths away from roads. They occupy their positions just before the attack. As a rule attached assault guns are employed in platoon and company strength; single commitment is avoided. Tank units are attached only in exceptional circumstances.

Organization of a defensive position in deep snow or on frozen ground takes considerable time, for it is necessary to move weapons into position, lay out foot paths and roads, and build strong outposts and strongpoints with all-around defense. Camouflage is particularly stressed under such conditions. Since normal units used as reserves in deep snow have only limited mobility, the Germans employ ski troops for reserves wherever possible. These ski units are used for immediate counterattacks which are directed, where possible, against the flank of the attacking enemy. The Germans also use the ski troops as raiding parties to harass the enemy's front and rear.

6. Partisan Warfare

a. GENERAL. In order to understand German anti-partisan measures, it is necessary to discuss briefly the characteristics of Allied partisan organizations and their fighting techniques. The following discussion is based entirely on official German sources. The principles involved may be accepted by the Germans and find their way into actual practice in the near future.

b. TASKS OF PARTISAN WARFARE. The Germans consider that the strategic mission of the Allied partisans was to inflict maximum injury on the German Armies of Occupation. Means employed to accomplish this task were as follows:

Raids on individual drivers, resting places, troop and supply trains, headquarters, airfields, and ammunition and supply dumps.

Demolition of bridges, roads, and railway tracks.

Destruction of wire communications and railway systems.

Destruction of industrial installations and crops.

Terrorization of collaborators.

Undermining the morale of locally recruited auxiliary troops.

c. ORGANIZATION OF PARTISANS. (1) *General.* Allied partisan forces were organized partly prior to German occupation and partly during the occupation when dispersed army personnel and civilians rallied around a common leader. The Germans list the following elements as sources for the recruitment of Allied partisan units:

Remnants of Allied units which escaped destruction during military operations.

Individual stragglers.

Smaller units or individual members of Allied forces who infiltrated through the German lines.

Allied parachutists.

Escaped prisoners of war.

Deserters from locally recruited auxiliary services.

Civilian volunteers.

Terrorized civilians.

Women, who may be employed either as combatants or auxiliaries in the supply, medical, or signal services.

(2) *Russian partisan units.* The Germans outline the composition of Russian partisan units as follows:

Diversion groups of three to ten men.

Combat units of 75 to 100 men, divided into

two or three companies, each of two or three platoons.

Battalions.

Regiments, consisting of several battalions.

Brigades of several hundred men.

Units of several thousand men, of varying composition and fighting value.

Divisional headquarters in command of operational groups.

Corps headquarters controlling a certain number of brigades or regiments.

Scouting and reconnaissance detachments.

Higher intelligence headquarters.

In addition the Russians had signal organizations and special formations for demolition works and bridging, mounted detachments, and in some cases even artillery and antitank guns. A special ground organization was set up to serve the air forces which supplied the partisans.

(3) *French partisan units.* The composition of the French partisan forces, according to the Germans, is:

The squad consisted of four or five men.

The platoon consisted of approximately 30 men.

The company had approximately 100 men.

A battalion consisted of three or four companies.

(4) *Weapons.* The weapons of the partisans included rifles, light machine guns, light mortars, pistols, machine pistols, hand grenades, explosives and incendiary material. Battle units also had heavy machine guns, heavy mortars, and guns.

(5) *Uniforms.* Partisans had no standard uniform. They wore civilian dress and the most diverse uniforms of their own and enemy forces. Stocks of uniforms were maintained by raiding German supply depots.

(6) *Camps.* The partisans located their camping areas in inaccessible terrain such as dense forests, marshes, wooded mountains, and caves. The camps usually were fortified with field works, dugouts, tree platforms, and minefields. Normally a number of camps were set up in adjacent areas with alternate camp sites prepared. The camps were complete with dumps, slaughtering facilities, bakeries, dressing stations, and weapon repair shops. These camps were well guarded, the personnel of the guard being composed of partisans or of volunteers from nearby communities.

d. PARTISAN TACTICS. (1) *General.* Higher headquarters would issue directives of a general nature, and the leader of the smaller detachments would determine the method of execution. In accordance with their strategic function, partisans almost always avoided pitched battles. If trapped and forced to fight, they would follow different courses according to their strength. Large bands would fight it out, whereas smaller units endeavored to disperse by small groups, infiltrating through the lines of the attackers or disguising themselves as harmless and peaceful civilians. Defensively, partisans fought with determination, even ferocity, from behind well fortified and camouflaged positions, allowing the attackers to approach to close range and then delivering concentrated surprise fire. In Warsaw, Polish partisans fought in building areas for weeks with much skill, inflicting considerable losses on the Germans.

(2) *Fighting methods.* The partisans carried out guerrilla operations by conducting surprise raids against headquarters, camps, and weapon depots of the occupation army or by ambushing military transportation facilities, columns, or convoys.

When raiding columns, the partisans constructed obstacles along the route and then destroyed the first and last vehicle of the column. Railway trains were destroyed by exploding the roadbed or removing trackage. Troops trying to escape from trucks or trains were taken under fire. Before an attack partisans usually destroyed all telephone communications.

Partisan bands often changed their field of operations in order to carry out a given task, to secure supplies, or to evade discovery and prevent encirclement. Strict discipline on the march was maintained. Marches were generally at night, by routes known only to the local population. Partisan bands have marched 40 to 45 miles daily.

A common ruse was to give the appearance of greater strength by disseminating false information concerning partisan strength and armament. Partisans frequently used military uniforms of the occupation army for purposes of reconnaissance and requisitioning.

For successful operation the partisans needed secret agents who could be found in almost every village. The intelligence service of the partisans, of necessity, employed large numbers of women and children. In addition to collecting information, they were used as messengers between various partisan groups. (Local civilian populations usually were summoned to give assistance to the partisans.)

e. GERMAN ANTI-PARTISAN MEASURES. (1) *General.* The Germans divide the measures to be adopted against partisans into offensive action and passive defense measures. Both constitute specialized types of activity, brought about by the particular methods employed by the opponent. Since the partisans are inferior in armament, regular troops are inclined to underrate them and to act without due care and precaution. According to German doctrine, dealing with partisans demands increased vigilance, boldness, and aggressiveness in order to meet their extraordinary cunning and cruelty. In addition, the Germans considered that special training was necessary for their own troops in order to overcome difficult types of terrain such as woods, marshes, mountains, and built-up areas as well as for fighting at night or under winter conditions. Experience taught the Germans that the success of their anti-partisan measures depended on proper coordination between the German Armed Forces, *SS,* police, and the civil administration, ignoring, when necessary, territorial boundaries.

(2) *Offensive. action.* The Germans centralized the command and control of their anti-partisan measures and made arrangements in regard to the fields of responsibility between the supreme command of the armed forces, the *SS Reichsführer* and the Chief of Police. While in 1942-1943 the responsibility for the organization and direction of these measures rested with the supreme command in operational areas and with the *SS Reichsführer* in the so-called *Reichskommissariat,* the latter, upon acquiring increased powers, assumed complete responsibility.

Subordinate to the *SS Reichsführer* were the Chief in Command of Anti-partisan Formations (*Chef der Bandenkämpfverbande*) and the senior *SS* and police commanders, under whose command Army and Air Force units occasionally are attached.

All German troops and, in emergency, civilian establishments were prepared to engage partisans. The Germans employed the following army units in combat against partisans: divisions, independent task forces, cavalry units, motorized units, armored trains, service troops, emergency units, and locally recruited units. In addition to these organizations, the Germans employed Navy and Air Force units, as well as *SS* and police formations, including the security service (*Sicherheits-*

dienst) and Secret Field Police (*Geheime Feldpolizei*).

The Germans emphasized the equipping of their anti-partisan units with easily transportable and quick-firing weapons, such as small arms, machine pistols, automatic rifles, rifles with telescopic sights, light and heavy machine guns, light and medium antitank guns, light infantry guns, light antiaircraft guns, and light flame throwers. Heavier artillery, antitank and antiaircaft guns, tanks, and armored cars, although they effectively strengthened the forces, could not be employed in all situations and terrain.

Clothing and equipage were designed to enable the unit to operate in all types of terrain and under all weather conditions.

The Germans realized the necessity of intensive intelligence work for successful anti-partisan measures. Higher commanders kept situation maps based on information concerning the partisans transmitted by all headquarters and units of the armed forces, and by civilian establishments. Systematic observations were made by security branches, such as the security service, the secret field police, and the military intelligence (*Abwehr*); information was disseminated and exchanged by adjacent establishments.

To provide all the necessary data for the tactical employment of anti-partisan forces, the Germans conducted intensive reconnaissance preceding their operations. This was carried out by collaborators, by mobile patrols, or by reconnaissance aircraft. Collaborators were the only means of reconnaissance employed when the projected operation had to be kept absolutely secret. The interrogation of prisoners was considered one of the best sources of information. The Germans therefore abandoned their original practice of shooting captured partisans on the spot.

When the Germans had adequate forces available they attempted to encircle and annihilate partisan units. The planning for this operation included the determination of the ground to be encircled, usually limited to the area actually known to be held by partisans. The assembly area was well removed from the areas to be encircled and was occupied in such a manner that the offensive intention was not disclosed. All forces taking part in the operation moved from the assembly area so that they reached the encircling lines at the same time. Lines were chosen which could be defended easily, such as lines of hills or forest paths across the direction of the advance.

The Germans normally kept sufficient local and mobile reserves armed with heavy support weapons. The consolidation of the encircling line was considered decisive for the outcome of the operation, because partisan fighting patrols tested the German lines with the object of breaking out through weak spots. The consolidation of the encircling line followed the usual principles for defense, such as disposing forward battle outposts, drawing up fire plans for light and heavy support weapons, fortifying strongpoints for all-around defense, and keeping mobile reserves in readiness. The precise method by which the encircled partisans were annihilated depended on the forces the Germans had available, on the terrain, and on the reaction of the trapped unit. One method employed was the gradual compressing of the encircled pocket, possible only in restricted areas, because in large areas the encircling forces could not advance at the same rate, thus creating gaps through which partisans could escape. Another method employed was to exert pressure from one side of the pocket while the troops on the opposite side confined themselves to defense. This method was used when the partisans held ground easy to defend, such as a river course, a ridge of hills, or edges of woods. The Germans also utilized powerful wedges and split up the defense pocket into several smaller pockets which were mopped up separately. Another method was to attack from the encircling line by strong assault groups formed from reserves, in cases where battle reconnaissance indicated that the partisans intended to defend their center position.

When time and forces for an encirclement were not available, the Germans attempted to defeat partisan bands by surprise attacks, intending to pursue and wipe out single detached groups. This method proved to be of value where a partisan formation had not been able to consolidate its position. The German actions therefore were dependent on the methods adopted by the partisans. When they committed their forces for battle, the German attack was carried out systematically with concentrated forces and fire. When the partisans attempted to avoid contact, the Germans pursued them frontally, while other units carried out enveloping movements. When the partisan formation dissolved, however, the Germans had to undertake reconnaissance to locate their new assembly area before a new action could begin. The primary target in such actions was the leader of the partisans, and the Germans usually placed a premium on the head of the leader to encourage his capture or death.

The Germans employed large numbers of heavy support weapons, tanks, assault guns, self-propelled antitank guns and heavy howitzers, when fighting the partisans in communities, and concentrated all available heavy weapons against a single objective. The tactics employed followed the German combat methods for street fighting and combat in towns.

The Germans also employed combat patrols against the partisans, copying the latter's methods with the object of harassing the bands and hindering their assembly and supply. Areas which were used regularly by the partisans for food requisitioning, or which they crossed on raids or sabotage expeditions, offered good opportunities for the deployment of German combat patrols. These patrols consisted of hand-picked, tough, well trained "Partisan Hunters". of platoon to company strength. They often wore civilian clothes or partisan uniforms.

(3) *Protection measures.* Offensive anti-partisan operations were supplemented by vigilant protective measures designed to safeguard troops; road, rail, and waterway communications and traffic; industrial, administrative, and signal installations; and growing crops and forest preserves.

The Germans designated the security of troops as a command responsibility. As a rule the Germans did not billet units of less then company strength in lonely districts. All billets and camps were organized for all-around defense, and all guard rooms were made into strongpoints. Maps showing the local partisan situation were consulted before the march.

To protect railway installations the Germans organized special protection forces whose task included patrolling in addition to the protection of communication centers. Strongpoints were constructed inside all installations and often along the tracks.

The Germans also organized special forces for the protection of roads and waterways. These forces, *"Sicherungstruppen"*, were supplemented by military police detachments on the roads and water police on the waterways.

The ruthless methods employed by the Germans to maintain law and order are too well known to be discussed in this book. From the killing of individual suspects to the wholesale slaughter of whole communities and the burning of villages there is one long line of German atrocities and brutality.

f. GERMAN PREPARATION FOR PARTISAN WARFARE. Beyond doubt the Germans prepared and are still preparing fanatical members of the National Socialist Party, *SS,* and armed forces for partisan activities as the territory occupied by the Allies increases. One of Heinrich Himmler's main duties as commander-in-chief of the Home Army is supervising the establishment of partisan organizations and stay-behind agents in areas about to be occupied by the Allies. The Germans have built up large stores of ammunition and supplies, particularly in the mountainous areas of the country, and have established at various localities training centers for future German *SS* Partisans. Women are included in this training program. As to the methods which the Germans are most likely to employ, no definite information can be revealed at this time. However, it is recommended that a study of the Allied partisan combat methods be made to obtain an approximate conception of possible German partisan activities.

7. Anti-Airborne Operations

The Germans consider the use of mines and wire obstacles particularly effective against enemy airborne operations. They block landing fields and areas where landings might be made with S-mines, stakes, ditches, piled earth, stone, and wood, nondescript vehicles without wheels, and other barricades. They also construct minefields and dummy minefields.

For the protection of important installations against airborne attack, the Germans organize an all-around defense, giving particular attention to covering avenues of approach with machine guns. Observation posts are set up on high points, such as church towers and terrain features to give early warning of hostile landings. Such posts are located also in rear areas, and are especially important in thinly populated localities, since wire communications are particular targets of enemy airborne troops. Special signals by church bells, drums, or bugles are arranged for alarming the German mobile reserve units. These units, specially organized for the task of counteracting enemy airborne invasions and partisan activities usually consist of motorized troops with machine guns and antitank guns mounted on their vehicles. Although the Germans consider it an error to delay in committing these units, they stress that care should be used to avoid enemy deceptive maneuvers such as the dropping of dummy parachutists.

The Germans usually withhold rifle fire until descending parachutists are at close range, using machine-gun fire at greater distance. They believe that fire is most effective immediately upon the landing of the hostile force, before a consolidation of position has been made. Enemy transport planes are considered particularly good targets since they must reduce speed just prior to the jump of the troops.

The Germans appreciate the importance of immediate action against airborne troops and when no alternative is possible they will commit inferior forces to combat the hostile aerial invasion, hoping to delay the attack until reserves can be brought up.

CHAPTER V

FORTIFICATIONS AND DEFENSES

Section I. DOCTRINE OF FORTIFICATIONS

1. Economy of Force

The Germans regard economy of force as a fundamental principle in designing fortifications. In conformity with this view, they employ defense works to permit a relatively smaller force to defend a line than otherwise would be required. German troops are taught that fortifications exist not for their personal safety but to enable them to fight more effectively, although fortified works, especially those of reinforced concrete, naturally make for a lower casualty rate. The German doctrine of offensive warfare therefore is not affected by the construction of strong systems of defense. Such systems in fact may be considered to be offensive rather than defensive in purpose, since they make it possible to concentrate a relatively large proportion of the field forces for action at any given point. In September 1939, the Westwall (Siegfried Line)[1] enabled the Germans to hold their Western Front with approximately 20 divisions, while employing 40 to 50 divisions against Poland. These latter troops, in turn, could be concentrated on the northern and southern parts of the Polish border for a double envelopment of the Polish forces, since the vulnerable central sector due east of Berlin was protected by the so-called Oder Quadrilateral, a zone of permanent defense works constructed between 1935 and 1939. Again, in May 1940, the Westwall played an important role—this time in the envelopment of the Maginot Line—for, while the French border was held with relatively weak forces, the bulk of the *Wehrmacht* wheeled through Belgium and Luxembourg.

2. Organization of Defenses

a. PRINCIPLE OF DEPTH. The Germans believe that a fortified line should consist of small works

organized in great depth. This principle, embodied in the Westwall, is directly opposed to that of the French Maginot Line, which was a continuous wall of mammoth forts with little, if any, depth. The German idea is that a fortified line should not be employed to present an unyielding front to an attacker, but rather to act as a shock absorber and gradually slow down the advance. Then, when the attack has lost its momentum, counterattacks can be launched to destroy the penetration before the attacker has reorganized and consolidated his gains. The importance the Germans attach to counterattack is shown by the fact that they keep their best assault troops for this purpose and man the concrete positions with inferior soldiers. In order to impede the enemy's advance as much as possible and to facilitate the counterattack, troops manning the fortifications are taught to continue fighting even though their positions are overrun.

b. ZONES OF DEFENSE. The Germans achieve depth in a fortified line by constructing successive zones of defense. In a typical segment of the Westwall, there are three independent zones from front to rear.

(1) The Forward Zone (*Vorfeldzone*) contains field fortifications including trenches, barbed-wire entanglements, machine-gun emplacements, and observation posts.

(2) The Main Defense Zone (*Grosskampfzone*) comprises fortified structures such as pillboxes, casemates and shelters, and antitank obstacles covered by antitank guns. In addition, this zone has intermediate areas, front and rear, in which isolated works are placed at critical points along natural avenues of enemy approach.

(3) The Rear Defense Zone (*Rückwärtige Zone*) is much the same as (2), but is not as strong.

c. STRENGTH. It is the German practice to provide the weakest terrain with the strongest and

---

[1] The Germans do not employ the term "Siegfried Line".

most numerous defense works arranged in the greatest depth. But the defended zone is everywhere made as strong as the available resources permit, and no terrain is left entirely without the protecting fire of some permanent defense works.

d. SITING OF DEFENSE WORKS. Pillboxes and casemates in a fortified line are so spaced as to provide interlocking fields of fire between adjacent works, yet they are not so close together that hostile artillery fire which misses one structure will hit another.

In view of the German theory as to the purpose of fortifications, the principle of "effect before cover" is applicable; that is, a wide field of fire is considered more important in siting a position than cover or concealment. When possible, pillboxes and casemates may be sited to permit both frontal and flanking fire. This is particularly important since German doctrine directs that fortified positions be held even after the defensive line is overrun by the enemy. The fire plan of field artillery may be coordinated with the belts of fire from the fortifications so that concentrations can be laid on the areas where fire coverage from the fortifications is relatively weak.

e. FIELD WORKS. In accordance with German doctrine, concrete and steel pillboxes, and casemates are supplemented by extensive field fortifications to lend flexibility and mobility to the defense, to engage the enemy before he gets close enough to assault the main works, and to facilitate counterattack. Such field works are interspersed liberally throughout the Westwall and include minefields, obstacles, fire trenches for infantry weapons, and open emplacements for field artillery. Although open gun emplacements are intended to give supporting fire to pillboxes and casemates, they also can cover dead areas between the main works.

f. SHELTER. The German practice is to provide all troops with adequate shelter against weather and hostile fire. Concrete pillboxes and casemates often have accommodations for the gun crews, and open field works have underground shelters or dugouts adjacent to the firing positions. In a fortified line, underground shelters are provided in the rear of the battle zone for the reserves who are assigned to the counterattack. This is in accordance with the German doctrine that reserves should be committed as a unit, fresh, and without having had to sustain casualties or endure the strain of hostile aerial and artillery bombardment while waiting to attack. Personnel shelters enable

the reserves to be kept close to the front so they can begin the counterattack with minimum delay.

g. COMMUNICATIONS. German fortified works commonly are linked together with communication trenches to facilitate relief of personnel, ammunition supply, and the care and evacuation of the wounded. In some cases a group of defense works is connected by a system of tunnels. Signal communication is provided by telephone cables buried in the earth, and often telephones communicate between the outside and the inside of a structure. Speaking tubes are installed in many of the works in case of failure of the telephone system.

Section II. CHARACTERISTICS OF FORTIFICATIONS

1. Principles of Design

The basic considerations in the design of German fortifications are fire effect, cover, and concealment. Fire effect has first priority; natural concealment is used as much as possible by blending positions with the surrounding terrain. Personnel and supply shelters, in the construction of which fire effect need not be taken into consideration, are completely below ground level, or as low as the water-table level permits. In order to present as small a target as possible to high-angle fire and bombing, emplacements, pillboxes, and casemates are built no larger than necessary to permit crews to operate their guns.

2. Construction

a. GENERAL. All permanent, fortress-type works and many field works are of concrete reinforced with steel. Some field works, however, are of masonry, brick, or timber. Steel also is used in concrete structures for beams, turrets, cupolas, gun shields, machine-gun loopholes, and doors. These installations are prefabricated and are assigned code or model numbers. The concrete works themselves are designated by type number and are constructed from plans prepared in the Army Ordnance Office.

b. THICKNESS OF CONCRETE. The usual thickness of concrete walls and roofs is 6 feet 6 inches (2 meters); smaller thicknesses are found as a rule only in the small field works. In casemates the minimum thickness of the walls and roof is 6 feet 6 inches, and generally increases commensurately with the caliber of the gun.

Figure 1—German three-way reinforcing rods and wooden forms ready for pouring in concrete.

c. REINFORCEMENT OF CONCRETE. Most German concrete fortifications are reinforced with steel bars running in three dimensions to form cubes of 10- or 12-inch sides. The diameter of the bars, which are hooked at both ends, varies from ⅜ inch to ⅝ inch, the most common size being ½ inch.

The roof over the interior compartments in most structures is supported by steel I-beams, encased in the concrete roof. The size of the beams depends on length of the span. Steel plates laid between the I-beams, and resting on the lower flanges, form the ceiling of the structure. These plates prevent the inside of the roof from spalling if the structure sustains a direct hit from artillery shells or aerial bombs. In some cases, the roof is supported by reinforced-concrete beams instead of the steel I-beams, apparently to save critical material.

3. Open Emplacements

a. "TOBRUK" TYPE. From experience in the North African campaign the Germans derived a type of open, circular pit lined with concrete, which they called a "Tobruk". Hitler subsequently ordered Tobruk pits to be used as defense works in the field, and instructions for building them were distributed down to divisions. A Tobruk pit, which consists of a concrete weapon chamber with a neck-like opening at the top, is built entirely underground. The concrete usually is reinforced. Tobruks vary in size, depending on the weapon mounted in them, but the diameter of the neck is kept as small as possible to reduce the risk of direct hits. Instructions to German troops insist that a Tobruk should not have a concrete roof, since this would reveal the position to the enemy. A board of irregular shape, used as a lid, camouflages the circular opening and keeps out rain.

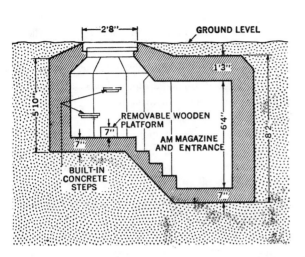
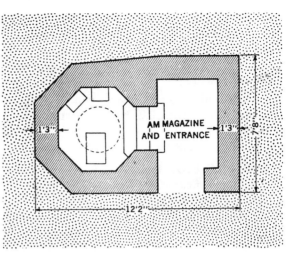

Figure 2.—Ringstand.

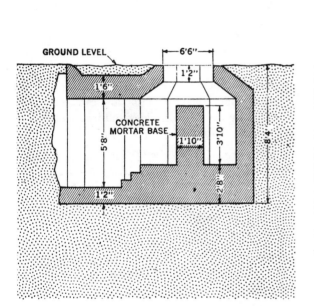
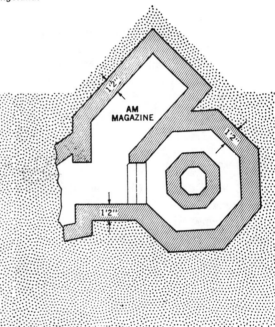

Figure 3.—Tobruk for 50-mm mortar.

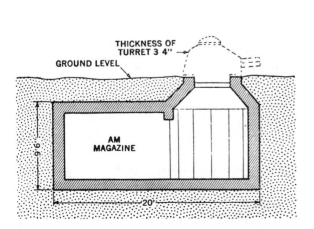
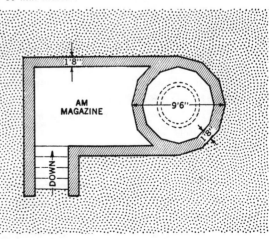

Figure 4.—Panzerstellung.

b. TOBRUK *58c*. The most common type of Tobruk is designated *58c* by the Germans (see *Figure 2*). It also is called a *Ringstand* from a rail that runs around the inside of the neck. The rail provides a track for rotating a machine-gun mount, thus giving the gun a 360-degree traverse. This type of Tobruk has an ammunition chamber, which also serves as an underground entrance.

c. MORTAR EMPLACEMENT. A Tobruk used as a mortar emplacement, such as Type *61a* (see *Figure 3*), is larger than a *Ringstand* and has a concrete base in the center of the pit for mounting the mortar. This type also is combined with an ammunition magazine.

d. *Panzerstellung*. The German also have used a Tobruk as a base for a tank turret, usually taken from a French *Renault 35* (see *Figure 4*). Such an installation, called a *Panzerstellung*, has a turret armed with an antitank gun and a machine gun coaxially mounted. The turret is bolted to a circular metal plate, which is rotated by hand on wheels around a track in the top of the pit affording a 360-degree arc of fire.

4. Pillboxes and Casemates

a. CONSTRUCTION. (1) *General*. Although the Germans have a number of types of pillboxes and casemates, most infantry and artillery weapons are installed in open rather than closed emplacements. In accordance with German doctrine, pillboxes and casemates are supported by open field works. Pillboxes may have wall and roof thicknesses of as little as 2 feet; indeed, some of the earliest examples built on the Westwall had thicknesses of only 1 foot. This was increased, however, until all pillboxes had at least the standard thickness of 6 feet 6 inches. Casemates, which house guns of large caliber, have at least the standard thickness of 6 feet 6 inches. Pillboxes and casemates usually have a stepped embrasure to prevent bullets from richocheting into the gun opening. In addition, a steel gun shield may close the opening.

(2) *Type 630 pillbox*. Figure 5 illustrates a newer type of pillbox for the light antitank gun, Type 630, which has 6 feet 6 inches of concrete in the roof, front wall, and side walls; and 6 feet 4 inches in the rear wall. A machine gun firing through a loophole in the rear provides close defense, and a loophole in the interior wall at the

foot of the stairs has an opening for a machine gun to keep attackers from entering the pillbox. A Tobruk pit is built into the front wall as an observation or machine-gun post.

(3) *Local designs*. Some pillboxes are found which do not conform to standard types and are apparently of local design. The Germans often construct a pillbox by mounting a steel turret on an open emplacement, and many pillboxes along the French coast were built by mounting a tank turret over a pit in the sea wall.

(4) *Type 685 casemate*. Figure 6 illustrates a typical German casemate, Type 685, for the 210-mm or 128-mm antiaircraft guns. Most casemates are of this simple design, consisting of a gun room with recesses for ammunition, but some may provide quarters for the gun crew. The walls and roof of Type 685 are 11 feet 5 inches (3.5 meters) thick. The embrasure permits a traverse of 60 degrees and an elevation of 45 degrees. A number of similar casemates (Types 683, 684, 686, 688, 689, 690, 692, and 694) have embrasures for a traverse of 90 degrees or 120 degrees. Additional protection and camouflage are afforded by banking the sides and by covering the top with a 2-foot 6-inch layer of earth.

(5) *Type 677 casemate*. The Germans often site a casemate to deliver flanking fire. For this purpose, a wing wall is provided on the side toward the enemy to shield the embrasure from hostile fire, as in Type 677 for 8-cm gun (*Figure 7*). The length of this wing wall depends on local ground conditions. The casemate can be built to fire to the right flank by constructing the wing on the opposite wall.

b. CAMOUFLAGE. To camouflage pillboxes and casemates, earth is banked over the sides and top, the entrance in the rear is covered by a flat-top, and a camouflage net may be hung in front of the embrasure while the gun is not in action. In the case of small pillboxes, branches may be placed over the embrasure. The Germans also conceal pillboxes and casemates by enclosing them in wooden structures resembling ordinary houses. The guns then are fired through false doors or windows, or a section of the wall over the embrasure is made to drop out of the way. Pillboxes also are built into the cellars of existing buildings. German instructions to troops insist that no cover or concealment should obstruct the field of fire of the gun.

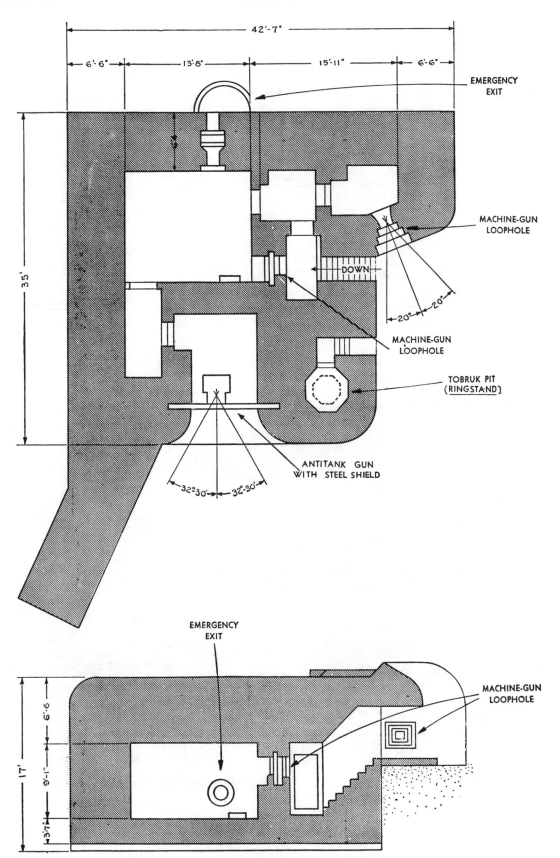

Figure 5.—Typical pillbox, Type 630 for light antitank gun.

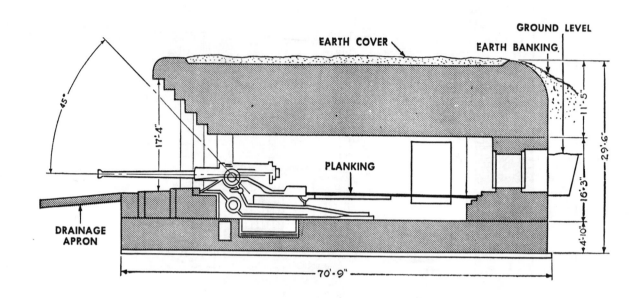

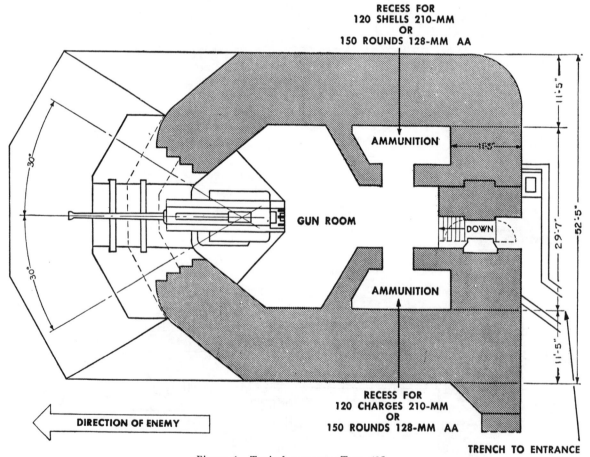

Figure 6.—Typical casemate, Type 685.

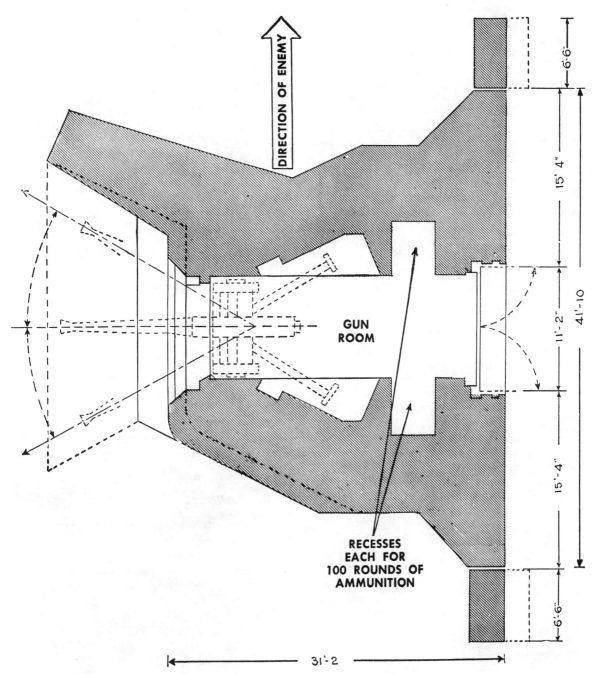

Figure 7.—Typical casemate, Type 677.

Figure 8.—Emplacing a mobile steel pillbox.

Figure 9.—German mobile steel pillbox.

*Figure 10.—Interior of mobile steel pillbox showing
machine-gun mount.*

*Figure 11.—View through doorway of mobile steel
pillbox.*

c. MOBILE STEEL PILLBOX. The Germans also have a mobile steel pillbox (*Figures 8, 9, 10, 11*) which is armed with a machine gun and manned by two men. The pillbox is constructed in two sections, a top half and a bottom half welded together. The top half contains the aperture, armament, air vents, and entrance door. Thickness of the armor varies from 5 inches at the aperture to 2 inches at the sides and top. The bottom half is only ¾ inch thick, but is entirely below ground level when the pillbox is in place.

The total weight of the pillbox without armament or ammunition is 6,955 pounds. The aperture, which is seen on the left side in the photograph, is divided into two parts: the lower part for the gun barrel; the upper for sighting. The machine gun has an arc of fire of approximately 45 degrees. The aperture cover is operated manually from the interior of the pillbox. Entry is through a door, 20 inches by 23 inches, in the back of the upper half. The door can be seen hanging open on the right in the photograph. There are two openings in the top for periscopes, one over each seat.

A blower operated by a pedal provides ventilation. The ventilation holes on both sides of the pillbox also enable an axle to be passed through the pillbox. Wheels are fitted to the ends of this axle and the pillbox can then be towed upside down. When installed for use, the sides and top are banked to blend with the surroundings.

5. Shelters

a. PERSONNEL SHELTERS. (1) *Purposes.* The Germans stress the desirability of adequate shelter for all troops. Personnel shelters are built in the rear of a fortified line to house the reserves and also in individual defense positions for the troops who man the installation. Some personnel shelters have accommodation for two sections, or 20 men, but it is the usual German practice to house no more than ten men in one shelter. A personnel shelter also may serve as a headquarters, a command post, a medical station, or a signal center. Types provided for these purposes are similar in design and differ mainly in size and number of interior compartments.

(2) *Type 621 shelter.* One of the most common personnel shelters (Type 621, for one infantry section) is illustrated in Figure 12. It is constructed of reinforced concrete, with the standard wall and roof thickness of 6 feet 6 inches (2 meters). It is entirely underground, with an earth covering of 1 foot over the roof. Seventeen steel I-beams, 13 feet 2 inches long, support the ceiling over the interior compartment. Steel plates resting on the bottom flanges of the I-beams provide an all-steel ceiling. Shorter I-beams support the ceiling over the doors and entrance stairs. A camouflage flat-top is stretched over the trench in the rear, which gives access to the entrance stairs, to conceal it from air observation. To secure one side of the flat-top, a row of hooks is cast into the roof along the rear side of the shelter. A Tobruk pit is built into one of the wings in the rear for observation. Although the shelter accommodates only ten men, two entrances are provided to enable the section to deploy rapidly when they are to man their positions nearby or launch a counterattack. Each of the entrance stairs is covered by a machine gun firing through a loophole in the interior wall at the foot of the stairs. Both entrances converge into a gas lock, sealed by three steel doors each about 1 inch thick. All doors open out. To make the chimney grenade-proof, the vertical shaft is continued below the stovepipe and curved outward into the space used for the emergency exit. A grenade dropped into the chimney thus will not enter the shelter but will fall outside the sidewall and explode harmlessly. There are four ventilation shafts opening into the rear wall between the entrance stairs. Two of these are dummies to mislead attackers who try to introduce smoke into the ventilating system to drive out the occupants. The blower is driven by an electric motor, but the Germans usually make provision for manual operation as well, in case of power failure. To communicate with the interior of the shelter, there is a telephone at the head of one of the entrance stairs, and both a telephone and a speaking tube in the Tobruk. A telephone cable, buried deep in the earth, leads to neighboring installations.

(3) *Modifications in design.* Modifications may be made in the plans in order to adapt the shelter to the terrain; for example, the Tobruk may be built into the other rear wing, or the emergency exit may be installed in the opposite side wall. Such changes are at the discretion of the local construction authorities. Some types of personnel shelters have a steel turret built into the roof for observation, and sometimes a machine gun is mounted in the Tobruk. However, the Germans insist that troops are not to fight from shelters, but are to use them merely as protection while not engaged in combat.

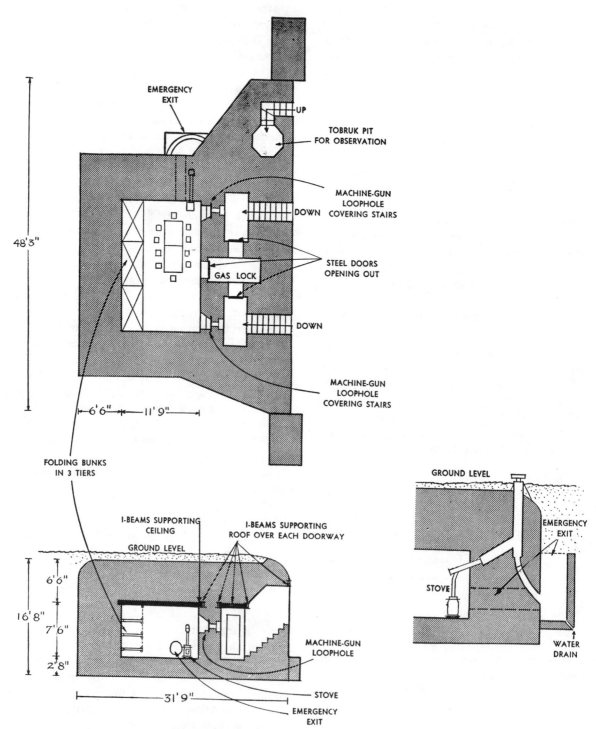

Figure 12.—Typical personnel shelter, Type 621.

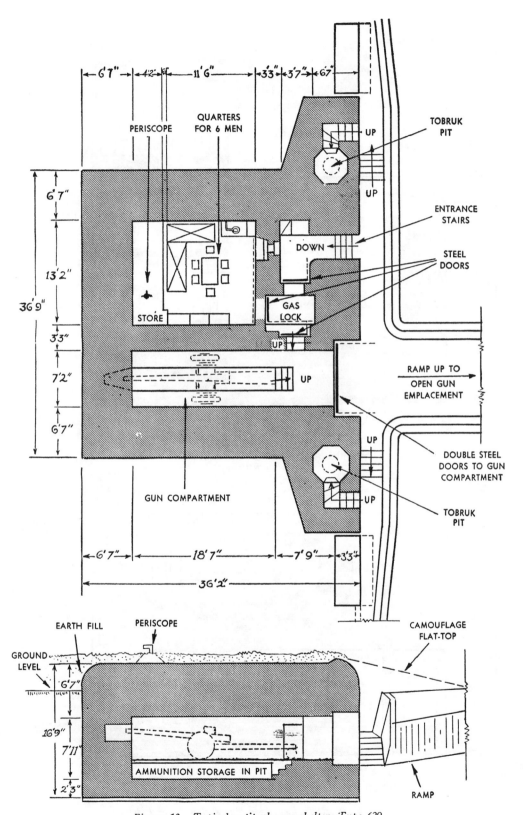

Figure 13.—Typical antitank-gun shelter, Type 629.

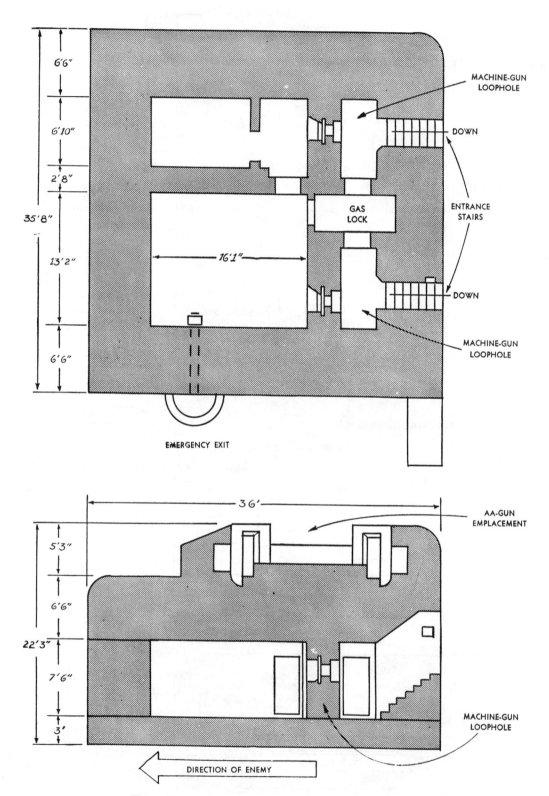

Figure 14.—Typical emplacement and shelter, Type L 409.

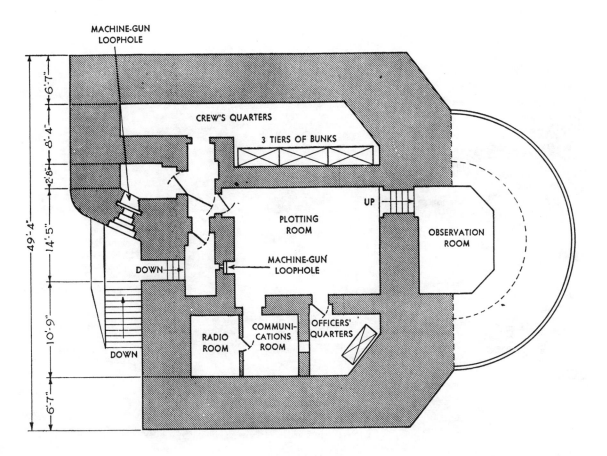

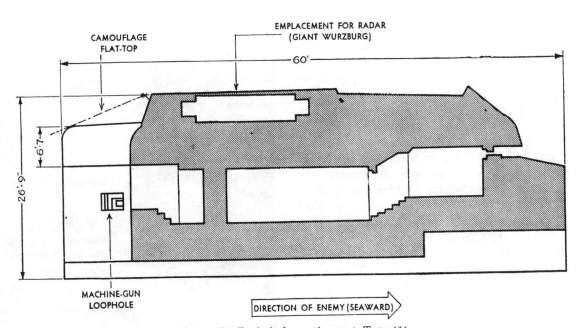

Figure 15.—Typical observation post, Type 636.

Figure 16.—Dragon's teeth showing concrete foundations.

b. ANTITANK-GUN SHELTERS. The Germans provide a special shelter for antitank guns and their crews. Figure 13 shows a typical antitank gun shelter, designated by the Germans as Type 629. Accommodation for the men is similar to that of other personnel shelters, but there is a separate compartment for the gun and ammunition. Double doors in this compartment enable the gun to be rolled out of the shelter and up a ramp (slope 1:6) to an open emplacement in the rear of the shelter from which it fires over the top of the shelter. The shelter has two Tobruk pits (*Ringstände*) in which machine guns appear to be installed to support the antitank gun. These Tobruks are connected by telephone and speaking tube to the crew's quarters. The shelter also is equipped with a periscope.

Figure 17.—German Elements "C" joined to form antitank obstacles.

c. COMBINED SHELTER AND EMPLACEMENT. Figure 14 shows a personnel shelter, with an open emplacement on the roof, known as Type L 409 ("L" stands for *Luftwaffe*). This type will accommodate nine men, and its details are similar to those of other personnel shelters. Type L 409 is for a light antiaircraft gun, but in others of the L 400 series the roof emplacement is used to mount a searchlight (L 411), or a radio direction finder (L 405). In some types, the shelter below the gun emplacement is used as a battalion command post (L 434) or an ammunition magazine (L 407).

d. SUPPLY SHELTERS. The Germans have designed a number of shelters for the storage of supplies, ammunition, and drinking water. Such types usually are entirely underground and may have a wall and roof thicknesses less than the standard 6 feet 6 inches. Shelters designed for supplies may have only one entrance; they ordinarily have no emergency exit, machine-gun loopholes, or Tobruk.

6. Observation Posts

The Germans have constructed special works of reinforced concrete as coast artillery observation and command posts. A typical observation post, Type 636 (for Army Coast Artillery), is shown in Figure 15. Separate rooms are provided for observation, plotting, radar, officers' quarters, and enlisted men's quarters. A Giant *Würzburg* radio direction finder is mounted in

Figure 18.—Slots in the concrete pillars hold steel bars across the road to serve as a block.

the emplacement on the roof. For close defense, there are two machine-gun loopholes covering the rear entrance: one in the exterior wall, and one in the interior wall at the foot of the stairs. There are quarters for two officers and nine enlisted men, but since this does not accommodate all the personnel on duty at the observation post, a personnel shelter for one section is built nearby.

Field artillery observation posts in a permanent defense line are similar to personnel shelters, with the addition of a steel cupola for the observer.

7. Obstacles

The German tactical use of obstacles differs from the U. S. Army in that they install them within the main battle positions. Obstacles are covered by fire from concrete pillboxes and open emplacements. The Germans employ both fixed and movable permanent obstacles, constructed for the most part of steel, concrete, or both. The most common types are described below.

a. ANTITANK OBSTACLES. (1) *Dragon's teeth.* A prominent feature of the Westwall is the antitank obstacle called by the Germans "dragon's teeth". These are truncated pyramids of reinforced concrete, arranged in irregular rows of four or five. The height of the teeth varies successively from 2½ feet in the first row on the enemy side to 5 feet in the rear row, so that a tank is made to belly on the obstacle. The teeth are cast in a concrete foundation running from front to rear, and sometimes also along each row, to prevent the teeth from being toppled over.

Dragon's teeth are usually sited in long continuous lines, broken only where roads pass through the line of obstacles and where the terrain is considered unsuitable for tank activity.

(2) *Elements C.* The Germans adopted the Belgian de Cointet antitank obstacle, more often called "Elements C", which is illustrated in Figure 17. Here a number of units have been fastened together to form a continuous antitank wall, but since the units have rollers in the front

Figure 19.—Concrete tetrahedra used as antitank obstacles.

*Figure 20.—Road passing through **Westwall dragon's** teeth. Note (right) uprights for horizontal steel bars which can be placed across the road as a block.*

Figure 21.—Line of dragon's teeth of Westwall. Note steel antitank barrier set at an angle in the road.

and rear, the Germans also use them singly as movable blocks.

(3) *Curved-rail obstacle.* Similar to the "Elements C" is the curve-rail antitank obstacle, which the Germans used extensively along the Westwall. The curved rail, which slopes upward to a steep angle at the rear, faces the enemy, so that tanks attempting to climb over the obstacle tip over backward. It usually is made in sections 6 feet high, 3 feet wide, and 10 feet long.

b. ROAD BLOCKS. (1) *Steel bars.* A road passing through a barrier may be closed by horizontal steel bars arranged successively higher in reinforced concrete slots or by steel rails set upright into the road.

(2) *Tetrahedra.* The Germans also block roads with tetrahedra, which consist of steel frames or solid concrete blocks with four faces. The height of a tetrahedron varies from 2½ to 4½ feet, and its purpose is to belly a tank.

c. BARBED-WIRE OBSTACLES. (1) A German double-apron fence is illustrated in Figure 22. The fence is 4 to 5 feet high. (2) Knife rests, or *chevaux de frise,* strung with barbed wire, can be seen to the right of the fence where the road passes through the obstacles. The Germans call knife rests "Spanish riders" and use them as road blocks. German knife rests are about 4 feet high and have angle-iron or timber frames. (3) Concertina wire (*S-Rolle*) often is used by the Germans either in single, double, or triple coils. Sometimes it is wired to concrete posts, fixed on top of walls, and interwoven with double-apron fences or between concrete dragon's teeth. (4) The Germans also use an obstacle consisting of trip wires (*Stolperdraht*) arranged about 30 feet in depth. The wire is stretched from 4 to 8 inches above the ground on irregular rows of wooden pickets. The interval between pickets in rows is 10 to 13 feet and between rows 7 to 10 feet.

Figure 22.—German double-apron barbed wire. Note knife rests in the background (right).

CHAPTER VI

SUPPLY, EVACUATION, AND MOVEMENTS

Section I. HIGHER ORGANIZATION OF SUPPLY

1. Government Direction of Production

Economic production in Germany is highly centralized and under complete governmental control. The Ministry for Armament and War Production (*Reichsminsterium für Rüstung und Kriegsproduktion*) under Albert Speer controls production of war material and ammunition; the Ministry for Economic Affairs (*Reichswirtschaftsministerium*) controls all other industrial production; the Ministry for Food and Agriculture (*Reichsministerium für Ernährung und Landwirtschaft*) controls food production. Among them these three ministries control production of the supplies for the German Armed Forces and, within the limitations imposed upon Germany by the insufficiency of her natural resources and the effects of the Allied advances and bombings, they are able to gear the production to the needs of the war machine.

2. Estimate of Needs and Placing of Orders.

These are essentially General Staff functions, since they involve present and future operations and capabilities. On the basis of High Command directives, the detailed estimates of the number or quantity of each article of supply are worked out by the technical branches concerned; they must be adjusted to the industrial, labor, and raw material potentialities of the nation.

The three branches of the Armed Forces and the *Waffen-SS* establish their procurement policies on an interservice basis and coordinate the use of railways, canals, and roads for military traffic. In addition, for a number of particularly critical items, the Armed Forces High Command has created special depots which are at its exclusive disposal (*Verfügungsdepots*).

Within the Armed Forces the lines of distinction between the Armed Forces High Command and the Army High Command are not always clearly drawn as far as procurement is concerned. The Army being by far the largest branch of service, the Army High Command (*OKH*) may in certain cases act for the Armed Forces High Command (*OKW*). In addition, the Army procures a proportion of the materiel used by the *Waffen-SS*. The bulk of this materiel is transferred to the *Waffen-SS* through Army channels of supply and not through the system of depots maintained by the *SS* High Command.

3. The Army

The Army High Command (*OKH*) has the direct responsibility for a well functioning army supply system. Its wartime supply functions are divided into two distinct phases. The first phase, centering in the Zone of the Interior, is supervised by the Chief of Army Equipment and Commander of the Replacement Army (*Chef der Heeresrüstung und Befehlshaber des Ersatzheeres*) who organizes the procurement of supplies, their storage in suitably placed depots, and their distribution to home and field units. It is his duty to interpret high command directives on an over-all nationwide basis. He determines what proportion of supplies is essential for use by garrison and training units, what amount can be sent to the front, and which areas are in the best position o issue supplies. The second phase, the Field Army (*Feldheer*) supply system, is controlled by the Chief of Field Army Supply and Administration (*Generalquartiermeister* or *Gen. Qu*) who administers the sending of requisitions to depots established by the Chief of Army Equipment and the receipt, storage, and distribution of supplies in the field.

Section II. SYSTEM OF SUPPLY WITHIN GERMANY

1. Production, Acceptance, and Distribution of Equipment* and Ammunition

a. DESIGN AND DEVELOPMENT. This is primarily the responsibility of the Army Ordnance Office (*Heereswaffenamt*). In particular, its Weapons and Equipment Manufacture Group (*Amtsgruppe für Industrielle Rüstung*) includes ten sections dealing with the main categories of equipment and known as armament sections one to ten (*Waffenrüstungsabteilungen 1-10*). The Ordnance Office also has a Research Branch (*Forschungsabteilung*) and a Development and Testing Branch (*Amtsgruppe für Entwicklung und Prüfung*). In addition, the Ordnance officer coordinates the activities of numerous army-owned and semi-private research institutes and experimental stations throughout the country. Suggestions for design and development are also received from all the technical branches of the Army.

b. PRODUCTION. On the production side the Ministry for Armament and War Production has, through its regional Armament Inspectorates, a decisive influence on the selection of firms, coordination of armament orders with other orders, labor questions, and scheduling and supervision of production.

c. ACCEPTANCE. The testing of weapons, equipment, and ammunition, and their acceptance at the armament factory is the responsibility of the Army Acceptance Organization (*Heeresabnahmewesen*), which is a branch of the Army High Command/Army Ordnance Office (*OKH/Heereswaffenamt*). There is one Acceptance Inspector (*Abnahmeinspizient*) in each corps area who acts through acceptance commissions located at the factories.

d. DISTRIBUTION OF EQUIPMENT AND AMMUNITION TO ARMY UNITS. After acceptance at the factories, the flow of equipment and ammunition to field and home units may take a number of routes:

By way of equipment and ammunition depots.
By way of equipment parks.
Direct from the factory.
Through *SS* depots.
Through special Armed Forces High Command (*OKW*) depots.

*The term "equipment" refers to the group of materials handled by equipment depots and equipment parks, in contrast to the individual equipment (*Ausrüstung des Mannes*) and clothing handled by clothing depots.

2. Main Army Equipment and Ammunition Depot Organization

a. ORGANIZATION. The agencies responsible for most of the storage, issue, and repair of equipment and for the storage, issue, and salvaging of ammunition belong to a separate branch of the Army, the Ordnance Branch (*Feldzeugwesen*). The branch is headed by the Chief Army Ordnance Officer (*Feldzeugmeister*), who works through his staff, the Ordnance Inspectorate (*Feldzeuginspektion*) in the General Army Office (*Allgemeines Heeresamt*). From the Ordnance Inspectorate the chain of command leads through three regional commands, called Ordnance Groups (*Feldzeuggruppen*), with headquarters in Berlin, Kassel, and Munich, to the Ordnance Headquarters (*Feldzeugkommandos*) which are at the level of the corps areas but not affiliated with the latter. There is one Ordnance Headquarters in each corps area, where it controls a varying number of equipment and ammunition depots. The Ordnance Headquarters is the lowest controlling agency for the storage and issue of equipment and ammunition, and it is important to note that below this level equipment and ammunition are handled by two separate types of depots. The Ordnance Headquarters is designated by the number of the corps area. It and the depots it controls are not, however, part of the corps area organization, although the auditing of their books is done by the Corps Area Administration.

In addition to the Ordnance Headquarters designated by the corps area numbers, there exist an Ordnance Headquarters XXX, which is in charge of a great number of subterranean ammunition depots in central Germany, and a special Tank Ordnance Headquarters (*Panzer-Feldzeugkommando*), created in 1943 in order to centralize the supply of all types of armored fighting vehicles and their spare parts throughout Germany.

b. EQUIPMENT DEPOTS. Army Equipment Depots (*Heereszeugämter* or *HZa*) and Army Branch Equipment Depots (*Heeresnebenzeugämter* or *HNZa*), controlled by the Ordnance Headquarters, handle weapons, tanks, tank spare parts, motor transport, assault boats, radio apparatus, anti-gas equipment, bridge materials, special clothing, concrete mixers, and manuals, as well as many other articles. They do not furnish ammunition, fuel, rations, clothing (other than special types), medical and veterinary equipment, horses, or most types of individual equipment.

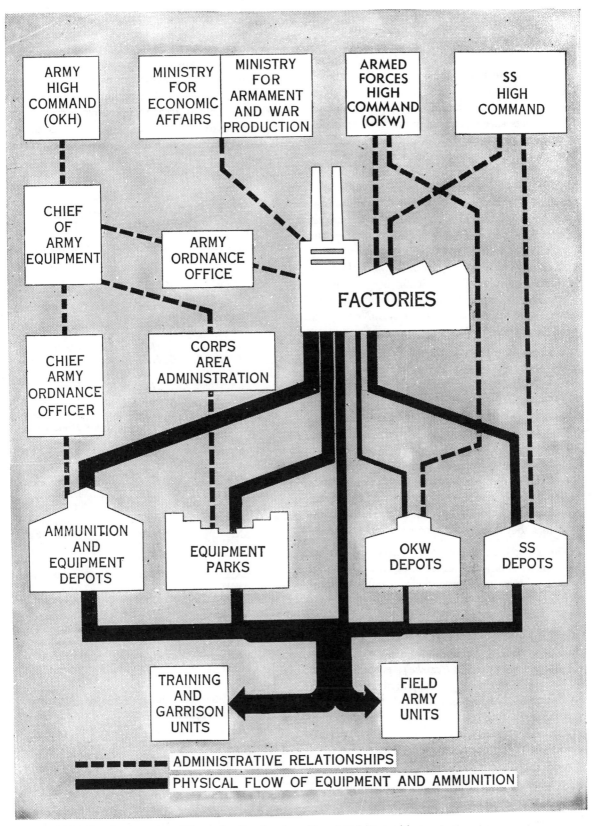

Figure 1.—Supply of equipment and ammunition.

Although the depots normally handle a great variety of items, they sometimes concentrate upon particular types. For example, air reconnaissance has revealed large concentrations of motor transport at the Chemnitz *HZa* and large artillery stores at the Berlin-Spandau *HZa*. It is known, however, that these centers also hold large stores of equipment which cannot be seen from the air. When depots specialize in only one type of equipment, they have their specialties incorporated into their names. This group includes the Army Tank Equipment Depot (*Heerespanzerzeugamt* or *HPZa*) at Magdeburg-Königsborn; the Army Branch Tank Equipment Depots (*Heerespanzernebenzeugämter* or *HPNZa*) at Frankfurt an der Oder, Naumburg, Bielefeld, Breslau, Oppeln, Kassel, Altengrabow, and Olmütz; the Army Signal Equipment Depot (*Heereszeugamtnachrichten* or *HZaNachr*) at Berlin-Schöneberg; and the Army Branch Signal Equipment Depot (*Heeresnebenzeugamtnachrichten* or *HNZaNachr*) at Wien-Strebersdorf (Vienna).

In addition to their storage functions, the *HZa* and *HNZa* adjust and test newly arrived materials and repair damaged equipment. Several of the *HNZa* are engaged almost entirely in repair functions, and most equipment depots maintain ordnance, signal, and engineer equipment servicing sections for inspecting newly manufactured equipment and repairing damaged equipment. Specialization in items repaired may occur: thus the tank equipment depots repair tanks and armored vehicles which have been so badly damaged that they cannot be repaired in the field.

The equipment depots are staffed by officers and noncommissioned officers of the Ordnance Branch who control the workers, usually civilians or soldiers serving a prison sentence.

An Army Equipment Depot is divided into two parts: the storage depot (*Lager*) and the workshop (*Werkstatt*). The storage depot is subdivided in departments (*Bezirke*), each of which specializes in one type of equipment. Depending on the type of equipment handled, the workshop will have separate sections like an arms workshop (*Waffen-Werkstatt*), an optical instruments workshop (*Optische-Werkstatt*), etc.

The Army Equipment Branch Depot is organized along the same lines as the Army Equipment Depot.

Associated with equipment depots are the Armed Forces depots attached to motor transport manufacturers. The main function of these is to facilitate transfer of vehicles from factories to equipment depots.

As the number of *HZa* is relatively limited and as they are perhaps the largest supply depots within Germany, they have been heavily bombed by Allied air forces. Despite much damage, the *HZa* have shown great recuperative powers. The importance of many *HZa*, however, has diminished, while that of the *HNZa* has increased through the dispersion of stores among the smaller supply centers.

List of known Army Equipment Depots (branch depots not included):

Corps Area	Installation	Location
I	*HZa*	Königsberg
II	*HZa*	Güstrow
II	*HZa*	Stettin
III	*HZa*	Berlin-Spandau
III	*HZaNachr*	Berlin-Schöneberg
IV	*HZa*	Chemnitz
IV	*HZa*	Naumburg
V	*HZa*	Ulm
VI	*HZa*	Unna
VII	*HZa*	Freilassing
VII	*HZa*	Ingolstadt
VII	*HZa*	München
VIII	*HZa*	Breslau
VIII	*HZa*	Brieg
VIII	*HZa*	Kotzenau
IX	*HZa*	Kassel
X	*HZa*	Hamburg-Glinde
XI	*HZa*	Hannover
XI	*HZa*	Magdeburg
XI	*HPZa*	Magdeburg-Königsborn
XII	*HZa*	Mainz-Kastel
XIII	*HZa*	Amberg
XVII	*HZa*	Wels
XVII	*HZa*	Wien
XVIII	*HZa*	Hall (in Tirol)
XVIII	*HZa*	Salzburg
XX	*HZa*	Graudenz
XXI	*HZa*	Posen

c. AMMUNITION DEPOTS. Army Ammunition Depots (*Heeresmunitionsanstalten* or *HMa*) and Army Ammunition Branch Depots (*Heeresmunitionsnebenanstalten* or *HMNa*) are the main German centers for the storage and issue of ammunition. Frequently they concentrate upon particular types of ammunition; for example, the *HMa* at Münsterlager, Celle, Dessau, Augsburg, and Neu Ulm are probably principal centers for the storage of chemical warfare ammunition.

Figure 2.—MUNCHEN MAIN EQUIPMENT DEPOT (HZA)

Photographed early in 1943 after a bombing. Chief features are four very large standard equipment buildings (averaging 590′ x 155′) typical of Main Equipment Depots; 21 smaller standard equipment buildings (about 270′ x 70′); a gun park containing about 300 guns; and about 55 miscellaneous buildings in the depot area.

In addition to storing and issuing ammunition, the *HMa* and *HMNa* participate in its production by assembling and filling shells and by manufacturing fuzes and other accessories.

Like the equipment depots, the ammunition depots are staffed by personnel of the Ordnance Branch. Employees include civilians, soldiers, prisoners of war, and large numbers of foreign laborers. An *HMa* usually has the following departments:

Administration
Manufacture (filling and packing of shells)
Shipping
Personnel administration
Motor pool

Because of the large number of well distributed ammunition depots, many of them undeground, Allied air attacks have not interfered materially with their functioning. But the increased number of foreign laborers employed by these depots undoubtedly has lowered their productivity.

d. AREA OF DISTRIBUTION. Generally a depot is allocated a definite geographical distribution area. The depot may be the exclusive German distributor of a particular item, or it may be merely the exclusive distributor within an allotted area. Thus the Ulm *HZa* distributes types of engineer equipment to all areas, while it issues Czech small arms to less than half of the corps areas. In addition, a depot may be assigned to a particular army for the supply of materiel replacements and the repair of its damaged materiel.

3. Corps Area Equipment Park Organization

a. GENERAL. The corps area parks complement the equipment depots in the handling of motor transport, engineer equipment, and anti-gas equipment, and form the principal centers for the distribution of horses, veterinary equipment, and medical equipment. Requisitions for repairs reach the parks from both home and field units. Primarily, a park is responsible for servicing its allotted area; usually it also is charged with the supply and maintenance of designated units of the Field Army.

b. MOTOR TRANSPORT PARKS. The Home Motor Transport Parks (*Heimatkraftfahrparke* or *HKP*) received damaged or impounded vehicles such as motorcycles, trucks, and staff cars, but do not handle tanks and armored vehicles, or any newly manufactured vehicles. There are several such parks in each corps area, controlled by the Home Motor Maintenance District Headquarters (*Heimatkraftfahrbezirk*) of the corps area.

Most of the vehicles repaired belong to the *Wehrmacht* and the *SS*; but vehicles from semi-military and civilian agencies are also repaired. The *HKP* vary widely as to the number of vehicles repaired daily and the average number held. At Berlin, where there are three *HKP*, each may hold as many as 1,000 vehicles and repair 30 daily. Most *HKP*, however, hold 60 to 100 vehicles and have a daily repair average of probably less than ten vehicles. Since many of the vehicles received are damaged beyond repair and must be scrapped or cannibalized, the daily repair averages are not as inefficient as may appear upon initial glance.

A typical *HKP* includes a reception point where vehicle defects are inspected, a large number of workshops, and final inspection points where vehicles are either dispatched to units or sent back for further repair. Frequently there are branch administrative offices (*Zweigstellen*) and workshops located as far as 40 miles from the Main Office (*Hauptstelle*). The number of *HKP* in a corps area varies greatly: at one time Corps Area VI was known to have nine *HKP*, while Corps Area V had only four.

Supplies of spare parts and tires are procured from Central Spare Parts Depots (*Zentralersatzteillager* or *ZEL*) and Tire Depots (*Reifenlager*) which are controlled by the *HKP*, or direct from factories.

c. MEDICAL PARKS. The Berlin Main Medical Park (*Hauptsanitätspark*) and the Corps Area Medical Parks (*Wehrkreissanitätsparke*)—one per corps area—receive all types of surgical apparatus, drugs, bandages, and dispensing equipment from factories and hold them for distribution to hospitals within their corps areas and to Medical Collecting Parks (*Sammelsanitätsparke*). The latter are subsidiaries of the Corps Area Medical Parks and serve as collecting points for medical supplies to the field forces. In certain cases the Main Medical Park and Corps Area Medical Parks may deliver their supplies direct to the field forces.

The Main Medical Park in Berlin occupies a special position as it holds critical drugs and hospital supplies for distribution to Corps Area Medical Parks and Medical Collecting Parks. In addition it tests newly developed pharmaceutical preparations and medical equipment and furnishes the Corps Area Medical Parks with "standard" samples of medical equipment. The Main Medical Park is subordinate to the Chief Army Medical Inspector, and the Corps Area Medical Parks are subordinate to the Corps Area Surgeons; there is thus no chain of command leading from the Main Medical Park to the Corps Area Medical Parks.

There is also a group of Medical Booty Collecting Points (*Sanitätsbeutesammelstellen*) that are centers for the collection of captured medical equipment. This is sorted and tested prior to shipment to the medical parks for distribution.

Although the medical parks participate in the repair of damaged medical equipment, it is very likely that much of the recovery work is done by the manufacturers.

d. VETERINARY PARKS. Veterinary supplies are procured through veterinary parks. The Army Main Veterinary Park (*Heereshauptveterinärpark*) is directly subordinate to the Veterinary Inspector. It is the central procurement agency for veterinary equipment. Upon orders from the Veterinary Inspector the Army Main Veterinary Park will supply the Home Veterinary Parks (*Heimatveterinärparke*) with veterinary equipment either directly or by ordering it for these parks from commercial manufacturers. Horseshoeing equipment is always ordered from civilian factories.

The Home Veterinary Parks, numbering one in each corps area, and the Army Main Veterinary Park receive veterinary equipment such as shoeing equipment and veterinary medicines from the manufacturers and issue it to units and horse hospitals, besides repairing and salvaging damaged veterinary equipment received from units.

e. HORSE PARKS. Young horses purchased by the Army are sent to Army Remount Depots (*Heeresremonteämter*) for their maintenance and training until they are suited for field use. They are then delivered direct to corps area riding schools, to home units, or to Home Horse Parks (*Heimatpferdeparke*) which forward horses to Field Army units.

As the occupied territories formerly furnished most of the horse replacements for the German Army, their loss will greatly aggravate the already noticeable animal shortage at a time when the German Army is becoming increasingly dependent on horse transportation.

f. OTHER PARKS. A sizeable number of Home Engineer Parks (*Heimatpionierparke*) have been reported functioning within the corps areas, supplying home and field units with engineer equipment. In addition, there are at least five special

Home Fortress Engineer Parks (*Heimatfestungspionierparke*), which supply fortress engineer units; a number of Home Railway Engineer Parks (*Heimateisenbahnpionierparke*); and a few Gas Defense Equipment Parks (*Gasschutzgeräteparke*).

4. Clothing and Individual Equipment* Supply Organization

a. PROCUREMENT AND ADMINISTRATION. Procurement of raw materials is the special function of the Armed Forces Clothing and Equipment Procurement Office (*Wehrmachtbeschaffungsamt Bekleidung und Ausrüstung*) at Berlin. The raw materials are then issued to the clothing depots of the three branches of the Armed Forces and the SS which manufacture, store, and issue clothing and various items of individual equipment. In addition, damaged, captured, or impounded clothing may be sent to the clothing depots for repair and reissue.

In the Army the highest administrative echelon is a section in the staff of the General Army Office (*Allgemeines Heeresamt/Stab/Bekleidung*) which issues all directives on clothing and equipment. It controls the work of the Army Clothing Depots (*Heeresbekleidungsämter* or *HBA*). Within each corps area the supply of clothing is directed by Section E (*Sachgebiet E*) of the Corps Area Administration (*Wehrkreisverwaltung*). Thus for all practical purposes the normal Army Clothing Depot is subject to a dual control.

b. CLOTHING DEPOTS. One or more Army Clothing Depots are generally found in each corps area. These *HBA* receive raw materials from which they manufacture clothing, insignia, shoes, tents, canteens, blankets, and other items of individual equipment. They exercise control over Testing and Repair Sections (*Verwaltungsund Instandsetzungabteilungen*), which repair damaged clothing, and Army Clothing Dumps and Branch Dumps (*Heeresbekleidungslager und Nebenlager*), which assist in the forwarding of clothing to the field forces.

Specialized types of clothing depots include Collecting Points for Winter Clothing (*Sammel-Stellen für Winterbekleidung*), Army Clothing Repair Workshops (*Heeresbekleidungsinstandsetzungswerkstätten*) which presumably do not handle newly manufactured clothing, and Clothing Processing Centers (*Durchschleusungsstel-*

* *Ausrüstung des Mannes.* See note on page 2.

len) which are believed to be centers to which reinforcements requiring refitting are routed before their departure for the front. In addition, rations depots may store and issue clothing for certain areas.

c. AREA OF DISTRIBUTION. The *HBA* issues clothing and individual equipment to units within its assigned territorial area. Many *HBA* are also responsible for the supply of particular armies in the field; to facilitate the transfer of clothing to field units, issues may be made to Army Clothing Dumps and Branch Dumps which in turn issue clothing and individual equipment to field units.

5. Rations Supply Organization

a. GENERAL. The German Army depends for its transportation to a large extent on horse-drawn vehicles; forage is therefore considered to be of equal importance to human rations, and the supply of both is handled by the same agencies. In the following description of the supply organization the term rations includes forage as well.

b. PROCUREMENT AND ADMINISTRATION. The over-all planning of rations and the laying down of policies for the procurement and organization of supplies is done for all branches of the Armed Forces at the Rations and Procurement Group (*Amtsgruppe Verpflegung und Beschaffung*) of the Army High Command/Administration Office (*OKH/Heeresverwaltungsamt*). At the same time the Rations and Procurement Group directs the supply of rations to the Field Army and to the Replacement Army. Regional control of supply is exercised by Section C (*Sachgebiet C*) of the Corps Area Administration.

Although all rations depots procure a proportion of their supplies direct from local producers, they draw most of them from the Higher Rations Stores (*Ersatzverpflegungsmagazine* or *EVM*) to which they are subordinate. In procuring rations for distribution, the *EVM* purchases food from all parts of the corps area in which it is located and arranges for the exchange of goods with other corps areas. In many instances procurement of a particular rations component, such as flour or fodder, may be delegated to one of the depots subsidiary to the *EVM*.

c. RATIONS DEPOTS. While in peacetime the troops purchased their rations mostly through commercial channels and only bread and forage were procured from the Army bakeries and rations depots, in wartime the supply of rations from Army depots has become the rule. To fulfil this task, the Higher Rations Stores or *EVM* were formed at the outbreak of war from many of the already existent Army Rations Main Depots (*Heeresverpflegungshauptämter*) or (*HVHA*).

The most important type of rations depot is the *EVM*. The *EVM* control Army Rations Main Depots (*HVHA*) which in turn control Army Rations Depots (*Heeresverpflegungsämter* or *HVA*) and Army Garrison Rations Depots (*Heeresstandortverwaltung Verpflegungsabteilungen*). Although the number of such installations in a corps area varies, one corps area is known to have two *EVM*, three *HVHA*, nine *HVA* and at least 12 Army Garrison Ration Depots. There are probably 40 *EVM* in Germany, 36 of which are listed below.

The echelon of the depot generally determines its size and stock. Each *EVM* is expected to maintain stock sufficient for one month's rations for 300,000 men; this would amount to over 10,000 tons of food. An *HVHA* retains food reserves of perhaps 3,000 tons, while an *HVA* usually stocks several hundred tons. An *EVM* almost invariably has a bakery and good rail facilities; lower echelon depots may lack bakeries and may have only road connections.

The rule as to size of depots is not inflexible. A large share of the stores normally retained by the *EVM* may be divided among *HVHA* and *HVA* for additional protection from air raids and to facilitate the loading of rations trains. In other instances, Army Garrison Rations Depots handle more stores than *HVHA* or *HVA* of the same corps area due to abnormal troop concentrations in their particular garrison areas.

While specialization is not typical of the rations depots, since both human and animal rations are found in all types, a limited number of *HVHA* and *HVA* tend to have concentrated stores of a particular rations component. As an example, one *HVHA*, now captured, maintained a reserve of thousands of tons of oats in addition to its stores of troop rations. In certain farming districts Fodder Collecting Points (*Rauhfuttersammelstellen*) specialize in the collection and storage of forage.

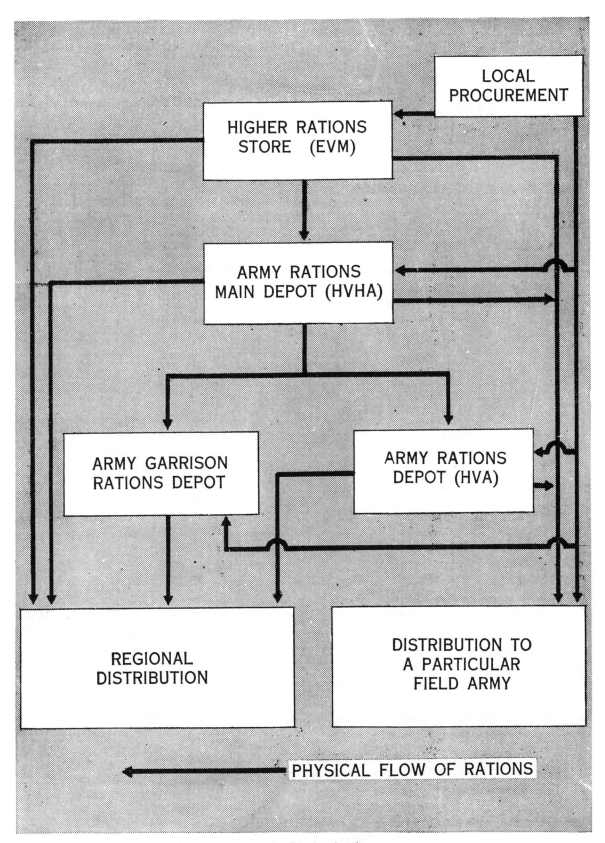

Figure 3.—Supply of rations.

List of known Higher Rations Stores (*EVM*):

Corps Area	Location
I	Insterburg
I	Königsberg
I	Lötzen
II	Stettin
III	Berlin
III	Potsdam
IV	Dresden
IV	Halle
IV	Leipzig
IV	Torgau
V	Aalen
V	Ulm
VI	Minden
VI	Münster
VII	München
VIII	Breslau
VIII	Liegnitz
VIII	Oppeln
IX	Erfurt
IX	Frankfurt am Main
IX	Kassel
X	Bremen
X	Hamburg
X	Rendsburg
XI	Hannover
XI	Magdeburg
XII	Mainz
XIII	Bamberg
XIII	Nürnberg
XVII	Linz
XVII	Wien
XVIII	Graz
XX	Danzig
XXI	Posen
B.u.M	Olmütz
B.u.M	Prag

d. AREA OF DISTRIBUTION. The depots maintained by the Army supply food and forage to Army, *SS,* and Air Force units present in their localities. Naval units generally are supplied by Naval Rations Depots (*Marineverpflegungsämter*). The process of local supply is relatively simple, as units contact the nearest rations depot and thereafter automatically are attached to a depot for their supply of rations. If a depot finds itself unable to provide full rations to all units in its area, it receives assistance from other depots in the corps area.

In addition to supplying local needs, the *EVM* are the principal centers for the supply of rations to the Field Army. Ordinarily, a group of *EVM* becomes responsible for the rations supply of a particular army; then the *EVM* must make certain that the army has about 10 days' supply of rations on hand at all times, based upon an esti-mate of the probable rations strength prepared by the army 28 days in advance.

Lower echelon depots may become involved in the supply of the field armies in a number of ways:

(1) When an *HVA* or *HVHA* is delegated to assist the *EVM* in storage of field army rations.

(2) When an *HVHA* is assigned the function of procuring and storing a particular component of the ration for the entire corps area.

(3) When any of the depots located in the theater of operations are turned over to a field army to be used as an Army Rations Depot (*Armeeverpflegungslager*).

6. Fuels and Lubricants Supply Organization

a. GENERAL. Because of the critical condition of German fuel supply, the collection and distribution of fuel have largely been retained by the Ministry of Economic Affairs through its Central Petroleum Office. Both the Central Petroleum Office and the Armed Forces High Command exercise authority over the *WIFO* (Economic Research Company), which is the organization responsible for the administration of depots supplying fuel to the armed forces.

b. PROCUREMENT. The Ministry of Economic Affairs, in collaboration with the Armed Forces High Command, establishes the proportional allotment of fuel to the Armed Forces and to civilian users. The refineries, producers, and importers then are directed to ship supplies either to the *WIFO* Depots or to air force, naval or commercial storage depots.

c. TYPES OF DEPOTS. The main *WIFO* depots controlled by the Central Petroleum Office consist of Main Strategic Depots (*Zentralhauptlager*), which are usually underground, and of Main Transit Depots (*Zentralumschlaglager*), which store supplies for transshipment. In addition to supplying the largest share of fuel received by army fuel depots, these depots handle a portion of the fuel used by the Air Force and Navy. The Main Strategic Depots have storage capacities ranging into hundreds of thousands of tons of oil. For this reason the Allied air forces have bombed them with great consistency. The importance of the Main Transit Depots has decreased since the cutting off of Rumanian petroleum imports.

The smaller *WIFO* depots, controlled by the Armed Forces High Command, consist of Army High Command Fuel Supply Depots (*OKH*

Nachschubtanklager) and subsidiary Army Fuel Supply Depots (*Heeresnachschubtanklager*). These depots are directed solely to the supply of Army units. Very likely, commercial storage depots situated in the Theater of Operations have been converted into *WIFO* depots of this sort.

Not controlled by *WIFO* are the depots situated near the producing plants (*Marschtanklager* or Fuel Replacement Depots) which send fuel supplies to the depots mentioned above as well as direct to the Field Army.

7. *Waffen-SS* Supply Organization

a. RELATION TO ARMY SUPPLY. While the *Waffen-SS* is generally self-sufficient in its Zone of the Interior supply, it depends upon the Chief of Army Equipment for most of its tanks, self-propelled guns, and other heavy equipment and for the repair of many of its vehicles. Indeed, *Waffen-SS* units have a higher priority on heavy equipment than do army units. To what extent the *SS* reciprocates by supplying army units has not been determined.

b. *SS* DEPOTS. Of the *SS* depot centers, Oranienburg is the most important as it contains the Main *SS* Equipment Depot (*SS-Zeugamt*), the *SS* Central Distribution Center (*SS-Zentralzulassungstelle*), the *SS* Signal Equipment Depot (*SS-Nachrichtenzeugamt*), and an *SS* Motor Transport Depot (*SS-Kraftfahrzeugdepot*). Other important *SS* depot centers are Berlin, Dachau, and Prague. Since the *SS* depots supply the other branches of the *SS* as well as the *Waffen-SS* with rations, clothing, and certain types of equipment, they cannot be considered as purely military depots.

8. Transportation

All military transportation by rail or on inland waterways comes under the direction of the Chief of Transportation (*Chef des Transportwesens*) at the High Command of the Armed Forces (*OKW*). He works through a chain of transportation headquarters which are usually subordinate to the Army but act for the whole of the Armed Forces. The activities of the transportation headquarters cover the occupied territories as well as Germany.

The Transportation Headquarters (*Transport-Kommandanturen*) are regional liaison offices of the Armed Forces with the German State Railways (*Deutsche Reichsbahn*) and the authorities controlling the transportation on inland water-

ways. The Transportation Headquarters are located at the seat of a Railway Directorate (*Reichsbahndirektion*) and control the area of one or more Railway Directorates.

The Transportation Headquarters are the basic units through which all military agencies must deal if they require rail or water transportation for units, freight, or casualties. The Transportation Headquarters make the transportation facilities available and issue orders as to how and when they are to be used.

The staff of the Transportation Headquarters is organized into:

Section Ia: Troop movements for the Armed Forces
                Auxiliaries of the Armed Forces
                Transportation of prisoners of war

Section Ib: Freight for the Armed Forces
                Armament goods
                Armed Forces travel

Section IVb: Hospital and convalescent trains

Subordinate to the transportation headquarters are railway station headquarters (*Bahnhofskommandanturen*) and officers stationed at inland harbors (*Hafenoffiziere*). These headquarters and officers are stationed there for the maintenance of order and as liaison officers with the local railway and harbor officials.

Section III. SYSTEM OF SUPPLY OF THE FIELD ARMY

1. General

The supply system of the Field Army is simple and flexible. Its main objective during combat is to replace all supplies used during one day of combat by the beginning of the next day. Rules and regulations are not mandatory; much discretion therefore remains with the supply officers who are encouraged to move supplies as far forward as possible without reloading, to salvage all usable materiel, and to limit expenditure of supplies as far as possible.

2. Staff Control

a. SUPPLY DIRECTIVES. The commanders of Field Army units conduct supply within their commands in accordance with directives laid down by the Army High Command. For this purpose their general staffs are provided with staff officers, analogous to our G-4's, who are called *Ib* and who are responsible for all matters of transport and supply. When the *Ib,* acting in the name of his commander, issues supply directives, their execution usually falls to the following:

(1) Arms and Equipment Section (*W* and *WuG*).

(2) Intendance Section (*IVa* or *Intendantur*), dealing with rations, clothing, and pay.

(3) Medical Section (*IVb*).

(4) Veterinary Section (*IVc*).

(5) Motor Transport Section (*V*).

(6) Supply Troop Commander (*Kommandeur der Nachschubtruppen*), commanding the organic or attached supply troops.

b. STAFF OFFICERS AND DUTIES. The staff officers concerned with supply in the Field Army and their duties are as follows:

(1) At Field Army headquarters, the Chief of Field Army Supply and Administration (*General Quartiermeister*) is directly responsible to the Chief of Staff of the Field Army and constantly is kept informed of the supply situation of the various armies. One of his main functions is forwarding the requirements of the armies to the Chief of Army Equipment. He regulates the evacuation of prisoners and wounded, and the use of communications in the theater of operations. Large stocks of materials, including captured materials and mobile supply trains, are under his control. Important repair centers are also maintained under his control.

(2) At army group headquarters, the Army Group *Ib* intervenes only when a critical situation requires action, since army groups are not in the normal chain of supply. Normally his most important function is the supervision of security units which safeguard supplies in the communications zones. Units attached to an army group are supplied through the army in whose area they are located.

(3) At army headquarters, the Army *Ib* (*Oberquartiermeister*) administers the collation and forwarding of requisitions, the receipt of supplies from Zone of the Interior depots, the distribution of supplies to lower echelons, and the maintenance of important dumps and repair centers.

(4) At corps headquarters, the Corps *Ib* (*Quartiermeister*), who always has been a link in the chain of requisitioning, recently has been assigned a role in the chain of supply, although the larger proportion of supplies still pass direct from army dumps to divisions. In addition to handling

the supply of organic corps troops, the Corps *Ib* supervises the distribution of supplies from corps dumps to lower echelons.

(5) At division headquarters, the Division *Ib* makes his requisition to the Corps *Ib* on the basis of requisitions and reports from the troop units. He controls the division services of supply and provides a systematic supply of reserves of all kinds for the troops. Like the Army *Ib,* he is in the normal chain of supply.

3. Requisitioning and Procurement

a. REQUISITIONING. (1) The normal channel of requisitioning is from troop units through regiment, division, and corps to army.

(2) An army generally sends requisitions for ammunition, fuel, motor transport, horses, weapons, spare parts, and most other types of equipment to the Field Army, while requisitions for rations, clothing, medical equipment, and veterinary equipment go direct to home depots assigned to the army. While these are the usual channels, many variations are known to occur. For instance, an army may send a requisition for certain special weapons and chemical warfare equipment directly to the Chief of Army Equipment, or an army may send a rations requisition to the Field Army in addition to forwarding the requisition to a home depot.

(3) Requisitions arriving at the Field Army usually are forwarded to the Chief of Army Equipment, who passes them down to a designated home depot. In some cases, however, the Field Army may send requisitions directly to a home depot without routing them through the Chief of Army Equipment.

(4) A requisition may be filled at any level by the echelon which has the necessary supplies available in its storage centers.

b. PROCUREMENT. Requisitioning is supplemented by two methods of field procurement: living off the land and the use of captured materiel.

(1) Living off the land may be accomplished either by local purchase or by outright confiscation of local supplies. Such procedure seldom is sufficient to supply all the requirements of units. In some areas, nevertheless, it has considerably lessened the German supply problem, as in Italy where much food, clothing, ammunition, and equipment is locally procured.

(2) The employment of captured materiel has always been a favored practice in the German Army. In the offensive beginning in December

1944, directed against the Americans holding the St. Vith-Bastogne area, the Germans apparently expected to keep their tanks operating by the seizure of American fuel dumps. The German soldiers frequently were clothed with American uniforms and operated with liberal amounts of captured Czech, British, French, and Russian, as well as American weapons and equipment.

4. Principal Installations

a. REARWARD OF RAILHEADS. (1) *Collecting stations (Sammelbahnhöfe)*. Shipments of less than a rail carload are sent to these stations and combined into carloads and train shipments before being routed to the railhead.

(2) *Forwarding stations (Weiterleitungstationen)*. Rail shipments that are not unit-loaded for one organization may be forwarded to the army through one of these stations.

(3) *Distributing stations (Verteilerbahnhöfe)*. When a large number of units are dependent upon a single railroad for their supply, a distributing station may be set up to regulate the dispatch of supplies to the proper railhead or unloading point; apparently the combined functions of the collecting, forwarding, and distributing stations approach the functions of the U. S. regulating station.

(4) *Supply collecting areas (Nachschubsammelgebiete)*. Reserves of ammunition, fuel, and rations are kept loaded in trains in these areas subject to disposition by the Chief of Field Army Administration and Supply.

(5) *Field Army parks, bases, and depots (Heeres Parke, Stützpunkte, und Lager)*. Primarily concerned with the maintenance, repair, and forwarding of vehicles, including tanks and armored vehicles, these Field Army installations may be located well to the rear of the railheads.

(6) *Army parks (Armee Parke)*. Some of the army equipment parks may be located to the rear of the army railheads.

b. RAILHEADS (*Kopfbahnhöfe*). Railheads are located as far forward as possible. While this generally results in army (*Armee*) railheads, each of which supplies a number of divisions or a corps (in the latter case the railhead may be called a corps railhead), a division railhead for each division is established whenever possible. On the Western Front, depending on the nature of the terrain and the effectiveness of Allied bombings, the railhead is found from 10 to 50 miles—usually about 25 miles—from the front. This is a great improvement over the conditions that existed in the early stages of the Russian campaign, when German railheads were on an average from 90 to 120 miles behind the front troops.

c. FORWARD OF RAILHEADS. (1) *Army parks and dumps (Armee Parke und Lager)*. Army fuel, rations, and ammunition dumps are almost invariably forward of army railheads, while army equipment parks generally are in the vicinity of the railheads.

(2) *Corps dumps (Korps Lager)*. If army installations are far to the rear, corps dumps may be set up between army and division; in such cases the corps dumps function as advanced army dumps distributing to divisions.

(3) *Division dumps (Divisions Lager)*. The dump system may be pushed forward even into the division area, but this is the exception rather than the rule.

(4) *Distributing points (Ausgabestellen)*. These are maintained by divisions and possibly other echelons in their areas for the distribution of rations, fuel, and ammunition. While stores are not generally retained at these points, small accumulations may occur.

(5) *Collecting points (Sammelstellen)*. Although called collecting points, these centers, which are maintained by army and division, serve as supply points for new and repaired equipment as well as collecting points for damaged and captured equipment.

(6) *Reloading points (Umschlagstellen)*. When long road movements are involved, reloading points may be set up by army or corps to facilitate supply movements.

(7) *Supply points*. Units lower than divisions have points analogous to collecting and distributing points.

5. Distribution of Supplies to Field Units

a. GENERAL SCHEME OF DISTRIBUTION. (1) Supplies are transported by rail from home depots to army railheads where they are picked up by army supply columns and transported to army dumps and parks. Division supply columns receive rations, fuel, and ammunition at army dumps, and equipment at army parks. They carry the rations, fuel, and ammunition to division distributing points, and the equipment to division collecting points. At these points, supplies are transferred to battalion supply columns and carried to battalion or company supply points where the supplies are turned over to the troops.

(2) While this is the usual flow of supplies, it may be modified in a number of ways, most of which are shown in Figure 2. Operational conditions are the cause of most modifications of the usual system of distribution. Hence, if the army and divisions are short of trucks or gasoline, columns from units as low as companies may be forced to go as far as 20 miles to receive supplies from army railheads and dumps; if the lower echelons lack means of transportation, army supply columns may be used to bring supplies to the troops; if Allied strafing is expected, supply movements may be limited to the hours of darkness; if units are stationed in the near vicinity of army dumps, they may draw their supplies direct from the dumps.

b. DISTRIBUTION OF RATIONS. Normally home rations depots ship supplies direct to Army Rations Dumps (*Armeeverpflegungslager*). A number of such dumps may be set up, each with stores of less than 100 tons. In some cases, these dumps have been known to store small amounts of clothing, individual equipment, and office equipment. As they are not permanent installations, they may move from time to time. Forward army dumps sometimes are controlled by corps and called Corps Rations Dumps (*Korpsverpflegungslager*); in such cases, the corps dumps supply the division and corps troops, while army dumps supply units and individual detachments attached to army headquarters, and form a permanent organization for the support of future military operations. Rations supply within the division is handled through a rations distributing point (*Verpflegungsausgabestelle*). Supplies are received at this point and are distributed to division units. Usually livestock is sent to field butchery platoons for dressing, and flour to field bakeries for bread production.

(1) A butchery platoon can process the following number of animals per day:

```
40 beef cattle........equal to 40,000 meat rations.
80 pigs ..............equal to 24,000 meat rations.
240 sheep ...........equal to 19,000 meat rations.
```

(2) A field bakery company can produce between 15,000 and 19,200 bread rations, according to the weather and the time of the year. After passing through the rations supply points of the division units, the supplies finally reach field kitchens and troops. Field kitchens of two types are found: large, with a capacity for supplying 125 to 225 men; and small, with a capacity for supplying 60 to 125 men.

c. DISTRIBUTION OF AMMUNITION. The home ammunition depots forward supplies to the Army Ammunition Dumps (*Armeemunitionslager*) which usually store from 3,000 to 6,000 tons. Any forward army dumps taken over by corps are called Corps Ammunition Dumps (*Korpsmunitionslager*). From these dumps, the ammunition is taken to Division Ammunition Distributing Points (*Divisionsausgabestellen*). One or more well camouflaged distributing points are established, located out of the effective range of Allied artillery and, if possible, on terrain protected from tank attacks. Ordinarily artillery ammunition and infantry ammunition are handled by different distributing points so as to facilitate the loading and unloading of supplies. In some cases Division Ammunition Dumps (*Divisionsmunitionslager*) are set up in the division area, especially if the front lines have been stabilized. From the divisions, ammunition is sent to infantry and artillery ammunition supply points maintained by regiments, battalions, and companies. As German regulations permit the setting up of temporary ammunition dumps at these points, small reserves may be present only a few miles behind the front lines.

Unused ammunition, empty shell cases, packing cases, and faulty ammunition must be returned by the troops to army dumps from where they are sent to the home areas. The rapid return of this material is considered as important as ammunition supply.

d. DISTRIBUTION OF FUELS AND LUBRICANTS. Fuel from home fuel depots or from Field Army mobile reserves is directed to the railheads. Sometimes the fuel is kept loaded in tanker trains (*Eisenbahntankstellen*) near the railhead and transferred from these directly to fuel columns, but preferably it is laid down in 20- and 200-liter containers in Army Fuel Dumps (*Armeebetriebsstofflager*) forward of the railhead. From these dumps the fuel is taken forward to Division Fuel Distributing Points (*Divisionsbetriebsstoffausgabestellen*) or, in the case of some motorized and armored divisions, to Division Fuel Dumps (*Divisionsbetriebsstofflager*). Fuel is forwarded from the division area to lower echelon supply points and to fuel points that are set aside for the use of single vehicles (*Tankstellen für Einzelkraftfahrzeuge*). The latter may also be supplied from the army fuel stores.

e. DISTRIBUTION OF CLOTHING AND INDIVIDUAL EQUIPMENT. Stores are dispatched from the Zone of the Interior to the field rations dumps

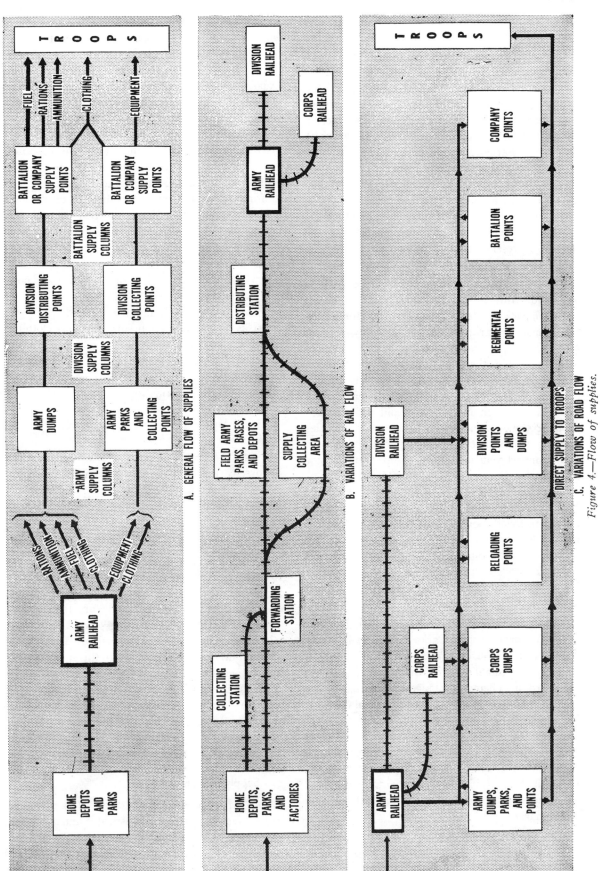

Figure 4.—Flow of supplies.

and to field equipment parks and collecting points, from which the stores are distributed to units.

f. DISTRIBUTION OF EQUIPMENT. (1) Equipment is handled by parks of two different categories: the *Herres,* or Field Army type, and the *Armee,* or army type. Although performing functions analogous to those of the Zone of the Interior Home (*Heimat*) and Corps Area (*Wehrkreis*) Equipment Parks, the field parks have a number of distinct characteristics. They are concerned only with military vehicles. Furthermore, they are dependent upon Zone of the Interior depots, parks, and factories for fifth echelon maintenance. Lastly, the field parks are responsible for the storage of reserve equipment as well as the distribution of new and repaired equipment.

(2) The most numerous *Heeres* type park is the Field Army Motor Transport Park (*Heereskraftfahrpark* or *HeKP*). Unlike the Home Motor Transport Park, the *HeKP* normally does all repairs itself, without farming vehicles out to workshops, with the already existing repair facilities which it customarily takes over. Usually a number of *HeKP* are established in each army group area. Each *HeKP* may hold a reserve of about 200 new vehicles in addition to vehicles arriving from home equipment parks and depots, and damaged vehicles coming from Army Motor Transport Parks (*Armeekraftfahrparke* or *AKP*). In conjunction with army parks, the *HeKP* establish and maintain gasoline stations at certain selected points, usually along important roads. Not ascertained are the functions of reported Motor Transport Repair Parks (*Kraftfahrinstandsetzungsparke*) and Winterization Parks (*Winterlager*) which may be specialized *HeKP* or *HeKP* branches.

(3) Perhaps even more important than the Field Army Motor Transport Parks are the Field Army Tank Parks or Bases (*Stützpunkte*). These presumably are established on the basis of one per army group. Their importance is increased by the fact that armies do not ordinarily maintain fixed installations for the repair of tanks, although armies may have semi-permanent tank workshops. The tank bases are reception or control centers from which tanks are dispatched to workshops in the near vicinity for repairs, or returned to home depots and factories for fifth echelon maintenance.

(4) Also under Field Army control are Spare Parts Depots (*Ersatzteillager*), Tire Depots (*Reifenlager*), Track Depots (*Gleiskettenlager*),

Tank Spare Parts Depots (*Panzerersatzteillager*), Armored Car Spare Parts Depots (*Panzerspähwagenersatzsteillager*), and Tractor Spare Parts Depots (*Zugkraftwagenersatzteillager*). The Depots furnish supplies to maintenance sections, workshop units, army parks, and Field Army parks.

(5) Army Parks (*Armee parke*) are primarily for repairs but they also are supposed to maintain a reserve of between 5 and 10 per cent of the arms and equipment of the army, and to forward equipment either directly or through collecting points to units. An army has the following parks:

(a) Infantry Park, for infantry weapons and trucks.

(b) Artillery Park, for artillery weapons and trucks.

(c) Anti-gas Equipment Park, for gas masks, decontamination suits, anti-gas clothing, and smoke equipment.

(d) Engineer Stores Park, for engineer materials.

(e) Signal Park, for radio and telephone materials.

(f) Motor Transport Park, for vehicles and spare parts.

(g) Army Equipment Park, for harness, horse carts. cooks equipment, and general items.

(h) Medical Park, for medical equipment.

(i) Veterinary Park, for veterinary equipment.

(j) Horse Park, for riding and draft horses.

(6) When equipment is forwarded from army to division, it passes either directly from the army parks to Division Equipment Collecting Points (*Divisionsgerätesammelstellen*) or through an Army Equipment Collecting Point (*Armeegerätesammelstelle*) to the division. In turn the division directs the equipment to the supply points maintained by its units. Equipment repaired by field maintenance sections and workshop units may be returned directly or through any of the collecting or supply points to the troops; because the procedure is greatly variant, Figure 6 pictures this latter flow as only direct to the troops.

6. Supply Movement

a. RAILROAD SUPPLY TRAINS. (1) *Standard supply trains.* German logistical manuals outline the use of standard rations, ammunition, and fuel supply trains with a maximum net load of 450 metric tons (or approximately 500 short tons) on a standard gauge (4 feet 8½ inches) railway. The text-book theory has generally been followed out in practice, although in some cases two or more locomotives have been sighted pulling unusually long fuel trains, and in some areas standard rations trains seldom are used. Standard equipment supply trains, with great variations in net loading weights, also are employed. In most cases, however, equipment of all kinds is loaded on the same train.

(2) *Rations supply trains (Verpflegungszüge)*, with an average of 40 cars per train may be composed as follows:

(a) Iron rations: 300,000 full and 300,000 half iron rations, totalling 442 metric tons.

(b) Full rations with fodder: 180,000 human and 40,000 animal rations, amounting to 454 metric tons. These may be loaded into three parts, each containing 3 days' supplies for 20,000 men and 4,000 animals.

(c) Full human rations with no bread but only baking materials: 300,000 rations, totaling 450 metric tons.

(d) Flour train (*Mehlzug*): 833,000 rations. amounting to 450 metric tons.

(e) Oat train (*Haferzug*): 90,000 rations, totaling 450 metric tons.

(f) Animal trains (*Viehzüge*): 360 cattle weighing 180 metric tons, 1200 pigs weighing 120 metric tons, or 1800 sheep weighing 72 metric tons.

(3) *Ammunition supply trains (Munitionszüge)*, with an average of 30 cars per train, are of three types:

(a) Unit-loaded trains, loaded according to the proportion of different types of ammunition needed by a particular division.

(b) Caliber unit trains, in which each car is loaded with approximately 15 metric tons (16½ short tons) of ammunition of a specific caliber.

(c) Single caliber unit trains, in which all cars are loaded with ammunition of the same caliber.

(4) *Fuel supply trains (Betriebstoffzüge)* of two types are used:

(a) 20 gasoline tank cars, holding between 340 cubic meters (around 89,800 gallons) and 440 cubic meters (around 116,200 gallons) of fuel.

(b) 25 cars, holding gasoline in 200-liter (53-gallon) and 20-liter (5-gallon) cans and carrying 400 cubic meters (105,600 gallons) of gasoline, and five cars with oil, engine oil, gear oil, paraffin, and (in winter) anti-freeze barrels and cans.

(5) *Horse supply trains (Pferdersatzzüge)* consist of 55 cars, each holding eight riding or light draft horses per car or 440 horses per train; six heavy draft horses per car or 330 horses per train; or four very heavy horses per car or 220 horses per train.

(6) *Signals and engineer construction materials trains (Baustoffzüge)* average 40 cars, of which 39 are open cars, with a net tonnage of about 820 metric tons (900 short tons).

(7) *Tank trains* carrying up to 25 medium tanks or up to 8 heavy tanks have also been reported. The average number of cars per tank train is about 33, with widely varying net loads.

(8) *Mixed equipment trains* are very frequent and may contain from 25 to 60 cars with a total net tonnage of up to 850 metric tons.

b. ROAD SUPPLY COLUMNS AND TRAINS. There are four types of road supply columns in the German Army:

(1) *Motorized columns (Kraftwagenkolonnen)* are, in general, employed on good roads. They can cover up to 125 miles per day. They are organized into very large, large, and small motor transport columns with a capacity of 120 metric tons, 60 tons, and 30 tons respectively for the transportation of supplies other than fuel. In addition, mountain divisions may have a special 10-ton capacity column. Fuel generally is transported in motorized fuel columns of two types —heavy columns with a minimum load of 50 cubic meters of fuel, and light columns with a minimum of 25 cubic meters. Motor transport columns are designated with reference to their employment as Field Army, army, corps, or division motor truck columns.

(2) *Animal-drawn columns (Fahrkolonnen)* normally have capacities of 30 or 17 metric tons, and mountain animal-drawn columns 15 metric tons. In general, they are equipped with one-team wagons; in cavalry units two-team wagons are used. According to German training instructions, well cared for and trained horses can cover 12 to 15 miles per day and under favorable conditions up to 20 miles, with a day of rest following. If oxen are employed, the rate of movement is slower. The Germans have been relying more and more upon animal-drawn columns for the movement of their supplies.

(3) *Pack trains (Tragtierkolonnen)*, generally consisting of 40 mules or horses each, usually are employed in mountainous terrain. A pack train can carry up to 5 tons, but its capacity and speed

are dependent on the trails and grade. Even in level country, pack trains usually march more slowly than foot troops.

(4) *Mountain carrier units* (*Gebirgsträgereinheiten*) consist of mountain carrier battalions and companies whose men are employed in terrain where not even pack animals can be used effectively. Each man can carry between 45 and 75 pounds of materiel on his back.

SUPPLY COLUMNS AND TRAINS

	Capacity (metric tons)	Capacity (short tons)
Very Large Motorized Column........	120	132
Large Motorized Column.............	60	66
Small Motorized Column....:........	30	33
Large Animal-Drawn Column........	30	33
Small Animal-Drawn Column.........	17	18½
Mountain Animal-Drawn Column.....	15	16½
Mountain Motorized Column..........	10	11
Pack Train	5	5½

	Minimum Amount (cubic meters)	Minimum Amount (gallons)
Large Motorized Fuel Column........	50	13,200
Small Motorized Fuel Column.........	25	6,600

c. SUPPLY ROADS. Whenever possible a supply road is designated for each self-contained unit such as a division. In general, the main route of advance of the unit is designated as its supply road. This principal route may be called a *Rollbahn,* or rolling road, to distinguish it from any secondary supply roads. When the main supply route is used for troop movements as well as for supply purposes, it generally will be called a *Durchgangsstrasse,* or through road. Great importance is attached to the upkeep of these routes and the placing of gasoline stations (*Tankstellen*) at strategic points close by the routes.

Section IV. MAINTENANCE REQUIREMENTS

I. Total Requirements

a. VARIABLES INVOLVED. The determination of the over-all requirements necessary to maintain German troops presents a number of difficulties. This is best shown by a review of the German supply expenditures in Russia in 1941. Armored divisions averaged some 30 tons daily when inactive and about 700 tons a day when engaged in heavy fighting; infantry divisions re-

quired 80 tons a day when inactive and some 1,100 tons during a day of heavy fighting. When engaged in defensive, mopping-up, or minor offensive activities, the divisions required supplies in amounts somewhere between the two extremes. By far the most important variable in this campaign was the amount of ammunition expended; requirements of fuel and equipment also varied considerably, while rations and clothing consumption remained relatively static. Expenditures depended upon the nature of the action involved, the types of units engaged, the zone of action, the season of the year, the amount of materiel available for consumption, and the facility with which supply movements could be made.

b. ESTIMATES OF TOTAL REQUIREMENTS. When the variables evident in the 1941 Russian campaign have become relatively constant, as is the case at present, the German supply requirements can be estimated with some degree of accuracy. Under present conditions the average total supply requirements per German soldier are estimated to vary as follows:

Character of fighting in area	Total pounds per man per day
Inactivity	5-10
Mopping-up	15-20
Defensive fighting (but not against a major Allied push)	20-25
Heavy defensive fighting	25-50
Offensive fighting	25-50

2. Rations

a. HUMAN RATIONS SCALES. The daily ration quantity (*Portionsatz*) is the amount of food consumed by one man for one day. It consists of three meals, the noon meal amounting to one-half of the total, the evening meal to one-third, and the next morning's breakfast to one-sixth. The Armed Forces High Command has laid down an over-all plan specifying the maximum amount of any ration item that may be served. The amount depends upon two factors: the duty class of the man receiving the ration, and the component class of the particular item being served.

There are four main types of rations served to troops. Ration I (*Verpflegungssatz I*) is for troops committed to combat, for those that are recuperating from combat, and for troops stationed in Norway north of 66° N. Lat. Ration II is for occupation and line-of-communication troops. Ration III is for garrison troops within Germany. Ration IV goes to office workers and

REPRESENTATIVE BREAKDOWN OF MAXIMUM RATION ALLOWANCES
IN GRAMS PER DAY

Item	Component Class	Duty Class			
		Ration I	Ration II	Ration III	Ration IV
Rye bread	(a)	700	700	700	600
Fresh meat with bones	(b)	136	107	90	56
Soy bean flour	(b)	7	7	7	7
Headless fish	(b)	30	30	30	30
Fresh vegetables and fruits	(c)	250	250	250	250
Potatoes	(c)	320	320	320	320
Legumes	(c)	80	80	80	80
Pudding powder	(d)	20	20	20	20
Sweetened condensed skim milk	(d)	25	25	25	25
Salt	(e)	15	15	15	15
Other seasonings	(e)	3	3	3	3
Spices	(f)	1	1	1	1
Fats and bread spreads	(g)	60	50	40	35
Coffee	(h)	9	9	9	9
Sugar	(i)	40	35	30	30
Supplementary allowances	(l)	2	2	2	2
Total Maximum Ration in grams		1,698	1,654	1,622	1,483
Total Maximum Ration in lbs		3.74	3.64	3.57	3.26
Wine (in summer) (quarts)	(j)	.026	.026	.026	.026
Cigarettes (pieces)	(k)	7	6	3	2

nurses within Germany. Hospital cases may fall within any of these classes depending on the seriousness of the cases.

The most important items of the component classes are as follows: (a) bread; (b) meats, soy bean flour, cheese, fish, and eggs; (c) vegetables; (d) puddings and milk; (e) salt, mustard, vinegar, and other seasonings; (f) spices such as pepper, cinnamon, and cloves; (g) butter, lard, marmalades, fats, and bread spreads; (h) coffee and tea; (i) sugar; (j) spirits and wines; (k) tobacco.

Substitute issues may be made within a component class but not among different component classes. Thus the daily maximum allowance of vegetables for a soldier is 60 grams* of dried vegetables, or 1200 grams of kidney beans, or 400 grams of salted vegetables, or equivalent quantities of any of about 30 other substitutes. It is not possible to predict which items will be served on any given day. The following chart, however, sets forth a likely breakdown of these maximum ration allowances.

b. SPECIAL TYPES OF HUMAN RATIONS. (1) *March ration (Marschverpflegung)*. The march ration is a cold food ration issued for not more than three or four consecutive days to units in transit either on carrier or by foot. It consists of approximately 700 grams of bread, 200 grams of cold meat or cheese, 60 grams of bread spreads, 9 grams of coffee (or 4 grams of tea), 10 grams of sugar, and six cigarettes. Thus it has a total weight of about 980 grams.

(2) *Iron ration (Eiserne Portion)*. An iron ration consists of 250 grams of biscuits, 200 grams of cold meat, 150 of preserved vegetables, 25 of coffee, and 25 of salt. Total weight is 650 grams without packing and 825 grams with packing. An iron half-ration is composed of 250 grams of biscuits and 200 grams of preserved meat; thus its total weight is 450 grams without packing and 535 grams with packing.

(3) *Combat Package (Grosskampfpäcken)* and *Close Combat Package (Nahkampfpäcken)*. The Germans have begun to use these types of rations for troops engaged in combat. They include chocolate bars, fruit bars, candies, cigarettes, and possibly biscuits.

c. ANIMAL RATIONS. An animal ration is the amount of food consumed by one horse, draft ox, dog, or carrier pigeon for one day. The quantity of an animal ration allowance (*Rationssatz*) depends on the type of animal, the area in which he is serving, and the content of the ration he is being fed. Horses, for instance, are divided into four groups: draft horses of the heaviest breed, draft horses of heavy breed, saddle-horses and light draft horses, and small horses. On the

*In dealing with captured German documents, the American soldier will invariably find the rations allowances computed in grams or kilograms. A gram equals .0353 ounce or .0022 pound. A kilogram (1000 grams) equals 35.3 ounces or 2.2 pounds.

Eastern front, draft horses of the heaviest breed receive a maximum ration allowance of 5650 grams of oats, 5300 grams of hay, and 5750 grams of straw (including 1500 grams of bedding straw). The allotments to other horse groups are proportionately less. On fronts other than the Eastern Front, the allotments for all horses are generally smaller. In addition, substitutes such as preserved forage, barley, corn, etc., may change the ration weight. If the horse is being fed an iron ration, he is given a single item such as oats or hay or straw.

d. RATIONS IN THE FIELD. Local stores obtained by purchase or confiscation play a greater part in the supply of rations in the field (*Feldportionen* for men and *Feldrationen* for animals) than is the case for any other class of supply. It is part of the German planning principle to live off the land as much as possible and to obtain only the remaining requirements from stocks procured through channels. The Germans fully appreciate the difficulty of employing such methods during periods of combat and do not count upon local stores during operative periods. Usually a normal reserve of about 10 days' rations for each man of an army is maintained within the army. The rations consist of full and iron rations, although the latter may be eaten only upon the receipt of special orders.

Rations carried in an army for each man:

	Full rations	Iron rations
With the man......	—	1 (half)
On a combat vehicle	—	1
In the field kitchen..	1	1
In the unit ration train	2	—
In the division train.	1	—
In the army dumps and train	a total of about 3	

Ordinarily there are two full and two iron horse rations carried either on the horse or in unit supply columns. Other rations are carried by the army and the division.

For staff planning purposes, the weights of rations are computed by the Germans as follows:

Type of Rations	Weight in grams	Weight in pounds
Human rations:		
Standard ration with packing.	1,500	3.3
Iron ration with packing....	825	1.82
Iron half-ration with packing	535	1.18
Horse rations:		
Standard ration	10,000	22.
Iron oat ration.............	5,000	11.
Iron hay ration.............	5,000	11.
Iron straw ration...........	2,500	5.5

3. Fuels and Lubricants

Distribution of fuel is calculated in the consumption unit (*Verbrauchssatz*) which is the amount of fuel that will move each vehicle in a formation 100 kilometers or 62 miles. The allowance of consumption units per formation is systematically replaced as it is expended. Under normal conditions it was standard for German formations to maintain three consumption units at army dumps; in addition, armored formations carried four units, reconnaissance elements carried six and a half units, and all other formations carried five units. Because of present fuel shortages, the allowances of consumption units are now determined by the amount of fuel which the General Staff believes is the minimum necessary for the desired tactical uses.

4. Equipment and Clothing

The replacement of equipment and clothing is based upon the allowances authorized for units and individuals in the table of organization (*Kriegsstärenachweisung*), the table of basic allowances (*Kriegsausrüstungnachweisung*), and the various annexes (*Anlagen*) to these tables. When the materials allotted under the tables are destroyed, damaged, lost, or worn out, they are repaired or replaced as quickly as possible.

5. Ammunition

a. AMMUNITION ALLOWANCES. The initial issue (*erste Ausstattung*) of ammunition is the total ammunition carried by a formation in columns, in dumps, and with the troops. The initial issue is systematically replaced as it is expended, on the basis of reports of ammunition remaining on hand sent from the divisions through corps to army, except as operational conditions modify the system. The allowance per formation is based on the number of weapons called for in the table of organization of the unit. Each weapon, in turn, has a number of rounds which is allotted to it as an ammunition quota or unit of issue (*Munitionsausstattung*). Two units of issue for all weapons of the division are carried within the division, while another unit of issue for all weapons in the army is held on army columns or trains as an army reserve. Thus each army has three ammunition quotas or units of issue for all weapons of the army.

b. AMMUNITION ISSUES. Of the two ammunition units of issue that are found within the division, over one unit is found forward on the men, with the guns, and as company and battalion reserves, while less than one full unit of issue is retained as a division reserve in division columns and dumps. The exact quantity issued to each man is largely determined by the amount held by the battalion and company as their reserves. The following charts exemplify the units of issue found in infantry and artillery units of an army.

Ammunition Issues (Rounds) for a Volks Grenadier Division:

Weapon*	Forward Issue	Division Reserve	Probable Army Reserve (Unit of Issue)
9-mm automatic pistol...	18	16	17
9-mm machine pistol....	690	512	601
7.92-mm machine pistol..	720	540	630
7.92-mm rifle	99	75	87
7.92-mm rifle (for troops other than infantry troops)	25	20	22
7.92-mm semi-auto rifle.	159	135	147
Rifle grenade launcher...	75	70	70
7.92-mm LMG	3450	2505	2977
7.92-mm LMG (for arty and AT troops)......	1350	1020	1185
7.92-mm HvMG	6300	4750	5525
88-mm bazooka	5	5	5
81-mm mortar	150	126	138
120-mm mortar	150	90	120
37-mm AA	1200	none**	?**
75-mm inf how	192	151	171
75-mm AT (mtz)......	150	100	125
75-mm AT (SP).......	255	—	—
105-mm gun how........	225	126	175
150-mm how	150	60	105

* Not included are 75-mm gun and flame thrower.
** AA ammunition reserves are usually kept by army and not by division.

Units of Issue for Artillery Units:

Weapon	Number of Rounds
37-mm AA	1,500
75-mm AA	300
88-mm AA	300
105-mm gun	125
150-mm how.	125
150-mm gun	75
210-mm how.	50

c. AMMUNITION EXPENDITURE. The unit of issue of ammunition is not to be confused with the daily expenditure amount of ammunition. The latter does not arrive at any constant figure, but varies with the type of action, the area of fighting, and the other factors mentioned in paragraph 1. By analogy with the reserve amounts of other expendable supplies, however, it is possible that three units of fire are judged by the Germans to be sufficient to maintain an army for a period of roughly eight to ten days.

Section V. EVACUATION

1. Maintenance and Repair of Equipment

a. GENERAL. Perhaps the fundamental German principle of repair and maintenance is that equipment should be repaired as far forward as possible.

Practically all the installations that deal with repair and maintenance of equipment also participate in the flow of supplies, both in transferring repaired equipment back to units and in moving newly manufactured equipment to units (see Sections II and III). In the following paragraphs, therefore, they will be treated solely from the point of view of rearward flow.

b. MOTOR TRANSPORT. Maintenance of an individual vehicle is the responsibility of the driver and the crew, but for repairs it is sent to one of a number of repair centers. While the procedure that determines which center shall undertake the repair has changed from time to time, it probably is determined by two factors: the number of working hours; and the facilities needed to effect the repair. Thus maintenance (Instandsetzungs) detachments and sections probably carry out repairs requiring less than four working hours with the tools at their disposal, while mobile field workshop (Werkstatt) units carry out repairs requiring less than 12 working hours. If the damage inflicted is too extensive for the facilities of the mobile workshops, the vehicle is sent to an Army Motor Transport Park (AKP) or to a Field Army Motor Transport Park (HeKP). The difference of functions between these two types of installations is not clear; it is likely, however, that the more difficult repair jobs are sent to the HeKP, while the AKP handle repairs that can be completed in less than 24 working hours. The disposition of the vehicle from these centers may be as follows: it may be repaired or scrapped; it may be forwarded to a Home Motor Transport Park (HKP), which is capable of carrying out all types of repairs; or, in the case of an AKP, the vehicle may be forwarded to a HeKP.

While the exact position of collecting points in the rearward movement of damaged vehicles is not certain, it is very likely that whenever possible vehicles move directly to repair and maintenance centers under their own power without passing through collecting points.

c. TANKS, ARMORED VEHICLES, AND SELF-PROPELLED WEAPONS. Minor repairs to armored vehicles (including tanks, self-propelled weapons, and other armored vehicles) are made by unit mechanics and by mobile tank-workshop units. If the repairs cannot be completed in the division area within three days, the vehicles may be sent to semi-permanent army tank workshops or to Field Army Tank Parks or Bases. When armored vehicles are so badly damaged that they cannot be repaired in the field, they are cannibalized or forwarded to tank equipment depots or factories in the home area. In the latter case the vehicles are no longer under Field Army control and are not returned to the units to which they were originally assigned.

Armored vehicles are repaired on the spot if possible. Otherwise they are moved rearward under their own power. Tank transporters are used only when long movements are contemplated or when vehicles cannot move under their own power.

d. OTHER EQUIPMENT AND CLOTHING. All types of equipment including weapons, signal equipment, bicycles, and clothing are repaired within the division area if possible. If the equipment (other than clothing and individual equipment) requires more specialized attention, it is forwarded either directly or through equipment collecting points or workshop units to one of the army parks. Equipment which cannot be repaired in the field is directed to a home equipment park, depot, or factory. Damaged clothing and individual equipment generally pass from collecting points direct to home clothing depots and dumps. Figure 6, which is largely compiled from German schematics, should be examined for other details of the German repair methods.

2. Evacuation of Installations

With the narrowing of the Zone of the Interior, the Germans have been faced with the problem of what to do with depots that were formerly part of the Zone of the Interior system of supply. Variant courses adopted have been the conversion of the installation into a field installation, the evacuation of the depot to the new Zone of the Interior, and the operation of the depot as though it were still within the Zone of the Interior.

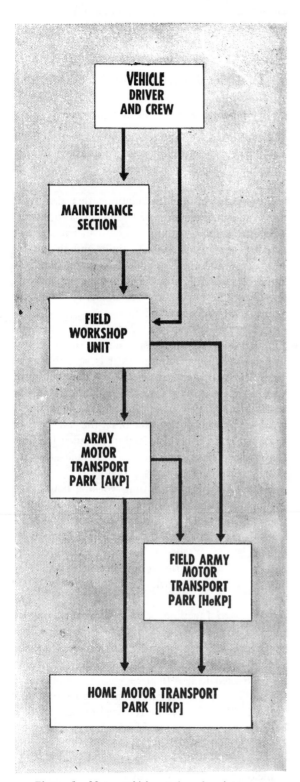

Figure 5.—Motor vehicle repair and maintenance.

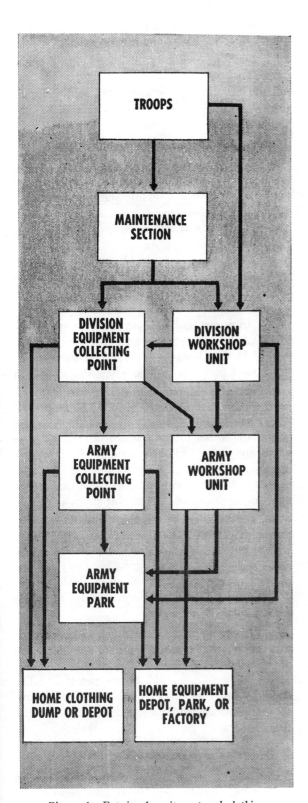

Figure 6.—Repair of equipment and clothing.

3. Evacuation of Wounded

a. GENERAL. The German system for the evacuation of casualties is based upon an immediate sorting of the wounded so that soldiers who are not seriously injured can be returned to their units as quickly as possible, and those who are severely wounded can receive medical care with maximum speed. Under combat conditions the accomplishment of these ends in many cases will cause deviations from the normal system. A good example of this was shown in the early part of the Russian campaign when the great distances between the combat zone and the Zone of the Interior forced the Germans to use a chain of Casualty Collecting Points to control and expedite the rearward movement of sick and wounded.

Now that the combat zone has moved into Germany proper, deviations of an integrating nature should be anticipated.

b. CHANNELS OF EVACUATION. (1) Casualties unable to walk are carried from the battlefield by battalion stretcher bearers, while those still capable of walking are directed to the Battalion Aid Station (*Verwundetennest*) which is located as close to the front line as is practicable. The Battalion Aid Station gives first aid in emergency cases. As quickly as movements can be made, it passes the wounded to the Regimental Aid Station (*Truppenverbandplatz*), which is generally some 200 to 500 yards to the rear of the front line. At this station the wounded receive first aid and are sorted into ambulatory cases and stretcher cases. Stretcher cases are carried by litter to an Ambulance Loading Post (*Wagenhalteplatz*) for rearward movement, while ambulatory cases are instructed to make their way rearward on foot.

(2) Usually the stretcher cases are sent to a Main Dressing Station (*Hauptverbandplatz*), whereas the walking wounded move to a Collecting Point for the Slightly Wounded (*Leichtverwundetensammelplatz*). The latter two installations, both controlled by the regimental medical officer, sometimes operate as a combined unit, and in practically all cases are located reasonably close to each other. Their functions are as follows:

The Main Dressing Station attends the serious cases. It contains a surgical unit which performs amputations, applies dressings and splints, checks hemorrhages, gives blood transfusions, and administers sedatives and preventative injections. After treatment the casualties are evacuated further rearward.

The Collecting Point for the Slightly Wounded administers to casualties whose treatment requires only a few days. When the treatment is completed, the men are returned to combat. If, however, a case has taken a more serious turn, the wounded soldier is evacuated rearward.

(3) From the regimental area casualties may be taken to any of the various types of hospitals (*Lazarette*) found in the field or at home. Casualty Collecting Points (*Krankensammelstellen*) usually are set up along the line of evacuation to facilitate the grouping of casualties and their distribution to the rear. These points are generally established at railheads and other traffic centers by ambulance units. They do not handle casualties whose condition will not permit movement. Mobile Field Hospitals (*Feldlazarette*) serve as way stations for casualties who cannot be moved through the Casualty Collecting Points. They may be operated either by an army or by a division. Wherever possible, the Field Hospital is set up in available permanent buildings. It is equipped to handle any casualty and has a capacity of 200 beds.

(4) Casualties who are physically able to be evacuated after treatment at the Main Dressing Station or the Field Hospital are moved either directly, or via the Casualty Collecting Points, to a Base Hospital (*Kriegslazarett*) or sometimes to a General Hospital (*Reservelazarett*).

Base Hospitals are large and relatively permanent installations which may be established by an army or the Field Army well to the rear of the combat zone. These hospitals are of two types: General Base Hospitals (*Kriegslazarette*), with normal accommodations for 500 cases, for casualties who require up to eight weeks' treatment before being discharged and for those who require a period of convalescence before moved to Reserve Hospitals; and Base Hospitals for Minor Cases (*Leichtkrankenkriegslazarette*), with accommodations for 1,000 patients, for casualties who need up to four weeks' of treatment or convalescence prior to discharge.

General Hospitals are permanent installations located inside Germany and are supervised by the Chief of Army Equipment; they are dealt with at length in Chapter I.

(5) A man may be pronounced fit for duty by any hospital. If he is in a forward hospital, he will be returned to his unit. If he is in a General Hospital for more than eight weeks, he will be returned to the Replacement Army for reassignment.

c. TRANSPORTATION FACILITIES. Hospital trains (*Lazarettzüge*) can carry between 358 and 386 lying cases or 920 sitting cases.

Standard German ambulances transport four lying cases, or two lying and four sitting cases, or eight sitting cases.

Horse-drawn vehicles, trucks, and hospital planes also may be used in evacuating the wounded.

4. Evacuation of Horses

a. CHANNELS OF EVACUATION. Sick and wounded horses are marched by foot from the battlefield to a Horse Dressing Station (*Pferdeverbandplatz*), where emergency cases are treated. They then are marched or transported in horse transport columns to a station set up by the Division Veterinary Company (*Veterinärkompanie*). This station can be established within a minimum of six hours and can treat 150 cases. If the horses require further treatment, they are moved by horse transport columns to the Army Horse Hospital (*Armeepferdelazarett*) or to the Field Army Horse Hospital (*Heerespferdelazarett*). Such field hospitals can be established within a minimum of 12 hours and can handle 500 sick horses. Horse Collecting Points (*Pferdesammelplätz*) are formed generally to expedite the evacuation of horses to the rear. Normally there is an Army Horse Collecting Point (*Armeepferdesammelplatz*), intermediate between division and army, and a Division Horse Collecting Point (*Divisionspferdesammelplatz*) at division. Evacuated horses may be moved either directly or through these collecting points to the rear. Horses which require special surgical operations and those not likely to be fit again for army use are moved by rail from the field hospitals to the Zone of the Interior Home Horse Hospitals (*Heimatpferdelazarette*).

b. TRANSPORTATION FACILITIES. Horse transport trains (*Pferdetransportzüge*) are composed of 55 cars, each carrying six sick or wounded horses, or a total of 350 horses per train. The standard horse transport road column can move 40 sick or wounded horses about 90 miles in one day.

5. Evacuation of Prisoners of War

Guard details drawn from the military police or from the combat unit itself take prisoners to the Division Prisoner of War Collecting Point (*Divisionsgefangenensammelstelle*). The Prisoners of War are next moved to the Army Prisoner of War Collecting Point (*Armeegefangenen-sammelstelle*), the guard details being drawn from military police, combat troops, or guard units. The Prisoners of War are lastly transferred from the jurisdiction of the Field Army to the Replacement Army Command. This is accomplished when the Prisoners of War are moved by rail to one of the Prisoner of War Camps within Germany. Officers are incarcerated in Officer Prisoner of War Camps (*Offizierlager* or *Oflag*); enlisted men are confined in Enlisted Men's Prisoner of War Camps (*Mannschafts-Stammlager* or *Stalag*).

Section VI. TROOP MOVEMENTS

I. Introduction

In movements of entire bodies of troops with their equipment, the space occupied, rather than the total weight, is the important factor. A very large proportion of the space is taken up by personnel, horses, and organic equipment; daily maintenance requirements that accompany the troops occupy much less space.

2. Rail Transportation

a. MAIN MILITARY ROUTES. German railways generally are used jointly for military and civilian traffic, although military trains are given priority. Perhaps the only instances of railways designated solely for military uses are found in the combat zone, either on already existent railways or on railways constructed by the Army.

Normally double-track standard-gauge (4' 8½") railways have a daily capacity of 30 military trains in each direction, while single-track standard-gauge railways can move 10 trains a day in each direction. Air damage can materially decrease these capacity figures.

b. STANDARD TROOP TRAINS. The Germans have found it desirable to use troop trains of a reasonably constant composition. The standard trains found in the Balkans, Italy, and Norway are composed of fewer cars than the base types in Germany, Denmark, and the Netherlands which are described below. All types are designed as far as possible to carry a self-contained unit such as a company or a battalion. Nonstandard trains also may be used for troop movements.

K-trains (*Kraftfahrzüge* or motor vehicle trains) average 51 cars per train and carry approximately 250 soldiers, 20 heavy vehicles (weighing up to 22 short tons per vehicle), and 20 light vehicles, plus other equipment. If lighter equipment is carried, the number of soldiers can be increased.

S-trains (*Sonderzüge,* or special trains) are made up for the movement of very heavy tanks and self-propelled guns. The number of men carried per train averages 125; the number of cars forming the train is between 30 and 35. An S-train usually carries from four to six Tiger tanks or from six to eight Panther tanks, interspersed with lighter equipment.

Sp-trains (*Sonderpanzerzüge,* or special tank trains) carry approximately 20 medium tanks together with personnel and other equipment. The standard Sp-train is composed of about 33 cars.

I-trains (*Infanteriezüge* or infantry trains) of about 55 cars per train hold some 350 officers and men, 10 light vehicles, 10 heavy vehicles of a maximum weight of 22 short tons per vehicle, and 70 horses, together with other equipment. If a minimum of equipment is carried, up to 800 troops can be moved. It is possible that the I-trains seldom are used by the Germans at present.

Replacement troop trains with 50 to 60 cars per train can hold over 2,000 replacements. The use of this type of train probably has been discontinued.

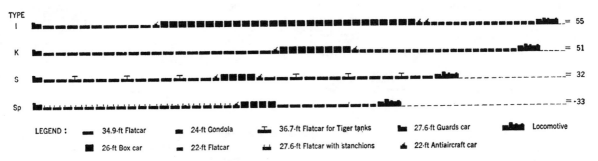

Figure 7.—German basic standard troop-train types.

c. ENTRAINMENT AND DETRAINMENT. Troop trains generally are formed at railroad stations. The speed with which entraining can be accomplished varies according to the number of units being loaded, the number of stations used, the facilities available at the stations, and the importance attached to speedy loading. Depending on these conditions, loading of a single train can be accomplished within 2 to 12 hours. If all the unit trains can be loaded simultaneously at the entraining stations, an entire division can be loaded within that time. In practice, however, the time taken to assemble trains and troops and the limited number of entraining stations will materially increase the loading time of divisions.

It is estimated that a troop train can be unloaded in about half the time taken to load. Detrainment of infantry units may occur far forward, while armored units usually are detrained in rear areas.

d. SPEED OF MOVEMENTS. The average German movement appears to average from 150 to 200 miles per day for long movements within Germany, and about 60 miles daily in areas near the combat zone.

e. TRAIN REQUIREMENTS. At present the number of trains required to transport an infantry division is about 35 to 40. An armored division needs about twice that number. If a large number of divisions are being moved, additional trains will be necessary for corps and army units.

3. Road Transportation

a. MAIN MILITARY ROUTES. Certain roads have been selected by the High Command to form a system of through routes (*Durchgangstrassen*) for military traffic in Germany and occupied areas. For the most part the through routes comprise the national highways and *Autobahnen*. In Denmark, however, the through routes more frequently consist of secondary roads than main arteries. Through routes generally run either east and west or north and south. When supply or troop movements are to be made over these roads, all civilian traffic is diverted to other roads.

b. MARCH SPEEDS. (1) The average speeds of division marches in miles per hour are as follows:

	By day	By Night
Infantry division	3	3
Motorized division	16	10
Armored division	12	7

(2) The average speeds of march columns in miles per hour are as follows:

Infantry (long marches)	3
Infantry (short marches)	4
Mounted troops	6
Cyclists	8
Motorcycles and cars	22
Trucks	22
Trucks with trailers	16
Half-track vehicles	16
Tanks	12

c. MARCH DISTANCES. The infantry division normally can march about 20 miles in a day; under adverse weather or road conditions the rate of march may fall to 10 miles a day. The motorized division can maintain an average daily march of between 90 and 150 miles; the armored division from 60 to 90 miles a day. In the near vicinity of the combat zone, road movements without motor transport average 10 to 15 miles a day, while movements by motor transport approximate 30 miles a day.

d. ROAD SPACES. While the road spaces occupied by divisions on the march are not constant, the road spaces of individual units may prove of some value. The following examples are from German sources and do not indicate the intervals maintained between elements:

INFANTRY DIVISION

(at 5 kilometers or approximately 3 miles per hour.)

	Yards	Meters
Inf Regt (each of three)	6,234	5,700
Rcn Bn	3,116	2,850
AT Bn	2,734	2,500
Arty Regt	7,382	6,750
Sig Bn	3,193	2,920
Engr Bn	2,570	2,350
Div Serv	4,155	3,800
Div Hq	1,553	1,420
Total Inf Div (approx.; without intervals between elements)	43,405	39,690
Total converted to miles	24.7	

ARMORED DIVISION

(at 20 kilometers or approximately 12 miles per hour.)

	Yards	Meters
Tank Regt	21,325	19,500
Pz Gren Regt (each of two) .	13,145	12,020
Pz Rcn Bn	9,154	8,370
AT Bn	3,838	3.510
Pz Arty Regt	14,458	13,220
Pz Sig Bn	3,762	3,440
Pz Engr Bn	6,365	5,820
Div Serv	11,702	10,700
Div Hq	1,444	1,320
Others	5,468	5,000

Total Armd Div (approx.; without intervals between elements) 103,806		94,920
Total converted to miles......	59.0	

If distances between the individual units are included, the average length of the infantry division would be about 30 miles (at 3 miles per hour), of the armored division 70 miles (at 12 miles per hour), and of the motorized division 80 miles (at 16 miles per hour).

4. Sea Transportation

a. GENERAL. In the sea movements referred to in the following text, the basic shipping measurement is the gross registered ton (G/T), which is 100 cubic feet of the entire enclosed space of a ship.

The Germans use all types of cargo and passenger vessels for the transportation of troops. Generally the depth of water of the embarkation and debarkation ports determines the size of ship to be used. Thus many of the Baltic ports are limited to cargo ships up to 2,000 G/T. Cargo between Norway and Germany, on the other hand, ordinarily can be carried on much larger vessels.

The average speed of a ship is estimated at 200 nautical miles per day, although fast ships may average much more.

b. LOADING AND UNLOADING TIMES. The time required for the loading of a vessel varies with a number of factors, such as the size of the vessel, the plan of the vessel, the port facilities, and the efficiency with which loading is conducted. The following average loading times are based upon German estimates. They apply for loading during day and night; considerable delays, however, may occur on account of adverse weather conditions.

Classification	Loading Time
100 men	8 minutes.
100 horses (led over a ramp)....	1 hour.
100 horses (lifted by cranes)....	6 hours.
100 light motor vehicles (lifted by cranes)	6 hours.
Supplies sufficient to load a 2,000 G/T vessel	16 hours.

c. TONNAGE REQUIREMENTS. Among other factors, the amount of tonnage required to transport troops depends upon the type of unit being transported, the efficiency of loading, the types of ships used, and the amount of nonmilitary stowage transported. Hence the following figures give only a general indication of the amount of space which is occupied by items when efficiently loaded.

Classification	Estimated G/T requirement
1 man	2
1 horse	8
1 light motor vehicle	10
1 truck	20
1 heavy field gun......................	20
1 medium tank	25

It is likely that an infantry division requires between 50,000 and 70,000 gross registered tons for its movement, or a mean average of five or six gross registered tons per man. If loading is inefficient or if light loading is used, the G/T requirements per man will rise considerably. Thus in short movements such as ferry crossing, as much as 15 gross registered tons per man and equipment have been employed.

CHAPTER VII

WEAPONS

Section I. INTRODUCTION

1. General

Before and during the first years of the present war it was the policy of the German army to use the smallest variety of weapons consistent with meeting operational requirements, while emphasis was maintained on developing weapons with a high degree of fighting efficiency. Recent developments in warfare, however, particularly in the last year, gradually have forced the Germans to adopt the opposite policy of experimentation with many innovations in weapon design.

2. Recent Trends

Within the last 12 months distinct trends in the development of German weapons have become apparent.

a. TANKS AND TANK DESTROYERS. First, there has been a tendency for tanks and tank destroyers to become armed and armored more heavily at the expense to some extent of mobility and maneuverability. This is compensated for by the ability to open effective fire at very long ranges.

b. INFANTRY ANTITANK WEAPONS. Second, there has been a striking increase in the ability of the German infantry to combat Allied tanks. This has been accomplished by the development and constant improvement of close-range grenade and rocket launchers employing the hollow-charge principle.

c. ROCKET WEAPONS. Third, German experiments which began before the war have materialized into a comparatively wide range of rocket weapons used to supplement orthodox artillery. These experiments with rockets are being continued, and improvements in range and accuracy may be expected. In the event of the outbreak of chemical warfare, rocket weapons will assume a greater significance than at present. The German recoilless gun (originally developed as an airborne gun) comes close to combining the lightness and mobility of the rocket weapon with the range and accuracy of the standard type of howitzer.

d. ARTILLERY. There have been some belated attempts on the part of the Germans at improvements in their standard artillery, but no basic redesign appears contemplated at present.

Section II. SMALL ARMS

1. General

The general trends in German small arms have been an increase in production of semiautomatic and fully automatic weapons and an increase in the rate of fire of machine guns. During 1944, additional close-quarter antitank weapons have been included among German small arms.

2. Pistols

a. GENERAL. The two standard pistols now in use in the German Army are the Luger, which was used in the last war, and a more modern weapon, the Walther; neither German weapon has the shock effect of the U. S. M1911 or M1911 A1 Colt .45. The Mauser pistol is seldom encountered.

Figure 1.—Luger Pistole 08, caliber 9 mm.

b. LUGER PISTOL (*Pistole 08*). (1) *General description.* This is a semiautomatic, recoil-operated pistol with a toggle-joint breech action (*Fig.

1). The safety is located on the left rear side of the body. The pistol is set on "safe" when "*Gesichert*" is showing. There is also a longer model of this pistol, provision being made on the rear side of the grip for a stock attachment. Construction is almost identical with the standard model except that the barrel is longer, and a leaf rear sight graduated up to 800 meters is attached.

(2) *Characteristics.*

    Caliber ......9 mm (actually 0.347 inch).
    Length of barrel............4¼ inches.
    Weight.....................2 pounds.
    Feed...........8-round grip magazine.

(3) *Ammunition.* The Luger pistol fires the standard German 9-mm Parabellum ammunition.

Figure 2.—Walther Pistole 38, caliber 9 mm.

c. WALTHER PISTOL (*Pistole 38*). (1) *General description.* The Walther weapon is a semiautomatic pistol with a grip magazine feed. It is recoil-operated, the breech mechanism sliding to the rear after each round has been fired. The pistol may be carried loaded with the hammer uncocked; the first shot may be fired by a double-action mechanism. The safety is a catch on the left-hand side of the body.

(2) *Characteristics.*

    Caliber......9 mm (actually 0.347 inch).
    Length of barrel............4¾ inches.
    Weight, loaded......2 pounds 5 ounces.
    Feed...........8-round grip magazine.

(3) *Ammunition.* German or British 9-mm Parabellum ammunition may be used in this weapon.

d. MAUSER PISTOL. (1) *General description.* The Mauser can be used as a semiautomatic pistol or as a carbine when attached to its wooden

holster, which is in the shape of a hollow stock. The safety is at the left rear above the trigger guard. The weapon is fed ammunition from a 10-round fixed magazine inserted forward of the trigger guard. Twenty-round magazines are used when the weapon is employed as a carbine.

(2) *Characteristics.*

    Caliber......9 mm (actually 0.347 inch).
    Length without stock..........12 inches.
    Length with stock..........25½ inches.
    Weight without stock. .2 pounds 8 ounces.
    Feed.........10- or 20-round magazine.

(3) *Ammunition.* Standard 9-mm ammunition is used.

3. Signal Pistols

a. LIGHT SIGNAL PISTOL (*Leuchtpistole*). This is the standard German signal pistol; it is 26.7-mm caliber, has a smooth bore, and fires a series of colored signal cartridges, as well as a whistling cartridge (*Pfeifpatrone*) used as a gas warning signal.

Figure 3.—Kampfpistole (grenade and signal pistol).

b. MODIFIED SIGNAL PISTOL (*Kampfpistole*). The Germans have modified the *Leuchtpistole* by rifling the bore and providing a small sight to produce the *Kampfpistole* (*Fig. 3*). With these alterations a small, nose-fused HE grenade, a smoke grenade, and an orange smoke grenade are fired in addition to the standard signal cartridges. The pistol has a maximum range of about 100 yards, firing a 5-ounce HE round.

c. DOUBLE-BARRELED SIGNAL PISTOL. This pistol is similar to the standard *Leuchtpistole* but has a double barrel and trigger mechanism. At the rear of the hammer action, and above the pistol grip, is a change lever of the type used on double-barreled shotguns. This may be set so either one or both of the barrels will fire when the trigger is squeezed. The standard signal cartridges are fired.

Figure 4.—Sturmpistole (modified light signal pistol).

Figure 5.—Sturmpistole (modified light signal pistol).

d. GRENADE AND SIGNAL PISTOL (*Sturmpistole*). This weapon consists basically of the standard *Leuchtpistole* to which a loose steel liner is fitted (*Figs. 4* and *5*). This liner is rifled and fitted with a base, which prevents firing a standard round through the liner. A combined front and rear sight is clamped around the barrel,

and a folding stock is attached above the pistol grip. The liner and the folding stock enable this pistol to fire a hollow-charge grenade as a close-quarter weapon against tanks (*Fig. 5*). With the steel liner removed this pistol will fire the standard signal cartridges fired from the *Leuchtpistole*.

4. Machine Pistols

a. M.P. (MASCHINENPISTOLE) 40. (1) *General description*. This blowback-operated machine pistol (*Fig. 6*) was developed from the *M.P. 38,* an earlier model designed for issue to parachute troops and still used. Distinctive features of both weapons are the folding stock and all metal and plastic construction. The safety recess at the rear of the cocking-handle stop is marked "S". To set the weapon on "safe", the operating handle is pulled back as far as it will go and then pushed upward into the safety notch. On later models, a safety stud is located on the cocking handle. The magazine is inserted in a vertical position on the underside of the receiver. The weapon has a 100-meter (109 yards) fixed rear sight and a 200-meter (219 yards) folding rear sight.

(2) *Characteristics.*

Caliber......9 mm (actually 0.347 inch).
Length, over-all............33½ inches.
Weight without magazine......9 pounds.
Feed...............32-round magazine.
Rate of fire
　(cyclic)........500 rounds per minute.
　(practical).....180 rounds per minute.

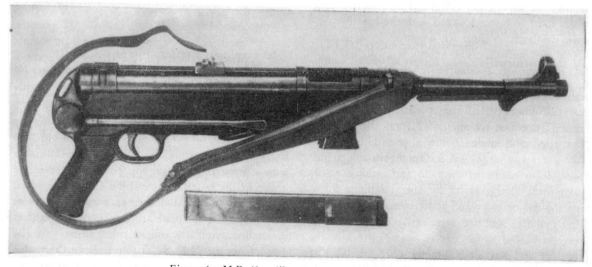

Figure 6.—M.P. 40, caliber 9 mm, showing magazine.

Figure 7.—M.P. 43/1, caliber 7.92 mm, showing magazine in place for firing.

Figure 8.—M.P. 44, (modified M.P. 43), caliber 7.92 mm, with grenade launcher attached.

(3) *Ammunition.* This weapon uses the standard 9-mm Parabellum ammunition.

b. MODEL 43/1 MACHINE PISTOL (*M.P. (Maschinenpistole) 43/1*). (1) *General description.* This gas-operated machine pistol (*Fig. 7*) is constructed almost entirely of metal stampings and can be stripped only to a limited degree. Although provision is made for both single-shot and automatic fire, bursts of more than five rounds are not recommended, and the pistol is best used as a single-shot weapon. This weapon has not proved very successful because it is impossible to repair in the field and because of its poor firing characteristics. The stampings forming the gas cylinder and body casings are made of thin material and are very easily damaged. The weapon is fed by a curved magazine below the receiver and has an 800-meter (876 yards) leaf rear sight.

(2) *Characteristics.*

Caliber . . . . .7.92 mm (0.312 inch).
Length. .37 inches.
Weight. .11 pounds.
Feed. . . . . .35- to 38-round magazine.
Muzzle velocity. . . .2,200 feet per second.

(3) *Ammunition.* A special type of short rifle caliber ammunition is used in this machine pistol.

c. M.P. (MASCHINENPISTOLE) 44. This weapon is the *M.P. 43/1* slightly modified to accommodate the standard rifle grenade launcher cup (*Schiessbecher*). The barrel is machined down at the muzzle end and the front sight block is smaller and located farther forward to allow the launcher cup to be attached. Although it is presumed that the standard rifle grenades can be fired from the *M.P. 44*, it is not certain that this has yet become an operational practice.

5. Rifles and Automatic Rifles

a. MODEL 98 RIFLE AND CARBINE (*Gewehr 98* and *Karabiner 98*). (1) *General description.* The standard German rifles and carbines are all of the same basic bolt-operated Mauser design (*Figs. 9* and *10*), but may be divided into three distinct types. These are the rifle Model 98 (*Gewehr 98*) which is 49½ inches long and has the sling fitted underneath; the long barrel carbine Model 98 b (*Karabiner 98 b*) which is approximately the same length as the rifle; and the short carbine Model 98 k (*Karabiner 98 k*) which is 43½ inches long. Each weapon has a safety catch at the rear of the bolt similar to the safety on the U. S. rifle M1903 and a blade front sight and V rear sight graduated from 100 to 2,000 meters (109 to 2,190 yards). The *Gewehr 98* fires rifle grenades from a grenade launcher cup or from a spigot launcher.

(2) *Characteristics.*

    Caliber...........7.92 mm (0.312 inch).
    Weight (each
       type) ......9 pounds (approximately).
    Feed....................5-round clip.
    Effective range.............800 yards.

(3) *Ammunition.* These weapons fire the standard German 7.92-mm rimless small-arms ammunition.

b. MODEL 33/40 RIFLE (*Gewehr 33/40*). The Germans have designed the *Gewehr 33/40* as a special short rifle for parachutists or for personnel carrying concealed arms. The weapon is fitted with a folding stock, hinged on the left and retained in position by a press catch on the right side. When the rifle is not in use, the stock can be folded along the left of the piece. Apart from the folding stock the rifle is normal in design and similar to the 98 models.

c. MODEL 41 RIFLE (*Gewehr 41*). (1) *General description.* This is a semiautomatic rifle (*Fig. 10*) which is made in two models, the *Gewehr 41 m* and *Gewehr 41 w,* similar in operation and differing only slightly in construction. Both models are gas-operated; the gases are compressed in a gas choke at the muzzle, forcing to the rear a floating piston mounted concentrically around the barrel. The movement of the piston is communicated to the bolt head, and the rifle is recocked automatically after each round has been fired. The weapon is fed through a magazine fixed in the receiver which holds two standard rifle clips. Both models have a blade front sight and leaf rear sight graduated from 100 to 1,200 meters (109 to 1,310 yards). When fitted with a telescopic sight this rifle can be used as a sniper's weapon.

(2) *Characteristics.*

    Caliber ....7.92 mm (0.312 inch).
    Length, over-all ....45 inches.
    Weight ....10 pounds 14 ounces.
    Feed...............Two 5-round clips.

(3) *Ammunition.* This weapon fires the 7.92-mm rimless ammunition.

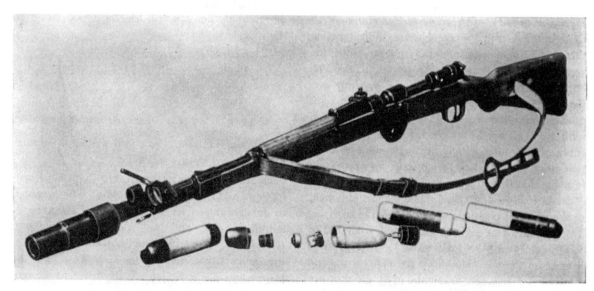

Figure 9.—Gewehr 98 with grenade launcher attached, showing rifle grenades.

Figure 10.—Gewehr 41, caliber 7.92 mm semiautomatic rifle.

Figure 11.—Fallschirmjägergewehr 42, caliber 7.92 mm automatic rifle.

d. MODEL 42 AUTOMATIC RIFLE (*Fallschirm-jägergewehr 42*). (1) *General description.* Although the German nomenclature indicates that this rifle (*Fig. 11*) is intended to be an automatic weapon for use by parachute troops, it also can be used as a light machine gun or a machine carbine. The weapon is designed more like a light machine gun than a rifle. It is gas-operated, fitted with a permanently attached folding bipod, and can be fired automatically or single shot. A compensator is attached to the muzzle, and provision is made for the attachment of a telescopic sight. A bayonet also is attached. The magazine is held in a horizontal position on the left of the receiver. The aperture rear sight is graduated from 100 to 1,200 meters (109 to 1,310 yards). The safety is located on the left side above the pistol grip, and the lever for selecting automatic or single-shot fire is placed above and to the rear of the trigger. A

later model of this weapon, slightly heavier and more solidly constructed, has the bipod closer to the muzzle.

(2) *Characteristics.*

Caliber ....7.92 mm (0.312 inch).
Length with bayonet ....43¾ inches.
Weight ....9 pounds.
Feed ....20-round magazine.

(3) *Ammunition.* Standard 7.92-mm ammunition is used in this weapon.

e. MODEL 43 SEMIAUTOMATIC RIFLE (*Karabiner 43*). (1) *General description.* This weapon, originally known as the *Gewehr 43*, is a semiautomatic rifle and was developed from the *Gewehr 41*. The trigger and bolt mechanisms are the same as those used on the *Gewehr 41*, but the piston and gas cylinder are of different design. The piston group is located on top of the barrel instead of concentrically. The rifle may be loaded by inserting either a fully loaded magazine or two cartridge clips into an empty magazine from the top. The leaf rear sight is graduated from 100 to 1,250 meters (109 to 1,365 yards).

(2) *Characteristics.*

Caliber .... 7.92 mm (0.312 inch).
Length, over-all .... 45 inches.
Weight .... 10 pounds.

(3) *Ammunition.* Standard 7.92-mm ammunition is used in this weapon.

6. Machine Guns

a. MODEL 34 MACHINE GUN (*M.G. 34*). (1) *General description.* This weapon (*Figs. 12* and *13*) was the original standard German dual-purpose machine gun and is still used, although it has been replaced largely by the *M.G. 42.* (*M.G.* is the German abbreviation for *Maschinengewehr,* which means "machine gun".) It may be used on a bipod, on single or dual AA mounts, or mounted on a tripod as a heavy machine gun. It still is used as the subsidiary armament of all German tanks. It is operated by short recoil, assisted by muzzle blast, and has a standard Solothurn-type breech mechanism. The gun has a leaf rear sight graduated from 200 to 2,000 meters (219 to 2,190 yards), an AA ring sight, and an optical sight for use with the tripod mount. It is fed either by 50-round metallic-link belts, which may be connected together, or by drums. The weapon is air-cooled by a perforated barrel jacket.

(2) *Characteristics.*

Caliber .... 7.92 mm (0.312 inch).
Length, over-all .... 48 inches.
Weight with bipod .... 26½ pounds.
Weight with tripod .... 42 pounds.
Feed .... Belt or drum.
Rate of fire
  (cyclic) .... 900 rounds per minute.
  (practical) .... As LMG 100 to 120 rounds per minute.
    As Hv MG 300 rounds per minute.
Effective range...... As LMG 600 to 800 yards.
    As Hv MG 2,000 to 2,500 yards.

(3) *Ammunition.* The *M.G. 34* fires 7.92-mm rimless small-arms ammunition.

Figure 12.—M.G. 34, caliber 7.92 mm, on bipod mount as light machine gun.

Figure 13.—M.G. 34, caliber 7.92 mm, on tripod mount as heavy machine gun.

Figure 14.—M.G. 42, caliber 7.92 mm, on bipod mount.

b. MODEL 42 MACHINE GUN (*M.G. 42*). (1) *General description.* This is the latest type of German machine gun known and in most cases has replaced the *M.G. 34* as a standard dual-purpose weapon (*Fig. 14*). Like the *M.G. 34,* it may be used on a fixed bipod, a tripod mount, or an antiaircraft mount. The square barrel casing makes this machine gun unsuitable as a tank weapon. The main features of the weapon are the extensive use of pressings in its construction, a greatly increased rate of fire, and a quick barrel change feature necessitated by the high rate of fire which causes the gun to heat rapidly. The weapon is fundamentally similar to the *M.G. 34* and has the same short recoil action. It has no provision for single-shot fire, however.

(2) *Characteristics.*

Caliber . . . . .7.92 mm (0.312 inch).
Length, over-all . . . . .49 inches.
Weight . . . . .23¾ pounds.
Rate of fire
  (cyclic) . . . . .1,200 to 1,400 rounds per minute.
  (practical) . . . . . . .As LMG 250 rounds per minute.
         As Hv MG 500 rounds per minute.
Effective range. . . . . .As LMG 600 to 800 yards.
        As Hv MG 2,000 to 2,500 yards.

(3) *Ammunition.* This machine gun fires the standard German 7.92-mm rimless ammunition.

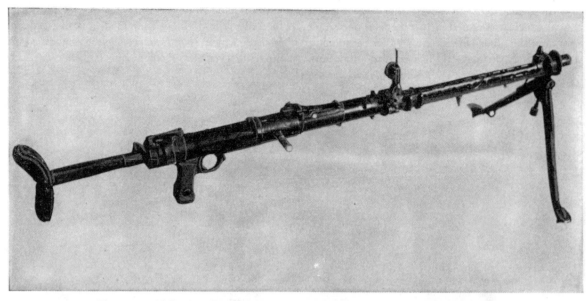

Figure 15.—M.G. 15, caliber 7.92 mm, aircraft machine gun adapted for ground use.

c. MODEL 15 MACHINE GUN (M.G. 15). (1) *General description.* Although primarily intended as an aircraft machine gun, the *M.G. 15* has been adopted as a ground weapon (*Fig. 15*), using an adapter, which clips around the barrel for attaching the standard bipod, and a butt extension. It is a light weapon and has short recoil action, firing automatic only.

(2) *Characteristics.*

Caliber ....7.92 mm (0.312 inch).
Length, over-all ....42 inches.
Weight ....15 pounds 12 ounces.
Feed ....75-round saddle magazine.
Rate of fire
  (cyclic) ......1,000 rounds per minute.
  (practical) .....300 rounds per minute.

(3) *Ammunition.* The standard 7.92-mm rimless ammunition is used in this machine gun.

d. MODEL 151/20 MACHINE GUN (*M.G. 151/20*). (1) *General description.* Although primarily an aircraft machine gun (*Fig. 16*), it also has been found on an improvised ground mount as an antitank weapon and triple-mounted on a half-tracked vehicle. When used on the ground, the gun is hand cocked and mechanically fired, instead of utilizing the electrical cocking and firing mechanism provided for its use in aircraft. The gun is entirely recoil-operated. The 15-mm *M.G. 151* is sometimes used instead of the *M.G. 151/20* on the triple mount. It often is supposed that these two are the same gun fitted with inter-

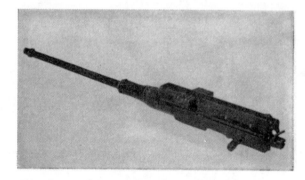

Figure 16.—M.G. 151/20, a 20-mm aircraft machine gun.

changeable barrels; this is not the case, although the guns are very similar in construction.

(2) *Characteristics.*

Caliber ....20 mm (0.787 inch).
Length, over-all ....69¾ inches.
Weight...................93½ pounds.
Feed.....Disintegrating metallic-link belt.
Rate of fire ....800 rounds per minute.
Muzzle velocity (HE),
                    2,656 feet per second.

(3) *Ammunition.* This gun fires HE, AP, and APHE ammunition.

7. Antitank Weapons

a. RIFLES. The original German antitank rifles were the *7.92-mm Panzerbüchse 38,* with automatic extraction mechanism, and the 7.92-mm *Panzerbüchse 39,* operated entirely by hand. These weapons were not very effective and are now obsolete. Next followed the 20-mm Solothurn, which was issued in two models: one single shot, and the other both single shot and automatic. The tendency during 1944 has been to adopt anti-tank grenade launchers in preference to rifles, and the only relic of these four models is the *Granatbüchse,* which is a *Panzerbüchse 39* modified to fire rifle grenades from a rifle launcher cup.

Figure 17.—Panzerbüchse 39, a 7.92-mm antitank rifle.

Figure 18.—Granatbüchse 39, a 7.92-mm antitank rifle modified for launching rifle grenades.

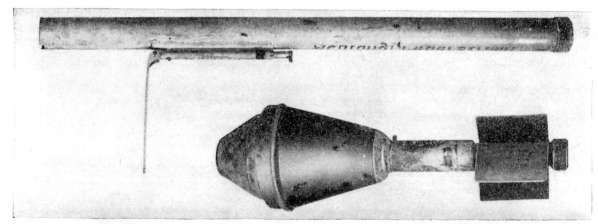

Figure 19.—Faustpatrone 2 (Panzerfaust), 44-mm recoilless antitank grenade launcher, showing launching tube and grenade.

b. RECOILLESS ANTITANK GRENADE LAUNCH-ERS—*Panzerfaust.* This is a series of antitank grenade launchers each bearing the name *Panzerfaust* but each having a different number after the name.

(1) *Panzerfaust 30*

(a) *General Description.* This weapon, also known as the *Faustpatrone 2,* was the first of the four models of recoilless antitank grenade dischargers to be produced. It is designed for use against armor at ranges of about 30 yards, at which range a penetration of just over 200 mm is obtained.

The weapon consists of a steel launching tube, containing a percussion fired propellent charge. A hollow-charge antitank grenade is fired from the tube.

The weapon is fired from the standing, kneeling or prone positions, aim being taken over the vertical sight and the forward end of the bomb.

(b) *Characteristics.*

Diameter of tube . . . . 1¾ inches.
Over-all length . . . . 41 inches.
Weight . . . . 11 pounds.

(c) *Ammunition.* The grenade is provided with spring steel fins which are wrapped around the tail for loading and which are released as the projectile leaves the tube and stabilize the bomb during flight.

(2) *Panzerfaust Klein 30*

This weapon, also known as the *Faustpatrone 1* or *Gretchen,* is a smaller version of the *Panzerfaust 30* and has a differently shaped projectile head. The system of operation is the same and the range is again about 30 yards. A penetration of 140 mm is claimed for this projectile.

(3) *Panzerfaust 60*

This launcher is similar in appearance to the *Panzerfaust 30.* A redesigned firing mechanism has been fitted and also a new sight, which has apertures for 30, 60 and 80 meters.

The tube of this weapon is slightly thicker than that of the *Panzerfaust 30* and the weight has been increased to 13½ lbs.

The penetration figure of 200 mm for the *Panzerfaust 30* will apply equally well to this weapon.

(4) *Panzerfaust 100*

This is the latest of the *Panzerfaust* series of antitank launchers to be encountered. In appearance it is similar to the *Panzerfaust 60,* though slightly increased in size and performance. A penetration figure of 200 mm is claimed for this weapon, which is sighted up to 150 meters.

c. ROCKET LAUNCHER (*Raketenpanzerbüchse 54*). (1) *General description.* This weapon, which is also known as the *Ofenrohr* (Stovepipe) or *Panzerschreck* (Tank Terror), is similar to the U. S. 2.36-inch rocket launcher (Bazooka) and fires a hollow-charge rocket projectile. The launcher consists of a steel tube provided with fore and back sights and a cocking lever and trigger which operate an electrical firing mechanism. For firing, the rocket is inserted in the rear of the tube, where it is retained in position by a catch and makes a contact with the electrical leads at the rear of the launcher. When the trigger is pressed, a magnetized rod passes through a coil located in a housing underneath the projector. This generates a current which provides the spark necessary to ignite the propellent charge in the tail end of the projectile. Later models of this projector are fitted with steel protective shields clamped around the barrel. In each shield there is an observation window on the left of the firer. These shields eliminate the necessity for the firer to wear protective clothing. The Germans claim

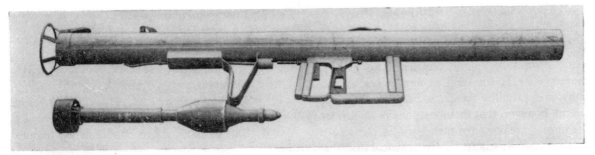

Figure 20.—Raketenpanzerbüchse 54, an 88-mm antitank rocket launcher.

an effective range of 120 meters (130 yards) for this weapon.

(2) *Characteristics.*

Caliber ....88 mm (3.5 inches).
Length, over-all ....5 feet 4½ inches.
External diameter ....3.7 inches.
Weight ....20½ pounds.
Maximum range ....132 yards.

(3) *Ammunition.* The projectile is a 7-pound hollow-charge rocket containing a propellant in the tail tube. The rocket is equipped with a nose fuze and a circular tail fin. It measures 2 feet 1¼ inches in length.

d. HEAVY ROCKET LAUNCHER (*Raketenwerfer 43* or *Püppchen*). (1) *General description.* A heavier version of the *Raketenpanzerbüchse,* this weapon fires hollow-charge rockets against tanks. The barrel, mounted on a two-wheeled, single-trail carriage with protective shield, has a simple hinged breechblock with striker mechanism. No traversing or elevating wheels are provided on the carriage; the gun must be held at the required

elevation by a spade hand grip and manually traversed on a traversing slide. The weapon has a front sight and an adjustable rear sight mounted on the barrel. The rear sight is graduated from 180 to 700 meters (195 to 765 yards). This may mean that the weapon can be used in an antipersonnel role as a mortar at long ranges.

(2) *Characteristics.*

Caliber ....88 mm (3.5 inches).
Length, over-all ....9 feet 2 inches.
Weight.....270 pounds (approximately).
Width of carriage......3 feet 3½ inches.
Height of barrel ....1 foot 6 inches.
Elevation ....—18° to + 15°.

(3) *Ammunition.* The projectile is an 88-mm hollow-charge rocket similar to that used with the *Raketenpanzerbüchse,* but with a flash cap in the center of a rimmed base fitting over the end of the stabilizing fins. The rimmed base serves as a cartridge case and remains in the breech after the projectile has been fired.

Figure 21.—Raketenwerfer 43 (Püppchen), 88-mm rocket projector.

Section III. MORTARS

I. General

The Germans began the war with two principal mortars: the 50-mm and 81-mm pieces as company and battalion weapons, respectively. They found, however, that these weapons did not match the mortar fire power of their enemies, particularly that of the Russians. Two principal measures were taken in an effort to correct this deficiency. A short 81-mm mortar was developed for use as a light weapon to supplement the 50-mm piece. A copy of the Russian 120-mm mortar, which far surpassed the performance of any German mortar, was adopted.

Figure 22.—5 cm leichter Granatenwerfer 36.

2. Light Mortars

a. 50-MM MORTAR (*5 cm Leichter Granatenwerfer 36*). (1) *General description.* This is a muzzle-loaded, trigger-fired weapon used solely for high angle fire. Elevation is adjusted by an elevating arm attached to the baseplate and supporting the tube, with provision for both coarse and fine adjustment. Traverse of about 15 degrees in either direction is controlled by a traversing arc of conventional design. Two cross-leveling handscrews, one on each side of the baseplate, are used for initial laying and to steady the mortar during firing.

(2) *Characteristics.*

```
Caliber ...........50 mm (1.97 inches).
Total weight ................31 pounds.
Maximum traverse ................34°.
Elevation ..................43° to 90°.
Maximum range .............570 yards.
Weight of shell.............2.2 pounds.
Rate of fire...12 to 20 rounds per minute.
```

(3) *Ammunition.* This weapon fires an HE shell weighing 2.2 pounds, including 4.5 ounces of TNT explosive filling.

b. 50-MM AUTOMATIC MORTAR (*5 cm Maschinengranatwerfer*). (1) *General description.* This power-operated automatic mortar is almost twice as long as the standard 50-mm weapon. Six-round clips are manually loaded into a rack on the left side. As each round is fed onto the breechblock, the tube slides down over the shell and locks, releasing the firing pin. The feeding, locking, and firing mechanisms are electrically operated. The mortar has been found only in special concrete turrets in fixed defensive systems. These emplacements, below ground except for the roof of the turret, incorporate ammunition storage, power plant, ammunition hoist, and living quarters for the crew.

(2) *Ammunition.* Standard 50-mm ammunition is fired and a range scale in the turret indicates a maximum range of 820 yards.

3. Medium Mortars

a. 81-MM MORTAR (*8 cm Schwerer Granatenwerfer 34*). (1) *General description.* This weapon is the German equivalent of the U. S. 81-mm mortar M-1. It is a smooth-bore, muzzle-loaded weapon with a fixed firing pin. The elevating, traversing, and cross-leveling mechanisms are of conventional design.

(2) *Characteristics.*

```
Caliber ..........81.4 mm (3.19 inches).
Total weight ...............124 pounds.
Maximum traverse .................14°.
Elevation ..................40° to 90°.
Maximum ranges firing HE shell
    Main propelling charge .....591 yards.
    Additional charge 1 .......1,094 yards.
    Additional charge 2 .......1,597 yards.
    Additional charge 3 .......2,078 yards.
    Additional charge 4 .......2,625 yards.
Weight of shell .............7.7 pounds.
Rate of fire...10 to 12 rounds per minute.
```

Figure 23.—8 cm schwerer Granatenwerfer (81-mm mortar) in action.

Figure 24.—8 cm schwerer Granatenwerfer 34 or 81-mm mortar.

(3) *Ammunition.* The HE shell contains 1.1 pounds of TNT, and the smoke shell contains 1 pound of sulphur trioxide. In addition to the standard smoke and HE ammunition, another shell known as the "bouncing bomb" was used with this mortar to provide air burst, but proved unsuccessful. This projectile weighed the same as the standard HE shell but contained only 0.8 pound of TNT.

Figure 25.—8 cm Kurzer Granatenwerfer 42 or short 81-mm.

b. SHORT 81-MM MORTAR (*8 cm Kurzer Granatenwerfer 42*). (1) *General description.* This weapon represents an attempt to combine the hitting power of a medium mortar with the mobility and lightness of a smaller weapon, such as the 50-mm mortar. It is a reduced version of the standard 81-mm mortar with modified elevating and traversing gears. The cross-leveling mechanism is similar to that used in the U. S. 81-mm mortar M-1.

(2) *Characteristics.*

Caliber . . . . .81.4 mm (3.19 inches).
Total weight . . . . .62 pounds.
Maximum traverse . . . . .10°.
Elevation . . . . .47° to 88°.
Maximum range . . . . .1,200 yards.

(3) *Ammunition.* This weapon fires the same ammunition as the standard 81-mm mortar, but only three increments may be used, giving a maximum range of 1,200 yards with HE.

4. Heavy Mortars

a. 105-MM SMOKE MORTAR (*10 cm Nebelwerfer 35*). (1) *General description.* This is an enlarged version of the standard 81-mm mortar. Issued originally to chemical warfare troops, it was intended primarily for firing smoke and chemical shells, although HE shells now are issued. In appearance the mortar is almost identical with the 81-mm mortar.

(2) *Characteristics.*

Caliber . . . . .105 mm (4.13 inches).
Total weight . . . . .231 pounds.
Maximum traverse . . . . .13°.
Elevation . . . . .45° to 80°.
Maximum range . . . . .3,300 yards.
   (with four increments)
Weight of shell . . . . .16 pounds.

(3) *Ammunition.* Both HE and smoke shells weigh 16 pounds. The HE shell contains 3.75 pounds of TNT.

b. CHEMICAL MORTAR (*10 cm Nebelwerfer 40*). (1) *General description.* This is a smooth-bore, breech-loaded weapon transported on a carriage from which it can be fired. The mortar is of monobloc construction. The unusual breech mechanism is so designed that the movement of the operating handle causes the rear of the mortar to ride over the breechblock, which is secured to the frame. A buffer cylinder is located internally on each side of the frame, the buffer pistons being attached to the sides of the breechblock. The carriage is constructed of steel tubing and provided with elevating and traversing gears and a sighting arrangement.

(2) *Characteristics.*

Caliber . . . . .105 mm (4.13 inches).
Total weight . . . . .1,708 pounds.
Maximum traverse . . . . .14°.

Figure 26.—10 cm Nebelwerfer 40.

Elevation ....45° to 85°.
Maximum range (HE shell)..6,780 yards.
Weight of HE shell.........19.1 pounds.

(3) *Ammunition*. This mortar fires both HE and smoke projectiles. The smoke shell weighs 0.5 pound more than the HE shell.

c. 105-MM FIXED DEFENSE MORTAR (*10 cm Leichte Haubitze Turm*). (1) *General description*. This mortar is incorporated in underground defensive systems. The mortar itself is located in the upper compartment of a large cylindrical emplacement and is completely enclosed except for a small firing aperture covered by a steel shutter. The lower compartment is used for storing ammunition and housing the crew. Ammunition is carried up to the mortar on a conveyor belt and is manually loaded. The mortar is a smooth-bore, breech-loaded weapon, fitted with a semiautomatic breech mechanism, horizontal sliding breechblock, and hydropneumatic recoil system. The mortar tube is held in a cradle which may be raised and locked into firing position. The traversing mechanism is arranged so that turning the traversing handle rotates the entire fighting compartment. Fire normally is controlled electrically from an observation post, but also can be controlled by means of a periscope in the fighting compartment.

(2) *Characteristics.* Details of the characteristics of this weapon are lacking. Limits of elevation are 45 degrees to 90 degrees.

(3) *Ammunition.* Ammunition fired is the same as that used with the 105-mm smoke mortar (*Nebelwerfer 40*) but with different charge weights.

Figure 27.—12 cm Granatenwerfer 42 or 120-mm mortar.

d. 120-MM MORTAR (*12 cm Granatenwerfer 42*). (1) *General description.* This is a virtually exact German copy of a standard Russian weapon. The mortar itself is of conventional construction and consists of a tube, a circular baseplate, and

a bipod. It has the advantage of being highly mobile, however, since it is equipped with a two-wheeled, quickly attached axle, and the bipod is carried clamped to the mortar ready for action. The weapon can be quickly towed or manhandled into a new firing position. The heavy shell and long range of this weapon provide a type of fire support comparable with that from the 105-mm field howitzer.

(2) *Characteristics.*

Caliber ....120 mm (4.7 inches).
Total weight ....616 pounds.
Maximum traverse ....16°.
Elevation ....45° to 85°.
Maximum range ....6,600 yards.
Weight of shell ....35 pounds.

(3) *Ammunition.* This mortar fires four types of HE projectiles.

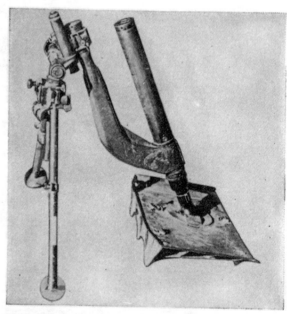

Figure 28.—20 cm leichter Ladungswerfer light spigot mortar.

e. 200-MM LIGHT SPIGOT MORTAR (*20 cm Leichter Ladungswerfer*). (1) *General description.* This weapon consists of a bipod, baseplate, spigot, and spigot arm. The baseplate is of conventional German design and is provided with a socket to receive the base-cap knob at the lower end of the spigot. The bipod is similar to that used with the 81-mm and 105-mm mortars but has more powerful shock absorbers. The spigot is in the form of a drawn steel tube reduced at the lower end where it is threaded to receive the supporting arm. Two insulated electrical contact plates are located above the supporting arm and are connected internally to a contact tube running to the upper end of the spigot to contact the electric primer of the propelling charge.

(2) *Characteristics.*

Diameter of spigot ....3.5 inches.
Total weight ....205 pounds.
Total traverse ....5°.
Elevation ....45° to 80°.
Maximum range ....766 yards.
   (three increments)
Weight of shell ....46 pounds.

(3) *Ammunition.* This mortar fires HE or smoke projectiles. The HE shell contains 15 pounds of amatol explosive. Reports indicate ammunition known as the "harpoon projectile" is also used. This shell is said to project a cord and grapnel with which to clear mines or networks of charges.

f. 380-mm HEAVY SPIGOT MORTAR (*38 cm Schwerer Ladungswerfer*). (1) *General description.* No details of this weapon are available, its existence having been established from identification of a 380-mm HE spigot shell. This mortar is probably an enlarged version of the 200-mm weapon.

(2) *Characteristics.*

Diameter of spigot ....6.25 inches.
Weight of shell ....331 pounds.

(3) *Ammunition.* Both HE and smoke ammunition are fired by this mortar. The HE shell bursting charge weighs 110 pounds.

Section IV. ARTILLERY

1. General

a. DEVELOPMENT. The Germans, comparatively speaking, neglected their artillery during the early stages of the war and since have been compelled to give increased thought to it. The German concept of modern war in 1939 was that of the *Blitzkrieg* or "Lightning War", in which armor and the dive bomber jointly were to dominate the battlefield. The enemy was to be softened up by bombing and smashed by the tanks, and artillery scarcely had more than a subsidiary role. The *Blitzkrieg* was successful against inadequately equipped armies, but the gradual recovery of Germany's enemies and the complete bankruptcy of the "Lightning War" theory have compelled the Germans to attempt a refurbishing of their artillery doctrine.

b. DIVISION ARTILLERY. The division artillery weapons with which Germany started the war were all of the "18" class (*10 cm le. F.H. 18, 10 cm K. 18, 15 cm s. F.H. 18*), and all these guns are still standard. Various experimental modifications may be standardized eventually as "42" series, but no fundamental redesign of any of their weapons appears to be contemplated at present.

2. Infantry Guns

a. 75-MM LIGHT INFANTRY GUN (*7.5 cm le. I. G. 18*). (1) *General description.* The *7.5 cm le. I. G. 18* is an infantry close-support weapon firing in both lower and upper registers. It has a box-type mount on pneumatic-tired disk wheels, and is fitted with a shield. A modification, the *le. Geb. I. G. 18,* has wooden-spoked wheels, a split tubular trail, and no shield; this version has similar performance and is used by airborne troops. Both models have an unusual tube, encased in a slipper block. Operation of the breech mechanism causes the rear of the tube to rise clear of the block for loading.

Figure 29.—7.5 cm le. I.G. 18 (75-mm light infantry gun) in action.

(2) *Characteristics.*

Caliber ....75 mm (2.95 inches).
Length of tube.........34.75 inches.
Weight in action.......880 pounds.
Maximum range.......3,900 yards.
Muzzle velocity........725 feet per second.
Traverse ....12°.
Elevation ....—10° to + 73°.
Traction ....Motor- or horse-drawn.
Mountain version......Six pack loads.
                      (heaviest 165 pounds).

(3) *Ammunition.* HE a n d hollow-charge rounds are fired by this gun. The HE rounds weigh 13.2 and 12.13 pounds.

b. 75-MM INFANTRY GUN (*7.5 cm le. I. G. 37*). (1) *General description.* The *7.5 cm le. I. G. 37,* formerly called *7.5 cm Pak 37,* consists of a 75-mm tube, 21 calibers long, on the *3.7 cm Pak* mount. The gun has a four-baffle muzzle brake which is square in cross section.

(2) *Characteristics.*

Caliber ....75 mm (2.95 inches).
Length of tube.........5 feet 1.95 inches.
Weight in action.......1,124 pounds.
Maximum range (with trails dug in 3 feet to increase elevation)...5,630 yards.
Muzzle velocity........1,165 feet per second.
Traverse ....Under 60°.
Elevation ....22° 30'.
Traction ....Horse- or motor-drawn.

(3) *Ammunition.* HE and hollow-charge projectiles are fired. They are identical to those used with the *7.5 cm le. I.G. 18.* The hollow-charge projectile will penetrate 75 mm (2.95 inches) at 30 degrees from normal.

c. 150-MM HEAVY INFANTRY GUN (*15 cm s. I. G. 33*). (1) *General description.* The *15 cm s. I. G. 33* is a standard infantry weapon, which can be used for high- or low-angle fire. The tube is monobloc, with a horizontal sliding breechblock and cartridge case obturation. The piece is mounted on a two-wheeled carriage with a box trail. Recently this gun has been issued with a stick bomb used against wire and minefields.

(2) *Characteristics.*

Caliber ....150 mm (5.9 inches).
Length of tube.........5 feet, 4.57 inches.
Weight in action.......3,360 pounds.
Maximum range (HE).5,140 yards.
Muzzle velocity........787 feet per second.
Traverse ....11° 15'.
Elevation ....0 to 73°.
Traction ....Horse- or motor-drawn.

(3) *Ammunition.* HE and smoke projectiles are fired, in addition to a stick bomb. Projectile weights are: HE, 84 pounds; smoke, 85 pounds; and stick bomb, 197 pounds.

Figure 30.—15 cm s. I.G. 33 (150-mm heavy infantry gun) showing box trail.

Figure 31.—7.5 cm Geb. G. 36 (75-mm mountain howitzer) with perforated cylindrical muzzle brake.

3. Mountain Guns

a. 75-MM MOUNTAIN HOWITZER (*7.5 cm Geb. G. 36*). (1) *General description.* The *7.5 cm Geb. G. 36* is the standard German light mountain howitzer. The monobloc tube may be fitted with either a baffled or a perforated cylindrical muzzle brake. Both the buffer and recuperator are below the tube. The breachblock is a horizontal sliding type, and the mount has split-box trails, solid rubber tires, but no shield. The howitzer may be quickly broken down into 11 pack loads, the heaviest of which are the tube (249 pounds), and the cradle and recoil system (250 pounds).

(2) *Characteristics.*

Caliber ....75 mm (2.95 inches).
Length of tube.........57.09 inches.
Weight in action.......1,650 pounds.
Maximum range.......10,100 yards.
Muzzle velocity.......1,558 feet per second.
Traverse ....40°.
Elevation ....—8° to + 70°.
Traction ....Horse-drawn, sledges, or pack.

(3) *Ammunition.* HE and hollow-charge projectiles are fired. The HE projectiles weigh 12.6 pounds, and 12.81 pounds. The hollow-charge projectile weighs 9.75 pounds.

Figure 32.—10.5 cm Geb. H. 40 (105-mm mountain howitzer) with double-baffle muzzle brake.

b. 105-MM MOUNTAIN HOWITZER (*10.5 cm Geb. H. 40*). (1) *General description.* This weapon is the latest German mountain artillery piece to appear. It is fitted with a double-baffle muzzle brake with wide side flanges, and has a horizontal sliding breechblock and cartridge case obturation. The split-trail carriage is mounted on light alloy wheels. For transport the weapon is disassembled into nine loads, the heaviest of which is the barrel and muzzle brake (551 pounds).

(2) *Characteristics.*

Caliber ....105 mm (4.14 inches).
Length of tube.........11 feet, 3.4 inches (including breech ring and muzzle brake).
Weight in action.......3,660 pounds.
Maximum range.......13,810 yards.
Muzzle velocity........1,870 feet per second.
Traverse ....50° 40′.
Elevation ....−4° 47′ to + 70°.
Traction ....Usually carried by horse-drawn cart.

(3) *Ammunition.* The *10.5 cm Geb. H. 40* fires semi-fixed HE, smoke, star, and hollow-charge ammunition. The HE projectile weighs 32.6 pounds.

4. Airborne Recoilless Guns

a. 75-MM AIRBORNE RECOILLESS GUN (*7.5 cm L. G. 40*). (1) *General description.* The *7.5 cm L. G. 40,* formerly known as the *7.5 cm L. G. 1 (L) Rh.,* needs no recoil mechanism. The breech is designed to eliminate recoil by emitting part of the propellent gases to the rear. Weight has been reduced considerably by constructing the carriage largely of light alloys, and the gun may be dropped by parachute in two wicker containers. The thin horizontal sliding breechblock is hand-operated. A Venturi tube extends from the rear of the breech which is bored to allow gases to escape. Light metal disk-type wheels are fitted to the mount.

Figure 33.—7.5 cm L.G. 40 (75-mm airborne recoilless gun) showing breech mechanism.

Figure 34.—10.5 cm L.G. 40 (105-mm airborne recoilless gun) in traveling position.

(2) *Characteristics.*

Caliber ....75 mm (2.95 inches).
Length of tube includ-
   ing breech ring and
   jet ....45.28 inches.
Weight in action.......321 pounds.
Maximum range (HE).8,900 yards (estimated).
Muzzle velocity (HE).1,238 feet per second.
Traverse with elevation
   —15° to + 42°......30° right and left.
Traverse with elevation
   —15° to + 20°......360° right and left.
Elevation with traverse
   of 360°.............—15° to + 20°.
Elevation with traverse
   of 30°, right and left.—15° to + 42°.
Traction ....Airborne.

(3) *Ammunition.* HE, APCBC, and hollow-charge projectiles are fired. Projectile weights are: HE, 12 pounds, APCBC, 15 pounds; hollow charge, 10.13 pounds. The hollow-charge projectile will penetrate 50 mm at 30 degrees from normal.

b. 105-mm Airborne Recoilless Gun (*10.5 cm L. G. 40*). (1) *General description.* The

10.5 cm L. G. 40, formerly known as the 10.5 cm L. G. 2 Kp., like the 7.5 cm L. G. 40, has a jet at the rear for the escape of part of the propellent gases instead of a recoil system. There is no breechblock. The firing mechanism is operated from the top of the breech ring and the striker hits a primer in the side of the cartridge. A modification of this weapon, the 10.5 cm L. G. 40/2, also exists

(2) *Characteristics.*

Caliber ....105 mm (4.14 inches).
Length of tube, includ-
   ing jet.............6 feet, 3 inches.
Weight in action.......855 pounds.
Maximum range.......8,694 yards.
Muzzle velocity (HE).1,099 feet per second.
Traverse ....80°.
Elevation ....—15° to + 40° 30'.
Traction ....Airborne.

(3) *Ammunition.* HE and hollow-charge projectiles are fired. The base of the cartridge case has a circular bakelite disk which is destroyed when the gun fires. Projectile weights are: HE, 32.63 pounds; hollow charge, 25.88 pounds.

c. 105-MM AIRBORNE RECOILLESS GUN *(10.5 cm L. G. 42).* (1) *General description.* The *10.5 cm L. G. 42,* formerly known as the *L. G. 2 Rh,* differs from the *10.5 cm L. G. 40* in that it has a horizontal sliding breechblock bored for the passage of gases to the rear. The mount is made of fairly heavy tubing, and is designed for rapid dismantling and reassembly. Both air and pack transport are possible. A variation, known as *10.5 cm L. G. 42/1,* differs in weight (1,191 pounds). It uses the same range tables.

(2) *Characteristics.*

Caliber ....105 mm (4.14 inches).
Length of tube.........6 feet, 0.28 inch (including jet).

Weight in action.......1,217 pounds.
Maximum range (HE).8,695 yards.
Muzzle velocity........1,099 feet per second.
Traverse ....360° at elevations up to 12°; 71° 15′ at elevations over 12°.
Elevation ....15° to 42° 35′.
Traction ....Airborne or pack.

(3) *Ammunition.* This weapon fires HE, hollow-charge, smoke, and HE incendiary projectiles. The projectile weights are: HE, 32.58 pounds; hollow charge, 26.62 and 27.17 pounds: smoke, 32.36 pounds, and HE incendiary, 33.52 pounds.

Figure 35.—Right front view (top) 10.5 cm le. F.H. 18 (M), the standard divisional field artillery howitzer with muzzle brake; left rear view (bottom).

Figure 36.—10.5 cm le. F.H. 18 (105-mm field howitzer), the standard divisional field artillery howitzer.

5. Field and Medium Artillery

a. 75-mm FIELD GUN 38 *(7.5 cm Feld Kanone 38)*. (1) *General description.* This gun is of conventional design, with a semiautomatic horizontal sliding breechblock. A slotted cylindrical muzzle brake is fitted to the monobloc tube. The hydropneumatic recuperator is above the tube, and the hydraulic buffer below. Equilibrators are spring type. The carriage has split trails of riveted box construction and artillery wheels.

(2) *Characteristics.*

Caliber ....75 mm (2.95 inches).
Length of tube.........9 feet, 3½ inches.
Weight in action.......3,136 pounds.
Maximum range......12,570 yards.
Muzzle velocity........1,985 feet per second.
Traverse ....50°.
Elevation ....—5° to + 45°.
Traction ....Tractor.

(3) *Ammunition.* Two types of HE shell and one hollow-charge shell are fired. The HE shells weigh 12.85 pounds and 13.88 pounds, and the hollow-charge, 10.07 pounds.

b. 105-mm FIELD HOWITZER *(10.5 cm Leichte Feld Haubitze 18)*. (1) *General description.* This is the standard divisional field artillery howitzer developed during the last war. It has a hydropneumatic recoil system and a heavy, simply designed breech mechanism with a horizontal sliding block and cartridge case obturation. The first modification of the original model appeared in 1941 when a muzzle brake of conventional design was fitted to permit a new long-

range charge to be fired, increasing the range by 1,800 yards. This version is known as the *le. F. H. 18 (M)*. By 1944 a second modification had appeared, the *le. F. H. 18/40*. The tube of the *le. F. H. 18 (M)* was mounted on the carriage already in large scale production for the *7.5 Pak 40* (75-mm AT gun). By modifying the elevating and firing mechanisms, the rate of fire was increased, and a more efficient muzzle brake decreased the recoil load. The *10.5 cm le. F. H. 18 (M)* and the *le. F. H. 18/40* are ballistically identical and have the same firing tables.

(2) *Characteristics* (of *10.5 cm le F. H. 18/40*).

Caliber ....105 mm (4.14 inches).
Length of tube.........10 feet, 8.252 inches.
  (including breech ring
  and muzzle brake)
Weight in action.......4,320 pounds.
Maximum range......13,480 yards.
Muzzle velocity........1,772 feet per second.
Traverse ....56°.
Elevation ....—6° to + 40°.
Traction ....Tractor.

(3) *Ammunition.* HE, smoke, incendiary, illuminating, propaganda, hollow-charge, HE sabot, and AP sabot shells are fired. (Sabot shells may not be fired from guns equipped with existing muzzle brakes, however.) The weight of HE projectiles is 32 pounds, 11 ounces.

c. 150-mm MEDIUM HOWITZER *(15 cm s. F. H. 18)*. (1) *General description.* The *15 cm s. F. H. 18* is the standard divisional artillery medium howitzer, with the same mount as the *10 cm*

Figure 37.—15 cm s. F.H. 18 (150-mm medium howitzer) in firing position.

Figure 38.—15 cm s. F.H. 18 (150-mm medium howitzer) in traveling position.

K. 18, the standard medium gun. The tube is solid, and loose in its jacket. The manually operated breech, with horizontal sliding block, has continuous-pull firing mechanism and cartridge case obturation. Spring equilibrators are fitted. The carriage has split-box trails, and double-disk, solid rubber-tired wheels. A new model of this weapon, called the *15 cm s. F. H. 18/40,* is fitted with a muzzle brake. The same ammunition is fired at higher muzzle velocity, 1,952 feet per second, increasing maximum range to 16,514 yards. An *s. F. H. 42,* a further modification, has also been reported.

(2) *Characteristics.*

Caliber ....150 mm (5.866 inches).
Length of tube.........14 feet, 5.16 inches.
Weight in action.......12,096 pounds.
Maximum range.......14,630 yards.
Muzzle velocity.......1,705 feet per second.
  (with charge 8)
Traverse ....60°.
Elevation ....—1° 30′ to + 45°.
Traction ....Horse- or tractor-drawn.

(3) *Ammunition.* HE, anti-concrete, AP, and smoke projectiles are fired. Projectiles weigh 95.7 pounds. The propellent charge consists of eight increments.

333

Figure 39.—s. 10 cm K. 18 (105-mm medium gun) in firing position.

Figure 40.—s. 10 cm K. 18 (105-mm medium gun) with tube in traveling position.

d. 105-MM MEDIUM GUN (*s. 10 cm K. 18*).

(1) *General description.* The *10 cm K. 18* is the standard medium gun. It has a mount interchangeable with that of the *15 cm s. F. H. 18*. The breech is hand-operated, with horizontal sliding block and cartridge case obturation.

(2) *Characteristics.*

Caliber .... 105 mm (4.14 inches).
Length of tube......... 17 feet 11.28 inches.
Weight in action....... 11,424 pounds.

Maximum range....... 20,850 yards.
Muzzle velocity........ 2,740 feet per second.
Traverse .... 60°.
Elevation .... —1° 30′ to + 45°.
Traction .... Horse- or motor-drawn.

(3) *Ammunition.* HE, AP, and APCBC projectiles are fired. Projectile weights are: HE, 33.5 pounds, AP, 31.25 pounds; APCBC, 34.63 pounds. Three charges, small, medium, and large, are used.

Figure 41.—15 cm K. 18 (150-mm heavy gun) in traveling position.

e. 150-MM GUN (*15 cm K. 18*). (1) *General description*. The *15 cm K. 18* has the characteristic features of German "18" class field artillery design, including the recuperator above and the buffer below the tube. A cartridge case accomplishes obturation, and the usual horizontal sliding breechblock is manually operated. Two hydropneumatic equilibrators are bolted to the tube jacket. The mount is sprung on two wheels, and has a box trail.

(2) *Characteristics*.

Caliber ....150 mm (5.9 inches).
Length of tube.........27 feet, 0.5 inch.
Weight in action.......14.22 tons.
Maximum range.......27,040 yards.
Muzzle velocity........2,838 feet per second.
Traverse ....12°.
Elevation ....—40° to + 45°.
Traction ....Motor-drawn.

(3) *Ammunition*. HE streamline, AP, and anti-concrete projectiles are fired. Projectile weights are: HE, 94.6 pounds and anti-concrete, 95.7 pounds.

f. 150-MM GUN (*15 cm K. 39*). (1) *General description*. The *15 cm K. 39,* a later version of the *15 cm K. 18,* is used either as a field gun on its split-trail, rubber-tired carriage, or as a coast defense gun, with its field carriage mounted on the turntable of an emplaced platform.

(2) *Characteristics*.

Caliber ....150 mm (5.9 inches).
Length of tube.........27 feet 0.84 inch.
Weight in action.......13.44 tons.
  (without platform)

Maximum range.......27,040 yards.
Muzzle velocity........2,838 feet per second.
Traverse on wheels....60°.
Traverse on platform..360°.
Elevation ....—4° to + 45°.
Traction ....Motor-drawn.

(3) *Ammunition*. The gun fires HE streamline, anti-concrete, semi-AP, and AP projectiles. Projectile weights are: HE 94.6 and 99.25 pounds; anti-concrete, 95.7 pounds; semi-AP 99.25 pounds; AP, 99.25 pounds.

g. 170-MM GUN (*17 cm K. in Mörser Lafette*). (1) *General description*. The *17 cm K. in Mrs. Laf.* is a long-range, mobile gun mounted on the *21 cm Mörser 18* (210-mm howitzer) carriage. It has a built-up tube, and a separate recoil mechanism for the upper carriage, which also moves in recoil. The breech mechanism is operated manually. The gun has a horizontal sliding block and cartridge case obturation. In spite of its weight, the gun can be put into and taken out of action very rapidly. A firing platform is lowered by jacks, and the wheels are raised for firing. One man, with a trail spike, can traverse the gun 360 degrees around this platform.

(2) *Characteristics*.

Caliber ....170 mm (6.79 inches).
Length of tube.........28 feet 3.6 inches.
Weight in action.......19.04 tons.
Maximum range.......32 370 yards.
  (HE streamline)
Muzzle velocity.......3,035 feet per second.
  (HE streamline)

Figure 42.—17 cm K. in Mrs. Laf. (170-mm gun mounted on 210-mm howitzer carriage).

Traverse (on traversing
    arc) ....16°.
Elevation ....70° (Actually limited to 50°
                   by a stop).

(3) *Ammunition.* HE streamline, HEBC streamline, and AP projectiles are fired. The HE projectile weighs 138 pounds, and the HEBC, 148 pounds.

h. 210-MM HOWITZER (*21 cm Mörser 18*). (1) *General description.* The *21 cm Mörser 18* is the standard heavy howitzer. The piece recoils in a cradle trunnioned to an upper carriage. This upper carriage also moves in recoil along a lower carriage. The breech mechanism is operated manually, and has a horizontal sliding block with cartridge case obturation. In action, a firing platform is lowered on jacks and the wheels are raised; the rear of the trail is supported by a traversing path. When traveling, a two-wheeled trailer is attached to and supports the trail, while a separate traveling carriage supports the tube.

(2) *Characteristics.*
    Caliber ....210 mm (8.27 inches).
    Length of tube........21 feet 4.37 inches.
    Weight in action.......36,740 pounds.
    Maximum range.......18,300 yards.
    Muzzle velocity........1,854 feet per second.

Figure 43.—21 cm Mrs. 18 (210-mm howitzer) with tube elevated.

Traverse ....16°.
Elevation ....70°.
Traction ....Motor-drawn.

  (3) *Ammunition.* HE streamline and anti-

concrete projectiles are fired, as well as a fin-stabilized, anti-concrete stick bomb. The HE projectile weighs 249 pounds, and the anti-concrete projectile 268 pounds.

Figure 44.—2.8 cm s. Pz. B 41 (28/20-mm tapered-bore antitank gun).

6. Antitank Artillery

a. 28/20-MM ANTITANK GUN (*2.8 cm s. Pz. B 41*). (1) *General description.* This first Gerlich high velocity tapered-bore antitank gun appeared in 1941. The monobloc tube has a semi-

Figure 45.—Airborne version of 2.8 cm s. Pz. B. 41 (28/20-mm tapered-bore antitank gun).

automatic breech with horizontal sliding-wedge block, and is fitted with a muzzle brake. An airborne version exists which consists of an identical tube on a light alloy cradle and two-wheeled tubular mount. This version weighs 260 pounds.

(2) *Characteristics.*

Caliber (initial).......28 mm (1.1 inches).
        (emergent)....20 mm (0.78 inch).
Length of tube.........5 feet 7.62 inches.
Weight in action......501 pounds.

Muzzle velocity........4,600 feet per second.
Traverse ....90°.
Elevation ....—5° to + 45°.

(3) *Ammunition.* HE and AP (tungsten carbide core) rounds are fired. Projectile weights are: HE, 3.1 ounces; and AP, 4.6 ounces. The AP ammunition will penetrate 53 mm (2.09 inches) at 400 yards, 30 degrees from normal.

b. 37-MM ANTITANK GUN (*3.7 cm Pak*). (1) *General description.* Formerly the main German antitank gun, this weapon is still likely to be met. AP 40 ammunition gives the gun a reasonable penetration performance at ranges up to 400 yards. The breechblock is horizontal sliding type, and the shield is 3/16-inch armor plate.

(2) *Characteristics.*

Caliber ....37 mm (1.45 inches).
Length of tube.........5 feet 5.52 inches.
Weight in action.......970 pounds.
Muzzle velocity (AP40).3,450 feet per second.
Muzzle velocity (AP)..2,625 feet per second.
Traverse ....60°.
Elevation ....—8° to + 25°.
Traction ....Motor-drawn; carried in
                       truck; airborne.

(3) *Ammunition.* HE, AP, and AP 40 projectiles are fired, as well as a hollow-charge stick bomb. Projectile weights are: HE, 1.38 pounds; AP, 1.5 pounds; and AP 40, 12.5 ounces. The stick bomb, 6.25 inches in diameter, weighs 18.75 pounds. Penetration of homogeneous armor at 400 yards, 30 degrees from normal, firing AP 40

Figure 46.—3.7 cm Pak (37-mm antitank gun), 5 cm Pak 38 (50-mm antitank gun), and 7.5 cm Pak 40 (75-mm antitank gun) (front to rear).

ammunition is 49 mm (1.93 inches). The stick bomb will penetrate about 6 inches of homogeneous plate. The range at which a moving target may be hit does not exceed 150 yards.

c. 42/28-MM ANTITANK GUN (*4.2 cm le. Pak 41*). (1) *General description.* The *4.2 cm le. Pak 41* is the second of the tapered-bore antitank gun series. The monobloc tube is long with obvious external as well as internal taper, and has no muzzle brake. The horizontal sliding breechblock is hand-operated. The mount is identical with that of the *3.7 cm Pak,* but with a double upper shield. A second shield, $\frac{3}{16}$-inch thick, is riveted to the standard shield, with an intervening space of approximately $1\frac{5}{8}$ inches.

(2) *Characteristics.*

Caliber (initial)......42 mm (1.65 inches).
      (emergent)....28 mm (1.1 inches).
Length of tube.........7 feet 4.5 inches.
Weight in action.......990 pounds.
Muzzle velocity........4,100 feet per second.
Traverse ....44°.
Elevation ....—8° to + 32°.
Method of traction.....Motor-drawn.

(3) *Ammunition.* HE and AP (Tungsten carbide core) rounds are fired. Projectile weights are: HE, 0.56 pound, and AP, 0.69 pound. At 700 yards this weapon, firing AP ammunition, will penetrate 68 mm (2.88 inches) of armor at 30 degrees from normal.

d. 50-MM ANTITANK GUN (*5 cm Pak 38*). (1) *General description.* This gun, introduced in 1941 to replace the *3.7 cm Pak,* is mounted on a split-trail carriage of conventional design. The monobloc tube is fitted with a muzzle brake, and

Figure 47.—4.2 cm le. Pak 41 (42/28-mm tapered-bore antitank gun) showing front of double shield.

the breech mechanism is semiautomatic with a horizontal sliding block. Solid rubber tires are fitted, and the shield consists of two 4-mm armor plates about 1 inch apart.

(2) *Characteristics.*

Caliber ....50 mm (1.97 inches).
Length of tube.........10 feet, 4.96 inches.
Weight in action........2,016 pounds.
Muzzle velocity (AP40) .3,940 feet per second.
Muzzle velocity (AP)..2,740 feet per second.
Muzzle velocity (HE) .1,800 feet per second.
Traverse ....65°.
Elevation ....—18° to + 27°.
Traction ....Half-tracked tractor.

(3) *Ammunition.* Projectile weights are: AP, 4.56 pounds; AP 40, 2.025 pounds; and HE, 3.94 pounds. Penetration, firing AP ammunition, is 56 mm (2.2 inches) of armor at 1,000 yards at 30 degrees from normal.

Figure 48.—7.5 cm Pak 41 (75/55-mm tapered-bore antitank gun).

Figure 49.—7.5 cm Pak 97/38 (75-mm antitank gun) with Solothurn muzzle brake.

e. 75-MM ANTITANK GUN (*7.5 cm Pak 40*). (1) *General description.* The *7.5 cm Pak 40* is similar in appearance to the *5 cm Pak 38.* The monobloc tube is fitted with a double-baffle muzzle brake, and the breech mechanism is semiautomatic with a horizontal sliding block. The carriage, with tubular split trail, has solid-rubber-tired wheels and torsion bar suspension and may be towed at about 25 miles an hour. The shield consists of two 4-mm armor plates spaced about 1 inch apart.

(2) *Characteristics.*

Caliber ....75 mm (2.95 inches).
Length of tube.........11 feet 4 inches.
Weight in action.......3,136 pounds.
Muzzle velocity (AP40) .3,250 feet per second.

Muzzle velocity
(APCBC) ....2,530 feet per second.
Muzzle velocity (HE) .1,800 feet per second.
Muzzle velocity (hollow
charge) ....1,476 feet per second.
Traverse ....65°.
Elevation ....—5° to + 22°.
Traction ....Motor-drawn.

(3) *Ammunition.* Weights of projectiles fired from this gun are: HE, 12.54 pounds; APCBC, 15 pounds; AP shot, 9.125 pounds; hollow charge, 9.97 pounds; and smoke 13.7 pounds. With APCBC ammunition, penetration of homogeneous armor is 102 mm (4.02 inches) at 30 degrees from normal, at 1,000 yards.

Figure 50.—7.62 cm Pak 36 (r) (3-inch antitank gun).

f. 75/55-MM ANTITANK GUN (*7.5 cm Pak 41*). (1) *General description.* This was the third tapered-bore antitank gun to be introduced. It has a muzzle brake, and a semiautomatic vertical sliding breechblock. A cylindrical cradle, covering the rear half of the tube, is attached to the shield by a spherical universal joint.

(2) *Characteristics.*

```
Caliber  ...............75 mm (2.95 inches).
  (initial)
Caliber  ...............55 mm (2.17 inches).
  (emergent)
Length of tube.........13 feet 7.375 inches.
Weight in action.......3,136 pounds.
Muzzle velocity........3,936 feet per second.
  (estimated)
Traverse ..............60°.
Elevation  .............—10° to + 18°.
Traction ..............Motor-drawn.
```

(3) *Ammunition.* AP and HE projectiles are fired. The AP projectile weighs 5.68 pounds, of which 2.01 pounds is tungsten carbide core. The AP projectile will penetrate 130 mm (5.12 inches) of homogeneous armor plate at 30 degrees from normal at 1,000 yards.

g. 75-MM ANTITANK GUN (*7.5 cm Pak 97/38*). (1) *General description.* This weapon, originally introduced in 1942, consists of the well known French 75-mm gun, Model 1897, mounted on the *5 cm Pak 38* carriage, and fitted with a long perforated muzzle brake. The breech mechanism is hand-operated with eccentric screw-type block.

(2) *Characteristics.*

```
Caliber  ...............75 mm (2.95 inches).
Length of tube.........9 feet 8 inches.
Weight in action.......2,624 pounds.
```

```
Muzzle velocity (HE).1,788-1,892 feet per
                        second.
Muzzle velocity (hollow
  charge)  ...........1,476 feet per second.
Muzzle velocity (AP)..1,870 feet per second.
Traverse ..............60°.
Elevation  .............—8° to + 25°.
Traction ..............Motor-drawn.
```

(3) *Ammunition.* AP, HE, and hollow-charge projectiles are fired. AP and HE projectiles weigh 14.8 pounds, and 13.4 pounds respectively.

h. 3-INCH ANTITANK GUN (*7.62 cm Pak 36 (r)*. (1) *General description.* The 76.2 cm *Pak 36 (r)* is a German modified antitank version of the 7.62-cm Russian field gun, 296 (r). The built-up tube is rebored to take a longer cartridge case, and a two-baffle muzzle brake is added. The breech mechanism is semiautomatic with a vertical sliding block.

(2) *Characteristics.*

```
Caliber  ...............76.2 mm (3 inches).
Length of tube.........12 feet 9.35 inches.
Weight in action.......3,564 pounds.
  (without shield)
Muzzle velocity
  (APCBC)  ..........2,430 feet per second.
Muzzle velocity (HE).1,805 feet per second.
Muzzle velocity (AP40).3,520 feet per second.
Traverse ..............60°.
Elevation  .............—5° to + 75°.
Traction ..............Motor-drawn.
```

(3) *Ammunition.* APCBC, AP 40, and HE projectiles are fired. Projectile weights are: APCBC, 16.72 pounds; AP 40, 9.24 pounds; HE, 12.64 pounds. Penetration, firing APCBC projectiles at 1,000 yards at 30 degrees from normal, is 83 mm (3.27 inches) of homogeneous armor plate.

i. 3-INCH ANTITANK GUN (*7.62 cm Pak 39*).

(1) *General description.* This 3-inch antitank gun is a modified version of the Russian field gun *7.62 cm F.K. 297 (r)*. The chamber is bored out, and a *7.62 Pak 36* muzzle brake is fitted. The breech mechanism is semiautomatic with a vertical sliding block. The mount has box-type trails and pneumatic tires.

(2) *Characteristics.*

    Caliber ....76.2 mm (3 inches).
    Length of tube.........11 feet 5 inches.
    Weight in action.......3,360 pounds.
    Muzzle velocity........2,230 feet per second.
    Traverse ....57°.
    Elevation ....−6° to + 45°.
    Traction ....Motor-drawn.

(3) *Ammunition.* This gun fires the same ammunition as the *7.62 cm Pak 36 (r)*, but has somewhat lower performance.

j. 88-MM ANTITANK GUN (*8.8 cm Pak 43*).

(1) *General description.* The *8.8 cm Pak 43* is an electrically fired, semiautomatic gun on a two-bogie cruciform mount. It may be fired from its wheels if the direction of fire is within 30 degrees of the longitudinal girders, but must be fired with its platform on the ground when used in an artillery role. With platform down, the top of the shield is only 5 feet 6⅞ inches high. An automatic firing cut-out restricts elevation when firing over the legs to 12 degrees on early mounts and 16 degrees on later mounts. The *8.8 cm Pak 43* is ballistically identical with the *8.8 cm Pak 43/41*.

(2) *Characteristics.*

    Caliber ....88 mm (3.45 inches).
    Length of tube.........21 feet 7.25 inches.
    Weight in action.......8,000 pounds.

    Muzzle velocity (HE) .2,460 feet per second.
    Muzzle velocity
      (APCBC) ....3,280 feet per second.
    Muzzle velocity (AP40) .3,705 feet per second.
    Traverse ....360°.
    Elevation ....−8° to + 40°.
    Traction ....Tractor.

(3) *Ammunition.* Weight of projectiles fired from this gun are: HE, 20.68 pounds; APCBC, 22 pounds, and 22.36 pounds; AP 40, 16 pounds; Hollow charge, 16.8 pounds. At 1,500 yards, the APCBC and AP 40 projectiles will penetrate approximately 130 mm (5.12 inches) of homogeneous armor plate at 30 degrees from normal.

k. 88-MM ANTITANK GUN (*8.8 cm Pak 43/41*).

(1) *General description.* This 88-mm gun, 71 calibers long, is mounted on an orthodox two-wheeled carriage. The legs of the split trail are hinged to a base which also mounts the upper carriage. The wheels, on stub axles, are sprung independently. The gun has a four-point support when firing. A muzzle brake is fitted, and the breech mechanism is semiautomatic with a horizontal sliding block.

(2) *Characteristics.*

    Caliber ....88 mm (3.46 inches).
    Length of tube.........21 feet 7.25 inches.
    Weight in action.......9,660 pounds.
    Muzzle velocity (AP40) .3,705 feet per second.
    Muzzle velocity
      (APCBC) ....3,280 feet per second.
    Muzzle velocity (HE) .2,460 feet per second.
    Muzzle velocity (hollow
      charge) ....1,968 feet per second.
    Traverse ....56°.
    Elevation ....−5° to + 38°.
    Traction ....Motor-drawn.

Figure 51.—8.8 cm Pak 43 (88-mm antitank gun) on a cruciform mount.

Figure 52.—8.8 cm Pak 43/41 (88-mm antitank gun).

(3) *Ammunition.* Projectile weights are : HE, 20.68 pounds; APCBC, 22.36 pounds, and 22 pounds; AP 40, 16 pounds; hollow charge, 16.8 pounds. At 1,500 yards, the APCBC and AP 40 projectiles will penetrate approximately 130 mm (5.12 inches) of homogeneous armor plate at 30 degrees from normal.

7. Antiaircraft Artillery

a. GENERAL. German antiaircraft guns have been increasingly developed as dual-purpose, or as with the 88-mm antiaircraft gun, multipurpose weapons. All standard German antiaircraft guns may be used against ground targets, and armor-piercing ammunition is available in all calibers. (Antiaircraft rocket weapons are described in Section VII.)

b. AUTOMATIC WEAPONS. (1) *20-mm Antiaircraft Gun (2 cm Flak 30).* (a) *General description.* The *2 cm Flak 30* was the standard light antiaircraft gun until the introduction of the *2 cm Flak 38* and the *Flakvierling 38*. It is recoil-operated, fed by a 20-round magazine, and may be fired either full or semiautomatic. A combined flash hider and muzzle brake is used The carriage consists of an undercarriage leveled by three adjustable feet, and a top carriage supported on ball bearings.

(b) *Characteristics.*

Caliber ....20 mm (0.79 inch).
Length of tube.........56.6 inches.
Weight in action.......1,064 pounds.
Effective ceiling.......3,500 feet.
Maximum horizontal
　range ....5,230 yards.
Rate of fire: practical..120 rounds per minute.
Muzzle velocity (HE).2,950 feet per second.
Muzzle velocity (AP)..2,625 feet per second.
Muzzle velocity (AP40).3,250 feet per second.
Traverse ....360°.
Elevation ....—12° to + 90°.
Traction ....Motor-drawn or SP.
Antiaircraft sights: *Flakvisier 35,*
　Linealvisier 21, Schwebekreisvisier 30/38.

(c) *Ammunition.* Projectile weights are : HE, 4.2 ounces; AP, 5.2 ounces; and AP 40, 3.6 ounces.

(2) *20-mm Antiaircraft Gun (2 cm Flak 38).* (a) *General description.* The *2 cm Flak 38* was introduced to replace the *2 cm Flak 30*. It is operated by short-barrel recoil, and the residual pressure of gas in the barrel. Except for a higher cyclic rate of fire, it does not differ in performance from the *Flak 30*. This gun also is mounted on a 760-pound carriage, which may be disassembled easily into 27 loads for mountain warfare. The total weight of the gun on this light mount is 1,013 pounds. This combination is designated *2 cm Geb. Flak 38*. (The normal *2 cm Flak 38* gun and mount weigh 1,650 pounds traveling.)

Figure 53.—2 cm Flak 30 (20-mm antiaircraft gun) on half-track.

Figure 54.—2 cm Flak 38 (20-mm antiaircraft gun).

Figure 55.—2 cm Flak 38 in firing position.

Figure 56.—2 cm Geb. Flak 38 (20-mm mountain anti-aircraft gun).

(b) *Characteristics.*

Caliber ....20 mm (0.79 inch).
Length of tube.........56.6 inches.
Weight in action.......896 pounds.
Effective ceiling........3,500 feet.
Maximum horizontal
    range ....5,230 yards.
Rate of fire: practical..180 to 220 rounds per
                   minute.
Muzzle velocity (HE).2,950 feet per second.
Muzzle velocity (AP)..2,625 feet per second.
Muzzle velocity (AP40).3,250 feet per second.
Traverse ....360°.
Elevation ....—20° to + 90°.
Traction ....Motor-drawn, RR, SP.
Antiaircraft sights: *Flakvisier 38,*
    Linealvisier 21, Schwebekreisvisier 30/38.

(c) *Ammunition.* Weights of projectiles fired by this gun are: HE, 4.2 ounces; AP, 5.2 ounces; and AP 40, 3.6 ounces.

(3) *20-mm Four-Barreled Antiaircraft Gun* (*2 cm Flakvierling 38*). (a) *General description.* The *2 cm Flakvierling 38* consists of four *2 cm Flak 38's* on a triangular-base mount with three leveling jacks. Muzzle preponderance is counteracted by an equilibrator bolted to the mount.

(b) *Characteristics.*

Caliber .... 20 mm (0.79 inch).
Length of tube .... 56.6 inches.
Weight in action .... 1.68 tons.
Effective ceiling ...... 3,500 feet.
Maximum horizontal
    range .... 5,230 yards.
Rate of fire: practical .. 700 to 800 rounds per
                   minute.
Muzzle velocity (HE) . 2,950 feet per second.
Muzzle velocity (AP) .. 2,625 feet per second.
Muzzle velocity (AP40) . 3,250 feet per second.
Traverse .... 360°.
Elevation .... —10° to + 100°.
Traction .... Motor-drawn, SP, or
                 static.
Antiaircraft sights: *Flakvisier 40,*
    Linealvisier 21, Schwebekreisvisier 30/38.

(c) *Ammunition.* Weights of projectiles fired are: HE, 4.2 ounces; AP, 5.2 ounces; AP 40, 3.6 ounces.

(4) *37-mm Antiaircraft Gun* (*3.7 cm Flak 18, 36, and 37*). (a) *General description.* The *3.7 cm Flak 18* has a monobloc tube, and an automatic action operated by barrel recoil and residual gas pressure. A combination muzzle brake and flash eliminator is fitted. The cruciform mount has two bogies, and screw-type leveling jacks. The *3.7 cm Flak 36* is identical ballistically with the

Figure 57.—2 cm Flakvierling 38 (20-mm four-barreled antiaircraft gun).

Figure 58.—3.7 cm Flak 36 (37-mm antiaircraft gun) mounted on half-track.

Flak 18. It is mounted on a triangular platform on three adjustable leveling feet. Piece and mount are carried on a two-wheeled trailer. Weight in action is 1.71 tons. The *3.7 cm Flak 37* consists of a normal *3.7 cm Flak 18* mounted on a modified carriage. Ballistically, it is identical with *3.7 cm Flak 18* and *36*.

(b) *Characteristics.*

Caliber ....37 mm (1.45 inches).
Length of tube.........10 feet 8.75 inches.
Weight in action.......1.93 tons.
Effective ceiling......5,000 feet.
Maximum horizontal
    range ....7,200 yards.
Rate of fire: practical..80 rounds per minute.
Muzzle velocity........2,690 feet per second.
Traverse ....360°.
Elevation ....—5° to + 85°.
Traction ....Motor-drawn.
Antiaircraft sights: *Flakvisier 33,*
   Flakvisier 37 (for Flak 37), Schwebedornvisier.

(5) *37-mm Antiaircraft Gun (3.7 cm Flak 43).* (a) *General description.* Although this gun does not differ externally from the *3.7 cm Flak 18, 36,* and *37*, it has a completely different, fully automatic, gas-operated action. The gun is fed by eight-round clips on a fixed loading tray in the left side. Using a fixed firing pin, it fires on the forward movement of the bolt. Of low build, the *3.7 cm Flak 43* has a pedestal mount with a shield. A twin version known as the *Flakzwilling* exists, with one gun mounted above the other. The guns may be fired together or independently. In action the twin version weighs 3.08 tons.

(b) *Characteristics.*

Caliber ....37 mm (1.45 inches).
Length of tube.........9 feet 8.16 inches.
Weight in action.......1.37 tons.
Effective ceiling......5,000 feet (approximate).
Maximum horizontal
    range ....7,200 yards
                   (approximate).
Rate of fire: practical...150 rounds per minute.
             theoretical.250 rounds per minute.
Muzzle velocity........2,750 feet per second.
Traverse ....360°.
Elevation ....—6° to + 90°.
Traction ....Static emplacement, mobile mount, or SP.
Antiaircraft sights: *Flakvisier 43,*
   Schwebedornvisier.

(c) *Ammunition.* HE-tracer, HE-incendiary-tracer, AP-HE, HE-incendiary, and HE projectiles.

(6) *50-mm Antiaircraft Gun (5 cm Flak 41).* (a) *General description.* The *5 cm Flak 41* is similar to the *3.7 cm Flak 36.* It is gas-operated, and is fired by the forward movement of the breech mechanism. Clips of five rounds are fed from the left. The mount is a triangular platform with two short outriggers forward.

(b) *Characteristics.*

Caliber ....50 mm (1.97 inches).
Weight in action.......3.42 tons.
Effective ceiling......10,000 feet.
Maximum horizontal
    range ....14,760 yards.
Rate of fire: practical..130 rounds per minute.
Muzzle velocity........2,755 feet per second.
Traverse ....360°.
Elevation ....—10° to + 90°.
Traction ....4-wheel trailer, motor-drawn.
Antiaircraft sight: *Flakvisier 41.*

(c) *Ammunition.* Projectile weights are: HE, 4.8 pounds; HE-incendiary-tracer, 4.8 pounds; AP, 4.87 pounds.

(7) *Miscellaneous.* The following antiaircraft automatic weapons possessed by the Germans in limited numbers may be encountered occasionally:

2 cm Flak 28 ....Oerlikon type.
4 cm Flak 28 ....Bofors type.
4.7 cm Flak ....Manufactured for the Czechslovakian Army by the Skoda works.

Figure 59.—3.7 cm Flak 18 (37-mm antiaircraft gun) being prepared for firing.

Figure 60.—8.8 cm Flak 36 (88-mm antiaircraft gun) in firing position.

Figure 61.—8.8 cm Flak 36 (88-mm antiaircraft gun) in traveling position.

c. HEAVY ANTIAIRCRAFT GUNS. (1) *88-mm Antiaircraft Gun (8.8 cm Flak 18, 36, and 37).* (a) *General description.* The 88-mm gun was produced first in 1934 as the standard mobile antiaircraft gun. The tube consists of either an outer tube with an inner locking tube and a loose three-

section liner, or of a loose barrel fitting into a jacket. A semiautomatic, horizontal sliding-wedge breechblock is used. The mount has two outriggers to steady the gun for firing other than directly front or rear. The *8.8 cm Flak 36* differs from the *Flak 18* only in having a slightly different mount, while the *8.8 cm Flak 37* is identical with the *Flak 36* except for a slightly different data transmission system.

(b) *Characteristics.*

Caliber ....88 mm (3.46 inches).
Length of tube.........15 feet 5 inches.
Weight in action.......5.49 tons.
Maximum ceiling......32,500 feet.
Maximum horizontal
    range ....16,200 yards.
Rate of fire: practical..15 to 20 rounds per
                                minute.
Muzzle velocity (HE).2,690 feet per second.
Muzzle velocity (AP)..2,600 feet per second.
Traverse ....360°.
Elevation ....—3° to + 85°.
Traction ....Motor-drawn.

(c) *Ammunition.* Projectile weights are: HE, 20 pounds; AP, 21 pounds.

(2) *88-mm Antiaircraft Gun (8.8 cm Flak 41).* (a) *General description.* The *8.8 cm Flak 41* is designed for use against air, ground, and sea targets. Although usually fired from the platform, it may be fired from its wheels, with the side members of the platform extended. The breech has a horizontal sliding-wedge block, and the gun has an automatic rammer. An electric firing mechanism is employed.

(b) *Characteristics.*

Caliber ....88 mm (3.46 inches).
Length of tube.........21 feet 5.75 inches.
Weight in action.......8.85 tons.
Maximum ceiling......49,200 feet

Maximum horizontal
    range ....21,580 yards.
Rate of fire: practical..20 rounds per minute.
Muzzle velocity (HE).3,280 feet per second.
Traverse ....360°.
Elevation ....—3° to + 90°.
Traction ....Motor-drawn (12-ton
                                half-track, *Sd. Kfz. 8*),
                                or static.

(c) *Ammunition.* Projectile weights are: HE, 20.68 pounds; APCBC, 22.45 pounds.

(3) *105-mm Antiaircraft Gun (10.5 cm Flak 38 and 39).* (a) *General description.* The 105-mm antiaircraft gun appears in two models. It is produced in static and mobile versions, and also is mounted on railway cars. The breech has a horizontal sliding block, which may be operated manually or automatically, and an electric firing mechanism. The buffer is hydraulic, the recuperator hydropneumatic, and the equilibrator of the spring type. Traverse and elevation may be accomplished either manually or by power. A remote control, power-operated fuze setter and a power rammer are part of the complete unit.

(b) *Characteristics.*

Caliber ....105 mm (4.13 inches).
Length of tube.........21 feet 9.6 inches.
Weight in action....:...11.03 tons.
Maximum ceiling......36,750 feet.
Effective ceiling......31,000 feet
                                (approximately).
Maximum horizontal
    range ....19,100 yards.

Figure 62.—8.8 cm Flak 41 (88-mm multipurpose gun) showing carriage lowered.

I MARCH 1945   RESTRICTED   TM-E 30-451

Figure 63.—105-mm Flak 38 (105-mm antiaircraft gun), top view showing elevating and traversing mechanism on right side of gun; bottom view showing left side with drill round in fuze setter tray.

Rate of fire: practical..10 to 15 rounds per
minute.
Muzzle velocity........2,890 feet per second.
Traverse ....360°.
Elevation ....—3° to + 85°.
Traction ....Motor-drawn, static,
or RR.

(c) *Ammunition.* HE (time fuze), HE (percussion fuze), and APCBC projectiles are fired. The HE time fuzed projectile weighs 33.2 pounds.

(4) *128-mm Antiaircraft Gun (12.8 cm Flak 40).* (a) *General description.* The *12.8 cm Flak* looks like the *10.5 cm Flak.* The breechblock slides horizontally to the right, and incorporates an electric firing mechanism. The recoil system is conventional, with hydropneumatic recuperator above the tube, and buffer below. Hydropneumatic equilibrators are used. Elevation and traverse are either manual or powered. Fuse setting is by director control, and loading is facilitated by a power rammer incorporating two horizontal rubber rollers at the entrance to the bore. The gun may be statically emplaced, transported on a mobile mount, or mounted on a railway car.

A twin-barreled version of this gun also exists, but it is produced only for a static role.

(b) *Characteristics.*

Caliber ....128 mm (5.04 inches).
Length of tube..... ...25 feet 8.5 inches.
Weight in action:
   mobile version.......18.75 tons.
   static version........14.34 tons.
Maximum ceiling......48,555 feet.
Maximum horizontal
   range ....22,910 yards.
Rate of fire: practical..12 rounds per minute.
Muzzle velocity (HE).2,886 feet per second.
Traverse ....360°.
Elevation ....—3° to + 88°.
Traction ....RR, motor-drawn, or
static.

(c) *Ammunition.* Projectile weights are: HE, 57 pounds; and APC, 58.13 pounds.

(5) *150-mm Antiaircraft Gun (15 cm Flak).* This large caliber gun exists in limited quantities, and apparently is manned by navy personnel. Its use is confined to Germany proper in a static role.

d. AA Fire Control. (1) *Automatic weap-*

351

Figure 64.—12.8 cm Flak 40 (128-mm antiaircraft gun) on static mount.

Figure 65.—12.8 cm Flak 40 (128-mm antiaircraft gun) on railway mount.

ons. (a) *General*. Antiaircraft fire control for automatic weapons is accomplished through the use of various types of on-carriage sights, ranging from the simple manually operated *Linealvisier* (linear sight) through various mechanical types and the complicated, electrical *Flakvisier*. Range must be set into some of the simpler sights, and this is obtained either through estimation or through the use of a one-meter base range finder. Tracer observation also is used for fire control.

(b) *Linealvisier (Linear sight) 21*. This is a simple, adjustable type of speed ring sight, used as an alternate for the more complicated sights designed for use on the 20-mm antiaircraft guns. Range, course, and speed of target, angle of dive or climb, and superelevation are set in through manual manipulation of the sight.

(c) *Flakvisier (Antiaircraft sight) 35*. This is a mirror sight with a computor mechanism operating on the course and speed, slant-plane-linkage principle. It depends on accurate setting of target range, course, and speed. It can engage level-flying, climbing, or diving targets. It normally is used on the *2 cm Flak 30*, but also may be found on the *2 cm Flak 38* and *2 cm Flakvierling* in place of the electrical *Flakvisier 38 and 40*.

(d) *Flakvisier 38 and 40*. The *Flakvisier 38* is an electrically operated, range-rate sight which computes lateral and vertical leads plus superelevation. The azimuth rate and elevation rate are measured through tachometer generators coupled to the gun's traversing and elevating gears. Slant range is introduced as a battery voltage, modified by a rheostat, calibrated in hundreds of meters. In tracking, the reticles of the sight head are displaced by the battery voltage and tachometer generator voltage in such a manner that the gun is trained automatically on the future position. The use of electric current eliminates mechanical time lag. This sight is used normally with the *2 cm Flak 38*. The *Flakvisier 40*, which is used with the *2 cm Flakvierling*, differs from the *Flakvisier 38* only in minor details of construction. The principle of operation is the same.

(e) *Flakvisier 33*. Used with the *3.7 cm Flak 18* and *36*, this sight is similar in operating principles to the *Flakvisier 35*.

(f) *Flakvisier 37 (43)*. This *Flakvisier* is a mechanical computing sight used with the *3.7 cm Flak 37*. When used with the *3.7 cm Flak 43*, it is known as *Flakvisier 43*. Computation for deflections is based upon the angular rates of quadrant elevation and azimuth. Ranges are estimated or obtained from a separate source, and are set into the sight by hand. A clock-work motor drives three disc and wheel mechanisms which perform the multiplications necessary in the computation of deflections. Uni-directional drives from the elevating and traversing mechanisms rewind the clock motor. In operation, the necessary deflection is obtained by mechanically offsetting the cross hairs of the reticle of a one-power telescope. Provision is incorporated for corrections for superelevation and temperature changes. The sight is of compact box-shaped construction, approximately 10 inches by 9 inches by 4½ inches in size and 23 pounds in weight. It is fitted to the sight bar of the gun by a suspension bracket and lug.

(g) *Schwebedornvisier*. This is a relatively simple antiaircraft sight recently developed for alternate use on the *3.7 cm Flak 37 and 43*. The sight works on the linear principle. Target speed, direction, and angle of climb or dive are set into the sight manually.

(h) *Schwebekreisvisier 30/38*. This is a recent type of relatively simple, pivoted ring sight designed for use with the *2 cm Flak* weapons. Its use is becoming more and more frequent on the later models of *2 cm Flak* in lieu of the more complicated electrical *Flakvisier 38 and 40*.

(i) *Flakvisier 41*. This is a completely automatic, tachometric clock-work, range-rate sight employed with the *5 cm Flak 41*. Operated by one man, range is introduced and angular velocities are calculated in such manner that superelevation and vertical and lateral deflections are applied automatically. The principle of operation is the same as that of the *Flakvisier 38* and *40*.

(2) *Heavy antiaircraft guns*. (a) *Kommandogerät 36*. (1) This instrument is the earliest standard German linear speed antiaircraft director, providing continuous data for the engagement of aerial targets by heavy antiaircraft guns. It employs a mechanical solution of the antiaircraft problem, and has facilities for making necessary ballistic corrections to gun data. The instrument is mounted on a four-wheel trailer for transport.

(2) The director has a main pedestal with three leveling feet and two suspension arms by which it is raised and secured to front and rear bogies for transport. The main pedestal supports a casting carrying the director mechanisms and supporting brackets on which a stereoscopic, four-meter range finder rests when the director is emplaced for action.

Figure 66.—Kommandogerät 36 (antiaircraft gun director) in operating position.

Figure 67.—Kommandogerät 36 (antiaircraft gun director) without range finder.

Figure 68.—Kommandogerät 40 (antiaircraft gun director) in trailer for traveling, without range finder.

(3) Firing data determined by the director (firing azimuth, quadrant elevation, and fuze) are transmitted electrically to appropriate dials on the guns.

(b) *Kommandogerät 40.* (1) This is a later and improved version of the *Kommandogerät 36*, which it has superseded to a very large extent for use with all heavy antiaircraft guns. The four-meter, stereoscopic range finder used with the "40" model is mounted on the director, and gun data is transmitted electrically to the guns. It also uses the linear speed method of data computation. However, the "40" model can be operated by five men, whereas 11 men are required to operate the "36".

(2) The "40" director incorporates a mechanism which copes with changes in target altitude and target course (curvilinear flight).

(3) This director can be used with the different types of heavy antiaircraft weapons by changing the ballistic cams. The *Kommandogerät 41* is a *Kommandogerät 40* fitted with cams for the *8.8 cm Flak 41*, the nomenclature apparently being a convenient way of distinguishing its use for this purpose.

(c) *Kommandohilfsgerät 35.* This is an older type of antiaircraft director used only for auxiliary purposes. It operates on the angular-rate method of data computation. The four-meter base range finder used with this instrument is mounted separately, and gun data provided by the director normally are transmitted to the guns by telephone.

(d) *Range finders.* Four-meter base stereoscopic range finders furnish slant range for the antiaircraft directors. Range Finder 34 is used with the *Kommandogerät 35* and is separately

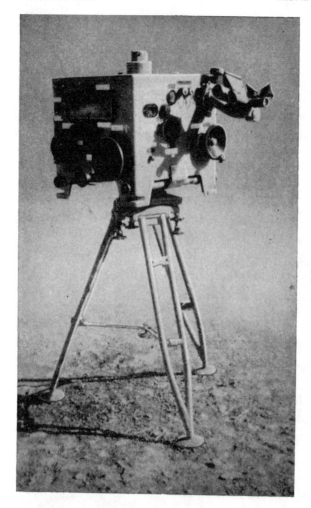

Figure 69.—Kommandohilfegerät 35 (antiaircraft gun director) used as an auxiliary.

emplaced. Range Finders 36 and 40 are used with *Kommandogerät 36* and *Kommandogerät 40*, respectively. Range Finders 36 and 40 are mounted in brackets on the directors.

(e) *Fire control radar.* Several types of radar, known as *Flakmessgerät*, are used by German antiaircraft artillery to furnish basic antiaircraft gun data to the directors. As radar is a fairly recent development, the directors have been modified to receive this basic data.

(f) *Flakumwertegerät Malsi 41, 42, and 43 (Flak Converter Malsi).* This is a plotting instrument used to convert antiaircraft fire control data received from a distant source into basic data suitable for use by individual batteries. It is reported that the latest type can deal with displacements up to 5 miles, and is more accurate than the two earlier models.

e. SEARCHLIGHTS. (1) *150-cm (60 inches) Searchlight 34 and 37.* (a) The standard antiair-

craft searchlight is 150 cm (60 inches) in diameter, and is equipped with azimuth and elevation receiver dials for receiving initial locator data. Normally hand-controlled, later versions of the 150-cm searchlight also are equipped with remote control gear.

(b) The high-current-density arc lamp is self-regulating and is fitted in an inverted position. The light is 990 million candle power and has a range, in favorable weather, of 8,800 yards at a height of 13,000 to 16,500 feet. The searchlight can be moved in azimuth through 360 degrees, and in elevation from —12 degrees through the vertical to —12 degrees on the other side. Current is supplied by a separate 24-kilowatt generator driven by an eight-cylinder internal combustion engine.

(c) For visual searching, a "dark search equipment" (*Dunkelsuchgerät 41*) is used. This consists of a pair of binoculars (having a few degrees of lateral and vertical movement) mounted on the searchlight. In operation, the searchlight and optical equipment are laid initially by location data furnished from a separate source.

(d) Sound locators are of the ring-trumpet type which work on the binaural principle, with provision for calculation of and correction for "sound lag". They also are equipped with electrical data transmitters for passing azimuth and elevation data to the receivers on the searchlight.

(e) Antiaircraft fire-control radar equipment is also used to furnish data for searchlights. *Flak* converter equipment known as *Flakumwertegerät* is used as an aid to the radar equipment and permits three searchlights at a distance from the radar to be supplied simultaneously with corrected azimuth and elevation.

(2) *200-cm (80 inches) Searchlight 40.* Many of the searchlight units are equipped at least partially with these larger searchlights. Although methods of location of initial data are similar in principle to those employed for the 150-cm searchlights, these larger 200-cm searchlights usually are equipped with necessary apparatus for remote control. For visual searching, a *"Flak* laying equipment" (*Flakrichtegerät*) is used, consisting of a pair of binoculars mounted on a control pillar. This light is reported to be 2,430 million candle power with a range effectiveness 60 per cent over that of the standard 150-cm searchlight.

(3) *60-cm (24 inches) Searchlight.* (a) The equipment consists of a 60-cm searchlight and an

8-kilowatt generator, and was designed for use without a sound locator against low-flying aerial targets. The searchlight is controlled manually in azimuth and elevation by a layer seated on the equipment. No separate location equipment is used. The beam can be exposed and covered by a shutter of venetian-blind type. This searchlight usually will be found in the vicinity of automatic weapons.

(b) The high-current-density arc lamp is self-regulating and is fitted in an inverted position. The light is 135 million candlepower and has a range under favorable weather conditions of 5,700 yards at a height of 5,000 feet. With beam dispersed the range is 3,500 yards.

(4) *Miscellaneous.* (a) In addition to the above, there are a few 150-cm searchlights employed on a special quadruple mount. These mounts, carrying four searchlights, are equipped with remote control gear.

(b) A few obsolete 110-cm (43 inches) searchlights, and a few French 200-cm and 240-cm (90

inches) searchlights, also may be found still in active use.

f. BARRAGE BALLOONS. Two main types of barrage balloons are employed by the Germans for added protection of vital installations against low-flying aircraft. The standard barrage balloon, which is reported to have a hydrogen gas capacity of 200 cubic meters (7,062 cubic feet), usually is flown at an altitude of 6,000 or 8,000 feet. A smaller barrage balloon, reported to have a gas capacity of 77 cubic meters (2,718 cubic feet), is capable of use at altitudes under 2,900 feet. A large type of German barrage balloon capable of being flown at altitudes of 18,000 to 20,000 feet has been reported, but this balloon has not been used extensively.

8. Heavy and Railway Artillery

Details available on German heavy and railway artillery are given in Figures 40 and 41.

Figure 70.—61.5 cm Karl Mrs. (24-inch gun), also known as "Thor".

Figure 71.—42 cm Gamma Mrs. (16.5-inch gun) being tested.

Caliber	Length of Tube	Weight in action (tons)	Maximum Range (yards)	MV (f/s)	Traverse	Elevation	Shell Type	Shell Weight (lbs.)	Remarks
21 cm K. 38	38' (55 cals)	28	36,000	2,970	16°	50°	HE	265	Box trail; mounted on platform containing recoil system. Transported in two loads.
21 cm K. 39	31' 3.6" (45 cals)	37.24	32,800	2,625	360°	45°	HE SAP AP AC	278	Platform mounted. Carriage in three parts on four-wheeled limber. Models K. 39/40 and K. 39/41 exist; performance and details similar.
24 cm H. 39	21' 11" (28 cals)	30.24	19,700	1,970	360°	70°	HE SAP	365	Platform mounted. Improved Model 24 cm H. 39/40 with similar performance exists.
24 cm K. 3		59.36	41,010	3,248			HE	331	Carriage in five sections.
24 cm K. 18	43' 1" (55 cals)	59.36	40,460	3,182	6°	56°	HE	334	Carriage in five sections. Box trail plus platform. Fires pre-rifled shell.
28 cm H.L/12	11' (12 cals)	55.33	11,370	1,148	360°		HE	770	Platform semi-static. Obsolete.
28 cm Kst. H.		40.88	12,470	1,243	360°		HE	770	Platform static. Obsolete.
35.5 cm M1		82.65	21,870	1,870			HE AC	827	Carriage in seven sections. Also fires AC fin stabilized stick bomb.
42 cm Gamma Mrs.	22' (16 cals)	15.43	15,530	1,483	45°	66°	AC	2,249	Semi-static platform. Obsolete.
54 cm Karl Mrs.	17' 8.5" (10 cals)	132	13,000? HE			70°(?)	AP AF[1] HE	3,310	S. P. tracked carriage. Known as "Thor".
61.5 cm Karl Mrs.	16' 2" (8 cals)	132	6,200? HE			70°(?)	AP HE	4,400	Carriage as for 54 cm Karl Mrs. Known as "Thor".

[1] Anti-fortification.

? Unconfirmed.

Figure 72.—German heavy guns.

	Caliber	Length of Tube	Weight in action (tons)	Range (yards)		MV (f/s)	Traverse	Elevation	Ammunition		Remarks
				Max.	Min.				Type	Weight (lbs.)	
15 cm K. (E)	5.9"	19' 8" (40 cals)	84	25,000?	12,360	2,800	360°?		HE AC	95	Top carriage traversing railway mount with outrigger.
17 cm K. (E)	6.7"	22' 4" (40 cals)	88.48	29,200?	14,770	2,870	360°?		HEBC	138	Same as above.
20.3 cm K. (E)	8"	39' 4" (59 cals)	95.2	40,000?		3,040?		45°?	HE,AP Star	247 (AP)	Car traverse. Usually fired from turntable. Carriage does not recoil.
21 cm K. 12 (E)	8.3"	135' 7"? (196 cals)	373?	126,800?	49,230	5,330?			HEBC	236	Fires pre-rifled shell.
24 cm Th. Br. K. (E)	9.4"	27' 5" (35 cals)	104.16	22,200?	10,940	2,210?	1°	25°	HEBC	328	Railway mount, car traverse.
24 cm Th. K. (E)	9.4"	31' 4" (40 cals)	105.28	29,000?	14,990	2,670?	1° 360°[1]	25°?	HEBC	328	Railway mount, car traverse. Carriage does not recoil. Usually fired from turntable.
28 cm Kz. Br. K. (E)	11"	36' 8" (40 cals)	130	32,300?	15,645	2,690?			HEBC AP	529	Same as above.
28 cm Lg. Br. K. (E)	11"	41' 3" (45 cals)	135.5	40,500?	18,380	2,820?			HEBC	626	Same as above. A 50 calibers long version, 28 cm s Br. K. (E), has estimated range of 40,500 (?) yds., a min. range of 18,380 yds. A 28 cm Bruno NK. (E) also exists.
28 cm K.5 (E)	11"	69' 8" (76 cals)	241	67,900	27,350	3,950?	1° 360°[1]	50°	HEBC	551	Shell splined instead of having driving bands. Double recoil system, turntable. Fires rocket assisted shell.
40.6 cm K. (E) Adolf	16"			49,200		2,657 3,445				2,271 1,323	
38 cm K. (E) Siegfried	15"	64' .5" (52 cals)	316?	60,900		2,690 3,445	360°[1]		HE	1,764 1,091	Projectile fitted with three driving bands. Double recoil system, turntable.
80 cm Gustav Geschütz	31.5"	94' 9" (36 cals)	1,344	51,400					AC	16,540	Also known as "Dora."

[1] On turntable.

(?) Unconfirmed.

Figure 73.—German railway guns.

Figure 74.—35.5 cm M.1. (14-inch howitzer) being emplaced.

Figure 75.—15 cm K. (E) (150-mm railway guns) in action.

Figure 76.—150-mm railway guns being emplaced.

Figure 77.—A large railway gun firing.

Figure 78.—A large railway gun.

Section V. SELF-PROPELLED ARTILLERY

I. General

a. DEVELOPMENT. German self-propelled artillery has now developed to a point where there is scarcely any artillery piece up to and including 150-mm caliber which has not appeared on at least one self-propelled chassis. Some of these have been experimental, but others have been standardized and have appeared in large numbers.

b. PRODUCTION METHODS. Self-propelled artillery has been produced in three different ways. First, there are the gun-chassis combinations which have been designed and engineered carefully to fill a particular role. These were produced in quantity by major armament factories in Germany and exist in large numbers. The 75-mm and 105-mm assault guns are examples of this type. Second, there are the standard guns fitted on standard tank chassis. Conversion has been carried out in accordance with well-engineered designs at considerable expense of time and skill. Among these are the *10.5 cm le. F. H. 18/2* on the *Gw. II* (*Wespe*) and the *15 cm s. F. H. 18/1* on the *Gw. III/IV* (*Hummel*). Third, there is a large class of self-propelled guns produced by field conversion, carried out in unit or base workshops, and requiring little skill, time, or material. An example of this is the *15 cm s. I. G. 33* mounted on the chassis of the *Pz. Kpfw. I*.

c. TACTICAL USES. German self-propelled artillery may be divided into four types from a tactical point of view, but the line of demarcation often is not clear, as many self-propelled artillery pieces have dual missions. These types are: close-support artillery, including assault guns; field and medium artillery; tank destroyers; and antiaircraft artillery.

(1) *Close-support and assault guns.* The development of close-support and assault guns was begun about 1940. Assault guns are designed for the close support of infantry, and normally consist of a gun of limited traverse on an armored self-propelled chassis carrying heavy frontal armor. They are inclined to be slower and less maneuverable than tanks but are suited particularly well for attacks on enemy infantry heavy weapons and main points of resistance.

(2) *Field and medium self-propelled artillery.* Field and medium self-propelled artillery was introduced first about the middle of 1942. Both types of howitzers (*10.5 cm. le F. H. 18* and *15 cm s. F. H. 18*) in the division artillery now may be found on self-propelled chassis.

(3) *Self-propelled antitank guns.* The first self-propelled antitank gun was the *4.7 cm Pak.* (*t*) mounted on the then (1941) obsolescent chassis of the *Pz. Kpfw. I b*. Antitank guns now form the numerically largest class of self-propelled artillery weapons.

(4) *Self-propelled antiaircraft artillery.* Self-propelled antiaircraft artillery actually was developed before any attempt was made to apply this principle to other types of weapons, but so far no serious effort has been made to mount anti-

Figure 79.—7.5 cm Stu. K.40.

aircraft guns larger than 37-mm on motor-driven carriages.

d. GUN AND CHASSIS MODIFICATIONS. Guns with the exception of assault guns, are mounted normally on their self-propelled carriages without any major alteration. Assault guns usually are fitted with electric firing devices and modified recoil systems. The chassis, however, particularly in cases where they are those of existing tanks, have undergone considerable modification. Not only have the superstructures been altered, but in some cases the engine has been moved from the rear to a central position to enable the gun crew to stand on the floor of the hull to serve the gun.

2. Close Support and Assault Guns

a. 75-MM ASSAULT GUN ON *Pz. Kpfw. III* CHASSIS (*Stu. G. III für 7.5 cm Stu. K. 40 (L/48)*). (1) *General*. The *7.5 cm Stu. K. 40 (L/48)* is the latest assault gun to be mounted on the chassis of the *Pz. Kpfw. III*. The *7.5 cm Kw. K. (L/24)* and the *7.5 cm Stu. K. 40 (L/43)*, which previously were mounted on this chassis, now have been superseded and are tending to go out of service. The *7.5 cm Kw.K. (L/24)* also has been mounted on an armored half-tracked vehicle and on the modified eight-wheeled armored car. The *7.5 cm Stu. K. 40 (L/48)* has an antitank role, as well as its anti-personnel role as a close-support weapon. It fires both high explosive and armor-piercing ammunition.

(2) *Specifications*.

General

Nomenclature ....*Stu. G. III für 7.5 cm*
                   Stu. K. 40 (L/48).
Type of carriage.......*Stu. G. III, Sd. Kfz. 142/1*.
Length over-all,
  Including gun.......22 feet 5½ inches.
  Excluding gun ......17 feet 9½ inches.
Width over-all ....9 feet 8 inches.
Height over-all ....7 feet.
Weight ....26.35 short tons.
Crew ....4 men.

Gun

Type ....*7.5 cm Stu. K. 40 (L/48)*.
Muzzle velocity ....APCBC 2,300 feet per
                     second.
Elevation ....—6° to + 17°.
Traverse ....10° each way.
Muzzle brake ....Yes.
Buffer ....Hydraulic.
Recuperator ....Hydropneumatic.

Ammunition:

Types fired.....	APCBC	HE	HC	AP 40	Smoke
Rounds carried...	22	27			5
Muzzle velocity... (feet per second)	2,300	1,800	1,475	3,248	1,771
Projectile weight. (pounds)	15	12.7	11	9	13.7

Carriage

Suspension:
  Number of bogies....6.
  Type of bogies...... Small rubber tired.
  Number of return
    rollers ....3.
  Track, length ....9 feet 2½ inches.
  Track, width ....8 feet 2½ inches.
  Width of link......1 foot 3¾ inches.

Hull armor:
  Front ....81 mm at 52°.
  Sides ....31 mm vertical.
  Rear ....51 mm at 23°.
  Belly ....20 mm.

Fighting compartment armor:
  Front ....53 to 71 mm at 15°.
  Sides ....30 mm vertical.

Power

Engine:
  Type ....Maybach HL 120 TRM.
  Cylinders ....V-12 at 60°.
  Fuel ....Gasoline.
  Location ....Rear.
  Horsepower ....295 at 3,000 rpm.
Transmission ....Synchromesh,
                  6 forward, 1 reverse.
Drive ....Front sprocket.

Performance

Trench crossing ....8 feet 6 inches.
Fording ....2 feet 9 inches.
Step ....2 feet.
Gradient ....30°.
Maximum speed ....20 miles per hour.

Armament

Type ....One *M.G. 34*.
Location ....Carried.

Remarks

Penetration of homogeneous armor at 30°, APCBC projectile:

500 yards ....84 mm.
1,000 yards ....72 mm.

b. 75-MM ASSAULT-ANTITANK GUN ON *Czech 38 (t)* TANK CHASSIS *7.5 cm le. Stu. G. 38 (t)*. (1) *General*. The gun mounted on this carriage, the *7.5 cm Pak 39 (L/48)*, has the same ballistic characteristics and is very similar to the *7.5 cm Stu. K. 40 (L/48)*. Despite the difference in nomenclature the guns are employed in exactly the

Figure 80.—7.5 cm Assault Gun (Stu. G. 7.5 cm K.).

Figure 81.—7.5 cm Pak 39 (L/48) on Pz. Jäg 38.

same way in both antitank and assault roles. The *7.5 cm Pak 39 (L/48)* is mounted low in a thick, sloping front plate. Previous guns mounted on this chassis, the *7.5 cm Pak 40* and the *7.62 cm Pak 36 (r)*, were fitted in a high superstructure which gave poor protection to the crew. In this case, however, the armor layout has been completely redesigned, and the vehicle has taken on the aspect of an assault gun. (See Paragraph 6 of this section for other vehicles on which the *7.5 cm Pak 40* and *7.62 cm Pak 36 (r)* have been mounted.)

(2) *Specifications.*

General

Nomenclature ....*7.5 cm le. Stu. G. 38 (t).*
Type of carriage.......*Pz. Jag. 38 (t).*
Length over-all:
   Including gun ....20 feet 7 inches.
   Excluding gun.......15 feet 11 inches.
Width over-all.........8 feet 7½ inches.
Height ....6 feet 10½ inches.
Weight ....17.65 tons.
Crew ....4 men.

Gun

Type ....*7.5 cm Pak 39 (L/48).*
Muzzle velocity........APCBC 2,300 feet per second.
Elevation ....—8° to + 20°.
Traverse ....10° each way.
Muzzle brake..........No.
Buffer ....Hydraulic.
Recuperator ....Hydropneumatic.

Ammunition:

Types fired.....	APCBC	HE	HC	AP 40	Smoke
Rounds carried...	41				
Muzzle velocity.. (feet per second)	2,300	1,800	1,475	3,248	1,771
Projectile weight. (pounds)	15	12.7	11	9	13.7

Carriage

Suspension:
   Number of bogies....**4.**
   Type of bogies......Christie.
   Number of return
     rollers ....1.
   Track, length........12 feet 10¾ inches.
   Track, width........6 feet 10½ inches.
   Width of link.......1 foot 1¾ inches.

Hull armor:
   Front ....60 mm at 60°.
   Sides ....20 mm at 15°.
   Rear ....20 mm at 15°.
   Belly ....10 mm horizontal.

Fighting compartment
   armor:
   Front ....60 mm at 60°.
   Sides ....20 mm at 40°.

Power

Engine:
   Type ....Czech EP4.
   Cylinders ....Six, in-line.
   Fuel ....Gasoline.
   Location ....Rear.
   Horsepower ....150.
Transmission ....Preselective
               5 forward, 1 reverse.
Drive ....Front sprocket.

Performance

Fording ....2 feet 11½ inches.
Radius of action.......124 miles.
Maximum speed.......23 miles per hour.

Armament

Type ....One *M.G. 34.*
Location ....Superstructure roof.
Ammunition carried....600 rounds.

Remarks

Penetration of homogeneous armor at 30°,
   APCBC projectile:
     500 yards........84 mm.
     1,000 yards........72 mm.

c. 75-MM ASSAULT-ANTITANK GUN ON *Pz. Kpfw. IV* CHASSIS (*Pz. Jäg. IV für 7.5 cm Pak 39 (L/48)*). (1) *General.* In this case the *7.5 cm Pak 39 (L/48)*, has been mounted on a modified *Pz. Kpfw. IV* chassis. It again is an assault gun in form, with a dual mission: antitank and anti-personnel.

(2) *Specifications.*

General

Nomenclature ....*Panzer Jäger IV für 7.5 cm Pak 39 (L/48).*
Type of carriage.......*Panzer Jäger IV.*
Length over-all:
   Excluding gun.......18 feet 2 inches.
Width over-all.........10 feet 4 inches.
Height over-all........6 feet 5 inches.
Weight ....27 short tons.
Crew ....4 men.

Gun

Type ....*7.5 cm Pak 39 (L/48).*
Muzzle velocity.......APCBC 2,300 feet per second.
Elevation ....—8° to + 22°.
Traverse ....12° left, 10° right.
Muzzle brake..........No.
Buffer ....Hydraulic.
Recuperator ....Hydropneumatic.

Ammunition:

Types fired.....	APCBC	HE	HC	AP 40	Smoke
Rounds carried...	79				
Muzzle velocity.. (feet per second)	2,300	1,800	1,475	3,248	1,771
Projectile weight. (pounds)	15	12.7	11	9	13.7

Figure 82.—7.5 cm Pak 40 on Pz. Kpfw. 38 (t) Chassis.

Figure 83.—7.5 cm Pak 40 on Pz. Kpfw. II Chassis.

Figure 84.—7.62 cm Pak 36(r) on 38(t) Chassis.

Carriage

Suspension:

Number of bogies....8.
Type of bogies......Small rubber tired.
Number of return
   rollers ....4.
Track, length.......11 feet 6 inches.
Track, width.......7 feet 11 inches.
Width of link.......1 foot 3 inches.

Hull armor:

Front ....60 mm at 45°.
Sides ....30 mm vertical.
Rear ....22 mm at 12°.
Top ....20 mm.
Belly ....12 mm.

Fighting compartment
   armor:

Front ....60 mm at 50°.
Sides ....30 mm at 30°.

Power

Engine:

Type ....Maybach HL 120 TRM.
Cylinders ....V-12 at 60°.
Fuel ....Gasoline.
Location ....Rear.
Horsepower ....295 at 3,000 rpm.
Transmission ....Manual synchromesh,
                sliding dog type, 6
                forward, 1 reverse.
Drive ....Front sprocket.

Performance

Trench crossing.......9 feet.
Fording ....3 feet.
Radius of action......160 miles.
Step ....2 feet 6 inches.
Gradient ....30°.
Maximum speed.......24 miles per hour.

Armament

Type ....Two *M.G. 42* with mounts.
Location ....Front superstructure.

Remarks

Penetration of homo-
  geneous armor at 30°,
  APCBC projectile:
     500 yards.......84 mm.
   1,000 yards.......72 mm.

d. 75-MM ASSAULT GUN ON *Pz. Kpfw. IV* CHASSIS (*Pz. Jäg. IV für 7.5 cm Stu. K. 42 (L/70)*. (1) *General.* This extremely long-barreled gun, in an assault gun mounting on the chassis of the *Pz. Kpfw. IV,* is a development from the *7.5 cm Stu. K 40 (L/48),* which has been mounted on the same chassis but is only 48 calibers long instead of 70. The long-barreled gun has the dual role of antitank and assault gun.

(2) *Specifications.*

General

Nomenclature ....*Panzer Jäger IV. für 7.5 cm
                Stu. K. 42 (L/70).*
Type of carriage.......*Panzer Jäger IV, Sd.
                Kfz. 162.*
Length over-all:
  Including gun........28 feet 2½ inches.
  Excluding gun......19 feet 9½ inches.
Width over-all........10 feet 4¾ inches.
Height over-all.......6 feet 5 inches.
Weight ....27 short tons (approxi-
                mately).
Crew ....5 men.

Gun

Type ....*7.5 cm Stu. K. 42 (L/70).*
Muzzle velocity.......APCBC 3,068 feet per
                second.

Elevation ....—5° to + 15°.
Traverse ....10° each way.
Muzzle brake.........Not encountered.
Buffer ....Hydraulic.
Recuperator ....Hydropneumatic.
Ammunition:

	APCBC	HE	AP 40
Types fired.........	APCBC	HE	AP 40
Muzzle velocity...... (feet per second)	3,068	2,300	3,674
Projectile weight..... (pounds)	15	12.7	10.7

Rounds carried.......Total of 55 rounds.

Carriage

Suspension:
   Number of bogies....8.
   Type of bogies......Small rubber tired.
   Number of return
      rollers ....4.
   Track, length.......11 feet 6 inches.
   Track, width........7 feet 11 inches.
   Width of link.......1 foot 3 inches.
Hull armor:
   Front ....80 mm at 45°.
   Sides ....30 mm vertical.
   Rear ....20 mm, 10° undercut.
   Belly ....10 to 20 mm.
Fighting compartment
   armor:
   Front ....80 mm at 50°.

Sides ....40 mm at 30°.
Top ....20 mm.

Power

Engine:
   Type ....Maybach HL 120 TRM.
   Cylinders ....V-12 at 60°.
   Fuel ....Gasoline.
   Location ....Rear.
   Horsepower ....295 at 3,000 rpm.
Transmission ....Manual, synchromesh,
              sliding dog type;
              6 forward, 1 reverse.
Drive ....Front sprocket.

Performance

Trench crossing........9 feet.
Fording ....3 feet.
Radius of action.......160 miles (estimated).
Step ....2 feet 6 inches.
Gradient ....30°.
Maximum speed.......20 miles per hour.

Armament

Type ....Machine gun on ball
              mounting.
Location ....Superstructure front.

Remarks

Penetration of homo-
   geneous armor at 30°,
   APCBC projectile:
      500 yards.......141 mm.
      1,000 yards.......121 mm.

Figure 85.—7.5 cm Stu. K.40 (L/48) on Pz. Jäg. IV.

Figure 86.—10.5 cm Stu. H. 42.

e. 105-MM ASSAULT HOWITZER ON *Pz. Kpfw. III* CHASSIS (*Stu. G. III für 10.5 cm Stu. H. 42*). (1) *General.* This close-support weapon has the usual characteristics of the assault guns mentioned in previous paragraphs, but is confined to a purely antipersonnel role and does not fire armor-piercing ammunition. Like most German howitzers, however, it is supplied with hollow-charge ammunition to give it some anti-armor performance.

(2) *Specifications.*

General

Nomenclature ....*Stu. G. III für 10.5 cm*
                         Stu. H. 42.
Type of carriage......*Stu. G. III, Sd. Kfz. 142/2.*
Length over-all:
   Including gun.......20 feet 2 inches.
   Excluding gun.......17 feet 9 inches.
Width over-all.........9 feet 8 inches.
Height over-all........6 feet 5 inches.
Weight ....25.8 short tons.
Crew ....4 men.

Gun

Type ....*10.5 cm Stu. H. 42.*
Muzzle velocity........HE 1,540 feet per
                        second.
Maximum range.......8,530 yards.
Elevation ....—6° to 20°.
Traverse ....10° each way.
Muzzle brake..........Yes.
Buffer ....Hydraulic.
Recuperator ....Hydropneumatic.

Ammunition:

Types fired..........	HE	HC	Smoke
Muzzle velocity....... (feet per second)	1,540		
Projectile weight..... (pounds)	32.6	25.9	32.4
Rounds carried......	Total of 36 rounds.		

Carriage

Torsion Bar Suspension:
  Number of bogie
    wheels ....6.
  Type of bogie wheels.Small rubber tired.
  Number of return
    rollers ....3.
  Track, length ....9 feet 2½ inches.

Track, width ....8 feet 2½ inches.
Width of link ....1 foot 3¾ inches.

Hull armor:
Front ....50 mm at 52°.
Sides ....30 mm vertical.
Rear ....50 mm.
Belly ....30 mm.

Fighting compartment
armor:
Front ....80 mm at 10°.
Sides ....30 mm vertical.

Power

Engine:
Type ....Maybach HL 120.
Cylinders ....V-12.
Fuel ....Gasoline.
Location ....Rear.
Horsepower ....295 at 3,000 rpm.
Transmission ....Synchromesh; 6 forward,
1 reverse.
Drive ....Front sprocket.

Performance

Trench crossing......8 feet 6 inches.
Fording ....2 feet 9 inches.
Radius of action......105 miles.
Step ....2 feet.
Gradient ....27°.
Maximum speed......25 miles per hour.

3. Field and Medium Self-Propelled Artillery

a. WASP (*Wespe*), *10.5 cm le. F. H.* (*18/2*) ON THE MODIFIED *Pz. Kpfw. II* CHASSIS. (1) *General.* The Wasp is the most common self-propelled version of the standard German light field howitzer, *10.5 cm le. F. H. 18.* With a maximum elevation of 42 degrees, it has only slightly less maximum range than the field-mounted version. Other modified versions of the *10.5 cm le. F. H. 18* may be found mounted on the French "Lorraine" chassis, the Hotchkiss 39 tank chassis, and the *Pz. Kpfw. IV B* chassis.

(2) *Specifications.*

General

Nomenclature ....*Wespe.*
Type of carriage.......*Gw. II (Wespe), Sd.
Kfz. 124.*

Length over-all:
Excluding gun......15 feet 9 inches.
Width over-all........7 feet 3½ inches.
Height over-all.......7 feet 10½ inches.
Weight ....12.33 tons.
Crew ....5 men.

Figure 87.—Wasp (10.5 cm le. F.H. 18/2 on Pz. Kpfw. II).

Figure 89.—15 cm Stu. H. 43 on Pz. Kpfw. IV Chassis (Brummbär).

Figure 90.—15 cm Heavy Infantry Howitzer (s.I.G. 33) on Pz. Kpfw. II Chassis.

Gun

Type ....10.5 cm le. F. H. 18/2.
Muzzle velocity.......HE 1,772 feet per second.
Maximum range.......13,500 yards.
Elevation ....—5° to + 42°.
Traverse ....10° each way.
Muzzle brake..........Yes.
Buffer ....Hydraulic.
Recuperator ....Hydropneumatic.

Ammunition :

Types fired..........	HE	HC	Smoke
Rounds carried.......	22	8	
Muzzle velocity...... (feet per second)	1,772 (supercharge)		
Projectile weight..... (pounds)	32.6	25.9	32.4

Carriage

Suspension :
  Number of bogie
    wheels ....5.
  Type of bogie wheels.large.
  Number of return
    rollers ....3.
  Track, length.......7 feet 10½ inches.
  Track, width........6 feet 2 inches.
  Width of link.......11¾ inches.

Hull armor :
  Front ....30 mm.
  Sides ....20 mm.

Fighting compartment
  armor :
  Front ....10 mm.
  Sides ....10 mm.

Power

Engine :
  Type ....Maybach HL 62 TR.
  Cylinders ....6.
  Fuel ....Gasoline.
  Horsepower ....140.
  Transmission ....Synchromesh; 6 forward,
                 one reverse.
  Drive .. ..Front sprocket.

Performance

Trench crossing........6 feet.
Fording ....3 feet.
Radius of action.......127 miles.
Step ....1 foot.
Gradient ....30°.
Maximum speed.......25 miles per hour.

b. GRIZZLY BEAR (*Brummbär*) or *Stu. Pz. 43* (*15 cm Stu. H. 43 (L/12) on Pz. Kpfw. IV* CHASSIS). (1) *General.* This is essentially a close-support weapon and mounts a very short-barreled howitzer in a high, armored superstructure. The 150-mm infantry gun (*s. I. G. 33*) performs a similar role on its various self-propelled mountings: the chassis of *Pz Kpfw. IB*, *Pz. Kpfw. II,* and the Czech *38 (t).* The Grizzly

Bear gives much better protection to the crew than any of these.

(2) *Specifications.*

General

Nomenclature ....*Brummbär* or *Stu. Pz. 43*.
Type of carriage.......*Stu. G. IV, Sd. Kfz. 166.*
Length over-all :
  Including gun.......19 feet 4 inches.
  Excluding gun......19 feet 4 inches.
Width over-all........9 feet 8 inches.
Height over-all........8 feet 2 inches.
Weight ....30.4 tons.
Crew .....　.......5 men.

Gun

Type ....*15 cm Stu. H. 43 (L/12).*
Muzzle velocity........HE 790 feet per second.
Maximum range.......HE 5,000 yards
                (approximately).
Elevation ....—8.5° to + 30°.
Traverse ....8° each way.
Muzzle brake.........No.

Ammunition :

Types fired.........	HE	HC	Smoke
Muzzle velocity...... (feet per second)	790	902	780
Projectile weight..... (pounds)	83.6	55	85.7
Rounds carried......Total of 38 rounds.			

Carriage

Suspension :
  Number of bogie
    wheels ....8.
  Type of bogie wheels.Small rubber tired.
  Number of return
    rollers ....4.
  Track, length.......11 feet 6 inches.
  Track, width........8 feet 1 inch.

Hull armor :
  Front ....45 plus 50 mm
                 armor at 15°.
  Sides ....30 mm vertical.
  Rear ....20 mm.

Fighting compartment
  armor :
  Front ....101 mm at 38°.
  Sides .... 50 mm at 18°.
  Roof .... 22 mm at 82°.

Power

Engine :
  Type ....Maybach HL 120 TRM.
  Cylinders ....V-12.
  Fuel ....Gasoline.
  Horsepower ....295 at 3,000 rpm.
  Transmission ....Synchromesh; 6 forward,
                 1 reverse.
  Drive ....Front sprocket.

Figure 91.—15 cm. s.F.H. 18 on hybrid Pz. Kpfw. III/IV Chassis (Hummel).

Performance

Trench crossing.......9 feet.
Fording ....3 feet.
Radius of action......130 miles.
Step ....2 feet 6 inches.
Gradient ....30°.
Maximum speed.......25 miles per hour.

Armament

Type ....One *M.G. 34,* ball mount.
Location ....Left of main armament.

c. BUMBLE BEE (*Hummel*) *15 cm s. F.H. 18/1*
ON *Gw. III/IV.* (1) *General.* This self-propelled medium howitzer employs a hybrid chassis
made up of the suspension of the *Pz. Kpfw. IV*
and various components of *Pz. Kpfw. III.* This
gun has the same mission in its self-propelled version as in its field version. The *15 cm S. F. H. 13,*
an older medium howitzer (obsolete on its field
mount), may be found in the same role, mounted
on the French "Lorraine" chassis.

(2) *Specifications.*

General

Nomenclature ....*Hummel.*
Type of carriage.......*Gw. III/IV, Sd. Kfz. 165.*

Length over-all:

Including gun.......21 feet 3⅞ inches.
Excluding gun.......20 feet 4⅛ inches.
Width over-all.........9 feet 8⅛ inches.
Height over-all........9 feet 7¾ inches.

Weight ....25.2 tons.
Crew ....6 men.

Gun

Type ....*15 cm s.F.H.18/1.*
Weight ....2.07 tons (barrel and
breech).
Muzzle velocity........HE 1,705 feet per second.
Maximum range.......HE charge eight 14,570
yards.
Elevation ....0° to 39°.
Traverse ....16° each way.
Muzzle brake.........No.
Buffer ....Hydraulic (under tube).
Recuperator ....Hydropneumatic (over
tube).
Ammunition:

	HE	HC	Smoke
Types fired.........	HE	HC	Smoke
Rounds carried......	12	6	
Muzzle velocity......	1,705		
Projectile weight....	95.9		86

Carriage

Suspension:

Number of bogie
wheels ....8.
Type of bogie wheels.Small rubber tired.
Number of return
rollers ....4.
Track, length........11 feet 6 inches.
Track, width........7 feet 10⅞ inches.
Width of link........1 foot 3 inches.

Hull armor:

Front ....30 mm at 22°.
Sides ....20 mm vertical.
Rear ....20 mm at 9°.

Figure 92.—15 cm Howitzer (s.F.H. 13) on French Lorraine Chassis.

Top ....17 mm horizontal.
Belly ....17 mm horizontal.

Fighting compartment
　armor:

Front ....10 mm at 37°.
Sides ....10 mm at 16°.
Top ....10 mm at 12°.

Power

Engine:

Type ....Maybach HL 120 TRM.
Cylinders ....V-12.
Fuel ....Gasoline.
Location ....Center.
Horsepower ....295 at 3,000 rpm.
Transmission ....Synchromesh; 6 forward,
　　　　　　　　　1 reverse.
Drive ....Front sprocket.

Performance

Trench crossing ....9 feet.
Fording ....2 feet 7½ inches.
Radius of action ....160 miles.
Step ....2 feet 6 inches.
Gradient ....30°.
Maximum speed .....25 miles per hour.

4. Tank Destroyers

a. RHINOCEROS (*Nashorn*), FORMERLY HOR-
NET (*Hornisse*), *8.8 cm Pak 43/1* ON THE *Gw.
III/IV*. (1) *General*. This is one of the versions of the *8.8 cm Pak 43,* the latest 88-mm
antitank gun, mounted on the hybrid chassis of
the *Pz. Kpfw. III* and *IV*. The vehicle's sil-
houette is very high and the armor protection
given to the crew by the thin-skinned superstructure is very poor. The gun, however, is able to
engage tanks at very long ranges.

(2) *Specifications.*

General

Nomenclature ....*Nashorn*.
Type of carriage ......*Gw. III/IV, Sd. Kfz. 164.*

Length over-all:

Including gun ....27 feet 8¼ inches.
Excluding gun ......20 feet 4⅛ inches.
Width over-all ....9 feet 8⅛ inches.
Height over-all ....9 feet 7¾ inches.
Weight ....27 tons.
Crew ....5 men.

Gun

Type ....*8.8 cm Pak 43/1 (L/71)*.
Muzzle velocity ....APCBC 3,280 feet per
　　　　　　　　　second.
Elevation ....—5° to + 20°.
Traverse ....15° each way.
Muzzle brake ....Yes.
Buffer ....Hydraulic.
Recuperator ....Hydropneumatic.

Ammunition:

Types fired ....APCBC HE　HC　AP 40
Muzzle velocity ....3,280　2,400　1,968　3,705
　(feet per second)
Projectile weight .....22.4　20.7　16.8　16
　(pounds)
Rounds carried ....Total of 48 rounds.

Carriage

Suspension:

Number of bogies....8.
Type of bogies ......Small rubber tired.
Number of return
　rollers ....4.
Track, length ....11 feet 6 inches.
Track, width ....7 feet 11 inches.
Width of link ....1 foot 3 inches.

Hull armor:

Front ....30 mm at 12°.
Sides ....20 mm vertical.
Rear ....22 mm.
Top ....17 mm.
Belly ....17 mm.

Fighting compartment
　armor:

Front ....10 mm at 30°.
Sides ....10 mm at 16°.

Power

Engine:

Type ....HL 120 TRM.
Cylinders ....V-12.
Fuel ....Gasoline.
Location ....Center.
Horsepower ....295 at 3,000 rpm.
Transmission ....Maybach synchromesh;
　　　　　　　　　6 forward, 1 reverse.
Drive ....Front sprocket.

Performance

Trench crossing ....9 feet.
Fording ....2 feet 7½ inches.
Radius of action ......160 miles.
Step ....2 feet 6 inches.
Gradient ....30°.
Maximum speed ....25 miles per hour.

Remarks

Penetration of homogeneous armor at 30°,
APCBC projectile:
500 yards ....184 mm.
1,000 yards ....169 mm.

b. ELEPHANT (*Elefant*), FORMERLY FERDI-
NAND, *8.8 cm Stu. K. 43* OR *Pak 43/2* ON THE
Panzer Jäger Tiger P. (1) *General*. This is another version of the latest model, long 88-mm
antitank gun. The gun is mounted on the Tiger
P chassis, a discarded early version of the Tiger,
incorporating twin gasoline generating units with
direct electric drive. Although protected by heavy
armor, this vehicle has been relatively unsuccess-

Figure 93.—8.8 cm Pak 43/1 on Pz Jäg. III/IV (Rhinoceros).

Figure 94.—8.8 cm Stu. K.43/1 on Tiger P Chassis (Elephant).

ful because it is ponderous and difficult to maneuver.

(2) *Specifications.*

General

Nomenclature ....*Elefant.*
Type of carriage ......*Pz. Jäg. Tiger P, Sd. Kfz. 184.*
Length over-all:
  Including gun ......26 feet 10 inches.
  Excluding gun ......23 feet 4 inches.
Width over-all ....11 feet 3 inches.
Height over-all ....9 feet 10 inches.
Weight ....73 short tons.
Crew ....6 men.

Gun

Type ....*8.8 cm Stu. K. 43 (L/71) or Pak 43/2.*
Muzzle velocity ....APCBC 3,280 feet per second.
Elevation ....—6° to + 25°
Traverse ....12° each way.
Muzzle brake ....Fitted.

Buffer ....Hydraulic.
Recuperator ....Hydropneumatic.

Ammunition:

Types fired	APCBC	HE	HC	AP 40
Rounds carried 20	70			
Muzzle velocity 3,280	2,460	1,968	3,705	
(feet per second)				
Projectile weight ...22.4	20.7	16.8	16	
(pounds)				

Carriage

Suspension:

Number of bogie
  wheels ....6, in pairs.
Type of bogie wheels. Large.
Number of return
  rollers ....None.

Hull armor:

Front ....200 mm at 32°.
Sides ....80 mm vertical.
Rear ....80 mm vertical.
Top ....30 mm horizontal.
Belly ....20 mm horizontal.

Fighting compartment
  armor:

Front ....170 mm at 30°.
Sides ....90 mm at 30°.

Power

Engines:

Type ....Two Maybach HL 120
                TRMs.
Location ....Center.
Horsepower ....590.
Transmission ....Electric drive.
Drive ....Rear sprocket.

Performance

Fording ....2 feet 4 inches.
Radius of action ......62 miles.
Gradient ....30°.
Maximum speed ......12.5 miles per hour.

Remarks

Penetration of homogeneous armor at 30°,
APCBC projectile:

500 yards ....184 mm.
1,000 yards ....169 mm.

c. *Jagdpanther, 8.8 cm Pak 43/3* OR *43/4*
(L/71) ON THE PANTHER CHASSIS. (1) *General*. This tank destroyer is intended for engaging armored targets at long ranges from stationary positions. A single, heavy, sloping plate protects the front of both hull and superstructure. The gun is mounted centrally in this plate, giving the vehicle the appearance of an assault gun, with the gun rather high.

(2) *Specifications*.

General

Nomenclature ....*Jagdpanther*.

Type of carriage ......*Pz. Jäg. Panther, Sd. Kfz. 173*.

Length over-all:

Including gun ....32 feet 4 inches.
Excluding gun ......22 feet 9 inches.
Width over-all ....10 feet 9 inches.
Height over-all ....8 feet 3 inches.
Weight ....51.25 short tons.
Crew ....5 men.

Gun

Type ....*8.8 cm Pak 43/3* or *43/4 (L/71)*.
Muzzle velocity ....APCBC 3,280 feet per second.
Elevation ....—8° to + 14°.
Traverse ....13° each way.
Muzzle brake ....Yes.
Buffer ....Hydraulic.
Recuperator ....Hydropneumatic.

Ammunition:

Types fired	APCBC	HE	HC	AP 40
Rounds carried 28	29			
Muzzle velocity 3,280	2,460	1,968	3,705	
(feet per second)				
Projectile weight.....22.4	20.7	16.8	16	
(pounds)				

Carriage

Suspension:

Number of bogies...8.
Type of bogies ......Double.
Number of return
  rollers ....1.
Track, length ....13 feet 5½ inches.
Track, width ....8 feet 7½ inches.
Width of link ....2 feet 2 inches.

Hull armor:

Front ....80 mm at 55°.
Sides ....30 mm vertical.
Rear ....40 mm at 30°.

Fighting compartment
  armor:

Front ....80 mm at 55°.
Sides ....45 mm at 30°.

Power

Engine:

Type ....Maybach HL 230 P30.
Cylinders ....V-12.
Fuel ....Gasoline.
Location ....Rear.
Horsepower ....690 at 3,000 rpm.
Transmission ....Synchromesh; 7 forward,
                1 reverse.
Drive ....Front sprocket.

Performance

Trench crossing ......8 feet.
Fording ....5 feet 1 inch.
Radius of action ......87 miles.
Step ....3 feet.
Gradient ....30°.

Figure 95.—8.8 cm Pak 43/3 on Panther Chassis (Jagdpanther).

Armament

Type ....One *M.G. 34,* ball mount.
Location ....Glacis plate.

Remarks

Penetration of homogeneous armor at 30°,
APCBC projectile:
   500 yards ....184 mm.
   1,000 yards ....169 mm.

d. *Jagdtiger, 12.8 cm Pak 44 (L/55)* ON THE
Pz. Jäg. Tiger MODEL B. (1) *General.* The
12.8 cm Pak 44 (L/55) is the largest caliber antitank gun the Germans have produced so far. It
is only found in a self-propelled version, mounted
on the *Pz. Jäg Tiger Model B,* which is an adaptation of the King Tiger chassis. The superstructure in which the gun is mounted, is very heavily
armored. The *Jagdtiger* supersedes the *12.8 cm
K. 40* mounted on a hybrid chassis, which was
employed in Russia and will probably not be encountered in the future.

(2) *Specifications.*

General

Nomenclature ....*Jagdtiger.*
Type of carriage ......*Pz. Jäg. Tiger* Model B,
                 Sd. Kfz. 186.
Length over-all:
   Including gun ....32 feet 2 inches.
   Excluding gun ......23 feet 10 inches.
Width over-all ....11 feet 9½ inches.
Height over-all ....9 feet 3 inches.
Weight ....77.2 short tons.
Crew ....6 men.

Gun

Type ....*12.8 cm Pak 44 (L/55).*
Muzzle velocity ....APCBC 3,020 feet per
                 second.
Muzzle brake ....Yes.

Ammunition:
   Types fired ....APC APCBC HE
   Muzzle velocity 2,890 3,020 2,886
     (feet per second)
   Projectile weight 58.1   62.5   57
     (pounds)
   Rounds carried ......Total of 40 rounds.

Carriage

Torsion Bar Suspen-
   sion:
   Number of bogie
     wheels ....9.
   Type of bogie wheels.Twin.
   Number of return
     rollers ....None.
   Track, length ....13 feet 4 inches.
   Track, width ....9 feet, 2 inches.
   Width of link ....2 feet 8½ inches.
Hull armor:
   Front ....150 mm at 50°.
   Sides ....80 mm vertical.
   Rear ....80 mm at 30°.
Fighting compartment
   armor:
   Front ....250 mm at 15°.
   Sides ....80 mm at 25°.
   Rear ....80 mm at 10°.

Power

Engine:
   Type ....Maybach HL 230 P30.
   Cylinders ....V-12.
   Fuel ....Gasoline.
   Location ....Rear.
   Horsepower ....595 at 2,600 rpm.
Transmission ....Preselector, hydraulic
               operation; 8 forward,
               4 reverse.
Drive ....Front sprocket.

Figure 96.—12.8 cm K.40 on Hybrid Chassis (Pz. Kpfw. III, IV, VI).

Performance

Fording ....5 feet 9 inches.
Radius of action ......106 miles.
Gradient ....35°.
Maximum speed ......26 miles per hour.

Armament

Mounted ....One *M.G.34.*
Carried ....One *M.G.42.*

Remarks

Penetration of homogeneous armor at 30°:

	APC	APCBC
500 yards	172 mm	212 mm.
1,000 yards	148 mm	200 mm.

5. Self-Propelled Antiaircraft Guns

a. GENERAL. The growth of Allied air power and the decline of the *Luftwaffe* have forced the Germans to devise self-propelled antiaircraft guns to defend transport columns from low-level air attack.

b. *Flakpanzer.* Light antiaircraft guns of 20-mm or 37-mm caliber mounted on half-tracked vehicles have been in existence for some time, but the appearance of the so-called *Flakpanzer* or antiaircraft tanks is a new development. These consist essentially of a tank with turret removed and replaced by a light antiaircraft gun protected by an armored shield. The following types of *Flakpanzer* have been identified so far:

(1) The *2 cm Flak 38* mounted on the chassis of the Czech *38 (t)* tank.

(2) The *3.7 cm Flak 43* mounted on the *Pz. Kpfw. IV* chassis.

(3) The *2 cm Flakvierling 38* (four-barreled antiaircraft automatic cannon) mounted on the *Pz. Kpfw. IV* chassis with a thin eight-sided shield.

c. HALF-TRACK CARRIAGES. The 15-mm or 20-mm *M. G. 151,* a standard aircraft machine gun, has been recently mounted on the 3-ton, lightly armored, half-tracked vehicle, *Sd. Kfz. 251/21,* in a triple mounting with maximum elevation of 49°. The maximum cyclic rate of fire for the three guns is 2,100 rounds per minute. (Details of antiaircraft weapons are given in Section IV.)

6. List of Self-Propelled Artillery

a. CLOSE SUPPORT AND ASSAULT SELF-PROPELLED ARTILLERY.

Gun	Carriage
7.5 cm Kw.K. (L/24)	Pz. Kpfw. III chassis (Sd. Kfz. 142)
7.5 cm Kw.K. (L/24)	Half-track (Sd. Kfz. 251/90)
7.5 cm Kw.K. (L/24)	8-wheeled armoured car (Sd. Kfz. 233)
7.5 cm Kw.K. (L/24)	Half-track (Sd. Kfz. 10)
7.5 cm Stu.K. 40 (L/43)	Pz. Kpfw. III chassis (Sd. Kfz. 142)
7.5 cm Stu.K. 40 (L/48)	Pz. Kpfw. III chassis (Sd. Kfz. 142)
7.5 cm Stu.K. 40 (L/48)	Pz. Kpfw. IV chassis
7.5 cm Stu.K. 42 (L/70)	Pz. Kpfw. IV chassis (Sd. Kfz. 162)

b. FIELD AND MEDIUM SELF-PROPELLED ARTILLERY.

Gun	Carriage
10.5 cm Stu.H. 42 (L/28)	Pz. Kpfw III chassis (Sd. Kfz. 142)
15 cm s.I.G. 33 (L/12)	Pz. Kpfw. I B chassis (Sd. Kfz. 101)
15 cm s.I.G. 33 (L/12)	Pz. Kpfw. II chassis (Sd. Kfz. 121)
15 cm s.I.G. 33/1 (L/12)	Gw. 38 (Sd. Kfz. 138/1)
15 cm Stu. H. 43 (L/12)	Pz. Kpfw. IV chassis (Sd. Kfz. 166)
10.5 cm le.F.H. 18/2	Gw. II (Sd. Kfz. 124)
10.5 cm le.F.H. 18/4	Lorraine (French) chassis
10.5 cm le.F.H. 18	Pz. Kpfw. H. 39 chassis
10.5 cm le.F.H. 18/1	Pz. Kpfw. IV B chassis
15 cm s.F.H. 13	Lorraine (French) chassis
15 cm s.F.H. 18/1	Gw. III/IV (Sd. Kfz. 165)

c. TANK DESTROYERS.

Gun	Carriage
2.8 cm Pak 41*	Half-track (Sd. Kfz. 250)
3.7 cm Pak*	Half-track (Sd. Kfz. 251)
3.7 cm Pak*	Renault "Chenillette" (French) armored carrier
4.7 cm Pak (t)*	Pz. Kpfw. I chassis
4.7 cm Pak (t)*	Pz. Jäg. I
4.7 cm Pak (t)*	Renault R.35 (French) tank chassis
5 cm Kw.K. 39/1**	8-wheeled armored car (Sd. Kfz. 234)
7.5 cm Pak 40	Pz. Kpfw. 38 (t) chassis
7.5 cm Pak 40/3	Pz. Jäg 38 (Sd. Kfz.138)

Gun	Carriage
7.5 cm Pak 39 L/48	Pz. Jäg 38 (t)
7.5 cm Pak 40	Pz. Kpfw. II chassis
7.5 cm Pak 40	Pz. Jäg. II (Sd. Kfz. 131)
7.5 cm Pak 40	Pz. Jäg. II (Ausf. D/E) (Sd. Kfz. 132)
7.5 cm Kw.K.*	Half-track (Sd. Kfz. 251/9)
7.5 cm Pak 40/1	Pz. Jäg. Lr. S. (Sd. Kfz. 135)
7.5 cm Pak 40	Truck
7.5 cm Pak 40	Schneider Kegresse Armored Car chassis (modified)
7.5 cm Pak 40	Hotchkiss H. 39 tank chassis
7.5 cm Pak 39 (L/48)	Panzerjäger IV (Sd. Kfz. 162)
7.62 cm Pak 36 (r)*	Half-track (Sd. Kfz. 6)
7.62 cm Pak 36 (r)	Pz. Kpfw. 38 (t) chassis
7.62 cm Pak 36 (r)	Pz. Jäg. 38 (Sd. Kfz. 139)
7.62 cm Pak 36 (r)	Pz. Kpfw. II chassis
7.62 cm Pak 36 (r)	Pz. Jäg. II (Sd. Kfz. 131)
7.62 cm Pak 36 (r)	Pz. Jäg. II Ausf. D/E (Sd. Kfz. 132)
7.62 cm F.K. (r)	Pz. Jäg. II Ausf. D/E (Sd. Kfz. 132)
8.8 cm Pak 43/1 (L/71)	Pz. Jäg. III/IV (Sd. Kfz. 164)
8.8 cm Pak 43/3 or Pak 43/4	Pz. Kpfw. Panther chassis (Sd. Kfz. 173)
8.8 cm Stu.K. 43/1 (L/71) or Pak 43/2 (L/71)	Tiger (P) chassis (Sd. Kfz. 182)
12.8 cm K.40	Hybrid chassis
12.8 cm Pak 44 (L/55)	Tiger II chassis

d. SELF-PROPELLED ANTIAIRCRAFT GUNS.

Gun	Carriage
2 cm Flak 30 or 38*	Half-track (Sd. Kfz. 10)
2 cm Flak 38*	Half-track (Sd. Kfz. 70)
2 cm Flakvierling 38*	Half-track (Sd. Kfz. 7)
3.7 cm Flak 18 or 36*	Half-track (Sd. Kfz. 6)
5 cm Flak 41*	
M.G. 151/15 or M.G. 151/20 Flakdrilling	Half-track (Sd. Kfz. 251 21) (3-ton half-track)
2 cm Flak 38	Pz. Kpfw. 38 (t) chassis
3.7 cm Flak 43	Pz. Kpfw. IV chassis
2 cm Flakvierling 38	Pz. Kpfw. IV chassis

* Obsolete
** See "Armored Cars" for description

Figure 97.—Pz. Kpfw..I, Model A.

(2) *Specifications.*

Specification Number .... *Sd. Kfz.** 101.
(Commander's Model .... *Sd. Kfz.* 265.)

		Model		
	A	*B*	*C*	*Commander's*
Weight in action (tons)	5.88	6.44	8.96	6.44
Crew	2 men	2 men		3 men
Armor, Hull front	13 mm	13 mm		32 mm
Hull sides	15 mm	15 mm	25 mm	15 mm
Front glacis plate	8 mm	8 mm		20 mm
Superstructure				
Sides	13 mm	13 mm		15 mm
Turret front	15 mm	15 mm	50 mm	
Turret sides·	13 mm	13 mm		
Armament	Two	Two	One	One
	M.G. 13	*M.G. 13*	AT Gun	*M.G. 34*
			One *M.G.*	
Dimensions				
Length (feet)	13	14		14
Width (feet)	6.75	6.75		6.75
Height (feet)	5.58	5.73		6.41
Clearance (inches)	9.75	10		10
Road speed (miles per hour)	12	15-16		15-16
Range on roads (miles)	112	87		87

**Sd. Kfz.* is the German abbreviation for *Sonderkraftfahrzeug,* meaning special motor vehicle.

Section VI. ARMORED VEHICLES

I. General

The story of German armored vehicle development is concerned principally with tanks, which have undergone considerable change since the beginning of the war. German tanks have shown, in the course of 5 years of war, a gradual change from the *Blitzkrieg* concept of battle to greater emphasis on defensive, or at least offensive-defensive, operations for which the latest German tank, the King Tiger, heavily armed and armored but relatively slow and unmaneuverable, is suitable.

German tank development began in 1934, ostensibly at the same time as the rest of the rearmament program, but there is no doubt that considerable thought and experimentation had been devoted to the subject before then. By 1939 the Germans had evolved four types of tanks: the *Pz. Kpfw.*[1] *I, II, III,* and *IV,* with which the *Blitzkrieg* campaigns were conducted. There is evidence that larger tanks were being developed in 1939, and specimens of what are assumed to have been a *Pz. Kpfw. V* and a *Pz. Kpfw. VI* in an experimental stage were employed in the invasion of Norway. These, however, must have proved unsatisfactory, since they were dropped, and the present *Pz. Kpfw. V* (Panther) and *Pz. Kpfw. VI* (Tiger) have no connection with them.

Meanwhile, the *Pz. Kpfw. I* and *II* gradually became obsolescent, first being relegated to reconnaissance roles and then finally disappearing in 1943 from the Table of Equipment of the *Panzer* regiment. The heavier tanks, *Pz. Kpfw. III* and *IV,* which had proven satisfactory under fire, were modified to meet new conditions by thicker armor and more effective guns.

In 1942, the *Pz. Kpfw. VI,* or Tiger, appeared in Russia, and later in Africa. The Tiger was designed in the direct German tradition, and simply was armed more heavily and armored more thickly than its predecessors. It appeared out of its proper order in the line of succession, for the *Pz. Kpfw. V,* or Panther, did not appear until nearly a year later. The Panther was somewhat of a surprise, since it marked a departure from the conventional lines of German design, and in the arrangement of its armor showed strong signs of Russian influence. Its great success in combat undoubtedly gave rise to the decision to redesign the Tiger, which to some extent had fallen short of expectations. The new version is the *Koenigstiger* or King Tiger.

2. Obsolete Tanks

a. GENERAL. The *Pz. Kpfw. I, Pz. Kpfw. II,* and *Pz. Kpfw. III,* although obsolete, are discussed here since they still may be met occasionally in the field.

b. LIGHT TANK (*Pz. Kpfw. I*). (1) *General.* This was the first tank to be standardized by the Germans, and the first ones were produced in 1934. Three models (A, B, and C) and a commander's version (based on model B) have been identified, but model C never has been encountered in action. The hull of the *Pz. Kpfw. I* was **used as a self-propelled mount** for several types of artillery weapons, but it no longer will be met even in this role. [(2) *Specifications* on page 76.]

c. LIGHT TANK (*Pz. Kpfw. II*). (1) *General.* This tank is manned by three men: a commander, who acts as the gunner; a radio operator; and a driver. A large number of models of this tank were produced before it became obsolete. In a very much modified form it has reappeared as the *Luchs* (Lynx) reconnaissance tank in Western Europe. The original experimental models of *Pz. Kpfw. II* were produced between 1934 and 1936; it finally was abandoned as a fighting vehicle in 1943. A flame-throwing version, *Pz. Kpfw. II (F),* also has become obsolete and probably will not be met again. Model F, not the flame-thrower tank, was the latest model encountered. The modified hull of the *Pz. Kpfw. II* is still in use as a self-propelled gun carriage, notably in the case of the *15 cm s. I.G. 33* and the *10 cm le. F.H. 18.*

(2) *Specifications.*

	Model F	Model L (Lynx)
Specification number	*Sd. Kfz. 121*	*Sd. Kfz. 123.*
Weight in action (tons)	11.5	13.2
Crew	3 men	3 men
Armor, Hull front	35 mm	30 mm
Hull sides	20 mm	20 mm
Front glacis plate	20 mm	20 mm
Superstructure		
Front	30 mm	30 mm
Sides	20 mm	20 mm
Turret front	35 mm	30 mm
Turret sides	15 mm	20 mm
Armament (coaxially mounted in turret)	One *2 cm Kw.K.30*	One *2 cm Kw.K.18*
	One *M.G. 34*	One *M.G.34*

---

[1] *Pz. Kpfw.* is the German abbreviation for *Panzerkampfwagen,* meaning armored fighting vehicle or tank.

Figure 98.—Pz. Kpfw. II.

Dimensions, Length	
(feet) 14.75	14.83
Width (feet) 7.33	8.25
Height (feet) 6.48	6.58
Ground clearance	
(inches) 13	16 (approximate)
Engine 6-cylinder	6-cylinder
In-line	In-line
133 HP	176 HP
Gasoline	Gasoline
Road speed (miles	
per hour) 15	40
Range on roads	
(miles) 118	155

Suspension: Model F: 5 bogie wheels each side; quarter-elliptic leaf springing. Front drive sprocket, rear idler.

Model L: 5 axles, torsion bar suspension; interleaved bogie wheels. Front drive sprocket, rear idler.

d. MEDIUM TANK (*Pz. Kpfw. III*). (1) *General*. This tank has appeared in many models but has retained basic characteristics throughout. The latest models to appear are armed with the long-barreled *5 cm Kw.K. 39 (L/60)*, which in 1942 displaced the shorter *5 cm Kw.K. (L/42)*. The original main armament, discarded late in 1940,

was a 37-mm gun. The *Pz. Kpfw. III* now is obsolete and rarely encountered. The excellent hull and suspension have been utilized as the carriage for self-propelled guns, and it is in this form that the vehicle remains in production. The *Pz. Kpfw. III* has been encountered armed with the short *7.5 cm Kw.K.* (the original armament of the *Pz. Kpfw. IV*), and also as a commander's vehicle, as a flame-throwing tank, as a wrecker tank, as an armored ammunition carrier, and as an armored observation post.

(2) *Specifications.*

Models L and M
Specification number ...*Sd. Kfz. 141/1.*
Weight in action......24.6 tons (approximately).
Crew ....5 men.
Armor, Front nose plate.50 mm.
  Glacis plate ....25 mm.
  Driver's front plate..50 and 20 mm spaced armor.
  Hull sides ....30 mm.
  Rear plates ....50 mm.
  Turret front ....57 mm.
  Turret sides ....10 mm.
Armament (coaxially mounted in turret)...One *5 cm Kw.K. 39* with one *M.G.34*.

Figure 99.—Pz. Kpfw. III.

In hull ....One *M.G.34.*

Dimensions, Length....17 feet 8 inches.
 Width .... 9 feet 9 inches.
 Height .... 8 feet 3 inches.
 Gun overhang....... 1 foot 3 inches.
                    (approximately).
 Ground clearance ... 1 foot 2 inches.

Performance, Maximum
 speed ....35 miles per hour
                    (approximately).
 Road speed ....22 miles per hour.
 Cross-country speed..10 to 15 miles per hour.
 Range on roads .....102 miles.
 Range cross-country..59 miles.
 Trench crossing .....8 feet 6 inches.
 Step ....2 feet.
 Gradient ....30°.
 Fording ....2 feet 9 inches.

Engine, Type ....Maybach HL 120 TRM.
 Fuel ....Gasoline.
 BHP ....296 HP at 3,000 rpm.

Transmission: SSG77 Maybach synchromesh
 gear box, sliding dog type, manual control.
 Six forward speeds, one reverse.

Suspension: Six small rubber-tired bogie wheels
 on each side. Torsion-bar suspension.

3. Medium Tanks

a. *Pz. Kpfw. IV.* (1) *General.* Of the four tank types with which the Germans started the war, only the *Pz. Kpfw. IV* survives in service, although its role has been changed and it now carries a main armament which resembles the original gun only in caliber. It was armed originally with a short-barreled 75-mm gun (*7.5 cm Kw.K. (L/24)*) and a machine gun mounted coaxially in the turret. In later models a hull machine gun was added. With this short, low-velocity gun the tank was primarily a close-support weapon. In 1942 it was re-armed with a long-barreled, high-velocity gun, the *7.5 cm Kw.K. 40 (L/43),* and thus changed its role from a close-support vehicle to a fighting tank and displaced the *Pz. Kpfw. III* as the main armament of the *Panzer* regiment. At the present time the *Pz. Kpfw. IV* is only a stop-gap for the Panther. If enough Panther tanks become available, the disappearance of the *Pz. Kpfw. IV* may be expected.

The latest version of this tank to appear is the Model H, which differs from the Model G, of which details are given, only in its 75-mm gun being 48 calibers long instead of 43. There is no change in the ballistic characteristics.

This tank also has appeared in a commander's model, as an observation-post tank, as an ammunition tank, and as an armored antiaircraft vehicle. The hull and suspension also have been employed for self-propelled guns.

(2) *Specifications.*

 Model G
Specification number ..*Sd. Kfz. 161/1.*
                    (Model H is
                    Sd. Kfz. 161/2).
 Weight in action ......26 tons.
 Crew .... 5 men.

Figure 100.—Pz. Kpfw. IV, Model F2, (Sd. Kfz. 161).

Armor, Front nose plate . . 60 mm.
  Front glacis plate . . . 25 mm.
  Driver's front plate . . 60 mm.
  Hull sides . . . . 30 mm.
  Hull rear . . . . 20 mm.
  Turret front . . . . 40 mm.
  Turret sides . . . . 30 mm.

Armament (coaxially
  mounted in turret) . . . One *7.5 cm Kw.K.40*
                (L/43) and one *M.G.34.*
  In hull . . . . One *M.G.34.*

Dimensions, Length . . . 19 feet 4 inches.
  (excluding gun)
  Width . . . . 9 feet 7 inches.
  Height . . . . 8 feet 6 inches.
  Gun overhang . . . . . . 1 foot 6 inches.
               (In model H, 2 feet
               9 inches).
  Ground clearance . . . 1 foot 3 inches.

Performance:
  Trench crossing . . . . . 9 feet.
  Step . . . . 2 feet 6 inches.
  Gradient . . . . 30°.
  Fording . . . . 3 feet.
  Road speed . . . . 20 miles per hour.
  Cross-country speed . . 10 to 15 miles per hour
  Maximum speed . . . . . 25 miles per hour.
  Range on roads . . . . . 130 miles.
  Range cross country . . 80 miles.

Engine, Type . . . . Maybach HL 120 TRM.
  Cylinders . . . . V-12 at 60°
  Fuel . . . . Gasoline.
  Fuel capacity . . . . 126 gallons.
  Fuel consumption
  (per 100 miles)
    On roads . . . . 93.6 gallons.
    Cross-country . . . . . 153 gallons.
  BHP . . . . 295 HP at 3,000 rpm.

Capacity . . . . 11.9 liters
                (725.9 cubic inches).

Transmission: Manual synchromesh, sliding-dog
  type; six forward speeds, one reverse.

Steering: Epicyclic clutch brake mechanism.

Suspension: Four bogie assemblies, each carrying two rubber-tired bogie wheels. Quarter-
  elliptic springing.

4. Heavy Tanks

a. Pz. Kpfw. PANTHER. (1) *General.* In this
tank, probably the most successful they have produced, the Germans have departed from their cus-
tomary lines and sought inspiration in the design
of the Russian *T34.* The tank weighs about 50
short tons, and the effectiveness of its armor is
enhanced by the fact that most of the plates are
sloping. It has powerful armament, and has a
high-powered engine which gives it a maximum
speed of about 30 miles per hour. Internally the
Panther is arranged in the standard German manner, with the driver's compartment in front, the
fighting compartment in the center section, and
the engine at the rear.

The Panther's design employs the double torsion-bar suspension. There are eight double, interleaved, large Christie-type bogie wheels. Each set
of bogie wheels is mounted on a radius arm on
the projecting end of a torsion bar which is
coupled in series to a second one lying parallel to
it. This ingenious device has the effect of doubling
the length of the torsion bars.

Figure 101.—Pz. Kpfw. "Panther".

Figure 102.—Pz. Kpfw. "Tiger".

The Panther first was met in action on the Russian front in the summer of 1943. Originally designated *Pz. Kpfw. V*, its nickname, Panther, was adopted as its official nomenclature in February 1944. The latest version to appear is the Model G. The principal reasons for the success of the Panther are its relatively high speed, maneuverability, dangerous armament, and good protection.

Variants of the Panther tank which have been identified are the commander's version, the wrecker tank (*Bergepanther*), and the self-propelled gun *Jagdpanther*, which consists of the *8.8 cm Pak 43/3* or *4* on the Panther chassis.

(2) *Specifications.*

Model G

Specification number ...*Sd. Kfz.171.*
Weight in action ......50 short tons
　　　　　　　　　　(approximately).
Crew ....5 men.
Armor,
　Front glacis plate ....80 mm at 55°.*
　Front nose plate .....60 mm at 35°.
　Rear plate ....40 mm at 30°.
　　　　　　　　　　(undercut)
　Hull sides ....40 mm vertical.
　Superstructure sides..50 mm at 30°.
　Turret front ....110 mm at 10°.
　Turret sides ....45 mm at 25°.
　Turret rear ....45 mm at 28°.
Armament (coaxially
　mounted in turret) .One *7.5 cm Kw.K.42
　　　　　　　　　　(L/70)* and one *M.G.34.*
　In hull ....One *M.G. 34.*

* All angle measurements given are from vertical.

Dimensions, Length ...21 feet 11½ inches.
　(excluding gun)
　Width ....10 feet 9½ inches.
　Height ....9 feet 4 inches.
　Gun overhang ....6 feet 5 inches.
　Ground clearance ....1 foot 7½ inches.

Performance,
　Trench crossing .....10 feet.
　Step ....3 feet.
　Gradient ....30°.
　Fording ....6 feet (Some sub-
　　　　　　　　　　mersible to 13 feet).
　Road speed ....20 miles per hour.
　Cross-country speed..15 miles per hour.
　Maximum speed .....35 miles per hour.
　Range on roads ....124 miles.
　Range cross-country..62 miles.

Engine, Type ....Maybach HL 230 P30.
　Cylinders V-12
　Fuel ....Gasoline.
　Fuel capacity ......193 gallons.
　Fuel consumption (per
　　100 miles)
　　　On roads ......149 gallons.
　　　Cross-country ...298 gallons.
　BHP ....690 HP at 3,000 rpm.
　Capacity ....23 liters (1,403 cubic
　　　　　　　　　　inches).

Transmission: Maybach synchromesh sliding-dog type; manually operated, giving seven forward speeds, one reverse.

Suspension: Eight load-carrying axles each carrying two large disced rubber-tired bogie wheels, interleaved. Twin torsion-bar suspension.

b. *Pz. Kpfw.* TIGER. (1) *General.* This tank,

Figure 103.—Pz. Kpfw. "Tiger", Model E (Sd. Kfz. 181).

originally the *Pz. Kpfw. VI,* first was encountered by the Russians in the last half of 1942, and by the Western Allies in Tunisia early in 1943. It's colloquial name, Tiger, was adopted officially in February 1944. The current version is Model E.

Unlike the Panther, the Tiger is designed on familiar German lines, but all the dimensions are increased. The main armament is the *8.8 cm Kw.K. 36,* which is essentially the *8.8 cm Flak 36* adapted for turret mounting. The mounting of such a heavy gun has raised considerable problems of rigidity, and consequently the hull is constructed of large plates entirely welded together. The superstructure is made up in one unit, and welded to the hull. The turrent wall is made from a single large piece of armor, 82 mm thick, bent into a horseshoe shape. Further, all the armor plates are interlocked, in addition to being welded. The armor of the Tiger, at the time of its appearance, was the thickest ever to be fitted on any German tank, the front vertical plate being 102 mm thick and the hull sides 62 mm.

The suspension, which employs interleaved, Christie-type bogie wheels with a very wide track, is reasonably simple and is an effective solution of the suspension problem for such a large and heavy vehicle.

The Tiger engine requires very skilled driving and maintenance to get the best performance, and in the hands of insufficiently trained crews mechanical troubles are apt to appear. This characteristic has been the tank's principal disadvantage.

(2) *Specifications.*

Model E

Specification number...*Sd. Kfz. 181*
Weight in action......62.75 short tons.
Crew ....5 men.
Armor, Front nose plate102 mm at 20°.
  Front glacis plate....62 mm at 80°.
  Lower nose plate.....62 mm at 60°.
  Driver's front plate..102 mm at 10°.
  Hull sides ....62 mm vertical.
  Superstructure sides..82 mm vertical.
  Rear plate..........82 mm at 20°
           (undercut).
  Turret front ....100 mm at 0° to 11°.
  Turret sides and rear.82 mm vertical.
Armament (coaxially
  mounted in turret).One *8.8 cm Kw.K.36
      (L/56). One M.G.34*
  In hull ....One *M.G.34.*
Dimensions, Length ...20 feet 8½ inches.
(excluding gun)
  Width with wide com-
    bat track ....12 feet 3 inches.

Width with narrow
  transport track ....10 feet 4 inches.
Height ....9 feet 4¾ inches.
Gun overhang ......7 feet ½ inch.
Ground clearance ....1 foot 5 inches.

Performance,
  Trench crossing .....10 feet.
  Step ....2 feet 6 inches.
  Gradient ....30°.
  Fording ....Submersible to 13 feet.
  Road speed ....15 miles per hour.
  Cross-country speed .5 to 10 miles per hour.
  Maximum speed .....25 miles per hour.
  Range on roads .....87 miles.
  Range cross-country.53 miles.

Engine, Type ....Maybach HL 230 P45.
  Cylinders ....V-12.
  BHP ....690 HP at 3,000 rpm.
  Fuel ....Gasoline.
  Fuel capacity ....150 gallons
             (approximately).

Transmission: Maybach-Olvar preselective gearbox, hydraulically operated with eight forward speeds and four reverse.

Suspension: Front driving sprocket and rear idler. Eight load-carrying axles each with three large bogie wheels. Bogie wheels are interleaved. Torsion-bar suspension, one torsion bar per axle.

c. *Pz. Kpfw.* TIGER, MODEL B (KING TIGER). (1) *General.* This tank is a development of the Tiger along the lines of the Panther and with a new main armament, the *8.8 cm Kw.K. 43 (L/71).* The armor is as thick as that of the Tiger—in some parts thicker—and the improved design and the slope given to the majority of the plates (as in the Panther) give the tank vastly improved protection.

The King Tiger is a tank designed essentially for defensive warfare or for breaking through strong lines of defense. It is unsuitable for rapid maneuver and highly mobile warfare because of its great weight and low speed. To accommodate the gun the turret has been made unusually long in proportion to the total length of the tank. When "buttoned up" the tank is extremely blind, and this is one of its weakest points.

Since the King Tiger first appeared in August 1944 in Normandy, modifications have been made in the turret to eliminate the excessive plate-bending involved in the original construction. The King Tiger virtually is invulnerable to frontal attack, but the flanks, which are less well protected, can be penetrated by Allied antitank weapons at most normal combat ranges.

Figure 104.—Pz. Kpfw. "Tiger", Model B.

Figure 105.—Pz. Kpfw. "Tiger", Model B (Sd. Kfz. 182)

(2) *Specifications.*

Model B

Specification number...*Sd. Kfz. 182*
Weight in action ......75 tons.
Crew ....5 men.
Armor
  Front glacis plate ....150 mm at 50°.
  Lower nose plate ....100 mm at 50°.
  Hull sides ....80 mm vertical.
  Superstructure sides..80 mm at 20°.
  Rear plate ....80 mm at 25°.
  Turret front ....180 mm at 10°.
  Turret sides and rear.80 mm at 20°.
Armament (coaxially
  mounted in turret)...One *8.8 cm Kw.K.43
                     (L/71)* and one *M.G.34.*
  In hull ....One *M.G.34.*
Dimensions, Length ...23 feet 10 inches.
  (excluding gun)
  Width ....11 feet 11½ inches.
  Height ....10 feet 2 inches.
  Gun overhang.......8 feet 10 inches.
  Ground clearance,
    Front ....1 foot 7 inches.
    Rear ....1 foot 8 inches.
Performance,
  Road speed ....24 miles per hour.
  Cross-country
    speed ....9 to 10 miles per hour.
  Maximum speed .....26 miles per hour.
  Range on roads .....106 miles.
  Range cross-country.74 miles.
Engine, Type ....Maybach HL 230 P30.
  Cylinders ....V-12.
  Fuel ....229 gallons.

Fuel consumption
  (per 100 miles)
    On roads ....213 gallons.
    Cross-country ...300 gallons
  BHP ....590 HP at 2,600 rpm.
Transmission: Maybach-Olvar preselector type
  gearbox, hydraulically operated; eight forward
  speeds, four reverse.

Suspension: Nine load-carrying axles each side,
  each carrying twin over-lapping bogie wheels.
  Single torsion-bar suspension. Front driving
  sprocket rear idler.

5. Armored Cars

a. GENERAL. Two main types of armored cars still are in use in the German Army; the light four-wheeled, and heavy eight-wheeled vehicles. These have persisted almost without modification throughout the course of the war, and are vehicles entirely satisfactory in their role. A series of six-wheeled armored cars which existed before the outbreak of war apparently was unsatisfactory or redundant, for this type never has been met in action.

b. FOUR-WHEELED ARMORED CAR (*Leichter Panzerspähwagen 2 cm*). (1) *General.* In addition to the normal four-wheeled armored car, which is armed with a 20-mm automatic cannon and an *M.G. 34,* there is a model (*Sd. Kfz. 221*) mounting a machine gun only, and a radio vehicle (*Sd. Kfz. 223*), also mounting one machine gun and having a rectangular, overhead, folding, frame aerial.

Figure 106.—Four-wheeled armored car (Sd. Kfz. 222).

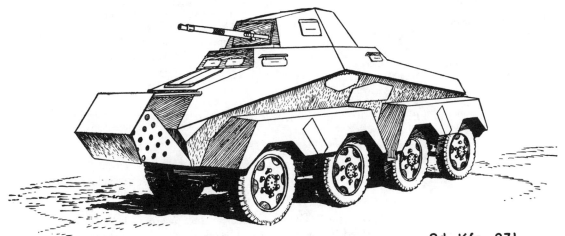

Sd. Kfz. 231

Sd. Kfz. 232

Sd. Kfz. 263

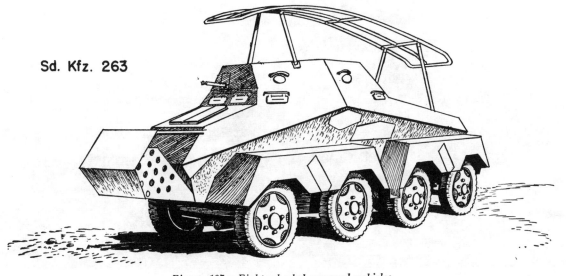

Figure 107.—Eight-wheeled armored vehicles.

(2) *Specifications.*

Specification number...*Sd. Kfz. 222.*
Weight in action.......5.25 tons.
Crew ....3 men.
Dimensions, Length....15 feet 7 inches.
   Width ....6 feet 3½ inches.
   Height ....5 feet 11½ inches.
   Ground clearance ....7¾ inches.
Armor ....8 mm.
Armament ....One *2 cm Kw.K. 30 or 38* and one *7.92 mm M.G.34* coaxially mounted.

c. EIGHT-WHEELED ARMORED CAR (*Schwerer Panzerspähwagen 8 Rad*). (1) *General.* The eight-wheeled armored car has appeared in a variety of subsidiary roles. In addition to the principal version (*Sd. Kfz. 231*), there are two radio vehicles (*Sd. Kfz. 232* and *263*), an armored car mounting the *7.5 cm Kw.K. 38* and having no turret, and the eight-wheeled armored car mounting a *5 cm Kw.K. 39* in a turret (*Sd. Kfz. 234/2*). The radio vehicles have large, rectangular, folding, frame aerials.

(2) *Specifications.*

Specification number...*Sd. Kfz.231.*
Weight in action ......8.35 tons.
Crew ....4 men.
Dimensions, Length....19 feet 1 inch.
   Width ....7 feet 3 inches.
   Height ....7 feet 10 inches.
   Ground clearance ...12 inches.

Armor, Turret front...15 mm.
   Turret sides and rear.8 mm.
   Superstructure front.18 mm.
   Superstructure sides..8 mm.
   Hull front nose plate.18 mm.
   Hull sides ....8 to 10 mm.
   Tail plate ....10 mm.
Armament ....One *2 cm Kw.K.30 or 38* and one 7.92-mm *M.G.34* coaxially mounted.
Engine ....8 cylinders
   155 BHP
   Gasoline.
Road speed ....51 miles per hour
Cross-country speed ...19 miles per hour.
Range on roads.......165 to 190 miles.
Range cross-country ..110 miles.
Suspension ....8 single wheels.
   (8-wheel drive).

Performance,
   Trench crossing .....5 feet.
   Step ....1 foot 7 inches.
   Fording ....2 feet.
   Maximum grade ....27°.

d. HALF-TRACKED ARMORED CAR (*Le. Schtz. Pz. Wg. 2 cm*). (1) *General.* This half-tracked armored car is armed with 20-mm automatic cannon and machine gun in a turret.

(2) *Specifications.*

Specification number... *Sd. Kfz. 250/9.*
Weight in action ......6.5 tons.
Crew ....3 men.
Dimensions, Length ... 15 feet
   Width ....6 feet 4½ inches.
Speed ....40 miles per hour.

Figure 108.—Armored 3-ton half-tracked vehicle mounting 2 cm Flak 36.

6. Armored Personnel Carriers

A great variety of vehicles of the armored personnel-carrier type are in use in the German Army. Two types of chassis have been used for these: the 1-ton half-tracked prime mover (*Sd. Kfz. 10*) and the 3-ton half-tracked prime mover (*Sd. Kfz. 11*). These vehicles are armored only lightly (5 to 15 mm) and the plates are sloped like those on the armored cars. There has been a recent tendency to mount artillery (antiaircraft or antitank) up to 37-mm caliber in these vehicles. The following are examples of these vehicles:

> On the 1-ton half-tracked
>   chassis:
> Light Armored Troop
>   Carrier ....*Sd. Kfz. 250.*
> Light Armored Am-
>   munition Carrier...*Sd. Kfz. 252.*
> Light Armored OP..*Sd. Kfz. 253.*
> On the 3-ton half-
>   tracked chassis:
> Medium Armored
>   Troop Carrier .....*Sd. Kfz. 251.*
> Armored Flame-
>   thrower Vehicle ...*Sd. Kfz. 251/16.*
> Self - propelled Anti -
>   tank Gun ....*3.7 cm Pak.*
> Self - propelled Anti -
>   aircraft Gun ......*2 cm Flak 36.*

Section VII. ROCKET WEAPONS

I. General

a. DEVELOPMENT. German rocket weapons have undergone considerable development since their first appearance in combat in 1941, after experiments over a period of several years. There are now about a dozen standard projectors, in addition to a number of non-standard weapons which either are of a specialized design or have not yet reached a stage of development warranting large-scale production. The Germans introduced rocket projectors for laying heavy concentrations of smoke and for massed fire on area targets. Because the projectors are comparatively light, they are far more mobile than field artillery weapons firing projectiles of similar weights. However, the rocket projectors do not have the accuracy of artillery.

b. TYPES OF ROCKET WEAPONS. The more common types of German rocket weapons are the 150-mm six-barreled projector (*15 cm Nebel-*

werfer 41), the 210-mm five-barreled projector (*21 cm Nebelwerfer 42*), and the 280-mm and 320-mm projector (*28/32 cm Nebelwerfer 41*), all mounted on two-wheeled tired carriages, and the 150-mm ten-barreled projector (*15 cm Panzerwerfer 42*), mounted on an armored half-track.

2. Field Projectors

a. 150-MM ROCKET LAUNCHER (*15 cm Nebelwerfer 41*). (1) *General description.* This is the original tube-type equipment and consists of six tubes mounted on a simple two-wheeled carriage with a split trail. It is provided with elevating and traversing gears and has an electrical firing contact at the breech end of each barrel. These contacts lead to a junction box on the upper right-hand side of the barrel assembly. To prevent the weapon from being over-turned by blast, the barrels are fired separately in fixed order (1, 4, 6, 2, 3, 5), all six rounds being discharged in 10 seconds. To escape the blast, the firer lies in a slit trench about 15 yards to the flank and operates the weapon by means of an electrical switch connected to the junction box. Since the crew must seek shelter during firing, it requires about 90 seconds to load and fire a series of six rounds. A single tube projector known as the *Do-Gerät* which fires the same ammunition is used by airborne troops.

(2) *Characteristics.*

> Caliber ....150 mm (5.9 inches).
> Length of barrels ....51 inches.
> Weight ....1,195 pounds.
> Traverse ....30°.
> Elevation ....44°.
> Maximum Range (HE) .....7,330 yards.
> Maximum Range (Smoke)...7,550 yards.
> Weight of Rocket (HE).....75.3 pounds.
> Weight of Rocket (Smoke)....78 pounds.
> Velocity...........1,120 feet per second.

(3) *Ammunition.* This projector fires HE and smoke projectiles, and there is some evidence that chemical rockets also exist for this weapon.

b. 210-MM ROCKET LAUNCHER (*21 cm Nebelwerfer 42*). (1) *General description.* This is a five-barreled projector on the lines of the *15 cm Nebelwerfer 41,* with similar carriage and electrical firing system. Removable internal rails are now supplied for this weapon to permit firing the 150-mm rockets.

Figure 109.—15 cm Nebelwerfer 41.

Figure 110.—21 cm Nebelwerfer 42.

Figure 111.—The Panzerwerfer 42 fires the same rockets as the 15 cm Nebelwerfer 41.

(2) Characteristics.

Caliber..........210 mm (8.27 inches).
Length of barrels......4 feet 3½ inches.
Maximum range ....8,600 yards.
Weight of rocket..........248 pounds.

(3) Ammunition. The projector fires an HE projectile with a 28-pound bursting charge.

c. 150-MM SELF-PROPELLED PROJECTOR (*15 cm Panzerwerfer 42*). (1) *General description.* The Germans have mounted this ten-barreled rocket projector on the rear of a lightly armored half-tracked vehicle with a *Maultier* suspension. Two horizontal rows of five barrels are mounted on a turntable with a 360-degree traverse. The weapon is fired electrically by a gunner who sits in the body of the vehicle immediately below the platform, his head protected by a shallow cupola. It is probable that the rate of fire of this weapon is higher than that of the *Nebelwerfer 41,* since the crew remains behind armor near the weapon and can reload in less time.

(2) Characteristics.

Caliber............150 mm (5.9 inches).
Traverse ....360°.
Maximum elevation................45°.
Maximum range ....7,330 yards.
Vehicle weight................7.1 tons.
Vehicle road speed......25 miles per hour.

(3) Ammunition. The ammunition is the same as that fired by the *15 cm Nebelwerfer 41.*

d. WOODEN RACK LAUNCHER (*28/32 cm Schweres Wurfgerät 40*). (1) *General description.* This is the original frame-type rocket projector and consists of a simple wooden frame upon which the projectiles are rested to be fired from the crates. The rockets are stabilized in flight by rotation imparted by the 26 jets which are inclined at an angle.

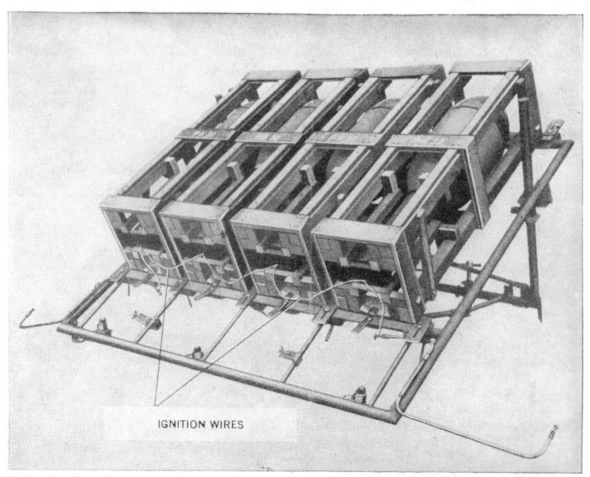

IGNITION WIRES

Figure 112.—The Wurfgerät 41 consists of a frame of steel tubing on which may be placed 280- or 320-mm rockets in either wooden or steel crates. (The wooden crates are illustrated above.) The rockets are fired from these crates.

Figure 113.—The Wurfrahmen 40 is here shown in action. Four wooden rocket-carrying crates are in place on the plates on the side of the half-track. The last of the four rockets has just been fired. Empty crates lie at the right.

Figure 114.—U. S. soldiers inspect a captured 28/32 cm Nebelwerfer 41. The weapon is loaded, but electrical leads are not connected to the bases of the rocket motors. Note the box (shown open) which protects the sight.

(2) *Ammunition.* Both high explosive 280-mm and incendiary 320-mm rockets can be fired from this frame.

High explosive 280-mm rocket.

Designation......*28 cm Wurfkörper Spr.*
Marking ....Pink band.
Weight ....184.5 pounds.
Bursting charge.....110 pounds of TNT.
Maximum range............2,100 yards.
Length of rocket.........3 feet 11 inches

Figure 115.—7.5 cm Multiple Fortress Rocket Projector.

Incendiary 320-mm rocket.

Designation..*32 cm Wurfkörper M. Fl. 50.*
Marking.........Green and yellow band.
Weight ....173 pounds.
Filling.................11 gallons of oil.
Maximum range............2,400 yards.
Length of rocket.........3 feet 4 inches.

e. STEEL RACK LAUNCHER (*28/32 cm Schweres Wurfgerät 41*). Metal instead of wood construction of the launching frame and crate distinguish this rocket launcher from the *28/32 cm Schweres Wurfgerät 40*. The same HE and incendiary projectiles are fired.

f. MOTORIZED LAUNCHER (*28/32 cm Schwerer Wurfrahmen 40*). (1) *General description.* Modified versions of the *Schweres Wurfgerät* are used on half-tracked armored vehicles. Six projectors are mounted on the vehicle, three on each side. Each projector consists of two parts: a carrier plate bolted on the side of the vehicle and a bracket to hold the crate from which the rocket is fired. This bracket is provided with an elevating scale and clamp.

(2) *Ammunition.* The same projectiles are fired as from the *Schweres Wurfgerät.*

g. MOBILE LAUNCHER (*28/32 cm Nebelwerfer 41*). (1) *General description.* This mobile version of the *Schweres Wurfgerät* consists of a framework designed to hold six projectiles mounted upon a two-wheeled carriage. The trail is detached after the carriage has been towed into position, and the launcher is laid like an artillery piece. The standard electrical firing mechanism is used.

(2) *Ammunition.* The projectiles fired are the standard 280-mm (HE) and 320-mm incendiary rockets.

h. 300-MM MOBILE LAUNCHER (*30 cm Nebelwerfer 42*). (1) *General description.* Similar to the *28/32 cm Nebelwerfer 41,* this six-frame projector launches the largest of the German high-explosive rockets.

(2) *Ammunition.* The 300-mm rocket is better streamlined than the 280-mm or 320-mm projectiles, has a higher ratio of propellent weight to total weight, and as a result has a much longer range.

High explosive 300-mm rocket.

    Designation.........*30 cm Wk. 42 Spr.*
    Weight ....277 pounds.
    Bursting charge....100 pounds of amatol.
    Maximum range............5,000 yards.
    Length of rocket........4 feet $7/16$ inches.

3. Antiaircraft Rocket Weapons

a. GENERAL. Despite persistent reports of some kind of high-altitude antiaircraft rocket in use by the Germans, only two such projectiles have been identified, and neither has a high vertical range. The two antiaircraft rockets known are the 86-mm free cable and parachute type and 152-mm rocket of similar type but with the cable tied to the ground. The cables emitted by the rockets are designed as a hazard to aircraft.

b. 86-MM ANTIAIRCRAFT PROJECTOR. (1) *General description.* The 86-mm antiaircraft parachute rockets are fired from this single type projector. The frame is enclosed in a square-sectioned sheet metal casing, enlarged at the forward end to form a flash hider. The casing is mounted on a vertical tube provided with elevating and traversing gears. The projector sight is graduated up to 2,625 feet.

(2) *Ammunition.* The rocket, which is percussion fired, weighs 11 pounds and contains 310 feet of thin wire cable with a parachute at one end and a circular counterweight at the other. This parachute is ejected by a small charge actuated by a delay train initiated by the propellant.

c. 152-MM ANTIAIRCRAFT ROCKET. (1) *General description.* The details of the launching device for this rocket are not known. The projectile contains an HE charge in the nose and a parachute and length of cable in the body. When the projectile is discharged it unwinds the cable which is anchored to the ground. The cable is fully unwound at an altitude of about 3,000 feet and pulls out the parachute. The projectile continues its upward flight until destroyed by the nose charge which is fitted with a delay action fuze. The cable, suspended by the parachute, will sink slowly to the ground.

4. Other Rocket Weapons

a. 75-MM MULTIPLE ROCKET PROJECTOR. The latest German frame-type projector consists of 28 frames mounted in four horizontal rows of seven each at the forward end of a long carriage. Each frame is built of a metal hoop and a T-shaped steel guide bar. Each row of frames is a separate assembly and is bolted to the inclined superstructure above the carriage. The four rows are connected by a system of links and are elevated simultaneously from the rear of the carriage, where a shield, 0.4 inch thick, protects the layer. The whole assembly may be traversed either about a forked center pivot or by moving the carriage itself, which is light enough to be manhandled. The limits of elevation are 4 degrees and 55 degrees. The rockets are fired by percussion through a multiple firing pin mechanism at the rear of each row of projectors. Each row is cocked separately, but all strikers are released by one pull on the firing cable. The rocket fired from this launcher has not been identified.

b. 73-MM PROPAGANDA ROCKET LAUNCHER (*7.3 cm Propagandawerfer*). (1) *General description.* This is a very simple launcher consisting of a single cage hinged to a framework base of tubular steel and supported at the front by an adjustable arm. The weapon is intended for close range delivery of paper propaganda.

(2) *Ammunition.* The rocket weighs 7.1 pounds and instead of bursting charge or chemical filling contains 8 ounces of propaganda leaflets.

c. 80-MM ROCKET (*8 cm Raketen Sprenggranate*). This high explosive rocket is provided with studs on the side for projection, which indicate that it possibly is used both as a ground and aircraft rocket. It is unrotated and is stabilized in flight by tail fins. The rocket weighs 15.2 pounds, and the maximum ground range is estimated at 6,300 yards.

d. 240-MM ROCKET PROJECTOR. The existence of this projector has been inferred from the use of a 240-mm rocket bomb. Details are not known.

Section VIII. GRENADES

1. Hand Grenades

a. HIGH EXPLOSIVE STICK GRENADE (*Stielhandgranate 24*). (1) *General description.* This grenade consists of a hollow wooden handle and a thin sheet metal head containing the bursting charge. A double length of cord connects a porcelain bead at the lower end of the handle to a friction igniter and detonator assembly screwed on the head of the grenade. The wooden handle is closed at its lower end by a metal screw cap. A fragmentation sleeve is sometimes used with this grenade to improve the antipersonnel effect. This is a metal collar split longitudinally so it can be clipped around the head of the grenade. The surface of the sleeve may be either smooth or divided by serrations to assist fragmentation.

Figure 116.—Stielhandgranate 24, HE Stick Grenade.

(2) *Characteristics.*

Weight of grenade . . . . 1.36 pounds.
Weight of bursting
　charge . . . . 0.365 pound.
Type of bursting charge. TNT.
Length over-all . . . . . . 14 inches.
Detonator . . . . Standard German No. 8.
Igniter delay . . . . 4 to 5 seconds.
Igniter B.Z.24

(3) *Operation.* To arm the grenade, unscrew the metal cap at the lower end of the handle and pull the porcelain bead. This initiates the friction igniter and the grenade will function at the end of the 4- to 5-second delay.

b. HIGH EXPLOSIVE STICK GRENADE (*Stielhandgranate 43*). (1) *General description.* This is a modified form of the *Stielhandgranate 24*. It has the same thin sheet metal head, but has a solid handle. A blue-capped pull igniter and detonator assembly screw into the top of the grenade head. Like the Model 24, this grenade is used with a smooth or serrated fragmentation sleeve.

(2) *Characteristics.*

Total weight . . . . 1 pound 6 ounces.
Weight of bursting
　charge . . . . 7 ounces.
Igniter . . . . *B.Z.f.Eihgr.*
Detonator . . . . No. 8.
Fuze delay . . . . 4½ seconds.

(3) *Operation.* To arm the grenade unscrew and pull the blue metal cap on the top of the explosive head. This initiates the 4½-second delay.

c. WOODEN IMPROVISED HAND GRENADE (*Behelfshandgranate-Holz*). (1) *General description.* This is an offensive-type grenade constructed entirely of wood. It consists of a cylindrical wooden head screwed on a hollow wooden handle. The head is bored to a depth of 4⅞ inches, and specimens of this grenade have been found to contain half a *Bohrpatrone* (standard 100-gram (3.527 ounces) demolition cartridge). The extra space is filled by a wooden plug. A fuze and detonator assembly is located in the forward end of the handle with the detonator inserted into the center of the *Bohrpatrone*. A pull igniter is attached by cord to a button in the recess under the metal cap at the lower end of the handle. These grenades are packed in wooden boxes holding 14 grenades. They are prepared with charges and delay igniters. The detonators, with a short length of fuze, are carried in a separate container inside the box.

(2) *Characteristics.*

Length over-all . . . . 15 inches.
Length of head . . . . 5¼ inches.
Diameter of head . . . . . 2¼ inches.
Diameter of handle . . . . 1¼ inches.
Total weight . . . . 12 ounces.
Weight of bursting
　charge . . . . 50 grams (1.763
　　　　　　　　　　　　　　ounces).
Detonator . . . . No. 8.

(3) *Operation.* To arm the grenade, unscrew the head and break the paper seal on the *Bohrpatrone*. Screw the detonator and fuze assembly into the igniter and slip the detonator into the head of the *Bohrpatrone*. Replace the head and

the grenade is ready for use. To use the grenade remove the metal cap on the lower end of the handle, pull the button attached to the friction igniter and throw. This grenade is designed to produce blast effect and may be used by troops advancing in the open.

d. CONCRETE IMPROVISED HAND GRENADE (*Behelfshandgranate-Beton*). (1) *General description.* This grenade is an offensive type grenade similar to the wooden improvised hand grenade, except the grenade head is made of concrete instead of wood and a full 100-gram *Bohrpatrone* is used as an explosive charge.

(2) *Characteristics.*

Igniter ...............*B.Z.4.5Sek.*
Detonator ....No. 8.

Figure 117.—Eihandgranate 39 HE Egg Grenade (left, older; right, later version).

e. HIGH EXPLOSIVE HAND GRENADE (*Eihandgranate 39*). (1) *General description.* This is an egg-shaped hand grenade constructed of thin sheet metal with high explosive bursting charge. This grenade and the *Stielhandgranate 24* are the standard German hand grenades and are used most. The explosive charge is initiated by a detonator and a friction igniter. The wire loop of the friction igniter is connected by a short cord to a blue metal cap screwed on the top of the grenade body. A model of this grenade containing chloracetophenone also exists. It may be recognized by a yellow ring painted around the grenade and four pear-shaped projections on the lower half of the body. It contains a 112-gram (3.95 ounces) TNT bursting charge and a small aluminum capsule containing 5 grams (0.176 ounce) of chloracetophenone.

(2) *Characteristics.*

Weight of grenade....8 ounces.
Weight of bursting
   charge ....4 ounces.
Detonator ....No. 8.
Igniter ...............*B.Z.f.Eihgr.*
Fuze delay ....4 to 5 seconds.

(3) *Operation.* Unscrew the blue metal cap

and pull the igniter. The grenade will explode after a delay of 4 to 5 seconds.

f. SMOKE STICK GRENADE (*Nebelhandgranate 39*). (1) *General description.* This grenade can be distinguished from the high explosive stick grenade (*Stielhandgranate*) by three grooves in the handle, which serve as recognition features in the dark, and by a white band painted around the center of the handle and an interrupted white band around the head, with the lettering "*Nb. Hgr. 39*", also in white. The head is made of thin metal and contains a filling of zinc-hexachlorethane. Instead of the detonator used in the high explosive grenade, an ignition tube is used. This is very similar in appearance to the No. 8 detonator, but may be distinguished by the closed end which is painted green. The smoke generated in the head escapes through holes around the handle socket. A pull igniter is located inside the handle.

(2) *Characteristics.*

Igniter ...............*B.Z.39.*
Ignition tube ....*N.4.*
Fuze delay ....7 seconds.

g. SMOKE STICK GRENADE (*Nebelhandgranate 39B.*) This grenade is a later model of the *Nebelhandgranate 39* and differs only in the composition of the smoke mixture. In the Model 39B more hexachlorethane and less zinc are used.

h. SMOKE HAND GRENADE (*Nebelhandgranate 41*). (1) *General description.* This grenade has a body which is very similar to that of the *Nebelhandgranate 39* but has, instead of a stick handle, a pull igniter inserted into a plastic adapter in the top of the body. There are only two smoke emission holes. The grenade may be recognized by the letters "*Nb. Hgr. 41*" and a broken line stencilled in white on the body.

(2) *Characteristics.*

Igniter ..........*B.Z.39.*
Ignition tube .....*N.4.*
Duration of smoke
   emission ....100 to 120 seconds.
Filling ....Berger mixture.
Fuze delay ....3 seconds.

(3) *Operation.* The grenade is initiated by unscrewing the igniter cap and pulling the igniter. This initiates the ignition tube and the grenade begins to emit smoke after about 3 seconds.

i. SMOKE EGG GRENADE (*Nebeleihandgranate 42*). (1) *General description.* The elongated egg-shaped body of this grenade is made of thin metal. At the lower extremity a small metal loop is welded or riveted to the body and at the top there is a threaded socket for the igniter assembly. Three holes allow the smoke to escape. A standard German pull igniter is screwed into the top. The igniter has a brass body and a steel ring attached to the top. The grenade is marked *"Nb. Eihgr. 42"* in white and has three short white bands stencilled around the body. A label near the base warns that the fumes can be dangerous in an enclosed space.

(2) *Characteristics.*

Length over-all ....5.3 inches.
Diameter over-all .....1.96 inches.
Body length..........4.1 inches.
Body diameter ....1.7 inches.
Igniter ....*Zd. Schn. Anz. 29.*

(3) *Operation.* Pull the ring on the igniter before throwing the grenade.

j. GLASS SMOKE GRENADE (*Blendkörper 1H*). (1) *General description.* This grenade consists of a sealed glass bulb in a hexagonal carton of corrugated cardboard. The glass is shaped like a somewhat elongated electric light bulb and is about the same size, but of thicker glass. The bulb contains 260 grams (9.17 ounces) of titanium tetrachloride. This grenade is intended for use against the crews of pillboxes and vehicles.

(2) *Operation.* The grenade is carried in the cardboard container and when required for use it can be withdrawn by a tape attached to the lid of the box; the lid is cemented to the neck of the bulb. Remove the lid and throw the grenade against the target. When the bulb bursts, the mixture will give off a dense smoke.

k. GLASS SMOKE GRENADE (*Blendkörper 2H*). (1) *General description.* The glass bulb of this grenade contains 250 grams (8.8175 ounces) of a yellowish liquid. The bulb is sealed at the neck with a sulphur plug which also holds in position a glass tube, orientated along the axis of the bulb. This tube contains 25 grams (0.882 ounce) of a calcium chloride solution. The smoke liquid consists of titanium tetrachloride with silicon tetrachloride added to lower its freezing point. The calcium chloride is used to lower the freezing point of the water which is included to increase the effectiveness of the smoke under conditions of low humidity.

(2) *Operation.* Throw the grenade at the target in the same way as the Model 1H. A notice on the side of the container, which holds four

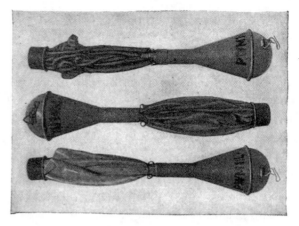

Figure 118.—Panzerwurfmine 1 (L), hollow-charge antitank hand grenade.

grenades, states that they are suitable for use at temperatures down to —40° centigrade.

l. HOLLOW-CHARGE ANTITANK HAND GRENADE (*Panzerwurfmine 1 (L)*). (1) *General description.* This is a recent type antitank grenade. It is of hollow-charge design and is thrown by hand at tanks from a distance of 20 to 30 yards. The grenade body is in the form of a metal cone with a hemispherical, thin, sheet-metal head. The cone contains an explosive charge, with a concave metal retaining plate at the forward end. An air space is formed between this plate and the sheet metal head of the grenade. The narrow end of the cone is located by setting screws around the circumference of a hollow wooden tailpiece containing picric rings and serving as a throwing handle. Around the outside of the tailpiece are four, cloth, triangular shaped fins. Along the outer end of each fin is a steel spring which retains the fins in the open position when the grenade is thrown. When the grenade is being carried, and up to the moment of throwing, these fins are wrapped around the tailpiece and retained in position by a cap. Located in the tail of the grenade is a striker mechanism fitted with a safety pin which has a cloth tab attached. The safety pin is retained in position by a metal clip attached to one of the fins.

(2) *Operation.* The grenade is held for throwing by the tailpiece, and immediately before throwing the metal cap is removed from the end of the tailpiece. When the grenade is thrown the fins fly outward and the clip attached to one of them comes away from the striker mechanism and releases the safety pin. Upon impact the striker mechanism functions and initiates the bomb.

m. HOLLOW-CHARGE STICKY GRENADE. The tapering steel body of this grenade contains the hollow-charge. A flat sticky pad at the nose is covered by a press-on lid with a small handle. A tapering fuze adapter terminating in a socket, threaded internally to receive an igniter, is attached to the base of the grenade. The igniter socket is closed during transit by a black plastic plug. Specimens of the igniter and detonator have not been received, but it is believed that a No. 8 detonator is used in combination with a standard 4½-second egg grenade igniter. It is not clear whether it is necessary to place the grenade on the tank or whether it may be thrown from short ranges.

2. Rifle Grenades

a. HIGH EXPLOSIVE RIFLE GRENADE (*Gewehr Sprenggranate*). (1) *General description.* This is a high explosive grenade which may be either fired from the standard rifle discharger cup (*Schiessbecher*) or thrown as a hand grenade. The projectile has a steel body containing a bursting charge, a base incorporating a flash pellet and delay train, and a point detonating fuze. The base is rifled to conform with the rifling of the discharger cup and fitted with a screwed-in base plug in which there is a flash hole communicating to a 6½-second delay flash pellet.

(2) *Characteristics.*

```
Length over-all........5.5 inches.
Diameter  ............1.17 inches.
Weight of grenade.....9 ounces.
Weight of bursting
    charge .............1.1 ounces.
Type of bursting charge.Penthrite-Wax.
Detonator .............Similar to No. 8 but
                          slightly larger and
                          perforated.
Maximum range.......265 yards.
```

(3) *Operation.* (a) *As rifle grenade.* When the grenade is fired from the launcher it will be initiated normally by the point detonating fuze, which consists of a striker, primer, and detonator assembly of conventional design. Should the point detonating fuze fail to operate, a flash pellet in the base will ignite a friction composition in the lower end of the projectile body. This will in turn ignite a 4½-second delay pellet which then initiates the detonator in the bursting charge.

(b) *As hand grenade.* A short cord located internally between the top of the base and the

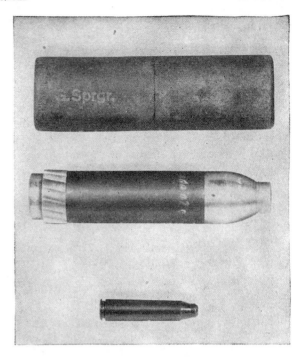

Figure 119.—Gewehr Sprenggranate, HE Rifle Grenade.

lower end of the body connects a friction wire below the 4½-second delay pellet to a washer resting freely in the base. When the grenade is to be thrown by hand, the base is unscrewed and the washer pulled. This operates the friction igniter and sets off the delay train. The grenade is thrown and functions at the end of 4½ seconds.

(4) *Modifications.* Modifications to this grenade have appeared. The pull igniter is sometimes omitted, permitting the grenade to be fired from the launcher but it cannot be thrown. The self-destroying device is sometimes omitted. An "all-ways" fuze is sometimes fitted instead of the standard point detonating fuze, setting off the charge no matter which way the grenade strikes.

b. HIGH EXPLOSIVE RIFLE GRENADE WITH INCREASED RANGE (*Gewehr Sprenggranate mit Gesteigerter Reichweite*). This is a later model of the standard rifle grenade. The self-destroying device has been eliminated and it is fired by a new propelling cartridge. It is claimed that the maximum range has been increased to 711 yards. The grenades may be identified by the box label (*Gewehr Sprenggranate mit Gesteigerter Reichweite*), by the unperforated base plate and fixed rifle base, or by the propelling cartridge with its bright yellow bullet.

c. ANTITANK RIFLE GRENADE (*Gewehr Panzergranate 30*). (1) *General description.* This

405

Figure 120.—*Gewehr Panzergranate, Antitank Rifle Grenade.*

is a rifle grenade incorporating the hollow-charge principle. It is fired from the 30-mm rifled discharger cup (*Schiessbecher*) which can be attached to most types of German rifles. The body of the grenade is in two parts. The forward section is made of steel and contains the bursting charge with the hollow charge cone, closed by a light metal cap. The rear portion is made of light aluminum alloy and contains the fuze and exploder system. A pre-rifled rotating band is located near the base of the grenade. The propellant is contained in a 7.92-mm blank cartridge, crimped at the mouth.

(2) *Characteristics.*

Total weight...........8.8 ounces.
Length over-all.......6.4 inches.
Weight of bursting
   charge ....1.75 ounces.
Maximum accurate
   range ....100 yards.

d. LARGE ANTITANK RIFLE GRENADE (*Gross Gewehr Panzergranate 40*). (1) *General description.* This is similar to the *Gewehr Panzergranate 30* except that the front portion is enlarged to accommodate a greater bursting charge. The propellant is contained in a standard 7.92-mm cartridge with a wooden bullet.

(2) *Characteristics.*

Weight ....13½ ounces (approximately).
Length over-all.......7 inches (approximately).
Weight of bursting
   charge ....4½ ounces.
Maximum accurate
   range ....100 yards.

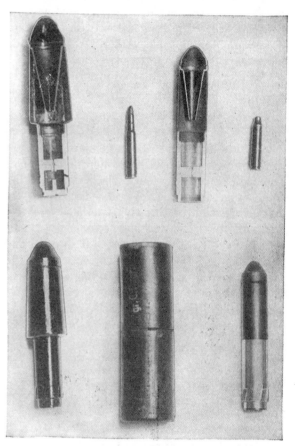

Figure 121.—*Gross Gewehr Panzergranate, Large Antitank Rifle Grenade.*

e. 46-MM HOLLOW-CHARGE RIFLE GRENADE (*S.S. Gewehr Panzergranate 46*). (1) *General description.* This rifle grenade has a streamlined body with a maximum diameter of 46 mm. The body is treated against corrosion and is closed by a conical unpainted impact cap. The stem is of steel and fits into the standard 30-mm discharger cup. It has a pre-rifled rotating band. The base plug is conical in shape. The propelling cartridge consists of a lacquered steel 7.92-mm cartridge case crimped at the neck and sealed with wax. The cap is yellow.

(2) *Characteristics.*

Weight ....15½ ounces (approximately).
Length over-all........7.7 inches.
Length of stem........4 inches.
Maximum diameter of head ....1.8 inches.
Diameter of stem......1.2 inches.
Type of bursting charge ....RDX-TNT.
Weight of bursting charge ....4.8 ounces.

(3) *Performance.* Static test indicates that the penetration at long ranges is approximately 90 mm of homogeneous armor. At short range (approximately 18 feet) the penetration was 70 mm. A ¼-inch mild steel plate, spaced 11 inches

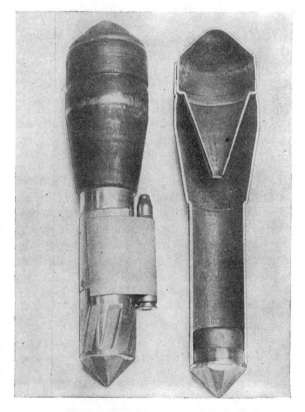

Figure 122.—S.S. Gewehr Panzergranate 46, 46-mm. Hollow-Charge Rifle Grenade.

in front of the armor, completely nullified the effect on the armor.

f. 61-MM HOLLOW-CHARGE RIFLE GRENADE (*S.S. Gewehr Panzergranate 61*). (1) *General description.* This is a hollow-charge rifle grenade similar to the *S.S. Gewehr Panzergranate 46* but having a streamlined body of larger dimensions.

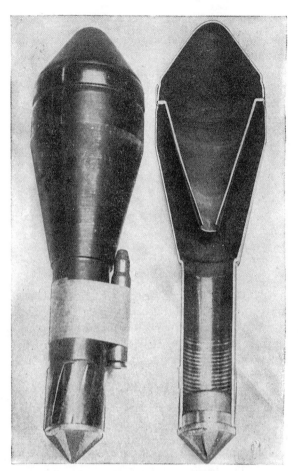

Figure 123.—S.S. Gewehr Panzergranate 61, 61-mm. Hollow-Charge Rifle Grenade.

(2) *Characteristics.*

Weight ....19 ounces (approximately).
Length over-all........9.4 inches.
Length of stem........4 inches.
Maximum diameter of head ....2.4 inches.
Diameter of stem......1.2 inches.
Type of bursting charge ....RDX-TNT.
Weight of bursting charge ....8.5 ounces.

(3) *Performance.* Static tests indicate that the maximum penetration of homogeneous armor at the extreme range of 220 yards will be approximately 126 mm. At a range of approximately 18 feet the penetration falls to 100 mm. A ¼-inch mild steel plate, spaced 11 inches in front of the main armor, completely defeats the grenade.

g. HOLLOW-CHARGE RIFLE GRENADE. This late type hollow-charge rifle grenade is similar in appearance to the *S.S. Gewehr Panzergranate 61*. It differs, however, in having an impact cap that is approximately hemispherical and unpainted. The grenade is 9.61 inches long and its greatest diameter is 2.4 inches. The base is rifled for firing from the standard grenade launcher.

Figure 124.—Gewehr Fellschirmleuchtgranate, Parachute Star Rifle Grenade.

h. ILLUMINATING PARACHUTE RIFLE GRENADE (*Gewehrfallschirmleuchtgranate*). (1) *General description.* This illuminating parachute grenade has a cylindrical steel body. At the front is a conical cap with round tip, and at the rear a base rifled to engage the rifling in the standard grenade launcher. Within the body is a delay pellet, an ejection charge, and a container holding the parachute, rigging, and star flare. This container incorporates a second delay pellet, and a second ejection charge for the parachute and flare. The grenade is fired by a cartridge case containing 1.5 grams (0.05 ounce) of propelling charge. The cartridge is closed by a wooden bullet.

(2) *Characteristics.*
Diameter ....1.18 inches.
Length ....6.88 inches.
Weight ....9.9 ounces.

(3) *Operation.* When the grenade is fired, the flash from the propellent gases ignites the delay pellet in the base of the grenade. After 6½ seconds an ejection charge explodes and ejects the container holding the parachute and star. Simultaneously a second delay pellet in the container is initiated. Two seconds later, the parachute ejection charge is set off and the parachute and star are ejected.

i. PROPAGANDA RIFLE GRENADE (*Gewehr Propagandagranate*). (1) *General description.* This grenade, which weighs 8 ounces when filled, is fired from the standard launcher. The grenade body is a cylindrical steel tube, closed by a loose-fitting ballistic cap. The propaganda leaflets are enclosed in two semi-cylindrical steel covers within the body and rest on a cup-shaped platform. The tail element, with the usual pre-rifled

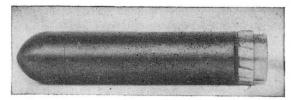

Figure 125.—Gewehr Propagandagranate, Propaganda Rifle Grenade.

base, contains the ejecting charge and a delay train. The propellant is contained in the usual type of blank cartridge, distinguished by a red band.

(2) *Operation.* The delay train is ignited by the flash from the propellant and detonates the ejecting charge. The platform, leaflets, leaflet covers, and ballistic cap are ejected during flight. The maximum range is approximately 500 yards.

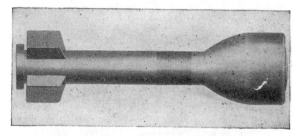

Figure 126.—Gewehr Granatpatrone, Rifle Spigot Grenade.

j. HIGH EXPLOSIVE ANTITANK HOLLOW-CHARGE RIFLE GRENADE (*Gewehr Granatpatrone 30*). (1) *General description.* This grenade consists of a streamlined bell-shaped body, closed in front by a slightly convex closing disc of aluminum, a graze fuze screwed into a projection on the base of the body, and a finned tail unit screwed to the fuze base. It is fired from the standard rifle (*Gewehr 98*) fitted with a spigot type launcher and using blank cartridges with wooden bullets. The bursting charge is cast cyclonite wax with hemispherical cavity in the head. This cavity has an aluminum liner.

(2) *Characteristics.*
Length over-all........9.3 inches (approximately).
Maximum diameter....2.4 inches.
Length of body........3.15 inches.

(3) *Operation.* When the grenade is fired, the propellent gases shatter the wooden bullet and shear a safety pin by forcing forward a cutting member. In the armed position, the striker is withheld from the detonator by a creep spring and initiates the grenade when it hits or grazes a target.

3. Grenades for Smooth Bore Signal Pistol (*Leuchtpistole*)

a. HIGH EXPLOSIVE PROJECTILE FOR SIGNAL PISTOL (*Wurfkörper 361, Leuchtpistole*). This projectile consists of the normal egg hand grenade with a stem screwed on in place of the powder train time fuze. The stem contains a powder train fuze (with a delay of approximately 4½ seconds) with a No. 8 detonator at the upper end. In the lower end the projectile carries the cartridge (propellent charge with percussion cap) which expels the grenade and sets off the time fuze. The projectile is secured to the stem by a split pin and ring which must be withdrawn before the projectile is loaded into the signal pistol. The projectile is then armed. A removable liner must be inserted in the tube of the signal pistol before firing this grenade. The liner is inserted from the breech end and held in place by a projecting stud engaging with the upper surface of the breech. (See Section II for a description of signal pistols.)

Figure 127.—Wurfkörper 361, Leuchtpistole, modified egg grenade for signal pistol.

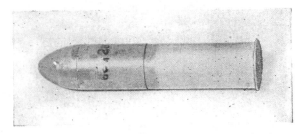

Figure 128.—Wurfgranatpatrone 326, Leuchtpistole, HE projectile for signal pistol.

b. HIGH EXPLOSIVE PROJECTILE FOR SIGNAL PISTOL (*Wurfgranatpatrone 326, Leuchtpistole*). (1) *General description.* This projectile, which is painted yellow, has the appearance of a small mortar shell. It is attached to a signal cartridge case by crimping. The head is hollow and contains a fixed needle which is separated from a pellet containing the detonator assembly and a 7-gram (0.247 ounce) TNT bursting charge by a creep spring.

(2) *Operation.* A pin inserted through the tail of the bomb pushes two metal balls into a groove and thus prevents the pellet from moving forward against the needle. On firing the projectile is automatically armed, since the pin is left behind. On impact the pellet is thrown forward onto the needle.

c. HOLLOW CHARGE GRENADE FOR SIGNAL PISTOL (*Panzerwurfkörper 42, Leuchtpistole*). (1) *General description.* This grenade is fired up to a maximum range of 75 yards from the *Leuchtpistole,* using the reinforcing sleeve, stock, and combined front and rear sight. The grenade has a pear-shaped head containing the hollow charge and is fitted with an impact cap. The grenade tapers to form a tail tube with pre-rifling for screwing into the reinforcing sleeve. A thinner tube, containing the propellant, percussion cap, and a shearing and propelling bolt, is inserted into the end of the tail tube.

(2) *Characteristics.*

Weight of grenade.....1 pound 5 ounces.
Diameter of head......2.4 inches.
Diameter of tail tube..0.875 inch.
Length of grenade.....8.56 inches.

(3) *Operation.* The complete grenade is loaded into the pistol from the muzzle end. The propellent tube fits freely into the bore until the pre-rifled band meets the muzzle of the reinforcing sleeve, when the grenade must be screwed into the rifling. On firing, the propellent gases drive the propelling and shearing bolt forward. This bolt breaks a shear pin in the front end of the propelling tube and discharges the grenade. The graze fuze in the tail tube is armed by setback as the grenade leaves the pistol.

d. SMOKE EGG GRENADE (*Nebeleihandgranate 42/II*). This grenade reportedly can be fired from the *Leuchtpistole.* No details are available, however. It seems probable that the *Nebeleigranate 42* has been modified for firing from the signal pistol, using the reinforcing sleeve, in the same way as the *Eihandgranate 39* was modified to produce the *Wurfkörper 361 L.P.*

e. TIME FUZED HIGH EXPLOSIVE ROUND FOR SIGNAL PISTOL (*Sprenggranatpatrone, Leuchtpistole Mit Z.Z.*). This is a new type of signal pistol ammunition designed for shooting from tanks or equivalent cover. The round consists of a heavy cased high explosive projectile with a 1-second time fuze in the base and a varnished steel cartridge case. Packing cases for these grenades bear the following inscription: "*Ach-*

tung! nur aus Panzer oder gleichwertiger Decken verfeuern. Brennzeit I Sek." ("Danger! Only to be fired from tanks or equivalent cover. Time of burning 1 second.")

4. Grenades for Modified Rifled Grenade and Signal Pistol

a. HIGH EXPLOSIVE GRENADE (*Sprengpatrone für Kampfpistole*). This round consists of a die-cast aluminum cartridge case into which the projectile is fitted. A percussion cap and propellant are in the base of the cartridge case. Ten holes in a plate above the propellent charge lead the gases to the base of the projectile. The projectile has a rifled aluminum body containing two bursting charges of penthrite wax and a point detonating fuze which is armed as the projectile leaves the muzzle of the pistol. The projectile may be recognized by the letters *"Spr. Z."* stencilled on the base.

b. SMOKE GRENADE (*Nebelpatrone für Kampfpistole*). (1) *General description.* Externally this projectile is similar to the high explosive projectile. Internally it contains a smoke generator. It is fitted with a point detonating fuze similar to that used in the high explosive projectile, except that there is a charge of gunpowder in place of the detonator below the flash cap.

(2) *Operation.* The projectile functions on

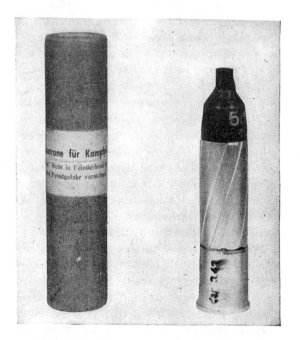

impact. The internal charge of gunpowder is ignited by the flash cap and blows off the nose. At the same time the smoke generator is ignited. The smoke generator is projected a considerable distance from the point of impact.

c. ORANGE SMOKE GRENADE (*Deutpatrone für Kampfpistole*). (1) *General description.* Externally this projectile is similar to the *Nebelpatrone*, except that it has no nose fuze. The head is parabolic. The grenade is filled with an orange smoke composition. In a central cavity are four strands of quick-match connected to a gunpowder pellet in the center of the projectile base. The smoke jets at the base are covered with a thick pad of compressed paper which is burst by the smoke pressure. *"Deut. Z."* is stencilled on the base.

(2) *Operation.* When the projectile leaves the cartridge case, the gunpowder pellet is ignited and, after a delay, the quick-match ignites and in turn ignites the smoke mixture.

d. PARACHUTE FLARES (*Fallschirmleuchtpatrone für Kampfpistole*). (1) *General description.* Externally this has the general appearance of the other types. It has a black bakelite head with a white spot in the center. The base of the projectile has a screwed-in plug which is perforated to hold a gunpowder pellet. Above this is a flare with parachute attached. *"F. Leucht. Z."* is stencilled on the base.

(2) *Operation.* On firing the flash from the propellant ignites the gunpowder pellet which, after a delay, ignites the flare. The bakelite head is blown off and the illuminating type flare ejected.

e. MESSAGE GRENADE (*Nachrichtpatrone für Kampfpistole*). (1) *General description.* This grenade consists of a pre-rifled aluminum body, with a plastic head, and an aluminum cartridge case. The black plastic head, which screws onto the body, contains a message form and pencil. The body contains a smoke generator, a colored silk streamer, and an ejecting charge. The body is closed by a screwed-in base plate with a gunpowder delay pellet. Stencilled on the base are the letters *"Nachr. Z"*.

(2) *Operation.* When the projectile is fired, the flash from the propellant ignites the delay in the grenade base plate. This in turn ignites the ejecting charge and expels the message container, smoke generator, and streamer.

Section IX. OTHER WEAPONS

I. Remote Controlled Demolition Vehicles

a. GENERAL. Three main types of remote controlled demolition vehicles in use by the German army have been identified. These are the Goliath which is line controlled, the B-IV controlled by radio, and the *N.S.U.-Springer* which has not been encountered in the field. These vehicles have been unsuccessful in action; they usually have been stopped by small arms fire.

b. GOLIATH. (1) *General description.* This vehicle has been produced in two models; one driven by a gasoline engine; the other by an electric motor. The two models have roughly the same external appearance and resemble miniature versions of the type of tanks used during the war of 1914-1918. The Goliath's hull is divided into three compartments by transverse bulkheads. The explosive charge is carried in the front compartment; the engine (in the gasoline driven version) and control gear are in the center, and the drum carrying the coiled cable is in the rear compartment. In the electrically driven model, a battery and motor are carried in sponsons on both sides. Hinged steel covers give access to the cable compartment and the engine space. The vehicle is driven by front sprockets. There are four bogie wheels, mounted on lever arms with simple coil springing, and a rear idler. A small jockey wheel is mounted between the driving sprocket and the first bogie wheel on each side.

(2) *Specifications.*

```
Length ...................5 feet 3 inches.
Height  .................2 feet.
Width ...................2 feet 10 inches.
Total weight ...........800 pounds (approxi-
                               mately).
Weight of explosive
    charge ...............200 pounds (approxi-
                               mately).
Speed ...................5 to 12 miles per hour.
Power plant:
    Gasoline engine Model..2-cylinder, 2-cycle in-line
                               engine with chain drive.
    Electric motor Model...Two 12-volt Bosch starter
                               motors geared to driving
                               sprockets.
```

(3) *Operation.* The Goliath is transported to the front line on a two-wheeled trailer. After it has been unloaded from the trailer and started toward its target it is controlled through the three-core cable, about 2,000 feet long, which unwinds from the rear and is connected to the operator's control panel. In the electrically driven type, this control is direct to the motors which drive each track individually. In the gasoline-driven model, the control operates magnetic clutches which control the tracks. There is no provision for reversing the vehicle. The charge is fired by a dry cell battery in the control unit. Firing is initiated by throwing a switch on the control panel; the firing circuit runs through the two outer wires in the three-core cable. The Goliath is expendable and is destroyed when its demolition charge is set off.

c. B-IV. (1) *General description.* This radio-controlled demolition vehicle, larger than the Goliath, also has been generally unsuccessful. The hull of the B-IV is constructed of poorly welded 8-mm armor plate. It is divided into an engine compartment at the rear, a driver's compartment on the right front, and a radio equipment compartment on the left front. The vehicle is fully tracked, with front driving sprocket, five bogie wheels, and a rear idler on each side. A six-cylinder gasoline engine is fitted in the left-hand side of the engine compartment; two gasoline tanks are on the right, and in the center is the hydraulic mechanism for operating the engine under radio control.

(2) *Specifications.*

```
Length .................12 feet.
Height .................4 feet 6 inches.
Width ..................6 feet.
Total weight ...........4.5 tons.
Weight of explosive
    charge ..............800 pounds.
Armor thickness ........8 mm.
```

(3) *Operation.* The B-IV is driven under its own power to the line of departure near the target, usually an emplacement or pillbox. The control transmitter of the radio equipment, retained by the driver when he dismounts, is used to steer the vehicle to its destination. In contrast to the Goliath the B-IV is not expendable, but deposits its load of explosive at the target and returns. The TNT demolition charge is in a container which rests on the sloping front of the vehicle. The charge is released either directly by radio control, or by a trip mechanism which operates when the vehicle is reversed.

d. N.S.U.-Springer. (1) *General description.* This vehicle has not been encountered in action, but it is known to be a remotely controlled demolition vehicle of intermediate size. Lightly armored, it probably is no less vulnerable to attack than the Goliath or B-IV.

Figure 130.—Demolition Charge (B1 Goliath). Top, front view; below, rear view.

Figure 131.—Radio Controlled Demolition Vehicle
(B-IV).

(2) *Specifications.*

Length ....9 feet 3½ inches.
Height ....3 feet 10½ inches.
Width ....3 feet 7 inches.
Total weight ....2.25 tons.
Weight of explosive
    charge ....661 pounds.
Armor thickness ....5 to 8 mm.
Remote control range ...2,200 yards (Approximately).
Manually controlled range:
    On roads ....149 miles.
    Cross-country ....87 miles.

2. Armored Trains

a. GENERAL. At the outset of the Polish and Dutch campaigns, German armored trains actually preceded the main forces and seized and held key railroad stations or bridges. More recently the Germans made extensive use of armored trains, particularly in Eastern Europe. Their main function has been to patrol and keep open railroads in areas of partisan and guerrilla operations, and their usefulness has been confined largely to operations against enemies who lack heavy weapons. Armored trains are under the direct control of the General Staff and are allotted to army groups. Each train carries a train commandant, who is usually also the infantry commander; an artillery commander; and a technical officer, responsible for the operation of the train itself.

b. COMPOSITION. The following details apply to a typical armored train with the nomenclature *Epz.Bp. 42:*

Composition	Armament
Two armored gun trucks (37 to 41.5 tons)	Each, one *10 cm le.F.H. 14/19(P).*
Two armored antiaircraft gun trucks (37 to 41.5) tons)	Each, one 20-mm quadruple antiaircraft guns and one *7.62 cm F.K. 295/1(r).*
Two armored infantry trucks (37 to 41.5) tons)	Each, two 81-mm mortars, one heavy machine gun, 22 light machine guns, and one flame thrower.
One armored steam locomotive (in middle of train)	No armament.

Other details:
    Total personnel ....113.
    Armor ....15 to 30 mm.
    Maximum speed ....35 miles per hour (approximately).
    Range ....110 miles.

In addition, composition of the train may include two tank transporter trucks, each carrying a Czech *38 (t)* tank; two light armored Panhard reconnaissance vehicles, capable of traveling either on railroad tracks or across country; and two spare-parts trucks. Various other types of armored trains may be encountered, some incorporating components of an improvised nature, and in these the armor may be anything from boiler plate to railroad ties.

3. Aircraft Armament

a. GENERAL. The aircraft armament described in this section is limited to weapons such as machine guns and cannon which form an integral part of aircraft. The numerous types of bombs and mines which are carried in and dropped from aircraft do not form part of the standard attached armament and are not included here. There has been an increasing tendency to use aircraft machine guns on ground mounts, as illustrated by the use of the *M.G.15* as a light machine gun and the *M.G.151/15* and *M.G.151/20* as triple, self-propelled, antiaircraft weapons. (See Section II, Small Arms, for details on use of aircraft machine guns in ground roles.)

b. 7.92-MM MACHINE GUN *(M.G.15).* (1) *General description.* This was the standard, rifle-caliber, free gun until superseded by the *M.G. 81.* It also is used by the infantry, with bipod and shoulder rest. The design is Solothurn. The gun fires only automatically.

(2) *Characteristics.*

Caliber ....7.92 mm (0.312 inch).
Length over-all ....42 inches.
Weight (without mount) .15.75 pounds.
Operation ....Recoil and residual gas pressure from muzzle blast.
Feed ....75-round saddle magazine.
Cocking ....Manual.
Firing ....Percussion.
Rate of fire ....1,000 rounds per minute.
Muzzle velocity:
  AP Incendiary ....3,000 feet per second.

c. 7.92-MM MACHINE GUN *(M.G. 17).* (1) *General description.* This is the fixed gun version of the *M.G.15.* It fires only automatically. Non-disintegrating, sectionally disintegrating, and full-disintegrating ammunition belts are used with the gun.

(2) *Characteristics.*

Caliber ....7.92 mm (0.312 inch).
Length over-all ....47.7 inches.
Weight (with control mechanism) ....27.69 pounds.
Operation ....Recoil and residual gas pressure from muzzle blast.
Feed ....Metal link belt.
Cocking ....Pneumatic, electrical control with mechanical interruption for synchronized firing.
Rate of fire:
  Unsynchronized ....1,100 rounds per minute.
  Synchronized ....1,000 rounds per minute.
Muzzle velocity:
  AP Incendiary ....3,000 feet per second.

d. 7.92-MM MACHINE GUN *(M.G.81).* (1) *General description.* This gun has superseded the *M.G.15* as the standard, rifle caliber, free gun. The high rate of fire of this gun, which is automatic only, precludes its use as a ground weapon.

(2) *Characteristics.*

Caliber ....7.92 mm (0.312 inch).
Length over-all..........35 inches.
Weight ....13.88 pounds.
Operation ....Recoil and residual gas pressure from muzzle blast.
Feed ....Disintegrating metal link belt.
Cocking ....Cable with finger pull at rear.
Firing ....Percussion.
Rate of fire ....1,200 to 1,500 rounds per minute.

e. 13-MM MACHINE GUN *(M.G.131).* (1) *General description.* This gun is compact and very light. Since it is electrically fired, there is no firing pin, and fire interruption or synchronization are facilitated greatly. The gun fires only automatically.

(2) *Characteristics.*

Caliber ....13 mm (0.512 inch.)
Length over-all ....46 inches.
Weight ....40 pounds.
Operation ....Recoil and residual gas pressure from muzzle blast.
Feed ....Disintegrating metal link belt.
Cocking ....Manual.
Firing ....Electric.
Rate of fire ....900 rounds per minute.
Muzzle velocity:
  HE Tracer and Incendiary Tracer ....2,370 feet per second.

(3) *Ammunition.* The gun fires tracer, high explosive tracer, high explosive incendiary tracer, and armor-piercing tracer projectiles.

f. 15-MM MACHINE GUN *(M.G.151/15).* (1) *General description.* This Mauser-designed gun is percussion fired by solenoid control and is cocked electrically. It is basically identical in design with the *M.G.151/20.* This gun, which fires only automatically, has been triple mounted on a half-tracked vehicle and employed in a self-propelled antiaircraft role.

(2) *Characteristics.*

Caliber ....15 mm (0.591 inch).
Length over-all ....75.5 inches.
Weight (including electrical control) ....84 pounds.
Operation ....Recoil.
Feed ....Disintegrating metal link belt.
Cocking ....Electrical.
Firing ....Percussion (electrical solenoid, manually operated trigger).
Rate of fire:
  With AP ....750 rounds per minute.
  With HE ....680 rounds per minute.
Muzzle velocity:
  AP Tracer ....2,715 feet per second.

(3) *Ammunition.* This gun fires tracer, armor-piercing tracer, and high explosive incendiary tracer.

g. 20-MM MACHINE GUN *(M.G.151/20).* (1) *General description.* This is the 20-mm version of the Mauser *M.G.151* design. It is only slightly different from the 15-mm gun. Barrels of the 15-mm and 20-mm models are not interchangeable. This gun also is issued in an electrically fired version, with a spring-loaded contact instead of a firing pin. Two types of ground mounts exist for the *M.G.151/20,* and there is a self-propelled antiaircraft version on a half-track.

(2) *Characteristics.*

Caliber ....20 mm (0.791 inch).
Length over-all ....69.75 inches.
Weight (including elec-
   trical control) ....93.5 pounds.
Operation ....Recoil.
Feed ....Disintegrating metal link
                          belt.
Cocking ....Electrical.
Firing ....Percussion (electrical sol-
                          enoid, manually oper-
                          ated trigger).
Rate of fire:
   Unsynchronized ....AP, 800 rounds per minute.
                          HE, 750 rounds per minute.
Muzzle velocity:
   HE Incendiary ....2,650 feet per second.
   AP Incendiary and
      APHE ....2,300 feet per second.

(3) *Ammunition.* Projectiles fired in this gun include high explosive, incendiary tracer, armor-piercing incendiary, armor-piercing high explosive, and high explosive incendiary.

h. 20-MM MACHINE GUN (*Oerlikon F.F. and F.F.M.*). (1) *General description.* This is the German air force version of the standard *Oerlikon* design. It is chambered to fit the short German 20-mm round, and the recoiling parts have been redesigned accordingly. The *M.G.F.F.* is a fixed gun. The *M.G.F.F.M.*, a later version, is mechanically identical, but may have a cooling cowling and hand firing device for use as a free gun. Both models fire only automatically.

(2) *Characteristics.*

Caliber ....20 mm (0.791 inch).
Length over-all ....52.75 inches.
Weight:
   Pneumatic cocking ....60 pounds.
   Hand cocking ....**55.75 pounds.**
Operation ....Recoil.
Feed ....60-round drum, 20-round
                        drum, or 15-round clip.
Cocking:
   Fixed gun ....Pneumatic, electrical con-
                       trol.
   Free gun ....Manual.
Firing ....Percussion.
Rate of fire (operation).400 rounds per minute.
Muzzle velocity ....1,900 feet per second.

(3) *Ammunition.* Ball tracer, high explosive, high explosive tracer, high explosive incendiary tracer, and armor piercing projectiles are fired from this gun.

i. 30-MM MACHINE GUN *(Mk.101).* (1) *General description.* This heavy machine gun is of Rheinmetall Börsig design. It may be fired single shot or automatically. Two heavy coiled springs around the barrel are necessary to check recoil. This 30-mm machine gun is being replaced by the Model 108.

(2) *Characteristics.*

Caliber ....30 mm (1.18 inches).
Length over-all ....96 inches.
Weight ....394 pounds.
Operation ....Recoil.
Feed ....10-round box magazine.
Cocking ....Pneumatic.
Firing ....Percussion, electrical sol-
                       enoid operated.
Rate of fire (estimated)..400 rounds per minute.

j. 30-MM MACHINE GUN (*Mk. 108*). (1) *General description.* The Model 108 is the latest 30-mm machine gun to be employed in aircraft and is replacing the Model 101.

(2) *Characteristics.*

Caliber ....30 mm (1.18 inches).
Length over-all ....3 feet 6 inches.
Weight ....265 pounds.
Operation ....Blowback.
Feed ....60-round disintegrating link
                       belt.
Cocking ....Compressed air.
Firing ....Electrical (sear is actu-
                       ated by compressed air).
Rate of fire ....500 rounds per minute.
Muzzle velocity ....1,650 feet per second.

(3) *Ammunition.* The high explosive tracer projectile fired from this gun weighs 11.22 ounces. Incendiary tracer projectiles are also fired.

k. 21-CM ROCKET. Single engine German fighters carry two of these rockets, while twin engined fighters carry four. The projectiles, 42.44 inches long and weighing 248 pounds, are projected from open end tubes 50.31 inches long. The rockets are fired by electricity. The launching tubes may be jettisoned by electrical detonator charges.

CHAPTER VIII

EQUIPMENT

Section I. INTRODUCTION

1. General

Current equipment of the German Armed Forces is generally good, despite more than five years of war. Although some German equipment does not reach Allied standards, in the majority of categories it has been found to be as good as, or better than, comparable U. S. items.

2. Design

Much German equipment differs radically in design from Allied counterparts. This does not mean that the functioning of the equipment is in any way inferior; the solution of the problem has been approached from another angle.

3. Shortages

Although acute material shortages sometimes force the employment of substitutes, redesigned German equipment seldom shows impaired efficiency. This is attributable to careful, meticulous planning, and to the production of a surprisingly versatile industry which is controlled completely by the state.

Section II. AUTOMOTIVE EQUIPMENT

1. General

In general, German military automotive equipment consists of adaptations of civilian types, and these in most cases do not reach the high standard of American or British vehicles either in reliability or performance. The German branches of Ford and General Motors appear to have been incapable of reproducing their prototypes with unimpaired efficiency. With half-tracked prime-

movers and personnel-carriers, however, the Germans have excelled; in this class they have produced vehicles which have given excellent service and which are unrivaled for cross-country performance.

2. German Cars

a. LIGHT ARMY CAR (*Volkswagen*). (1) *General*. This four-seat vehicle was developed from the famous "People's Car", which in fact never came into the hands of the German people. The military version has a touring body with a folding top instead of the civilian sedan type body. The *Volkswagen*, the German equivalent of the American "Jeep", is inferior in every way except in the comfort of its seating accommodations.

(2) *Chassis*. The chassis consists of a central, welded-steel tube bifurcating at the rear to support the engine and transmission. The steel floor on both sides of the central member provides the means of supporting the body. The front axle consists of steel tubes which house the two torsion bars of the suspension. The body is of sheet steel.

(3) *Power*. The engine, mounted at the rear, develops 24.5 brake horsepower at 3,300 revolutions per minute. Its capacity is 985 cubic centimeters (60 cubic inches). It is air-cooled and has four cylinders, horizontally opposed in pairs. The gasoline tank is below the instrument panel in front of the right seat. There are four forward speeds, and one reverse. The maximum speed in high gear is about 50 miles per hour. The *Volkswagen* is a four-wheeled vehicle with two-wheel drive.

(4) *Amphibious version*. An amphibious version, known as the *Schwimmwagen* or *le.P.Kw. K.2s,* has an engine of slightly increased capacity (1,131 cubic centimeters or 69 cubic inches). The crankshaft is extended to the rear of the

Figure 1.—Small personnel carrier, Volkswagen.

Figure 2.—Amphibious Volkswagen, Schimmwagen.

body and engages with the propeller-shaft by means of a dog clutch. When traveling overland, the propeller and shaft fold over the back of the vehicle. The body, which resembles a civilian sports car, is of thin welded sheet metal.

b. STANDARD CHASSIS I FOR LIGHT ARMY CAR. (1) *Chassis.* This chassis is of normal type, with a frame of rectangular section, side, and cross members and bracing to support the engine, transmission, and body. The hood is hinged down the center and fastened on each side by two clips. This chassis is used for the four-seat light car (*Kfz. 1*) and for a variety of radio and other special purpose vehicles.

(2) *Engines.* The engine is mounted at the front and may be any of the following types:

(a) *Hanomag 2-Liter (122 cubic inches) Type 20 B.* This is a water-cooled, four-cylinder O.H.V. gasoline engine with dry sump lubrication. It generates 50 brake horsepower at 3,500 revolutions per minute. Water pump, fan, and dynamo are driven by one V-belt from the camshaft.

(b) *B.M.W. 2-Liter (122 cubic inches) Type 325.* This engine is a water-cooled, six-cylinder (in-line) O.H.V. gasoline engine with dry sump lubrication, generating 45 brake horsepower at 4,000 revolutions per minute.

(c) *Stoewer Types R 180 W and AW 2.* These are both water-cooled, four-cylinder O.H.V. gasoline engines with dry sump lubrication. The R 180 W is a 1,750 cubic centimeter (106.75 cubic inches) model generating 43 brake horsepower at 3,600 revolutions per minute, and the AW 2 is a 2-liter (122 cubic inches) engine giving 50 brake horsepower at the same speed.

(3) *Power.* The power train is geared to all four wheels. The vehicle also has four-wheel steering, but the rear wheel steering mechanism may be locked. The gears give five forward speeds and one reverse. Maximum speed is 50 miles per hour. Ignition is by a 12-volt battery and coil. The main gasoline tank (13.25 gallons) is mounted at the rear, and the reserve tank (2.4 gallons) is in the engine compartment.

c. STANDARD CHASSIS I TYPE 40 FOR LIGHT ARMY CAR. This chassis, used for light staff cars and various special purpose vehicles, is practically the same as the Standard Chassis I, but has front wheel steering only. The engine is the Stoewer 2-liter (122 cubic inches) AW 2. The vehicle has a maximum speed of about 50 miles per hour.

d. LIGHT CAR, MERCEDES BENZ TYPE 170 V. (1) *Chassis.* The chassis, used for light staff

Figure 3.—Medium personnel carrier.

cars and specialized vehicles, is X-shaped and supports the engine at the front. The front wheels are independently sprung by two parallel, semi-elliptic springs crossing the front of the vehicle. The rear wheel suspension is by coil springs. The engine is fitted beneath the hood, which is of normal type.

(2) *Engine.* The engine is the water-cooled, four-cylinder, 1,700 cubic centimeters (103.7 cubic inches) Mercedes Benz Type M 136. This is a side-valve, gasoline engine with an L-shaped cylinder head, with the camshaft and valve gear on the right side. The engine develops about 38 brake horsepower at 3,400 revolutions per minute. The fuel tank, located in the engine compartment, contains 11.5 gallons.

e. STANDARD CHASSIS FOR MEDIUM CAR. (1) *Chassis.* This is a conventional chassis used for staff cars, radio vehicles, and other specialized types and consisting of two parallel side members and various cross members and brackets. The engine is fitted at the front, and the wheels are sprung independently by two coil springs with double-action, hydraulic shock absorbers

The spare wheels are carried one on each side of the chassis on stub axles to prevent bellying when traveling over rough ground.

(2) *Engines.* The engine may be either of two types: Horch V-8 Type 901 (a water-cooled, 3.5-liter (213.5 cubic inches) gasoline engine developing 82 brake horsepower at 3,600 revolutions per minute), or an Opel straight-six (a water-cooled, 3.6 liter (219.6 cubic inches) O.H.V. gasoline engine developing 68 brake horsepower at 2,800 revolutions per minute). There are two gasoline tanks. The main tank, holding 18.7 gallons, is suspended in the center of the chassis frame, and the reserve tank holding 10.8 gallons, is at the rear. The main gear box has four forward speeds and one reverse, with an auxiliary gear box giving two ratios: normal and cross-country. All four wheels are driving wheels.

f. STANDARD CHASSIS II FOR HEAVY CAR. (1) *Chassis.* There are actually three known models of this chassis, all being similar in general appearance. Model EGa has stub axles carrying the spare wheels to assist in crossing rough ground, and four-wheel steering. The steering

Figure 4.—Medium Half-tracked prime mover (8-ton).

mechanism for the rear wheels can be locked. Model EGb has front wheel steering only. Model EGd has no anti-bellying support axles. The body usually fitted is a four-door touring type of clumsy appearance. The vehicle is used for a variety of purposes, including an artillery prime mover for light guns.

(2) *Engine.* The engine is the Ford 3.6-liter (219.6 cubic inches) V-8, developing 78 brake horsepower at 3,600 revolutions per minute. This is a side-valve model with L-type cylinder heads. There are five forward speeds and one reverse. The main (14.5 gallons) and subsidiary (17 gallons) gasoline tanks are supported within the chassis frame.

3. German Trucks

a. Opel "Blitz" 3-Ton Truck Type 3.6-36 S. (1) *Chassis.* This vehicle, employed principally as a general purpose truck, has a variety of specialized bodies. There are actually three models: the 3.6-36 S, the original Chevrolet-type commercial vehicle; the 3.6-36 S (army model), which is modified to meet army specifications; and the 3.6-47 which is intended primarily for coaches and has a lengthened chassis. The vehicle has a normal rectangular type chassis, supporting the engine at the front.

(2) *Power.* The engine is a water-cooled, straight-six O.H.V. gasoline unit of 3.6 liters

(219.6 cubic inches) capacity, developing about 68 brake horsepower. The gasoline tank (21.6 gallons) is situated under the driver's seat. The gear box gives five forward speeds and one reverse. The two rear wheels are the driving wheels.

b. Opel "Blitz" 3-Ton Truck (Type 6700 A). This is essentially the four-wheel drive version of the type 3.6-36S. The drive is taken from the five-speed main gear box to a transfer case. The transfer gears have two positions: one for roads and one for cross-country travel.

c. Ford 3-Ton Truck (Types G 917 T and G 997 T). These are both commercial models with two-wheel drive, slightly modified to meet army specifications. Both are powered by V-8 water-cooled gasoline engines developing about 78 brake horsepower. In the model G 917 T the capacity is 3.6 liters (219.6 cubic inches), increased to 3.9 liters (237.9 cubic inches) in the G 997 T by enlarging the bore. The gear box gives four forward speeds and one reverse. There is also a type G 987 T, a purely commercial model but very similar to the two army models.

d. Mercedes Benz 3-Ton Truck (Type LCF 3000). (1) *Chassis.* The chassis is of welded construction with pressed steel cross-members. The engine is mounted at the front beneath a hood of normal type. Both front and rear axles are supported by two longitudinal, semi-elliptic

Figure 5.—22-ton tank transport trailer.

springs, each of which has a two-way shock absorber.

(2) *Power.* The Diesel engine is a four-cylinder, O.H.V., water-cooled model of about 5 liters (305 cubic inches) capacity. The gear-box gives four forward speeds and one reverse. There is an auxiliary gear box for selecting road or cross-country gear ratio. The driving power is carried to only two of the four wheels. Similar vehicles of Mercedes Benz manufacture also exist up to the 10-ton class. Some of the smaller ones may be found with gasoline engines, but in all the larger sizes only Dicsels are used.

e. Büssing-N.A.G. 4½-Ton Diesel Truck. This is a conventional type of truck which performs satisfactorily under test. At the governed speed of 1,740 revolutions per minute, 93 brake horsepower was developed. Over a 100-mile road circuit with heavy traffic, the vehicle averaged 21.1 miles per hour, and the fuel consumption averaged 8.72 miles per gallon. The vehicle, during the test, carried a load of 6¾ tons without any difficulty.

f. Heavy Wheeled Prime Mover *Radschlepper Ost.* (1) *Description.* This is a heavy prime mover with four large wheels, intended for use on the Russian front. This vehicle should not be confused with the *Raupenschlepper Ost,* a fully-tracked prime mover also intended for use on the Russian front.

(2) *Specifications.*

Length	20 feet.
Width	7 feet 4 inches.
Height	10 feet.
Wheels (steel)	Four, 4 feet 10 inches in diameter.
Engine	4-cylinder, in-line, air-cooled, 90 horsepower.
Fuel	Gasoline.
Capacity	6,024 cubic centimeters. (367.46 cubic inches.) (with 2-cylinder, air-cooled, 12 horsepower auxiliary starter engine).
Drive	4 wheel, with locking differential.
Gears	Five forward, one reverse.
Speed, road	6 miles per hour (average).
Weight unloaded	9 tons.
Useful load	4.5 tons.
Trailed load	5.6 tons.
Winch capacity	5.6 tons.

g. Half-Tracked Prime Movers and Personnel Carriers. These vehicles form the most successful series produced by the Germans, and have multifarious uses. Figure 60 gives brief comparative details of each. The dates given in column 3 refer to the presumed date of introduction. In the same column, the initial letters in the manufacturer's type are the initials of the original manufacturer. Thus DB stands for Daimler Benz, Bn for Büssing N.A.G., HL for Hansa-Lloyd (Borgward), D for Demag, H for Hanomag, and F for Famo. The original manufacturer may not be the exclusive maker of a particular type of vehicle, for certain types may be manufactured by several firms.

COMPARATIVE TABLE OF VARIOUS TYPES OF GERMAN HALF-TRACKED VEHICLES.

Zg.Kw. TYPE	Sd. Kfz. No.	Manufacturer's type	Maybach Engine type	Gearbox type	Braking system	Suspension	Clutch
1 ton	10	D7 (1938/9)	NL 38 TRKM or HL 42 TRKM	Maybach pre-selective semi-automatic SRG 102128H.	ATE Hydraulic foot brakes. Hydraulic steering brakes. Handbrake works mechanically on the steering brakes.	Full torsion-bar. (Idler not sprung, but fitted with shear-bolt safety device).	Fichtel and Sachs Mecano type PF 220 K.
1 ton	10	D7 (1940)	as above	Maybach Variorex VG102128H	as above	as above	as above
Light armored carrier on Zg.Kw. 1-ton chassis.	250 252 253	D7p (1940)	HL 42 TRKM	as above	as above	Note:- One pair of bogies less than on Zg.Kw. 1-ton (Sd Kfz. 10).	as above
3 ton	11	kl 6 (1938)	NL 38 TUKR or HL 42 TUKRM	Normal 4-speed type with auxiliary gearbox.	Mechanical hand and steering brakes. Mechanical servo-assisted footbrake.	Full torsion-bar. (Idler not sprung, but fitted with shear-bolt safety device).	Fichtel and Sachs Mecano type PF 220.
Medium armored carrier on Zg.Kw. 3-ton chassis.	251	kl 6p (1938)	NL 38 TUKRRM or HL 42 TUKRRM	as above	as above	as above	
as above	251	kl 6p (1940)	HL 42 TUKRRM	as above	as above		
as above	251	H kl 6p (1940)	NL 38 TUKRRM or HL 42 TUKRRM	as above	as above		
5 ton	6	BNL7 (1936)	NL 38 Spezial.	Zahnradfabrik Aphon gearbox type G.45 V. (non-synchromesh).	Mechanical steering brakes. Bosch pneumatic hand and footbrakes.	Bogies with leaf-springing in pairs. Idler sprung with 2 short torsion-bars, fixed in center of tube.	Fichtel and Sachs Mecano type PF 220 K.
5 ton	6	BNL8 DBL8 (1938/39)	NL 38 TUK or NL 38 TUKRM		Mechanical hand and steering brakes. Bosch pneumatic footbrake.	Full torsion bar. (Idler not sprung, but fitted with shear-bolt safety device).	as above

Footnote at end of table.

COMPARATIVE TABLE OF VARIOUS TYPES OF GERMAN HALF-TRACKED VEHICLES.—Continued

Zg.Kw. type	Sd. Kfz. No.	Manufacturer's type	Maybach Engine type	Gearbox type	Braking system	Suspension	Clutch
5 ton	6	BN 9 (ca. 1940)	HL 54 TUKRM		Bosch pneumatic foot brake. ATE hydraulic steering-brakes. Mechanical handbrake.	as above	as above
8 ton	7	KM m 8 (1935)	HL 52 TU	Zahnradfabrik ZG 55.	Mechanical steering and hand-brakes. Knorr pneumatic foot-brakes.	Bogies with leaf-springing in pairs. (Spiral springing on idler).	
8 ton	7	KM m 11 HL m 11 (ca. 1939)	HL 62 TUK	"Non-synchronized".	Mechanical hand and steering brakes. Bosch pneumatic foot brake.	Bogies with leaf-springing in pairs. (Torsion-bar springing on idler). Note: This model was being made up to 1942. but some later models have full torsion-bar suspension.	Mecano type K 230 K.
12 ton	8	DBs 8 (1938)	DSO/8		Bosch pneumatic foot brake. (Mechanical steering brakes).	Bogies with leaf-springing in pairs. Torsion-bar springing on idler.	Mecano type LA 80 H.
12 ton	8	DB 9 (1939)	HL 85 TUKRM.		Bosch pneumatic foot brakes. ATE hydraulic steering brakes.	as above	
12 ton	8	DB 10 (1939/40)	HL 85 TUKRM		Mechanical hand-brake. Bosch pneumatic foot-brake. Hydraulic steering brakes.	Full torsion-bar. (Idler not sprung, but fitted with shear-bolt safety device).	Mecano LA 65/80 B.
18 ton	9	F-2 (1938)	HL 98 TUK	Zahnradfabrik Type G 65 VL230.	Mechanical hand and steering brakes. Bosch pneumatic foot brake.	as above	Mecano LA 65/80.
18 ton	9	F-3 (1939)	HL 108 TUKRM	as above	as above	as above	Mecano LA 80.

Figure 60.

Section III. ARTILLERY FIRE CONTROL EQUIPMENT

1. On-Carriage Fire Control Equipment

a. GENERAL. German on-carriage fire control devices for field artillery, antitank artillery, self-propelled artillery, and tanks, are generally similar for all pieces of each class. All are characterized by excellent workmanship and ease of operation.

b. FIELD ARTILLERY. (1) *General.* Field artillery on-carriage fire control equipment is designed for both direct and indirect laying. Eight mounts of azimuth compensating type automatically allow for trunnion cant when cross-leveled. The angle-of-site mechanism is graduated from 100 to 500 mils, 300 mils representing normal. The gun is laid at the quadrant elevation on the sight by matching two arms, one moving with the gun, the other with the sight bracket. Fire adjustment depends on the accuracy of this rather difficult pointer matching. Range drums, graduated to suit the particular pieces on which they are mounted, are operated by handwheels.

(2) *Panoramic telescope M.32.* This is the

Figure 8.—Panoramic Telescope M32K.

standard German field artillery sight, and consists of the following:

(a) *Stem.* A stem fits into a tubular socket on the sight bracke of the gun.

(b) *Rotating head.* Main and slipping azimuth scales are attached to the rotating head. It can be rotated by operating a quick release, or, for finer adjustment, by micrometer heads.

(c) *Azimuth scales.* The main scale is fixed relative to the rotating head. It is graduated in hundreds of mils, numbered by twos, from zero to 6,400. The slipping scale follows every movement of the main scale, but can be rotated independently. It is graduated in hundreds of mils, numbered in twos from zero to 32 right and left. A micrometer drum, with fixed and movable scales, works in conjunction with main and slipping scales. Both are graduated in mils, numbered by tens. The index is on a fixed ring between the two scales.

(d) *Elevation micrometer.* Turning this micrometer head tilts the object glass, raising or

Figure 7.—Panoramic Telescope M32.

425

GERMAN TANK AND ARMORED CAR SIGHTS—TURRET SIGHTING TELESCOPES

TYPE	USED ON	GUNS AND AMMUNITION	Range Scales (Meters)	Magnification (X)	Field (Degrees)	Overall length (less eye guard) (inches)	Weight (pounds)	Exit Pupil distance (mm.)	Entrance Pupil diameter (mm.)	REMARKS
T.Z.F. 2 and 2X.	Pz.Kpfw.I. Models A and B.	7.92 mm MG 13.	800	2.5	28	19	19	5.5	—	It is not known with what gun the T.Z.F.2 was used, nor in which vehicle. Monocular.
T.Z.F. 3a.	4-wheeled armored car. Sd.Kfz.222 and semi-tracked A.C. Sd.Kfz. 250/9.	2 cm Kw.K. 38. 7.92 mm M.G. 34.	1200	—	—	—	—	—	—	Little is known about this telescope. Monocular.
T.Z.F.4.	Pz.Kpfw. II Models A to C.	2 cm Kw.K. 30. 7.92 mm M.G. 34.	1200	2.5	25	22.5	20	7	17.5	First confirmed Leitz design. Monocular.
T.Z.F.4/36 and 4/38.	Pz.Kpfw.II Model F.	2 cm Kw.K. 30. 7.92 mm M.G. 34.	1200 800	2.5	25	22.5	21	7	17.5	The range of 800 metres applies to T.Z.F. 4/36 and that of 1200 metres to T.Z.F. 4/38. Monocular.
T.Z.F. 5a.	Pz.Kpfw. III Models A to D.	3.7 cm Kw.K. (AP and HE). 7.92 mm M.G. 34.	2000 800	2.5	25	32.25	24	5	12.5	Monocular.
T.Z.F. 5a. (Vorf). 5 cm.	Pz.Kpfw. III Model E, etc. Kw.K. IV Models B to F.	5 cm Kw.K (AP and HE). 7.92 mm M.G. 34.	2000 1500	2.5	25	32.25	21.5	5	12.5	Monocular. Modified T.Z.F. 5a, superseded by T.Z.F. 5d.
T.Z.F. 5b.	Pz.Kpfw. III with 7.5 cm. Kw.K. Models J to N. Pz.Kpfw. IV Models B to F.	7.5 cm Kw.K. 7.92 mm M.G. 34.	2000 800	2.4	23.5	32.25	21.5	5	12.5	Monocular.
T.Z.F. 5b/36.	Pz.Kpfw. IV. Models B to F.	7.5 cm Kw.K. 7.92 mm M.G. 34.	2000 800	2.4	23.5	32.25	23	6	14.4	Monocular.
T.Z.F. 5d.	Pz.Kpfw. III. Models F and J.	5 cm Kw.K. (APC and HE) 7.92 mm M.G. 34.	3000 1500	2.4	25	31.8	20.13	5.5	13.2	Monocular.
T.Z.F. 5.	Pz.Kpfw. III Models L and M.	5 cm Kw.K 39 AP or APCHE 7.92 mm M.G. 34.	1500 3000 1200	2.4	25	31.8	20.13	5.5	13.2	Monocular.
T.Z.F. 5f (Vorf)	Pz.Kpfw. IV Models F2 to H.	7.5 cm KwK. 40 APCBC HE AP40 7.92 mm M.G. 34.	2500 3300 1500 (See Remarks)	2.4	25	31.8	20.13	5.5	13.2	Monocular. The HE scale serves for the machine gun also.

Figure 9.

GERMAN TANK AND ARMORED CAR SIGHTS—TURRET SIGHTING TELESCOPES—Continued

TYPE	USED ON	GUNS AND AMMUNITION	Range Scales (Meters)	Magnification (X)	Field (Degrees)	Overall length (less eye guard) (inches)	Weight (pounds)	Exit Pupil distance (mm.)	Entrance Pupil diameter (mm.)	REMARKS
T.Z.F. 5f. 1.	Pz.Kpfw. IV Models G to K.	7.5 cm Kw.K. 40 APCBC HE AP 40 7.92 mm M.G. 34.	3000 4000 1500 (See Remarks)	2.4	25	32	26	5.8	13.9	Monocular. The HE scale serves for the machine gun also.
T.Z.F. 6.	8-wheeled armored car and Pz. Sp. Wg. II (Luchs) Sd. Kfz. 123.	2 cm Kw K. 30 and 38, and 7.92 mm M.G. 34.	1200	2.4	22	28.4	21	5	12	Monocular.
T.Z.F. 6/38.		2 cm Kw.K. 38 and 7.92 mm M.G. 34.	1200	2.5	25					Little known about this telescope but known dimensions agree with those for the T.Z.F.6. Monocular.
T.Z.F. 9b.	Pz.Kpfw. Tiger Model E.	8.8 cm Kw.K. 36. 7.92 mm M.G. 34.	4000 1200	2.4	26	32.5	37	6	15	Binocular. Adjustable interocular distance.
T.Z.F. 9d.	Pz.Kpfw. Tiger Model B.	8.8 cm Kw.K. 43 APCBC HE 7.92 mm M.G. 34.	3000 5000 (See Remarks)							Monocular. The HE scale is believed to serve for the machine gun also.
T.Z.F. 12.	Pz.Kpfw. Panther Model D.	7.5 cm Kw.K. 42 APCBC (L/70) HE AP 40. 7.92 mm M.G. 34.	3000 4000 2000 (See Remarks)	2.5	29	45.1	63.88	6.2	15	Binocular. Light and dark filters fitted. The HE scale serves for the machine gun also.
T.Z.F. 12a.	Pz.Kpfw. Panther Models A and G.	As above.	3000 4000 2000 (See Remarks)	2.5 5	19 15	44.5	44	6.2 3.1		Monocular, dual magnification.

HULL MACHINE GUN TELESCOPES

K.Z.F. 1.	Early models of most tanks.	7.92 mm M.G. 34. (gimbal mountings).	200 (fixed)	1.8	18			5	—	Cranked, monocular, moving-eyepiece type.
K.Z.F. 2.	Pz.Kpfw. I, Commander's. Fz.Kpfw. II, Flamethrower. Pz.Kpfw. III, Commander's and Models F to J. Pz.Kpfw. IV, Tiger and Panther.	7.92 mm M.G. 34. (gimbal and ball mountings).	200 (fixed)	1.75	18	14.13	7	5	—	Cranked, monocular, moving-eyepiece type.

Figure 10.

lowering the line of sight. The elevation scale is graduated in hundreds, from 100 mils to 500 mils, with 300 as normal. The micrometer is graduated in single mils numbered in tens.

(e) *Eyepiece.* This is at the end of an arm and can be turned in any direction. The recticle which may be illuminated has an interrupted vertical line with an inverted "V" for elevation. Late models of the *M.32* as well as *M.32 K* sights have a horizontal scale added to the reticle.

(f) *Characteristics, M.32 and M.32 K.*

Power ....4 x.
Field of view...........10°.
Diameter of exit pupil...1.8 inches.
Overall length ....6.25 inches.
Weight ....5 pounds.

Figure 11.—Panoramic Telescope M16/18.

(3) *Panoramic Sight M.16/18.* (a) *Description.* The *M.16/18* sight differs from the *M.32* as follows:

It has no slipping scales.

When the azimuth scale is set at zero, the rotating head forms an angle of 90 degrees with the eye piece.

A cross-level vial asembly is secured to the shank. It is adjusted by turning an eccentric plug.

(b) *Characteristics.*

Power ....4 x.
Field of view ....10°.
Diameter of exit pupil....1.5 inches.
Length Over-all ....6.25 inches.
Weight ....4 pounds 5 ounces.

c. ANTITANK GUNS. (1) *General.* All German antitank-gun sight mounts have facilities for applying range, and most have a means for applying lateral deflection. Characteristics of various sights are:

(a) *2 cm S.Pz. B41.* Open sights "U" and acorn. Graduations for range, but no mechanical arrangement for applying deflection. Telescope sight fits into a trigger housing on sight mount.

(b) *5 cm Pak 38.* The sight incorporates lateral deflection gear and means for adjusting line and elevation. Range drum is graduated to 2,400 meters (HE) and 1,400 meters (AP).

(c) *7.5 cm Pak 40.* As for *5 cm Pak 38* but graduated to 2,800 mils (HE) and 1,400 mils (AP).

(d) *7.62 cm Pak 36 (r).* Rocking bar reciprocating; range indicator graduated to 6,000 meters (APCBC) and 2,000 meters (AP 40). Elevation indicator graduated in meters for three types of projectiles and in mils up to 800.

(e) *7.5/5.5 cm Pak 41.* Range drum with five scales. The first is graduated in mils, the remaining four in meters with decreasing range limits; believed used as muzzle velocity decreases with rapid wear of the tapered bore. A deflection mechanism is located below the range setting handle.

(f) *8.8 cm Pak 43/41.* There are two telescopic mounts side by side on the left. One, of rocking bar type, is for antitank use, and the other, similar to the sight mount of the *10.5 cm le. F.H.18* is for indirect laying.

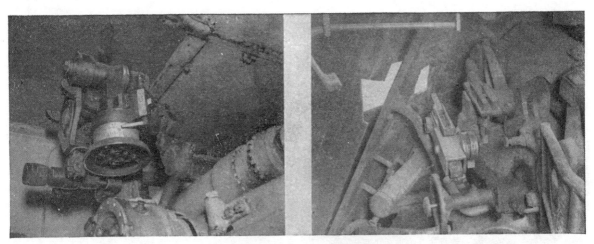

Figure 12.—Sight mounts. (Left) For 10.5 cm Howitzer on Pz. Kpfw. III chassis (Stu. H42). (Right) For 7.5 cm Pak 40 on Czech (38t) tank chassis.

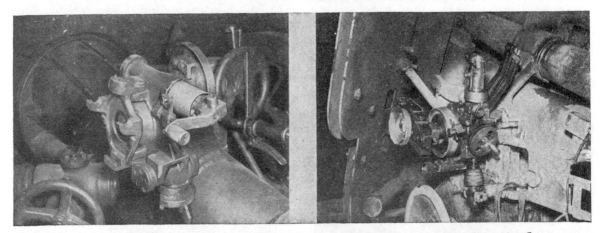

Figure 13.—Sight mounts. (Left) For 75/55 mm Pak 41 Gun. (Right) For 8.8 cm Pak 43/41 Gun.

Figure 14.—Sight mounts (Left) For 7.5 cm (Stu. K40) Pz. Kpfw. III chassis. (Right) For 7.5 cm on Pz. Kpfw. III w/o rotary cupola.

(2) *Zielfernrohr, Z.F. 38/II S.v.o.4* This is the sight now used with all antitank guns. It has one main graduation with three secondary graduations on each side, and a vertical line between the conical reticles. The angle from conical to vertical reticle is 4 mils, giving a maximum lay-off of 24 mils on each side. The field of view is 8 degrees, and magnification three-fold.

Figure 15.—Sight mounts. (Top) For 7.5 cm Howitzer. (Center) For 10.5 cm LFH 18 Howitzer. (Bottom) For 15 cm SIG 33 Howitzer.

(3) *Aushilfsrichtmittel 38.* This is the sight used for indirect laying of antitank guns. It consists of a tangent elevation drum, bearing ring, and telescopic sight with 10-degree field of view and 3-power magnification. The tangent elevation drum is graduated from zero to 1,300 mils by hundreds, and the bearing scale from zero to 6,400 mils in hundreds. Both have micrometer adjustments for zero to 100 mils.

d. SELF-PROPELLED ARTILLERY. Most German self-propelled assault and antitank guns of 75 mm or more caliber use the *Sfl. Z.F.* series of direct-laying telescopes. Excepting the *Sfl. Z.F. 5,* on the *8.8 cm Pak 43/3 (L/71)* on *Pz. Jag. Panther,* they are mounted on a *Zieleinrichtung 37 (Z.E. 37)* sight bracket. This sight bracket has cross-levelling deflection and range adjustments. Since 1942 panoramic sights issued for self-propelled artillery have been reduced to one for each two guns.

e. TANK AND ARMORED CAR SIGHTS. (1) *General.* German tank and armored car sights are of articulated stationary eyepiece type, with vertically moving reticles. They are for direct laying, and consist of two main parts: objective tube and reticle box, which move with the gun; and the eyepiece tube, carrying the range control, which remains stationary. (Details of tank and armored car sights are given in Figure 9.)

(2) *Range scales.* Range scales (including an allowance for jump) consist of a series of small circles about the optical axis, graduated in hundreds of meters, and numbered every 200 meters. Those for various projectiles are marked accordingly. Ranges are read against a fixed translucent pointer at the top of the field of view.

(3) *Reticle markings.* Reticle markings consist of a large central triangle, or inverted V, with three smaller triangles on each side at 4-mil intervals. The center apex is the normal aiming point. Zeroing knobs for line (*"Seite"*) and elevation (*"Höhe"*) and reticle illumination are provided. The optical and mechanical joint is a dust proof, water-tight prism system, usually limited to —20 degrees depression and +30 degrees elevation.

(4) *Machine-gun sights.* Machine-gun sights on tanks and armored cars are fixed in gimbal or ball mounts, with the optical axis offset so that the line of sight is close to the machine gun when it passes through the ball. The reticle has no range or deflection settings. Zeroing adjustments are provided, however, as well as illumination.

Figure 16.—Aiming Circle, Rkr 31, with case and illuminating apparatus.

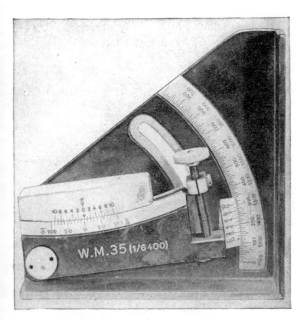

Figure 17.—Gunner's quadrant.

2. Off-Carriage Fire Control Equipment

a. GENERAL. Like their other optical instruments, German off-carriage fire control equipment is superior in design and workmanship. Most instruments which are quite similar to our own could be used effectively by Allied troops.

b. *Winkelmesser 35* (*W.M. 35*), GUNNER'S QUADRANT. (1) *General.* This gunner's quadrant is simple and well constructed. The frame contains an elevation arc with a scale graduated in ten-mil units from zero to 1,000 mils in black numerals, and from 600 to 1,600 mils in red. The quadrant arm carries a spirit level and is provided with coarse and fine screw-type adjustments.

(2) *Characteristics:*

Weight ....1.75 pounds.
Height ....4.63 inches.
Width ....0.94 inch.
Length ....4.63 inches.

c. *Richtkreis 31* (*Rkr. 31*), AIMING CIRCLE. (1) *General.* Material, workmanship, and design of the *Rkr. 31* are excellent, and no expense has been spared in its production. It is con-

431

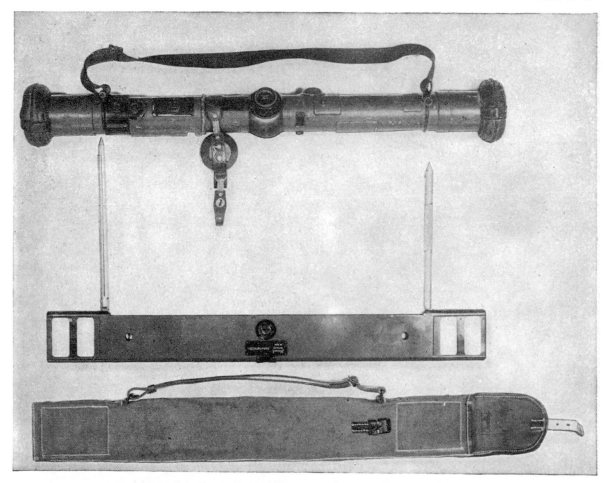

Figure 18.—70 cm Range Finder with adjusting lath and carrying case.

structed in three major parts: the periscope, the telescope, and the angle-of-site mechanism. When assembled, these can be mounted on the spindle of a tripod. The instrument can be used to measure vertical and horizontal angles; by using the magnetic needle, magnetic bearings can be taken. When disassembled, part of the instrument can be used for plane table work.

(2) *Description.* The periscope is fitted to the aiming circle by means of a dovetailed slide. Its function is merely to raise the line of sight. It has no magnifying power. The telescope has an adjustable focussing eyepiece, with a leveling bubble on top. A lighting attachment is provided on the left side. To the left of the telescope is a spherical level by which the head can be leveled. The angle-of-sight mechanism can be rotated through a total of 1,400 mils, the horizontal being 300 mils. The smallest graduation is 1 mil. The traversing mechanism is graduated in mils

from zero to 6,400. A quick release mechanism is provided.

The tripod is adjustable in height and has a traversing mechanism. A spindle projecting from the traversing head forms the support for the aiming circle. Two rings in which the spindle is mounted eccentrically control its vertical position, and by rotating these rings the spherical level can be centered.

d. RANGE FINDERS. (1) *General.* In general, German range finders are of the stereoscopic type, but a 70-cm base coincidence range finder, though no longer in production, is still in use. Range finders are known to exist in the following sizes:

70-cm base.
1-meter base.
1.5-meter base.
4-meter base.
6-meter base.
10-meter base.
12-meter base.

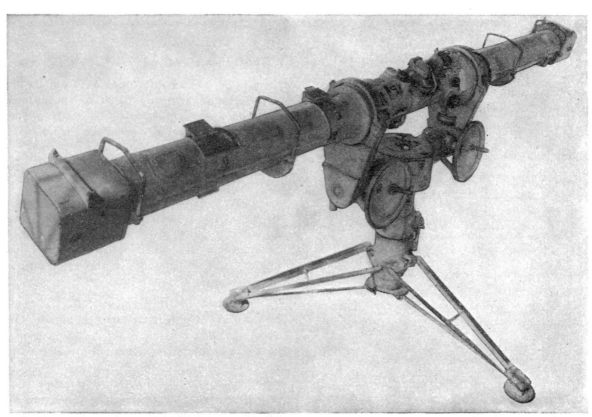

Figure 19.—4-meter Range Finder, Model Em 4m R40.

Figure 20.—Range Finder, 1.5 meter-Base. (Top) Assembled view. (Bottom) Assembled ready for use.

(2) *70-cm Range Finders 14 and 34 (Entfernungsmesser 14 and 34).*

(a) *General.* The 70-cm (27.56 inches) co-incidence range finder is used by German machine-gun and mortar units, and by airborne troops for obtaining the ranges of ground targets. It also is used with the *M.G.34* for antiaircraft fire. For adjustment an artificial infinity is used. There is no adapter for mounting on a tripod.

(b) *Characteristics.*

```
Base length ..............70 cm (27.56 inches).
Magnification ...........11 x.
Range ..................219 to 10,930 yards.
Weight of Range finder..10 pounds.
Weight of case complete..4.5 pounds.
```

(3) *1-Meter (39.37 inches) Stereoscopic Range Finders.* (a) *General.* These portable 1-meter base range finders are used largely by light antiaircraft units manning 20-mm and 37-mm guns.

(b) *Characteristics.*

	Em.R. 1 m.	Em.R.36 1 m.
Base length	39.37 inches	39.37 inches.
Magnification	7.8 x	6 x.
Range	275 to 8,740 yards.	545 to 10,930 yards.
Weight	9.9 pounds	16 pounds.

(4) *1.5-Meter (59.06 inches) Stereoscopic Range Finder (Em.R.1.5 m).* (a) *General.* This range finder is provided with a tripod and is only used against fixed targets.

(b) *Characteristics.*

```
Base length .............59.06 inches.
Magnification ...........11 x.
Range ..................435 to 21,860 yards.
Weight .................20.9 pounds.
Weight of tripod.,......39.6 pounds.
```

(5) *4-Meter (157.48 inches) Range Finder (Em.R. 4 m).* (a) *General.* This is the standard instrument for use with heavy antiaircraft guns. It may be employed either as an independent range finder, or incorporated into an antiaircraft detector. As a range finder it is served by a crew of four: rangetaker, layer for line, layer for elevation, and reader.

(b) *Characteristics.*

```
Range .............from 2,200 feet.
Weight ...........420 pounds.
```

(6) *6-, 10-, and 12-Meter Range Finders.* These instruments are used for range measurement for seacoast artillery.

Section IV. SIGNAL EQUIPMENT

I. Constructional Features

a. GENERAL. Two features stand out in the construction of Germany Army communications equipment: the unit construction methods employed and the material from which the units are made.

b. UNIT CONSTRUCTION METHODS. Practically every piece of radio equipment is constructed in units, which are secured to panels and to each other, electrical connections being made by plug and socket strips or by screwing tags or soldering wires to a terminal strip. In most cases this permits quick dismantling for servicing and repair.

c. MATERIALS USED (1) *General.* The metal from which radio sets are made is almost universally an alloy of about 90 per cent magnesium; 8 per cent aluminum; and 2 per cent zinc, copper, and other metals. Each unit consists of a die-casting of this alloy. Not only is the main sub-chassis cast, but also the screening plates, bosses, and recesses for mounting components. The castings are accurately made, requiring little machining, thus establishing excellent mechanical rigidity and improved electrical performance.

(2) *Tuning condensers.* Main tuning condensers are made from the standard alloy. Both rotors and stators are machined from a block casting. Thus, there can be no deterioration in performance due to corrosion between individual plates and their mountings.

(3) *Insulation.* Extensive use is made of ceramic materials for insulating; they are used for tag strips, tube holders, tube bases, coil formers, and almost universally as the main bearing for ganged condensers. Where coil formers are not made from ceramics, porcelain or pressed bakelised paper is used.

(4) *Condensers.* Trimmer condensers are usually either small, air-spaced ones, or of the silvered ceramic-disc type (Philips), which are used to some extent in British and American equipment. Small, fixed condensers are the tubular ceramic type or flat mica type in a bakelite shroud. Except in older versions of the *100 W.S.,* mica is used sparingly. Larger condensers are paper-dielectric Mansbridge type. No color coding is used, the values being printed on the condenser in mF, pF, or centimeters.

(5) *Resistors.* Resistors are usually of the noninductive carbon type, although a few wire-wound ones are employed purely for direct current purposes, such as voltage dividers. No color coding is used, the values being printed on the resistor in ohms.

(6) *Coils.* Low frequency coils and chokes are wound with single-strand, enamel-insulated wire, or with silk-covered *liztendraht* wire. High frequency coils usually are wound with bare copper or copper strip. Alternatively, the coil former has a helical groove in which a thin layer of copper is deposited, apparently by electrolysis. The inductance of most high frequency coils can be varied within small limits by adjustment of a co-axial iron dust core, or copper ring. Intermediate frequency transformers not only have iron dust cores, but are in many cases completely enclosed in an iron dust shrouding.

(7) *Tubes.* German radio receivers of modern design have only one type of tube throughout, usually a pentode. These tubes are not always used in an orthodox fashion—for instance a pentode may be used as a diode—but the method considerably facilitates the supply of spares.

2. Power Supplies

Power supplies vary according to the purpose for which the piece of equipment is used. Vehicle sets employ separate rotary converters driven from the 12-volt vehicle storage batteries. These converters are of heavy rugged construction, and therefore remain serviceable for long periods without attention. Ground stations employ storage batteries and dry batteries, pedal operated generators, or small gasoline electric sets. Pack sets employ storage batteries with dry batteries or synchronous vibrators.

3. Simplification

a. CONDENSERS. Great pains are taken to make the working of the sets as simple and reliable as possible. Tuning condensers are driven through a chain of precision gearing, using fiber and spring-loaded metallic wheels to remove backlash.

b. DIALS. The dials are of a large size, with calibration spaced over 300 degrees or more. They are accurately marked out, permitting the frequency to be set to very close limits without the use of a wavemeter. Most dials are marked with one or more check points, allowing initial calibration to be accurately set or checked by means of **an** external or internal crystal oscilla-

tor or by means of an internal "glow crystal" (*leuchtquarz*).

c. NUMBERING. As an aid to both construction and servicing, each component in a set has a number, and in many cases the wiring is numbered also. Any two points bearing the same number are directly connected.

4. Armored Vehicle Radio Sets

a. GENERAL. Complete sets in armored vehicles include transmitter, receiver, power units, and accessories, referred to by the designation *Fu.*, followed by a number. An exception is the voice transmitting set *Fu. Spr.f.* used in self-propelled field and medium artillery vehicles and certain armored cars. This set has no *Fu.* number. Transmitters and receivers individually are referred to by a description and a letter, such as 10 watt transmitter "c".

b. RADIO SETS USED. The following tabulation shows what complete radio sets are likely to be installed in various types of armored and self-propelled artillery vehicles. Details on these sets will be found in the accompanying tables.

Vehicle	Radio
Commander's tank	*Fu.8* and *Fu.5; or Fu.7* and *Fu.5.*
Fighting tanks, all types	*Fu.5* and *Fu.2; or Fu.5* only.
Assault guns (in armored formations)	*Fu.5* and *Fu.2; or Fu.5* only.
Armored OP vehicles (artillery)	*Fu.8* and *Fu.4; or Fu.8, Fu.4,* and *Fu.Spr.f.*
Assault guns (artillery)	*Fu.8, Fu.16,* and *Fu.15; or Fu.16* and *Fu.15; or Fu.16 only.*
Self-propelled antitank guns (light and medium chassis)	*Fu.8* and *Fu.5; or Fu.5* only.
Self-propelled antitank guns (heavy chassis)	*Fu.8* and *Fu.5; or Fu.7* and *Fu.5; or Fu.5* and *Fu.2.*
Antitank-assault guns	*Fu.8* and *Fu.5; or Fu.5* only.
Lynx (reconnaissance)	*Fu.12* and *Fu.Spr.f.* or *Fu.Spr.f.* only.
Antiaircraft tanks (*Flakpanzer*)	*Fu.5* or *Fu.2* only.
Self-propelled heavy infantry gun	*Fu.16* only.
Wasp and Bumble Bee	*Fu.Spr.f.* only.
Armored cars (except eight-wheeled vehicle) and semi-tracked vehicles with armament.	*Fu.Spr.f.* only.
Armored cars	*Fu.12* and *Fu.Spr.f.*
Eight-wheeled armored car	*Fu.12* and *Fu.Spr.f.* or *Fu.Spr.f.* only.

Figure 21.—Short Wave Receiver Kw.E.a.

Figure 22.—Radio TFuG. k.

Figure 23.—Relaiskasten T39 Teletype Repeater.

Figure 24.—Transmitter 15 W.S.E.b.

Figure 25.—Transmitter 5 W.S.c.

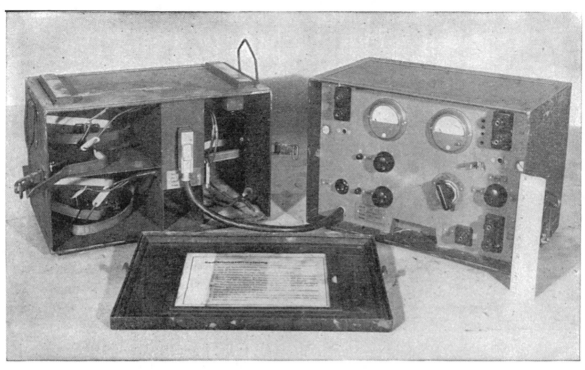

Figure 26.—Feldverstarker with battery case.

Figure 27.—Transmitter 100 W.

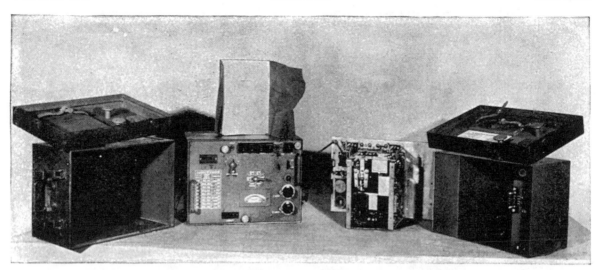

Figure 28.—Attenuator Meter Dampfrugmesser 39.

Figure 29.—Feldfernschreiber.

Figure 30.—Transmitter/Receiver (Torn.Fu. bl) with case for battery and accessories.

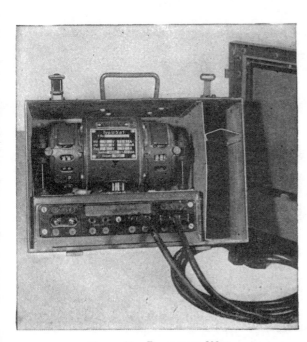

Figure 31.—Dynamotor U5a1.

Figure 32.—Fixed emplacement wall telephone.

Figure 33.—10-Line switchboard.

Figure 34.—Teleprinter terminal unit.   Figure 35.—TFb 1 carrier frequency unit.

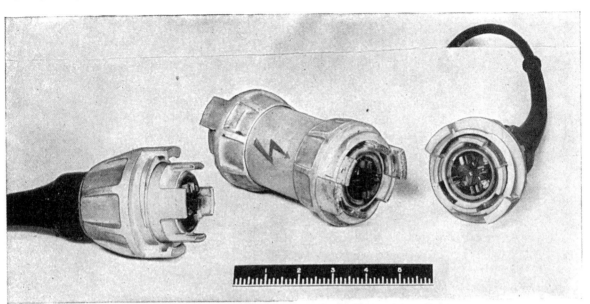

Figure 36.—"Spiral-Four" field telephone cable assembly.

Figure 37.—Torn. Fu. g.

Figure 38.——Direction finding receiver E.P.2a.

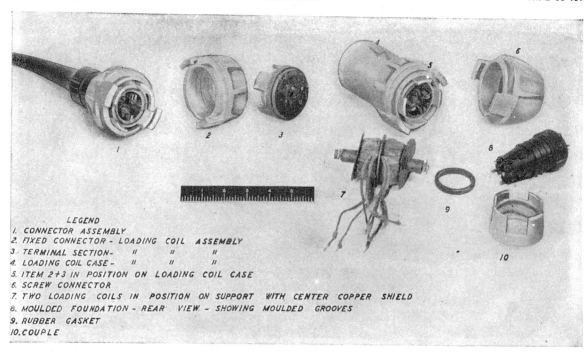

LEGEND
1. CONNECTOR ASSEMBLY
2. FIXED CONNECTOR - LOADING COIL ASSEMBLY
3. TERMINAL SECTION-   "   "   "
4. LOADING COIL CASE-   "   "   "
5. ITEM 2+3 IN POSITION ON LOADING COIL CASE
6. SCREW CONNECTOR
7. TWO LOADING COILS IN POSITION ON SUPPORT WITH CENTER COPPER SHIELD
8. MOULDED FOUNDATION - REAR VIEW - SHOWING MOULDED GROOVES
9. RUBBER GASKET
10. COUPLE

Figure 39.—"Spiral-Four" field telephone cable unassembled.

Figure 40.—30W. S. a.

Figure 41.—Field telephone central (10 lines).

Figure 42.—Vibrator power supply EW.E.

Figure 43.—Walkie Talkie Feldfu.f.

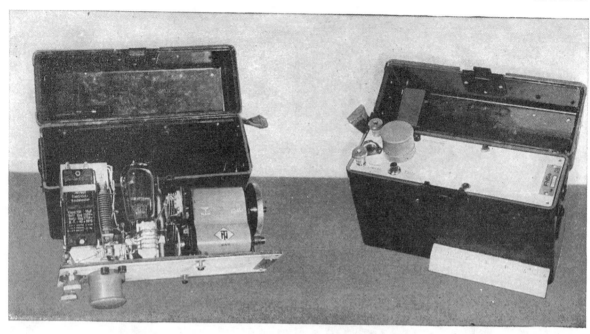

Figure 44.—Fortress emergency transmitter.

Figure 45.—Receiver Ukw. E.e. Transmitter 10 WS.c.

Figure 46.—Leitungsabschluss Kasten line terminal equipment.

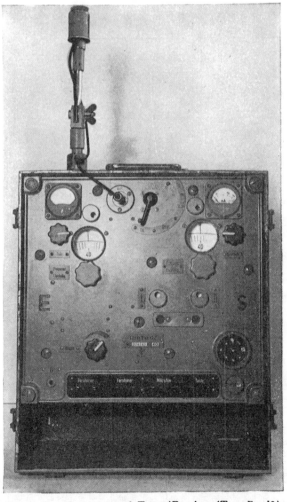

Figure 47.—Two-man pack Trans/Receiver (Torn.Fu. d2).

SPECIFICATIONS OF VACUUM TUBES USED IN GERMAN ARMY SIGNAL EQUIPMENT

NUMBER	TYPE	CATHODE TYPE AND RATING C.T.	VOLTS	AMP.	USE AND APPLICATION	Plate Voltage *Maximum VOLTS	Grid Voltage *Maximum VOLTS	Screen Voltage *Maximum VOLTS	Plate Current at Plate Voltage Indicated M A	Screen Current at Screen Voltage Indicated M A	Plate Resistance OHMS	Transconductance umhos	Amplification Factor u	Allowable Plate Dissipation WATTS	Allowable Screen Dissipation WATTS	Load Output OHMS	Maximum Grid-Plate Capacity uufds
A32 Telefunken AB2 Valvo 4D1 Loewe	Duo-Diode Receiver Tube	Ind.	4 A.C.	0.65	H.F. Rectifier												
AC2 Telefunken AC2 Valvo AC2 Tungsram	Triode Receiver Tube	Ind.	4 A.C.	0.65	Audio and H.F. Tube Oscillator L.F. Amplifier	250*	−5.5		6		12,000	2,500	30	2.0			1.7
AF3 Telefunken	Variable mu Pentode Receiver Tube	Ind.	4 A.C.	0.65	Variable mu H.F. Tube	250*	−3	100	8		1.2M	1,800	2,200	2.0			0.003
AF3 Valvo AF3 Tungsram 4H2 Loewe							−55	100	.015		10M	2					
AF7 Telefunken	Pentode	Ind.	4 A.C.	0.65	H.F. Tube	300*	−2	100	3		20M	2,100	4,000	1.0			0.003
AF7 Valvo AF7 Tungsram	Receiver				Audio Frequency Amplifier (Resistance Coupling)				0.9								
4H1 Loewe	Tube				Audio Tube												
AL4 Telefunken AL4 Valvo 4EI Loewe	Pentode	Ind.	4 A.C.	1.75	Output Pentode	250	−6	250	36	5	50,000	9,500		9		7,000	
AZ1 Telefunken AZ1 Valvo TAZ1 Tungsram A21 Phillips VG5007 Hoges	Duo-Diode Rectifier Tube		4	1	Full Wave Rectifier	Maximum A.C. Input 500 Volts per Plate 300 Volts per Plate					Maximum D.C. Output 60 M A 100 M A						
DAF11	Variable mu Pentode Diode		1.2 D.C.	0.05	Variable mu Pentode Low Frequency Amplifier H.F. Rectifier	150*	0	120	0.29		.9M			0.6			
DCH11	Triode Hexode		1.4 D.C.	0.075	Oscillator Convertor Variable mu												
DDD11	Duplex Triode		1.2 D.C.	0.1	Output Tube	120 150*	−4.5		6 per Plate							14,000	

Figure 48.

SPECIFICATIONS OF VACUUM TUBES USED IN GERMAN ARMY SIGNAL EQUIPMENT—Continued

NUMBER	TYPE	CATHODE TYPE AND RATING C.T.	VOLTS	AMP.	USE AND APPLICATION	Plate Voltage *Maximum VOLTS	Grid Voltage *Maximum VOLTS	Screen Voltage *Maximum VOLTS	Plate Current at Plate Voltage Indicated M A	Screen Current at Screen Voltage Indicated M A	Plate Resistance OHMS	Transconductance umhos	Amplification Factor u	Allowable Plate Dissipation WATTS	Allowable Screen Dissipation WATTS	Load Output OHMS	Maximum Grid-Plate Capacity uufds
DF11	Variable mu Pentode		1.4 D.C.	0.025	H.F. Tube	150* 120	0 −3.5	120			1M 10M	700 7		105			
G407 Tungsram					Refer to RE074												
H406D Valvo RES094 Telefunken	Screen Tetrode Receiver Tube	Dir.	4 D.C.	0.062	H.F. Tube	200*	−2	80	4		4M	700	280				0.02
S406 Tungsram																	
HL2/0.5 a					Ballast Tube												
LD 1	Triode				H.F. Tube												
LD 2	Triode (Transmitting)				H.F. Tube I.F. Stages												
LG 1	Diode				H.F. Tube												
LS50	Pentode (Transmitting)				H.F. Tube	2,100											
RE074 Telefunken G407 Tungsram H406 Valvo	Triode Receiver Tube	Dir.	4 D.C.	0.06	Audio and H.F. Tube Low Frequency Amplifier (Transformer Coupling)	150*	−9		3.5		11,000	900	10				4
RE084 Telefunken LD408 Tungsram A408 Valvo	Triode Receiver Tube	Dir.	4 D.C.	0.08	Audio Tube Low Frequency Amplifier	150*	−4		4		10,000	1,500	15				4.5
RE084K	Triode	Dir.	4	0.08	Audio Tube Low Frequency Amplifier (Transformer Coupling)	120					11,000	1,200	13.5				3
RE134 Telefunken L414 Tungsram L413 Valvo	Triode Output Tube	Dir.	4 D.C.	0.15	Output Triode	250	−17 12*		12			2,000		3		12,000	
REN904 Telefunken AG495 Tungsram A4110 Valvo LA203 Loewe	Triode Receiver Tube	Ind.	4 A.C.	1.0	Audio and H.F. Tube Low Frequency Amplifier	150*	−9		3.5		11,000	900	10	1.5			2

Figure 48 (Continued).

SPECIFICATIONS OF VACUUM TUBES USED IN GERMAN ARMY SIGNAL EQUIPMENT—Continued

NUMBER	TYPE	CATHODE TYPE AND RATING			USE AND APPLICATION	Plate Voltage *Maximum VOLTS	Grid Voltage *Maximum VOLTS	Screen Voltage *Maximum VOLTS	Plate Current at Plate Voltage Indicated M A	Screen Current at Screen Voltage Indicated M A	Plate Resistance OHMS	Trans-conductance umhos	Amplification Factor u	Allowable Plate Dissipation WATTS	Allowable Screen Dissipation WATTS	Load Output OHMS	Maximum Grid-Plate Capacity uufds
		C.T.	VOLTS	AMP.													
RENS1264 Telefunken AS4120 Tungsram H4111D Valvo	Screen Tetrode Receiver	Ind.	4 A.C.	1.0	Audio and H.F. Tube Low Frequency Amplifier (Resistance Coupling)	200*	−2	100	3		45M	2,000	900	1.0			0.006
RES094					Refer to H406D												
RES164 Telefunken PP416 Tungsram L416D Valvo LAP513 Loewe	Pentode	Dir.	4 D.C.	0.15	Output Tube	250	−11.5	80	12	1.9	60,000	14,000		3		10,000	
RGN2004 Telefunken PV4200 Tungstram G2004 Valvo VG3512 Hoges 1561 Philips VG420 Sator	Duo-Diode	Dir.	4	2.0	Full Wave Rectifier	Maximum A.C. input 300 Volts Per Plate — Maximum D.C. Output 160 M.A.											
RL2P3 Telefunken	Pentode	Dir.	1.9 D.C.	0.28	H.F. Tube Oscillator	200*		150*			75,000	1,000	75	2.0			0.1
RL 2.4P2																	
RL2T2 Telefunken	Triode	Dir.	1.9	0.30		150*					5,000	2,400	12	2.0			2.85
RL 2.4T1																	
RL 12P10																	
RL 12T15																	
RL12P35 Telefunken	Pentode (Transmitting)		12.6														
RS 241V			3.8														
RS242																	
RS337 Telefunken	Pentode (Transmitting)		12														

Figure 48 (Continued).

SPECIFICATIONS OF VACUUM TUBES USED IN GERMAN ARMY SIGNAL EQUIPMENT—Continued

NUMBER	TYPE	CATHODE TYPE AND RATING			USE AND APPLICATION	Plate Voltage *Maximum	Grid Voltage *Maximum	Screen Voltage *Maximum	Plate Current at Plate Voltage Indicated	Screen Current at Screen Voltage Indicated	Plate Resistance	Trans-conductance	Amplification Factor	Allowable Plate Dissipation	Allowable Screen Dissipation	Load Output	Maximum Grid-Plate Capacity
		C.T.	VOLTS	AMP.		VOLTS	VOLTS	VOLTS	M A	M A	OHMS	umhos	u	WATTS	WATTS	OHMS	uufds
RV2P700 Telefunken	Pentode	Dir.	1.9	0.09	Audio and H.F. Tube Short Wave Tube	200*		120*			1.2M	900	850	1.0			0.01
RV2P800 Telefunken	Pentode	Dir.	1.9	0.18	Audio and H.F. Tube	200*		150*			1M	900	800	1.5			0.01
RV2.4P700																	
RV12P2000 Telefunken	Pentode	Ind.	12.6	0.065	Audio and H.F. Tube Short Wave "Universal" Receiving Output Pentode	220*		140*			1.5M	1,500	2,000	1.0			0.005
RV12P4000 Telefunken	Pentode	Ind.	12.6	0.2	Audio and H.F. Tube "Universal" Receiving	200*		125*			1.8M	2,300	4,000	1.5			0.004
STV280/80																	
STV150/40Z					Voltage Regulator												

Figure 48 (Continued).

POWER SUPPLIES FOR GERMAN RADIO SETS

Type of Equipment	Exact Nameplate Nomenclature	Input From	Input Volts	Input Amperes	Input Watts*	Revolutions per minute	HV Volts	HV Amperes	HV Watts	LV Volts	LV Amperes (max)	LV Watts*	Used With (German Sets)
Dynamotors	U. 1500	3-phase motor	380γ	17.3	9,100	2,900	3,000	0.8	2,400	27	37	1,000	**1000 W. S.**
			220Δ	30			1,000	0.8	800	440	2	80	**1500 W. S.**
	U. 100 or U. 100a			33/40		3,000	1,000	0.24	240	12	7.3	87.6	**100 W. S.**
	U. 80a			35	420	2,600	800/300	0.3/0.005	240				**80 W. S. a**
	U. 30			16.5	195	3,200	330	0.35	115	12	3.3	39.6	**30 W. S./24b-120**
	U. 30b			12	144	4,000	400	0.175	70				**30 W. S. a**
	U. 20a, U. 20a2, U. 20a3	12-volt storage battery	12	10	120	2,800	370	0.16	60	12	2.75	33	**20 W. S. c** **20 W. S. d**
	U. 20a1S												**20 W. S. b**
	U. 15a			14.6	175	5,500	320	0.19	60	4.8	2.6	12.5	**15 W. S. E. a** **15 W. S. E. b**
	U. 10 and U. 10a1			6.7	80	3,500	350	0.115	40				**10 W. S. c** **10 W. S. h**
	U. 5a1			7.5	90	4,000	330	0.140	46	5	1.2	6	**5 W. S./24b-104**
	E. U. a1, a2, a3			2.3	26	4,000	130	0.026	3.4	12			**U. Kw. E. d. U. Kw. E. e**
	S. E. U. a			5.2	62	8,000	300	0.070	21	12			**Radiotelephone sets a. d. f**
Vibrator units (Consumption figures include receiver, low-voltage)	E W b	2-volt storage battery	2	1.5	3			0.010	1	2	0.75	1.5	**Torn. E. b**
	E W c			1	12								
	E W d	12-volt storage battery	12	2.5	30		100	0.014	1.4	2	1.5	3.0	**Lw. E. a**
	E W e			1	12			0.024	2.4		2.0	4.0	**Kw. E. a**
	E W f	2.4-volt storage battery	2.4				100	0.010	1	2.4	0.6	1.44	**15 W. S. E.** (Receiver only)

Footnotes at end of table.

Figure 49.

POWER SUPPLIES FOR GERMAN RADIO SETS—Continued

TYPE OF EQUIPMENT	EXACT NAME-PLATE NOMENCLATURE	INPUT				OUTPUT						USED WITH (GERMAN SETS)
		From	Consumption			Revolutions per minute	High voltage			Low voltage		
			Volts	Amperes	Watts*		Volts	Amperes	Watts	Volts	Amperes (max)	Watts*	
Pedal generators	T 5 †	Foot driven				65	330	0.140	46	5	1.2	6	5 W. S./24b-104.
	T 15 †	Foot driven											SE469A
	T 20 †					70							20 W. S. c / 20 W. S. d
	Heavy engine generator set a.	4-stroke gasoline engine, 4 cyl, 26 hp.	Gasoline/oil........			1,500	220 / 380 3-phase a-c	40 / 23	15 kva				1,500 and 1,000 watt transmitters and workshop machines.
	Light engine generator set C100.						1,000 a-c		300	12.8		90	100 W. S.
Engine generator sets (H. G. N. 100)	Light engine generator set C30 (H. G. N. 20a1).	2-stroke gasoline engine, 1 cyl, 1.8 hp.	1-¾ pints per hour (oil/gasoline) 1/25			3,000	350	0.3	105	15	7	105	Special sound ranging equipment.
	Light engine generator set C20 (H. G. N. 20a).	2-stroke gasoline engine, 1 cyl, 1.8 hp.											
	Engine generator set F (WG3000).	4-stroke gasoline engine, 2 cyl, 9 hp.	Gasoline/oil........			1,500	220 a-c	13.6	3,000				
	Engine generator set (WG570a).	2-stroke gasoline engine, 1 cyl, 1.8 hp.	1¾ pints per hour (oil/gasoline) 1/25).			3,000		2.6	572				
	Charging set C (LG650).									15/50 65	15/10 10	650	Storage battery charging with charging board C.
	Charging set D (LG3000).	2-stroke gasoline engine, 1 cyl, 6.5 hp.	5¼ pints per hour (oil/gasoline)..			2,000				65	46	3,000	Storage battery charging (storage battery charging vehicle (Kfz. 42).
	Charging set E (LG800).	2-stroke gasoline engine, 1 cyl, 1.8 hp.	1¾ pints per hour (oil/gasoline) 1/25			3,000				15	53	800	Float charging of radio storage battery while set is working (with charging board C).
Engine generator charging sets	Engine generator (GG400).	2-stroke gasoline engine, 1 cyl 0.9 hp.	1¾ pints per hour (oil/gasoline) 1/25).			4,800				12 / 16	33.5 / 25	400	
	Engine generator (GG600).									12 / 15.5	25-50	600	

Footnotes at end of table.

Figure 49 (Continued)

POWER SUPPLIES FOR GERMAN RADIO SETS—Continued

TYPE OF EQUIPMENT	EXACT NAME-PLATE NOMENCLATURE	INPUT From	Consumption Volts	Consumption Amperes	Consumption Watts*	Revolutions per minute	OUTPUT High voltage Volts	High voltage Amperes	High voltage Watts	Low voltage Volts	Low voltage Amperes (max)	Low voltage Watts*	USED WITH (GERMAN SETS)
Hand charging sets	HLSa	Hand driven				82				4	4	16	Charging 2- and 2.4-volt radio storage batteries
Charging rectifiers (with metal rectification)	T 506b†	A-c mains		10/9/7/5							10	560	Storage battery charging
	T 200†	A-c mains	110/125, 155/220	3.6/3.2, 2.6/1.8						12/24, 36/48	3.5	200	
	T 48†	A-c mains		1/0.9/0.7/0.5							1	48	
Transmitter rectifiers (with metal rectification)	T 1500†	3-phase a-c mains	220/380	22/12.7			440/1,000/ 3,000 d-c	2/0.5/0.9	4,100	24	36	864	**1000 W. S. 1500 W. S.**
	T/100†	A-c mains	110/125, 155/220	8.8/7.8, 6.3/4.4			1,000	0.3	300	12	7.5	90	**100 W. S.**
	T5/10/20/30†	A-c mains	110/125, 155/220	3.2/2.8, 2.3/1.6			330	0.3	100	5 / 12	1.2/1.5	6 / 18	5-, 10-, 20-, and 30-watt transmitters
Receiver rectifier	N A 6	A-c mains	110/150, 220/240				100	0.045	4.5	2-2.4	2.5-8	4	Long- and short-wave receivers
Lead-acid storage batteries	12 B 150	Charged by engine generator charging sets or charging rectifiers	12	15	*150					12	15	*120	For vehicle or radio use
	12 B 105				*105							*180	
	12 B 100			10	*100						10	120	
	12 B 60			6	*60						6	*72	
	12 B 75				*75								
	4 B 25		4	3.5	*25					4	3.5	*14	Obsolete radio storage battery
	2 B 38		2	8	*38					2	8	*16	For pack wireless sets
	2 B 19		2	2	*19					2	2	*4	For modulated-light speech equipment

Footnotes at end of table.

Figure 49 (Continued)

POWER SUPPLIES FOR GERMAN RADIO SETS—Continued

TYPE OF EQUIPMENT	EXACT NAME-PLATE NOMENCLATURE	INPUT				OUTPUT							USED WITH (GERMAN SETS)
		From	Consumption			High voltage				Low voltage			
			Volts	Amperes	Watts*	Revolutions per minute	Volts	Amperes	Watts	Volts	Amperes (max)	Watts*	
Nickel-cadmium storage batteries.	4.8 NC 10	Charged by engine generator charging sets or charging rectifiers	4.8	3.5	*10					4.8	2.5	*12	For pack wireless sets, field telephony sets, RDF and intercept sets
	4.8 NC 5			1.5	*5						1	*5	
	2.4 NC 58		2.4	12	*58					2.4	12	*30	
	2.4 NC 28			6	*28						6	*15	
	2.4 NC 20			2	*20						2	*5	
B batteries	90-volt DIN/VDE 1600						90	0.021	2				Pack wireless sets and receivers
	30-volt						30		0.5				Long and medium wave RDF sets
Field cells	Wet cell EL 1.5 KZF 30									1.5	0.3	*0.5	Field telephones and switchboards

*For watts column, items marked with an asterisk (*) indicate ampere hours, and are for batteries only.   †Letter T designates German word "TRAGFAHIGKEIT," meaning *carrying capacity.*

Figure 49 (Continued)

PARTICULARS OF RADIO EQUIPMENT USED IN GERMAN ARMORED VEHICLES, SELF-PROPELLED ARTILLERY AND ARMORED HALF-TRACKED VEHICLES

Equipment No.	Designation of sets	Frequency range (kilocycles)	Aerial	Range Kilometers (Miles) Key	Range Kilometers (Miles) Voice	Remarks
Fu. 1	Pack receiver "b" (Torn.E.b.)	100–6970				Receiver only.
Fu. 2	Ultra short wave receiver "e" (Ukw.E.e)	27200–33300				Receiver only.
Fu. 3	Ultra short wave receiver "dl" (UKw.E.dl)	42100–47800				Receiver only.
Fu. 4	Medium wave receiver "c" (MW.E.c)	835–3000				Receiver only.
Fu. 5	10 watt transmitter (10 W.S.c.) Ultra short wave receiver "e" (UKw.E.e)	27200–33300	2-Meter Rod (Stationary) (On the move)	6 (3.7) 4 (2.5)	4 (2.5) 2 (1.3)	This is the standard tank equipment.
Fu. 6	20 Watt transmitter (20 W.S.c) Ultra short wave receiver "e" (UKw.E.c)	27200–33300	2-Meter Rod (Stationary) (On the move)	10 (6.2) 8 (5)	8 (5) 6 (3.7)	This equipment may sometimes be found in Commander's tanks instead of Fu. 5, where extra range is required. The 20-watt transmitter "c" is no longer issued.
Fu. 7	20 watt transmitter (20 W.S.d) Ultra short wave receiver "dl" (UKw.E.dl)	42100–47800	2-Meter Rod	50 (31)	50 (31)	This is standard ground-air cooperation equipment.
Fu. 8	30 watt transmitter "a" (30 W.S.a) Medium wave receiver "c" (Mw.E.c)	1120–3000 835–3000	Roof aerial (Stationary) (On the move)	50 (31) 40 (24.8)	15 (9.3) 10 (6.2)	With 8-meter winch mast and star aerial the range increased to approximately 93 miles (key), 31 miles (voice).
Fu. 11	100 watt transmitter (100 W.S.) Pack receiver "b" (Torn.E.b)	200–1200 100–6970	Roof aerial (Stationary) (On the move)	80 (49.6) 50 (31)	20 (12.4) 10 (6.2)	With 9-meter winch mast and umbrella aerial range can be increased to approximately 124 miles (key), 43 miles (voice).
Fu. 12	80 watt transmitter (80 W.S.a) Medium wave receiver "c" (Mw.E.c)	1120–3000 835–3000	Roof aerial (Stationary)	80 (49.6)	25 (15.5)	With 8-meter winch mast and star aerial range is approximately 124 miles (key), 43 miles (voice)
Fu. 13	20 watt transmitter (20 W.S.c)	27200–33300	2-Meter Rod (Stationary) (On the move)	10 (6.2) 8 (5)	8 (5) 6 (3.7)	Fu. 13 is the same as Fu 6. extra receiver "c". See remarks under Fu. 6.
Fu. 15	Ultra short wave receiver "h" (UKw.E.h)	23000–24950				Receiver only.
Fu. 16	10 watt transmitter "h" (10 W.S.h) Ultra short wave receiver "h" (UKw.E.h)	23000–24950	2-Meter Rod	4 (2.5)	2 (1.3)	This equipment is similar to Fu. 5 with different frequency range.
Fu. 17	Pack set (transmitter/receiver) "h" (Torn. Fu. h)	23000–24950	Rod	6 (3.7)	2½ (1.5)	Voice only portable set, not fitted in the vehicle.
Fu. 19	15 watt transmitter/receiver "a" (15 W.S.E.a)	3000–7500	Roof aerial			Range given as 19 miles (key), 16 miles (voice), but these figures probably only hold good when using rod aerial fixed at top of high mast (7 meters) (stationary).
Fu.Spr.f.	Transmitter/receiver Fusprech. "f"	19997.5–21472.5	1.4 or 2 Meter Rod (Stationary) (On the move)	—	5 (3.1) 2 (1.3)	Voice only. Equipment includes loud speaker.

DETAILED DESCRIPTION OF GERMAN ARMY LINE COMMUNICATION EQUIPMENT INCLUDING FIELD TELEPHONES AND SWITCHBOARDS

NOMEN-CLATURE	DIMENSIONS AND WEIGHT	DESCRIPTION	REMARKS
Field Telephone 33	8.5″x11″x4″—12 lbs	This general purpose telephone for local battery operation only, with magneto system for calling, is equipped with magneto system. Provision is made for extra plug in headphones and testing of line and bell circuits, and two jacks connected in parallel with line circuit for connection as exchange. It can be connected to a post office exchange by a special adaptor. The power supply is 1.5 volts; either inert or dry cells may be used.	The instrument case is a bakelite moulding approximately 0.2 inch thick. The lid has a self locking fastener which is pressed to open. The shoulder strap has a hook on it from which the telephone head set can be hung if required operation of the instrument is conventional.
The German Wall Telephone for Field Emplacements.	15″x7¼″x5½″	A telephone of extremely sturdy construction and used apparently where moisture and vibration are excessive. These telephones are local battery operated, mounted on concrete walls, and interconnected through ducts. The telephone is of heavy waterproof construction and the handset is connected to the main assembly by a heavy rubber-covered waterproof cord. The receiver is covered with a rubber earpiece. Both the main assembly case and the handset frame cover plate is fastened by means of 4 bolts with triangular shaped heads recessed in each corner of the face. This case plate is attached to the body by chains to prevent its falling off when loosened.	The ringing generator of this set is the same type as that employed in the field telephone 33; may be employed by Allied troops in locations where its qualities are desirable.
Endverstarker (*f. Feldfernsprecher 33*) (Terminal Amplifier for Field Telephone 33)	9″ x7¾″x4¼″ A.C. Set 8½″x6½″x3½″ Battery Set	AC powered unit: This is an audio-frequency amplifier employing one triode tube, type RE 084. The receiver circuit of the field telephone 33 is opened and the incoming signal is fed to the grid of the amplifier. The amplified signal is returned to the earphone receiver. Power is supplied through a transformer, having high and low voltage windings for plate and filament supplies. The plate supply is rectified (half-wave) by rectifier GL$_0$ and the filament supply by a full wave rectifier GL$_1$. Battery operated unit: The principle of operation is very nearly the same.	This piece of equipment is an audio-frequency amplifier to increase the range operation of field telephone 33. They may be either powered by AC or by batteries. These sets are employed in place of, or in conjunction with field repeaters. When using the AC set, the handset of the field telephone 33 is used, but with the battery set there is already one provided.

Line Intercept Receiver LE. 35.	17½″x13½″x11″—78 lbs.	Provision for tapping to several telephone or telegraph lines and monitoring any one required. No Contact need be made as a loop brought to within a foot of the line may be sufficient. The equipment can be used to pick up earth currents between two earthed lines.
		The amplifier consists of a three-stage resistance capacity coupled circuit using three pentodes, all RV2 P800's. The amplifier has a gain of 72 db.
		Three fillers are incorporated in the set:
		  (a) Storsieb: a special filter for alternating the odd harmonics of 50 cycles where main interference reduces intelligibility.
		  (b) A band-pass filter normally in circuit.
		  (c) Additional filter sections which reduce the band filter to 400 c/s-2200 c/s.
			A portable line intercept amplifier, complete with batteries; may be either manpack or vehicle.

10-Line Exchange	8″x14″x6″—20 lbs.	The exchange will take up to 10 single or double line circuits. In case of mixed circuits (double and single lines to exchange) where the double lines are numerically superior, the single wire circuits should be connected via a cordless transformer, or vice versa if single lines preponderate. Subscribers lines may be connected either direct to the terminals 1 a.b. to 10 a.b. on top of the exchange or through a connection rack; or via 30-way plug and line system to a line terminal unit.	The exchange is roughly comparable with the British 10-line U.C. switchboard, although it is smaller and more compact.

Figure 51.

DETAILED DESCRIPTION OF GERMAN ARMY LINE COMMUNICATION
EQUIPMENT INCLUDING FIELD TELEPHONES AND SWITCHBOARDS—Continued

NOMEN-CLATURE	DIMENSIONS AND WEIGHT	DESCRIPTION	REMARKS
German 10 Line Cordless Exchange (Exact German Nomenclature unknown)	9½"x17½"x7½"—	This set was designed for common battery operation, the line terminals being marked negative and positive, but may be used for local battery operation. It accommodates 9 lines besides operator's phone and can handle only two conversations at one time. Provision for night alarm circuit has also been made. Toggle switches for cross connection of the subscribers are utilized in conjunction with line drops which are located about the keys. May be paralleled with similar type of exchange.	Is well made, easy to use and maintain, but has the disadvantage of being unable to accommodate more than two calls at one time, though ideal for conference calls.
Small telephone exchange Box (*Vermittlungskästchen*)	4"x4"x1½"	One line switchboard unit with an attachable visual indicator used with other such units to serve from two to ten or more telephone subscribers.	The set is well built and sturdy. Its simplicity and portability are outstanding characteristics.
The small fortress switchboard OB 36(*Kleine Festungsvermittlung*)	48"x39"x8"—	The switchboard is extremely heavy and housed in a cast iron box; brackets are provided at the back of the box for fastening the switchboard on a wall. Can accommodate 30 lines and 12 interconnections are possible. Provision has been made for connecting ten of the 30 lines on the OB 36 to common battery trunks. (Lines 21 to 30 being fitted with a 4 mfd condenser).	Because of its weight and size obviously could only be used in fixed installations. Is very similar to the OB 37 with the exception of two principle differences in circuit.
Large Field Switchboard for 60 lines		This is made up of three types of standard sections combined in multiple until desired size is reached. Is designed for local battery operation with ground return or metallic circuit. By adding a commercial adapter, connections may be established with civil exchanges using C.B. or automatic dial system. Is made up of 4 sections: (1) assembly "A" including plug cord holders and conference jack panel, (2) answering jack panel unit (ten jacks), (3) conference call panel, (4) adapter for use with automatic dial exchange.	With the use of multiple jack field this board can be built up to 300 lines. Knowing this, whether the term 60-line switchboard is applicable as a separate piece of equipment is a matter for further consideration.

Figure 51 (Continued).

DETAILED DESCRIPTION OF GERMAN ARMY LINE COMMUNICATIONS EQUIPMENT INCLUDING SWITCHBOARDS AND KINDRED EQUIPMENT

NOMENCLATURE	DIMENSIONS AND WEIGHT	DESCRIPTION	REMARKS
10-300 Line Switchboard	Operating Unit 9½"x13"x21½"—52 lbs. 10 Line Unit 4½"x13"x 7" —11 lbs. 50 Line Unit 15½"x13"x 7" —37 lbs. 100 Line Unit 15½"x13"x 7" —31 lbs. 150 Line Unit 15½"x13"x 7" —27 lbs. Bunching Unit 2½"x13"x 7" — 5 lbs. Dialing Unit 7" x13"x 7" —12 lbs. Superimposing Unit 7½"x13"x 7" —21 lbs.	The apparatus consists of several units built up to form the whole exchange: the operating unit, 10-line answering unit, 50-line answering unit, 100-line multiple unit, 150-line multiple unit, 10-jack bunching unit, dialing unit, and superimposing unit. Line connections are made at the rear of each unit by a 30-way connector with a 30-pin plug at each end. The drop-flap indicators are automatically restored when the associated jack has a plug inserted. A night alarm is also provided.	Very neat, light and compact, probably used in line of communication formations.
Teleprinter Terminal Unit Incorporating Single Channel V.F. Equipment. (*Springschreibanschlussgerat*)	24"x21"x9½"—93 lbs.	The terminal unit and teleprinter are operated from 110-220 volts AC (total consumption 150 watts). Provides for single and double current working (simplex or duplex) and remote control operation. (VF working.) Intercommunication between teleprinter and similar equipment over a line or radio link.	Used in line of communication companies.
Teleprinter Terminal Unit Incorporating Single Channel V. F. Equipment. (*Springschreibanschlussgerat*)	24"x21"x9½"—96 lbs.	This is for simple working only and operates on the same type of power supply as above.	Both types can be worked with American and British teleprinter with the inclusion of their respective T.T. Units. For line of communication purposes.
Telewriter Tbs/24a-32	17½"x15½"x9½"—57 lbs.	Sends figures 1 to 9 and 0, the characters +, −, /, ?, and the 26 letters of the alphabet. Works directly into a telephone line. Field telephone can be plugged in for speech working. A 900-cycles filter can be switched in to reduce interference. When the interference is too great, 900/c/s morse code can be sent and received on headphones. 12-pt socket on panel is for connection to radio set through an intermediate unit. Tube system 900 c/s sender oscillator—Rec amplifier—Rec rectifier speed control. All tubes are type RV12P400. Power supply 12-volt storage battery to motor. coupled to dynamo for H.T. for tube.	The mechanism of the set is simple but precision made, and the keyboard is continental type.
Telewriter Tbs/T 36 L.O. (Tape Teleprinter) *Fernschreiber*	20"x16½"x12"—63½ lbs.	The receiving and transmitting mechanisms are similar to those in the American Teletype machine described in detail in the Teletype Manual No. 11. All cables are permanently attached to the teleprinter. Schematic and wiring diagrams will be found mounted on the meter base plate.	Associated equipment T.T.U., e.g. (*Springschreibar-schussgerat*).
Speech Scrambler 9K III b.	17"x13"x9" (approx.)—70 lbs.	These are used to provide two-way security on a wire or radio-telephone circuit. It is powered by a 2-volt storage battery and one, 90-volt dry battery. The set is compactly built and is very sturdy in construction. The individual circuit components are separated according to their functions and completely screened. 3RV2P800 are used. Two of these are used as audio amplifiers, one on each side of the two-way circuit. The other is used as a 2000-cycle audio-oscillator. If not required the scrambler circuit may be switched on and the input and output circuits directly connected.	Use for security purposes over telephone lines. Is portable and can be carried by 1 man.

Figure 52.

DETAILED DESCRIPTION OF GERMAN ARMY LINE COMMUNICATIONS EQUIPMENT INCLUDING SWITCHBOARDS AND KINDRED EQUIPMENT—Continued

NOMENCLATURE	DIMENSIONS AND WEIGHT	DESCRIPTION	REMARKS
Tonschreiber Models b and b1		Both models with the exception of one employing a synchronous speed control system are identical. They are divided physically into two sub units known respectively as the *Lanfwerke* and the *Verstarker*. It offers the facility of recording an audio signal on a magnetic ribbon. During the recording process, the quality and ware of the signal impressed on the tape may be monitored. Provision has also been made for playback and for rewinding and wiping the tape used. This recording tape is made of paper; one side of it has been covered with a coating of material having high magnetic properties. The apparatus was designed to be supplied from AC mains. DC cannot be used. While the voltage may vary from 110 to 250 volts the permissable frequency variation is not known.	High speed recording apparatus. The Germans have designed and manufactured a series of magnetic tape recorders. There are in existence 2 other models known; they are: the *Tonschreiber c* which is a spring-driven recorder for rough field use; and the *AEG Type K4*, which is a studio type device.
German Teleprinter SWBD (T39) *Vermittlungsschrank*	21″x18½″x8¾″—50 lbs.	This teletypewriter switchboard is housed in a metal cabinet with folding tubular legs. It has four pairs of cords for handling simultaneous complete circuits and provisions for terminating one to ten teletypewriters. The construction is rugged and will withstand considerable abuse, although it is not moisture proof; the wiring is neat and sturdy. The answering and calling cords are each coiled on an individual wound reel. This method of storing excess cord lengths is same as that employed on the German 20-line, local battery telephone switchboard.	Line of communication companies.
German SWBD. 20 line.			
German *Relaiskasten T39.* Teletype Repeater.			
Leitungsabschlusskasten (Line Terminal Equipment)			

Figure 52 (Continued)

PERFORMANCE CHARACTERISTICS AND SPECIFICATIONS OF TWO-WAY RADIO SETS USED IN THE GERMAN ARMY GROUND FORCES

NOMEN-CLATURE	FREQUENCY RANGE (mcs) a. Send b. Receive c. Crystal	TYPE OF SIGNAL RANGE IN MILES	CIRCUIT AND TUBES (a) Send (b) Receive	POWER OUTPUT (watts)	POWER SUPPLY AND CONSUMPTION (a) Send (b) Receive	TYPE OF AERIAL	DIMENSIONS AND WEIGHT	ALLOCATION	REMARKS
Transceiver *Torn.Fu.bl*	a. 3–5 b. 3–6.7	C.W. 25 R/T 10	a. MO-PA RV2 P800-RL2P3 b. RF-M-LO-IF-DET-AF 6RV2 P800	.65-C.W. .35-R/T.	a. 2-volt storage battery b. 130-volt H.T. dry battery.	12-ft. (max.) rod or 50-ft. horizontal wire and counterpoise.	18"x15½"x8" —43 lbs.	Short range communication by all arms except infantry.	This set is identical with the *Torn.Fu. f.* except for frequency rangt of sender.
Transceiver *Torn.Fu.a2.*	a. 33.8–38 b. 33.8–38	C.W.:9 R/T :4	a. MO-B-PA-MOD to PA grid 2, RV2P8000,-RL2T2 (Mod is rec. AF Tube). b. RF-M-LO-IF-REAC: DET-AF 6RV2 P800	1	a. 2-volt storage battery and 130-volt H.T. dry battery. b.	6-ft. rod (sectional) or wire on masts.	14½"x12½"x4½" —37 lbs.	Communication from infantry regt. (brigade) to battalion, and from battalion to corps.	
Transceiver *Torn.Fu.f.*	a. 4.5–6.7 b.				Same as for *Torn.Fu.bl.*			Communications from field artillery troops to their observation posts.	
Transceiver *SE 469A.*	a. 3–5 b.	C.W.:60 R/T :20	a. MO-PA (2 tubes in parallel) RS242-REO84. b. RF-Fc-2,IF-DET-AF 4,RESO94-,2 REO84.	15-C.W. 7-R/T.	Pedal generator, or 12-volt storage battery and dynamotor. (6-volt battery and 150-volt H.T. battery for receiver only).	Inverted L, 40-ft. long,10-ft. high with two 20-ft. counterpoise cables.	19½"x16"x8½" —44 lbs.	For fire control in artillery units.	
Transceiver *Feldfu.b*	a. 90–110 b. 90–110	R/T :3/4	a. MO-PA b. RF-DET-AF (Super-regenerative). RV2.4 P700-RL2.4T1-RL2. 4P2.	.15	a. Storage battery type 2.4 b. NC28 driving an internal vibrato pack.	32"-vertical rod; later models have laminated steel tape.	14"x13½"x7" —28 lbs.	Short range patrol set, used by infantry in forward areas.	This set is a modern pack set. The tubes used are of small dimensions and the whole set is compactly constructed. The *Feldfu c.* is a similar set covering a different frequency range. They are distinguished by a color code, the "b" having red markings and the "c" green.

Figure 53.

PERFORMANCE CHARACTERISTICS AND SPECIFICATIONS OF TWO-WAY RADIO SETS USED IN THE GERMAN ARMY GROUND FORCES—Continued

NOMENCLATURE	FREQUENCY RANGE (mcs) a. Send b. Receive c. Crystal	TYPE OF SIGNAL RANGE IN MILES	CIRCUIT AND TUBES (a) Send (b) Receive	POWER OUTPUT (watts)	POWER SUPPLY AND CONSUMPTION (a) Send (b) Receive	TYPE OF AERIAL	DIMENSIONS AND WEIGHT	ALLOCATION	REMARKS
Transceiver *Fusprech a.*	a. 24.1-25 b.	R/T -2	a. MO (Rec osc)-PA (Rec output (Grid MOD (Rec 1st AF) to PA. b. M-OSC-2,IF-DET-2,AF-	8	a. 12-volt storage battery to b. dynamotor SEUa. 12 volts @ .5 amps.	6½-ft. rod connected via feeder.	11"x8"x6" —15 lbs.	Inter-communication between armored reconnaissance cars	
Transceiver *SEG2T*	a. 454–508 b.	M.C.W. R/T 125.	a. MO-Anode Modulator DS310 (acorn) RL2T2. b. Quench-DET-AF RL2T2-DS310 (acorn) RV2P800.	40-60 m/W.	a. 2-volt storage battery, and two 90-volt H.T. dry batteries, tapped at 9, 60, 90, 130, and 180 volts. b.	Saw tooth reflective aerial.	13½"x8¾"x8⅛" —24 lbs.	For quasi optical point to point working. Not known which troops use it.	
Transceiver *Torn.Fu.g.*	a. 2.5–3.5 b. 2.5–3.5	C.W :15 R/T : 8	a. MO-PA. 2.RL24P3. b. RF-FC-IF-DET-AF 5,RV2.4P700		a. 2.4-volt storage battery and built in vibrator. b.	On move whip aerial 5-ft. long with loading coil at base.	15"x13"x7"	As a pack set on the move or as a ground station.	This set is provided with "Break" in working.
Transceiver *Feldfu.f.*	a. 28–33 b. 28–33				Same as for *Feldfu.b.*	4-ft. rod.		By troops supporting armored fighting vehicles.	Main features distinguishing this set from the *Feldfu.b.* are: (1) tuning is continuous, not in fixed channels; (2) aerial base is tilted so that aerial is 40° out of vertical; (3) a large white spot.
Transceiver *Feldfu.al.*	a. 120–156 b. 120–156	R/T 11		.15 watts	a. 2-volt storage battery, type 2B19. b. and 90-volt H.T. battery	Rod: short, 2 ft.; long, 6 ft.	14"x13"x4¾" —26½ lbs.	By infantry.	The name of this set is also abbreviated to *Fusp al.*
Transceiver *Fusprech.f.*	a. 19.9975–21.4725. b.	R/T: 2			Same as for *Fusprech.a.*	4'7"-vertical rod.		Intercommunication between self-propelled guns.	This set is practically identical with the *Fusprech.a.* except that the *Fusprech.a.* has a receiver fire control.
Transceiver *Fusprech.d.*	a. 23.11-24.01 b.								
Transceiver *Torn.Fu.c.*	b. 1.5–2.3 b. 1.5..2.3	C.W.:15 R/T : 7			Same as for *Torn.Fu.bl.* and *Fu.f.*			For artillery observation.	

Figure 53 (Continued).

PERFORMANCE CHARACTERISTICS AND SPECIFICATIONS OF TWO-WAY RADIO SETS USED IN THE GERMAN ARMY GROUND FORCES—Continued

NOMEN-CLATURE	FREQUENCY RANGE (mcs) a. Send b. Receive c. Crystal	TYPE OF SIGNAL RANGE IN MILES	CIRCUIT AND TUBES (a) Send (b) Receive	POWER OUTPUT (watts)	POWER SUPPLY AND CONSUMPTION (a) Send (b) Receive	TYPE OF AERIAL	DIMENSIONS AND WEIGHT	ALLOCATION	REMARKS
Transceiver S.E.a.2/24b-202.	a. 3-6.67 b. 3-6.67	M.C.W.:15 R/T. : 5	a. MO-PA. b. (3.REO84K.-2RE134.-1.4406D or 1.RESO94.)	5	a. 2-volt storage battery (NC-10). b. Two 90-volt dry batteries.	Rod or wire.	18"x14"x8" —35 lbs.	Used in defensive positions.	This is an old Lorenz commercial set designed before the war.
Transmitter-Receiver 15.W.S.E.a.	a. 3-7.5 b. (2 Bands).	C.W.:60 R/T :20	a. 3,RL4.8P15-1,RV2.4P700. b. 8,RV2.4P700.		a. Pedal generator type b. 15A and rectifier with storage battery 2.4NC58: 12-volt storage battery in vehicle with convertor type 15A and rectifier.	High rod antennae with counterpoise or vehicle roof antennae.	39½ lbs.	From artillery division down to lower formations.	
Transmitter-Receiver DMG 4K DMG 5K	a. 500-600 b. 500-600	N.C.W.:60 R/T :30		0.5-1	a. 220 volts AC supply or b. 220-volt, 50-cycle, gasoline driven alternator.	Two broad-band directional arrays, 1 for Xsmtter, 1 for Rec. DMG 4K. 3 rows of dipoles.	Rack— 46"x20½"x12½" Base— 25½"x26"x20" Cases for antennae 66x51x10. Total weight 900 lbs.	These sets are used for multichannel communication over limited distances.	
Transceiver Form.Fu.G.k.	a. 4.5-6.7 b. 3-6.7	a. C.W.:15 R/T : 7 b. (C.W.M.C.W. R/T.)	a. MO-PA (2 tubes in parallel) RI2.4P2-2,RI2.4P2 b. RF-M-LO-IF-DET-AF 6,RV2.4P700 (IF amplifier used for transmitter modulation).	1.5	a. Two nickel iron 2.4-volt b. storage batteries (type N.C.58a) and vibrator-power pack SEWg.	12-ft. vertical rod or horizontal 33-ft. wire.	17.2"x13½"x7½" —45.5 lbs.	Is replacing Form.Fu.bl. in artillery units.	Very similar to Fu.bl. except for frequency range and transmitter construction.
Transmitter 120.	a. 42.1-54	C.W. M.C.W. R/T		120		70-ft. mast with vertical stub aerial on top.		Army corps and Hq.	
Transmitter AS-59.	a.	C.W. M.C.W. R/T	a. MO-B-PA (Push-Pull) RLT15-RS391-2.RS391.				25"x21"x18¾" —100 lbs.	Not known.	
Transceiver PH11.UK43	a. 37.5-462.2 b.	R/T	a. 2.K.D.D.-2,DF25. b.	1.	a. Three 4.5 volt batteries in parallel. b. One 150-volt H.T. batteries. .3 amps. @ 4.5 volt. 40 m/a @ 150 volt.	¼ wave pole (1.75 meters) ½ wave pole (2.40 meters)	11¾"x15¾"x14" (approx.) 33 lbs.	Not known.	

Figure 53 (Continued).

PERFORMANCE CHARACTERISTICS AND SPECIFICATIONS FOR GERMAN GROUND RADIO TRANSMITTERS

NOMENCLATURE	FREQUENCY RANGE (mcs) a. Send b. Receive c. Crystal	TYPES OF SIGNAL RANGE IN MILES	CIRCUIT AND TUBES (a) Send (b) Receive	POWER OUTPUT (watts)	POWER SUPPLY AND CONSUMPTION (a) Send (b) Receive	TYPE OF AERIAL	DIMENSIONS AND WEIGHT	ALLOCATION	REMARKS
Transmitter 5WS/24b-104	a. .95-3.15	C.W.:36 R/T:10	a. MO-PA 2, RS 241	5-7	a. Pedal generator. Storage battery and dynamotor U.S.A.L., or gasoline motor generator. 3.8 Volts @ 1.2 amps. 300-330 volt @ .14 amps.	Horizontal wire. vehicular rod. Counterpoise 50 ft. long.	18"x14⅛"x7⅝" —52 lbs.	Regimental and Divisional nets may be employed for vehicular or ground use.	A general medium frequency low power transmitter.
Transmitter 10W.S.c.	a. 27.2-33.3	M.C.W.:4 R/T :2½	a. MO-MOD-PA RL12, P.55-RV 12. P.4000-RV 12.P. 35.	6.5 (10 Max.)	a. 12-volt storage battery and dynamo U-10AL 12 volts @ 2 amps. 350 volts @ 100 m/a.	6½-ft. rod on move. Mast sections and gear provided for ground use.	7½"x12½"x7" —22 lbs.	Armored vehicles. Generally tank units. Usually in Commander's tank.	This is similar to the 10W.S.b. but for calibration and frequency range 10W. S.b. frequency range is 23–24.95 mcs.
Transmitter 8W.S.	a. 1-3	C.W. R/T	a. MO-PA 2, R1 12 TI5	8 (Can be reduced to ¼ power)	a. Pedal generator, engine generator or 12 volt storage battery and dynamotor. 12 volts @ 1.25 amps. 350 volts @ 75 m/a.	66-ft. "L" type or 33-ft. T type.	20"x12"x11" —48½ lbs.	Regimental command and reconnaissance nets.	
Transmitter 20W.S.c.	a. 27.2-33.3	M.C.W.-3 R/T -2	a. MO-D-MOD-PA; (PA-Push pull) 5, RL 12 TI5	20	a. 12-volt storage battery and dynamotor U-20A. U-20A2 or U-20A3. 12 volts @ 2.75 amps. 370 volts @ 130 m/a.	4½-ft.—6½-ft. whip type.	19"x8½"x10" —30 lbs.	Tank formations generally.	A similar set is the 20W.S.d. but which has a frequency range of 42.1-47.8.
Transmitter 20W.S.b.	a. 25-27	R/T		20	a. 12-volt storage battery to dynamotor U-20A3.	8-ft. vertical rod via feeder.	19¼"x8¾"x9¼" —35 lbs.	By sound ranges in artillery units.	Very similar to 20.W. S.c. except for modulator control and indicator.
Transmitter AKS 25.	a. 3-6	C.W.:50 R/T :15	a. MO-D-MOD-PA; (PA-Push pull). 5 RL 12 TI5.	25	a. Engine driven or pedal driven generator. 12.5 volts @ 2.5 amps. 350 volts @ 250 m/a.	33-ft. wire on one 33-ft. mast with 4-33-ft. counterpoise.	17½"x12"x14½" —60 lbs.	In infantry divisions and artillery regiments.	
Transmitter 30W.S.a.	a. 1.1-3.01 (3 Bands)	C.W.:50 R/T :16	a. MO-MOD-PA (2 tubes in parallel) (Mod: 2 tubes in parallel) 2 RL 12, P 35-2, RV 12 P.20001.RL12TI5.	30	a. 12 volt storage battery to dynamotor U-30 b.	Vehicular rod or roof antennae. Open wire antennae.	19"x9¾"x9¼" —42 lbs.	Small signal units and signal troops in armored corps.	Medium powered field transmitter. This set is identical with the 80W.S.a. as regards its circuit.

Figure 54.

PERFORMANCE CHARACTERISTICS AND SPECIFICATIONS FOR GERMAN GROUND RADIO TRANSMITTERS—continued

NOMENCLATURE	FREQUENCY RANGE (mcs) a. Send b. Receive c. Crystal	TYPES OF SIGNAL RANGE IN MILES	CIRCUIT AND TUBES (a) Send (b) Receive	POWER OUTPUT (watts)	POWER SUPPLY AND CONSUMPTION (a) Send (b) Receive	TYPE OF AERIAL	DIMENSIONS AND WEIGHT	ALLOCATION	REMARKS
Transmitter *30W.S./24b-120*	a. .95–1.68	C.W.:25 R/T:10		30	a. 12-volt storage battery to dynamotor U-30A.		19"x11¾"x11" —56 lbs.	Armored cars and other vehicles and reconnaissance nets of division troops.	
Transmitter *70W.S.*	a. 3–16.667	C.W. 36		70	a. 12-volt storage battery to dynamo U-30A.	Rod, or 25-40-ft. single wire.	21¼"x11¾"x19⅜" —78 lbs.	Used by all reconnaissance units within command nets.	
Transmitter *80W.S.a.*	a. 1.12–3.0 (3 Bands)	C.W. 125 R/T 45	a. MO-MOD-PA (PA-2, tubes in parallel) MOD 2, tubes in parallel (3RL 12. P.36, 2 RV 12 P2000.)	80 (or 10)	a. 12-volt storage battery to dynamo U-80A.	8-meter vertical mast vehicular rod or roof aerial.	18½"x11¾"x10" —48 lbs.	In tank division to tank brigade sets.	
Transmitter *100W.S.*	a. 0.2–1.2	C.W.:200 R/T: 70	a. MO-MOD-PA RS-237-RS 241-RS 237.	100 (or 10)	a. Storage battery to dynamotor U-100 or U-100A 12 volts @ 30.8 amps. Field gasoline division D-C generator. 12 volts @ 7.3 amps. 1000 volts @ 240-300 m/a.	1-33-ft. mast with 4-spoke antennae (medium frequency) or one 20-ft. sectional mast with 3-spoke umbrella (higher frequency)	18½"x18"x10" —76 lbs.	Administrative control set for large areas. Can be used in vehicle or as a fixed station.	A commercial design adapted for military use. Provision made for local or remote control and picture transmitter. High-low power switch for C.W.
Transmitter *1000W.S.b.*	a. 1.090–6.7 (4 Bands)	C.W. –700 M.C.W.–700 R/T–150–300	a. MO-B-PA MO and Buffer RS 282. PA. RS 329G Keying Section 2, RS 282 and 3 RGN 2004 Amp. Section 2, RS282 and 3RE 084K.	1,000	a. Dynamotor U-1000 to AC line, or M.G. gas engine set.	(2) Two 80-ft. masts supporting single wire antennae 83-ft. for medium frequency and 33-ft. long for high frequency.	5'2"x3'4"x6'¾" —1630 lbs.	Army and corps staffs, also used for liaison as ground set to *Luftwaffe*.	

Figure 54 (Continued).

PERFORMANCE CHARACTERISTICS AND SPECIFICATIONS FOR GERMAN GROUND RADIO TRANSMITTERS—continued

NOMEN-CLATURE	FREQUENCY RANGE (mcs) a. Send b. Receive c. Crystal	TYPES OF SIGNAL RANGE IN MILES	CIRCUIT AND TUBES (a) Send (b) Receive	POWER OUTPUT (watts)	POWER SUPPLY AND CONSUMPTION (a) Send (b) Receive	TYPE OF AERIAL	DIMENSIONS AND WEIGHT	ALLOCATION	REMARKS
Transmitter *1500W.S.a.*	a. 0.1–66 (4 Bands)	C.W. :725 M.C.W.:725 R/T :18–340	a. As for 1000 W.S. b. Except that P.A. tubes are RS 239.	1,500	a. Dynamotor to V-1500 AC line or M.G. gas engine set.	80-ft. mast with 6- or 12-ft. spoke "umbrellas."	5'2"x3'3"x6'¾" —1430 lbs.	For communication between corps ground headquarters, and army staff.	A 3-stage transmitter for installation in motor cars and fixed stations. It is divided into several components for speedy removal assembly and replacement.
Transmitter *60W* (Jamming)	a. 18.75–61.25	C.W. Freq. Mod.	a. MO/D-PA (Freq. Mod.) 3, PE 06/40-(EL 2)	60	AC single phase, 50 cycle, 110 volts.		20"x12½"x12½"		A special type of transmitter designed for jamming.
Transmitter *600H.* (S.W. Jamming)	a. (a)17.75–17.85 (b)15.1–15.35 (c)11.7–11.9 (d)9.5–9.7 (e)7.2–7.3 (f)6.–6.2	M.C.W. Freq. Mod.	a. MO/D-(Freq. MOD/PA) 2, PE 06/40-PB 3/1000	6,004	a. AC three phase, 50 cycle, 180/200 volts.		75"x27"x27" —880 lbs.		This special S.W. jamming apparatus is made in 6 models corresponding to the 6 models as shown in column 2. Each. band has a variable frequency.

Figure 54 (Continued).

PERFORMANCE CHARACTERISTICS FOR RADIO TRANSMITTERS USED AS GERMAN ARMY MESSAGE CARRIER EQUIPMENT

Nomenclature or Designation	No. of Channels	Frequency Range Kcs.	Carrier Frequencies Kc.	Ringing Frequency	Max. Line Attenuation. db. and Nepers	2mm C. Open Wire	Ranges (Km. and Miles) 3 mm Cu Open Wire	Field Cable (FFK)
T.f. a	1	3.4–8.2	5.8	500/20	4.0 np. 34.76 db.	400 Km. 250 Miles	520 Km. 325 Miles	25–60 Km. 16–37 Miles
T.f. b 1.	1	3.5–7.5	5.5	500	3.6 np. 31.28 db.	400 Km. 250 Miles	500 Km. 325 Miles	25–50 Km. 16–31 Miles
T.f. b 2.	1	9.0–13.0	11.0	500	3.6 np. 31.28 db.	320 Km. 200 Miles	400 Km. 250 Miles	15–30 Km. 9–19 Miles
T.f. b 3.	1	16.5–20.5	18.5	500	3.6 np. 31.28 db.	220 Km. 137 Miles	280 Km. 175 Miles	
T.f. b 4.	1	22.0–26.0	24.0	500	3.6 np. 31.28 db.	160 Km. 100 Miles	200 Km. 125 Miles	
E. 1.			Same as for T.f. a.					
E. 2.	1	3.4–8.2	5.8	500/20	2.0 np. 17.38 db.	230 Km. 144 Miles	290 Km. 181 Miles	10–30 Km. 6–19 Miles
E. 3.	1	3.7–10.0	6.4; 10.3.	500	3.75 np 32.49 db.	350 Km. 219 Miles	450 Km. 281 Miles	18–45 Km. 11–28 Miles
T. 1.	3	6.6–28.2	6.3; 9.4; 12.9 20.7; 24.4; 28.5	500/20	4.0 np. 34.76 db.	270 Km. 169 Miles	350 Km. 219 Miles	
T. 3	3	8.8–30.4	7.7; 10.9; 14.3 19.8; 23.7; 27.7	500/20	4.0 np. 34.76 db.	270 Km. 169 Miles	350 Km. 219 Miles	
T.f.R. (Rundf) (Broadcasting)	1	34.0–42.8	42.8					
MEK	8.	6.0–60.0	6:9:12:15:18 21:27:36:39: 42:45:48:51 54:57		4.0 np. 34.76 db.		250 Km. 156 Miles	

LINE EQUIPMENT—German Carrier Equipment (Army and Commercial)

The German carrier equipment, both commercial and army is listed above. It is similar to the American in design, channel frequencies, and use Diagrams (not shown here) authenticate this, and show that the carrier practice in line and repeater set up are practically identical.

Within the German army the most common sets for field use are the *Tragerfrequenzgerat a* (*Tf.a.*) and the *Tragerfrequenzgerat b* (*T.f.b*), including b1, b2, b3, and b4. Other sets in use by the Germans are: *Mehrfach* (*MEK*) *MG, MK, T1, T3, E1, E2,* and *E3*; the *MG* and *MEK* carrier systems are apparently more recent additions.

The "L" and "U" carrier systems for cable, are used by the German PO. The "L" system is installed on lightly loaded cable, and the "U" on non-loaded cable. The German broadcasting carrier system is the *Tragerfrequenzgerat Rundfunk* (*TfR*—"Carries Broadcasting."

Differentiation is made with multiple Tf (carrier) systems between single channel systems (transmission channels for EW and WE traffic lie directly next to one another, as in the case of sets T.f.a. and T.f.b.) and group systems (the channels for each carrier direction are adjacent and they form therefore, two separate groups, e.g. sets MEDK and MG).

Abbreviations and Nomenclature:—

   a. Carries Equipment:—

     (1) *T.f. (a or b)*, *Tragerfrequenzgerat*, Carrier Frequency Set.

     (2) *MEK.*, *Mehrfach-Einzelkanal*, Multiple Channel.

     (3) *T.f.R.*, *Tragerfrequenz Rundfunk*, Carrier Frequency Broadcasting.

     (4) *E (1, 2, 3)*; *T (1, 3)*; *MG*; *M (1-7)*; *MK EK*; *L*; *U*:—Meanings not known.

      On the chart above, kilometers are converted to miles and nepers (standard German power level unit) to decibels.

        1 neper equals. 8.6858 decibels.

        1 decibel equals. 0.11513 nepers.

Figure 55.

PERFORMANCE CHARACTERISTICS FOR RADIO TRANSMITTERS USED AS
GERMAN ARMY MESSAGE CARRIER EQUIPMENT—Continued

Nomenclature or Designation	No. of Channels	Frequency Range Kcs.	Carrier Frequencies Kc.	Ringing Frequency	Max. Line Attenuation, db. and Nepers	2mm C. Open Wire	Ranges (Km. and Miles) 3 mm Cu Open Wire	Field Cable (FFK)
MG	15.	48–156		500/20	4.0 np. 34.76 db.		100 Km. 62 Miles	
M 1	3	5.8–38.4						
M 2 (M3)	4	5.2–39.7						
M 4 (M5)	3	12.2–29.7						
M 6 (M7)	4	8.7–43.7						
MK (K 1)	5	57.6–142.4	60:68:76:84:92: 108:116:124: 132:140		4.0 np. 34.76 db.			
MK (K 2)	5	53.6–138.4	56:64:72:80:88 104:112:120: 128:136:		4.0 np. 34.76 db.			
MEF	5.	10.3–57.6	10:20:30:40:50 15:25:35:45:55					
EK	1	41.5–54.5	44:52.					
Erickson (12 Kanal)	12	49.3–154.4						
L-(Kabel-System) DRP	1	3.3–5.8	6					
U-(Kabelsystem) DRP	12	12.3–60.0						

Figure 55 (Continued).

PERFORMANCE CHARACTERISTICS AND SPECIFICATIONS FOR GERMAN INTERCEPT
GENERAL PURPOSE, AND SPECIAL PURPOSE RADIO RECEIVERS

NOMEN-CLATURE	FREQUENCY RANGE (mcs) a. Send b. Receive c. Crystal	TYPES OF SIGNAL	CIRCUIT AND TUBES (a) Send (b) Receive	POWER SUPPLY AND CONSUMPTION (a) Send (b) Receive	TYPE OF AERIAL	DIMENSIONS AND WEIGHT	ALLOCATION	REMARKS
Receiver *Fu.HE.c.*	b. 3.0–25.8 (4 bands)	C.W. M.C.W. R/T	b. 2.RF-M-LO-3, IF-DET-OBFO-AF 10, RV 2P800	b. 2-volt storage battery and 90-volt H.T. dry battery. 2-volts @ 1.7 amps. 90-volts @ 12 m/a.		18"x14"x10" —56 lbs.	Intercept service. Monitoring for security.	It is very difficult to service. Is one of a series of four intercept receivers.
Receiver *K.w.E.a.*	b. .98–10.2	C.W. R/T	b. 2RF-M-LO-3, IF-DET-BFO-AVC-AF. 11, RV 2P800	b. 2-volt storage battery and 90-volt H.T. dry battery, or Convertor unit *EU.d.* or main unit *N/46.*		27"x10½"x13½" —91 lbs.	For stationary or semi-mobile services. All arms.	
Receiver *UKw.E.f.*	b. 42–48	M.C.W. R/T	b. RF-FC-IF-DET-AF. 5, RV2-4P700	b. 2.4-volt storage battery for internal H.T. vibrator.	6½-ft. vertical rod when used as pack set.	14"x12½"x6½" —17 lbs.		The associated sender is the *20 W.S.d.* When used alone the aerial base and rod are mounted on top of the case.
Receiver *Torn Eb.*	b. .096–7.095 (8 bands)	C.W. M.C.W. R/T	b. 2, RF-DET-AF. 4, RV 2P800'	b. 2-volt storage battery and 90-volt H.T. battery, or 12-volt storage battery and vibrator unit *E.W.c.* 2-volts @ 0.75 amps. 12-volts @ 1 amp.		9½"x14¼"x8¾" —29 lbs.	General purpose receiver.	
Receiver *L.M.W. H.E./240-316*	b. .075–3.333 (5 bands)	C.W. M.C.W. R/T	b. RF-M-LO-IF-DET-AF. (RF-M-IF-RES 094) (LO-DET-AF RE 084K)	b. 4.8-volt storage battery; four 30-volt or 90-volt plus one 30-volt H.T. batteries. 4.8-volt @ 0.45 amps. 100 volt @ 18 m/a.	Open wire and counterpoise.	18½"x15½"x9" —44 lbs.	Intercept receiver.	This set is an old design and is being replaced by intercept receivers *Fu.H.E.d.* and *b.*
Receiver *Fu.H.E.d.*	b. 25–60 (4 bands)	C.W. M.C.W. R/T	b. 2, RF-M-LO-3, IF-DET-BFO-2,AF A11 RV2 P800	b. 2-volt storage battery and 90-volt H.T. dry battery. (2.4-volt storage battery may be used after internal adjustment to set.)	15-ft. open wire on sectional masts and counterpoise.	18"x14"x10" —56 lbs.	Intercept receiver for U.H.F. signals.	This receiver is similar in every respect to the *Fu.H. E.c.* except in frequency range and number of tubes.
Receiver *WR IP.*	b. .15–15.5	M.C.W. R/T	b. FC-2,IF-DET/AF-Driver Class 'B' Output DCH 25-2,DF25-DAC25-DC25-DDD25 DF26	b. AC or DC mains supply 90-250. Volts (voltage need not be known), or, two 1.25 dry cells *ENL DIN VDE.* 1210 plus 90-volt A.T. battery from mains 0.25 amps.		19½"x16"x11½" —57 lbs.	For broadcast reception. With the aid of a microphone it can be used for oral transmission of orders.	Can be used as a microphone amplifier.
Receiver *UKW.E.e.*	b. 27.2–33.3	M.C.W. R/T	b. RF-M-LO-2, IF-DET-AF 7 RV 12 P4000.	b. 12-volt storage battery to dynamotor *EU.a2.*	6½-ft. vertical rod.-	12½"x8"x7" —22 lbs.	Communication throughout a tank battalion.	

Figure 56.

PERFORMANCE CHARACTERISTICS AND SPECIFICATIONS FOR GERMAN INTERCEPT, GENERAL PURPOSE, AND SPECIAL PURPOSE RADIO RECEIVERS—Continued

NOMEN- CLATURE	FREQUENCY RANGE (mcs) a. Send b. Receive c. Crystal	TYPES OF SIGNAL	CIRCUIT AND TUBES (a) Send (b) Receive	POWER SUPPLY AND CONSUMPTION (a) Send (b) Receive	TYPE OF AERIAL	DIMENSIONS AND WEIGHT	ALLOCATION	REMARKS
Receiver M.W.E.c.	b. .835-3	C.W. M.C.W. R/T	b. RF-M-LO-2, IF-BFO/Calibrator DET-AF (2 tubes in push pull) ALL RV12 P200	b. 12-volt storage battery to dynamotor EU a.1, 2, or 3. 12-volts @ 4-5 amperes.	Open wire or roof aerial.	12½"x8"x7" —24 lbs.	Communication receiver for medium waveband.	
Receiver Fu.H.E.u.	b. .5-25 (5 bands)	C.W. M.C.W. R/T	b. 1 9-tube superhetrodyne.	b. As for Fu.H.E.c.		17"x13½"x10 —56 lbs.	Intercept services.	Very similar to Fu.H.E.c. but for frequency range and circuit.
Receiver L.W.E.e.	b. .072-1.525 (5 bands)	C.W. R/T	b. RF-M-LO-2, IF-DET-BFO-AF 8, RV2 P 800	b. 2-volt storage battery and 90-volt dry H.T. battery or convertor unit E.U.a. or mains unit NA6.		27"x13½"x10½" —87 lbs.	Long range communication at army and command hq.	Similar in construction to K.W.E.a. except that the K.W.E.a. has fewer stages and no A.V.C.
Receiver Spez.445b.	b. .1-6.7	C.W. R/T	b. RF-REG DET-2,AF 4, REO 74	b. 4.8-volt nickel-iron storage battery and 90-volt H.T. dry battery.	Long wire or rod.	18"x14"x8½" —55 lbs.	General purpose receiver.	
Receiver UKW.E.d I.	b. 42.1-47.8	M.C.W. R/T	b. RF-M-LO-3, IF-2nd DET-AVC-AF 9 RV12 P2000	b. Dynamotor E.U.a.2 or 130-volt dry H.T. batteries and 12-volt storage battery.	6½-ft. rod connected via feeder.	15½"x10"x8" —19 lbs.	By signal and armored troops for ground-air cooperation.	Very accessible for servicing.
Receiver UKW.E.h.	b. 23-24.95	M.C.W. R/T	b. RF-M-LO-2, IF-DET-AF 7; RV12 P4000	b. 12-volt storage battery to dynamotor E.U.a. 1, 2, or 3.	6½-ft. rod.	12½"x8"x6½" 22½ lbs.	Armored troops in cars and assault guns, model G.	Very similar to the U.KW.-e. except for frequency range.
Receiver D/F Ground L.M.W.P./24b-315.	b. .075-3.333 (5 bands)	C.W. M.C.W. R/T	b. RF-M-LO-IF-DET-BFO-AF 2.RES094,-RE084K-RES094,-2,RE084K respectively.	b. 4.8-volt storage battery (NC-10); four 30-volt or one 90-volt plus one 30-volt H.T. dry battery. 4.8-volts @ .45 amps. 100-volts @ 18 m/a.	Goniometer loops. about 1 square meter each, and auxiliary aerial (1-meter rod or 3-meter horizontal wire).	21"x14½"x8⅝" —51 lbs.	Used by subsection of intercept company.	The circuit is the same as the intercept receiver L. Mw. HE/246-316.
Receiver (Radio Controlled Tank) Set B 4 Fu.E.6.	b. 24.6 c. Crystal	R/T	b. FC-IF-IF,AVC, DET-AF-AF ECH 11-EF 13-EBF 11-2, EF12.	b. Dynamotor with 12-volt storage battery.	4-ft. flexible rod.	7.1"x10.6"x3.1"	For radio controlled tank in conjunction with an audio filler unit which is not listed here.	

Figure 56 (Continued).

PERFORMANCE CHARACTERISTICS AND SPECIFICATIONS OF TWO-WAY RADIOS AND EMERGENCY TRANSMITTERS USED IN GERMAN AIRCRAFT

NOMENCLATURE	FREQUENCY RANGE (mcs) a. Send b. Receive c. Crystal	TYPES OF SIGNAL RANGE IN MILES	CIRCUIT AND TUBES (a) Send (b) Receive	POWER OUTPUT (watts)	POWER SUPPLY AND CONSUMPTION (a) Send (b) Receive	TYPE OF AERIAL	DIMENSIONS AND WEIGHT a. Send b. Receive	ALLOCATION	REMARKS
Transmitter-Receiver Fu.G3. (Airborne)	a. .3–.6 and b. 3–6	C.W., M.C.W. R/T	a. 3, RS31-3, R2074 & 1, R.2134.	100 (High) 20 (Low)	a. Air driven generator (G3) b. Two 90-volt batteries, one 4-volt Edison.	Both fixed and trailing		Bomber aircraft; found in some but not all specimens of the following types of aircraft: Ju 52, FW 58, HE 114, DO 11, 13, & 17E & F; AR 66, AR 96, W 33 and 34.	Similar sets Fu.G3 A. and Fu.G3 AU. Both the above sets are still in use in transport aircraft, flying boats, and second-line aircraft generally.
Transmitter-Receiver Fu.G7, 7a, 7c. (Airborne)	a. 2.5–3.75 b.	a. C.W./RT –15 b. M.C.W. R/T	a. 2, REN 904,–2, RENS 1664. b. 5, RENS 1264.	20	a. Dynamotor U4A/24. b.	Fixed antennae in fighter aircraft: In dive bombers a trailing antennae manually reeled.	a. 14"x9"x8" —20 lbs. b. 14"x9"x8" —25 lbs.	In fighter aircraft and dive bombers. Prior to 1943,7A was fitted in ME 109, ME 109 F, FW 190. It is still fitted in JU 87 and HS 129.	Was replaced by Fu.G16Z. Is still used, however, in twin seater aircraft particularly the JU 87.
Transmitter-Receiver Fu.G8. (Airborne)	a. S.W. 3–6: L.W. b. .3–.6	a, (L.W:C.W.) (SW:CW.R/T) R/T) b. (C.W.M.C.W., R/T)	a. 9, RS 242 b. 4, NF 2 and 3NF 3	20 (S.W.) 40 (L.W.)	a. Dynamotor (U5) b. Dynamotor (U6)	Common T and R. Fixed or trailing antennae may be used.		Air-to-air-to ground (intercommunication).	Intended originally for bomber aircraft but was superseded by Fu.G10.
Transmitter-Receiver Fu.G10. (Airborne)	a. As for Fu.G8 b.	a. C.W.–R/T. 300–500 b.	a. 6, RL 12P35-25, RV12 P2000 b.	40 (S.W.) 70 (L.W.)	a. Dynamotor U-10/S b. Dynamotor U-10/E	Both fixed and trailing. Aerial tuning units, AAAG-2 and AAAG-3 are provided.	a. 9"x8¾"x8" —16½ lbs. b. 7¼"x8¾"x8" —16 lbs.	Current equipment for all first line multiple engine aircraft.	
Transmitter-Receiver Fu.G16. (Airborne)	a. 38–42.5 b.	a. R/T. 20–100 20 ground level 100 in the air b.	a. 2, RL12P35-11, RV12 P2000 b.	10	a. Dynamotor U-17 b.	Fixed single wire 6'11" long	a. 15"x8¼"x8" —26½ lbs.	All bombers. Air-to-air and ground liaison.	Is fitted in large aircraft in addition to the Fu.G10. The design was taken from the Fu.G17.

Figure 57.

PERFORMANCE CHARACTERISTICS AND SPECIFICATIONS OF TWO-WAY RADIOS AND EMERGENCY TRANSMITTERS USED IN GERMAN AIRCRAFT—Continued

NOMEN-CLATURE	FRE-QUENCY RANGE (mcs) a. Send b. Receive c. Crystal	TYPES OF SIGNAL RANGE IN MILES	CIRCUIT AND TUBES (a) Send (b) Receive	POWER OUTPUT (watts)	POWER SUPPLY AND CONSUMPTION (a) Send (b) Receive	TYPE OF AERIAL	DIMENSIONS AND WEIGHT a. Send b. Receive	ALLOCATION	REMARKS
Transmitter-Receiver *Fu.G16 Z,ZE.* (Airborne)	a. b. As for *Fu.G16*	a. M.C.W. b. R/T. 20 ground level 100 in the air	a. 2, RL 12P35 b. 9, RV 12P2000 7, RV 12P2000 in navigational aid equipment.	As above	a. Dynamotor U-17 b.	Fixed single wire 6'11" long. Matching units AAG16-2 and AAG-16-3 permit use of leading edge of the tail fin as antennae 8" single loop is used for D/F homing.	a. 15"x8¾"x8" —26½ lbs.	Used in all single seater fighters.	Also incorporates D/F homing apparatus.
Transmitter-Receiver *Fu.G17 17E and Z.* (Airborne)	a. 42.1–47.9 b.	a. M.C.W. b. R/T. 30 at ground level 185 in the air	a. 2 RL 12P35,-13,RV12 P2000 b.	As above	a. Dynamotor U-17 b.	Vertical rod about 39" long terminating in matching unit AAG7.		In twin seater, close supporting aircraft. Air-to-air-to ground liaison.	*Fu.G17* was the original design from which *Fu.G16* was copied.. *Fu.G 72* is used alternatively with D/F homing apparatus.
Transmitter-Receiver *Fu.G1 and G2.* (Airborne)	a. .6–1.667 b.	a. C.W. b. C.W. M.C.W. R/T.	a. 3, RS-31G-3,R2074+ b. 1 R 2134	20–100	a. Air driven generator b. Batteries	Fixed.		For bombers.	
Transmitter-Receiver *Fu.G6, 6A* (Airborne)					As for *Fu.G7*			Interrogation and command. Air-to-air-to ground.	
Transmitter-Receiver *Fu.G10 K-1* (Airborne)	a. 5.3–10 b.	a. R/T. b. M.C.W.-R/T.	a. 2, RL 12P35-11 RV 12P2000 b.	10	a. Dynamotor U-17 b.	Single wire 6'11" long.		Command liaison set.	

Figure 57 (Continued).

PERFORMANCE CHARACTERISTICS AND SPECIFICATIONS OF TWO-WAY RADIOS AND EMERGENCY TRANSMITTERS USED IN GERMAN AIRCRAFT—Continued

NOMEN-CLATURE	FRE-QUENCY RANGE (mcs) a. Send b. Receive c. Crystal	TYPES OF SIGNAL RANGE IN MILES	CIRCUIT AND TUBES (a) Send (b) Receive	POWER OUTPUT (watts)	POWER SUPPLY AND CONSUMPTION (a) Send (b) Receive	TYPE OF AERIAL	DIMENSIONS AND WEIGHT a. Send b. Receive	ALLOCATION	REMARKS
Transmitter-Receiver *Fu.G10 K-2* (Airborne)	a. 6–12 b.							Command and liaison set. Used in small aircraft.	
Transmitter-Receiver *Fu.G10 K-* (Airborne)	a. 6–18 b.							Voice communication air-to-air-to-ground.	
Transmitter-Receiver *Fu.G21.* (Airborne)	a. .3–.9 b.	a. M.C.W.–R/T. b.	a. 3, RS 241-1, RESO94–2, RESO74 b.	10				Communication (general) for flying boats and seaplanes.	
Transmitter-Receiver *Fu.G25 a.*	a. 152.2–161 b. 123–128		a. L550 b. 6, RV12P2000,-2,LD1.	440	a. Dynamotor b.	14″ Stub, common to Trans.-Receiver. (Antennae tuning unit AAG25 a).	14″x8″x8″ —33 lbs.		
Transmitter NS2. ("Notsender") (2a, 2b)	a. 0.5.	C.W.: M.C.W.: 250 at sea, 120 overland	a. AL5N-RE13A.	8	a. Hand generator	Steel antennae wire235 feet long with ground wire and sender raised by box kite or hydrogen filled balloon.	11″x10″x7½″ —15 lbs.	Emergency transmitter for dinghy use.	Carried loose in aircraft. Forerunner of *N.S.I.*
Transmitter NS4. ("Notsender")	a. 53.5–61.0	C.W. at 200 feet to aircraft 9, at 1000 feet is 14, 40,000 feet 40.	a. 2, LS 1 and LS2	1–2	a. 11 midget storage cells—3 used in parallel for 2-volt filament, 8 used in series parallel for 8-volt vibrator supply.	Strip of copper plate steel tape 3′5″ long and 1′ in diameter tapering to 3/16″ at end.	6¼″x6¼″x3″ —3½ lbs.	Emergency transmitter for dinghy use.	Replaces the *N.S.2.* Standard equipment on all twin engine and larger aircraft.

Figure 57 (Continued).

PERFORMANCE CHARACTERISTICS AND SPECIFICATIONS OF RADIO EQUIPMENT INSTALLED IN GERMAN AIRCRAFT FOR DIRECTION FINDING, BLIND LANDING, BLIND BOMBING AND HEIGHT FINDING

NOMEN-CLATURE	FREQUENCY RANGE (mcs) a. Send b. Receive c. Crystal	TYPE OF SIGNAL RANGE IN MILES	CIRCUIT AND TUBES (a) Send (b) Receive	POWER OUTPUT (watts)	POWER SUPPLY & CONSUMPTION (a) Send (b) Receive	TYPE OF AERIAL	DIMENSIONS AND WEIGHT	ALLOCATION	REMARKS
D/F Receiver *Peil: 4.*	b. 0.25–0.4	C.W. M.C.W. R/T 150 (approx.)	b. 8 Tube superhetrodyne 8 RV 12 P200		b. Dynamotor U-8 and aircraft battery.	Fixed loop 13″ long and 3½″ in diameter, carries 13 turns of Litz wire crosswound in series.	b. 11″x9½″x6″ —22½ lbs.	Homing receiver used in single seater fighters prior to introduction of *FUG 16Z.*	
D/F Receiver *Peil: 5.*	b. .165–1	C.W. M.C.W. R/T 250	b. 6 Tube superhetrodyne 6 NF 2		b. Dynamotor U-8 and aircraft battery.	Oval loop with powder Ironb. cone: 8 turns of Litz wire connected in series.	24″x10″x8″ —24 lbs.	D/F and homing receiver in twin engine and larger aircraft for above purpose.	A pre-war commercial set.
D/F Receiver *Peil: 6*	b. .15–1.2	C.W. M.C.W. R/T	b. 6 Tube superhetrodyne 6 RV 12 P2000		b. Dynamotor U-11A	Oval loop: sense antenna is metal paint on loop housing.	b. 9½″x8½″x7″ —20 lbs.	Used in bombers. May be used as a separate receiver in *FUG 10.*	One of the few German sets that uses crystals.
D/F Receiver *Peil: 7.*	b. .15–1.2	C.W. M.C.W. R/T			b. Dynamotor U-11A	Same as above.			
Navigation Receiver *FU 1 EB1.*	b. 28.5–35	R/T 250	b. 2NF2 TRF		b. Dynamotor U-8	39-ft. vertical rod.			Carried loose in aircraft for blind landings.
Navigation Receiver *FU 2H.*	b. 30–33.3		b. 7 Tube superhet: 7RV12 P4000		b. Dynamotor U-8	39-ft. vertical rod.			For blind landings.

Figure 58.

PERFORMANCE CHARACTERISTICS AND SPECIFICATIONS OF RADIO EQUIPMENT INSTALLED IN GERMAN AIRCRAFT FOR DIRECTION FINDING, BLIND LANDING, BLIND BOMBING AND HEIGHT FINDING—continued

NOMEN-CLATURE	FREQUENCY RANGE (mcs) a. Send b. Receive c. Crystal	TYPE OF SIGNAL RANGE IN MILES	CIRCUIT AND TUBES (a) Send (b) Receive	POWER OUTPUT (watts)	POWER SUPPLY & CONSUMPTION (a) Send (b) Receive	TYPE OF AERIAL	DIMENSIONS AND WEIGHT	ALLOCATION	REMARKS
Navigation Receiver FU 2 EB12.	b. 38		b. 5NF 2 TRF		b. Dynamotor U-8	Dipole under fuselage.			For blind landings.
X Gerät	b. 66.5–75 (2 on the same range)	Visual Dot-Dash left-right beams.	b. 7 Tube superhetrodyne 20 RV12 P4000		b. Dynamotor	Two vertical ¼ wave rods in streamlined housing.		Bomber aircraft.	A special blind bombing device operating on three main beams: one for pilot and two for observers. (Believed to be obsolete.)
Y Gerät (with FUG 17E and FUG 28A.	a. b. 42.1–47.9	M.C.W. R/T R/T 250	a. 2 RL P35-13, RV12 b. P4000	10	a. Dynamotor U-17	Vertical rod above and retractable antennae below fuselage.		Bomber aircraft.	A later development than the X-Gerät employing one instead of three beams.
Radio-Altimeter FUG101-101A.	a. 351–389 b. (Operating Frequency) 370	F.M.C.W. 0-150 meters 100-1500 meters	a. 1, LD 2-1, RV 12 P2001 b. 1, LV5-6, RV12 P2001		a. Dynamotor U-101 b.	Two separate ½ wave dipoles horizontally polarized: one each for transmitter and receiver.		Multi-engined aircraft for height finding.	
Radio Altimeters FUG 103.	a. 370 b.								An improvement on FUG 101 and 101A. Does not interfere with other wireless equipment on board.

Figure 58 (Continued).

GERMAN CABLES

Description	Conductor Strands	Insulation Material	Outside Diameter	Estimated Talking Range (Mls.)	Weight (Lbs. per 1,000 Feet)	Tensile Strength (Lbs.)	Insulation Abrasion Resistance	D-C Resistance Single Conductor per 1,000 Feet	Attenuation at 1,000 CPS. db. per Mile
Two-conductor cable with black rubber jacket applied over one white and one black rubber-insulated conductor.	0.024-inch solid copper.	Rubber type.	0.115-inch (single-conductor).	Dry, 16.3; wet, 10.1.	20.5	275	High.	25.9	Dry, 1.84; wet, 2.97.
Twisted-pair field wire, each conductor of which has a black braid over a white rubber insulation.	6, 0.013-inch steel; 2, 0.013-inch copper; 1, 0.021-inch copper.	Rubber type.	0.128-inch.	10.3 (2-wire metallic circuit).	12.9	400	Very high.	11.6	2.91
Single-conductor field wire with a stiff red synthetic insulation over 8 steel and 1 copper strands.	8, 0.015-inch steel; 1, 0.028-inch copper.	Polyvinyl, Chloride type.	0.135-inch.	....	....	400	Very high.	11.6	....
Single-conductor field wire with a wax-impregnated cotton braid over a black rubber insulation. The conductor consisting of 8 steel, and 1 copper, strands.	8, 0.015-inch steel; 1, 0.028-inch copper.	Rubber type.	0.128-inch.	8.5 (2-wire metallic circuit).	11.8	400	Very high.	16.9	3.53
Single-conductor field wire with a stiff red synthetic insulation and a conductor consisting of 8 steel and 1 aluminum strands.	8, 0.015-inch steel; 1, 0.028-inch aluminum.	Polyvinyl, Chloride type.	0.130-inch.	4.9 (2-wire metallic circuit).	9.2	...	High.	51.4	6.12
Single-conductor assault wire with a yellow synthetic insulation over a conductor consisting of 7 aluminum strands.	7, 0.016-inch aluminum.	Polyvinyl, Chloride type.	0.055-inch.	....	2.5	...	....	83.5	
Single-conductor assault wire with a cotton braid over a blue cellophane insulation. The conductor has 6 steel and 1 copper strands.	6, 0.008-inch steel; 1, 0.010-inch copper.	Cellophane type material.	0.425-inch.	Dry, 25.6; wet, 25.6 (not loaded). Voice frequency.	127	510	....	3.52	Dry, 1.17; wet, 1.17.
Long range field cable having four rubber-insulated conductors spirally twisted about a rubber-covered synthetic core. Over this quad is placed a tinsel shielding tape and a black rubber jacket.	19, 0.0125-inch copper.	Rubber type insulation and jacket.				...	....	....	
108-conductor cable composed of 12 tinned copper strands. Insulation of cotton covered with impregnated cotton tape and rubber outer jacket.	12 copper	....	0.875-inch.		525			....	....

Figure 59.

DESCRIPTION OF EQUIPMENT USED IN THE GERMAN ARMY FOR TESTING RADIO SETS

NOMENCLATURE	DIMENSIONS AND WEIGHT	DESCRIPTION	REMARKS
Wavemeter *Fremes a.*	17½"x14"x10"—46 lbs.	Frequency range: —30 kcs —30 mcs in 20 switched bands. Facilities: will emit modulated or unmodulated signal. (Loose or tight coupling to receiver.) Circuit as receiver: RF-oscillating detector—2AF RES 094. RE134W: RE. 134 Circuit as sender: oscillator—anode modulator. Power supply: 4-volt storage battery. 3-volt grid bias, 150-volt H.T. batteries.	The outstanding feature in the construction of the wavemeter is the massive turret for waveband switching, which takes up most of the space inside the case.
Frequency Tester *F. pruf. dl.*	—29 lbs.	Frequency range —120 —156 mc (26 fixed frequencies). Power supply: storage battery 2 N/9 and one 90-volt H.T. Battery.	For frequency calibration of fixed sets within its range.
Field Test Set 18 (*Das Feldmesskastchen*)	6.3"x4.7"x2.9"—2¾ lbs.	A field test set similar to the U. S. army's EE65.	A general purpose field Test Set.
Attenuation Meter.—39 (*Dampfungsmesser 39*)	13¼"x10¼"x9½"—	Is capable of measuring the amplification (in nepers) of 2 and 4 wire repeaters and the attenuation at 300 cycles over any type of line. Can measure crosstalk attenuation between the lines. Is powered with 90-volt H.T. battery and a 2-volt 2B19 storage battery.	Used in conjunction with telephone repeaters in testing and adjusting input and output levels.
German Tube Checker (*Rohrenprufgerat RPG4*)	16"x15"x9"—30 lbs.	Will test all European and a small number of American tubes. It may be used as a milliammeter, ohmeter, and capacity meter. Can only be used for DC voltages and currents.	
German Exploring Coil		This apparatus can be used to locate grounds, shorts, crosses and wet spots in cables. (However, it will not locate "opens" in cable pairs.)	
German Frequency Test Set *F. prufg. f.*	—25 lbs.	Crystal controlled oscillator fundamental output frequency of 26 mcs. Power supply: 2.4-volt storage battery for vibrator, one tube RL2 4T1. Consumption: 2.42 @ 6 amperes.	A field pack servicing and calibration unit for the *Feldfu. b* and *c.*

Figure 60.

Section V. ENGINEER EQUIPMENT

I. Instruments

a. GENERAL. In general the instruments used in the field by the engineers of the German Army are identical with our own, particularly their transits, theodolites, and surveyor's levels. The main differences occur in compasses and gap-measuring instruments.

b. GERMAN FIELD COMPASS (Marschkompass). (1) Description. The German field compass is a black, pocket-sized instrument. The housing is of aluminum-like metal. A brass outer ring is attached with a carrying handle. A hinged, linear, centimeter scale unfolds from the base of the compass housing. The letters MKZ(KZ) are marked on the body of the compass.

(2) Operation. The swinging of the magnetic needle can be stopped by pressing the damper button. When the destination is visible, open the cover and raise the mirror half way, so the magnetic needle can be seen clearly. Sight the point through the rear V sight and the front aperture at the base of the mirror. Hold steady until the point is in line with the eye, then with the free hand turn the azimuth circle until the magnetic needle falls on the magnetic declination mark. Read the azimuth from the dial. The German compass is numbered counter-clockwise, and the graduations are in mils. To simplify compass reading, the dial has been abbreviated so the last two zeros have been omitted; thus, 6,000 mils is shown as 60. The markings for directions are the same as our own, with the exception of East which is marked "O" for Ost. The adjustments for magnetic declination are marked directly on the azimuth dial; two luminous dots indicate 150 mils East and West.

c. NEW TYPE FIELD COMPASS (Marschkompass "A"). It is now known that a new type compass is in use in the German Army. This compass is numbered clockwise in mils.

d. GAP-MEASURING INSTRUMENT. This is a simple device to measure the width of streams and similar gaps. It is designed on the principle of similar right-angled triangles and consists of two parts: a fixed mirror and a measuring mirror.

2. German Demolition Equipment

a. SAFETY FUZE BLASTING CAP AND ACCESSORIES (Sprengkapsel No. 8). (1) Description. This blasting cap is similar to the U. S. and British types. It is designed to fit over the safety fuze and be initiated by it. The initiator of the cap consists of lead azide and lead styphnate.

(2) Characteristics.

Length ....2.36 inches.
Diameter ....0.28 inch.
Packing ....15 in wooden box.

(3) Bakelite Holder (Zünderhälter). This holder serves the double purpose of connecting the cap and fuze and permitting the cap to be screwed into the charge. It consists of a tube which covers the junction of the cap and fuze, and is enclosed in a bakelite cover. At one end of this cover is an externally threaded sleeve; the other end is covered by a bakelite cap with a central hole for passage of the fuze.

(4). Blasting Cap Igniter Set (Sprengkapsel-zünder). This is a prepared set with a cap in a bakelite holder, with a 3- to 6-foot safety fuze attached, and a safety fuze igniter. This provides a convenient short-delay demolition igniter.

b. SAFETY FUZE (Zeitzündschnur). The black powder train of this fuze is enclosed in strands of jute-like fibre and white cotton-like fibre alternately, the whole being covered with a bituminous paint, over which goes the black rubber outer covering. This safety fuze burns in air or under water at the rate of approximately 2 feet a minute. It can be initiated in the same way as U. S. and British safety fuzes.

c. ELECTRIC BLASTING CAPS. (1) Glühzünder 28. This consists of a cap, with twin leads of copper or iron, and a wire bridge. The whole fits into a standard bakelite cap holder. The copper leads have a resistance of 2 ohms; iron, 3 ohms.

(2) Delay Electric Blasting Cap (Glühzünder mit Verzögerung). These electric caps, which fire with a delay of 2, 4, 6, 8, or 10 seconds after electrical initiation, are similar to ordinary electric caps except that there is a pyrotechnic delay pellet between the wire bridge and the cap proper. These caps have the number of seconds delay marked on a disc attached to the leads.

(3) Spark Gap Electric Blasting Cap (Spalt-zünder). In these caps, the wire bridge has been replaced by a spark gap.

d. INSTANTANEOUS FUZE (Knallzündschnur). This fuze has a soft, pliable, green, outer covering with a waterproof varnish finish, surrounding an explosive core. It will detonate under water, initiated by a cap, but the ends must be water-proofed.

e. 100-GRAM CARTRIDGE *(Bohrpatrone 28)*. There are two types of this cartridge; one in waxed paper, and one in compressed paper. Both cartridges may be marked *Bohr-Patr. 28,* identifying the cartridge, and *Fp.02* or *Grf.88,* identifying the explosive as TNT or picric acid.

f. 200-GRAM SLAB *(Sprengkoerper 38)*. This slab is provided in two forms: in waxed paper and in a bakelite case. The waxed paper slab may contain either TNT or picric acid. Pressed picric acid is contained in the casing of two bakelite mouldings. The bakelite slab actually weighs 250 grams or 8¾ ounces.

g. 1-KILOGRAM (2.2 POUNDS) SLAB *(Sprengbüchse 24)*. (1) *Description.* This slab may be made either of TNT or picric acid, in a pressure-resisting zinc container which permits it to be used at any depth of water. There are three sockets for standard caps and holders, or igniters —one on each face of the slab, excluding the base. Each socket is covered with a paper disc marked *Sprengbüchse 24* and either *Fp.02* (TNT) or *Grf.88* (picric acid).

(2) *Characteristics.*

Weight ....2.2 pounds.
Length ....7.9 inches.
Width ....2.9 inches.
Thickness ....2.2 inches.

h. 3-KILOGRAM (6.6 POUNDS) SLAB *(Geballte Ladung 3 Kg.)*. (1) *Description.* This slab, in a zinc container with a carrying handle at one end, has either three or five sockets for standard caps and holders or igniters. The container is pressure-resisting, and the slab may be used under any depth of water. This slab is often used with igniters for improvised mines. It is marked *3 Kg.* on the side.

(2) *Characteristics.*

Weight ....6.6 pounds.
Height ....7.7 inches.
Width ....6.5 inches.
Thickness ....3 inches.

i. 3-KILOGRAM BALL CHARGE. (1) *Description.* The spherical body of the charge is constructed in two hemispherical sections of pressed mild steel, seamed together by a rolled joint. The securing lugs are welded to the top half of the body, and to them are attached the two ends of a canvas carrying strap. The charge has the standard threaded igniter socket and is marked *3 Kg.*

(2) *Characteristics.*

Weight of explosive .....6.6 pounds.
Diameter ....6.25 inches.
Filling ....Amatol.

j. HOLLOW DEMOLITION CHARGE (400 GRAMS OR 14 OUNCES). This charge is a cup-shaped, aluminum case, painted field gray, with the standard threaded cap socket in the top. A plate is recessed into the base. The central part of this plate forms a hemispherical wall surrounding the hollow space in the base of the charge. The main filling is penthrite.

k. 12.5-KILOGRAM HOLLOW CHARGE *(Hohlladung)*. (1) *Description.* This charge is designed to blast holes in steel plates in permanent fortifications or for special tasks. It is enclosed in a sheet iron cover with a carrying handle. In the base of the charge is a hemispherical cavity, and in the top is a standard threaded cap socket. This charge is usually part of the equipment of airborne troops.

(2) *Characteristics.*

Outside diameter ....11 inches.
Diameter of cavity ......5.3 inches.
Weight ....28 pounds.
Filling ....TNT.

l. 13.5-KILOGRAM HOLLOW CHARGE *(Hohlladung)*. (1) *Description.* This hollow charge rests on three telescopic legs, which ensure proper "stand-off". The charge is provided with a pellet contained in a standard detonator socket.

(2) *Characteristics.*

Outside diameter ....13½ inches.
Diameter of cavity ......9¾ inches.
Weight of charge ....30 pounds.
Filling (RDX-TNT) ....21 pounds.

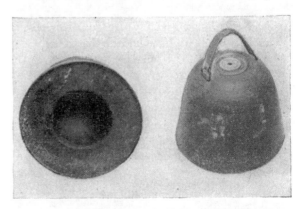

Figure 61.—Hohlladung 12.5-kg Demolition Charge.

m. 50-KILOGRAM HOLLOW CHARGE *(Hohlladung)*. (1) *Description.* For convenience in

transport, this charge is made in two parts. The lower part, which is provided with a separate carrying handle, contains a hemispherical cavity. The upper part contains both an explosive charge and a standard cap socket. This charge is part of the equipment of airborne troops.

(2) *Characteristics*.

Outside diameter ....20 inches.
Diameter of cavity ......8 inches.

Figure 62.—Hohlladung 13.5-kg Demolition Charge (Top: showing hemispherical cavity and stand-off legs in collapsed position. Bottom: in firing position).

Height of cavity ....4 inches.
Weight of charge ....110 pounds.
Filling ....TNT.

n. HOLLOW RING CHARGES (*Hohlringladung*).
(1) *Description*. These charges, used principally for the destruction of gun barrels, contain TNT, in a thin annular metal casing which is slipped over the gun barrel and fired by a cap. There is an annular, hollow space of semi-circular cross section on the inside of the ring, designed to increase the cutting effect. The fragmentation effect of these charges is negligible, which makes them suitable for use by raiding parties and patrols.

(2) *Characteristics*.

Hollow ring charge for antitank and machine-gun barrels:

Weight ....2 pounds 11 ounces.
Outside diameter ....7.1 inches.
Inside diameter ....3.9 inches.
Width ....3.1 inches.

Hollow ring charge for field guns:

Weight ....7 pounds 1 ounce.
Outside diameter ....10.4 inches.
Inside diameter ....6.7 inches.
Width ....3.4 inches.

Figure 63.—Shaped Demolition Charge (50 kg).

o. BANGALORE TORPEDO (*Gestreckte Ladung*). This torpedo is made up of units of 16-gauge steel pipe lengths, with a sleeve welded to one end to form a socket for the adjoining unit. Units are packed with blasting gelatine or other suitable explosives. Detonating fuzes run the lengths of the tubes. The torpedo is initiated at one end by two independent caps, using a cap igniter set

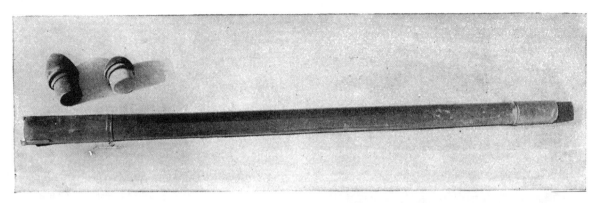

Figure 64.—Bangalore torpedo.

for one and a length of safety fuze and match for the other. Other sections carry a cap fitted to the end of the tube. When assembling sections, the free end of the fuze at the socket end of one section is tied to the cap at the spigot end of the next section.

p. GERMAN FIELD EXPLODERS. (1) *Exploder 1942, six-barrelled (Nebelwerfer).* This exploder is 6 inches high and has two sockets in the core. One socket is for winding, and the other for a seven-pin plug providing six circuits with a common central return. On the outside of each of the six outer plug holes are six numbered windows which glow in turn as their circuit is completed. The exploder thus can fire six circuits rapidly, one after another; the operator can see the glow lamps recording the firing in succession. Since this exploder has a low capacity, with 20 detonators the maximum number it will handle, its use for demolitions is restricted.

(2) *Small Exploder 1940 (Glühzündapparat 40).* This exploder forms part of the portable demolition kit *(Zündgerät 40).* It is 5.3 inches high and has an oval-shaped top, mounting the firing terminals and the winding socket. It will fire through 90 ohms external resistance, and the generator is turned directly by the handle in the winding socket. Only when the maximum current is generated is the circuit closed; for firing, the handle must be turned as fast as possible to the "stop". The exploder has an internal resistance of 30 ohms and generates a current of 1 ampere at 80 volts. Before using the exploder, it must be tested with a special neon test tube, which not only tests the exploder but also excites the magnetism in the generator.

Figure 65.—Exploder 43 (6-barreled).

Figure 66.—Exploder 39 (Glühzündapparat 39).

(3) *Field Exploder 1939 (Glühzündapparat 39)*. This exploder is packed in a leather carrying case. It fires through a maximum resistance of 300 ohms and has an internal resistance of 40 ohms. The winding key is kept in the carrying case, which also holds the test resistance, a spare spring, and a screw driver. On the top of the exploder are the winding socket, the spring socket, and the spring terminals.

(4) *Field Exploder 1937 (Glühzündapparat 37)*. This exploder generates 300 volts and fires through a maximum resistance of 300 ohms. The internal resistance is 43 ohms. The exploder has a winding key kept in the carrying case, which also holds the test resistance. On top of the exploder is a winding socket marked *Aufziehen* and a firing socket marked *Zünden*. The firing terminals are on an insulated step below the level of the cover. The spring driving the generator cannot be released unless it has been fully wound. To use the exploder, wind the spring clockwise until the "stop" is reached. To fire, turn the socket marked *"Zünden"* with the key.

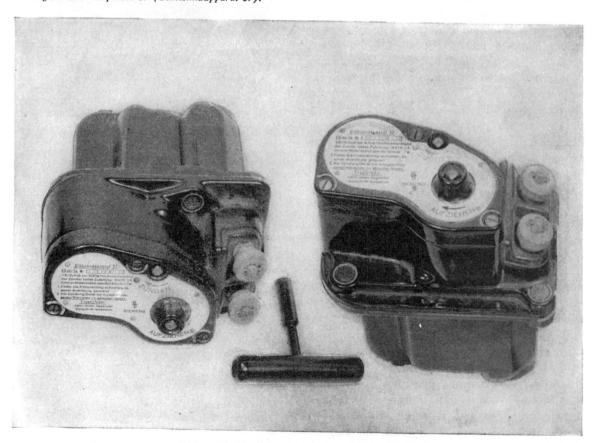

Figure 67.—Exploder 37 (Glühzündapparat 37).

Figure 68.—Exploder 26 (Glühzündapparat 26).

(5) *Field Exploder 1926*. This exploder weighs 14.5 pounds and is packed in a leather case. The exploder is of the low tension type (hot wire as opposed to spark) with an internal resistance of 45 ohms. Maximum resistance through which it will fire is 255 ohms.

q. PORTABLE DEMOLITION KIT 1940. This is a pack containing everything needed to fire charges electrically. It weighs 51 pounds, and can be carried by a handle or by shoulder straps on the back. It contains a small exploder (1940) and neon test tube, a continuity tester (galvanometer) (1926), 40 electric detonators, two spools of single cable and two drums of double cable, metal sleeve for crimping over electrical joints, a notched pocket knife, crimpers, and insulating tape.

r. CONTINUITY TEST (GALVANOMETER) 1926. This tester not only tests continuity but also measures resistance of circuits and detonators. It contains an ohmeter, resistance, and battery (1.5 volts). The battery is housed in a cylinder 4.7 inches high with the ohmeter on top. Adjusting screws for setting the ohmeter needle to zero and infinity are midway between the testing terminals. A built-in resistance protects caps from being initiated while being tested for continuity.

s. TEST RESISTANCE AND NEON LAMPS. The resistance is for testing the Field Exploder 1926 for firing through 250 ohms resistance. The neon lamp, designed for testing the Field Exploder 1937 and 1939, has a screw head which may be set to test for firing either 50 or 100 detonators. There is another neon lamp for

testing the small Exploder 1940. It is part of the portable Demolition Kit 1940.

t. MAGNETIC DEMOLITION CHARGE ANTITANK (*Panzerhandmine*). This charge is spherical and completely covered by pressed cardboard. This cardboard casing, held in shape by two metal bands, extends 4 inches below the base of the explosive. Primarily designed as a demolition charge, it also can be used against tanks. The explosive filler is 1 pound 12 ounces of cyclonite and TNT. The booster consists of two pellets of cyclonite and wax in which there is a fitting for a standard igniter of the *BZ* type.

Figure 69.—Resistance and neon test lamp.

u. GERMAN ANTITANK MAGNETIC HOLLOW CHARGE. This charge is painted field gray. The three attached magnets are strong enough to hold the charge against a vertical surface. The main filling is in a pressed metal container, conical in shape, with an elongated apex to act as a hand grip and to accommodate the detonator. The igniter has a delay of only 4½ seconds. However, a new type igniter with a yellow head and a 7½-second delay has been introduced.

3. Booby Traps

a. MATERIALS. The following standard materials have been used in German booby traps:

Tellermines.

S-Mines.

C.V.P.I. Mines.

Improvised wooden mines.

Prepared charges.

Mortar bombs.

Hand grenades.

Italian B.4 mines.

Italian hand grenades.

French antitank mines.

British G.S. mines Mks. II, IV, and V.

British gun cotton slabs.

British aircraft bombs.

b. METHODS OF SETTING. The booby traps are set ordinarily in the following ways:

Tellermines with anti-lifting devices.

Tellermines connected by prima cord to two or more E.P. mines and fitted with an anti-lifting device.

S-Mines with pull igniters.

C.V.P.I. mines with setting at "K" and a trip or pull wire.

Prepared charges, concealed in rubbish, fitted with pull igniters and pull wires.

Charges inside a water bottle fitted with a pull igniter to detonate on the withdrawal of the cork.

Mortar bombs fitted with S.Mi.Z.35 igniter.

Egg and stick grenades fitted with pull igniters.

Italian B.4 mines with trip wires.

French antitank mines with pull igniters.

British aircraft bombs with pull igniters and trip wires.

Empty German mine cases with pull igniters attached to the bottom of the crate or inside of the lid.

c. EMPLOYMENT IN BUILDINGS. Pull igniters inserted in prepared charges, grenades, and standard mines commonly are used as booby traps in buildings. The friction igniter ZDSCHN. ANZ.

29, attached to a prepared detonator, also is used with a pull cord. The trip or pull wires may be laid across entrances and doorways, across stairways, or attached to doors of rooms, cupboards, or to windows. Both ends of wires should be investigated for traps. If wires are in tension, they must not be cut until this investigation has been carried out. Pressure igniters commonly are found under loose boards and door mats. The DZ.35 type is the igniter usually employed.

4. German Mine Detectors

a. MINE DETECTING ROD, 1939 PATTERN. (1) Description. This detector consists of a length of light alloy tubing, one end of which carries a steel point, while the other carries a bayonet joint permitting a second length of tubing to be added when the operator is standing. The weight of the main tube and point is approximately 10 ounces.

(2) Employment. This detector is used as a probe, the point being dropped vertically into the ground from a height of about 4 inches. It is claimed that the nature of any underground object encountered can be recognized by the characteristic sound coming from the tube.

b. MINE DETECTOR BERLIN 40 TYPE B. (1) Description. This detector consists of a detector unit carried in a pack on the operator's back, a search coil, sectionalized pole, headphones, and cable connections.

(2) Employment. The variable condenser is adjusted to produce a suitable note in the earphones. Proximity of a metal object to the search coil produces a change of tone.

c. MINE DETECTOR Tempelhof 41. (1) Description. This is a portable detector provided with a loud speaker instead of earphones. The whole instrument can be carried in an infantry pack.

(2) Employment. The tone control is turned to the right until the loudspeaker produces its maximum volume. In presence of a metal object the tone will rise in pitch.

d. MINE DETECTOR Frankfurt 40. (1) Description. This detector is contained in a wooden box which fits into a canvas pack. The pack also has a compartment in which the search coil can be carried when not in use. The box is divided into two compartments, one for the batteries and one for the detector. The wiring is exposed by removal of a sliding panel which is held in position by one screw. The tubes and batteries are acces-

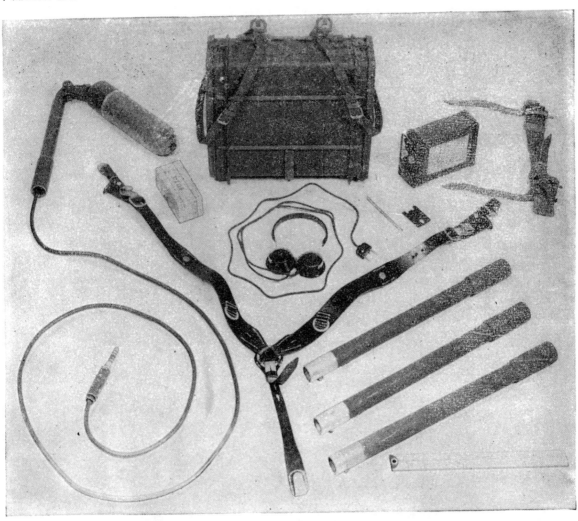

Figure 70.—Mine Detector (Wien 41).

Figure 71.—Mine Detector (Frankfurt 42).

sible after removal of the front panel. The pole is in three sections. The search coil is housed in a bakelite moulding.

(2) *Employment.* The circuit is adjusted for zero balance. A tone is produced in the earphones by proximity of a metal object.

e. OTHER MINE DETECTORS. Other mine detectors in general use are:

Pentagrid tube type.
M.S.F. 1007.
Frankfurt 42.
Pram Mine Detector.
Wiesbaden Mine Detector.

5. Antipersonnel Mines

a. S-MINE 35. (1) *Description.* This antipersonnel mine may be operated by direct pressure on an igniter in the head, or by a pull on one or more trip wires attached to pull igniters. The mine may also be fired electrically. The pressure igniter, *S.Mi.Z.35,* functions under a weight of about 15 pounds. When set with trip wires, pull igniters *ZZ.35* or *Zu.ZZ.35* are used, with a two- or three-way adapter screwed on the mine in place of the transit cap. The mine is cylindrical with a close-fitting cover. For transport three are carried in a wooden box or watertight pressed metal case. In the space between the outer case and inner cylinder of each mine there are approximately 360 steel balls, mild steel rods in short lengths, or small pieces of scrap steel. These constitute the loading of the mine. The base plate has a recess to hold the propellent charge. The central steel tube is threaded externally to take the adapters or igniters, and internally to take any standard German igniter or electric detonator for deliberate firing. At its lower end, the tube passes through the base plate and is secured by a union. Inside the main steel tube is another short tube, containing a delay element (about 4½ seconds). There have been cases where the delay holder has been replaced by a detonator, causing the mine to explode without jumping. Equally spaced in the base plate are holes leading into the bottom of the three detonator tubes and containing short-delay elements. When the igniter functions, the delay pellet provides a short delay before igniting the propellent charge in the base of the mine. The burning of this charge projects the main elements of the mine into the air. Simultaneously, the powder delays in the bottom of the detonator tubes are ignited and explode the mine some 3 to 5 feet above the ground.

Figure 72.—S-Mine with Y Adapter and Z.Z. 35 Igniter.

Figure 73.—S-Mine with S. Mi.Z. 35 Igniter.

Figure 74.—Jerrican booby-trapped to S-Mine.

(2) Characteristics.

Height (less igniter) ....5 inches.
Diameter ....4 inches.
Weight ....9 pounds.
Weight of filling:
    Poured TNT ....14 ounces.
    Powdered TNT ....8 ounces.

(3) *Performance.* The delay between firing the igniter and the ejection of the mine varies according to age and condition of the mine. However, tests have shown an average of 3.9 seconds. The delay between the ejection of the mine and the detonation also varies; tests have shown that it averages 0.6 second.

(4) *Neutralization.* Anti-handling devices first are neutralized. Then uncover the mine, identify, and neutralize the igniters.

(5) *Disarming.* After neutralizing, cut the trip wires of the pull igniters. Unscrew the igniters and unscrew the plugs from the three holes in the cover and remove the detonator by turning the mine over.

b. S-MINE 44. (1) *Description.* The S-Mine 44 is an antipersonnel mine of the bounding type similar to the S-mine 35. The igniter well is toward one side of the cover plate, and the height at which the mine explodes is controlled by an internal pull-igniter arrangement. The igniter is the combination push-and-pull type, and its neutralization demands extreme care. The employment of this mine is the same as for the S-mine 35. The lethal range is 22 yards, and the casualty range 110 yards.

(2) *Operation.* The igniter initiates the 4½-second delay pellet firing the propellant, which throws the mine upward. When the coiled wire is fully extended it pulls the release pin from the igniter, exploding the mine.

c. *Schü-Mine 42.* (1) *Description.* The *Schü-mine 42* with the Z.Z. 42 igniter is an easy, handy obstacle to employ against infantry, cavalry, and light vehicles. In small-scale obstacles, it conveniently can be substituted for the S-mine 35. In almost all minefields it can be used in conjunction with Tellermines. The mine consists of a casing of impregnated plywood, or hardened compressed fibrous cardboard, painted dull black; one 1928 pattern demolition charge weighing 200 grams or 7 ounces; and one Z.Z.42 pull igniter with No. 8 detonator. The total weight is 1.1 pounds. The igniter is prepared for use by unscrewing the safety cap and inserting the detonator (open end to open end). The pin is held in position by the spring-loaded striker.

(2) *Lifting and Neutralizing.* After locating the mine, search for and neutralize any anti-handling devices, then lift the lid without exerting any pressure. See whether the pin of the igniter is still seated firmly in the striker. If this is the case the mine may be lifted, after determining that there are no anti-lifting devices. Mines on which pressure has been exerted and the pin disturbed from its normal position should be destroyed in place.

d. WOODEN ANTIPERSONNEL MINE 43(N). (1) *Description.* In its operation this mine, with an impregnated wood body, is very similar to the standard German *Schü-mine 42.* The lid, hinged to the back of the body, is fitted with a metal operating flange at the front. This flange, in the armed position, rests on two wooden dowels and is secured by a safety pin. The center of the flange is slotted to clear the striker of the igniter, but two small tongues rest in the loop of the igniter pin. The igniter, *Z.Z.42,* is screwed into a zinc socket. The main filling is cast TNT, with pressed TNT around the detonator socket.

(2) *Characteristics.*

Length ....8¼ inches.
Width ....6⅞ inches.
Height open ....4¼ inches.
Height closed ....3¼ inches.
Weight of filling ....3 pounds 5 ounces.

(3) *Operation.* The mine is fired by pressure on the lid. The metal flange will first shear the dowels and then push out the pin, thus releasing

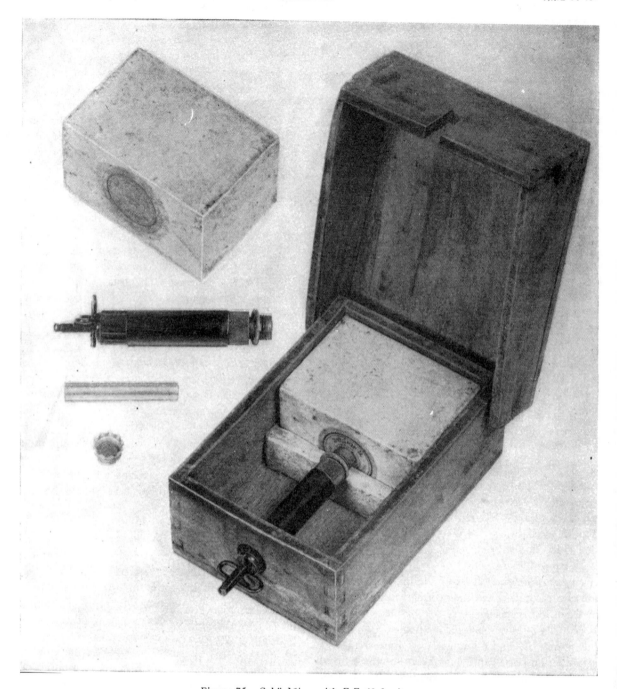

Figure 75.—Schü-Mine with Z.Z. 42 Igniter.

the striker. The operating load is approximately 75 pounds.

(4) *To Neutralize*. The same as for the *Schü-mine 42*.

e. WOODEN MINE 42(N). (1) *Description*. The body is made of impregnated wood, with a zinc socket in the top to take a detonator and igniter. Across the top is a shaped block of wood drilled to allow the igniter to be screwed down on the top of the body. The igniter is the stand-ard *D.Z.35*. The main filling is cast TNT with pressed TNT primer.

(2) *Characteristics*.

Length	6¼ inches.
Width	6¼ inches.
Over-all height	5⅛ inches.
Height of body	2¾ inches.
Weight of filling	3 pounds 5 ounces.

(3) *Operation*. The mine is fired by pressure on top of the *D.Z.35* igniter, or by pressure on a

Figure 76.—Glass Mine 43 with (a) Hebelzünder Igniter, and (b) Buck Igniter.

cover board over the head of the igniter. Without the cover board, the mine is practically insensible to blast, but the probability of operating the mine is reduced considerably. The functioning load of the igniter fitted to this mine is 75 pounds. It appears that the igniter is being manufactured with a weaker spring for use in this mine, since the pressure required to function a standard D.Z.35 is 130 to 165 pounds.

f. ANTIPERSONNEL PRESSURE MINE (ITAL-IAN). (1) *Description.* This mine consists of a rectangular bakelite box, with a wedge-shaped, hinged lid, containing a TNT charge held in place by a projection and surrounded on the remaining three sides by deeply grooved fragmentation plates. The igniter mechanism consists of a metal tube which contains a spring-loaded striker, fitted with an actuating pin and a cocking ring. The outer end of the striker tube is secured against

the wall of the box by a flange. The striker assembly slips into the side of the mine, in a recess cut out to receive it. A corresponding slot in the lid enables the mine to be completely closed when the igniter is not cocked.

(2) *Characteristics.*

Length of box ....5.35 inches.
Width of box ....2.56 inches.
Depth of box ....1.5 inches.
Length of charge ....2.6 inches.
Width of charge ....1.97 inches.
Depth of charge ....1.18 inches.
Weight of charge ....5¼ ounces.

(3) *Method of arming.* To arm the mine the igniter is cocked by pulling out the ring and inserting the actuating pin. The detonator is then inserted in the striker tube and secured by locking the ring. The whole assembly is inserted in the box, the detonator fitting into a recess in

the explosive charge. Finally, the lid is gently closed until it rests on the actuating pin.

(4) *Operation.* A slight pressure on the lid will cause it to push out the pin and release the striker.

(5) *To Neutralize.* Avoid all pressure on the lid of the mine. Search for and neutralize any anti-handling devices. Lift the lid clear of the actuating pin. Insert a wire or nail in the safety-pin hole and lift out the striker assembly. Unscrew the locking ring and remove the detonator.

g. ANTIPERSONNEL GLASS MINE 43. (1) *Description.* This antipersonnel mine is made almost entirely of glass. It is armed with the chemical igniter or with the *Hebelzünder.* The bottom of the glass container is recessed to hold a *Sprengkorper 28.* On top of the mine rests a glass shear plate, and, on top of that, a thick glass pressure plate.

(2) *Operation.* A pressure of 20 to 25 pounds breaks the thin shear plate and applies pressure on the lever of the *Hebelzünder,* thus firing the igniter and exploding the mine.

(3) *To Neutralize.* If the mine is fitted with a *Hebelzünder,* remove the two glass plates, insert safety pin, and unscrew the igniter. Then remove the detonator. If it is fitted with a chemical igniter, unscrew the igniter by gripping it as low as possible. Do not grip the corrugated portion which crushes easily.

h. GERMAN ANTIPERSONNEL "POT MINE". (1) *Description.* A crush igniter is screwed into the top of the cylindrical body of this mine by means of an adapter. The pressed steel body contains an explosive filling of approximately 4 ounces of powdered picric acid.

(2) *Operation.* A moderate pressure on the top of the igniter explodes the mine.

(3) *To Neutralize.* Unscrew the igniter, grasping it as low as possible. If the detonator does not come out with the igniter, remove it by turning the mine upside down. If it does not then drop out, unscrew the adapter and remove the detonator. The total weight of the mine is $12\frac{1}{2}$ ounces.

i. MODIFIED *Schü-Mine.* (1) *Description.* This modified *Schü-mine* may be used with the *Z.Z.35* igniter. The large lid has a sloping front through which the igniter plunger head protrudes.

(2) *Operation.* Pressure on the lid causes the sloping front to push on the actuating pin. This pulls out the plunger of the igniter, causing it to fire. A hole is bored in the lid directly above the safety pin of the igniter. A cord attached to the ring of the safety pin is used to draw the pin out through the hole to arm the mine.

6. Antitank Mines

a. GENERAL. The Germans use about 40 types of antitank mines, but the four types of Teller-mines are used most extensively.

b. TELLERMINE 43 (MUSHROOM). (1) *Description*. In place of the usual cover, this mine has a mushroom head pressure plate which screws into the igniter socket. Two threaded sockets are provided for subsidiary anti-lifting igniters, one in the side of the mine and the other in the base. The positions of these two sockets vary, although they always have been found on a diameter of the mine.

(2) *Characteristics*.

Diameter over-all ....12.5 inches.
Depth of body ....2.6 inches.
Maximum height of mine.3.5 inches.
Diameter of mushroom
   head ....7.5 inches.
Depth of mushroom head.1 inch.
Total weight of mine ...17 pounds 5 ounces.

c. TELLERMINE 1942 (*T.Mi.42*) (1) *Description*. This mine consists of a cylindrical, pressed-steel body, containing a central detonator pocket which is surrounded by a priming cylinder of a composition resembling penthrite. Two pull ig-

niter sockets are provided, one in the side of the mine 4 inches from the carrying handle, and the other in the base 2 inches from the center of the mine. These sockets are screwed into the body of the mine and waterproofed by rubber washers. A cylindrical cavity on the top of the mine contains the pressure-plate assembly. This pressure plate carries a rubber washer or aluminum strip, which is secured to it by a steel ring spot-welded to the plate and forming a seal where it passes under the lower edge of the flanged ring. A strong spring provides the resistance which must be overcome to depress the pressure plate. A central, threaded socket serves for the insertion of the igniter assembly, *T.Mi.Z.42(15)*, consisting of a spring-loaded striker retained by a shear pin. The detonator resembles that used in the Teller-mine 35, but it screws into the body of the mine.

(2) *Characteristics*.

Diameter of base ......12¾ inches.
Diameter of case ......12½ inches.
Diameter of pressure
   plate ....5¾ inches.
Maximum height ......4 inches.
Type of filling ....TNT.
Weight of filling ......12 pounds.
Weight of mine ....18 pounds (approximately).

Figure 77.—Tellermine 43 (mushroom).

Figure 78.—Tellermine 42.

Figure 79.—Tellermine 35 (steel).

(3) *Functioning.* The mine functions when a minimum pressure of 495 pounds on the pressure plate causes the hexagonal cap to descend on the head of the plunger and shear the pin which retains the striker in the body of the igniter.

d. TELLERMINE 35 (STEEL) (*T.Mi.35 Stahl*). This mine, 12½ inches in diameter, weighs 21 pounds. Painted a mat gray, it is marked *T.Mi.S 31 T Vii. 242* on the top in white paint; *S88 12 42A,* on the top in black paint; and *WO 42,* stamped on the top. In this model the pressure plate which extends over the entire mine is fluted, probably to prevent sand from blowing off when the mine is buried. In the center of the pressure plate is a threaded socket, closed by a screwed plug with a milled head. This socket will take the standard *T.Mi. Z.35* igniter, but the mine can also be used with the igniter assembly of the Tellermine 42. The subsidiary igniter sockets are located on the bottom and side of the mine.

e. TELLERMINE 35 (*T.Mi.35*). (1) *Description.* This is a circular mine with a flat base and slightly convex cover. A strong spiral spring inside the mine holds the cover against the turned-in flange of a skirt screwed to the outside of the main body. The central hole for the main igniter

Figure 80.—*Tellermine 35 with anti-lifting devices.*

(*T.Mi.Z.35* or *T.Mi.Z.42*) is provided with a rubber washer to make a close joint with the body. When the *T.Mi.Z.42* is used, a steel plug must be placed in the central well. Two holes for additional igniters are provided. The central tube, which takes the exploder system, contains the detonator, above which are two metal collars. Above these is a rubber ring, capable of compression to make the assembly watertight. The igniter screws into the cover of the mine, so that

Figure 81.—*Tellermine 35.*

the lower face of the igniter presses hard against the rubber ring. One collar is a retaining collar for the detonator; the other is an adjusting or positioning collar for the igniter. The igniter is screwed into the correct position by a special tool, and when positioned it is secured by a small grub passing through the collar. If this collar has been removed, it cannot be replaced correctly unless the special tool is available. Incorrect positioning makes the mine either too sluggish or too sensitive.

(2) *Characteristics.*

Diameter ....12.6 inches.
Weight of mine ....19.2 pounds.
Weight of filling ....11 pounds.
Type of filling ....TNT.

(3) *Functioning.* The mine functions when the pressure on the cover compresses the mine spring, causing the body of the igniter to descend and shear the pin holding the striker. Pressure of 175 to 400 pounds will explode the mine.

(4) *To neutralize.* Examine the sides and bottom of the mine for anti-handling igniters. Identify the igniters and neutralize. Remove the main igniter from the mine, manipulate the safety device, and immediately replace the igniter.

f. TELLERMINE 29 (*T. Mi. 29*). (1) *Description.* This mine was the first of the Tellermine series and was thought to have become obsolete, but it has been found in France since D-Day. It consists of a cylindrical body the lid of which is provided with three sockets for the reception of three *Z.D.Z. 29* push-pull igniters. These igniters, according to a German document, are to be set at the heavy pressure setting (marked S or 125 kg.). Three additional sockets, two in the side and one in the base provide means of attaching anti-handling igniters.

(2) *Characteristics.*

Diameter ....10 inches.
Height ....2.7 inches.
Weight ....13.2 pounds.
Weight of filling ......10 pounds.
Type of filling ....TNT.
Firing pressure ....100-275 pounds.

(3) *Neutralization.* Search for and neutralize anti-handling devices. Unscrew the three igniters. The mine is now safe.

g. L. Pz. ANTITANK MINE. (1) *Description.* This is a circular mine with flat top and bottom, enclosed in two saucer-shaped covers. In the center of the top is a small cover plate secured by bayonet catches under which is a safety screw.

Figure 82—Tellermine 29.

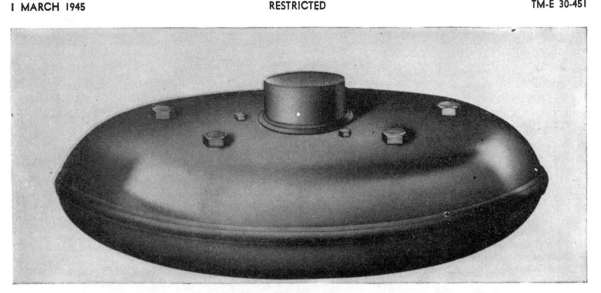

Figure 83.—L. P. Z. Mine.

which when screwed tightly clockwise closes the entry to the detonator. Above the blasting cap is a small chamber from which fire tubes lead radially to the five special pressure igniters action of which is similar to that of the *D.Z. 35* pressure igniter.

(2) *Characteristics.*

Diameter of mine .....1 foot.
Height ....3 inches.
Weight of mine ....8 pounds.
Weight of filling.......5 pounds.
Nature of filling.......TNT.

(3) *Functioning.* Pressure on the lid causes one or more of the igniters to fire, setting off the mine.

(4) *Neutralization.* Search for and neutralize any anti-handling devices. Remove cap and screw safety screw clockwise until line marked *SICHER* coincides with white mark on case. If all the nuts on the bottom of the mine are present and screwed up, mine is safe.

h. *Topf* MINE. (1) *Description.* The mine body is a hollow cylindrical disc of plastic material filled with HE. Its top face is formed as a circular pressure plate surrounded by a shear groove. The cylindrical recess in the center of the mine body accommodates the primer plug. The carrying handle is fixed to the mine bottom by two glass screws.

The primer plug assembly consists of a glass screw cap and the cylindrical igniter seating, made of bituminous cardboard material.

(2) *Action.* Under a load of 330 pounds, the pressure plate shears along its shear groove and comes to rest on the pressure head of igniter, crushing it and causing the mine to explode.

(3) *To neutralize:*

(a) Search for and neutralize any anti-handling devices.

(b) Ensure that the mine is undamaged.

(c) Lift carefully, rest on one side, and unscrew the primer plug.

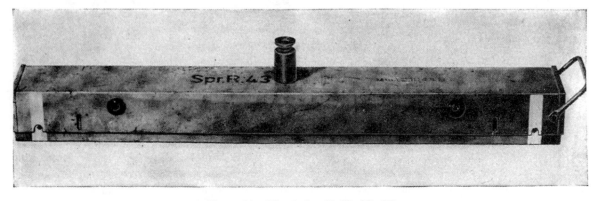

Figure 84.—Riegelmine 43 (R. Mi. 43).

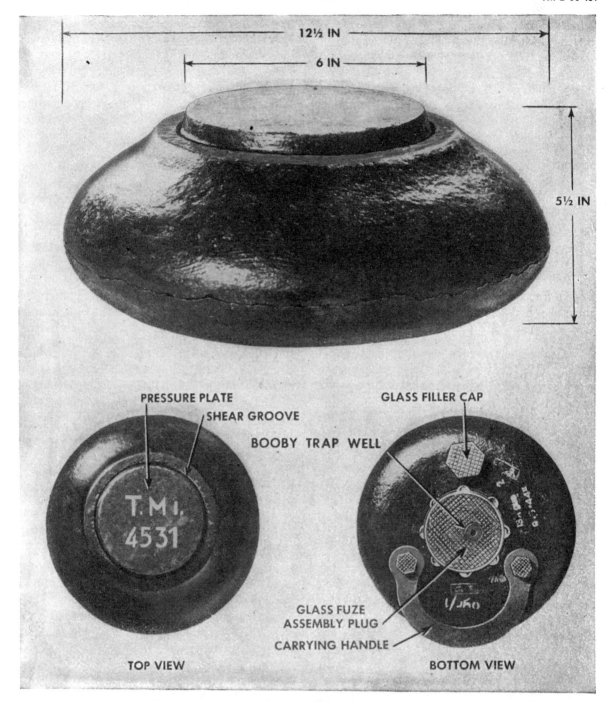

Figure 85.—Topf Mine.

(d) Remove the igniter.

(e) Unscrew protective detonator pocket.

(f) Remove the detonator and replace the protective pocket on the igniter.

i. *Riegel.* ANTITANK MINE (*R. Mi. 43*). (1) *Description.* The mine consists of an encased explosive charge and of an outer box in two parts, lid and tray. The charge is provided with five standard igniter sockets, one on top, two on one side, and one at each end. Holes in the box correspond with the sockets on top and on the side, enabling igniters to be inserted from outside and fitted as anti-handling devices.

Z.Z. 42 igniters are inserted in the end sockets and their pins rest on shoulders at each end of the tray and are covered by swivel clips. The charge is supported in the tray by two shear wires. For transport, two safety bars are inserted which take the weight of the charge off the shear wires. When the safety bars are withdrawn, spring-loaded shutters close the holes. These shutters can be opened by pushing a pencil or large nail through a hole in the base of the tray.

The lid rests on the charge, and the ends of the shear wires are led up over the lid and windlassed together to keep it on.

(2) *Characteristics.*

Length ....31.5 inches.
Width ....3¾ inches.
Height ....3½ inches.
Weight of mine ......20.5 pounds.
Weight of explosive...8.8 pounds.
Nature of explosive....Amatol 50/50.

(3) *Functioning.* Pressure on the lid of the mine shears the shear wires and the pins of the *Z.Z 42* igniters are pushed out, thus setting off the mine.

(4) *Neutralization.* Search for and neutralize any anti-handling devices. Turn the mine on its side and by pushing a pencil or nail through the hole in the base raise the shutters covering the safety bar holes. Insert safety bars. Cut shear wires and remove lid. Open swivel clips and, having seen that the pins of the *Z.Z. 42* igniters are resting on the shoulders and not beneath, take out the charge case. Unscrew the *Z.Z. 42* igniters.

NOTE: The charge case can be inserted with one *Z.Z. 42* igniter pin reversed and beneath the shoulders. In this case the charge case must be slid out by lifting the end in which the *Z.Z. 42* igniter is used normally.

j. FRENCH LIGHT ANTITANK MINE. (1) *Description.* The mine body consists of a rectangular steel body filled with 5¾ pounds of HE. In the top of the mine are two igniter pockets, one at either end. The body is covered with a slip-on rectangular cover the top of which is corrugated. There is a square hole in either end of the cover

Figure 86.—French light antitank mine.

through which passes a safety bar which is removed when the mine is laid.

(2) *Action.* A pressure of from 300 pounds to 500 pounds in the lid causes it to descend on the igniters, exploding the mine.

(3) *Characteristics.*

Length	9½ inches.
Width	5½ inches.
Height	4½ inches.
Weight	14½ pounds.

(4) *To neutralize:*

(a) Search for and neutralize any anti-handling devices.

(b) Lift cover and remove both igniters.

(c) Replace the cover.

k. WOODEN-BOX MINE 42 (*Holzmine*). (1) *Description.* The body of the mine is a rectangular wooden box containing 11½ pounds of HE. A pressure block protrudes through the lid of the mine, which inside the mine rests on a shear flange secured to the side of the mine by wooden dowels.

The mine is gray or unpainted, with a red band on one side and on the face of the pressure block.

(2) *Action.* Pressure of 200 pounds or more on the pressure block shears the dowels securing the shear flange, which when forced down pushes out the pin in the *Z.Z. 42* igniter, exploding the mine.

(3) *Characteristics.*

Length	13 inches.
Width	12 inches.
Height	4½ inches.
Weight	18 pounds.

(4) *Neutralizing.* Search for and neutralize any anti-handling devices. Remove the lid avoiding all pressure on the pressure block. Lift pressure block clear of the shear flange. Place the pressure block so it bears on the supporting block in the unarmed position. Replace the lid.

Figure 87.—Wooden Box Mine 42.

ANTITANK MINES IN USE BY THE GERMANS

NAME	Length (Inches)	Width (Inches)	Height (Inches)	Weight (Pounds)	Igniter	Firing load (Pounds)	REMARKS
Tellermine 35.	12.5 (diam.)		3.2	20	T.Mi.Z. 35 or T.Mi.Z. 42	175– 400	Fitted for anti-handling devices.
Tellermine 35 (steel).	12.5 (diam.)		3.5	20	T.Mi.Z. 35 or T.Mi.Z. 42	175– 400	Fitted for anti-handling devices.
Tellermine 42.	12.5 (diam.)		4	20	T.Mi.Z. 42	250– 400	Fitted for anti-handling devices.
Tellermine 43 (Mushroom).	12.5 (diam.)		4	20	T.Mi.Z. 42	440– 600	Fitted for anti-handling devices.
Tellermine 29.	10 (diam.)		2.7	13.2	Z.D.Z. 29	100– 275	Three igniters used.
L. PZ. AT Mine.	10.25 (diam.)		2.25	9	Five special pressure igniters.		Paratroop mine.
Topf Mine.	12.5 (diam.)		5.5	21.775	Chemical Non-metallic.	330	Non-metallic mine.
Riegel Mine (R.Mi.43).	32.75	4	3.5	20.5	ZZ.42	400	Fitted for three external igniters for anti handling.
Wooden Box Mine (42). Holzmine 42.	12	12	4½	18	ZZ.42	200	
Wooden Box Mine V.B.1. Holzmine V.B.1.	12	12	4	20	ZZ.42	200	
Heavy Wooden AT Mine.	17	15.75	10.5	37	DZ.35	200	Fitted for anti-handling devices.
Panzer Schnellmine Type A.	20.75	13	5	16 (approx.)	ZZ.42		Locally produced improvised mine.
Type B.	20.75	13	5	16 (approx.)	Buck igniter.		
Improvised Aluminum Mine.	12.5 (diam.)		4.75	14 to 16½	DZ.35 or T.Mi.Z. 42	130– 390	
C.V.P. 1 AT & Apers. Mine (Hungarian)	10 (diam.)		3	8		60	
French Light AT Mine.	9.5	5.5	4.5	14.5	Rod 35 Rod 36	420– 500	
Dutch AT Mine T. 40.	11 (diam.)		3.5	13.2	Pressure ball release type.	100	Oval section.
AT Mine Type N. (Norwegian).	15.75	5.5	5	10	Pressure	?	
Belgian Heavy AT Type HA.	9	8.75	8.5	33	Shear Pin and Striker.	400	

Figure 88.

7. Igniters

a. PULL IGNITERS. (1) *Bakelite Z.Z.42* (*Zug-zünder 42*). The pin, the striker, and the actuating spring of this igniter are steel. The body and the collar are plastic mouldings, and the cap holder is brass. Between the lower end of the spring and the striker head are a metal washer and a felt washer which act as a guiding gland. The over-all length is $3\frac{7}{16}$ inches, and the diameter is $\frac{1}{2}$ inch.

(2) *Zugzünder 35* (*Z.Z.35*). (a) *Description.* This igniter is used with trip wires to operate S-mines, improvised mines, and booby traps. The heavy antitank mines have this igniter as a booby trap against lifting the lid, and it also is used as an extra igniter in Tellermines and as the main igniter in the drifting mine. The brass body of the igniter contains a sliding cylinder, a compressing spring, the striker, and the striker spring. In the unarmed position, the safety pin is prevented from falling out by a nut on the end of the pin and by a spring clip. When the nut is removed prior to arming, the clip still holds the pin in place until it is pulled away by a cord.

(b) *Operation.* In the armed position the striker is held only by two small cotters, which project into the groove behind the head of the striker. When the sliding cylinder is pulled up about $\frac{3}{16}$ inch, the cotters are freed and move outwards, releasing the striker. The pull required to fire the igniter is 9 to 13 pounds.

(c) *To neutralize.* The igniter is made safe by pushing a small nail through the hole in the striker. The trip wire then may be cut.

(d) *To disarm.* When the igniter is fitted into a mine or charge, unscrew the igniter with the nail in place and remove the detonator.

(3) *Zug-und Zerschneidezünder 35* (*Zu. Z.Z.35*). (a) *Description.* This igniter is used chiefly in places where tension wires are easily concealed. It functions in two ways—either by pull on a wire or by cutting the wire. In both cases it is set by securely fastening a wire through the hole in the head of the movable cylinder. The body of the igniter contains a movable cylinder, a striker spring, and the striker. The striker is held in position by two cotters. The movable cylinder slides inside a sleeve fitted in the end of the main housing. This sleeve has two slots through which the safety pin passes. These slots allow for adjustment of the igniter when setting the charge. When the igniter is to be armed, the

wire is attached to the cylinder and given enough tension to hold the safety pin near the center of the slot. This ensures easy withdrawal of the safety pin after the charge or mine has been laid. Before withdrawal of the pin the nut is removed from the end of it.

(b) *Operation.* When properly armed the igniter will function if the tension wire is pulled or cut.

(c) *To neutralize.* If the safety pin has been removed, and the tension wire is intact, push a small nail through the safety-pin hole, and, after determining that there is no igniter on the other end of the wire, the wire may be cut.

b. PRESSURE IGNITERS. (1) *Druckzünder 35* (*DZ.35 Type A*). (a) *Description.* This is a mechanically-acting, push igniter, designed for use with improvised mines and booby traps. It is also the main igniter of the heavy antitank mine. It consists of an aluminum body and a plunger which carries the $1\frac{1}{4}$-inch pressure head. The plunger is held away from the cap by a strong spring. Within the plunger is a recess for the striker and spring. Two steel balls rest partly in two holes in the plunger and retain the striker in the cocked position. When in the safe position, the plunger is prevented from moving by a safety pin.

(b) *Operation.* After withdrawal of the safety pin the igniter is fired by pressure on the head, which depresses the plunger until the steel balls are free to escape into the space in the guide. The striker then is released and fires the cap. A pressure of 130 to 160 pounds (corresponding to a depression of about $\frac{1}{3}$ inch) is sufficient to fire the igniter.

(c) *To neutralize.* Push a nail into the safety pin hole and secure it in place to prevent its falling out.

(d) *To disarm.* After neutralizing the igniter, unscrew it from the charge and remove the detonator.

(2) *Druckzünder 35* (*DZ.35 Type B*). (a) *Description.* This igniter functions exactly the same way as type A, though its construction differs in a few minor details. The body is made of unpainted brass, and the diameter of the pressure head is 1 inch. The retaining steel balls are replaced by two small cotters, placed below the head of the striker. The cap is located in the base plug.

(b) *Operation.* After withdrawal of the safety pin, the igniter is fired by pressure on the head.

When the plunger is depressed about ⅓ inch, the two small cotters escape from the guide into the space below. The striker then is released and fires the cap. The pressure required in some cases is as low as 50 pounds.

(c) *To neutralize.* Same as for Type A.

(d) *To disarm.* Same as for Type A.

(3) *S-Minenzünder 35 (S.Mi.Z.35).* (a) *Description.* This igniter is used to initiate the S-mine when set as a pressure operated charge. The body of the igniter is made of aluminum and holds a pressure spring, plunger, striker, and striker spring. A central part of the body acts as a distance piece and guide for the plunger. Three steel antennae, 1¼ inches long, are screwed to the head of the plunger. This hollow plunger takes the striker, which is held in position against its spring by two steel balls. The balls are held partly in two holes in the plunger and partly in a groove in the striker. The safety pin is retained in its hole by a spring-loaded and milled nut. When the safety pin is withdrawn, the mine is armed.

(b) *Operation.* Pressure on the antennae causes the plunger to descend, and after moving approximately 0.2 inch the steel balls fall away releasing the striker. The firing pressure is approximately 15 pounds.

(c) *To neutralize.* Push a nail into the safety pin hole. Care must be taken in handling this igniter as a slight steady pressure may cause it to function.

(4) *Tellerminenzünder 42 (T.Mi.Z.42).* This igniter consists of a simple steel striker retained against the pressure of a steel spring by a shear wire. The striker is in a steel casing. A percussion cap is at the base of the casing. The pressure necessary on the head of the striker is approximately 400 pounds.

(5) *Tellerminenzünder 43 (T.Mi.Z.43).* (a) *Description.* The chief feature of this igniter, which can be used in Tellermines 35, 35 (steel), 42, and 43, is that once it has been placed in the mine and armed it cannot be removed without exploding the mine. The head of the *T.Mi.Z.43* is approximately ¼ inch higher than that of the *T.Mi.Z.42.* The upper shear pin is ¼ inch above the body of the igniter. The outer ends of the arming shear pins can be seen on the sides of the igniter body, either ½ inch or ⅞ inch below the top of the igniter body. The igniter consists of a body into which is pressed a cap retainer. Inside is a pressure sleeve, which protrudes above the casing. The upper part of the sleeve is fitted with a strong shear pin, and the lower part is connected to the igniter body by a weak brass arming wire. Inside the pressure sleeve is a plain tubular striker guide containing the striker, held in place by two retaining balls.

(b) *Operation.* The igniter is inserted in the normal manner, and the top of the mine is screwed on. This depresses the pressure sleeve, which in turn shears the weak arming pins with an audible snap. The anti-lifting device of the igniter now is armed. The igniter can be set off in either of two ways. When the pressure plate is crushed or depressed, the sleeve is pressed down until the strong shear pin is cut. The retaining balls escape into the recess above the shoulder of the sleeve, freeing the spring-loaded striker which fires the percussion cap. Any attempt to unscrew the pressure plate or cap of the mine will cause it to explode. Under pressure of the spring the sleeve follows any upward movement of the plate or cap and after about ⅛ inch upward travel the balls escape below the sleeve, again releasing the striker.

(c) *Disarming.* Since there is no way to determine whether a Tellermine is armed with this igniter, no pressure plate or screw caps should be removed from these mines. They should be lifted and destroyed. However, should it be necessary to determine the type of igniter, wind a rope or tracing tape counter-clockwise around the pressure plate or screw cap four complete times. Then pull from a safe distance to unscrew the plate or cap.

(6) *T.Mi.Z.35.* (a) *Description.* This pressure igniter has only been found in Tellermines. The brass body contains a floating striker assembly. The striker head is stepped to fit a projection on the spindle. This is a secondary safety device to keep the weight of the striker off the shear pin until the igniter is armed. A white mark with the word *Sicher* (safe) above it, and a red mark with the word *Scharf* (armed) above it are inscribed on the head of the igniter. When the screw head is turned so the red spot moves from the safe to the armed position, the projection moves clear of the striker head.

(b) *Operation.* In the mine the lower face of the guide compresses the ring situated above the adjusting collar. Pressure on the cover of the mine moves the body of the igniter down against the rubber on the collar and so exerts a force on

B.Z. 24   B.Z. 39   NB.B.Z. 38   B.Z. 39   B.Z. EXP.   B.Z. 4.5   Feld Schlag   Reisszün-
           Mod.   SEC.   Rohr.   der.

B.Z.E.

Reibzünder West.   ZDSCHN ANZ. 29.   ZDSCHN ANZ. 39.   B.Z.   N.B. Z. 29.

Figure 89.—Friction Igniters.

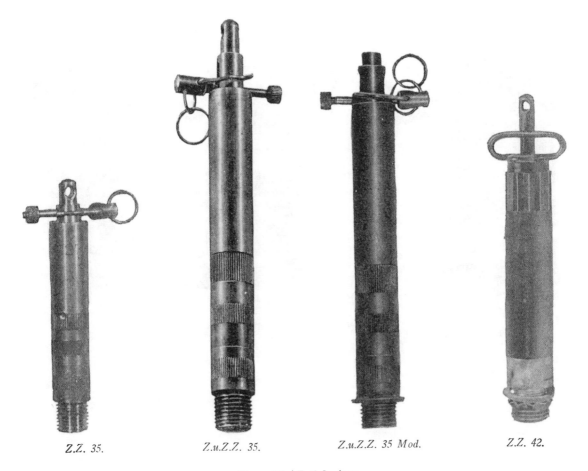

Z.Z. 35.   Z.u.Z.Z. 35.   Z.u.Z.Z. 35 Mod.   Z.Z. 42.

Figure 90.—Pull Igniters.

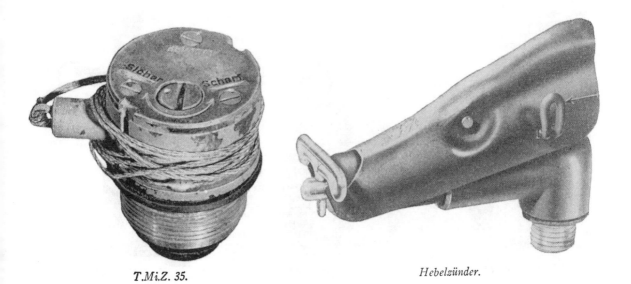

T.Mi.Z. 35.   *Hebelzünder.*

Figure 91.—Pressure Igniters.

D.Z. 35(A).

D.Z 35(B).

French A.T.

T.Mi.Z. 42.

T.Mi.Z. 43

S.Mi.Z. 35.

Figure 91 (Continued).

top of the striker, shearing the pin. The striker then moves under the pressure of the spring.

(c) *To neutralize.* If the mines have been subjected to blast, unscrew the igniter gently. Hold the igniter clear of the mine with the cap pointing away. Turn the red spot on the screw head from *Scharf* to *Sicher.* Fix the claw attached to the wire, or a similar improvisation, into the slotted end of the safety bolt, and press the safety bolt home. Replace the igniter in the mine, screwing it in hand tight. If the mines are known to be in good condition, turn the red spot from *Scharf* to *Sicher,* using a coin, not a screwdriver. Fix the claw attached to the wire into the slotted end of the safety bolt and press the bolt home.

Figure 92.—Pressure Release Device E.Z. 44.

c. OTHER IGNITERS. (1) *Pressure Release Device, E.Z.44 (Entlastungszünder 44).* (a) *Description.* This device is intended primarily for booby-trapping Tellermines. Any attempt to remove the mine permits a plunger to rise, setting off an 8-ounce charge of TNT-PETN. A weight of 10 pounds is sufficient to hold the device in the armed position, and a built-in clockwork, time-delay protects the person setting it from premature detonation. The device is housed in a steel body crimped at the base. The operating mechanism fills one-half of the container, while the explosive occupies the remaining space. The operating mechanism includes the pressure release assembly, including plunger, plunger spring, and striker retaining arm; the clockwork mechanism; and the firing assembly, including striker,

striker spring, percussion cap, detonator holder, and detonator.

(b) *Operation.* The clockwork mechanism is wound. A weight of at least 10 pounds is placed on the plunger. The safety bar is released, permitting the clockwork mechanism to function for 1½ minutes with a loud buzzing sound, withdrawing the internal safety pin. The device now is armed.

(c) *To neutralize.* Once this device is armed it cannot be neutralized.

(2) *Tilt Igniter, Ki.Z.43 (Kippzünder 43).* (a) *Description.* The tilt igniter is designed to fire whenever the tilt rod is moved in any direction. This tilt rod is on top of the igniter, which contains a sliding pressure piece, pressure spring, hollow striker, striker spring, and two retaining balls. The detonator assembly includes percussion cap and detonator. An extension rod, 24¾ inches long, is connected by pushing the sleeve over the tilt rod.

Figure 93.—Tellermine with Tilt Igniter attached.

(b) *Operation.* The igniter is armed by removing the safety pin. When the tilt rod is moved in any direction, the tilt-rod base is tilted inside the igniter body, depressing the pressure piece, thus freeing the striker. A lateral pressure of 15 to 23 pounds on the end of the tilt bar will fire the igniter. Use of the extension rod reduces the pressure needed to explode the igniter to 1½ pounds.

(3) *S-Mine Igniter 44.* (a) *Description.* This igniter is a combination push-and-pull type, with the standard German igniter thread. It can be used in mines and charges other than the *S.Mi.*

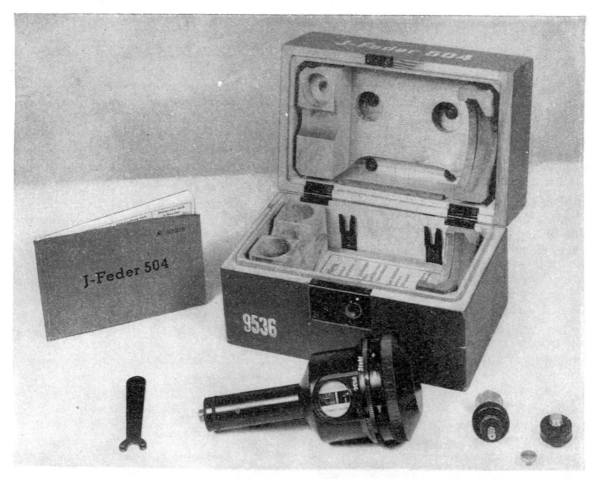

Figure 94.—Clockwork Long-delay Igniter (J-Feder 504).

44. The steel case of the igniter contains a spring-loaded striker above a percussion cap and detonator socket. The striker protrudes through the top of the igniter. Two flat, winged, actuating pieces are held together at the top by a safety pin. Holes in these pieces serve for the attachment of trip wires.

(b) *Operation.* The igniter is armed after the safety pin is withdrawn. A pressure of 21 pounds on the wings of the actuating pieces, or an outward pull of 14 pounds on the trip wires, opens the winged actuating pieces sufficiently to release the striker and fire the percussion cap.

(c) *To neutralize.* This igniter requires extreme care in neutralization. In place the igniter is completely covered, leaving only the wings exposed. Carefully locate the wings and remove enough earth to insert a safety pin or nail through the pin holes. If trouble is encountered in inserting the pin or nail, the mine is dangerous and should be destroyed in place. Unscrew the igniter, lift the mine, and remove the detonator.

(4) *Clockwork long delay igniter (J-Feder 504).* This igniter is a clockwork mechanism that may be set to function at any desired delay from 10 minutes to 21 days. It is used for special demolitions.

(5) *Crush Type Chemical "Buck" Igniter.* (a) *Description.* This igniter is a chemical, crush-actuated type, consisting of a thin metal drum, with circumferential grooves to reduce its resistance to vertical pressure. It contains a glass ampule half filled with acid, surrounded by a white, powdered, flash composition. It weighs 1 ounce.

(b) *Operation.* A moderate pressure on top of the igniter crushes the metal drum and the glass ampule inside it. The acid pours into the white powder, and a flash results, setting off detonator and mine.

8. Bridging Equipment

a. GENERAL. (1) *Development.* Apart from the introduction of a 60-ton type in the armored division bridging column, German bridging equipment has undergone few important changes since the beginning of the war. Standard types are not numerous; particular emphasis is placed upon the construction of improvised bridges at the earliest possible stage of a river crossing.

(2) *Bridging operations.* The initial stage of an assault crossing is carried out by storm boats. These may be supplemented by pneumatic boats supplied in three sizes. Once a bridgehead has been established, pneumatic boats play an important part, either in ferrying personnel and stores, or in construction of rafts and light bridges. The superstructure for these light bridges consists of standard timber members carried ready for construction. Ready made timber bridges for crossing dry gaps also are carried, and some engineer units carry a light box girder and ponton equipment known as bridging equipment "D". In the third stage of a river crossing, when the bridge is required for normal traffic of approximately 24 tons, bridges from the divisional bridging column are used. Of these, there are two types: bridging equipment "B", a ponton trestle bridge; and bridging equipment "K", a box girder bridge supported on pontons and trestles. A third type, bridging equipment "J", designed to accommodate the heavier German tanks, replaces the "K" equipment in armored divisions.

(3) *Heavy bridges.* Heavier semi-permanent bridges includes the *L.Z.* bridge, a sectionalized, through-girder type which is launched from a roller bed; the Herbert, with a girder superstructure supported on large sectionalized pontons, and the "S" equipment, used for heavy traffic over wide rivers and consisting of a double-way superstructure on sectionalized pontons similar to those of the Herbert. Railway bridges are represented by the Roth-Wagner, Krupp, and Ungaw bridges.

b. BOATS USED IN RAFTING AND BRIDGING.

(1) *Small pneumatic boat.*

Length ....9 feet 10 inches.
Beam over-all ....3 feet 9 inches.
Weight ....116 pounds.
Capacity ....3 armed men or 660
                        pounds.

(2) *Pneumatic boat assault bridge.* This bridge can be built in any lengths in a current up to 2¼ knots and will carry infantry in single file.

Weight of superstructure—12.8 pounds per foot.

Total weight of bridge—23.7 pounds per foot.

(3) *Medium pneumatic boat.* (a) *Description.* These pneumatic boats can be used as supports for the standard German 2¼-ton, 4½-ton, and 9-ton rafts. The 2¼-ton raft consists of two boats; the 4½-ton raft has four boats in the form of two pairs in tandem, and the 9-ton raft has three pairs in tandem.

(b) *Characteristics.*

Length over-all ....18 feet.
Beam over-all ....6 feet 1 inch.
Weight ....330 pounds.
Crew ....7 men.
Capacity, not including
    crew ....1.35 tons.

(4) *Motor boat.* (a) *Description.* This craft is used primarily for pushing and towing rafts and bridge sections in bridging operations. It also can be used for river reconnaissance and barge towing. It is transported on a special two-wheel trailer, which is provided with gear so the boat can be launched and recovered direct from the trailer. The motor boat is a broad-beamed craft constructed of steel plates with copper-nickel rivets.

(b) *Characteristics.*

Length over-all.......23 feet.
Beam over-all.........6 feet 7 inches.
Depth amidships.......4 feet.
Draught, fully laden...2 feet (approximately).
Weight of boat un-
    loaded ....2 tons (approximately).
Capacity, when not
    towing ....6 men, including crew,
                       or 1.7 tons evenly dis-
                       tributed on floor boards.
Speed, towing tension
    1.4 tons ....5½ knots.
Speed, towing tension
    1,900 pounds ....7 knots.
Capacity of fuel tank..33 gallons.
Maximum running time
    on full tank........6 hours (approximately.

(c) *Engine.* The boat is driven by a six-cylinder, Maybach-type, S5, water-cooled, gasoline engine.

Horsepower ....80 at 1,400 rpm.
Total engine capacity...7 liters (427 cubic inches)
                       (approximately).

Maximum permissible
    revolutions in still
    water ....1,400 rpm.

(d) *Trailer.* The two-wheel trailer includes chassis, extensible tipping slipway, traveling cradles, winch, and hoisting cable. It has the following characteristics:

```
Weight, unloaded.....2¼ tons.
Length over-all........24 feet 9 inches.
Length with boat.......28 feet 6 inches.
Length extended.......32 feet 4 inches.
Width over-all........6 feet 7 inches.
Length of hoisting
    cable ..............49 feet 3 inches.
Working party........6 men.
```

(5) *Storm boat.* (a) *Description.* This boat, when in operation, is carried and launched by eight men, while four men are required to carry and install the motor. The boat is steered by pivoting the motor on the bracket which attaches it to the stern. The helmsman stands in the stern gripping two handles at the front of the motor.

(b) *Characteristics.*

```
Length ..............19 feet 9 inches.
Beam ................5 feet 2 inches.
Depth amidships.......2 feet 1 inch.
Weight ..............475 pounds.
Material ..............Wood.
Crew ................2 men.
Capacity ..............7 men in addition to crew.
Maximum speed, loaded.15 to 16 knots.
Transport .............3 boats with motors on
                        special trailer.
```

(c) *Engine.* This is a "mechanical oar" propulsion unit: a propeller attached to a long shaft running through a casing bolted to the engine. The propeller revolves several feet behind the boat.

```
Length ..............13 feet 6 inches.
Width ................2 feet 9 inches.
Height ..............2 feet.
Weight (without oil
    and fuel)...........375 pounds.
Weight (with oil and
    fuel) ..............412 pounds.
BHP ................30.
Cylinders ............4, horizontally opposed.
Running time on full
    tank ...............1½ hours.
Propeller ...........3 blade, 10¾ inches in
                        diameter.
```

(6) *Large pneumatic boat.* This is the largest of the three standard pneumatic boats and is generally used singly.

```
Length over-all.......26 feet.
Beam over-all.........9 feet 9 inches.
Weight ..............637 pounds.
Maximum buoyancy....13.5 tons.
```

c. PONTON AND TRESTLE BRIDGES. (1) *Training ponton bridge.* (a) *Description.* There is little evidence of this equipment being used operationally; it is thought to be kept for training. There are two types of light ponton and trestle bridges: one with half pontons having a load capacity of 4 tons, and the other with double-ponton piers having a load capacity of 5½ tons. The decking used for this bridge also is used in bridging and rafting with pneumatic boats.

(b) *Characteristics.*

```
Half ponton:
    Length ............12 feet.
    Beam ..............5 feet.
    Depth .............2 feet 6 inches.
Superstructure:
    Timber with decking.20 feet by 2 feet.
    Track width........8 feet.
    Bay length.........20 feet.
```

(2) *Ponton and trestle bridge (Czech).* This equipment consists of steel half pontons and center sections. Two types of bridges are built.

(a) Roadways built on piers of one half ponton and one center section, with a capacity of 8.2 tons and the following characteristics.

```
Pier length:
    Half ponton........16 feet.
    Center section......8 feet.
Beam ................4 feet 6 inches.
Track width..........8 feet.
Bay length...........21 feet.
```

(b) Roadway built on piers of two half pontons and one center section, with a capacity 16.5 tons and the following characteristics:

```
Track width..........8 feet.
Bay length...........21 feet.
Complete pier:
    Width ............4 feet 6 inches.
    Length ...........40 feet.
```

(3) *Light ponton and trestle equipment* *(Brückengerät C)*. The three following types of bridges can be built with this equipment.

Detail	Type 1	Type 2	Type 3
Type of bridge	Footway on half pontons.	Bridge of two pier raft.	Bridge of three pier raft.
Capacity	Single file.	4.5 tons.	5.9 tons.
Floating unit	Timber of aluminum non-reversible half pontons.	Two half pontons clipped together to make pier.	
Unit length	12 feet 9 inches (approximately).	25 feet 6 inches (approximately).	
Unit beam	4 feet 6 inches (approximately).	4 feet 6 inches (approximately).	
Superstructure	Single decking strips.	Four decking strips.	
Track width	2 feet 1½ inches.	8 feet 6 inches.	
Bay length	22 feet 11½ inches.	22 feet 11½ inches.	

(4) *Medium ponton and trestle equipment* *(Brückengerät T)*.

Detail	Type 1	Type 2	Type 3
How used	Bridge with road bearers spanning from center of one ponton to center of next ponton.	As in Type 1 but with an extra ponton in center of span.	A three-pier raft.
Capacity	4.5 tons.	11 tons.	10 tons.
Floating unit	Timber reversible ponton with distinct bow and stern.	As for Type 1.	
Length	29 feet 6 inches.	Same as Type 1.	
Beam	5 feet 11 inches.	Same as Type 1.	
Superstructure	Timber decking on six timber road bearers.	Timber decking on nine timber road bearers.	
Track width	8 feet 6 inches.	Same as Type 1.	
Bay length	22 feet 1½ inches.	Same as Type 1.	

(5) *Heavy ponton and trestle equipment* *(Brückengerät B)*. This is the standard combat equipment of the German Army.

Detail	Type 1	Type 2	Type 3	Type 4
Type of bridge	Roadway spanning from center of ponton to center of ponton.	Whole ponton piers.	Two pier rafts on half pontons.	Two pier rafts on whole pontons.
Capacity	4.5 tons.	10 tons.	10 tons.	20 tons.
Floating units	Non-reversible steel or alloy pontons with upswept bows.			
Length	49 feet 11 inches.		24 feet 11½ inches.	49 feet 11 inches.
Beam	5 feet 9 inches.		5 feet 9 inches.	
Superstructure	Steel 1 section road bearers with single timber decking.			12 road bearers with double decking and double raft connectors.
Track width	All types: 8 feet 6 inches.			
Bay length	All types: 20 feet 9 inches.			
Capacity of Divisional Bridge Column	400 to 430 feet.	250 feet.	250 feet.	170 feet.

Figure 95.—Small pneumatic boat.

Figure 96.—Track bridge and medium pneumatic boat.

Figure 97.—K Bridge.

Figure 98.—L.Z. Bridge.

(6) *Light timber bridges on fixed supports.*
(a) *Folding single span foot bridges.* This
equipment is made up of two single members,
hinged together, and consisting each of two 3-
inch round timber roadbearers supporting three
cross bearers to which are wired two planks (9
foot 10 inches by 10 inches by 3½ inches. This
bridge is trussed by means of a timber strut **a**
short distance off center and a system of ties. The
total length of the bridge is 19 feet 8 inches.

(b) *Light tracked bridge.* This is a light
tracked timber bridge, constructed in two load
ratings: 6 tons and 9.5 tons. It generally is
supported by simple framed trestles, but if floating supports are needed the large pneumatic boat
is used. The following tables give the cross
sections of the roadbearers for varying spans
and loads:

	Span		
Bridge	*13 feet*	*16 feet 6 inches*	*20 feet*
6-ton	7 x 7 inches	8 x 7 inches	9 x 8 inches.
9.5-ton	8 x 8 inches	9½ x 8 inches	10½ x 9½ inches.

(7) *27-Ton heavy tracked bridge.* (a) *Description.* This bridge is a variation of the light
tracked bridge, with a capacity of 27 tons, it
consists of two bays and a span of 29 feet 6
inches. A single bent framed trestle is used
as a central support.

(b) *Components.*

Bridge seats:
    Length ....13 feet.
    Width ....11 inches.
    Depth ....8 inches.
Ramps:
    Length ....5 feet.
    Width ....4 feet 9 inches.
Roadbearers:
    Length ....14 feet 9 inches.
    Width ....7 inches.
    Depth ....9½ inches.
Track section:
    Length ....4 feet 11 inches.
    Width over-all.......4 feet 9 inches.
    Useful width........4 feet 3 inches.
Trestle:
    Capsill and
        Groundsill:
        Length ....13 feet.
        Width ....7 inches.
        Depth ....8½ inches.

Figure 99.—Herbert Bridge.

d. FIXED BRIDGES. (1) *Small box girder (Brückengerät K).* This equipment is capable of carrying heavy vehicles and light tanks over short gaps. It is essentially an assault bridge and can span gaps of 31 feet 6 inches, 47 feet 3 inches, or 63 feet with box girders alone. The bridge always is built with three girders and has a carrying capacity of 27 tons. Trestles and pontons are supplied to span wet or dry gaps with a series of bridges.

(2) *Light sectional bridge (Leichte Z Brücke).* This is a through bridge with a timber roadway, approximately 12 feet wide, slung between two main girders of braced steel panels 8 feet 2 inches long and 7 feet 10 inches high. The normal bridge cannot span a gap greater than 147 feet 6 inches, and is rated over this and all lesser spans at 33 tons for tanks. With special underslung bracing the span may be increased to 172 feet without altering its rating.

(3) *Herbert Bridge.* This bridge is sometimes called the "Italian Meccano Bridge". It is through-girder type with a 10-foot clear roadway. Each girder is constructed of steel lattice pyramids, made of angle iron and channel struts. The decking is of 6-inch timber plank. The German classification of this bridge is 18 tons over 82 feet. This bridge also may be used in conjunction with trestles or pontons.

e. HEAVY BRIDGING EQUIPMENT. *J 42 and J 43 Bridging Equipment (Brückengerät J 42 and J 43).* The *J 42* equipment consists of steel box-girder sections, of which any number up to four can be bolted together to form a maximum span of 64 feet. Each section is about 16 feet 6 inches long. A decking of stout chesses is laid on these main bearers and held down by two similar box girders used as vibrants. The girders are launched over rollers. Trestles and four-section pontons are used as supports. The single track width of the bridge is believed to be 13 feet 9 inches, but it also can be constructed in double track width. The *J 43* bridge is a strengthened version of the *J 42.*

9. Mechanical Equipment

a. 6-TON MOBILE CRANE *(Sd. Kfz. 9/1) (Drehkran Kraftwagen 6 t.).* This crane is mounted on the chassis of the 18-ton semi-tracked vehicle *(Sd. Kfz. 9).* It has a telescopic jib mounted on a ball-bearing base, which permits a traverse of 180 degrees and an adjustment for ground slope up to 12 degrees in any direction.

The jib has two radii of operation according to the lifting capacity: 6 tons for the smaller radius and 4 tons for the larger radius.

b. WIRE CUTTERS. (1) *Large type.* These cutters are approximately 2 feet in length and weigh 5 pounds. The two jaws of special steel are pivoted on two links and operated by a pair of tubular steel handles. These are hinged together and covered with insulated grips which are secured by terminal caps and locking rings. A short pin acts as a stop.

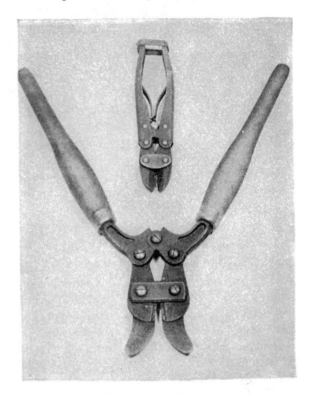

Figure 100.—Wirecutters.

(2) *Small type.* These cutters are 1 foot 4 inches long and weigh 2¾ pounds. There are minor variations in construction among samples manufactured by different firms. The general design is similar to that of the large cutters, but the shape of the jaws is different, one jaw being bent over in the form of a hook to aid in holding the wire. The handles have insulated grips.

c. BLAST DRIVE ROD. This equipment is designed for the rapid production of small diameter vertical holes in the ground for telegraph poles or similar supports. The equipment includes a drive rod; two tabular hand levers; a long, thin, metal rod; and a propellent charge, safety fuze, and igniter.

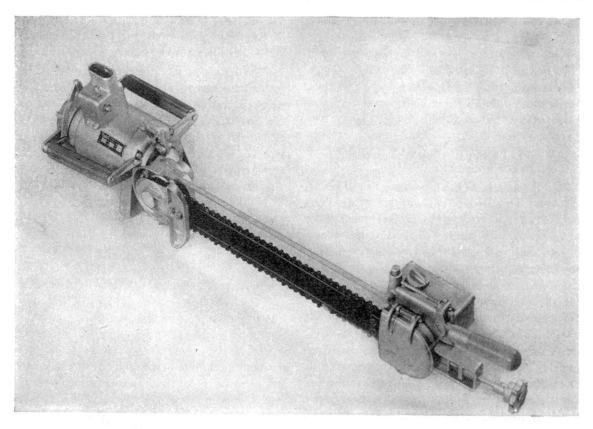

Figure 101.—Electric chain-saw.

d. GERMAN PORTABLE POWER SAWS. (1) *Light power saw.* (a) *Description.* The main components are the gasoline motor with its gearing, the clutch, saw blade, and saw chain. The saw blade can be turned through 90 degrees for horizontal or vertical cutting and is locked in position by a lever.

  (b) *Characteristics.*

    Weight including fuel..111 pounds.
    Effective length of
      blade ....3 feet 3 inches.
    Revolutions per minute.2,600.
    Speed of cutting chain.21 feet per second.
    Fuel consumption......1¾ to 2½ pints per hour.

  (2) *Heavy power saw.* (a) *Description.* This is similar to the light power saw. It is too heavy for hand use and is provided with three adjustable legs and a large bogie for wheeling into position. The saw blade can be swivelled about the axis of the chain drive wheel, as well as vertically of horizontally.

  (b) *Characteristics.*

    Weight including fuel..172 pounds.
    Effective length of
      blade ....3 feet 3 inches.
    Revolutions per minute.2,300.
    Speed of cutting chain.23 feet per second.
    Fuel consumption......2½ to 3 pints per hour.

e. ELECTRIC GENERATORS AND ELECTRIC POWER TOOLS. (1) *Field generating set.* (a) *Description.* This field generating set is used by German army engineers in mobile workshops for power driven tools. It is also used for charging storage batteries.

  (b) *Characteristics.*

    Designation ....*Maschinensatz 220/380.*
    Weight ....507 pounds.
    Motor ....2 cylinder, 2 stroke.
    Type of generator.....AC.
    Kilowatts ....6.
    Volts ....220/330.

  (2) *German electric two-speed drill.* This machine is used for boring holes in the construction of improvised bridges. The drill normally uses its own detachable mounting but, for boring wood, it may be held by hand. The drill consists of a 50-cycle AC motor, consuming 800 watts, fitted with a Morse taper sleeve and a two-speed gear box giving 200 to 400 revolutions per minute.

f. GERMAN PILE DRIVERS. (1) *Field Pile-Driving Frame 1939.* (a) *Description.* This equipment consists of a guide mast with a double block at the top, supported on a base by two back stays. For pile-driving from land the frame is mounted on four wheels. These wheels are replaced by beams when pile-driving is carried on from a raft. A two-drum, hand winch serves to raise and lower the pile driver. The following can be operated on the frame:

(b) *Characteristics.*

Three-piece hand-
  operated monkey.....440 foot pounds.
Compressed air pile
  driver ....360 foot pounds.
Compressed air pile
  driver ....1,440 foot pounds.
Diesel pile driver......992 foot pounds.
Diesel pile driver......1,323 foot pounds.

(2) *Pneumatic pile driver (360 foot pounds).*
(a) *Description.* The main components are a stationary part, consisting of the piston, piston rod, and piston base; a moving part (monkey) consisting of driving block, cylinder, and screw-in cylinder head; a spring-loaded clamping device, and a guide for use with the pile-driving frame 39. The driver is the fast hitting type and attains its high rate because the acceleration of the moving portion is due not only to its own weight but also to the compressed air operating downwards on an internal flange at the base of the bore of the cylinders.

(b) *Characteristics.*

Weight of monkey.....121 pounds.
Cylinder base..........2.5 inches.
Stroke ....1 foot 5⅜ inches.
Force per blow........360 foot pounds.
Striking rate.........105 per minute.

(3) *Pneumatic pile driver (1,440 foot pounds).*
(a) *Description.* This pile driver is similar to the lighter one, but it has a heavier monkey and a longer stroke. This driver is the free falling type. The monkey is lifted up by compressed air, falls freely onto the base plate, and gives up its kinetic energy to the pile after covering a stroke of little more than a yard.

(b) *Characteristics.*

Weight of monkey.....448 pounds.
Cylinder base..........3⁹⁄₁₆ inches.
Stroke ....3 feet 3½ inches.
Force per blow........1,440 foot pounds.
Striking rate.........54 per minute.

(4) *Diesel pile driver (992 foot pounds).*
(a) *Description.* The main components are the piston with anvil, the monkey, the guide tubes, the headpiece, and the fuel tank. This diesel pile driver works on the two-stroke principle: an explosion takes place on each hitting stroke.

The required ignition temperature is reached through the compression of the air trapped between the top of the falling piston and the monkey.

(b) *Characteristics.*

Weight of monkey.....980 pounds.
Total weight..........2,100 pounds.
Stroke ....4 feet 7 inches.
Striking rate.........56 per minute.

(5) *Heavy diesel pile driver.*
(a) *Characteristics.*

Weight of monkey.....1,100 pounds.
Cylinder base.........8¼ inches.
Stroke ....7 feet 2⅝ inches.
Energy per blow.......8,255 foot pounds.
Striking rate.........50 per minute.

g. WATER SUPPLY AND WATER PURIFICATION.
(1) *Portable haversack filter.* This filter, issued on a company basis, is a standard item of equipment in the German Army. Performance is said to be from 22 to 55 gallons of water per hour, according to the amount of solid matter in suspension. Although the action of the filter is purely one of clarification, it is claimed by the Germans that it effectively will treat "naturally" contaminated water, that is water in which corpses

Figure 102.—Haversack water filter.

have been lying. However, it will not rid the water of objectionable smell, nor is it effective against water containing chemical agents or substances in solution.

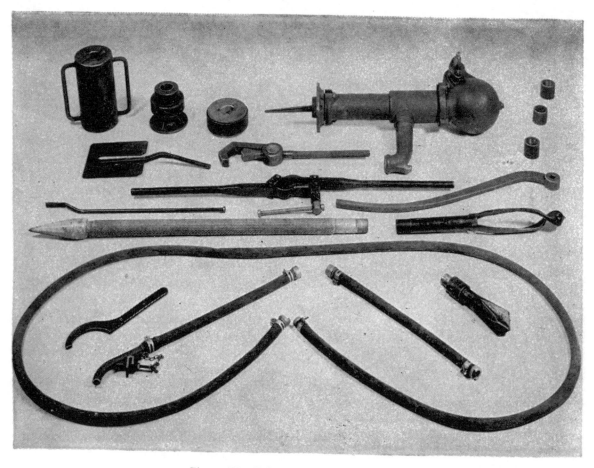

Figure 103.—Tube well set with accessories.

(2) *German Tube Well 1937 Pattern, with Accessories "A" and "B".* This tube well is a suction pump capable of lifting water from a depth of 26 feet. Accessory "A" extends the depth to about 33 feet. Accessory "B" permits the pump to be used for pumping surface water.

h. MARKINGS OF CYLINDERS OF INDUSTRIAL GASES. The Germans always stamp the type of gas their cylinders contain into the metal itself as guide in case the paint should change color or disappear through weathering.

Cylinder color	German name	English name
Red	*Wasserstoff*	Hydrogen
Blue	*Sauerstoff*	Oxygen
Green	*Stickstoff*	Nitrogen
Yellow	*Azetylen*	Acetylene
Gray (with red band)	*Propan*	Propane
Gray	*Pressluft*	Compressed air
Not given	*Kohlen Säure or Kohlen Dioxid*	Carbon dioxide
" "	*Schwefel Dioxid*	Sulphur dioxide
" "	*Chlormethyl*	Methyl chloride

i. EARTH MOVING EQUIPMENT. *Trench plows.* Small and large trench plows are used by the German Army. The small trench plow consists of a double plowshare on the hooked end of a girder which is supported on a two-wheeled trailer and towed behind a semi-tracked vehicle. The large plow consists of the plow, anchor, pulley assembly, tow wire, and support.

j. AIR COMPRESSORS AND PNEUMATIC TOOLS. (1) *Sinker rock drills.* There are two types of sinker rock drills used by the German Army: the "D" handle and the "T" handle types. Both, judged by American standards, fall into the lightweight class (40 to 50 pounds). These tools are similar in design but the internal parts are not interchangeable. Both of these rock drills can be used by attaching American standard air lines with the universal coupling used on the German drills.

(2) *German F.M.A. Air Compressor.* (a) *Engine.* This is a four-cylinder gasoline engine with magneto ignition. The horsepower rating is

Figure 104.—F.M.A. Air Compressor.

27 at 950 revolutions per minute. The main shaft is connected to the compressor by a single disc clutch with a rotating collar and a manual engaging lever. There are two water pumps, one attached to the engine and one to the compressor.

(b) *Compressor.* The compressor is a two-cylinder, single-stage mechanism. The operating pressure is presumed to be approximately 90 pounds per square inch. The air tank is of unusual design. It consists of three short sections of steel tubing welded into a "V" shape with the open ends sealed off. This air tank is used as the base for mounting the engine and compressor.

Section VI. CHEMICAL WARFARE EQUIPMENT

1. General

The German military organization is thoroughly prepared for chemical warfare. Germany's chemical industry is highly developed; equipment and stocks of war gases in storage and production are ample, and adequate well trained personnel are available. Offensively or defensively, the German Army is in a position to wage chemical warfare at any time. Unusual activity in research and manufacture has taken place in German chemical plants since the beginning of the war, and from time to time movements of war gases from one area to another have been reported. Military depots are believed to be amply stocked with gas shells of all calibers. Construction of anti-gas shelters in German cities, issue of gas masks to civilians, and a constant examination and replacement of gas mask canisters have been regularly carried out.

Figure 105.—German gas mask, GM 30.

2. Defensive Equipment

a. GAS MASKS. (1) *General.* Most German gas masks are of the snout type, in which the canister is connected directly to the facepiece. Types *GM 30* and *GM 38* are in general use, and in addition to the standard masks there are several special types. Generally, German gas masks provide good protection against the common war gases, and fair protection against such gases as arsine, hydrocyanic acid, and cyanogen chloride. The Germans also have three types of gas masks for horses and one for dogs.

(2) *Gas mask, GM 30.* The facepiece is of four-layer, field gray fabric, with a suede leather fitting band, a leather chin support, and plastic eyepieces. The head harness has seven points of attachment. There is a cotton strap for suspending the mask from the neck in an alert position. Some *GM 30* facepieces are fitted with an adapter for microphone.

Figure 106.—German FE 41 and FE 42 Canisters (larger is the FE 42).

Canisters normally used with this mask are the *FE 41* and the *FE 42*. The *FE 41* canister is drum-shaped and painted green. It measures $2\frac{1}{2}$ inches by $4\frac{1}{4}$ inches in diameter and weighs 11.9 ounces. It is being replaced by the *FE 42*, the canister of which is the newest and most efficient of the service canisters. Externally, it is similar to the *FE 41*, but is larger and heavier, measuring $3\frac{1}{2}$ inches high by $4\frac{1}{4}$ inches in diameter, and weighing 16.3 ounces.

The standard carrier is a corrugated cylindrical metal case with a hinged cover and cotton carrier straps. It is painted drab, field gray, or blue-gray. Parachutists are provided with a padded, canvas, satchel-type carrier, having a snap fastener at the top and a zipper along one side.

(3) *Gas mask, GM 38.* This mask began replacing the *GM 30* in 1938. It is similar in de-

Figure 107.—German gas mask, GM 38.

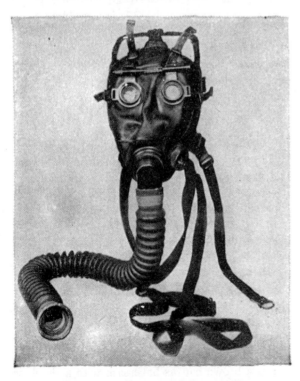

Figure 108.—German optical gas mask.

sign, but the facepiece, made of synthetic rubber has a rubber fitting band and a simpler head harness with only five points of attachment. The same canisters and carrier are used with this mask as with the *GM 30*.

(4) *Gas mask, cavalry.* The facepiece is of conventional German construction, similar in most respects to that of the *GM 30*. It has a hose-tube assembly, approximately 17 inches long, for connecting canister to facepiece. The brownish-gray canister has a generally elliptical cross-section, and measures $8\frac{1}{2}$ inches high by $4\frac{7}{8}$ inches by $2\frac{11}{16}$ inches. Its weight is 27.7 ounces. The facepiece carrier is lightweight duck, and measures 20 inches long by 8 inches wide at the upper end. Its sides are tapered to a width of about 3 inches throughout the 9-inch hose portion. The canister carrier, of dark brown saddle leather, fits snugly over the canister and is attached to the lower end of the facepiece carrier.

(5) *Gas mask, optical.* The facepiece, made of leather, has round, glass eyepieces, held in place by screw-type adapters. The interpupillary distances of eyepieces may be varied by means of an adjustable screw. A hose-tube connects the facepiece to the canister which is carried over the shoulder. In the left cheek of the facepiece is an adapter for a microphone. Standard canisters, as well as carbon monoxide canisters, may be used with this facepiece. The carrier is a rectangular metal box.

(6) *Gas mask, oxygen breathing set.* This is a self-contained, oxygen-breathing apparatus, effective for somewhat over an hour. The facepiece is of the usual service type. The carrier is a metal knapsack, designed to rest on the user's back. It contains an alkali canister, an oxygen bottle, a valve, and a breathing bag with two breathing tubes, an "in" and an "out". The mechanism operates automatically on breathing. The apparatus is designed for use in cellars, dugouts, gun turrets, and ship holds in the presence of high concentrations of toxic gas, such as carbon monoxide.

(7) *Plastic emergency breathing device.* This is an emergency breathing device enabling a canister to be used without a facepiece. Made of either transparent or yellow plastic, it consists of a circular piece to which are attached a tube for mouthpiece and a T-bar for chin rest. The circular piece is threaded internally to receive standard German canisters. A nose clip is at-

tached to the circular piece by a cord, which also may serve to hold the device in an alert position. Apparently intended for protection against rapidly acting gases in sudden concentration, it can be put into use in less than 5 seconds. Its existence may partly explain why the German soldier is supposed to carry a spare canister.

(8) *Gas mask, combat engineers.* This is a leather helmet, with a leather drop curtain fitted with eyepieces. The curtain normally is rolled up, but it may be dropped quickly over the face and held in place by a tape tied around the back of the head and neck. Flat filters cover the nose and mouth, possibly to provide limited, but speedy, protection against transient high gas concentrations. The face also would be protected against incendiary or corrosive materials.

(9) *Gas mask, headwound.* Designed for men with headwounds, this is a hood made of sheet rubber, with one oval window large enough to see out of with both eyes. It is provided with inlet and outlet valves and a fitting to receive the standard canisters. The carrier is a metal case.

(10) *Gas mask, carbon monoxide.* The Germans have several types of special canisters which provide very good protection against carbon monoxide. These canisters are attached to the normal facepieces by means of long hose-tubes. The canisters normally are larger and heavier than the standard canisters. An example is the *CO FB 38* canister, measuring 11 inches high by 5 inches in diameter and weighing 5.2 pounds.

(11) *Gas mask, horse.* (a) *Model 38.* This is a black rubber facepiece which fits over the nostrils and upper jaw. The bottom of the facepiece is reinforced to provide a biting pad. On

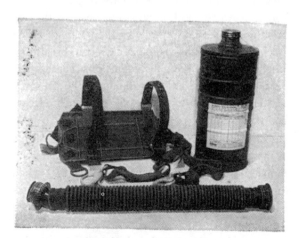

Figure 109.—German CO FB 38 Canister for protection against carbon monoxide.

Figure 110.—German horse gas mask, PFE 41.

Figure 111.—German dog gas mask 41.

each side of the facepiece is a canister, and on the front is an outlet valve. Near the top of each side, in the rear of the facepiece, are two heavy metal buckles for attaching the head harness. The canister, drum-shaped and painted green, measures approximately 2.1 inches high by 5 inches in diameter.

(b) *Model 41.* This consists of a pair of hollow cones with large slots near the apex, each with an outlet valve in the base and a threaded side opening into which a flat canister is screwed. The cones are placed up the nostrils of the horse and held in place by a harness over the head.

(c) *Damp mask, Model 41.* This consists of a large paper-fabric bag with padded lip and biting pad to fit over the upper jaw. Before it is used, the mask must be impregnated with a special salt solution.

(12) *Gas Mask 41, dog.* The facepiece, of a black, rubber-like compound, is made in four sizes. It has circular eyepieces, a valve assembly in the nose, and a canister on each side. The head harness consists of a throat strap, a fastener strap, and four head straps. The valve assembly consists of an air inlet knob and an outlet valve. The canister of thin green-painted metal, is 2 inches high by 3¼ inches in diameter. The carrier is a brown canvas haversack with a shoulder sling.

b. PROTECTIVE CLOTHING. (1) *General.* For troops there are the impermeable light and heavy protective suits and several types of protective capes. No impregnated clothing has been reported. There are leggings and protective covers for horses, and leggings and gas clothing for dogs.

(2) *Light protective suit.* This suit consisting of boots, shorts, gloves, and a neck cover, is made of a fabric coated with a synthetic rubber (opanol). Components of the normal suit vary in color from grayish-green to dark blue-gray, with light tan or khaki for tropical use. Boots are rubber soled. The gloves are of either elbow or shoulder length. In some cases shorts have a bib in front. When deemed necessary, an extra pair of shorts may be used to protect the upper part of the body. The suit is carried in a small case of the same material.

(3) *Heavy protective suit.* This comprises a jacket with hood, pants of the over-all type, gloves, and boots. Jacket and pants are made of fabric coated on both sides with gray rubber. Boots of knee length, are of heavy black rubber. Gloves are of gray or black molded rubber.

(4) *Protective sheet.* This rectangular sheet is approximately 78 inches long and 48 inches wide. It may be made of paper, opanol-coated fabric, or nylon.

(5) *Eyeshields.* Made of celluloid-type material, these consist of four separate sections sewed together to form an eyeshield with side panels. The eyeshield—two amber or green and two colorless—are carried in a green fabric case.

(6) *Horse cover.* Made of an impermeable opanol-coated fabric, black inside and tan outside, this cover is in two halves, one for the right side and one for the left. Each half is rectangular, 62 inches long and 45 inches wide. On the front end is a sleeve-like projection of double thickness to fit over the leg. The cover is designed to protect the underbelly parts of the horse.

(7) *Horse legging.* Sleeve-like in shape, of gray or green rubberized fabric, it is made in two sizes to fit front and hind legs.

(8) *Horse goggles.* These comprise a pair of plastic eyepieces trimmed with leather, held together by an adjustable cloth strap, with another cloth strap attached to the outside of each eyepiece. A red line on one eyepiece, and a blue line on the other, apparently are to mark the right and left eyepieces.

Figure 112.—Gloves, German heavy protective clothing.

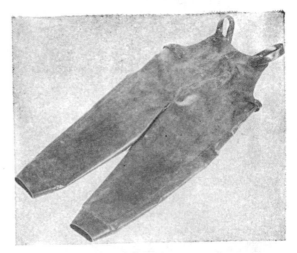

Figure 113.—Pants, German heavy protective clothing.

Figure 114.—Jacket, German heavy protective clothing.

LIGHT BULK CONTAMINATION VEHICLE
(Sd. Kfz. 10/3)

MEDIUM BULK CONTAMINATION VEHICLE
(Sd. Kfz. 11/3)

LIGHT DECONTAMINATION VEHICLE
(Sd. Kfz. 10/2)

MEDIUM DECONTAMINATION VEHICLE
(Sd. Kfz. 11/2)

VEHICLE FOR DECONTAMINATION OF CLOTHING
(Kfz. 93)

VEHICLE FOR DECONTAMINATION OF PERSONNEL
(Kfz. 92)

SMOKE VEHICLE (Sd. Kfz. 11/1)

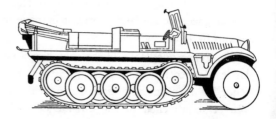

GAS–DETECTION VEHICLE (Sd. Kfz. 10/1)

Figure 115.—Decontamination vehicles.

(9) *Gas Clothing 41 for dogs.* This consists of a hood and suit, to which are sewed rubber footcovers. Suit and hood are made of thin, field-gray, impregnated fabric. The suit, made in three sizes, is carried inside the facepiece of the dog gas mask.

(10) *Dog Legging 41.* This is made of rubber in only one size and consists of foot and leg parts, fitted with fastening straps.

c. DECONTAMINATION. (1) *Equipment.* (a) *Mobile decontamination plant.* This plant for the decontamination of clothing and equipment may take the form of motor trucks mounting a water-tube boiler for the rapid generation of steam, a steam chamber, and a drying chamber.

(b) *Vehicle for decontamination of personnel.* A six-wheeled motor vehicle fitted with a large box body which contains bathing facilities for 150 men per hour. Completely equipped, it weighs about 9 tons.

(c) *Vehicle for decontamination of clothing.* A six-wheeled vehicle fitted with a large closed body which is equipped with a boiler, fans, and water tanks. Completely equipped, it weighs about 9.7 tons.

(d) *Light decontamination vehicle.* This open, semi-tracked, 1-ton motor vehicle, equipped with a distributing hopper on the rear, carries about 1,675 pounds of bulk decontaminant and 16 decontamination canisters (22 pounds) for use by hand.

(e) *Filter for decontamination of water.* The apparatus consists of two parts: the filter proper and a tank containing water for cleaning the filter. Both are of sheet iron covered with enamel. The filter proper is a tall, cylindrical tank filled with activated charcoal.

(f) *Decontamination plow.* This is a large, fish-hook-shaped, ditching plow, mounted on a two-wheeled carriage with pneumatic tires. Over-all length is 11 feet 6 inches; over-all width is 6 feet 1 inch. The plow produces a furrow 20 inches wide.

(g) *Decontamination pump.* This is a metal stirrup pump, approximately 24 inches in length, with about 9 inches of rubber hose.

(h) *Decontamination canisters.* These canisters consist of metal cylinders, 6.7 inches high by 3.3 inches in diameter, and a quadrangular metal or cardboard container, 14.6 inches high by 8.2 inches wide. Each has a perforated screen in the top for sprinkling the contents, normally Losantin, on a contaminated surface.

(2) *Decontaminants.* (a) *Losantin.* This high quality, stabilized, white bleach powder is used for decontamination of standard blister gases. It is packed in steel drums of 55 and 110 pounds capacity.

(b) *Decontaminant 40.* This is a fine white or pale cream powder, packed in steel drums holding 132 pounds. Especially designed for nitrogen mustards, it is also a powerful decontaminant for all blister gases.

(c) *Decontaminant N.* A powdered or flaked white solid, supplied in wooden boxes of 175 pounds capacity, this is a substitute for Decontaminant 40, which is difficult and expensive to produce.

(d) *Weapon decontamination agent.* This individual issue is a small bottle of liquid agent in a dark brown, bakelite container. It is used for the decontamination of small arms and individual equipment.

(e) *Weapon decontaminating agent set.* This is a company issue. It consists of two bottles of liquid in a cardboard container 14 inches high by 4.7 inches in diameter. The red-capped bottle contains the decontaminating agent, and the black-capped bottle contains a substance to counteract the corrosion caused by the agent.

(f) *Horse decontamination canister.* A quadrangular cardboard box, with a perforated screen at one end, type 40 holds about 20 ounces of decontaminant. It is intended for a team of horses; type 41 which holds only about 10 ounces is designed for an individual horse. The canister is carried in the horse gas-mask carrier.

(g) *Dog decontamination canister 42.* This is a quadrangular cardboard box holding about 10 ounces of decontaminant.

d. PROTECTIVE AGENTS. (1) *Losantin.* Ten tablets of Losantin are issued in plastic boxes for

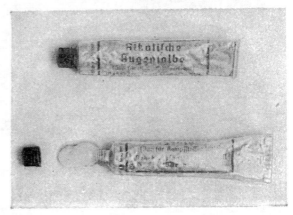

Figure 116.—German alkaline eye salve.

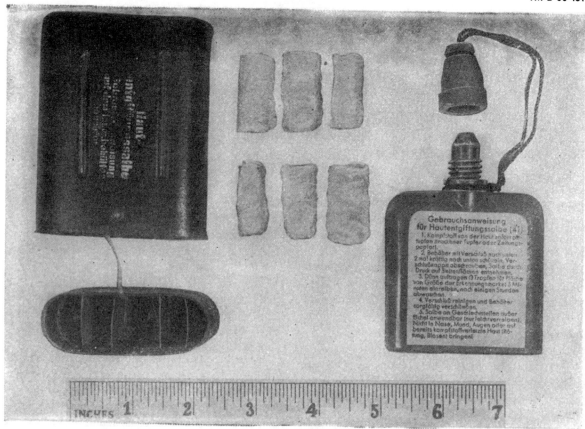

Figure 117.—German weapons decontaminating set, individual issue.

Figure 118.—German weapons decontaminating agent set, company issue.

decontamination of the skin. Adhesive strips of different colors indicate the year of manufacture. The issue is four boxes to a soldier, but reports state that it is being replaced by Protective Ointment 41.

(2) *Protective Ointment 41*. This is issued in bottles, with six swabs in an orange bakelite container, for decontamination of the skin.

(3) *Alkaline eye salve*. This is a creamy white salve in either a metal foil tube or a white jar. It is used for the treatment of eyes contaminated with blister gases.

(4) *Inhalant ampoules and swabs*. Five inhalant ampoules and six swabs are packed in a

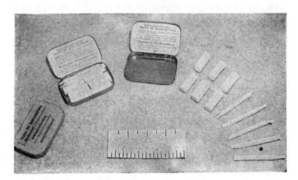

Figure 119.—German inhalant ampoules and swabs.

green metal box. The ampoules are for inhalation upon exposure to toxic smokes, and the swabs are for wiping off liquid blister gases.

e. GAS DETECTORS. (1) *Detector powder*. This is ochre or pink powder which changes color in contact with certain war gases in liquid form. The pink powder is reported to be obsolescent. Either a detector canister or a detector pump is used to spread the powder.

(2) *Carbon Monoxide Detector Paper 42*. Two bottles of testing liquid, 400 detector papers, and one holder for the detector paper comprise this set. When moistened with the testing liquid, the paper changes color in the presence of carbon monoxide.

(3) *Arsine detector paper*. This equipment is packed in a cardboard box, containing 100 bottles of detector paper and 30 holders for the detector paper. Each booklet which holds 10 sheets is inclosed in airtight packing. Arsine in the air changes the color of the paper.

(4) *Detector Canister 42.* This metal cylinder, with a perforated screen in one end, holds about 4 pounds of detector powder.

(5) *Gas detector*. This is for detection of gas vapors. It comprises an air-sampling pump

in a metal holder and five types of testing tubes in a metal carrier.

(6) *Carbon monoxide detector set*. (a) *Army type*. This consists of a field gray, wooden box, containing an air pump, 32 detector tubes, a tube holder, and accessories.

(b) *Commercial type*. Essentially, this consists of an air pump and detector tubes in a metal cylindrical carrier. Though a commercial detector, it is used in army fortifications. When air containing carbon monoxide is drawn through a tube from either set, the contents of the tube changes color.

(7) *Gas detector equipment set*. This consists of a metal carrier containing an air pump, a few detector tubes of each type, arsine detector paper, a small detector canister, and accessories.

(8) *Spray detector cards*. These stiff paper cards, packed 20 to a carton, are coated on both sides with a paint containing a dye which changes color in contact with liquid blister gases.

(9) *Detector powder pump*. This is a ribbed, sheet-metal box container having an internally

Figure 120—German gas detector set.

Figure 121.—German detector powder pump.

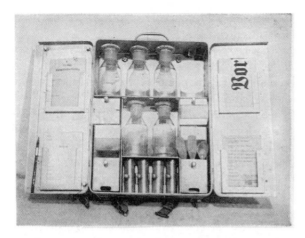

Figure 122.—German gas detector and sampling kit.

built pump, with a handle on one end and an adjustable spray nozzle on the other.

(10) *Gas detector and sampling kit.* This aluminum chest contains six sample bottles, four small detector canisters, war gas warning cards, spray detector paper, and accessories.

(11) *Detector paint.* This paint contains a dye which changes color in contact with certain liquid war gases. It is used to make smears on surfaces for detection of war gas spray.

(12) *Gas detector for fortifications.* A metal case contains an electric motor, air pumps, six pairs of metal and glass detector tubes, seatings for the tubes, and necessary connections for drawing air through all of the tubes at the same time.

(13) *Field laboratory.* This laboratory includes equipment for testing for war gases, in addition to necessary equipment for accomplishing its main function of food and drug analysis.

(14) *Gas detection vehicle.* This is an open, semi-tracked, 1-ton vehicle used for carrying gas detection personnel and their equipment.

f. MISCELLANEOUS. (1) *Ear plugs.* These are square tablets of yellow wax, packed six in a metal box, for protection of men with damaged ear drums.

(2) *Anti-dim disc.* This occurs in sets of two. The disc, 2.3 inches in diameter, has one side coated with gelatin. It is fitted over the inside of the eyepieces, with the gelatin-coated side next to the wearer's eyes. The gelatin rapidly absorbs moisture and prevents fogging of the eyepieces.

(3) *Anti-dim sheet.* This is an oval celluloid-type disc to fit over the window of a headwound gas mask to prevent fogging. The disc is believed to have one side coated with gelatin. Ten discs are packed in a tin box.

(4) *Gas mask tester.* This includes a rectangular chest containing an electric motor, a pressure gage, a head-form for the gas mask facepiece, and accessories.

(5) *Canister testing apparatus.* This is a portable tester in a wooden case. The case contains a pump, a canister resistance gage, and accessories.

Figure 123.—German gas mask testing equipment.

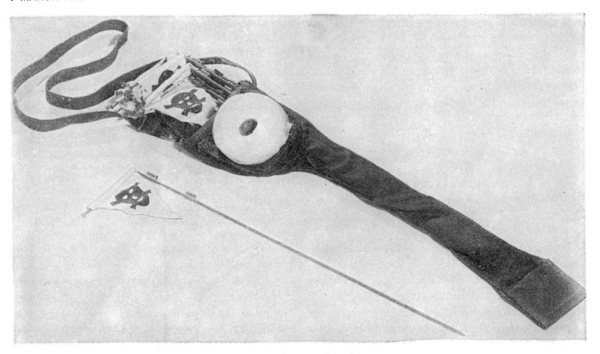

Figure 124.—Gas warning flag set.

(6) *Gas alarm device*. This is a whistling cartridge which is fired from a signal pistol. It rises about 50 feet, giving off either a whitish or green light and emitting a high-pitched whistle audible for about 400 yards.

(7) *Anti-gas pathway material*. This strong paper, impregnated with a tar-like substance, is prepared in rolls, approximately 4 feet wide and 55 yards long. It is stated to be of sufficient strength to allow 200 men to cross a contaminated area in safety.

(8) *Gas warning flag set*. This is a pistol-shaped case containing 20 L-shaped iron rods, 20 warning flags (yellow with black skull and crossed bones imprinted), and a roll of yellow marking tape.

Figure 125.—Set of German collective protectors.

(9) *Collective protector*. This is installed in air raid shelters and other fixed installations. It consists of a pump, either electrically or hand driven, a mechanical canister, a chemical canister, and necessary connections for drawing outside air through the canisters.

(10) *Gas protective case for pigeons*. This is a case of four compartments, each with an inlet tube and filter.

3. War Gases

a. GENERAL. German war gases, generally speaking, have retained their World War 1 classification. However, "crosses" are believed to have been superseded by the terms "rings" or "bands" for purposes of nomenclature. The appearance of the *FE 42* canister suggests that the Germans are aware of the potentialities of hydrocyanic acid (AC), cyanogen chloride (CK) and arsine (SA). Tests show that this canister affords fair protection against these gases. The Germans are known to favor the combination of gases. Thus, a vesicant toxic smoke is a combination of "blue"- and "yellow"-band gases, and the nature of the chemical filling would be indicated by two bands of the corresponding colors. "Green" and "yellow" bands would indicate a choking gas with vesicant properties. A double "yellow" band would indicate a vesicant gas of enhanced persistence.

527

b. NITROGEN MUSTARDS. In addition to the more or less standard agents, there is documentary evidence to show that the Germans possess a nearly odorless gas designated as "Green Band I." It is only one of several gases with like characteristics that may be referred to as "nitrogen mustards."

Generally speaking, the nitrogen mustards are either liquids or low-melting solids, pale yellow to colorless, and are practically odorless. Their volatility varies, some being less volatile than mustard gas and some more volatile. They are fairly readily hydrolyzed by water, but the products of such hydrolysis are toxic.

Nitrogen mustard gas has a low freezing point, and might, therefore, be used for high-altitude bombing or spray (if thickened). It may be three or four times as volatile as mustard gas and therefore less persistent. Since higher concentrations are possible, it is more dangerous as a gas, though not so powerful in its vesicant effect. It would require special stabilization if used in hot climates.

The principal danger from the nitrogen mustards lies in the fact that their vapors are not easily detected by smell. Munitions which contain these gases and have a high bursting charge (20 to 30 per cent HE) are indistinguishable from HE on detonation. Under such conditions, reliance must be placed on the usual U. S. detector methods: that is, detector paint or paper and the vapor detector kit, M-9.

Nitrogen mustard is likely to be used to achieve surprise by being included in a normal HE bombardment in order to capture key positions. It is also possible that this gas would be used as a spray from airplanes, or in aerial bombs.

Common name	German name
Blister gases (Vesicants)—"Yellow Cross"	
Mustard (H).............*Lost; Senf; Gelbkreuz*	
Lewisite (L).............*Gelbkreuz II* (?)	
Ethyldichlorarsine (ED)..*Dick; Gelbkreuz III*	
Nitrogen Mustard (HN)..*Stickstofflost*	

(Mixtures of mustard gas and Lewisite may be used in cold weather to reduce the freezing point. A 50-per cent mixture of mustard and Lewisite is called *Winterlost*. The mustard gas is likely to be an improvement over that of World War I; it is probably more persistent, possibly more vesicant, and more difficult to decontaminate.)

Choking gases (Lung Irritants)—"Green Cross"
Phosgene (CG).......*D-Stoff; Grünkreuz*

Diphosgene (DP).....*K-Stoff; Perstoff; Brunkreuz I, II*
Chlorpicrin (PS)......*Klop*
Chlorine (Cl)........*Chlor*

(There have been frequent references to mixtures of these choking gases.)

Vomiting gases (Sternutators)—"Blue Cross"
Diphenylchlorarsine (DA).. *Clark I; Blaukreuz*
Diphenylcyanarsine (DC)... *Clark II; Cyan Clark*
Adamsite (DM).......... *D. M. Adamsit*

Tear gases (Lacrimators)—"White Cross"
Chloracetophenone (CN)..............*T-Stoff*
Brombenzylcyanide (BBC)............*T-Stoff*

(Neither of these gases was used by the Germans in the last war. They relied upon a number of bromine compounds, which are less powerful than the two substances listed. It is thought that Germany attaches little importance to tear gases alone, but the possible use of other gases camouflaged by tear gases must not be overlooked.)

4. Ground Weapons

a. GENERAL. The Germans have a large number of weapons capable of firing chemical warfare munitions—guns, mortars, howitzers, and projectors—with varying calibers and ever-increasing types.

b. GUNS. No less than 12 guns of 75-mm caliber, including a self-propelled model, fire smoke shells. The limitations of gas shells for artillery are clearly recognized by the Germans. Although thus far no German gas shells have been captured, reports indicate that for some time they have been building up extensive stocks of gas-filled shells, 105-mm and 150-mm being the favored calibers. Smoke shells for several types of 105-mm guns, two of which are self-propelled, are known. Smoke shells weighing

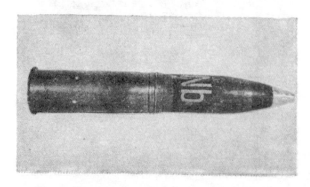

Figure 126.—75-mm smoke projectile for tank gun.

Figure 127.—15 cm Nebelwerfer 41 being loaded.

SMOKE PROJECTILES FIRED BY GERMAN WEAPONS

Smoke Shell	Weapon Firing the Munition	Color Markings and Remarks
8 cm Wgr. 34 Nb. 8 cm Wgr. 38 Blau.	8 cm Mortar (S. Gr. W. 34).	Red body. Nb. in white. Blue band. Ejects blue smoke for target indication.
10 cm Wgr. 35 Nb.	10 cm Smoke Mortar (Nb. W. 35).	Brick red or olive green; Nb in white.
*10 cm Wgr. 40 Nb. *10 cm Wgr. 40 Wkb. Nb.	Nb. W. 40. Nb. W. 40.	Brick red or olive green; Nb in white with long burster tube.
20 cm Wgr. 40 Nb.	20 cm Spigot Mortar (le. Ldg. W. 40).	Used by the Engineers. Electrically fired. Range 700 meters.
38 cm Wgr. 40 Nb.	38 cm Spigot Mortar (S. Ldg. W. 40).	Used by the Engineers.

* It should be noted that the HE shell for the 10 cm mortar 40 has stencilled on the tail *"10 cm Nb. W. 40"*, due to the fact that the mortar is the *"Nebelwerfer 40"*, i.e., "smoke" projector.

Figure 128.

approximately 86 pounds are provided for 150-mm self-propelled guns, known as the "Grizzly Bear" and the "Bumble Bee". There are also smoke and incendiary shells for the 150-mm heavy infantry gun.

c. MORTARS. The basic weapon of German chemical warfare troops is the 105-mm mortar, two models of which are known. In addition to the 81-mm mortar, the Germans have a 12-cm mortar that is identical with the Finnish 12-cm mortar made by Tampella. They also have copied the Russian 12-cm mortar. Revolutionary in design are the 20-cm and 38-cm spigot mortars. While these mortars are primarily intended for the destruction of obstacles, minefields, and gun emplacements, smoke shells are provided and there is apparently no reason why gas or incendiary fillings could not be substituted for HE.

d. HOWITZERS. Smoke shells are provided for two types of light field howitzers of 105-mm caliber and three types of 150-mm heavy field howitzers. Projectiles weighing 80 pounds filled with blister and choking gases, for the heavy field howitzers are reported.

e. PROJECTORS. Two general types of rocket projectors have made their appearance during the current war: the *Nebelwerfer* (literally, smoke projector) and the *Schweres Wurfgerät* (heavy throwing apparatus). For details of these weapons see Section VII of Chapter VII.

f. SMOKE GENERATORS. (1) *General.* Smoke generators are often referred to as "thermo-generators" due to the fact that they produce smoke by the "hot" process, namely, by the combustion of the smoke materials. They may be stationary, thrown by hand or rifle, or by dischargers mounted on tanks. Also, they may be fastened on floats or buoys for amphibious operations.

(2) *Smoke Candle 39 (Nb.K.39).* This smoke generator consists of a metal can, 5¾ inches high by 3½ inches in diameter, provided with holes in the top for smoke emission. It weighs approximately 4¾ pounds and is painted green, with two white bands around the body. The Berger-type smoke mixture, consisting of two parts of zinc dust to three parts of hexachlorethane, is fired by a pull type igniter and burns from 4 to 7 minutes.

(3) *Smoke Cylinder (Rauchrohr).* Designed primarily for use against tanks, this munition consists of a cylinder 10 inches long with a diameter of 1 inch. It contains 7½ ounces of a smoke mixture composed of zinc, magnesium, and hexachlorethane. Its total weight is 11 ounces. Ignited by a pull type igniter, it burns 3 to 4 minutes, emitting a dark gray smoke.

(4) *Long-Burning Smoke Generator (Langekerzer 42, Nb.KL 42).* This long burning smoke generator is a green, cylindrical metal container with an over-all height of 19 inches and a diameter of 6⅝ inches. It contains approximately 36 pounds of a smoke mixture consisting of zinc, zinc (or ammonium) chloride, and hexachlore-

Figure 129.—28/32 cm Schweres Wurfgerät 41 emplaced for launching incendiary rockets.

Figure 130.—Smoke candles: Nb.K.39B, Nb.K.S.39B, and Nb.K.39.

thane. Its total weight varies from 35 to 49 pounds. The ignition is electrical or by means of a pull wire. The generator burns 15 to 30 minutes, emitting a whitish gray smoke sufficient to provide a screen 200 yards wide, 400 to 500 yards long and 40 yards deep under favorable conditions.

(5) *French smoke floats.* German E-boats are reported to have used French 132-pound smoke floats consisting of a container, filled with Berger Mixture, a flotation device, a lid, and an igniter. The emission period is 4 to 5 minutes.

Figure 131.—Smoke cylinders, Rauchröhre Nb. 39.

Figure 132.—German smoke apparatus, drum and cylinder.

g. Smoke Generator Projectors for Armored Vehicles. The *Pz.Kpfw.III* and *Pz. Kpfw.VI* are provided with smoke generator projectors (dischargers), which are mounted on each side of the turret. They consist of three cylindrical tubes, 6 inches in length by 3.7 inches in diameter, mounted on a bracket one above the other at a fixed elevation of 45 degrees, but slightly splayed to give a lateral spread to the generators. *Nb.K.39* smoke generators are fired from inside the turret. Panther and Tiger Model B tanks are fitted with smoke generator dischargers mounted flush in the right rear top of the turret, at an angle of 60 degrees to the turret roof. They are mounted in a circular ring in such a manner that they may be traversed through 360 degrees. The barrel, 7½ inches long by 3⅝ inches in diameter, is fitted with a breechblock. The firing mechanism is operated by a trigger from within the tank, projecting the *Nb.K.39* smoke generators.

h. Smoke Sprayers. Smoke sprayers (*Nebelzerstäuber*) disseminate a liquid smoke-producing material by the application of compressed air. The smoke liquid, generally chlorsulfonic acid, is atomized or dispersed as minute particles which vaporize and quickly condense again as very fine droplets by absorption of water vapor from the atmosphere. The process is "cold" as distinct from the "hot" process of the smoke generator. The Germans have a variety of smoke sprayers for diverse uses: stationary, portable, mounted on vehicles or tanks, carried on board ship or aircraft, and floating on buoys.

i. Grenades. *Nebelhandgranate 39* and *41* are smoke hand grenades containing a hexachlorethane mixture. They are of similar design. Both are painted green and are distinguished by the inscription *Nb. Hgr. 39* (or *41*) in white, with a white broken line beneath the lettering. The Germans have two types of glass hand grenades, known as *Blendkorper 1H* and *Blendkorper 2H*, charged with a mixture of titanium tetrachloride (FM) and silicon tetrachloride. They also have incendiary frangible hand grenades of the Molotov-cocktail type, consisting of a pint glass bottle filled with a mixture of benzene and creosote oil. This type is intended primarily for use against tanks.

j. Gas Mines. The German gas mines are referred to as spray canisters (*Spruhbüchse*). They are used by the ground forces for contaminating ground, roadblocks, buildings, or in-

Figure 133.—Egg type smoke grenade.

Figure 134.—Frangible smoke grenade, Blenkörper 1H.

accessible places. They are also used for harassing landing parties on tidal beaches and for delaying armored vehicles and troops. The mines can be laid at the sides of roads, under bridges, in woods, or in other convenient locations and may be actuated by time mechanism or pressure fuzes. One mine can contaminate an area of 20 to 25 square meters.

k. Bulk Contamination. Any liquid-spraying apparatus (*Spruhgerät*) may be used for bulk contamination. Tanks, armored cars, and trucks may be equipped with apparatus for spraying gas and smoke. Chemical trucks are included in the equipment for the special gas companies. The special spraying apparatus of the decontamination battalions is a potential contaminating apparatus as well, since it may readily be used for offensive purposes, spraying liquid "gases" instead of decontaminating liquids.

l. Mobile Flame Throwers. A flame thrower is a pressure-operated apparatus which projects a jet of liquid ignited as it leaves the gun. Its essential features are: a fuel container, a device

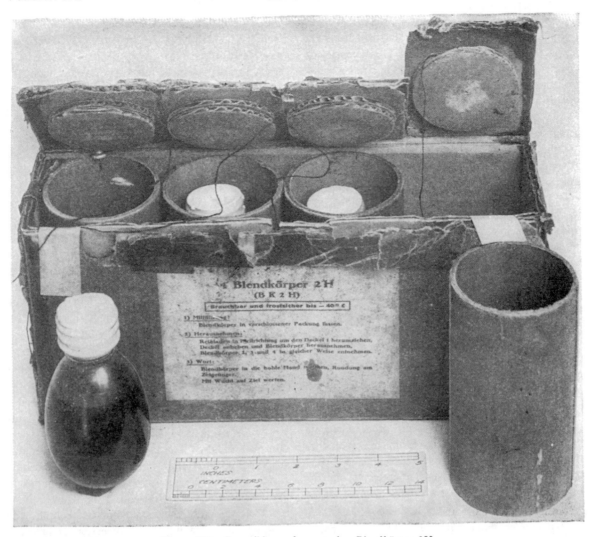

Figure 135.—Frangible smoke grenades, Blendkörper 2H.

for forcing the fuel out of the container, a projecting tube with a nozzle at its end, and an igniting system to set the jet of fuel aflame. The principle types developed by the Germans are as follows:

(1) *Flame thrower, portable, Model 35.* This is the type with which Germany started the present war. It is a modified version of the 1918 model. Both fuel and compressed nitrogen containers are housed in one cylinder. The nitrogen is used for propulsion of the fuel, which is ignited at the nozzle by a jet of hydrogen flame. Both ejection and ignition of the fuel are controlled by the same trigger placed on the top of the gun. It can fire ten one-second bursts as far as 30 yards. Weighing 79 pounds it is too heavy for a single man in action.

(2) *Flame thrower, portable, Model 40.* This is a "lifebuoy-type" flame thrower, weighing only 47 pounds. However, the decrease in weight has been accomplished by a one-third reduction in fuel, as compared with the Model 35. The range is unaltered.

(3) *Flame thrower, portable, Model 41.* This consists of two cylinders, one for fuel and the other for compressed nitrogen. The complete apparatus weighs 35 to 40 pounds. Ignition is by hydrogen, which flows over an electrically heated wire at the nozzle, where it is lighted and in turn sets the oil afire. Firing is by the "hot" method: the oil is ignited each time the trigger is pulled: thus, the target can not be first sprayed with oil and then set afire. Five blasts can be fired, producing a flame of 700 to 800 degrees centigrade.

(4) *Flame thrower, portable, Model 42.* In appearance it is similar to Model 41, but is slightly shorter and differing in one essential point:

the ignition system. The hot-spot hydrogen jet ignition system of the older model has been replaced by the cartridge system. This consists of a cartridge magazine in which there are ten rimless, blank, 9-mm pistol cartridges, loaded, fired, and ejected in automatic succession at each pull of the trigger. Since the fuel ejection and the firing mechanisms are operated by the same trigger the result is the "hot-firing", wherein prior drenching of the target with oil is impossible. The jet of the fuel is set afire at the instant it leaves the nozzle. The apparatus weighs about 30 pounds empty and up to 40 pounds full. It holds approximately 7½ gallons of fuel, a black oil smelling like creosote. The fuel ejection is by compressed nitrogen gas under a pressure of 441 pounds per square inch. There is no reducing valve on the nitrogen line. The oil is sufficient for 5 to 6 blasts, each lasting 3 seconds, reaching a range of 25 to 35 yards.

(5) *Para-Flame Thrower (Einstoss Flammenwerfer)*. This is another variety of the portable flame thrower. It is the standard one used by the paratroops and also is used to a great extent by the *SS*. It weighs 23¾ pounds. The fuel is the usual black liquid used in other German flame throwers. It is fired from the shoulder, throws a flame 38 yards long, lasting 2 to 3 seconds. It is said to possess a constant, steady pressure producing an even flame. Also, it is claimed that it can be aimed accurately.

(6) *Trailer flame thrower.* This is a flame thrower that bears a resemblance to a "field gun", since it is mounted on a chassis and is towed by a motor vehicle. Fitted on the frame is a box-shaped sheet metal body which contains the fuel tank, the pump, and the engine. The fuel tank is 4 feet 11½ inches by 1 foot 9½ inches, and holds 40 gallons of creosote oil. The pump is a gasoline engine-driven, centrifugal pump. The flame gun is mounted on a spigot on top of the fuel tank to facilitate traversing; the gun itself is carried on trunnions to permit elevating and depressing. It can be traversed 45 degrees each way and elevated between +30 degrees and —10 degrees. The fuel is ignited by an electric spark and the flame will last 24 seconds at a range of 45 to 50 yards, using 1.46 gallons of fuel per second. It has an over-all length of 7 feet 11 inches and weighs 900 pounds. When operating it makes a noise which can be heard easily at a distance of 300 yards.

(7) *Flame thrower on armored car (half-track) (Sd Kfz 251.)* Two flame throwers are mounted on the rear of an ordinary 3-ton half-track armored vehicle, but are controlled from the front seat next to the driver. The flame throwers may be traversed 160 degrees. Length of hose is 11 yards. The tank holds 185 gallons of the usual German flame thrower-fuel. A centrifugal pump propels fuel with a consumption rate of 2 gallons per second. The fuel is sufficient for 80 bursts of 1 to 2 seconds each at a range of 40 to 50 yards. The weapon is fired by an electro-gasoline system.

(8) *Flame thrower on Panzerjäger 38 Chassis. (le. Pz. Jäg. 38 Chassis).* The flame thrower is mounted offside on the front of the self-propelled *Panzerjäger 38*. The fuel capacity is 154 gallons, with a consumption rate of 1.8 gallons per second. Fuel release is controlled by hand through a 14-mm nozzle. The range is 55 to 66 yards.

m. STATIONARY FLAME THROWERS. (1) *General*. These are called *Abwehr Flammenwerfer* by the Germans, a nomenclature that implies the defensive nature of the weapons. They are also known as static flame throwers, emplaced flame throwers, fougasse flame throwers, and flame thrower mines. The latter name is probably due to the fact that they are buried directly behind minefields or are dispersed among the mines to "thicken up" the defense and fired by remote control. Usually they are emplaced behind wire entanglements facing in the direction of probable attack to cover road blocks, landing beaches, harbor walls, and to act as movable obstacles at a gap in defense walls. They are buried at intervals of 12 to 30 yards, well camouflaged, leaving only the horizontal muzzle projecting above the ground. Groups of emplaced flame throwers are controlled from a central point, usually a small pillbox, and are operated either by remote electric control or by trip-wire mechanism.

(2) *Emplaced flame thrower (Abwehrflammenwerfer 42)*. (a) *General*. This apparatus consists of fuel container, flame tube, and propellent container. Necessary accessories are slow burning powder propellant, electric squibs, wire, storage battery, and fuel. It has an over-all height of 2 feet 6 inches.

(b) *Fuel container.* The fuel container is a cylindrical tank 21 inches high and 11¾ inches in diameter. It has iron carrying handles, and a capacity of 8 gallons. The fuel is a black viscid liquid smelling like coal tar. It is a mixture of

Figure 136.—German static flamethrower.

pitch and light, medium, and heavy oils. It is a little thicker than the usual flame-thrower oil. The fuel tank holds 7.7 gallons.

(c) *Flame tube.* The flame tube is a 2-inch metal pipe rising vertically and centrally from near the bottom of the fuel container; after passing through the top it curves and extends horizontally a distance of 20 inches. This gives the apparatus a total height of 30 inches.

(d) *Propellent container.* This is a cylinder 10 inches high by 2⅝ inches in diameter. It contains slow-burning powder, an ignition squib, and firing wires. The propellent powder is either black powder or a mixture of nitrocellulose and diethylene glycol dinitrate. The pressure pro-

duced by the explosion of the propelling charge ejects the fuel.

(e) *Performance.* Both electrical squibs fire simultaneously into the pressure chamber. One ignites the propellent powder which generates pressure to force the fuel out through the flame tube; the other ignites the fuel as it passes out of the nozzle. There is an ignition composition of aluminum and barium nitrate at the nozzle. The flame, 5 yards wide and 3 yards high, lasts 1½ seconds. The range is 30 yards.

n. FLAME-THROWER TANKS. (1) *General.* These are tanks in which flame throwers are mounted. The flame thrower and its accessories, the fuel tanks, projecting hose, gas cylinders, pump, engines, and ignition system are all so

Figure 137.—Pz. Kpfw. III, Model L, flamethrowing tank.

housed in the turret that the vehicles preserve the external appearance of ordinary tanks. They have undergone several modifications and some are obsolescent.

(2) *Flame-Thrower Tank Pz. Kpfw. II (F) (Sd. Kfz. 122).* This tank has two flame throwing projectors, each mounted in a small turret well forward on the track guards but operated electrically from panels in the turret. The turrets have a traverse of 180 degrees, elevation of 20 degrees, and depression of 10 degrees. Seventy gallons of fuel are kept in two tanks mounted externally on the track guards. The fuel tanks are protected by shields. Fuel is projected by compressed nitrogen. It is sufficient for 80 shots of 2 to 3 seconds duration at a range of 35 yards. Ignition is by acetylene flame.

(3) *Flame-Thrower Tank Pz.Kpfw.III, Model L.* A flame thrower in the turret replaces the normal 50-mm gun (*5 cm Kw.K.39*), which it resembles outwardly. Traverse is 360 degrees, and elevation is from —10 degrees to +20 degrees. The fuel is a black, sticky oil smelling of creosote and is sufficient for 70 to 80 shots of 2 to 3 seconds duration. The range is 55 to 65 yards. The fuel, 225 gallons, is carried in tanks mounted inside the right and left side.

5. Aerial Weapons

a. CHEMICAL BOMBS. (1) *10-Kilogram (22 pounds) Fragmentation Bomb (GC 10).* This is a toxic smoke and high explosive bomb. It con-

tains an arsenic filling, identified by the Germans with a blue cross.

(2) *50-Kilogram (110 pounds) Mustard Gas Bomb (GC 50).* This bomb has a highly sensitive impact fuze, with either a small bursting charge for ground contamination or a large bursting charge for antipersonnel effect.

(3) *250-Kilogram (550 pounds) Mustard Gas Bomb (KC 250 GB).* This bomb has a time fuze which is set to function about 330 feet above the ground. The bomb will contaminate an area of about 6,000 square yards. It is possible that the Germans have gas bombs of larger caliber. A "green cross" (*KC 500*) bomb has been reported with a choking-gas filling.

b. SMOKE BOMBS. (1) *NG 50 Smoke Bomb.* This bomb has a field gray body with white nose. It may have four white vertical stripes or two white bands painted on the body. Its over-all length is 2 feet 7 inches.

(2) *NC 50 WC.* This bomb is for use on water. It has a field gray or silver body with yellow nose. Four yellow vertical stripes may appear on the body. It is 3 feet 7 inches long and 7¾ inches in diameter. The filling is a Berger Mixture or hexachlorethane.

(3) *NC 250 S.* This bomb is similar to the *Flam. C 250.* It is painted silver with a white band and *NC 250* painted between the filling plug and suspension socket. The nose is white, and the tail is olive drab. There are two sizes of this bomb, one weighing 242 pounds and the other

418 pounds. The filling is chlorsulfonic acid and sulphurtrioxide.

c. INCENDIARY BOMBS. (1) *1-Kilogram Bomb.* Specimens of this bomb may bear designations *B1 E1, B1 E1 Z,* and *B1 E1 ZB.* All types weigh about 2.75 pounds each. The body is painted aluminum or green. The diameter is 2 inches, and over-all length 13½ inches. The filling is 0.44 pounds of thermite.

(2) *2-Kilogram Bomb.* This bomb has the designation *B2 E1 Z* and weighs about 4½ pounds. The body color is aluminum or light green. The filling includes TNT or amatol in addition to thermite. The diameter is 2 inches, and the over-all length is 20.7 inches.

(3) *Oil Incendiary Bomb (Brand C 50 A).* This bomb weighs 99 pounds. It is painted field gray, with red under the tail, a red band encircling the body, and a yellow stripe on the tail cone. The body diameter is 8 inches, and the over-all length is 43.2 inches. The filling is 15 liters (3.3 gallons) of a mixture of 86 per cent benzene, 10 per cent rubber, and 4 per cent phosphorus. It has a bursting charge of picric acid.

(4) *Incendiary Bomb C 50 B.* This is identical in marking, dimensions, and body color with the *C 50 A.* However, it is filled with white phosphorus, and this is indicated by a small red bottle painted on the bomb.

(5) *Flam. C 250.* This bomb weighs 240 pounds. It is painted green with a red nose, two blue tail rings, and two red bands. The diameter of the body is 2 inches, and over-all length is 64½ inches. It contains 16 gallons of oil, weighing 110 pounds, composed of crude oil, aluminum, magnesium powder, and woodmeal-petroleum igniting mixture. The bursting charge is 2.65 pounds of picric acid and TNT.

(6) *Flam. C 250 B* and *Flam. C 250 C.* These bombs are identical with the *Flam. C 250* except markings. The type B and C bombs are painted dark blue or gray and have two red bands encircling the body.

(7) *Brand C 250 A.* This bomb is painted field gray with a red undertail. It measures 14½ inches in diameter and 64½ inches in length. The filling, 15.8 gallons, is a mixture of 87.7 per cent petroleum solvent, 11.7 per cent polystyrene, and 0.5 per cent phosphorus. The bursting charge is picric acid.

(8) *Flam. C. 500 C.* This bomb is painted blue or gray and weighs 440 to 460 pounds.

d. SPRAY TANKS. All German aircraft smoke sprayers, *S 100, S 125, S 200,* and *S 300,* are similar in construction. They make use of a smoke acid mixture and are operated by gas pressure. The sprayer is a cylindrical apparatus housing an acid container, a small cylinder or bottle of compressed air, air lines with valve, and emission pipe, and nozzle. It is carried externally on the aircraft and can be jettisoned at will. The smoke acid is ejected by compressed air at 45 pounds per square inch. It may be filled to two levels. When charged at low level, it has a weight of 551 pounds; charged at high level it weighs 827 pounds, holding 482 and 758 pounds respectively. The firing is done electrically by operating a magnetic valve. Emission may be interrupted and re-started at will.

Section VII. FIELD RANGES AND COOKING EQUIPMENT

I. General

Various types of field ranges and other cooking equipment are issued to units of the German Army. The most important of these include: rolling field kitchens, field ranges, fireless cookers, and cooking outfit, 15.

2. Rolling Field Kitchens

a. GENERAL. Horse-drawn rolling field kitchens are issued to non-mechanized units. The large rolling field kitchen will serve 125 to 225 men; the small rolling field kitchen, 50 to 125 men. Smaller units do not receive field kitchens but get either fireless cookers or cooking outfits, 15.

Figure 138.—The rolling field kitchen ready for traveling.

Figure 139.—German field bakery.

Figure 140.—German dough mixer.

Figure 141.—Small field range mounted in truck.

Figure 142.—Large field range mounted in truck.

b. LIMBER AND TRAILER. The rolling field kitchen consists of two parts: the detachable limber and the trailer, on which the field range is mounted. It is drawn either by two or four horses. The limber, on which the driver and cook may ride only during rapid marches, is used to transport most of the supplies, including the extra iron rations which are carried for emergency use only. After the kitchen has been set up, the limber may be used alone to get additional supplies. Under some circumstances the rolling field kitchen without the limber is issued to motorized units, and additional supplies are carried in the light truck used to move the kitchen.

c. COOKING UTENSILS. (1) *Range.* The range itself, mounted on the trailer, can burn either coal, coke, briquettes, or wood. The following is considered the normal issue of fuel:

	Large Field Kitchen	Small Field Kitchen
Briquettes	187 pounds	66 pounds
or Wood	82 pounds	29 pounds
or Briquettes	77 pounds	33 pounds
and Wood	48 pounds	13 pounds

The range normally is used as a fireless cooker, especially when underway. Fires are built in the fire boxes, but as soon as steam starts to escape from the safety valve the fire is banked and allowed to go out. This practice both saves fuel and prevents revealing the unit's position by the smoke.

(2) *Stew kettle.* The main part of the range is a large stew kettle, a kind of double boiler which has a second slightly larger shell around the food kettle. A special liquid between the inner and outer kettles keeps the heat evenly distributed and prevents burning. The double shell cover is provided with a safety valve. The actual capacity of the kettle of the large range is 200 liters (53 gallons), and its cooking capacity is 175 liters (46 gallons). The small range holds 125 liters (33 gallons) and can cook about 110 liters (29 gallons) of soup, stew, boiled meat, or vegetables at one time.

(3) *Coffee kettle.* The coffee kettle has a single shell but a double cover with a safety valve. Ninety liters (24 gallons) of coffee can be pre-

pared at one time in the large range, and 60 liters (16 gallons) in the small one. There is a faucet to draw off the coffee. There is also a broiler in some of the ranges. All have a separate fire box, but use the same chimney.

(4) *Food containers*. After the food has been prepared, it may be transported forward in insulated food containers, six of which are provided with each large rolling field kitchen, four with each small one. These containers hold 12 liters (about 12½ quarts) and weigh about 18 pounds. They consist of an inner and an outer container with air space between them to act as insulation. Special carrying harnesses may be attached to the rings at the four corners of the back.

3. Field Ranges

Field ranges are provided for motorized units. These consist of the same type ranges as used with the rolling field kitchen mounted on a stand in the back of a truck. The supplies which accompany the range are packed in a special chest.

4. Fireless Cookers

Either large or small fireless cookers may be provided for units of less than 60 men. The large fireless cooker outfit, which weighs 77 pounds, has an insert kettle of 25 liters capacity, while the small one, weighing 53 pounds, has a pot of 15 liters capacity. A cooking fork, butcher's knife, and ladle, as well as a coffee sieve complete the outfit.

5. Cooking Outfit, 15

This 29-pound cooking outfit is issued to groups smaller than those using the fireless cooker. It consists of three nesting pots of 9, 10, and 12 liters (2 to 2½ gallons) capacity, with a ladle, 10 plates, and 10 combination fork-spoons.

6. Bakery Equipment

a. BAKE OVEN TRAILER. The German field bake oven consists of a trailer with draw-hearth type ovens, heated by the steam-pipe principle. Seven trailers are issued per bakery company.

b. DOUGH MIXER. The German dough mixer, mounted on a single axle trailer, is operated by a gasoline engine. Two are authorized per bakery company.

CHAPTER IX

UNIFORMS, INSIGNIA, AND INDIVIDUAL EQUIPMENT

Section I. ARMY UNIFORMS

I. General

a. PREWAR DEVELOPMENTS. In peacetime the German Army provided its personnel with both a service and a field unifom. The service uniform is an extremely gaudy form of dress. Its purpose was to promote enlistments, and to induce soldiers to vie for the various embellishments awarded for skills, service, and rank. The field uniform was designed to retain these advantages as far as possible, while at the same time providing a practical field uniform. Its designers bore in mind considerations of comfort (fit, warmth in cold weather, coolness in hot weather, body ventilation), utility (adequate pockets, and support for individual equipment, arms, grenades, and ammunition), and security (relative inconspicuousness in different seasons and in different types of terrain). Because of anticipated strategic and production conditions, economic factors had great influence on the field uniform. In particular, the necessity of stockpiling wool and cotton against probable wartime shortages caused the Germans to mix about 30 per cent of rayon with the wool of the uniform cloth. So carefully was this material prepared that the resultant uniforms suffered little actual loss of thermal efficiency and wearing quality.

Armored and mountain troops were provided with special uniforms, while special clothing items were furnished personnel engaged in various other special tasks or on duty in unusual weather conditions. Nevertheless, prior to 1939, there was a remarkable degree of standardization in German Army uniforms, and an equally remarkable emphasis upon retention of traditional features and appurtenances designed to improve individual morale and to cultivate arm and unit *esprit de corps*.

b. WARTIME DEVELOPMENTS. The prolongation of the war into 1942 resulted in a need for simplification of the field uniform, and in the use of a poorer quality cloth. By the winter of 1943-44, the average wool content of the field uniform cloth had sunk to approximately 50 per cent, with some uniforms dropping as low as 40 per cent. The wool itself was of low quality because it had been re-worked. These recent field uniforms present a shoddy appearance even when new; they also have very poor thermal insulation, and when wet lack strength. The press of economic conditions resulted in the introduction on 25 September 1944 of an entirely new field uniform—the Model 1944. This uniform will replace that designed in 1936 as stocks of the latter are exhausted. The new field uniform is designed to conserve resources and to permit production by relatively unskilled labor.

As the quality of the uniform has decreased, the German High Comand has sought to bolster morale by exploiting to the utmost the esteem-building effect inherent in badges, awards, decorations, and arm bands, as well as marks of special units, rank, and specialty. German troops have prized these various symbols so highly that they usually wear them on the field of battle, even though personal security is compromised by nullification of protective coloration, by permitting the singling out of key or expert personnel by enemy observers and snipers, or by facilitating the operations of Allied intelligence. Indeed, such has been the disregard for security on the part of noncommissioned officers and men that they have worn silver instead of dull gray insignia whenever the former has been procurable.

Further recent developments include the provision of additional special uniforms required by the development of specialized troops and the necessity of campaigning under unforeseen conditions of extreme heat and cold. The service uniform has been confined to officers already owning them, officer candidate battalions, higher staffs in the rear, permanent parties of service schools, and similar personnel.

2. Service Uniform

a. GENERAL. Whereas many armies have both dress and service uniforms, in the German Army the service coat (*Waffenrock*) and trousers serve as the basis for the following varieties of dress:

(1) *Gesellschaftanzug*. This is the dress uniform, which in turn is divided into *grossen* (ceremonial) and *kleine* (ordinary) *Gesellschaftanzug*. Long trousers and high black shoes always are worn with this type of uniform. Officers may wear white jackets during appropriate seasons.

(2) *Ausgehanzug*. This is a type of uniform which might be termed "walking-out dress". In the peacetime Army, it was a most important uniform, since it gave noncommissioned officers and enlisted men an opportunity to display themselves while on pass. It includes service cap, service coat, long piped trousers, high black shoes, and black belt with saber (for senior noncommissioned officers) or decorative bayonet (for junior noncommissioned officers and men). Decorations and awards may be worn, together with a colored tassel on the sword or bayonet. For officers and senior noncommissioned officers, this tassel indicates rank; for others, it indicates by its color the wearer's unit within the regiment.

(3) *Meldeanzug*. This uniform, much like "walking-out dress", is worn on minor occasions.

(4) *Dienstanzug*. This is the service dress proper, worn when attending classes, on duty in an office, or performing other duties not calling for the field uniform.

(5) *Paradeanzug*. This uniform is similar to "walking-out dress", but resembles the field uniform in that steel helmet, boots, and (for enlisted men) cartridge pouches are worn.

b. SERVICE COAT. The service coat (Plate I), which forms the basis for all these uniforms, is highly decorative. The same basic formfitting coat

is used for all ranks. The base color is the warm, field green known to the Germans as "field gray" (*feldgrau*). Collar and cuffs are covered with a dark bluish-green imitation velvet, which also appears as the base for any sleeve insignia that may be worn. The front edge of the eight-button coat opening, the lower edge of the collar, and the upper part of the cuffs are piped in the color of the wearer's arm. Fancy silver patches with buttons are worn on the cuffs. These patches, together with the collar patches, are each mounted on a velvet base dyed in the color of arm. Noncommissioned officers wear silver braid on the upper edge of collar and cuffs, and around the shoulder straps. They therefore present an even gaudier appearance than commissioned officers. Officers and noncommissioned officers of the *Reichswehr* may wear *Reichswehr* coats with proper insignia as service dress (Plate II). These coats also are worn sometimes in the field. Though service coats are of wool, officers may have cotton ones privately tailored for summer wear.

c. SERVICE TROUSERS. The service trousers or breeches made of bluish-gray wool cloth, are piped along the sides in the color of arm. On both sides of this piping General Staff and general officers add a broad stripe in the proper color. Officers may wear service breeches in the field.

d. SERVICE CAP. The service cap is similar to the U. S. Army service cap, but is upswept to give the wearer the appearance of height. The visor is black, with a silvercorded chin strap for officers, and a black leather strap for noncommissioned officers and men. The cap band is of dark, bluish-green imitation velvet (blue-gray for *Sonderführer*), piped top and bottom in the color of arms. Piping also appears around the crown of the cap. The cap cover is field-gray. The national emblem (an eagle, stylized differently for the different Armed Forces and Party organizations), and below it the national colors (black, white, and red) surrounded by oak leaves, are worn on the cap front. Officers often wear service caps in the field.

3. Field Uniform

Since anticipated economic conditions precluded the provision of both service and field uniforms for all German Army personnel, the German Army field uniform was designed to perform the dual purpose of field and service uniform. It therefore retains as many of the morale-raising features of the service uniform as possible. In

Figure 1.—Army national emblem, worn on the right breast of the field and service coat and on the front of caps. The eagle is silver or gray, on a dark green background. The background is black for the black uniform. Navy personnel wear a similar gold eagle.

wartime, the field uniform is worn in combat and on all occasions except those that call for a fatigue or work uniform. As the war has progressed, the number of embellishments worn on the field uniform has tended to increase, except where economic conditions have interfered. The field uniform includes the following components (some of which have undergone changes during the war as noted):

a. HEADGEAR. (1) *Steel helmet.* The present steel helmet, M1935, is used by all branches of the German Armed forces, although some World War I helmets as well as Czech and Italian helmets still are in use. The M1935 is a smaller and lighter version of the World War I German helmet, from which it can be differentiated by the absence of facepiece lugs which characterized the old helmet. It comes in five basic sizes, which weigh from 1.8 to 2.7 pounds. Two ventilation holes are furnished at the sides. The suspension consists of an adjustable, leather-padded, spring-aluminum band, secured at the sides and rear of the helmet by three cotter keys. The chin strap is leather. Prior to the war, the national colors were worn on the right side of the helmet and the national emblem on the left side. These emblems are no longer worn.

(2) *Old-style field cap.* The old-style field cap (Plate I) is of field-gray wool-rayon cloth. It is cut similarly to the U. S. WAC garrison (oversea) cap, except that the turn-up is scalloped downward in front. This scallop is provided so that the eyes are left uncovered when the turn-up is lowered to protect the neck and ears. The front of the cap is decorated with the national emblem and the national colors. An inverted "V" in the color of arm at one time enclosed the national colors. Officers wear silver braid around the top of the crown and along the edge of the scallop (Plate II). The cap is designed to be worn under the steel helmet.

(3) *M1942 field cap.* The M1942 cap is an early type of field cap, tried out in 1936, and re-issued in 1942 as a new type. It resembles the old-style field cap, except that the turn-up is buttoned in front (Plate III). The turn-up flaps may be buttoned across the chin.

(4) *M1943 field cap (Einheitsmütze).* In 1943 a visored wool-rayon cap was introduced (Plate III) for all types of troops. Like the mountain cap and M1942 field cap, the turn-up may be used to protect the ears and back of the neck, with the buttoned flaps securing across the chin. The turn-

Figure 2.—*Field Cap M1942. The mountain cap and the Field Cap M1943 may be worn with the turn-down buttoned across the chin. The toque is shown worn under the cap.*

Figure 3.—*Believed to be the M1944 Field Uniform coat. The material incorporates a large amount of rayon.*

Figure 4.—Latest type of field uniform trousers with built-in cloth belt, known as Rundbundhosen. The belt buckle shown is that of the Waffen-SS.

up feature is unhandy and ineffective, even if the winter wool toque is worn underneath the cap. National emblem and colors are worn as on the other types of cap.

(5) *Toque.* A wool-rayon knit toque is issued to protect the head and neck in cold weather. It may be worn under the cap or helmet (*Figure 2*). This toque is not a balaclava helmet, but consists of an unshaped sleeve with neck and face openings.

b. Body Clothing. (1) *Coat.* The coat (*Feldbluse*) has appeared in several models.

(a) *Prewar coat.* The prewar coat was designed to be as handsome as possible, while at the same time providing a comfortable, practical, field coat affording maximum security and utility. Four pleated patch pockets are provided, with an inner pocket along the lower part of the right front flap for the first-aid kit. The gray-painted, stamped metal buttons are quickly removable, and are standard for all Armed Force uniforms. The sleeve ends are split so that they may be buttoned fairly snugly around the wrist. The collar is built like the collar of a U. S. shirt, except that it is stiff and is worn without a tie. Until 1943 the coat collar was protected by a sweat band (*Kragenbinde*) which buttoned to the inside of the collar. The coat collar was designed to be worn closed, although the collar hooks and top coat button might be freed in the field. Support for personal equipment is furnished by two adjustable metal belt holders in both front and rear. These coats were furnished with dark, bluish-green, imitation velvet collars and shoulder straps. Similar material was used as a backing for the national emblem worn on the right breast (often mistaken for an aviator's wings), and for chevrons and specialty badges.

Officers' prewar field coats are similar to those for noncommissioned officers and men, except that cuffs are worn. Officers, however, may wear the issue coat with proper insignia. General officers wear gold buttons and a gold national emblem. Chaplains' coats always have been distinguished by lack of shoulder straps. Since officers purchase their uniforms privately, some officers have acquired cotton field uniforms of field-gray color for summer wear.

(b) *Wartime changes.* As mentioned above, material shortages and production difficulties resulted in a lowering of the quality of the coat material. Besides the shoddy appearance of the newer coat, the most noticeable differences are the

Figure 5.—Field gray uniform for crews of self-propelled guns. These units now wear death's head collar patches.

absence since mid-1943 of pocket pleats, and the use of straight-edge instead of pointed pocket flaps. The color of the cloth also tends towards a gray rather than a warm green. (Compare in Plate I the private in field uniform, who wears the prewar coat, with the first sergeant in mountain uniform, who wears the later type of coat.) Necessity finally has compelled adoption of the Model 1944 coat (see *Figure 3*), the main apparent differences of which are tailoring modifications permitting the use of less skilled labor and the conservation of materials.

(2) *Trousers.* (a) *Prewar trousers.* Until 1943, full trousers of the same field-gray material as the field uniform coat were issued to the German Army. Suspenders are used with this type of trousers which have two sets of suspender buttons sewn in place. Many of these trousers have reinforcements in the seat. Many have semi-breeches legs, so that the leg ends easily may be fitted into the marching boot. Two slanting buttoned front pockets, a buttoned hip pocket, and a watch pocket with ring are provided. The trousers may be tightened at the waist by means of two tapes and a metal buckle in the rear.

(b) *Belted trousers (Rundbundhosen).* In 1943 the German Army was issued field uniform trousers with built-in cloth belt after the style of *Afrika Korps* clothing. The decision to drop suspender trousers was governed by two considerations: the impracticability of suspenders when only shirt and trousers are worn, and the inconvenient and, under combat conditions, dangerous necessity of removing the coat and battle equipment to let down the trousers. These trousers are still cut high. Like ski or mountain trousers, the legs are tapered to fit into leggings or shoe-tops.

(3) *Overcoat.* The double-breasted six-button, wool-rayon overcoat is standard for all ranks, except that general officers wear gold buttons and have red lapel facings (and administrative officials in general-officer grades wear dark green facings). Collars, once of dark, bluish-green imitation velvet, now tend to be plain field-gray wool. The coat, which is cut narrow at the waist, flares at the bottom, and has two side slash pockets. The ordinary leather belt may be worn, run through slits on the side so that it runs inside the rear of the overcoat without interfering with the cloth belt at the back. Overcoats have degenerated in quality of material in the same manner as the field coats.

Figure 6.—Cotton- or linen-twill fatigue and work uniform in the cut of the field uniform coat.

(4) *Sweater*. A light-weight wool-rayon, V-neck sweater always has been furnished as part of the field uniform. It is worn under the coat. A green band around the neck distinguishes Army sweaters; Air Force sweaters have a gray-blue band.

(5) *Gloves*. A pair of field-gray knit wool-rayon gloves is furnished in the winter with the field uniform.

(6) *Underwear*. (a) *Prewar type*. The type of Army underwear issued until 1943 consists of a long-sleeved undershirt and long underdrawers, worn in all seasons. They are made of medium-weight, tricot (machine-knit) cotton cloth, which gradually has incorporated increasing amounts of rayon. Since the war began, an increasing proportion of Army underwear has been dyed green for camouflage.

(b) *1943 shirt*. In 1943 the collarless undershirt was replaced by a green tricot combination shirt-undershirt with collar and two buttoned breast pockets. The shirt remains a pullover type. The collar obviates the need for a sweatband inside the coat collar. When worn with the coat collar closed, the shirt shows slightly above the edge of the coat collar. When the coat is worn with the collar hooks and top button open, the shirt collar is worn outside the coat collar (see the 1st sergeant in mountain uniform, Plate I). The provision of a fairly presentable shirt-undershirt makes possible a coatless summer uniform.

c. Footgear. (1) *Footwraps and socks*. The German soldier is furnished with long, wool-rayon socks and with footwraps. The latter are of the best quality wool or of cotton flannel, cut in large squares. One square is wrapped around each foot over the socks before the shoe or boot is put on. Boots are fitted to two pair of socks, or one pair of socks and one pair of footwraps.

(2) *Jack boots (Marschstiefel)*. Short boots have been the traditional footgear of German soldiers for centuries. This type of footgear, however, both requires an inordinate amount of leather and causes unnecessary wear on the heel during the march. The traditional marching jack boot therefore has received much adverse criticism in the German military press. By 1941 its use was limited to infantry, engineers, and motorcyclists. Issue finally has been completely suspended, although existing stocks will be used up.

(3) *Anklet leggings*. Short leggings worn with high shoes now replace the jack boot. The leggings are of cotton or linen duck, with the

lower edge rimmed with leather. Each legging is secured on the outside with two leather straps with metal buckles.

(4) *High shoes (Schnürschuh).* High laced leather service shoes have always been part of the field uniform issued by the German Army. They now replace the boot entirely, instead of serving as alternate footgear.

d. FATIGUE OR WORK CLOTHING. Prior to the war and during its first 2 years, individuals might be issued both a work suit and a fatigue suit with the field uniform. Generally only one was issued each man, the work suit being reserved for those with heavy tasks, such as motor maintenance. Both are cut in the same style, but the work suit is of unbleached linen woven as herringbone twill, while the fatigue suit is of a lighter linen herringbone twill dyed a rush green (Plate III). In 1943 a fatigue coat, cut in the style of the field uniform coat, was issued. This latter type, often of a cloth containing a high percentage of rayon, may serve as a summer uniform.

e. ISSUE. The field uniform as described above is issued to all troops except those requiring special uniforms or special clothing issue because of unusual tasks or because they are expected to operate under abnormal terrain or weather conditions.

4. Special Uniforms and Clothing

Special clothing issued to German Army troops varies from minor changes or additions to the field uniforms, to uniforms of completely different cut, color, and material.

a. BLACK UNIFORM. Prior to the war, a black uniform was furnished crews of German Army tanks and armored cars. This uniform, which has undergone slight changes, now is worn by crews of "Elephants", by tank-destroyer and assault-gun crews in *Panzer* and *Panzer Grenadier* divisions, and by tank and armored-car crews.

(1) *Headgear.* (a) *Beret.* Until the winter of 1939-40, troops wearing the black uniform wore a black beret, which served as a crash helmet. This helmet type of headgear proved unnecessary.

(b) *Black field cap.* During the winter of 1939-40, a black, wool-rayon field cap, in the style of the old-style Army field cap, replaced the black beret.

(c) *1934 black field cap (Einheitsmütze).* Simultaneously with the introduction of the field-gray *Einheitsmütze* for the normal field uniform, the black uniform received a similar visored cap

in black cloth. Insignia and braid for officers follow the field-gray cap pattern.

(2) *Body clothing.* (a) *Coat.* The black, double-breasted, wool-rayon coat issued with the black uniform is known as the "field jacket" (*Feldjacke*). It is illustrated in Plate II. Recent jackets lack the piping on the edge of the collar, and some may have large pockets on the left breast. The coat is made of the same quality of wool-rayon cloth as the field uniform. It is dyed black to conceal dirt and grease stains. A metal death's head is worn on each collar patch.

(b) *Trousers.* The black, wool-rayon trousers of the black uniform are referred to as "Field trousers" (*Feldhosen*). They resemble the later type of normal field uniform trousers in cut, with ski-pant legs. They are fitted with tapes, however, so that they may be bound to the leg at the ankle.

(c) *Underwear.* Underwear consists of long drawers and a collared tricot shirt-undershirt with black necktie. Until 1944, this shirt was gray. Issue since that date has been green, and therefore identical with underwear for the normal field uniform.

(d) *Two-piece coverall.* For camouflage purposes, for a summer uniform, and for a work garment a two-piece coverall of rush-green cotton or rayon is issued. It is cut identically with the black wool uniform.

(3) *Footgear.* Standard black service shoes, long socks, and footwraps are worn. The use of boots with the black uniform is contrary to German regulations.

b. FIELD-GRAY UNIFORM FOR ARMORED-VEHICLE CREWS. A wool-rayon field-gray uniform, identical in cut with the black uniform, was issued in the spring of 1940 to crews of assault guns. This uniform is worn by the crews of the assault guns and tank destroyers of infantry, light infantry, and mountain infantry divisions. The uniforms bear a death's head on each collar patch. Crews of armored trains and of self-propelled infantry and antiaircraft guns wear the same uniform with the usual field uniform collar patches (Plate II). A two-piece, rush-green coverall, identical with that issued to troops wearing the black uniform, also is issued to those wearing the field-gray uniform for armored-vehicle crews.

c. MOUNTAIN UNIFORM. The mountain uniform is similar to the normal field uniform with the following exceptions:

Figure 7.—White cap cover for the mountain cap.

(1) *Cap.* The visored mountain cap, derived from the visored Austrian cap of the last war, is the original model for the M1943 *Einheitsmütze.* The mountain cap may be distinguished by a metal *Edelweiss* sewn to the left side of the cap (Plate I). A white camouflage cap cover is furnished with the cap.

(2) *Coat and overcoat.* Field uniform coats and overcoats are worn, but are embellished by an *Edelweiss* on the upper right sleeve (Plate I).

(3) *Windjacket.* The mountain windjacket is a light, double-breasted, long jacket of olive-colored, windproof, water-repellent duck (Plate III). This is less common now than the parka, which appears to be superseding it.

(4) *Sweater.* The mountain sweater, heavier than the normal field uniform sweater, has a turtle neck for added warmth.

(5) *Trousers.* Baggy trousers, designed and fitted so as not to bind the mountaineer at any point, are provided German mountain troops. These trousers are of the usual field-gray, wool-rayon cloth. Their ski-pant bottoms tie with tapes at the ankles. Special mountain suspenders are issued with these trousers.

(6) *Parka and overpants.* Until 1942, a white parka was issued on the basis of 10 per cent of unit strength. By the time of the Caucasus campaign, a new and improved type of parka, with overpants of the same material, was furnished to mountain divisions. The parka is reversible, with a tan and a white side, and is distinguished by three buttoned breast pockets. The cloth is unusual, in that the rayon fibers are designed so that some provide strength, while others swell when wet. The swelling action renders the garment water-repellent to a high degree. When dry, the fiber shrinks, permitting proper ventilation through the garment. The objective of the designers was to avoid the accumulation of sweat, which, if the wearer should rest after heavy exertion, would cause undue dampness and cooling and result in colds, pneumonia, and frostbite.

(7) *Canvas overmittens.* These mittens with leather palms are furnished in addition to the field uniform wool gloves to provide extra insulation against cold and to keep the wool gloves dry.

(8) *Ski-mountain boots.* Heavily-hobnailed, high laced shoes are provided as ski-mountain boots.

(9) *Leggings.* Until October 1944, short, wrap leggings of field-gray wool, such as those used by Austrian mountain troops in World War I, were standard for German mountaineers. Now these are being replaced by the canvas leggings isssued with the normal field uniform.

(10) *Rock-climbing shoes.* High climbing shoes with rope or felt soles are issued when necessary.

(11) *Camouflage clothing.* Prior to 1941, white parkas or white suits were issued to mountain troops for operations in snow-covered regions. The present mountain parka and windproof trousers have a tan and a white side.

d. SPECIAL CLOTHING FOR MOTORCYCLISTS. Motorcyclists receive as supplementary clothing a raincoat; a pair of goggles; a pair of gauntlets; and, in winter, an extra sweater, wool oversocks, and a special coat. The gauntlets are of overcoat cloth with trigger finger, and may have leather palms. The footless oversocks come up high on the leg. The raincoat is a special, long, rubber coat, designed to be buttoned in a variety of ways to improve protection and to facilitate operation of the motorcycle (see motor vehicle coat in the color plates). This rubber coat also may be worn by drivers of light vehicles. In winter, a surcoat may be furnished—a heavy wool garment cut like the overcoat, but sufficiently large to be worn over all clothing including the overcoat. Recent surcoats have wool hoods.

e. SPECIAL CLOTHING FOR DRIVERS. Drivers of all types of vehicles receive motorcyclists' gauntlets, and for cold weather the surcoat. Drivers of horse transport also receive felt overboots with wooden soles.

f. SUMMER UNIFORM. Prior to 1941, no uniform for field summer wear was issued. Since that date, uniforms developed for the *Afrika Korps* have been made available to troops operating in arid and tropical climates, such as prevail in Italy, Greece, the Crimea, and the Kuban delta. Mention already has been made of the adaptation of the normal field uniform and normal fatigues as a summer uniform. The summer field uniform proper includes the following items:

(1) *Headgear.* The first *Afrika Korps* troops were provided with tropical helmets and khaki cotton field caps in the cut of the old-style field uniform cap. These soon were replaced by a visored khaki cotton field cap copied from the mountain cap.

(2) *Body clothing.* Body clothing consists of loose-mesh rayon or cotton undershorts and short-sleeved undershirt; a two-pocket, grayish-green or khaki cotton shirt carrying shoulder-strap insignia; and khaki shorts or long trousers with built-in cloth belts. Though shirtsleeves may be the uniform of the day, a roll-collar, V-necked, khaki coat is furnished. In spite of cotton shortages, the coat and trousers continue to be of good quality cotton twill. Since late 1942, however, the four pleated pockets of the coat have been modified in the same fashion as those of the normal field uniform coat. The cotton twill breeches furnished in the very early days of the *Afrika Korps* are worn only by those still possessing them.

(3) *Footgear.* Desert boots with cloth tops are no longer necessary, but still may be encountered. High brown leather shoes are now the standard wear. Wool socks, rather than footwraps, are worn.

g. WINTER UNIFORMS. (1) *Pre-1941 winter clothing.* Prior to the winter of 1941-42, the German Army made little provision for winter warfare. Mountain troops were the best equipped to fight under conditions of extreme cold and snow; the remainder of the Army received special clothing only for special missions and duties, as noted above. Sentries were the only soldiers, besides drivers and motorcyclists, who received specially designed clothing. To them were issued surcoats and felt overboots, or, if the latter were lacking, straw overboots. Ordinary troops wore the wool toque, gloves, sweater, and overcoat in winter.

(2) *Post-1941 winter clothing.* As soon as the necessity for great quantities of winter cloth-

ing became obvious, the German Army attempted numerous improvisations based on many varieties of civilian, military, and captured clothing. Even

Figure 8.—Improvised winter clothing. The ordinary overcoat has been wrapped around the legs and the lower part of the coat bound with strips of cloth secured by cords.

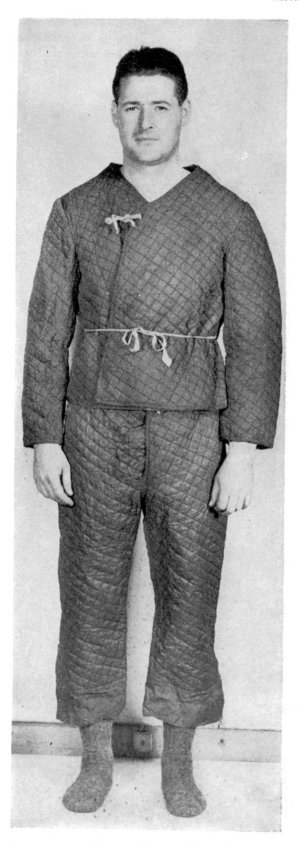

Figure 9.—Padded coat and trousers worn under the new winter uniform.

Figure 10.—The toque. Two toques are shown, one colored white to show the manner of wearing two in extreme cold.

though a standard winter uniform was developed in 1942 and issued for the winter of 1942-43, stocks have been inadequate. The necessity of providing heavy winter clothing for other than combat troops has required continued improvisations. These include rabbit-fur jackets and vests, as well as sleeveless and sleeved pile jackets of rayon known as "breastwarmers". Soviet pile caps and felt boots often are used. For sentries and others who are compelled to remain fairly motionless in the cold, overcoats and surcoats with extra linings are available. Heavy sheepskin surcoats, originated by the German Air Force, also may be used. However, a most important development is the new winter uniform.

(3) *New winter uniform.* The new winter uniform is designed to provide a confortable combat uniform giving freedom of movement and use of equipment, yet offering protection against extreme cold and overheating during periods of exertion. The uniform is worn over the normal field uniform. Cartridge pouches are worn on the normal leather belt, under the skirt of the parka. This feature aids in providing essential body ventilation to prevent the accumulation of sweat. Several clips of ammunition are kept available in the parka pocket. The hooded parka has a waist belt, bottom drawstring, and double-buttoned flaps up the front that provide a windproof

Figure 11.—Improvised camouflage coat in the cut of the Army field uniform coat. The cloth is taken from shelter duck material of an Italian shelter half.

closure. A toque is worn under the steel helmet, and when the wind is strong, a stiff, felt face mask may be fitted. The trousers have two side pockets, and fairly short legs. These legs fit over special, white, rayon-canvas boots which have fabric soles and three-layer walls. The latter may be stuffed with straw or paper as added protection against cold and moisture. Since these boots are not suited for mud conditions, ski-mountain boots or felt boots with leather soles and facings may be used instead. The parka, toque, and trousers are issued in three weights. The most common is the medium weight, in which the material consists of two layers of windproof cloth with a rayon-wool in-

Figure 12.—New winter uniform with mottled side out.

Figure 13.—Flak personnel in summer uniform.

terliner. The windproof cloth has the same water-repellent features as the latest mountain parka. Since the complete uniform contains only 9 per cent wool, the clothing is heavy for its warmth, and therefore not as efficient as the Germans had planned. The uniform originally had a white and a field-gray side, but by 1943 the need for better camouflage had become so apparent that a mottled design was substituted for the field-gray. Two designs of mottle are used— one is that of the normal shelter half, and the other is that of the Army camouflage jacket (Plate III). Both types are in use. To facilitate

recognition, cloth bands in the color of the day may be buttoned to the sleeves of the parka.

h. CAMOUFLAGE CLOTHING. The original prewar issue of a camouflage shelter half proved insufficient for the camouflage of individuals. After considerable improvisation on the part of field units, particularly in Italy, a standard Army light-rayon camouflage jacket (Plate III) was issued and put into use in 1943-44. Various types of field-made jackets, using German and Italian shelter halves, are widely employed. Snipers may wear complete camouflage suits, including face masks. Headgear camouflage often is improvised, since the Army did not provide a standard camouflage helmet cover until the issue of the camouflage jacket. But a very practical elastic band to fasten camouflage materials to the helmet was furnished to all troops. Camouflage clothing is usually organizational, and is issued to snipers, personnel of outposts, and like troops.

Section II. GERMAN ARMY INSIGNIA

1. General

German Army insignia are intended to establish clear differentiation between ranks and types of service, and at the same time to encourage individual combat efficiency and proficiency in military arts. Direct appeal is made to vanity and to the human tendency to show off military prowess as expressed in terms of insignia and decorations. Many of these insignia are based on traditional German military insignia selected from units famous in German popular and military history.

2. Insignia of Rank

Insignia of rank mainly are determined by shoulder-strap devices (Plate IV and V). While there are many minor complexities having to do with fine differentiation among various ranks, services, and functions, these do not concern the average case. A clear distinction is made among commissioned officers (*Offiziere*), noncommissioned officers (*Unteroffiziere*), and enlisted men of various grades (*Mannschaften*). Because of the importance of noncommissioned officers in combat and on the drill field, they are accorded special distinguishing marks beyond the normal insignia of rank. Along the lower edge of their coat collar they have a silver or gray braid .4 inch wide. First sergeants, as senior company or battery noncommissioned officers, wear two bands of similar braid on each coatsleeve. Distinction is made between the upper three and the lower two grades of noncommissioned officers. The former are known as *Portepeeunteroffiziere;* the latter as *Unteroffiziere ohne Portepee.* The former are entitled to special considerations and privileges, as are the first three grades of U. S. Army noncommissioned officers. These include wearing on certain occasions an officer's saber

Figure 14.—Tank destroyer uniform of the Hermann Goering Division (shoulder insignia of rank is missing on the uniform shown).

and a tassel known as the *Portepee,* hence the title. Fatigue clothing carries the type of non-commissioned-officer insignia used on *Reichswehr* uniforms.

3. Insignia of Arm and Specialty

In order to clarify an individual's duties, to afford easy recognition of line troops, and to avoid jealousy arising from rapid promotion of qualified specialists, the German Army has made a somewhat ill-organized effort to distinguish line personnel of the arms; personnel of special and administrative services, and personnel of both preceding categories who are so proficient or qualified that rapid promotion to suitable rank is necessary. The first group wear insignia of the line arms (normal insignia of rank and of arm); the specialists and administrative officials tend to be designated by varied insignia (usually by introducing a basic dark-green color); the third group (*Sonderführer*) wear modifications of normal insignia. *Sonderführer* insignia for line duty is shown in color plates; insignia for *Sonderführer* of the Corps of Administrative Officials is somewhat similar as regards the collar patch, but the shoulder strap is more difficult to differentiate. In peacetime and during the early part of the war, further differentiation was made to indicate reserve officers, *Landwehr* officers, officers recalled to active duty, and officers over the retirement age who might be required from time to time for consultation.

4. Fourrageres

All German officers are entitled to wear the fourragere shown on the officer's service dress in Plate II. Adjutants wear a single cord. The adjutant's fourragere must not be mistaken for one of the 12 grades of markmanship awards (Plate VII), and 1st sergeant in service dress (Plate I). The marksmanship awards sometimes are worn in combat.

5. Use of Numbers and Letters on Shoulder Insignia of Rank

Although the wearing of numbers and letters furnishing unit identification is forbidden in forward areas, German soldiers do not always observe this regulation. Soldiers of the Field Army, however, usually wear such identification in the form of slip-over cloth strips, with the numbers running across the shoulder strap with the length of the strip. In rear areas, numbers are worn as shown in Plates IV and V. Arabic numerals indicate the number of the regiment or battalion to which the wearer belongs. Enlisted men and the lower two grades of noncommissioned officers wear numbers in the color of their arm; other noncommissioned officers wear silver numbers, as do officer candidates. Officers wear gold numbers. Letters may be combined with Arabic numerals. In some cases (See Plate VI), these indicate units of special arms or of special branches of arms. In other cases, the letter D and an arabic numeral indicate division headquarters personnel. Since regulations have changed frequently since 1939, the system of identification by numbers and letters is difficult to follow without the aid of complex guides.

Section III. GERMAN AIR FORCE UNIFORMS AND INSIGNIA

1. General

Although many items of uniforms and clothing of special Air Force design are provided, many items are procured from the Army in suitable colors. There is not, however, the degree of standardization in Army and Air Force clothing that would appear desirable, particularly in view of the number of Air Force ground troops performing the same functions as comparable Army troops. This is especially true in regard to the uniforms provided for Africa, and now used as summer field uniforms. Characteristic of most Air Force uniforms is the gray-blue color of much of the uniforms and equipment. Comments made on the decline of cloth quality in Army uniforms are equally applicable to Air Force uniforms.

Figure 15.—Air Force national emblem, worn on the right breast of coats, overcoats, jackets, jump suits, and summer shirts.

2. Uniforms

a. SERVICE AND DRESS UNIFORMS. The German Air Force no longer has service uniforms, except for a white summer coat and a dress mess jacket for officers, and a service coat for generals. A service coat for all personnel was already in the process of being replaced in 1939. This coat (Tuchrock) resembles the present uniform coat (Waffenrock), except that it is not designed to be buttoned up to the neck. (Compare the private's and the colonel's coats on Plate VIII.)

b. NORMAL FIELD UNIFORM. (1) Headgear. The Air Force field cap (Fliegermütze) is a simple wool-rayon cap similar in cut to the present U. S. WAC garrison cap. The national colors are worn below the national emblem. Officers wear silver braid around the edge of the turn-up. The Army Einheitsmütze, in Air Force color and with proper insignia, has begun to replace the Fliegermütze. The Army M1935 steel helmet, painted gray, is issued when required.

(2) Body clothing. (a) Coat. The standard Air Force coat (Waffenrock) is a five-button coat, designed to be worn either with the collar closed at the neck, or as a roll-collared, V-neck coat with the collar hook and top button open (Plate VIII). Four pleated patch pockets are furnished, with the national emblem appearing over the right breast pocket. Two adjustable metal belt holders of Army style are located toward the sides of the uniform. The sleeves end in large cuffs. The collar at one time carried piping on the lower edge in the color of the arm. Though this feature was discontinued in 1940, such coats still may be found. Insignia of rank are worn on the shoulder and on patches located on the ends of the collar. In 1944 this coat was issued in cotton-rayon instead of wool.

(b) "Flight blouse" (Fliegerbluse). Air Force troops more commonly wear a short, cuffless, fly-front, wool-rayon jacket with slash pockets (Plate VIII). The jacket's collar may be worn open or closed. Belt holders, insignia, and piping (if the latter is worn) are placed as on the coat. The jacket is intended for crews of aircraft, and therefore is designed so that there will be no buttons, patch pockets, or cuffs to catch on projecting parts of aircraft interiors. The jacket is sufficiently convenient and smart-looking, however, to be popular with all Air Force troops.

(c) Trousers. The gray-blue, wool-rayon, Air Force trousers are similar in cut at the waist to Army suspender trousers. Air Force trousers, however, are always slacks, and are not fitted with narrow or ski-pant bottoms except in the case of mountain trousers.

(d) Shirt. Gray shirts of mottled gray-blue thread are worn with black tie. The shirts may be fitted with shoulder straps to indicate rank.

(e) Underwear. Army underwear is worn.

(f) Sweater. The Air Force sweater is identical with the Army's, except that the colored band at the neck is Air Force gray-blue.

(g) Overcoat. A blue-gray version of the Army overcoat is worn. Patches are placed on the collar. First sergeants wear their sleeve bands (Plate VIII).

(3) Footgear. The Air Force uses Army-type jack boots, shoes, socks, and footwraps. Leggings, when used, are Army leggings dyed blue-gray.

c. MOUNTAIN UNIFORM. Normal Air Force uniforms are combined with Army issue, properly colored when necessary, to make up mountain clothing (Plate VIII). The Waffenrock and mountain trousers are used, together with blue-gray, ankle-wrap leggings and ski-mountain boots. The Air Force mountain cap, which had but one button securing the turn-up in front, largely has been replaced by a cap in the style of the Army mountain cap. Army Edelweiss badges may be worn.

d. FATIGUE AND WORK SUITS. Flak crews and aircraft mechanics may be furnished with a cotton-linen-rayon, herringbone twill, black or dark blue-gray coverall with fly front (Plate IX). Two-piece work suits of various colors are also used (Plate X).

e. SUMMER UNIFORMS. Air Force issue resembles that of the Army both in history and in the nature of the items provided, except for slight modifications in all pieces of clothing. Peculiar to the Air Force are bright aluminum, built-in trouser belt buckles, and the long, baggy trousers with ankle buckles illustrated in Plate IX. As in the case of the Army, the tropical helmet no longer is worn except by those who still retain the original issue. The Air Force national emblem appears on all coats and shirts.

f. PARACHUTE TROOPS UNIFORMS. Parachute troops are issued several distinctive items. They are:

(1) Helmet. The parachute helmet, resembling a cut-down version of the M1935 steel helmet, is fitted with large sponge-rubber pads and leather suspension shaped to the skull.

(2) *Jump suit.* The older types of jump suit used in 1939-40 were of the pullover, coverall variety. The present types button up the front like coats, and have snap closures to secure the bottom tightly around the legs—a feature borrowed from the older types. Ample zipper-closed pockets are provided. The material is a light shelter duck, originally olive in color (Plate IX), but in present versions always mottled. The present jump suit, like older types, is worn over the wool or summer uniform, but can quickly be removed.

(3) *Camouflage jacket.* Usually peculiar to parachute troops (and worn by the 1st Parachute Division during the Battle of Cassino—hence the appellation "Green Devils") is a greenish, mottled camouflage jacket about the length of the jump suit. This is a fly-front, cotton, herringbone twill garment with two pockets (Plate IX).

(4) *Footgear.* Several types of jump boots have been issued. The earlier types laced along the sides and had heavy corrugated-rubber soles. Later types resemble the U. S. parachutist's boot. In battle, Army-type high service shoes may be worn.

g. WINTER CLOTHING. The Air Force uses the Army winter uniform, and improvises in the same way as the elder service. Often worn by *Flak* sentries in very exposed positions is the very heavy sheepskin surcoat shown in color plates. This coat may be worn by the entire gun crew, if necessary. It is, however, too heavy for infantry combat use.

h. UNIFORMS OF THE *Fallschirmjäger-Panzer Division Herman Goering.* This division follows unusual practices in the issue of uniforms and insignia. The collar patch is white for all ranks, while the color of the shoulder strap varies according to type of service. Tank crews and crews of self-propelled guns wear Army black or field-gray jackets and field trousers, but with Air Force insignia.

3. Insignia

Air Force insignia are extremely complex. There are four systems of indicating rank: that used on the shoulder straps and on sleeve chevrons; that used on the collar patch; that used on flying suits; and that used on both sleeves of the motor vehicle coat and on fatigue coveralls. The collar patches of noncommissioned officers' overcoats, and their coat collars, are edged with silver braid in the manner of Army noncommissioned officers' coats. The awards for combat flights (see color plates) easily may be mistaken for pilots' insignia because of their shape. The pilot's insignia, however, is worn as a metal or cloth badge on the lower left breast, whereas the awards for combat flights are worn above the left breast pocket. Not illustrated under awards in the color plates is that for night fighters, which consists of the award for fighters with a black instead of a silver winged arrow. Air Force personnel are awarded marksmanship badges of a design similar to that of Army awards. Other fourrageres are worn, indicating commissioned rank, adjutant, or merely length of service.

Figure 16.—National emblem of the Armed Party Elite Guard (Waffen-SS). This emblem is worn on the left sleeves of coats, overcoats, and jackets, and appears either on the front or on the left side of caps.

Section IV. ARMED ELITE GUARD UNIFORMS AND INSIGNIA.

I. Uniforms

The Armed Elite Guard (*Waffen-SS*) has followed the Army closely in the provision of uniform clothing. When first sent into the field, *Waffen-SS* units were distinguished in part by the type of roll-collar V-neck coat shown in Plate XVIII. Also distinctive were their camouflage jacket (Plate XVIII), and their brown shirts with black ties. For some time stocks of the *SS* coat have been practically exhausted, and Army coats have been used. Army shirts also are issued. There remain slight differences between the high grade shelter-duck, water-repellent, windproof *SS* camouflage jacket and the similar Army jacket; the *SS* jacket has two slant, buttoned pockets at its side in later versions, and a different camouflage pattern.

A new *Waffen-SS* uniform is a linen-cotton, herringbone twill, two-piece suit (Plate XIX).

SS regulations forbid wearing insignia on the collar of this uniform, but troops have shown an increasing tendency to include all possible insignia devices. However, no insignia are worn on the one-piece tank coverall (Plate XVIII). In general, *Waffen-SS* uniform clothing differs from that of the Army only in respect to the above items, and in the more complete authorized issue to *Waffen-SS* troops. Moreover, when complete issue cannot be made, the *Waffen-SS* troops always receive fuller issue than their Army neighbors. *Waffen-SS* troops now also receive the army winter uniform, which replaces the special *SS* pullover parka illustrated in Plate XIX.

2. Insignia

Waffen-SS troops wear shoulder insignia of rank similar to those of the Army, but wear collar patches of the *General-SS*. The sleeve insignia of rank, worn on camouflage jackets, coveralls, and similar clothing, is the same as that worn by corresponding Army grades. The grades of snipers' badges, shown in color plates, are issued to *Waffen-SS* as well as to Army personnel. Rifle regiments of *SS*-Police divisions wear collar patches similar to those worn by officers and men of the Army. The distinctive insignia of the *Waffen-SS* is the *SS* national emblem worn on the upper left sleeve. Noncommissioned officers wear silver braid along the edge of the collar in the manner of Army noncommissioned officers.

3. Uniforms and Insignia of the Security Service of the *Waffen-SS*

This uniform consists of the ordinary *SS* field uniform with Police shoulder straps to indicate rank, *SS* collar patches, and an *SD* badge (for *Sicherheitsdienst*) on the lower left sleeve.

Figure 18.—Uniform of the Security Service (Sicherheitsdienst) of the Waffen-SS.

Section V. GERMAN DECORATIONS

German decorations for valor consist of the various grades of Iron Cross shown on Plate XXII, together with the Honor Roll Clasp. In actuality, iron crosses of the first and second classes may be allotted in bulk to combat units, whether or not the personnel are individually deserving of such decorations. At one time there appeared to be some plan on the part of German authorities to keep locations of the various types of decorations, combat service, and ordinary service, and ordinary service awards distinct and recognizable as such even to the relatively uninitiated. In brief, this plan seemed to be to locate campaign and ordinary service awards above the left breast pocket in the form of ribbons, with participation in notable campaigns indicated by badges on the sleeve. Combat and wounds would be indicated by badges of bronze, silver, and gold located on the left breast, while actual decorations

Figure 17.—Waffen-SS camouflage jacket with buttoned pockets.

Figure 19.—German Air Force officers wearing decorations and awards.

would be worn as ribbons in the buttonhole, at the neck, or in the form of the easily recognizable actual metal medal pinned on the uniform. This rule holds as a rough guide, but there are many exceptions, notable among which are the various foreign ribbons for valor worn with other ribbons above the left breast pocket. Marksmanship awards are worn in the form of fourrageres across the right breast.

The German Armed Forces place much emphasis on the morale effect of the various decorations and awards, the numbers of which are almost incredibly large because of the authorization of the wearing of Nazi Party and Police badges, as well as foreign decorations and those of minor German states under the German Empire. Much of the paper-work of the German Army is concerned with the awarding of various types of medals and badges and their certificates. The German troops themselves prize these honors highly, and wear them on the field uniform even in combat.

Section VI. AUXILIARY FORCES AND SEMI-MILITARY ORGANIZATIONS

I. General

There are a host of puppet and auxiliary forces and semi-military organizations which may take part in combat alongside the Army, Navy, and Air Force. Included among these are the various units raised from former citizens of the Soviet Union. While many of these troops were intended to have insignia peculiar to their organization, it has not been possible in practice to manufacture and issue the necessary uniforms and insignia. The insignia for these forces may be grouped into three sets: those for the Eastern Legions (*Ostlegionen*), those for the Russian and Ukranian Armies of Liberation (with rank insignia after the Russian style), and those for Cossack units. In practice, German Army uniforms and insignia often are used. Military organizations with uniforms and insignia also were formed from men recruited from the former Baltic states. A Czech puppet Army, with its own uniforms and insignia, also exists. The Italian Republican Army also may use German uniforms and *Waffen-SS* insignia, although Italian Republican insignia may be worn on German-made uniforms. Women's uniformed auxiliary forces include signal services for the Army, Navy, and Air Force; antiaircraft personnel for the Air Force; and remount units for the Army. Such personnel have uniforms, insignia, and titles of rank peculiar to their organizations. Many uniformed Party organizations of a semi-military nature exist, as well as Frontier (Customs) Guards, Railway Police, State Railway Personnel, the Forestry Service, and other uniformed state organizations. Uniforms and insignia of several of the more important auxiliary organizations serving with the armed forces are briefly described below. These organizations usually wear an arm band inscribed *Deutsche Wehrmacht* when in forward areas. The Germans state that such arm bands indicate that the wearers are members of the German Armed Forces.

Figure 20.—Labor Service private (left), sergeant (center), and general officer (right).

Figure 21.—Uniform of an enlisted man of the German State Police.

2. *Volkssturm* Uniforms and Insignia

The German *Volkssturm* has no authorized uniform or insignia except for an armband variously stenciled *Deutscher Wehrmacht* or *Deutscher Volkssturm* with *Wehrmacht* directly underneath the upper two words. These bands may be in a variety of colors: black letters on red or white cloth, or white letters on yellow cloth. Clothing is issued according to what is available in the area. *Volkssturm* personnel are reported to be unwilling to fight if furnished only with armbands for fear of being arrested as *franc tireurs*. Efforts have therefore been made to provide Army issue when possible. This issue is supplemented by captured clothing: Italian, Czech, French, and so on. Uniforms of Nazi party organizations may also be worn. It is reported that personnel with civil and party uniforms such as street car crews, zoo keepers, postmen, *SA* men, etc. will have such uniforms dyed military field gray. The only known insignia of rank is the following:

German Rank	English Equivalent	Collar Patch Insignia
Volkssturmmann	Private	No pips
Gruppenführer	Squad Leader	One pip
Zugführer	Platoon Leader	Two pips horizontally
Waffenmeister	Ordnance Officer	Same as above
Zahlmeister	Paymaster	Same as above
Kompanieführer	Company Commander	Three pips diagonally
Ordonnanzoffizier	Administrative Officer	Same as above
Adjutant	Adjutant	Same as above
Bataillonführer	Battalion Commander	Four pips in square

3. Labor Service Uniforms and Insignia

Members of the Labor Service (*Reichsarbeitsdienst,* or *RAD*), wear uniforms with chocolate-brown collars. The coats generally are cut in the style of the Army field uniform coat. The rank insignia resemble and roughly follow those of the Army, although distinctive titles are employed. A stylized spade is used for the cap badge, and appears on the belt buckle.

4. Police Uniforms and Insignia

German State Police uniforms may readily be differentiated from Army uniforms by proper identification of the Police coat. This coat has four

Figure 22.—Company commander of the Volkssturm. The overcoat is the standard Army issue, worn with the field cap M1943. The man at right wears an Italian Army overcoat.

patch pockets, the lower two being pleatless (Fig. 21). The frontal closure is secured by eight buttons. Both collar and cuffs are brown in color, the latter each bearing two buttons. While the collar insignia for lower ranks resemble those of the Army, the collar patch rectangle is surrounded by a silver cord. However, police officers of general's rank wear *SS* collar patches (color plates), since they hold ranks in both *SS* and Police. Field and company grade police officers wear shoulder straps and collar patches similar to equivalent Army ranks, and are addressed by Army titles of rank. A national emblem similar to the sleeve insignia for Army Military police (color plates) is worn on the upper left sleeve, but no other national emblem is worn on the coat. This emblem is repeated on Police caps. The back of the police coat has a decorative double fly embellished with four buttons.

Section VII. INDIVIDUAL EQUIPMENT

1. Field Equipment

a. BELT. The German soldier habitually wears his belt, with or without field equipment. Normally the enlisted man wears a black leather belt, but a web belt goes with the tropical uniform. The belt always is worn with a steel buckle bearing the branch of service emblem. All ground forces of the Army (*Heer*) have a buckle embossed with a circular crest in the center of which appears an eagle. The circle is formed by the words "Gott mit uns" above the eagle and a wreath below. The Air Force (*Luftwaffe*) buckle carries an eagle in flight with a swastika in its claws. The figure is encircled by a wreath. The Armed Elite Guard (*Waffen SS*) buckle bears

an eagle whose outstretched wings extend across the top of the buckle. The words "Meine Ehre heisst Treue" make a nearly complete circle below the eagle's wings. The bird rests on another smaller circle which bears a swastika. Officers wear brown leather belts with a simple tongue-and-bar type buckle. In the field the soldier carries his cartridge pouches, bayonet, entrenching tool, and "bread bag" suspended from this belt. When not wearing field equipment he wears the belt and buckle alone. Metal hooks in the field blouse help hold the belt in place.

b. CARTRIDGE POUCHES. The usual German cartridge pouch is made of leather. It has three separate pockets, each holding 10 rounds of rifle ammunition in two clips. The uniform belt slips through loops on the back of the ammunition

Figure 23.—Field equipment of the German infantry soldier (front view). The cartridge pouches on the belt are partially held by leather suspenders. The "bread bag" and canteen with cup are carried on the right hip, and the entrenching tool and bayonet are carried on the left hip. The "bread bag" is hung on the belt, and for demonstration purposes is shown further forward than usual.

Figure 24.—Field equipment (rear view). Messkit, shelter quarter, and a small bag (concealed under the shelter quarter) are strapped to the combat pack. The canteen hangs from the "bread bag." (Mounted troops carry the canteen on the bread bag's right-hand fittings). The upper end of the metal gas mask carrier is suspended by a sling over the shoulder, while the rear end is hung on the belt.

pouch, which also has a ring into which the cartridge belt suspenders may be hooked to help support the equipment worn on the belt. Normally two pouches are worn, one on each side of the belt buckle, allowing the rifleman to carry 60 rounds of ammunition. However, soldiers who are not expected to use a great deal of ammunition receive only one pouch, and a leather loop with a ring is substituted for the second pouch to hold the cartridge belt suspenders. Other types of cartridge carriers include submachine-gun ammunition pouches, engineer assault pack pouches, and bandoleers. The submachine-gun pouches, now usually made of webbing, hold six clips. They are about 9 inches long and are carried in a manner similar to the ordinary pouch. The 120-round bandoliers, usually of camouflage pattern, are worn by paratroops slung across the chest. They are held in place by loops slipped over the belt. Medical soldiers receive single-pocket, leather, first-aid pouches which are somewhat deeper and about two-thirds as wide as the ordinary cartridge pouch.

c. ENTRENCHING SHOVEL. Although some of the old-style German entrenching shovels, which are like the old U. S. army shovel, still exist, most German troops are equipped with the standard folding shovel, similar to the standard U. S. entrenching tool. The German shovel consists of a 6 by 8½-inch pointed steel blade hinged to an 18-inch wooden handle. The hinge is provided with a threaded plastic nut which locks the blade in any one of three positions: in line with the handle for use as a shovel, at right angles to the handle for use as a pick, or folded back against the handle for carrying. A leather case for carrying the shovel is suspended from the cartridge belt on the left hip. Since the shovel serves as an adequate pick, few entrenching pick-mattocks are used.

d. BAYONET FROG. The bayonet hangs from the cartridge belt in a leather frog just ahead of the folding entrenching shovel or directly over the old-style entrenching shovel. A loop on the shovel case holds the scabbard in place.

e. BREAD BAG. The German soldier carries the bread bag (*Brotbeutel*) on his right hip, suspended from the belt. This duck bag holds toilet articles, the field cap when not worn, a towel, and other necessities of the combat soldier. Dismounted personnel carry the canteen snapped into the left hook on the flap of the bread bag. It is held securely in place by slipping the strap which

Figure 25.—Parachutists bandolier, holding 120 rounds of ammunition in rifle clips.

runs around the canteen through the loop on the lower part of the bread-bag flap. Mounted personnel carry the canteen on the right side of the bread bag. Formerly a special strap was used more frequently to allow the bread bag to be slung over the shoulder.

f. CANTEEN. The canteen, which holds nearly one quart, has a felt cover. The canteen cup, either round or oval, is strapped upside down over the mouth of the canteen. The first of these German canteens were made of aluminum, but about 1942 a few were made of a plastic impregnated wood and recent ones have been made of enameled steel. Mountain troops receive a slightly larger canteen. Special medical canteens are issued to medical troops.

g. GAS MASK. The only other item which commonly is suspended in part from the belt is the gas mask in its metal carrier. The top of the carrier is held by a strap which runs around the right shoulder. The bottom is hooked to the back of the belt. Paratroops receive a special fabric gas-mask carrier to reduce the danger of injuries in landing.

2. Combat Equipment

a. CARTRIDGE-BELT SUSPENDERS. There are a number of different types of leather cartridge-belt suspenders issued to German troops and webbing counterparts for use with the tropical uniform. The commonest of these are the infantry suspenders. These are issued to combat troops of infantry divisions who also receive the combat pack and the Model 39 haversack. The infantry suspenders consist of straps with hooks on the front to attach to the cartridge pouches and a single broad hook in back, which is slipped under the cartridge belt. D-rings on the back of the shoulder straps may be used to hold the top of the combat pack, the haversack, or other equipment. The bottom of these suspenders are held by auxiliary straps riveted to the suspenders in front just below the shoulders. Other common types include officers' cartridge-belt suspenders and cavalry suspenders.

b. COMBAT PACK. The normal infantryman's combat pack is a webbing trapezoid with a removable bag buttoned to the bottom. A single strap on the top half of the web frame is used to attach the mess kit and two straps at the bottom hold the shelter quarter, tightly rolled, over the small bag. There are hooks at all four corners so that the combat pack may be attached to the infantry cartridge-belt suspenders. A small pocket on the inside of the bag flap holds the rifle-cleaning kit. Normally the tent rope, one day's iron rations, and a sweater are carried in the bag. However, many times the rope, tent pole, and pins are carried rolled inside the shelter quarter. If necessary a horseshoe roll of overcoat or possibly a blanket may be attached to the combat pack by three straps, which run through the rectangular eyelets on the top and on each side of the pack.

c. MESS KIT. The mess kit, formerly aluminum but now made of enameled steel, is usually carried on the combat pack, although it is sometimes attached to the bread bag in the same way as the canteen. Similar to the Russian and Japanese mess kit, it consists of a kind of deep pot with a cover which may be inverted for use as a plate.

d. SHELTER QUARTER. The German shelter quarter serves both as a tent and as a poncho. It is highly water-repellent duck cut in the form of

Figure 26.—Four shelter quarters pitched as a pyramidal tent. These carry the Waffen-SS camouflage pattern.

an isosceles triangle about 6 feet 3 inches along the base and 8 feet 3 inches along the other two sides. There are buttons and buttonholes on all three edges. The shelter quarter is covered with a camouflage mottle, either the characteristic army camouflage pattern or the usual *Waffen SS* pattern. Some have different patterns on each side, greens predominating on one side and browns on the other. Each soldier also is issued two tent pins and one tent-pole section for use when the shelter quarter is made into a tent. Ordinarily four men pitch their sections together to make a small pyramidal tent, but other combinations are possible, the most common of which are eight- and 16-man tents. The eight-man tent is constructed by erecting two three-sided pyramids and buttoning an inverted shelter half in the space between them. The 16-man tent is made by joining four of the long sides of the eight-man tent. A regular, four-section, pyramidal tent is erected on this base. This tent stands over 9 feet high. Worn as a poncho, the shelter quarter provides good protection from rain because of its excellent water-repellent property. The soldier's head can be thrust through a slit with the narrow point of the triangle in front. The two rear points are brought forward and buttoned together. Slits are left open for the arms, around which the poncho drapes almost as if it has sleeves. Motorcyclists can fasten the shelter quarter around the thighs.

3. Other Packs

a. MODEL 39 HAVERSACK. Troops to whom the combat pack is issued also receive the Model 39 haversack. This square-shaped canvas pack, reinforced with leather, has no attached shoulder

Figure 27.—The shelter quarter worn as a poncho. A Waffen-SS quarter is shown.

straps. It is attached to the infantry cartridge-belt suspenders by four hooks like those on the combat pack. Service shoes, twill trousers, a set of brushes, and other necessary items are carried in the main section of the pack. Towel, socks, sewing kit, and shirt are carried in the flap pouch. The tent-pole section and two tent pegs are carried at the top of the pack between the main pouch and the flap pouch. The overcoat or a blanket may be carried on the pack in a horseshoe roll. If for some reason both the haversack and the combat pack have to be carried at the same time, the combat pack is hooked into the rings on the upper edge of the haversack flap and secured by the button stap on the flap.

b. MODEL 34 HAVERSACK. An older type of haversack still being issued to some German soldiers is the Model 34. This is similar to the Model 39, but is intended to carry all the soldier's equipment.

c. MOUNTAIN RUCKSACK The duties and equipment of mountain troops require a more versatile pack than the haversack. The mountain rucksack is a large olive-drab sack with attached shoulder straps. There is a large pocket on the outside below the cover flap. Leather loops facilitate attaching articles to the outside. The rucksack rests lower on the back than the haversack.

d. *Luftwaffe* RUCKSACK. The design of the *Luftwaffe* rucksack is similar, though not identical, to that of the mountain rucksack. The chief difference is in color: the Air Force rucksack is blue-gray.

e. TROPICAL RUCKSACK. The tropical rucksack is simpler than the mountain and *Luftwaffe* rucksack. Hooks at the corners snap into rings on the cartridge belt suspenders.

f. ARTILLERY RUCKSACK. Artillerymen receive the artillery rucksack, consisting of a full marching pack and a combat pack.

g. SADDLEBAGS. Until July 1944 a pair of saddlebags was issued to each mounted soldier, but since then saddlebags are considered organizational equipment. It is probable that the supplies of the old Model 34 now are nearly exhausted. It is being replaced by large and small saddlebags. The large saddlebag is the "horse" pack. Its contents include mess kit, horseshoe, eight nails, four calks, calk fastener and hoof cleaner, surcingle, curry comb, horse brush, and pail. The small saddlebag, carried on the right just behind the rider, carries the soldier's personal equipment. Sweater, iron rations, rifle-cleaning kit, toilet articles, tent rope, shoe-cleaning gear, and towel are carried inside the bag, while the shelter quarter is strapped to the outside. Fifteen rounds of ammunition are carried on the cover flap. This small saddlebag may be used as a combat pack if the rider must dismount. The hooks on the four corners snap into the rings of the cavalry cartridge-belt suspenders. The mess kit is removed from the large saddlebag and strapped to the outside of the small saddlebag when it is used as a combat pack.

h. ENGINEER ASSAULT PACK. One engineer assault pack is authorized for every five combat engineers. It is used with the infantry cartridge-belt suspenders and consists of a canvas pack worn on the back and two canvas pouches used in place of the regular cartridge pouches. Two smoke pots are carried in the top of the pack and a 3-kilogram boxed demolition charge in the bottom. In addition, the mess kit, which fits in a special pocket, and shelter quarter are carried in the pack. The pouches hold egg-shaped grenades with rifle ammunition in side pockets. There is a special pocket on the right pouch for a gas mask without carrier. The men to whom this assault pack is issued also receive Model 39 haversack.

4. Special Mountain Equipment

Special equipment issued to German mountain troops is very similar to civilian mountaineering equipment. Manila rope about ½ inch in diameter is issued in 100-foot lengths for mountain climbing, but it, of course, serves many other purposes. The equipment of German mountain troops also includes ice axes, 10-point crampons which are strapped to boots for better traction on ice, pitons, snaplinks, steel-edged mountain skis with Kandahar type bindings, and small oval snowshoes. Small, light-weight, A-shaped tents are issued to mountain troops. Red avalanche cords, avalanche shovels, and avalanche probes are provided for rescue work.

5. Special Winter Equipment

Ski troops in flat country are issued lighter skis than those given mountain troops. Their skis are not steel-edged and have a special binding designed for cross-country travel. This binding clamps securely to a metal plate screwed to the bottom of a special wooden-soled canvas overboot. Since all the plates are the same size, the

Figure 28.—A Waffen-SS mountain sergeant teaches the use of ice ax and crampons while simulating the descent of an ice slope. The crampons are strapped to ski-mountain boots.

Figure 29.—German pack frames for heavy weapons specially designed for the loads they are intended to carry.

binding fits all men, making the skis interchange-able. Small sleds, known as akajas and looking like small 7-foot, flat-bottomed canoes, are used to transport supplies and heavy weapons and evacuate wounded across snow. There are three types: the double-end boat akaja, the weapons akaja, and the plywood akaja. Also, other types of sleds are improvised.

6. Miscellaneous Equipment

a. DISPATCH CASE. Platoon and squad leaders, master sergeants, messenger carriers, and similar personnel wear a black leather dispatch case on their belts. Previously this case was issued to a greater number, but in 1943 the issue was re-stricted to conserve leather. A leather map case with a plastic window fits inside the dispatch case. Several pockets are sewn on the front of the case to accommodate seven pencils, rules, map-reading instruments, and other equipment.

b. PACK FRAMES. Pack frames, which are used by German troops to carry heavy weapons and other heavy or clumsy loads, particularly in difficult terrain, are somewhat similar in appear-ance to the metal tube frames sometimes used with frame rucksacks. There is no universal type but rather special ones for each type of load with special tubes and shelves to accommodate the particular type of equipment carried.

c. GOGGLES. The commonest German goggles are the plastic-lens folding type, made with both clear and amber lenses, one of each type fre-quently being issued to each man. These are the "sun and dust goggles" which are issued to all members of motorized or mechanized units except vehicle drivers and motorcyclists, who receive a heavier model with smoke-colored lenses and leather, synthetic rubber, or felt frames. The heavier goggles are also issued to some anti-aircraft gunners and sometimes to mountain troops, although mountain troops frequently get the plastic goggles.

d. FORK-SPOON. A combination aluminum fork-spoon is issued to each German soldier. The handles of the fork and spoon are riveted together so that when extended the fork is on one end and the spoon on the other, but when folded the handles lie together and the tines of the fork rest in the bowl of the spoon. Since the over-all length folded is only 5½ inches, this

Figure 30.—Fuel tablet stove (Esbit Kocher) in half-open position. When closed, the box of Esbit fuel tablets fits inside and is fully protected against breakage.

combination utensil is easily carried. It is much simpler and lighter than a combination strainless steel knife, fork, spoon, and sometimes can-opener issued to German troops during the Afri-can campaign.

e. RATION HEATERS. A small gasoline stove, weighing a little over a pound, is issued to special units such as mountain troops who must operate under difficult conditions but keep a high degree of mobility. This stove works by burning vapor-ized gasoline, but it has no pressure pump. Pres-sure is built up by heating the burner with gaso-line or fuel tablets burnt in a small cup below the tank and maintained by the heat generated by the stove itself. More widely issued are fuel tablets, the commonest of which is *Esbit:* tablets of hexamethylene tetramine. The fuel is packed in a paper carton which is carried in the fuel-tablet stove (*Esbit Kocher*). In the carton there are four cakes of five tablets each, one or more of which may be broken from the cake and and burned at a time. This fuel is extremely efficient. The fuel-tablet stove is made of three sections of zinc-coated steel. Two identical sec-tions, which form the cover in the closed posi-tion, and the sides and mess kit support in the two open positions, are attached to a third section, by a grommet hinge. This third section is a shallow pan on which the tablets are burned. Dimples in the metal at appropriate positions hold the stove in either the closed, half-open, or open positions.

GERMAN ARMY UNIFORMS

FIELD UNIFORM, ENLISTED MAN
Pvt; NCOs add braided edging to collar as shown on
1st sgt of Mountain Infantry.

MOUNTAIN UNIFORM, NCO
1st sgt; double sleeve braid on sleeves differentiates 1st
from master sergeants.

OVERCOAT, ALL RANKS
Tech sgt pyrotechnician; general officers wear red lapel
facings and gold buttons.

SERVICE DRESS, ENLISTED MAN
Pvt 1st class; parade uniform consists of same uniform
with marching boots.

MOUNTAIN TROOPS' CAP BADGE
Worn on the left side of the cap.

MOUNTAIN TROOPS' SLEEVE BADGE
Worn on the right sleeve of coat and overcoat.

PARADE DRESS, NCO
Cavalry mr sgt; cord is markmanship award for non
commissioned officers and men.

PLATE I

GERMAN ARMY UNIFORMS

SERVICE DRESS, OFFICER

Lt Col; coat is re-made Reichswehr coat; normal service coat resembles EM's.

FIELD UNIFORM, OFFICER

Maj artillery; the Reichswehr coat may also be worn as an ordinary field coat.

BLACK PANZER UNIFORM

2nd Lt; worn by tank crews and by certain tank destroyer and "Elephant" crews.

FIELD GRAY JACKET

As worn by SP infantry gunners; TD and assault gunners wear skulls on collar patches.

FATIGUE UNIFORM

Master sergeant; fatigues are issued in several colors, including white and black.

MOTOR VEHICLE COAT

Sgt; motorcycle riders may button the lower part of the coat around both legs.

GERMAN ARMY UNIFORMS

JAGER TROOPS CAP BADGE
Worn on the left side of the cap.

JAGER TROOPS SLEEVE BADGE
Worn on the right sleeve of the coat and overcoat.

SUMMER UNIFORM
1st sgt of Jager troops; uniform may consist of shorts, shirt and tropical helmet.

CAMOUFLAGE JACKET
This jacket resembles the SS pullover jacket, but is different in color scheme.

MOUNTAIN WINDJACKET
Worn by mountain and Jager troops and by mountaineers of the German Labor Service.

MOUNTAIN PARKA
This reversible windproof, water-repellant uniform has a white and tan side.

WINTER UNIFORM
This reversible uniform has the reverse side in plain or in various color patterns.

PLATE III   569

GERMAN ARMY: INSIGNIA OF RANK

Shoulder straps are the main indication of rank. Noncommissioned officers (Unteroffiziere) are further distinguished by a braided edge to the collar of their service, field, and fatigue coats. Certain noncommissioned officers may wear officers' uniforms and dispense with the braided collar edging. Illustrated below are (top to bottom) collar patch, shoulder strap, and the type of rank insignia worn on both sleeves of coveralls, winter suits and like uniforms.

GENERAL OFFICERS (Generale)

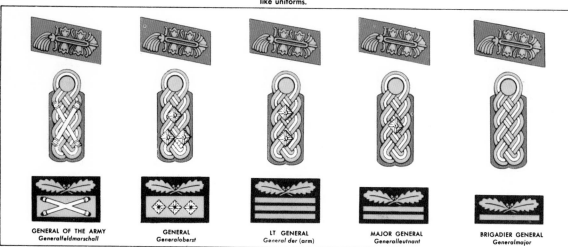

GENERAL OF THE ARMY	GENERAL	LT GENERAL	MAJOR GENERAL	BRIGADIER GENERAL
Generalfeldmarschall	Generaloberst	General der (arm)	Generalleutnant	Generalmajor

FIELD OFFICERS (Stabsoffiziere)

COMPANY OFFICERS

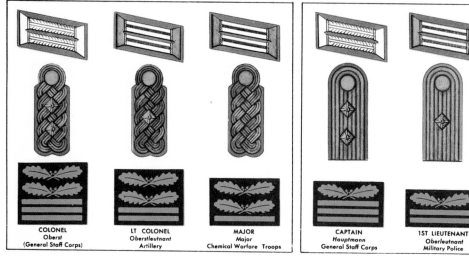

COLONEL	LT COLONEL	MAJOR
Oberst	Oberstleutnant	Major
(General Staff Corps)	Artillery	Chemical Warfare Troops

CAPTAIN	1ST LIEUTENANT	2D LIEUTENANT
Hauptmann	Oberleutnant	Leutnant
General Staff Corps	Military Police	Infantry

NONCOMMISSIONED OFFICERS (Unteroffiziere)

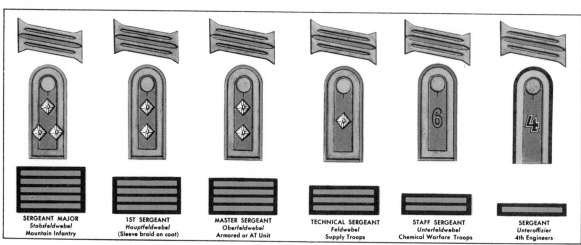

SERGEANT MAJOR	1ST SERGEANT	MASTER SERGEANT	TECHNICAL SERGEANT	STAFF SERGEANT	SERGEANT
Stabsfeldwebel	Hauptfeldwebel	Oberfeldwebel	Feldwebel	Unterfeldwebel	Unteroffizier
Mountain Infantry	(Sleeve braid on coat)	Armored or AT Unit	Supply Troops	Chemical Warfare Troops	4th Engineers

PLATE IV

GERMAN ARMY: INSIGNIA OF RANK

Corporals in the German Army are not rated as noncommissioned officers, but are placed among what amount to several grades of privates. These grades may wear the sleeve insignia shown below (chevrons or pip) on the coat, overcoat, fatigues, and on other types of uniform. There are many classes of administrative officials; examples of a few typical ranks and classes are shown. Such officials may be distinguished by their basic color of arm, which is dark green.

ENLISTED MEN

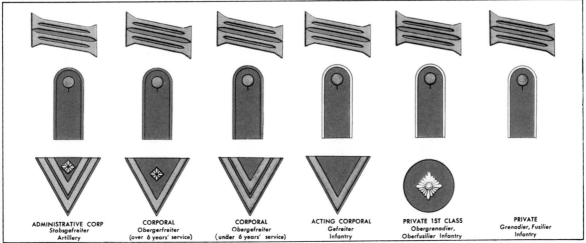

ADMINISTRATIVE CORP	CORPORAL	CORPORAL	ACTING CORPORAL	PRIVATE 1ST CLASS	PRIVATE
Stabsgefreiter	*Obergefreiter*	*Obergefreiter*	*Gefreiter*	*Obergrenadier,*	*Grenadier, Fusilier*
Artillery	(over 6 years' service)	(under 6 years' service)	Infantry	*Oberfusilier* Infantry	Infantry

OFFICER CANDIDATES

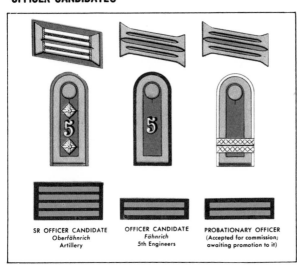

SR OFFICER CANDIDATE	OFFICER CANDIDATE	PROBATIONARY OFFICER
Oberfähnrich	*Fähnrich*	(Accepted for commission;
Artillery	5th Engineers	awaiting promotion to it)

NONCOMMISSIONED OFFICER CANDIDATES

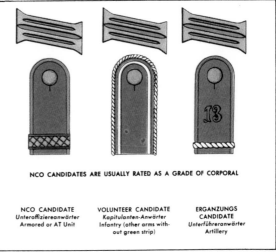

NCO CANDIDATES ARE USUALLY RATED AS A GRADE OF CORPORAL

NCO CANDIDATE	VOLUNTEER CANDIDATE	ERGANZUNGS CANDIDATE
Unteroffiziereanwärter	*Kapitulanten-Anwärter*	*Unterführeranwärter*
Armored or AT Unit	Infantry (other arms without green strip)	Artillery

ADMINISTRATIVE OFFICIALS — *Typical rank insignia*

GENERAL OFFICER	FIELD OFFICER	COMPANY OFFICER	NONCOMMISSIONED OFFICER
Ministry Director	Pharmacist (Maj)	Remount Official (Capt)	Saddler (Mr Sgt)
(Maj Gen)	*Oberstabsapotheker*	*Remonteamtsvorstehr*	*Heereswerkmeister T*
Ministerial Direktor			

CHAPLAINS

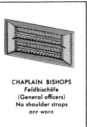

CHAPLAIN BISHOPS
Feldbischöfe
(General officers)
No shoulder straps
are worn

CHAPLAINS
Heeresoberpfarrer
No shoulder straps
are worn

OBSOLETE COLLAR PATCHES

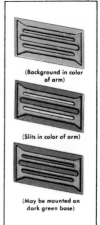

(Background in color of arm)

(Slits in color of arm)

(May be mounted on dark green base)

PLATE V

GERMAN ARMY: COLORS OF THE ARMS

Colors are the basic indication of arms (there are no services in the German Army). Color of arm is usually to be found on shoulder straps, on the service cap, on old-style field caps, and on collar patches of line officers' field uniforms, and on collar patches of service and dress uniforms. Piping in the color of arm appears on service and dress coats and trousers. In the instances recorded at right, letters on the shoulder strap indicate either a separate arm using the same color as another arm, or else a further subdivision of function within an arm. Numbers and letters may also be used to designate units.

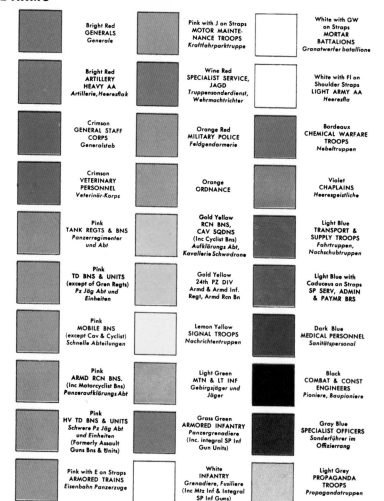

Color	Arm
Bright Red	GENERALS — Generale
Bright Red	ARTILLERY, HEAVY AA — Artillerie, Heeresflak
Crimson	GENERAL STAFF CORPS — Generalstab
Crimson	VETERINARY PERSONNEL — Veterinär-Korps
Pink	TANK REGTS & BNS — Panzerregimenter und Abt
Pink	TD BNS & UNITS (except of Gren Regts) — Pz Jäg Abt und Einheiten
Pink	MOBILE BNS (except Cav & Cyclist) — Schnelle Abteilungen
Pink	ARMD RCN BNS. (Inc Motorcyclist Bns) — Panzeraufklärungs Abt
Pink	HV TD BNS & UNITS — Schwere Pz Jäg Abt und Einheiten (Formerly Assault Guns Bns & Units)
Pink with E on Straps	ARMORED TRAINS — Eisenbahn Panzerzuge
Pink with J on Straps	MOTOR MAINTENANCE TROOPS — Kraftfahrparktruppe
Wine Red	SPECIALIST SERVICE, JAGD — Truppensonderdienst, Wehrmachtrichter
Orange Red	MILITARY POLICE — Feldgendarmerie
Orange	ORDNANCE
Gold Yellow	RCN BNS, CAV SQDNS (Inc Cyclist Bns) — Aufklärungs Abt, Kavallerie Schwadrone
Gold Yellow	24th PZ DIV Armd & Armd Inf. Regt, Armd Rcn Bn
Lemon Yellow	SIGNAL TROOPS — Nachrichtentruppen
Light Green	MTN & LT INF — Gebirgsjäger und Jäger
Grass Green	ARMORED INFANTRY — Panzergrenadiere (Inc. integral SP Inf Gun Units)
White	INFANTRY — Grenadiere, Fusiliere (Inc Mtz Inf & Integral SP Inf Guns)
White with GW on Straps	MORTAR BATTALIONS — Granatwerfer batallione
White with Fl on Shoulder Straps	LIGHT ARMY AA — Heeresfla
Bordeaux	CHEMICAL WARFARE TROOPS — Nebeltruppen
Violet	CHAPLAINS — Heeresgeistliche
Light Blue	TRANSPORT & SUPPLY TROOPS — Fahrtruppen, Nachschubtruppen
Light Blue with Caduceus on Straps	SP SERV, ADMIN & PAYMR BRS
Dark Blue	MEDICAL PERSONNEL — Sanitätspersonal
Black	COMBAT & CONST ENGINEERS — Pioniere, Baupioniere
Gray Blue	SPECIALIST OFFICERS — Sonderführer im Offizierrang
Light Grey	PROPAGANDA TROOPS — Propagandatruppen

SPECIALIST INSIGNIA: OFFICERS AND NCOs

Specialist officers and senior NCOs of the arms may wear special symbols on their shoulder straps in addition to the color of their arm. Specialist officers appointed because of special qualification (Sonderführer) wear such symbols only if they are medical officers; otherwise they wear the collar patch shown above, and the type of insignia of rank shown at right.

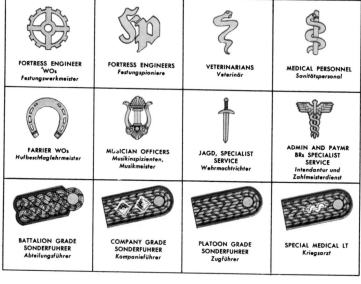

FORTRESS ENGINEER WOs — Festungswerkmeister	FORTRESS ENGINEERS — Festungspioniere	VETERINARIANS — Veterinär	MEDICAL PERSONNEL — Sanitätspersonal
FARRIER WOs — Hufbeschlaglehrmeister	MUSICIAN OFFICERS — Musikinspizienten, Musikmeister	JAGD, SPECIALIST SERVICE — Wehrmachtrichter	ADMIN AND PAYMR BRs SPECIALIST SERVICE — Intendantur und Zahlmeisterdienst
BATTALION GRADE SONDERFUHRER — Abteilungsführer	COMPANY GRADE SONDERFUHRER — Kompanieführer	PLATOON GRADE SONDERFUHRER — Zugführer	SPECIAL MEDICAL LT — Kriegsarzt

GERMAN ARMY: SPECIALTY BADGES (NCOs and Enlisted Men)

The following badges are worn on the lower right arm of the coat and overcoat. The system of designation illustrated on the first three farrier badges applies to the various other specialty badges, the lozenge insignia being peculiar to farrier instructors. The new specialty badge for supply sergeant is based on unconfirmed reports, but the design is believed to be approximately accurate.

FARRIER
NCO specialist
within organizational quota
Hufbeschlagmeister

FARRIER
Who has passed his tests
Hufbeschlagmeister

FARRIER
NCO over unit specialist
quota; EM specialist within quota
Hufbeschlagmeister

FARRIER INSTRUCTOR
Hufbeschlaglehrmeister

**MEDICAL ENLISTED
PERSONNEL**
Sanitätsunterpersonal

ORDNANCE SERGEANT
Waffenunteroffizier

PYROTECHNICIAN
Feuerwerker

TRANSPORT SERGEANT
Schirrmeister

RADIO SERGEANT
Funkmeister

PIGIONEER
Brieftaubemeister

**FORTRESS ENGINEER
SERGEANT**
Festungspionier-Feldwebel

**FORTIFICATION
MAINTENANCE SERGEANT**
Wallfeldwebel

PAYMASTER CANDIDATE
Zahlmeisteranwärter

SADDLER CANDIDATE
*Truppensattelmeister-
anwärter*

**FORTRESS CONSTRUCTION
SERGEANT**
Festungswerkfeldwebel

SUPPLY SERGEANT
(Inf and Arty Equipment)
Gerätverwaltungsunteroffizier

The following specialty badges are also worn on the lower right arm of the coat and overcoat. While candidates may wear the strip of candidate's braid (see farrier candidate above), they do not follow the same system of designation by braided edging as do the specialists above. The sniper's badges are partly insignia of specialty, and partly rewards for actual achievement in combat. They are to be worn over any other specialty badges worn on the lower right arm.

**MOTOR OR ARMD
MECHANIC 2D CLASS**
*Kraftzeug,
Panzerwarte II*

**MOTOR OR ARMD
MECHANIC 1ST CLASS**
*Kraftzeug,
Panzerwarter I*

**MOTOR OR ARMD
CRAFTSMAN**
Handwerker

**SKILLED MOTOR OR
ARMD CRAFTSMAN**
Vorhandwerker

SNIPER
Scharfschütze
(At least 20 enemy killed)

SNIPER
Scharfschütze
(At least 40 enemy killed)

SNIPER
Scharfschütze
(At least 60 enemy killed)

GAS DEFENSE SERGEANT
Gasschützunteroffizier

SIGNAL MECHANIC
Nachrichten-Mechaniker

**SIGNAL MECHANIC
SERGEANT**
*Nachrichten-
Mechanikerunteroffizier*

WORN ON LOWER LEFT ARM   ## UPPER LEFT ARM

GUNNER
(Artillery)
Richtkanonier

GUNNER
(Chemical Warfare Troops)

SIGNAL PERSONNEL
Symbol color changes
with arm
(Here Artillery)

RADIO MECHANIC
(Armored Troops)
Panzerfunkwarte

**ENGINEER ASSAULT BOAT
COXWAIN**
Steurermann

MILITARY POLICE
Feldgendarmerie
(Officers: silver eagle)

MUSICIAN'S BADGES (On both shoulders)   ## MARKSMANSHIP AWARDS: (Pz Tps substitute tank for swords)

BUGLER
Bataillionshornist
Signal Troops

MUSICIANS
Musiker
Artillery

**FIFE AND DRUM
CORPSMAN**
Spielleute
Transport Troops

Cord color, shield design, and number of acorns (shells for artillery) vary to produce 12 grades. Fourth grade shown.

PLATE VII

GERMAN AIR FORCE UNIFORMS

FIELD UNIFORM, EM, FRONT
Pvt; older style coat as shown may be worn by officers, NCOs, and enlisted men.

FIELD UNIFORM, EM, REAR
Pvt; equipment carried is similar to that of the German Army, except for color.

MOUNTAIN UNIFORM, NCO
Staff sgt; officers wear silver piping along top edge of the mountain cap turnup.

PARACHUTIST'S UNIFORM
Staff sgt; the "flight blouse" shown may be worn by all types of GAF personnel.

SERVICE DRESS, OFFICER
Colonel; GAF personnel may wear this coat with the collar buttoned at the neck.

OVERCOAT
1st sgt; this overcoat is worn with appropriate insignia by all GAF personnel.

GERMAN AIR FORCE UNIFORMS

SUMMER UNIFORM

Sgt; breeches may replace trousers shown. Shirt and shorts may also be worn.

WINTER OVERCOAT

This heavy sheepskin overcoat is worn by sentries and men manning static defenses.

SUMMER UNIFORM, OFFICERS

Lt. col; this uniform, either whole or with gray trousers may be worn by fliers.

PARACHUTIST JUMP SUIT

Tech sgt; other similar types, both plain and camouflaged, may be encountered.

FIELD JACKET

First sergeant; this jacket is usually worn by members of parachute divisions.

FATIGUE SUIT

Acting corp; this uniform is issued in cream, green, tan, and blue-covered cloth.

PLATE IX　　　　　　　575

GERMAN AIR FORCE UNIFORMS

LIGHT FLYING SUIT

Master or 1st sergeant; insignia of rank is worn on both sleeves of flying suits.

LINED FLYING SUIT

1st lieutenant; the suit illustrated is typical of the various lined flying suits.

FATIGUE COVERALL

Tech sgt; mr sgt, 2 bars; 1st sgt, 3 bars; sgt maj, 3 bars with pip below the bars.

SUMMER MOTORING COAT

2d lieutenant; NCOs wear the type of rank insignia worn on their fatigue coveralls.

STANDARD MOTORING COAT

This coat may be buttoned in the same manner as the summer motoring coat at left.

FLIER'S LEATHER JACKET

1st lt; senior NCOs and officers may wear leather flying jackets of this type.

GERMAN AIR FORCE: INSIGNIA OF RANK (Collar patch, shoulder strap, and coverall insignia)
GENERAL OFFICERS (Generale)

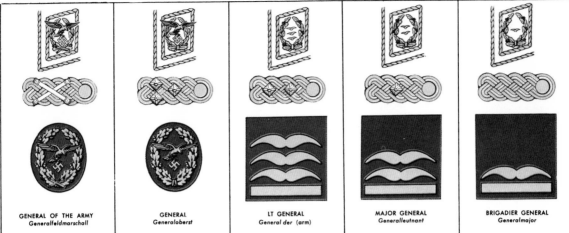

GENERAL OF THE ARMY	GENERAL	LT GENERAL	MAJOR GENERAL	BRIGADIER GENERAL
Generalfeldmarschall	*Generaloberst*	*General der (arm)*	*Generalleutnant*	*Generalmajor*

FIELD OFFICERS (Stabsoffiziere)　　　　COMPANY OFFICERS

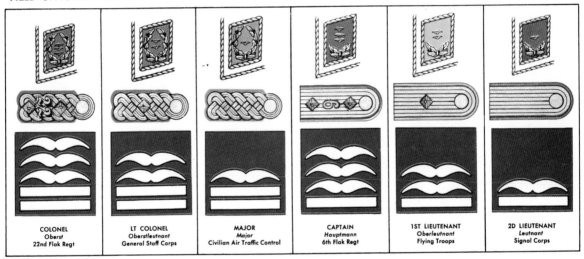

COLONEL	LT COLONEL	MAJOR	CAPTAIN	1ST LIEUTENANT	2D LIEUTENANT
Oberst	*Oberstleutnant*	*Major*	*Hauptmann*	*Oberleutnant*	*Leutnant*
22nd Flak Regt	General Staff Corps	Civilian Air Traffic Control	6th Flak Regt	Flying Troops	Signal Corps

NONCOMMISSIONED OFFICERS—TITLES:
{ Antiaircraft: *Hauptwachtmeister, Oberwachtmeister, Wachtmeister, Unterwachtmeister*
  Other Units: *Hauptfeldwebel, Oberfeldwebel, Feldwebel, Unterfeldwebel* }

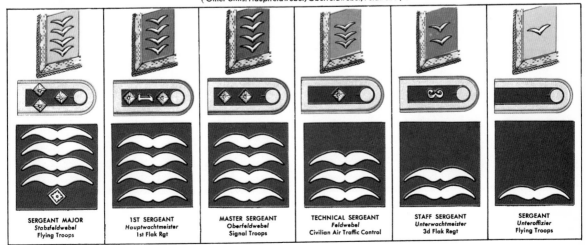

SERGEANT MAJOR	1ST SERGEANT	MASTER SERGEANT	TECHNICAL SERGEANT	STAFF SERGEANT	SERGEANT
Stabsfeldwebel	*Hauptwachtmeister*	*Oberfeldwebel*	*Feldwebel*	*Unterwachtmeister*	*Unteroffizier*
Flying Troops	1st Flak Rgt	Signal Troops	Civilian Air Traffic Control	3d Flak Regt	Flying Troops

PLATE XI

GERMAN AIR FORCE: INSIGNIA OF RANK
ENLISTED MEN

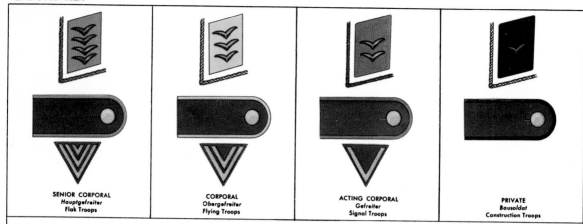

| SENIOR CORPORAL
Hauptgefreiter
Flak Troops | CORPORAL
Obergefreiter
Flying Troops | ACTING CORPORAL
Gefreiter
Signal Troops | PRIVATE
Bausoldat
Construction Troops |

OFFICER CANDIDATES   NCO CANDIDATES

| SENIOR OFFICER CANDIDATE
Oberfähnrich
Construction Troops | OFFICER CANDIDATE
Fähnrich
5th Flak Regt | VOLUNTEER OFFICER
CANDIDATE
Fähnenjunker
(May be any rank) | NCO CANDIDATE
Unteroffizieranwärter
(Here Gefreiter) | ERGANZUNGS NCO
CANDIDATE
Unterführeranwärter |

GERMAN AIR FORCE: ENGINEERING CORPS
(ADMINISTRATIVE OFFICIALS)

Engineers having to do with mechanical engineering in the German Air Force belong to a special corps and are distinguished by special rank insignia and special designations of rank. All ranks wear pink as color of their service.

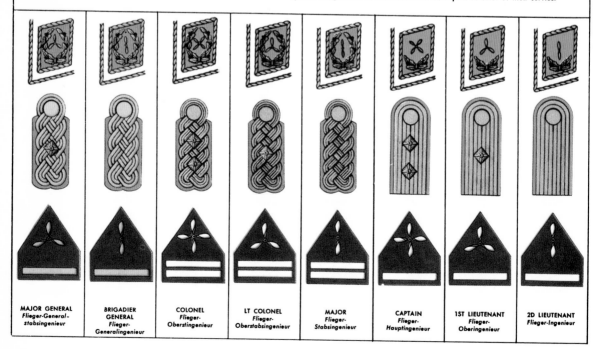

| MAJOR GENERAL
Flieger-General-stabsingenieur | BRIGADIER GENERAL
Flieger-Generalingenieur | COLONEL
Flieger-Oberstingenieur | LT COLONEL
Flieger-Oberstabsingenieur | MAJOR
Flieger-Stabsingenieur | CAPTAIN
Flieger-Hauptingenieur | 1ST LIEUTENANT
Flieger-Oberingenieur | 2D LIEUTENANT
Flieger-Ingenieur |

PLATE XII

GERMAN AIR FORCE: COLORS OF THE ARMS AND SERVICES

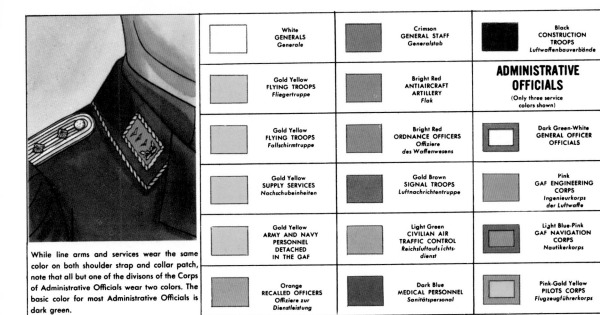

White GENERALS Generale	Crimson GENERAL STAFF Generalstab	Black CONSTRUCTION TROOPS Luftwaffenbauverbände
Gold Yellow FLYING TROOPS Fliegertruppe	Bright Red ANTIAIRCRAFT ARTILLERY Flak	**ADMINISTRATIVE OFFICIALS** (Only three service colors shown)
Gold Yellow FLYING TROOPS Fallschirmtruppe	Bright Red ORDNANCE OFFICERS Offiziere des Waffenwesens	Dark Green-White GENERAL OFFICER OFFICIALS
Gold Yellow SUPPLY SERVICES Nachschubeinheiten	Gold Brown SIGNAL TROOPS Luftnachrichtentruppe	Pink GAF ENGINEERING CORPS Ingenieurkorps der Luftwaffe
Gold Yellow ARMY AND NAVY PERSONNEL DETACHED IN THE GAF	Light Green CIVILIAN AIR TRAFFIC CONTROL Reichsluftaufsichtsdienst	Light Blue-Pink GAF NAVIGATION CORPS Nautikerkorps
Orange RECALLED OFFICERS Offiziere zur Dienstleistung	Dark Blue MEDICAL PERSONNEL Sanitätspersonal	Pink-Gold Yellow PILOTS CORPS Flugzeugführerkorps

While line arms and services wear the same color on both shoulder strap and collar patch, note that all but one of the divsions of the Corps of Administrative Officials wear two colors. The basic color for most Administrative Officials is dark green.

SONDERFÜHRER
Specialist officers and NCOs, awarded commissions or ratings because of special qualifications.

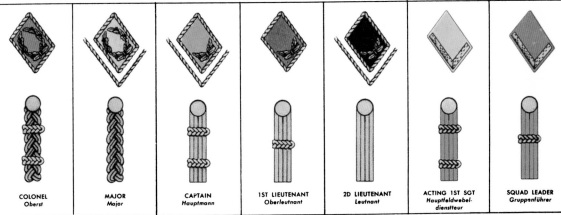

COLONEL Oberst	MAJOR Major	CAPTAIN Hauptmann	1ST LIEUTENANT Oberleutnant	2D LIEUTENANT Leutnant	ACTING 1ST SGT Hauptfeldwebeldienstteur	SQUAD LEADER Gruppenführer

TYPICAL ADMINISTRATIVE OFFICIALS

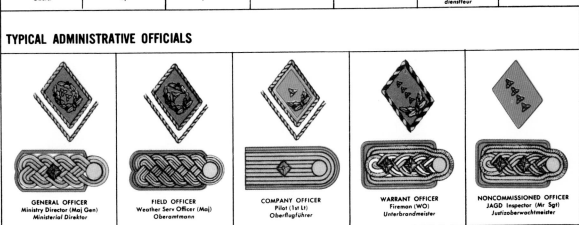

GENERAL OFFICER Ministry Director (Maj Gen) Ministerial Direktor	FIELD OFFICER Weather Serv Officer (Maj) Oberamtmann	COMPANY OFFICER Pilot (1st Lt) Oberflugführer	WARRANT OFFICER Fireman (WO) Unterbrandmeister	NONCOMMISSIONED OFFICER JAGD Inspector (Mr Sgt) Justizoberwachtmeister

PLATE XIII

GERMAN AIR FORCE: BADGES OF SPECIALTY—*Worn on lower left breast*

PILOT	OBSERVER	PILOT AND OBSERVER	AIR GUNNER-RADIO OPERATOR	AIR GUNNER FLIGHT ENGINEER	AIR CREW MEMBER (Uncertified as gunner)
		AWARDS			
GLIDER PILOT	AIR FORCE PARACHUTIST	The following awards are for the type of service indicated. They are worn in the same place as the specialty badges above.	WORLD WAR I FLIERS	GROUND COMBAT BADGE	ANTIAIRCRAFT BADGE

AWARDS FOR OPERATIONAL FLIGHTS—*Worn on upper left breast. Awarded in gold, silver, bronze; laurel pendant may be added to gold awards, as shown.*

RECONNAISANCE	BOMBER	ATTACK	FIGHTER	TRANSPORT

SPECIALTY BADGES—*Worn on lower left sleeve by NCOs and men*

AUTOMOTIVE EQUIPMENT ADMINISTRATORS (Band for candidates)	MEDICAL PERSONNEL *Sanitätspersonal*	SEARCHLIGHT EQUIPMENT ADMINISTRATORS *Scheinwerfergerätverwalter*	SIGNAL EQUIPMENT ADMINISTRATORS *Luftnachrichtengerätverwalter*	PYROTECHNICIANS *Feuerwerker*	FLAK ORDNANCE SGTS *Waffenunteroffiziere*

OTHER ORDNANCE SGTS *Waffenunteroffiziere*	AIRCRAFT EQUIPMENT ADMINISTRATORS *Flugzeuggerätverwater*	GRADS OF TECH PREP SCHOOLS	TELEPHONE OPERATORS *Fernsprecher*	TELEPHONE SERGEANTS *Fernsprechunteroffiziere*	TELETYPE OPERATORS *Fernschreiber*

TELETYPE SERGEANTS *Fernschreibunteroffiziere*	AIR RAID WARNING PERSONNEL *Flugmeldpersonnel*	RADIOMEN *Funker*	RADIO SERGEANTS *Funkunteroffiziere*	RADIO DIRECTION FINDERS *Peilfunker*	RADIO DIRECTION FINDER SGTS *Peilfunkunteroffiziere*
RADIO INTERCEPTORS *Horchfunker*	RADIO INTERCEPTION SGTS *Horchfunkunteroffiziere*	TECHNICAL AVN PERSONNEL *Fliegertechnisches Personal*	PERSONNEL OF TENDERS, CRASH BOATS, ETC *Seemännisches Bootspersonal*	FLYING PERSONNEL *Fliegendes Personal*	FLAK PERSONNEL (For 9 months' service)
RANGEFINDER CREWS *Entfernungsmessleute* (Gold border for 1 yr serv)	SOUND LOCATOR CREWS *Horcher*	SOUND LOCATOR CREWS (For over 1 year's service)	MOTOR VEHICLE DRIVER *Kraftfahrer*	ADMIN SGTS & TECH SGTS *Verwaltungsunteroffiziere und feldwebel*	SIGNAL PERSONNEL NON-SIGNAL UNITS *Truppennachrichtenpersonal*

PLATE XIV

GERMAN NAVY UNIFORMS

BLUE UNIFORM

Worn by officers, warrant officers, chief and 1st class petty officers; Lt (jg) shown.

OVERCOAT

Worn by officers, warrant officers, chief and 1st class petty officers; BM 1/C shown.

BLUE UNIFORM

Worn by 2nd and 3d class petty officers and seamen. May be fitted with striped collar.

PEAJACKET

Worn by 2d and 3d class petty officers and seamen. Note collar patch for BM 2/C.

KHAKI UNIFORM

Worn by all personnel of the German Navy. Rank insignia for BM 1/C is shown on shirt.

ADMINISTRATIVE OFFICIAL

Administrative officials wear normal blue uniform with silver replacing gold insignia.

PLATE XV

GERMAN NAVY—INSIGNIA OF RANK FOR BLUE AND WHITE UNIFORMS

ADMIRAL *Admiral* Line	VICE ADMIRAL *Vizeadmiral* Medical	REAR ADMIRAL *Kontreadmiral* Engineering	COMMODORE *Kommodore* Line	CAPTAIN *Kapitän zur See* Technical Communications	COMMANDER *Fregattenkapitän* Administration	LT COMMANDER *Korvettenkapitän* Defensive Ordnance

CHIEF BOATSWAIN *Stabsoberbootsmann*	BOATSWAIN *Oberbootsmann*	CHIEF BOATSWAIN'S MATE *Stabsbootsmann*	BOATSWAIN'S MATE 1/C *Bootsmann*

LIEUTENANT *Kapitänleutnant* Naval Coast Artillery	LIEUTENANT (jg) *Oberleutnant zur See* Communications Reserve	ENSIGN *Leutnant zur See* Line

CHEVRONS—For seamen

SEAMAN 1/C 4½ years' service *Hauptgefreiter*	SEAMAN 2/C *Obergefreiter*	SEAMAN 2/C *Gefreiter*

PETTY OFFICERS 2 AND 3/C

These POs wear their corps insignia on oval badges as below. These are their insignia of rank. Boatswains wear single anchors and quartermasters wear crossed anchors as corps insignia; other corps wear devices shown at right. Note that in seaman's branch, a star replaces the boatswain's anchor.

BOATSWAIN'S MATE 2/C *Oberbootsmannsmaat*	COXWAIN *Bootsmannsmaat*

SEAMAN'S SPECIALITY BADGES— Mounted on ovals for POs 2 and 3/C; selection only is shown

SEAMAN *Bootsmanns-Laufbann* *(Matrose)*	ORDNANCE ENGINEER *Artillerie-Mechaniker*	AIRCRAFT SPOTTERS *Flugmeldpersonal*	MOTOR TRANSPORT DRIVER *Kraftfahrer*
NAVAL ARTILLERY *Marine Artillerie*	STOREKEEPER *Verwalter*	MINE MACHINIST *Speer-Mechaniker*	TORPEDOMAN *Torpedo-Mechaniker*

PLATE XVI

GERMAN NAVY: FIELD GRAY UNIFORMS

FIELD GRAY UNIFORM, OFFICERS
Lieutenant (jg)
Leutnant zur See

FIELD GRAY UNIFORM, WOs, POs
Warrant Officer, Coast Artillery
Oberfeldwebel

FIELD GRAY UNIFORM, SEAMEN
Seaman, 2d Class
Gefreiter

INSIGNIA OF RANK FOR FIELD GRAY UNIFORM: OFFICERS

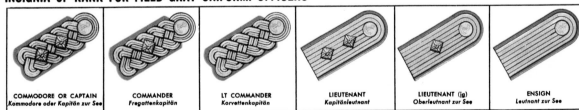

COMMODORE OR CAPTAIN	COMMANDER	LT COMMANDER	LIEUTENANT	LIEUTENANT (jg)	ENSIGN
Kommodore oder Kapitän zur See	*Fregattenkapitän*	*Korvettenkapitän*	*Kapitänleutnant*	*Oberleutnant zur See*	*Leutnant zur See*

WARRANT OFFICERS, PETTY OFFICERS, AND SEAMEN OF NAVAL COAST ARTILLERY

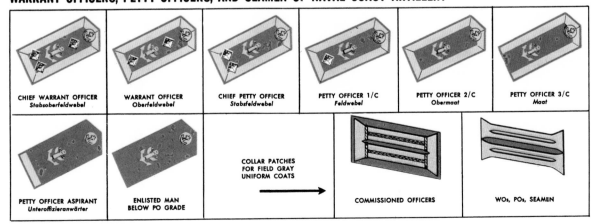

CHIEF WARRANT OFFICER	WARRANT OFFICER	CHIEF PETTY OFFICER	PETTY OFFICER 1/C	PETTY OFFICER 2/C	PETTY OFFICER 3/C
Stabsoberfeldwebel	*Oberfeldwebel*	*Stabsfeldwebel*	*Feldwebel*	*Obermaat*	*Maat*

PETTY OFFICER ASPIRANT	ENLISTED MAN BELOW PO GRADE	COLLAR PATCHES FOR FIELD GRAY UNIFORM COATS ➔	COMMISSIONED OFFICERS	WOs, POs, SEAMEN
Unteroffizieranwärter				

PLATE XVII

ARMED ELITE GUARD (WAFFEN-SS) UNIFORMS

FIELD UNIFORM, EM

Most Waffen-SS troops wear Army coats, but some still
wear the style of coat shown.

MOUNTAIN UNIFORM

The coat is the SS coat at left, which may be worn with
collar turned down as above.

SP GUN CREW UNIFORM

This uniform is the same as the field gray jacket uniform
worn by similar Army troops.

TANK UNIFORM

This uniform is the same as the black uniform worn by
certain troops in the Army.

TANK COVERALL

Tank crews of the Waffen-SS may also wear this
camouflage non-reversible coverall.

CAMOUFLAGE JACKET

New SS jackets have buttoned pockets, unlike Army
jackets. Note breeches for cavalry.

ARMED ELITE GUARD (WAFFEN-SS) UNIFORMS

SERVICE DRESS, OFFICER

Waffen-SS officers may wear Army coats instead of the
type of SS coat illustrated.

SERVICE DRESS, NCO

1st sgt; the coat shown is the Army coat, which may
appear with pleatless pockets.

OVERCOAT, NCOs AND EM

This overcoat is the same as the Army overcoat. Note
the placement of insignia.

OVERCOAT, GENERALS

Note the gray lapel facings. Other officers wear plain
lapels on their overcoats.

CAMOUFLAGE SUIT

Waffen-SS regulations forbidding the wearing of insignia on this suit are ignored.

WINTER UNIFORM

Some Waffen-SS armored troops have been furnished
with this special type of parka.

PLATE XIX

ARMED ELITE GUARD (WAFFEN-SS): COLORS OF THE ARMS

Waffen-SS troops wear collar patches similar to those of the General SS (Allgemeine SS), but Waffen-SS shoulder straps are after the German Army pattern, except for that of the Reichsführer-SS

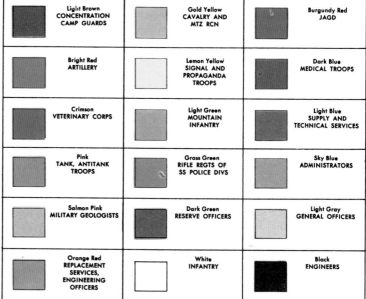

Light Brown CONCENTRATION CAMP GUARDS	Gold Yellow CAVALRY AND MTZ RCN	Burgundy Red JAGD
Bright Red ARTILLERY	Lemon Yellow SIGNAL AND PROPAGANDA TROOPS	Dark Blue MEDICAL TROOPS
Crimson VETERINARY CORPS	Light Green MOUNTAIN INFANTRY	Light Blue SUPPLY AND TECHNICAL SERVICES
Pink TANK, ANTITANK TROOPS	Grass Green RIFLE REGTS OF SS POLICE DIVS	Sky Blue ADMINISTRATORS
Salmon Pink MILITARY GEOLOGISTS	Dark Green RESERVE OFFICERS	Light Gray GENERAL OFFICERS
Orange Red REPLACEMENT SERVICES, ENGINEERING OFFICERS	White INFANTRY	Black ENGINEERS

INSIGNIA OF RANK: GENERAL OFFICERS

SS generals once wore collar patches with the following insignia:

General —3 leaves, 2 pips

Lt Gen —3 leaves, 1 pip

Maj Gen —3 leaves

Brig Gen —2 leaves, 1 pip

Police generals now wear the same collar patches as SS generals

REICHSFÜHRER-SS
Chief of Genl and Waffen-SS
(Heinrich Himmler)

GENERAL
Generaloberst der Waffen-SS
(Oberstgruppenführer in Genl SS)

LT GENERAL
General der Waffen-SS
(Obergruppenführer in Genl SS)

MAJOR GENERAL
Generalleutnant der Waffen-SS
(Gruppenführer in Genl SS)

BRIGADIER GENERAL
Generalmajor der Waffen-SS
(Brigadeführer in Genl SS)

FIELD OFFICERS

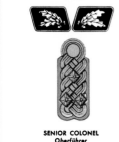

SENIOR COLONEL
Oberführer
Mountain Troops

COLONEL
Standartenführer
Infantry

LT COLONEL
Obersturmbannführer
Artillery

MAJOR
Sturmbannführer
Engineers

COMPANY OFFICERS

CAPTAIN
Hauptsturmführer
Supply Troops

1ST LIEUTENANT
Obersturmführer
Artillery

2D LIEUTENANT
Untersturmführer
Infantry

PLATE XX

ARMED ELITE GUARD (WAFFEN-SS): INSIGNIA OF RANK—NONCOMMISSIONED OFFICERS

| SERGEANT MAJOR *Sturmscharführer* Artillery | 1ST AND MR SERGEANT *Hauptscharführer* Cavalry | TECHNICAL SERGEANT *Oberscharführer* Infantry | STAFF SERGEANT *Scharführer* Artillery | SERGEANT *Unterscharführer* Artillery |

INSIGNIA OF RANK: ENLISTED MEN

| CORPORAL *Rottenführer* Infantry | ACTING CORPORAL *Sturmmann* Artillery | PRIVATE 1ST CLASS SS-Obershütze or SS-Obersoldat Medical Troops | PRIVATE SS-Schütze or SS-Soldat |

SPECIALTY BADGES—Worn on lower left arm by officers, NCOs, and men. See also Army sniper badges.

| SECURITY SERVICE *Sicherheitsdienst* | FARRIER PERSONNEL *Hufbeschlagpersonal* | TECHNICIAN OFFICERS *Führer im technischen Dienst* | SIGNAL PERSONNEL *Nachrichtenpersonal* (Blitz color changes with arm) | TRANSPORT SERGEANTS *Schirrmeister* | MEDICAL PERSONNEL *Sanitätspersonal* |

| ORDNANCE NCOs *Waffenunterführer* | VETERINARY OFFICERS, NCOs *Führer und Unterführer im Veterinärdienst* | OFFICERS IN LEGAL WORK *Führer im Gerichtsdienst* | MUSICIAN OFFICERS *Musikzugführer* | ADMINISTRATIVE OFFICERS *Führer im Verwaltungsdienst* | MEDICAL OFFICERS *Führer im Sanitätsdienst* |

TYPICAL ARM BANDS   INSIGNIA FOR VETERANS

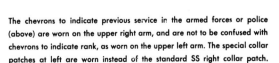

| TOTENKNOPF DIV & UNITS | GERMANIA DIVISION | DAS REICH DIVISION |
| NORD MOUNTAIN DIVISION | LIEBSTANDARTE ADOLPH HITLER DIV | PRINZ EUGEN MTN DIVISION |

VETERANS OF SERVICE IN ARMED FORCES OR IN POLICE   NAZI PARTY MEMBERS PRIOR TO 30 JAN 1933 *Alter Kampfer*

SPECIAL COLLAR PATCHES

| BOSNIAN-CROATIAN MTN DIV | TOTENKNOPF DIV & UNITS | PRINZ EUGEN MTN DIV |

The chevrons to indicate previous service in the armed forces or police (above) are worn on the upper right arm, and are not to be confused with chevrons to indicate rank, as worn on the upper left arm. The special collar patches at left are worn instead of the standard SS right collar patch.

PLATE XXI

GERMAN DECORATIONS AND AWARDS

The above figures illustrate the manner of wearing some of the more common German decorations and awards. The officer at left wears two tank destruction badges; the one at right has Crimea shield on arm, assault and wound badges on breast, 1939 bar to 1914 Iron Cross in buttonhole, and the Knight's Cross on ribbon at neck.

KNIGHT'S CROSS OF THE IRON CROSS
With gold oak leaves, swords, and diamonds

KNIGHT'S CROSS OF THE IRON CROSS
With oak leaves, swords, and diamonds

KNIGHT'S CROSS OF THE IRON CROSS
With oak leaves and swords

KNIGHT'S CROSS OF THE IRON CROSS
With oak leaves

KNIGHT'S CROSS OF THE IRON CROSS

THE GERMAN CROSS
Gold or silver

IRON CROSS 1ST CLASS
Worn without ribbon

IRON CROSS 2D CLASS
Usually ribbon only worn

1939 BAR TO 1914 IRON CROSS
Worn in buttonhole

WAR SERVICE CROSS WITH SWORDS
Silver or bronze

WAR SERVICE CROSS WITHOUT SWORDS
Silver or bronze

HONOR ROLL CLASP
Worn in buttonhole

PLATE XXII

GERMAN DECORATIONS AND AWARDS

TANK DESTRUCTION BADGE
Gold for 5 tanks

WOUND BADGE
Gold, silver, and black

INFANTRY ASSAULT BADGE

TANK ASSAULT BADGE

GENERAL ASSAULT BADGE

CLOSE COMBAT BADGE
Gold, silver, and bronze

GUERILLA WARFARE MEDAL
Gold, silver, and bronze

WINTER DEFENSIVE CAMPAIGN IN EAST, 1941-42

NARVIK SHIELD
Gold for the Navy

CHOLM SHIELD

CRIMEA SHIELD

DEMJANSK SHIELD

GERMAN-ITALIAN MEDAL

ARMY ANTIAIRCRAFT BADGE

MOTOR VEHICLE DRIVER'S BADGE

PLATE XXIII

RESTRICTED

RIBBONS FOR VALOR AND SERVICE— *These ribbons are a selection of those which may be worn above the left breast pocket by German military personnel.*

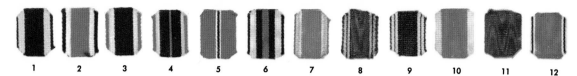

1. IRON CROSS, 1914
2. IRON CROSS, 1939
3. WAR SERVICE CROSS
4. WAR SERVICE MEDAL

5. EASTERN WINTER CAMPAIGN, 1941-42
6. WAR CROSS OF HONOR (Front Line Fighter)
7. PARTY SERVICE BADGE (24 Years)
8. PARTY SERVICE BADGE (15 Years)

9. PARTY SERVICE BADGE (10 Years)
10. GERMAN SOCIAL SERVICE
11. MEDAL FOR LENGTH OF MILITARY SERVICE
12. ENTRY INTO AUSTRIA

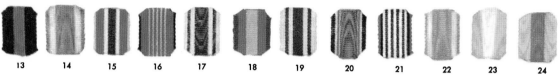

13. ENTRY INTO SUDETENLAND
14. WESTWALL SERVICE, 1939-40
15. MEMEL RIBBON
16. OLYMPIC GAMES MEDAL

17. GERMAN MOTHER'S CROSS
18. FIREMAN'S RIBBON
19. BALTIC CROSS (1919-20 Freikorps Service)
20. A.R.P. MEDAL

21. PRUSSIAN WAR EFFORT CROSS
22. PRUSSIAN LIFE-SAVING MEDAL
23. SILESIAN EAGLE (1919-20 Fighting vs. Poland)
24. BADEN MILITARY SERVICE CROSS

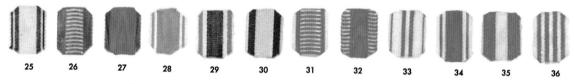

25. BAVARIAN MILITARY SERVICE CROSS
26. KING LUDWIG CROSS
27. PRINCE REGENT LUITPOLD MEDAL
28. BAVARIAN MILITARY SERVICE BADGE

29. BAVARIAN MEDAL OF VALOR
30. WURTTEMBERG MILITARY SERVICE CROSS
31. AUSTRIAN MEDAL OF VALOR
32. KARL TROOP CROSS

33. AUSTRIAN WAR SERVICE MEDAL
34. TIROL SERVICE MEDAL
35. HAMBURG HANSA WAR CROSS
36. BREMEN HANSA WAR CROSS

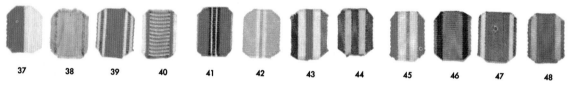

37. LUBECK HANSA WAR CROSS
38. BULGARIAN MEDAL OF VALOR
39. BULGARIAN WAR SERVICE MEDAL
40. HUNGARIAN WAR SERVICE (Horthy)

41. CROATIAN MEDAL OF VALOR
42. SLOVAKIAN MEDAL OF VALOR
43. AFRICA RIBBON
44. ITALIAN MEDAL OF VALOR

45. ITALIAN SERVICE MEDAL
46. FINNISH SERVICE MEDAL
47. FINNISH LIBERATION CROSS I CLASS
48. FINNISH LIBERATION CROSS II CLASS

49. FINNISH LIBERATION CROSS III CLASS
50. SPANISH MILITARY MEDAL OF VALOR
51. SPANISH RED MILITARY SERVICE CROSS
52. SPANISH WHITE MILITARY SERVICE CROSS

53. SPANISH CAMPAIGN MEDAL
54. SPANISH WOUND MEDAL
55. SPANISH SURVIVORS RIBBON
56. SPANISH COMMUNIST RIBBON

57. RUMANIAN MEDAL OF VALOR AND LOYALTY
58. RUMANIAN FAITHFUL SERVICE CROSS (Peace)
59. RUMANIAN MEDAL OF VALOR
60. RUMANIAN ORDER OF THE CROWN (Post 1932)

61. RUMANIAN ORDER OF THE CROWN (Pre-1932)
62. RUMANIAN FAITHFUL SERVICE CROSS (War)
63. RUMANIAN MEDICAL SERVICE CROSS
64. RUMANIAN FAITHFUL SERVICE MEDAL (War)
65. RUMANIAN ANTI-COMMUNIST SERVICE

66. CROSS OF QUEEN MARIE OF RUMANIA
67. RUMANIAN FLIERS' MEDAL OF VALOR
68. RUMANIAN FLIERS' ORDER OF VALOR
69. STAR OF RUMANIA

70. BRONZE CROSS OF VALOR AND SERVICE
    (For Eastern Volunteers)
71. SILVER CROSS OF VALOR AND SERVICE
    (For Eastern Volunteers)
72. GOLD CROSS OF VALOR AND SERVICE
    (For Eastern Volunteers)

PLATE XXIV

CHAPTER X

GERMAN AIR FORCE

Section I. AIR FORCE HIGH COMMAND

I. General

The German Air Force (*Luftwaffe*), one of the three branches of the German Armed Forces, is organized and administered independently of either the Army or the Navy. Its three main branches are the flying troops, antiaircraft artillery, and air signal troops. It also includes parachute and airborne troops, air engineers, air medical corps, and air police, and a number of special divisions formed of Air Force personnel for service as regular fighting troops. It is organized on a territorial rather than a functional basis, with separate operational and administrative commands. This division of responsibilities has made for a high degree of mobility among the flying units and thus has been responsible for much of the success of the German Air Force.

2. Commander-in-Chief

Reichsmarschall Goering serves in the dual capacity of Minister of Aviation (*Reichsminister der Luftfahrt*) and Commander-in-Chief of the Air Force (*Oberbefehlshaber der Luftwaffe*). As Commander-in-Chief he is charged with the administration and operations of the Air Force. As Minister of Aviation he is a member of the Cabinet and is responsible for the coordination and supervision of civil aviation. Since Goering has many other duties in the German Government, however, the supreme command usually is exercised by the State Secretary in the Ministry of Aviation and Inspector General of the Air Force.

3. Air Ministry (*Reichsluftfahrministerium* or *R.L.M.*)

At the Air Ministry—the highest administrative and operational authority of the Air Force—are found the departments which control all Air Force activity. These departments fall into two groups:

those of the General Staff and those concerned with administration and supply.

Section II. CHAIN OF COMMAND

I. General

The role of the Air Force in the conduct of the war, and to a certain extent in particular operations, is determined by the High Command of the Armed Forces (*Oberkommando der Wehrmacht*). The chain of command is from the Supreme Commander (Hitler), through the *OKW* to the Commander-in-Chief of the Air Force (Goering). The latter directs the actual employment of the Air Force through the Air Ministry and through his subordinate commanders of air combat units. However, when Air Force units are used in conjunction with Army or Navy units, all the forces involved come under a single operational control, in accordance with the German doctrine of unity of command. In such circumstances, a commanding officer is chosen from whichever of the three branches predominates in the operation, and he becomes directly responsible to the *OKW*.

2. *Luftflotte*

All Air Force units are organized into tactical and territorial air commands known as *Luftflotten*. Each *Luftflotte* is assigned a particular command area, although this assignment is not necessarily permanent, for an entire *Luftflotte* at any time may be moved from one area to another at the direction of the Air Ministry. Within its area, however, each *Luftflotte* not only controls all operations of the flying units, but also supervises the activities of all ground service units. Thus, in addition to a large operations department, each *Luftflotte* has its own adjutant, legal, administration, signal, and supply departments. All com-

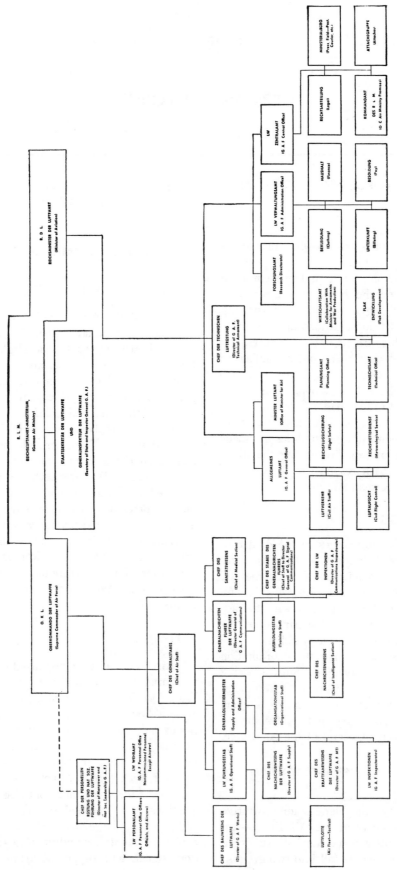

Figure 1.—The German Air Force High Command.

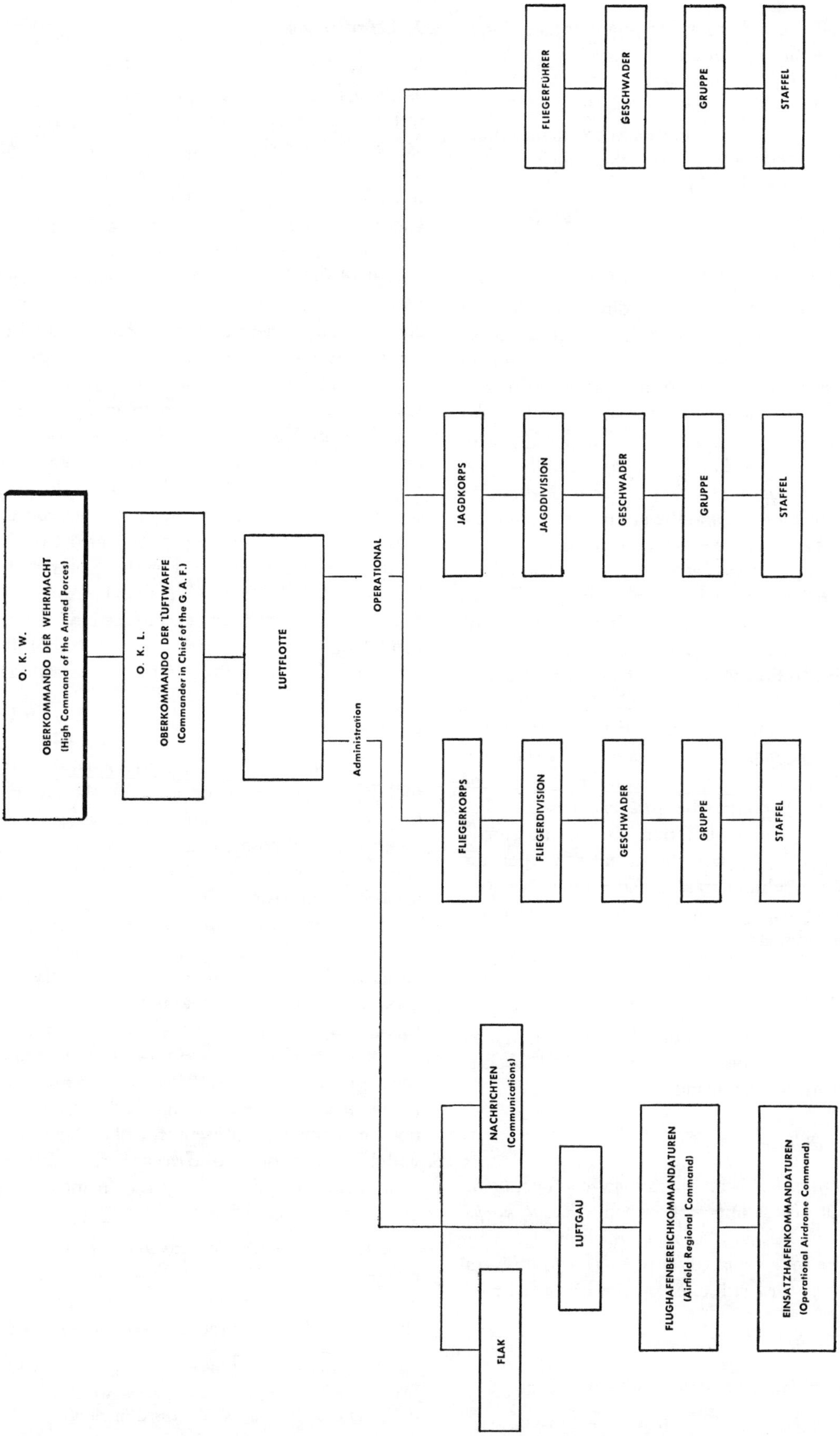

Figure 2.—German Air Force chain of command.

mands and formations subordinate to the *Luft-flotte* are either essentially operational (*Flieger-korps, Jagdkorps, Geschwader, Gruppen,* and *Staffeln*) or administrative (*Luftgaue*). Thus the administrative and operational commands meet at the *Luftflotte* headquarters, where their respective activities are coordinated.

3. *Fliegerkorps*

Operational units within the *Luftflotte* command area are organized into subordinate operational commands known as *Fliegerkorps*. Through these *Fliegerkorps,* the *Luftflotten* execute the operational directives received from the Air Ministry. Each *Fliegerkorps* is a composite, mobile command with its own geographical area of control and operations. A *Luftflotte* may command one or several *Fliegerkorps,* depending upon the size of the command area and the nature of operations. A *Fliegerkorps* may be detached at any time for operations in another *Luftflotte* area. The make-up of a *Fliegerkorps* is very elastic, both as to number and type of aircraft. It may consist of several bomber *Geschwader,* several fighter *Geschwader,* in addition to a varying number of short- and long-range reconnaissance *Gruppen.* On occasion it may be limited to one function such as that of a bomber command. The most important department of the *Fliegerkorps* command is that of operations. Although the *Fliegerkorps* also has adjutant, legal, administration, signal, and supply departments, it depends almost entirely upon the *Luftgau* for administrative and supply services. The *Fliegerkorps* are numbered nonconsecutively in Roman numerals.

4. *Jagdkorps*

A *Jagdkorps* is an operational command, similar to a *Fliegerkorps* but whose function is limited to that of a fighter command.

5. *Fliegerdivision*

A *Fliegerdivision* is an operational command similar to but of less importance than a *Fliegerkorps.* Most of the *Fliegerdivisionen* which existed prior to the war were replaced by *Fliegerkorps.* Several *Fliegerdivisionen* still exist on the Eastern Front.

6. *Jagddivision*

A *Jagddivision* is a command subordinate to a *Jagdkorps.*

7. *Lehrdivision*

This division is unnumbered and is known simply as the *Lehrdivision.* Its primary function was to test the latest types of aircraft, antiaircraft defenses, and air signals equipment from a tactical and operational point of view. *Lehr* units are incorporated directly into the combat commands and function as a part of the command's operational strength. *Lehr* personnel are supposed to have had previous combat experience. This system, by giving the *Lehr* units an operational status, enables them to experiment in actual combat operations, rather than under simulated conditions. The *Lehrdivision* was organized into a variety of formations and commands. There were two *Lehrgeschwader* composed of bomber, fighter, and reconnaissance *Lehrgruppen.* Recently, however, only a few bomber *Lehr* units have been operational and they no longer appear concerned with experimentation. There are also two *Lehr-regimenter,* one concerned with antiaircraft defenses and the other with signal developments. *Lehr* units are not to be confused with experimental units whose duties are of a technical nature, such as the testing of prototype aircraft.

8. *Geschwader*

a. GENERAL. The *Geschwader* is the largest mobile, homogeneous formation in the Air Force, and is used for long-range bombers, ground attack units, and both single- and twin-engine fighters. It normally consists of about 100 aircraft, organized into three *Gruppen.* A fourth and, in a few instances, a fifth *Gruppe* have been added to several single-engine fighter *Geschwader.*[1] Apparently the original intention was to have each *Geschwader* operate as a unit by stationing all three *Gruppen* at adjacent airdromes. However, although all *Gruppen* are now usually found on the same battlefront, all three of them are unlikely to operate from neighboring fields. In fact, it is not uncommon at present for the Air Force to withdraw one or two *Gruppen* for rest or re-equipment and subsequently return them to operations in another theater.

b. COMMAND. A *Geschwader* is generally commanded by an *Oberst* or *Oberstleutnant* known as the *Geschwaderkommodore.* He has a small staff of officers for the adjutant, operations, or-

---

[1] These fourth and fifth *Gruppen* are not to be confused with the *Ergänzungsgruppen,* which are devoted to operational training as discussed in Section VII.

ganization, technical, signal, navigation, meteorological, and intelligence branches. Some staffs also have a photographic officer. The staff has its own headquarters flight (*Stabs-Schwärm*) of three to six aircraft of the same type as those which make up the *Geschwader*. This *Geschwader* staff is always maintained, even when the subordinate *Gruppen* are separated for operations on different fronts.

c. TYPES. There are several types of *Geschwader*, known according to aircraft complement and/or operational employment as follows:

German title	Aircraft type	Abbreviation
Kampfgeschwader	Bomber	K. G.
Schlachtgeschwader[1]	Ground attack and antitank	S. G.
Jagdgeschwader	Single-engine fighter	J. G.
Zerstörergeschwader	Twin-engine fighter	Z. G.
Nachtjagdgeschwader	Night fighter	N. J. G.
Lehrgeschwader	Tactical experimental	L. G.

Each *Geschwader* is designated by its abbreviation followed by an Arabic numeral: for example, *K.G.77*, *N.J.G.26*, *Z.G.111*, etc. The numerals are not necessarily in consecutive order.

d. EQUIPMENT. Although all *Gruppen* in a *Geschwader* specialize in similar air tactics and are equipped with the same type of plane, the make and model may differ among the *Gruppen*. This variation is most prevalent in fighter *Geschwader*, but also occurs in a few of the bomber *Geschwader*. Thus a *Kampfgeschwader* may have one *Gruppe* equipped with the Dornier 217 and the other two *Gruppen* with the Heinkel 111, Junkers 88, or the Focke-Wulf 200. Or the entire *Geschwader* may be equipped with the same make of plane, such as the Messerschmitt 109, although one *Gruppe* may have a newer model while the other *Gruppen* have earlier ones.

9. *Gruppe*

a. GENERAL. The *Gruppe* is the basic combat unit of the Air Force for both administrative and operational purposes. It is a mobile homogeneous unit which is largely self-contained and which may be detached from its parent *Geschwader* for operations in any command area. In fact, directives for the movement of flying units are almost

---

[1] *Sturzkampfgeschwader* (Dive bomber) and *Schnellkampfgeschwader* (Ground attack) have been incorporated into, or superseded by the *Schlachtgeschwadern*.

always issued in terms of *Gruppen*. Usually the entire *Gruppe* is based at the same airdrome.

b. COMMAND. The *Gruppe* normally is commanded by a major or captain known as the *Gruppenkommandeur*. He has a small staff, consisting of the adjutant, operations officer, technical officer, and medical officer. There apparently is no special intelligence officer, since prisoners are sent directly to interrogation centers. Each *Gruppe* also has its own air signal platoon (*Luftnachrichtenzug*), known as a Technical Ground Station, and a staff flight (*Stabs-Kette*) of three aircraft generally of the same type with which the *Gruppe* is equipped.

c. EQUIPMENT. The *Gruppen* are organized into three *Staffeln*, with the exception of single-engine fighter *Geschwadern* which recently have been organized into four *Staffeln*. Thus, most *Gruppen* are considered to have a table of organization of 27 aircraft each (exclusive of the three aircraft of the *Gruppen-Stab*) and *Jagdgruppen* a table of organization of 36 aircraft (also exclusive of the *Gruppen-Stab*). Actual strength, however, is likely to differ substantially from authorized strength; on many occasions it has been found well below or above such figures. *Gruppen* attached to a *Geschwader* are numbered in Roman numerals in consecutive order. Thus *I/K.G.77*, *II/K.G.77*, and *III/K.G.77* are the first, second, and third *Gruppen*, respectively, of long-range bomber *Geschwader 77*.

10. *Staffel*

a. GENERAL. The *Staffel* is the smallest Air Force operational unit, and is generally commanded by a captain or lieutenant known as the *Staffelkapitän*. One officer serves as adjutant; the signal, technical, and navigation branches are supervised by the flying personnel in their spare time.

b. EQUIPMENT. A *Staffel* is considered to have a table of organization of nine aircraft. Its actual strength, however, may be as low as five or six aircraft or as much as 18 or 20 aircraft. For tactical purposes, it may be subdivided into *Schwärme* of five planes; into *Ketten* of three planes; or into *Rotten* of two planes. Each *Staffel* usually will have its own mobile repair shop for minor repairs in the dispersal areas; other motor vehicles must be drawn from the organization of the parent *Gruppe*.

c. NUMBERING. All *Staffeln* in the *Geschwader* are numbered consecutively in Arabic numerals. Thus, in all but *Jagdgeschwader,* the first, second, and third *Staffeln* constitute *Gruppe I;* the fourth, fifth and sixth *Staffeln, Gruppe II;* and the seventh, eighth, and ninth *Staffeln, Gruppe III.* Where a fourth or fifth *Gruppe* exists, the *Staffeln* will be numbered *10, 11,* and *12,* or *13, 14,* and *15,* respectively. In *Jagdgeschwadern* having four *Staffeln,* the *Gruppe I* thus will contain *Staffeln 1, 2, 3,* and *4; Gruppe II, Staffeln 5, 6, 7,* and *8; Gruppe III, Staffeln 9, 10, 11,* and *12,* etc. In unit designations, the *Gruppe* numeral is omitted whenever the *Staffel* number is indicated. Thus the fourth *Staffel* of *K.G.77* is known as *4/K.G.77,* and no other reference to its position in *Gruppe II* of *K.G.77* is necessary.

11. Semiautonomous Units

a. GENERAL. Reconnaissance and Army cooperation aircraft operate and are organized as semiautonomous units, as *Staffeln* or *Gruppen.* These semiautonomous units fall into three general categories, all of which are numbered nonconsecutively in Arabic numerals of one, two or three digits.

b. LONG-RANGE RECONNAISSANCE. Long-range reconnaissance aircraft are organized into *Fernaufklärungsgruppen,* which are known as (*F*) or *FAG* units. Thus *3(F)123* is the third *Staffel* of *Fernaufklärungsgruppe 123.*

c. SHORT-RANGE RECONNAISSANCE. Short-range reconnaissance and Army cooperation aircraft are organized into *Nahaufklärungsgruppen,* which are known as *NAGr* or (*H*) units (due to former name of *Heeresaufklärungsgruppen*). Under the old nomenclature still applying to some units, the first *Staffel* of *Nahaufklärungsgruppe 32* is therefore *1(H)32.* Under the more recent *Gruppen* organization and numbering, the third *Staffel* of *Nahaufklärungsgruppe 1* for instance, is *3/NAGr 1.*

d. COASTAL RECONNAISSANCE. Coastal reconnaissance and naval cooperation aircraft were originally organized into *Küstenfliegergruppen* (abbreviated *K.F.Gr.*). They are now known as *Seeaufklärungsgruppen* (abbreviated *SAGr.*). Thus the third *Staffel* of *Seeaufklärungsgruppe 196* is known as *3/SAGr. 196.*

e. MISCELLANEOUS UNITS. Miscellaneous units also are similarly organized and operated.

(1) *Nachtschlachtgruppen* (Night Harassing) represent the relatively recent grouping of previously loosely organized *Staffeln.* Most of them are equipped with obsolete aircraft, although coincidentally with their reorganization in *Gruppen,* these units have been modernized to some extent. Though some units in the East still have such aircraft as Arado 66, GO145, HE50, etc., those in the West are equipped with modern JU87 and FW190. These *Nachtschlachtgruppen* are numbered in Arabic numbers and thus abbreviated—*NS1, NS2, NS3,* etc.

(2) The *Luftbeobachter Staffeln* (Air Observers).

(3) A number of specialized units such as minesweeping *Staffeln,* etc.

12. Special Commands

a. *Jagdführer.* Separate fighter commands known as *Jagdführer,* or more commonly as *Jafü,* have been established in each *Luftflotte* since the outbreak of war. At first a *Jafü* was concerned primarily with matters of policy and controlled operations only on specific occasions. Yet, for a period, the *Jafüs* in France and Germany appeared to have had an overriding authority in directing all defensive fighter operations. Lately, however, it is believed that their functions have become virtually administrative.

b. *Fliegerführer.* Highly specialized operations on certain fronts have been put under the control of special commanders known as *Fliegerführer.* These *Fliegerführer* control operations in a particular area only and are directly responsible to the *Luftflotte* commander in whose area they operate. For instance, the three *Fliegerführer* (3, 4, 5) in *Luftflotte* V, although primarily concerned with antishipping operations and weather reconnaissance, controlled all types of combat aircraft in their area of operations.

13. *Luftgau*

a. GENERAL. The *Luftgaue* are the actual administrative and supply organizations of the *Luftwaffe.* They are stationary or immobile commands whose authority is limited to certain well defined and permanently fixed geographical areas. A *Luftgau* commander is usually a *General der Flieger* or *General der Flakartillerie,* and theoretically is responsible to the *Luftflotte* commander within whose command area the *Luftgau* lies. In actual practice, however, the *Luftgau* commanders receive most of their instructions direct from the Air Ministry, and the *Luftflottenchefs* interfere little with *Luftgau* administration. The *Luftgaue* permanently established in Germany are numbered non-consecutively by Roman numerals;

those in occupied countries are generally designated by their location: for example, *Luftgau Norwegen.*

b. FUNCTIONS. Each *Luftgau* is responsible for the following services within its command area:

(1) Administration, supply, and maintenance of all flying units.

(2) Active and passive defense against air attack.

(3) Operations of signal units.

(4) All training other than that of auxiliary units.

(5) Recruitment, mobilization, and training of reserve personnel.

c. SECTIONS. Each *Luftgau* has its own operations, adjutant, legal, administration, signal, and supply sections. It also has a department for prohibited and restricted flying areas which has no known counterpart in the *Luftflotte* or *Fliegerkorps* headquarters. All training within the *Luftgau* area is directed by a Higher Commander of Training. This officer is usually a *Generalmajor* and is subordinate only to the *Luftgau* commander. All other *Luftgau* services are maintained through subordinate section commands which are designated by Arabic numerals preceding the *Luftgau* unit designation. Thus *4/VIII* is the fourth section command in *Luftgau VIII.*

d. AIRDROME COMMANDS. The main channels through which the flying units draw on the services of the *Luftgaue* are the airdrome commands. Each *Luftgau* area is divided into about five airdrome regional commands (*Flughafenbereichkommandanturen*). The regional commands are in turn subdivided into five or more operational airdrome commands (*Einsatzhafenkommandanturen*). The regional command is essentially administrative and is not necessarily located at an airfield. The operational airdrome command, however, exists only to serve the flying units at their stations and is thus always found at an airdrome. The manner in which the *Luftgau* has decentralized its authority through these commands is as follows:

(1) The airdrome regional commands are charged with the *Luftgau's* responsibility for supply and maintenance of supplies and equipment within their respective areas; meeting the physical needs of the flying units; defense of aircraft, equipment, and motor transport against air attack; airdrome development; and air movements. These duties are discharged by specialized units which the *Luftgau* allots to the regional command and which the regional command then redistributes among the operational commands. For example, the Field Works Office (*Feldbauamt*) at the regional command handles airdrome maintenance through its subsidiary Works Superintendent's Offices which are stationed at the airdromes. Similarly, the Air Signal Company at each regional command is divided into platoons which are stationed at the operational commands. A senior technical officer supervises aircraft maintenance in the region through his subordinate technical officers at the operational commands. The airdrom regional command is thus largely self-contained and calls on the *Luftgau* for assistance only when the units already assigned prove inadequate.

(2) The airdrome regional command also acts as the intermediary between the *Luftgau* headquarters and the operational airdrome command. All orders, requests, reports, etc., traveling between the two must pass through the regional command staff. This staff numbers from 50 to 150 officers and enlisted men and is headed by a commandant who usually holds the rank of *Generalmajor.*

(3) The airdrome regional command's primary practical task is that of transporting supplies and equipment from the depots to its subordinate operational commands. For this purpose it is generally assigned a supply company (*Nachschubkompanie*) composed of a supply column staff (*Nachschubkolonnenstab*), some four transport columns (*Transportkolonnen*), and two or three fuel columns (*Flugbetriebsstoffkolonnen*).

(4) The commander of the operational airdrome command normally holds the rank of major, captain, or first lieutenant. His adjutant handles personnel matters. The personnel complement of an operational command numbers about 350 officers and enlisted men, and the motor transport allotment is between 50 and 100 vehicles.

(5) Airdrome maintenance at each operational command is handled by a Works Superintendent's Office (*Bauleitung*), subordinate to the Field Works Office at the regional command. The *Bauleitung* has charge of most of the construction done at the airdrome (buildings, dispersal areas, defense works, camouflage, etc.), as well as the laying of runways, extension of landing grounds, and installation of lighting systems. Reports on serviceability and bomb damage are radioed through the regional command to the *Luftgau,* and thence to the Air Ministry for broadcast over

the Air Force Safety Service network. The *Bauleitung* personnel is composed of civil servants and technical staffs. Any other specialized construction units which may be attached to the airdromes to repair bomb damage or enlarge facilities are also directed by the *Bauleitung*.

(6) The operational airdrome command is also responsible for defense against air attack, for which it has both heavy and light *Flak* units. These guns and other aerial defense units are commanded by the airdrome commander only when there is no flying unit stationed at the field. Otherwise, defense is controlled by the commander of that flying unit which is occupying the airdrome.

(7) The telephone, teleprinter, and radio at each operational airdrome command are operated by an air signal platoon (*Fliegerhorst-Luftnachrichtenzug*) and commanded by a signal officer who is subordinate to the senior signal officer at the airdrome regional command. The signal platoon also transmits the meteorological and airdrome serviceability reports and operates the Air Movements Control. This control directs only nonoperational flying. Signal communications with aircraft in operations are controlled by the tactical ground station attached to the flying unit.

(8) Aircraft maintenance at the operational airdrome command—except for servicing and minor repairs which are performed by the ground staff of the flying unit—is the responsibility of a technical officer. This officer not only handles overhauls and major repairs, but also is responsible for maintenance of motor vehicles; for bomb, fuel, and other supply stores; and for equipment stores and the armory. He is subordinate to the senior technical officer at the airdrome regional command.

(9) The requests by the operational airdrome command for equipment and spare parts reach the regional command through the technical officer. Requisitions for bombs, fuel, and ammunition are made by the supply section. The operational command also has an administrative section which handles clothing, food, pay, billeting, and other accommodations; a record office; a photographic section; a medical section; and a welfare section.

(10) *Luftgaustäbe z.b.V.* During campaigns the *Luftgaue* provide the advancing air formation with supplies and services through a system of subordinate commands known as *Luftgaustäbe zur besonderer Verwendung* (*Luftgau*

staffs for special duty) or, simply, *Luftgaustäbe z. b. V.* units. These units may be designated by an Arabic numeral (*Luftgaustäb z. b. V. 3*) or by their location (*Luftgaustäb Kiev*). They are sent into the forward battle areas by their controlling *Luftgau* and are normally responsible for all services in an area occupied by a *Fliegerkorps*. After conditions have become relatively stabilized—for example, when operational airdrome commands have been established and supply stations and fuel and ammunition field depots have been set up—the *Luftgaustäb z. b. V.* unit is withdrawn and the parent *Luftgau* assumes direct command.

Section III. AIR FORCE ARMS AND SERVICES

I. Antiaircraft Defenses

a. GENERAL. The bulk of the German antiaircraft artillery, inclusive of antiaircraft searchlight units, is an organic part of the German Air Force. The German Army has antiaircraft artillery units of its own, but these units are only for the organic use and protection of the Army units against air attack.

For organizational charts of *Luftwaffe* and Army antiaircraft units see Sections V and VI, Chapter II. For a discussion of antiaircraft weapons and equipment see Chapter VII, Section IV.

b. ANTIAIRCRAFT DEFENSE OF GERMANY AND REAR AREAS. The Chief of the German Air Force is responsible for the air defense of territorial Germany as well as important installations in occupied countries. The Aircraft Warning Service as a part of the Air Force is tied in with the coordinated use of aviation, antiaircraft artillery, and barrage balloons. All air raid precaution measures also are the responsibility of the Chief of the German Air Force.

Antiaircraft defense of rear areas is carried out through the *Luftgaue* mentioned above. *Luftgaue* coordinate their defenses with each other in accordance with regulations published by the Chief of the Air Force. The commander of each *Luftgau* has a specialist under him who exercises command over the antiaircraft artillery units, including searchlights, assigned to the district. Other specialists include the commanders of barrage balloon units and of units responsible for carrying out special defense measures. In actual operations, in most cases the commands above the actual operating units act mainly in a coordinating capacity, feeding information to the operating units which act in turn on their own initiative in accordance with prescribed standing operating procedure.

Within certain of the air districts there are special air defense commands. Each of these covers special areas or cities of vital importance, defense of which, under one command, is laid out with a concentration of coordinated defense facilities inclusive of antiaircraft guns and searchlights, fighter aviation, barrage balloons, warning facilities, and the use of special devices such as smoke generators.

Operation of the antiaircraft defense system calls for close cooperation between fighter planes and air warning systems, and the antiaircraft guns with supporting searchlights are considered the backbone of the static defense. For operational control, the antiaircraft command in a *Luftgau* is usually divided into groups known as *Flakgruppen,* and these groups in turn are divided into sub-groups known as *Flakuntergruppen.* The headquarters of the group is normally the control center of the *Flak* defenses, and acts downward through the sub-groups.

In deployment of heavy antiaircraft guns in important static areas, there is a tendency toward the use of concentrated sites known as *Grossbatterien.* These usually consist of three 4-, 6-, or even 8-gun batteries grouped together at one site, with fire control for all guns emanating from one central source.

Antiaircraft searchlights are used in cooperation with night fighters, as well as in their normal role of illuminating targets for the gun units.

c. USE OF ANTIAIRCRAFT WITH FIELD FORCES. For operation in the field, *Luftwaffe* antiaircraft units are allotted to field task forces for protection of Army and Air Force installations. Even in moving situations, a certain amount of antiaircraft is present for the defense of important semi-permanent installations such as depots, parks, railroads, bridges, and airdromes. No hard and fast rule is laid down for this use of antiaircraft artillery. The size of the antiaircraft force defending such areas will depend to a large extent on importance of the areas to be defended, plus availability of *Luftwaffe* antiaircraft units for such assignment. *Luftwaffe* antiaircraft organizations and units operating with the Army are subordinated operationally and for command pur-

poses to the Army unit concerned, and administratively (for replacements, etc.) to their parent Air Force Organization.

Employment and composition of the higher *Flak* units will vary in accordance with local conditions. For a fuller discussion of the organization and employment of higher antiaircraft units in the field, see Section V, Chapter II.

d. DEFENSE OF RAILWAY TRAINS. The mounting of antiaircraft materiel on railway mounts for the protection of railway trains and as a means of furnishing a highly mobile defense of lines of communication has been highly perfected by the Germans. Antiaircraft guns on railway mounts can be used either in rear areas for protection of trains operating there, or for the protection of trains carrying troops or supplies to forward combat areas. Although the 20-mm single- or four-barreled *Flak* is normally employed for this purpose, the 37-mm, 88-mm and 105-mm guns will also be encountered mounted on railway cars.

2. German Air Force Signal Service (*Luftnachrichtenwesen*)

a. GENERAL. The importance of a comprehensive and efficient air signal service in aerial warfare is obvious. Neither offensive nor defensive air operations could be conducted without a complete network of signal communications, or without radio and radar equipment for the direction and control of aircraft, particularly in fighter defense. So vital is the role of the German Air Force Signal Service that it has had a greater proportionate wartime expansion than any other arm of the German Air Force, and now has an estimated personnel strength of between 175,000 and 200,000.

b. FLEXIBILITY. The efficiency of the German Air Force has been enhanced by the flexibility of its signal organization. This was particularly true when the Germans were advancing into new territory, usually well prepared, on a temporary basis, for the reception of flying units. As soon as the captured territory was firmly occupied, signal units then established a more permanent land-line communications system. Under present circumstances, with the Germans on the defensive, the flexibility and mobility of the German Air Force are no longer dependent to the same extent on its signal organization. However, a workable German Air Force Signal Service is still of paramount importance in the defense of Germany against air attacks.

c. FUNCTIONS. These include the transmission of all orders and communications necessary for the operation and functioning of the German Air Force, if possible both by landline and by wireless; the establishment and supervision of all navigational aids to aircraft; the manning of Observer Corps and radar in connection with air defense; control of air traffic, air safety and rescue services; and the interception of enemy signals.

d. ORGANIZATION. (1) *General.* One of the departments of the German Air Ministry is the Director General of Signal Communications (*Generalnachrichtenführer der Luftwaffe*). To handle its multiple duties, a flexible organization has been developed, consisting of many self-contained specialist companies. The bulk of these companies are allocated to the major operational and administrative commands, and the others are grouped into battalions or remain as individual companies attached to minor commands.

(2) *Section platoon* and *company.* The basic operational unit is the section (*Truppe*) of 10-20 men. Each section specializes in one particular signal activity such as telephone, teletype, cable laying, construction, etc. Five to ten sections of the same type are organized into a platoon (*Zug*) of 80 to 100 men. Three to six platoons are grouped into a company (*Kompanie*) of 200 to 300 men. All platoons in a company specialize in the same branch of signal activity, so that each company is a self-contained specialist unit.

(3) *Battalion and regiment.* Three to four companies usually make up a battalion (*Abteilung*), although some have many more. The strength of a battalion, aside from its staff, depends on the number of companies. Three to five battalions normally form a regiment (*Regimenter*), with a strength between 1,500 and 9,000 and varying functions.

(4) *Allotment and numbering of units.* Signal regiments and smaller units are allotted to the several different types of operational and administrative commands requiring a permanent allocation of signal personnel. Allocation is on the basis of the size and requirements of the command. The relationship of the signal units to their assigned commands often is indicated by the terminal number of the unit designation; e.g. *Luftflotte* 2 had Signal Regiments 2, 12, and 22. However, with the creation of many new commands and the renumbering of others, the numbering

system for signal units is not as readily workable as formerly.

(5) *Special units.* In addition to the standard units, there is a special Research Regiment charged with the development of new types of signal equipment and its employment. Aircraft specially equipped for signal activities have also in many instances been allotted to various commands and have proved extremely useful in conducting air operations in mobile situations.

(6) *Command.* The supreme signal command of the above units is exercised by the Director General of Signals of the Air Ministry. Signal command of a *Luftflotte* is under a Chief Signal Officer (*Höhere Nachrichtenführer* or *Höhere Nafü*) who controls the senior Signal Officer (*Nafü*) of the *Fliegerkorps, Luftgaue, Flak-Korps* and *Flak Division,* and *Airfield Regional Command.* Subordinate to these are the Signal Officers (*Nachrichten Offizier* or *N. O.*) who exercise command in the lower subdivisions such as Operational Airfield Command signal platoons, and *Geschwader* signal companies.

e. SIGNAL EQUIPMENT. (1) *General.* German signal equipment, generally speaking, has been characterized by standardization of design, relatively few major types, and a high quality of components and workmanship. During the first years of the war, the Germans did not fully appreciate the tactical possibilities of radar[1] and for a time Allied radar development was well ahead of the German. However, the Germans have made tremendous efforts to match Allied technical progress and to overcome the various tactical problems resulting from Allied superiority.

(2) *Ground radar.* German ground radar falls into three general categories: Early warning set (*Freya, Mammut* or *Wassermann*) for long range detection; *Giant Würzburg* primarily for aircraft interception control; and *Small Würzburg* designed for flak control, but also used for height finding in the Aircraft Reporting Service. These various types of ground radar equipment play a large part in the German system of air raid warning and control of fighter interception. Many devices have been developed by the Allies to nullify the effectiveness of the German equipment, but at the same time the Germans have

---

[1] The basic principle of radar is the transmission of a wireless pulse of very short duration, the reflection of the pulse by the object to be detected, and the reception of both the original and reflected pulses by a receiver adjacent to the transmitter. Electrical measurement of the time interval between the two pulses gives a direct indication of the distance of the reflecting object. Means are also provided whereby direction of the object from the transmitter, and in some cases its height, can be obtained.

developed numerous countermeasures. These measures and countermeasures have led to extremely rapid development of new techniques and equipment both by the Germans and by the Allies.

(3) *Airborne radio and radar.* German airborne radio and radar equipment may be classified in four general categories: *Funkgerat (FuG)*, or radio and radar equipment involving transmitters and receivers; *Peilgerat (PeG)*, or navigational equipment; *Notsender (NS)*, or emergency transmitter; and other types of miscellaneous equipment. Airborne equipment is an absolute necessity for the successful conduct of air operations. Throughout the war, the Germans have developed navigational, bombing, and fighter control equipment. The latter is particularly important at the present time for the Germans who must depend on adequate warning of Allied air attacks and efficient control of fighters and flak for effective opposition.

f. FIGHTER DEFENSE. (1) *General.* During 1941 and early 1942, the German Air Force fighter organization was concerned mainly with defense of targets in Northern France and the Lowlands. The bulk of aerial combats then were taking place in the relatively small area over those countries and over the English Channel; and a warning system, consisting of a coastal radar belt and visual observers, was adequate. But the greater depth of penetration by Allied bombers in 1943 required that the German Air Force protect targets in Germany as well as in occupied territory, and the defensive problem thus became infinitely more complex. Additional radar belts and observer posts were required. German fighters had to be placed in tactically favorable positions, and they were forced to enlarge the scope of their activity to cover all areas subject to attack. Such developments naturally led to considerable changes in the German Air Force fighter organization and the methods of fighter control. The liberation of France and part of the Lowlands in 1944 further complicated the German defensive problem by depriving the German Air Force of a large and efficient part of its early warning system, as well as many excellent airfields at a time when the weight of the Allied air assault was increasing.

(2) *Reporting and warning system.* The Aircraft Reporting Service is a part of the German Air Force. Long-range radar sets determine the range and bearing of the approaching aircraft, and short-range sets measure height. Other types of equipment distinguish between friendly and hostile aircraft. An Observer Corps network with strategically located posts also supplies aircraft warning information, while in some instances patrolling aircraft shadow the attacking aircraft. On the basis of the information from these various sources, hostile aircraft are plotted in a central headquarters, and the Germans in the past have been able to construct a fairly accurate and current picture of Allied air operations. Proper warning then is given to all interested agencies, and defensive fighters are put in the air to intercept the attackers. Information on the course and expected target of the bombers is passed by radio to the airborne fighters until contact is made. The specific aerial tactics used by the German fighters have varied considerably throughout the war, but in general the precise method becomes the responsibility of the fighter pilots after contact is made. In spite of the excellent equipment and control methods the Germans have developed, their defensive warnings and operations are considerably handicapped by the loss of territory in Western Europe.

3. Airborne Forces

See Chapter X, section VII.

4. Air Force Fighting Units

See Chapter II, sections V, VI.

5. Air Transport

a. GENERAL. German transport aircraft and gliders are controlled by a General Staff Department at the Air Ministry. This department, headed by a *Kommodor und Lufttransportführer*, allocates and adminsters all transport units in the Air Force. The majority of the transport planes consist of the JU 52. This old type has been retained because of its adaptability to varied tasks and its ability to operate under difficult conditions. Since the production of JU 52's has been inadequate to meet present transport needs, the German Air Force has drawn upon Italian aircraft, such as the SM 82. Production of new types specifically designed as transports, such as the JU 252, JU 290 and the ME 323, has been almost negligible. The HE 111 has been adapted to extensive employment as a freight carrier, and lighter planes, such as the Fieseler Storch (FI 156), frequently are used for passenger-carrying and liaison work. Transport and communications aircraft are organized for the following services:

b. FOR OPERATIONAL UNITS. The Air Force maintains several minor air transport units which are more or less permanently allocated to various commands. These units are not intended to perform any particularly heavy or large-scale transport work such as airborne operations or long-term supply. They are used rather for the numerous odd jobs of communications, liaison, and passenger-carrying within the *Luftflotte* area, or between the *Luftflotte* and Air Force headquarters in Germany. These units are distributed among the commands as follows:

(1) The staff of each *Luftflotte* and *Fliegerkorps* is allotted a transport *Staffel,* with 12 or 13 aircraft to be used for transport within Germany proper as well as in forward areas.

(2) Each *Fliegerkorps* is allotted a transport *Staffel* of 10 to 15 JU 52's in addition to a *Kurier-Staffel* (communications) of lighter planes. The *Fliegerkorps* then may temporarily re-allot part or all of the JU 52's to the subordinate *Geschwader* and *Gruppen* whenever the transport of personnel, equipment, and/or supplies becomes particularly urgent.

(3) Each operational *Gruppe* is allotted several lighter types of communication aircraft. Formerly, each *Gruppe* also had at least one JU 52 for transport purposes. Now, however, the *Gruppen* usually rely on JU 52's temporarily lent to them by the *Fliegerkorps* headquarters.

(4) Each *Aufklärungsgruppe* (reconnaissance group) has a *Kurier-Staffel* within the *Fliegerkorps* organization which is primarily intended for liaison with Army commanders. These aircraft are at the disposal of Army personnel as well as the Air Force reconnaissance officers.

(5) Allotted to each *Flivo* is a *Verbindungs-Staffel* (liaison) of communication aircraft which is used for contact work between Army headquarters and those Air Force units which are providing close or direct support for the Army.

(6) The main air signal regiments of each *Luftflotte* and *Fliegerkorps* have their own *Staffeln* or transport aircraft. Some of these planes are equipped as flying signal stations, but many are used simply for transporting equipment and personnel.

(7) The higher commands, including the *Oberkommando der Wehrmacht,* the *Oberkommando des Heeres,* the *Oberkommando der Marine,* and the *Oberkommando der Luftwaffe,* each have

their own *Kurier-Staffel* to carry mail and personnel. These aircraft operate on a fixed schedule over all of Germany and remaining occupied territory. Individual aircraft may also be detailed on special urgent tasks.

c. FOR CIVIL AIRLINES. A small number of transports, primarily JU 52's, still are used on those civil air routes which the *Deutsche Lufthansa A. G.* operated before the war and continues to maintain under strict military supervision for high priority communication.

d. FOR *K. G. z. b. V.* UNITS. The *Kampfgeschwader zur besonderer Verwendung* (for special duty), known more simply as *K. G. z. b. V.* units, include over two-thirds of the German transport aircraft and are actually the mainstay of the Air Force transport organization. For limited operations these aircraft still may be subordinated to and receive their directives from the *Luftflotten* and *Geschwader.* In the past they occasionally were allotted by the Air Ministry to the *Luftflotten* on a fairly permanent basis (for example, to a *Luftflotte* headquarters). Now, however, they usually are so allotted for a specific operation only (for example, an airborne operation or supply mission). If only one or two units are allotted to a *Luftflotte,* the chief quartermaster department of the *Luftflotte* will handle administration, personnel, and aircraft serviceability. If several units are operating under the *Luftflotte,* however, the Air Ministry usually will detail an air transport officer to the *Luftflotte.* This officer, who normally holds the rank of *Oberst,* generally is assisted by a staff, which may include a technical officer, a personnel officer or adjutant, and an operations officer, in addition to a transport officer who apportions the loads.

The organization of the *K. G. z. b. V.* units is extremely fluid, and although the original intention apparently was to set up the units in *Geschwader,* the actual strength of most *z. b. V.* units rarely exceeds that of a *Gruppe.* These *Gruppen* normally number 53 aircraft organized into four *Staffeln* of 12 aircraft each plus a *Gruppenstab* of five planes.

For purposes of transporting parachute troops and air-landing infantry in airborne operations, transport aircraft are organized into *z. b. V. Geschwader.* Each such *Geschwader* consists of about 200 aircraft organized into four *Gruppen* of four *Staffeln* each. Each *Staffel* has 12 aircraft organized into four *Ketten* of three aircraft each. The organization of the *Kampfgeschwader* thus closely parallels that of the parachute troops which they transport. A JU 52 can carry 10 to 12 fully equipped parachutists. Thus one section of parachutists is carried by one aircraft; a platoon of 36 men is carried by a *z. b. V. Kette;* a company of 120 to 144 men is carried by a *z. b. V. Staffel;* and an entire parachute battalion is carried by a *z. b. V. Gruppe.* Whenever possible, the men are moved by units, that is, a *z. b. V. Kette* carrying a parachute platoon.

e. SPECIALLY EQUIPPED TRANSPORTS. A number of JU 52's have been designed for highly specialized transport services. For example, many JU 52's, a number of which are attached to Air Force medical units, are fitted as ambulance planes with a capacity of 12 stretcher patients and five sitting patients. Some JU 52's temporarily have been equipped with skis, and others with pontoons for transporting men and supplies into areas made inaccessible by snow or separated by bodies of water.

f. GLIDERS. The Germans also are using towed gliders for air transport. Since they combine a high load capacity with comparatively small fuel consumption for the towing aircraft (or of the glider itself in the powered version), they first were used in the Lowlands in 1940. The DFS 230 and the Gotha 242 carried troops and supplies from Italy and Sicily to Africa from mid-1941 until the conclusion of the Tunisian campaign. In the fall of 1942, the ME 323 powered glider caused wide comment in its operations between Sicily and Tunisia. At the same time it was revealed that each dive-bomber *Staffel* operating from Tunisia had its own DFS 230 to carry supplies from Sicily to Africa. Critical supply situations on the Russian Front and in the Balkans forced the Germans to employ gliders in many instances. Though they have seen little service in the West to date, disruption of transportation lines through Allied aerial attacks may compel further use of unpowered gliders.

6. Sea Rescue Service

The Air Force Sea Rescue Service (*Seenotdienst*) was first established to take care of airmen shot down over the North Sea area and the English Channel. Its services were extended to the Mediterranean, the Black Sea, and the Baltic. Rescues are performed normally by the service's own aircraft, but where the hazards of water landing are too great, the actual rescue is made by surface craft. These craft may be attached to the service or may be simply lent to it for a particular rescue.

Seenotdienst units were subordinated to the *Luftflotte* within whose area they serve. These units were organized into three sea rescue commands (*Seenotflugkommandos*), each of which is headed by a *Seenotdienstführer* with the rank of colonel. Subordinate to these commands are regional commands, known as *Bereichkommandos,* which control the various *Staffeln* and detachments. Single rescue planes were often attached to combat units which operated over water.

7. Meteorological Services

a. GENERAL. The Air Force Meteorological Service (*Flugwetterdienst*) is controlled by the Air Ministry. The chief responsibility of the *Flugwetterdienst* is to provide all flying units with dependable weather forecasts as well as all long-term forecasts for strategical planning. The two main sources of Air Force meteorological information are weather stations and weather aircraft.

b. WEATHER STATIONS. At each airfield there is a relatively small *Wetterstelle* (weather station) which reports on conditions in its immediate vicinity. These reports are collected at regular intervals (usually hourly) by a *Wetterberatungszentral* (weather reporting center) which then coordinates the reports of all the *Wetterstellen* within its area and prepares maps for the flying units. A center usually serves an area covered by a *Fliegerkorps* and frequently is motorized. Some centers carry a *Luftgau* unit designation, such as *W. Z. B./XIII.* The chain of command from the airfield to Air Ministry is completed through meteorological officers stationed at *Luftgau, Fliegerkorps,* and *Luftflotte* headquarters.

c. WEATHER AIRCRAFT. Attached to each *Luftflotte* is a *Wetterkündigungstaffel* (weather reconnaissance squadron), commonly known as a *Westa* unit. These units normally have nine to 12 aircraft equipped with automatic recording instruments. The crews include a meteorological officer and a specially trained wireless operator.

Combat aircraft often are detailed to report on weather conditions encountered during their operations. The outstanding example of this type of reporting is that of the long-range bomber units operating from Norway. Weather reconnaissance performed by these units has become almost as important as their anti-shipping reconnaissance.

Section IV. ARMY AND NAVY COOPERATION

Air Force cooperation may be of three types: direct or close support (tactical support); indirect support (strategic missions); and liaison.

1. Direct or Close Support

Close support usually is confined to the actual battle front and the area immediately behind it. It consists of bombing and strafing enemy ground forces, tanks, artillery, pillboxes, field defense works, antiaircraft defenses, forward dumps, and supply columns. It also includes air cover as protection for ground and Air Force units against enemy air attacks, and against enemy air reconnaissance. All types of aircraft may be used for these operations.

2. Indirect Support

Indirect support involves attacks on targets beyond the battle area such as rear maintenance and supply depots, enemy airfields, railroads, industrial centers, etc.

3. Liaison

Liaison between the Army and Air Force for both army cooperation and tactical reconnaissance is provided by specially trained Air Force officers known as *Flivos* (*Fliegerverbindungsoffiziere*). The German Air Force support is requested by the Army units through their superior commands. The armies transmit the request to the competent headquarters authority where a German Air Force liaison officer (*Flivo*) is stationed. Such headquarters are generally those of Army groups. German Air Force Signal Liaison officers (*Fliegerverbindungsoffiziere* (*Ln*)) are stationed with Army corps headquarters and in some particular cases with division headquarters. A German Air Force Liaison Officer is specially assigned to Army Headquarters for the purpose of directing close cooperation between the Army and German Air Force reconnaissance units (*Fliegerverbindungsoffiziere* (*Aufklärung*)). For the control of the close support missions, which as a result of these requests are ordered by the German Air Force Command (*Fliegerkorps* or *Luftflotte* HQ), special German Air Force officers are stationed at the front line. These control officers (*Fliegerleitoffiziere*) direct the flying formations to their targets by radio from advanced observation posts on the ground.

Section V. EQUIPMENT

!. Aircraft

a. CONVENTIONAL TYPES. (1) *General*. The decision of the German Air Ministry to concentrate on mass production of a few selected types has led to the development of versatile aircraft capable of performing several duties. Therefore, certain types of aircraft fall into more than one category; i. e., the Junkers 88 is both a twin-engine fighter and bomber. The German Air Force has relied chiefly on the Focke-Wulf 190, Messerschmitt 109, and Junkers 88 to perform the major part of all fighter, day and night bomber, and reconnaissance missions. During the course of the war, however, improvements became necessary, and many sub-types have been produced. It was important to prevent these changes from interfering seriously with production schedules, and especially to avoid the substitution of entirely new types. Therefore most of the improvements consisted of modernizations and adaptations of existing types rather than the creation of completely new models. The most favored improvements were the installations of more powerful engines, additional armament, and heavier armor plate. When these modifications did not achieve the desired end, the plane's structure was changed. One of the outstanding weaknesses of early German planes—their lack of defensive armament and protective armor—received increased attention, and in many cases has been adequately remedied.

(2) *Single-engine fighters* (a) *General*. The German single-engine fighter force is made up of only two plane types—the Messerschmitt 109 and the Focke-Wulf 190. Both types are produced in several versions and series, but the basic design of each has remained unchanged. Improvements have been achieved mainly by installation of more highly powered engines and heavier armament. The principal developments in these fighters have been the introduction of special high-altitude versions and the conversion of the FW 190 into a fighter-bomber.

(b) *Important operational aircraft*. (1) *Messerschmitt 109*. This plane was the standard single-engine fighter at the beginning of the war. At present, it is one of two standard single-engine fighters and is used primarily for high-altitude defensive duties.

(2) *Focke-Wulf 190*. This is the first single-engine fighter in the Air Force to use an air-cooled, radial engine. Of a more recent design than the ME 109, the FW 190 is a larger, cleaner plane. Its armor, armament, and simplified electrically operated controls are essential features that make it an exceptionally good medium-altitude fighter. It also is extensively used as a fighter-bomber with a normal bomb load of 550 pounds.

(3) *Twin-engine fighters*. (a) *General*. The Germans started the war with but one operational twin-engine fighter, the Messerschmitt 110. Attempts at introducing improved models (ME 210 and 410) encountered production difficulties, and these aircraft have not proved very successful as twin-engine fighters or been operational in large numbers. However, the German Air Force has adopted two of its long-range bombers as twin-engine fighters, the JU 88 and the DO 217. The fighter version of the JU 88 appeared in 1941, and this type since has been used in increasing numbers, now constituting a very substantial part of the German twin-engine fighter force. The DO 217 fighter is used primarily for night fighting, but has not achieved the success of the JU 88. Generally speaking, the night fighter branch of the German Air Force has constituted its most effective arm throughout the war.

(b) *Important operational aircraft*. (1) *Junkers 88*. Similar in appearance to its bomber prototype, except for the metal-panelled nose, the fighter version of the JU 88 is currently the most formidable German night fighter. It is relatively fast, heavily armed, and well protected. This type is employed for intruder and ground attack operations in addition to night fighting.

(2) *Dornier 217*. Likewise a modified bomber model, the DO 217 is used as a night-fighter, but has not proved as effective as the JU 88 in this category.

(4) *Ground attack aircraft*. The original JU 87 "Stuka" dive bomber, while still in limited use for night ground attack duty, has been largely superseded by faster single-engine fighters, equipped with bomb racks and known as fighter-bombers. The latter aircraft, of which the FW 190 is the best example, have the greater speed and maneuverability required by all ground attack operations without the necessity of strong fighter escort. The ME 262 jet plane also is being used for this type of operation.

(5) *Multi-engine bombers*. The long range bomber force has been relegated to a minor role

in German Air Force operations. Allied fighter superiority, combined with the necessity of increased German fighter production, largely has restricted bomber activities to mine laying and occasional night bombing. Principal types used are the JU 88, DO 217 and HE 111.

(6) *Transport planes*. Although a pre-war model, the Junkers 52 three-engine, low-wing monoplane is still the standard freight and troop carrying transport of the German Air Force. It also is used extensively for carrying and dropping parachute troops and as a glider tug. Other operational transport types include the six-engine Messerschmitt 323 and the four-engine Junkers 290. Converted bombers, such as the HE 111, also are employed frequently for heavy transport duty.

(7) *Gliders*. Gliders are of two types: powered and tow. Both resemble a conventional monoplane, but the tow glider lacks an engine and landing gear. The tow glider generally uses wheels during take-off and then jettisons them, subsequently landing on a skid. Both types of gliders are equipped with landing flaps and dive brakes, as well as navigation and landing lights.

The principal types of tow gliders are the DFS 230, GO 242 and ME 321. Principal powered gliders are ME 323 and GO 244.

(8) *Army cooperation and reconnaissance aircraft*. The standard type of Army cooperation plane, typified by the Henschel 126, has proved very vulnerable to modern fighters and antiaircraft fire. This has resulted in the employment of converted fighters, sufficiently fast, maneuverable, and armed to undertake short-range reconnaissance without fighter protection. Such conversion usually consists of replacing some of the armament with cameras. Recent development of high-speed jet aircraft has furnished the German Air Force with a highly desirable reconnaissance plane.

b. GERMAN COMPOSITE OR "PICK-A'BACK" AIRCRAFT. This innovation, still in the experimental stage, consists of a multi-motored plane with a large amount of explosive in the nose, surmounted and controlled by a single-engine aircraft. The latter directs the former in a dive towards the target and then releases it. Thereafter its operation is apparently by remote control. The usual components observed have been the JU 88 and the ME 109, but there is no reason to believe that other similar types could not be adapted for this purpose.

c. JET- AND ROCKET-PROPELLED. (1) *General*. The perfection and application of jet and rocket propulsion as motive power for aircraft are outstanding German aeronautical developments of the current war. To counter this new type aircraft, if it is employed on any appreciable scale, might well necessitate a general revision of defensive and offensive aerial tactics. Required changes or improvements also might extend to include ground defenses against attacks by these aircraft. To date the Germans have not employed jet or rocket aircraft on a sufficient scale to permit full and accurate assessment of their characteristics and possibilities. Those currently in use, however, appear to possess significant advantages over conventional types. In level flight, dives, and rate of climb all known conventional types have been surpassed by aircraft with this type of motive power. The propellerless power unit is capable of operation on the lowest grade fuels, and the absence of many intricate parts, necessary in conventional types, probably greatly simplifies assembly and repair methods.

(2) *Types*. Operational types of German jet and rocket aircraft thus far have been limited to those powered by single or twin-units. They have been employed to date as defensive fighters, as ground-attack or low-altitude bombers, and for reconnaissance. For the latter purpose they have proved to be very effective because of their speed.

(a) The only rocket-propelled aircraft known to be operational by the German Air Force is the Messerschmitt 163 (ME 163). It is a very fast, single-seat fighter. Although it has only a single power unit, it has a remarkable rate of climb. Because of its present limited endurance, to date it has seen comparatively little use, particularly in forward areas.

(b) The Messerschmitt 262 (ME 262), a twin-unit, jet-propelled aircraft, has proved to be the most successful of the German jet or rocket types thus far developed. Employed as a fighter, as a ground-attack or low-level bomber, and for reconnaissance duties, it is the most versatile of the jet or rocket aircraft yet introduced by the Germans.

(c) Other German twin-unit jet aircraft, either currently operational on a limited scale or expected to become operational in the near future, are the Arado 234 (AR 234) and Heinkel 280 (HE 280). Both of these aircraft are somewhat similar to the Messerschmitt 262 in appearance and are expected to be about equal in performance.

d. NAVAL AND MARINE. At present, naval and marine aircraft are operated by the German Air Force on a limited scale. The use of the BV 138 for reconnaissance in the Norway and Denmark areas is the principal duty performed by this type of aircraft. Other types, such as the HE 115 and AR 196, are employed for general reconnaissance and liaison with the various naval testing units operating in the Baltic Sea, and for the performance of air/sea rescue service. In addition, naval aircraft such as the BV 222 are occasionally used for marine supply and transport duty.

2. Power Units

a. ENGINES. The German Air Force has equipped practically all operational aircraft with engines manufactured by three large companies: Daimler-Benz (D.B.); the *Bayerische Moteren Werke* (*B.M.W.*); and the Junkers (Jumo). The trend of aeronautical engine development has been toward more powerful engines with increased altitude performance. German aero-engine designers have obtained this by modifying existing engines to use GM-1 (nitrous oxide) and MW-50 (methanol injection) apparatus and, in certain instances, by coupling two existing engines together. Lack of time for experimentation with new engines has led to the modification of existing types which could be more quickly put into service in war time.

b. JET PROPULSION UNITS. An outstanding achievement in the field of aircraft power units has been the development of jet propulsion, an example being the Junkers Jumo 004. This unit often is referred to as a jet-propulsion turbine, or turbo jet. Propulsion is developed through the reaction to ejected hot gases which have been created by compressed air igniting with liquid fuel. As these gases pass out to the vents they traverse a turbine, which in turn operates the air compressor. Original momentum of the turbine is created by an auxiliary engine which disengages when the turbine has developed sufficient speed to create the required compression. German aircraft using jet propulsion turbines include the Messerschmitt 262, Arado 234 and Heinkel 280.

c. ROCKET-PROPULSION UNITS. A closed unit in which fuel is burned or gasified, a rocket does not require air from the atmosphere for combustion. The gases leave through a nozzle at the rear to provide thrust by jet propulsion. Fuels are of three types: solids, (e. g., cordite); two liquids, one a fuel, (e. g., gasoline), and the second an oxidizing agent (e. g., liquid oxygen); or a single liquid with or without liquid as a catalyst, (e. g., hydrogen peroxide with potassium or sodium permanganate).

3. Armament

The Germans started the war with only a few types of aircraft armament, in order to standardize manufacture and achieve large-scale production. As the war progressed, improvements became necessary and many changes and additions have been made. In addition to increasing the rate of fire, muzzle velocity, and caliber of aircraft armament, the number of guns on German Air Force fighters has been greatly increased. The addition of the Model 108 30-mm cannon, a new weapon in aircraft armament, to FW 190's, ME 262's, ME 110 G's and ME 109 G's stands out as a great advancement, in terms of striking power. A detailed discussion of the various types of aircraft armament can be found in Chapter VII, Section IX.

4. Armor

The armor protection in German planes varies in thickness from 4 to 20 mm. The total weight per plane may vary from 100 pounds or less in some army cooperation types to over 1,000 pounds for a ground-attack plane. The demands of modern warfare have necessitated increased protection of the pilot as well as of the engine and accessory equipment. Other crew members are normally protected by plates on the sides and floor of the plane.

5. Tabulated Data

Specifications given are for the principal types in current operation. The following type abbreviations are used:

LWM—Low Wing Monoplane.
HWM—High Wing Monoplane.
MWM—Mid-Wing Monoplane.
TT—Twin tails.
TB—Twin tail booms.

FIGHTERS

Aircraft Manufacturer and Model	Type	Normal Crew	Engines, Model and Rated HP	Wing Span	Max. Speed MPH	Radius of Action (40% Normal Range) (Miles)	Typical Armament	Bomb or Freight Load (Pounds)	Normal Weight (Pounds)	Service Ceiling (Feet)
Single-Engine										
(1) Focke-Wulf FW 190	LWM	1	1xBMW 801D 14 cyl. twin-row, air-cooled radial—1755 HP	34'6"	385 at 19,000 ft.	175	*Forward fuselage* 2x7.9-or 13-mm. *Forward wings* 2/4x20-mm.	2x21-cm rockets under wings	8,600	36,000
(2) Focke-Wulf FW 190 (Long nose)	LWM	1	Jumo 213—12 cyl. liquid-cooled —1700 HP or DB603—12 cyl. liquid-cooled—1800 HP	34'6"	435 (est.)	160 (est.)	*Forward fuselage* 2x7.9- or 13-mm. *Forward wings* 2/4x20-mm.		9,000 (est.)	36,000 (est.)
(3) Messerschmitt ME 109	LWM	1	1xDB 605A/1 12 cyl. liquid-cooled—1460 HP	32'8"	400 at 22,000 ft.	175	*Forward fuselage* 2x7.9- or 13-mm. *Forward wings* 2 x 20-mm. *Prop. hub* 1x20-mm.	2x21-cm rockets under wings	6,820	38,500
Twin-engine										
(1) Dornier DO 217 J	HWM	3	2xBMW 801D 14 cyl. twin-row, air-cooled radial—1755 HP	62'5"	328 at 20,000 ft.	470	*Forward fuselage* 4x7.9-mm plus 4x20-mm. *Dorsal* 1x13-mm. *Ventral* 1x13-mm.		27,500	29,000
(2) Heinkel HE 219	MWM	2 (est.)	2xDB 603 12 cyl. liquid-cooled—1800 HP	60'6"	400 at 22,000 ft. (est.)	600 (est. max.)	*Forward wings* 2x20-mm. *Dorsal* 2x20-mm. *Ventral* 4x24- or 30-mm.		26,100	32,800

FIGHTERS—Continued

Aircraft Manufacturer and Model	Type	Normal Crew	Engines, Model and Rated HP	Wing Span	Max. Speed MPH	Radius of Action (40% Normal Range) (Miles)	Typical Armament	Bomb or Freight Load (Pounds)	Normal Weight (Pounds)	Service Ceiling (Feet)
(3) Junkers JU 88 C-6	LWM	3	2xJumo 211J 12 cyl. liquid-cooled—1380 HP	65'11"	295 at 14,000 ft.	285	*Forward fuselage* 1/3x20-mm plus 3x7.9-mm. *Dorsal* 2x7.9-mm plus 2x20-mm. *Ventral* 2x7.9-mm.		24,000	24,200
(4) Messerschmitt ME 110	LWM	2	2xDB 601F 12 cyl. liquid-cooled—1395 HP	53'11"	360 at 20,000 ft.	275	*Forward fuselage* 4x7.9 mm plus 2/4x20-mm. *Dorsal* 2x7.9-mm.		16,200	34,000
(5) Messerschmitt ME 410[1]	LWM	2	2xDB 603 A-2 12 cyl. liquid-cooled—1680 HP	53'7"	395 at 22,000 ft.	415	*Forward fuselage* 2/4x20-mm or 2x30-mm plus 2x47-mm or 1x37- or 50-mm plus 2x7.9-mm. *Dorsal* 2x13-mm.		24,000	30,000

[1] No technical data available for the rocket-and jet-propelled fighters Messerschmitt ME 163 and ME 262, Arado AR 234, and Heinke HE 280.

BOMBERS

Aircraft Manufacturer and Model	Type	Normal Crew	Engines, Model, and Rated HP	Wing Span	Max. Speed MPH	Radius of Action (40% Normal Range) (Miles)	Typical Armament	Bomb or Freight Load (Pounds)	Normal Weight (Pounds)	Service Ceiling (Feet)
Single-Engine (1) Junkers JU 87 (Stuka) (Dive-bomber)	Inverted Gull Wing	2	1xJumo 211 J 12 cyl. liquid-cooled—1335 HP	45'4"	255 at 13,500 ft.	280	*Forward fuselage* 2x12.7-mm. *Forward wings* 2x7.9-or 37-mm. *Dorsal* 2x7.9-mm.	2,200	12,600	18,500
(2) Focke-Wulf FW 190 (Fighter-bomber)	LWM	1	1xBMW 801D 14 cyl. twin-row, air-cooled radial—1755 HP	34'6"	370 at 19,000 ft.	165	*Forward fuselage* 2x7.9-or 13-mm. *Forward wings* 2/4x20-mm.	550	9,800	31,500
Twin-Engine (1) Henschel HS 129	LWM	1	2xGnome-Rhone 14M 04/05, 14 cyl. twin-row, air-cooled radial—800 HP	44'6"	275 at 9,000 ft.	220	*Forward fuselage* 2x7.9-mm plus 2x15-or 20-mm **plus** 1x30-mm or 6x7.9-mm. *Dorsal* Possibly 2x20-mm.	220	11,400	25,000
(2) Dornier DO 217 K-2	HWM	4	2xBMW 801 A-2 14 cyl. twin-row, air-cooled radial—1595 HP	80'6"	325 at 20,000 ft. (est.)	470	*Forward fuselage* 2x7.9-mm or larger caliber *Dorsal* 1x13-mm. *Lateral* 2x7.9-mm. *Ventral* 1x13-mm. *Tail* 4x7.9-mm.	6,600	35,000	25,000

BOMBERS—Continued

Aircraft Manufacturer and Model	Type	Normal Crew	Engines, Model, and Rated HP	Wing Span	Max. Speed MPH	Radius of Action (40% Normal Range) (Miles)	Typical Armament	Bomb or Freight Load (Pounds)	Normal Weight (Pounds)	Service Ceiling (Feet)
(3) Heinkel HE 111	LWM	5/6	2xJumo 211F 12 cyl. liquid-cooled—1230 HP	74'	252 at 14,000 ft.	215	Forward fuselage 1x20-mm plus 1/2x7.9-mm. Dorsal 1x13-mm. Ventral 2x7.9-mm.	2,020	25,500	26,000
(4) Heinkel HE 177	MWM	7	2xDB610 (DB 605 doubled) 24 cyl. liquid-cooled—2800 HP	103'6"	300 at 20,000 ft.	460	Forward fuselage 1x7.9-mm. Forward dorsal 1/2x13-mm. Rear dorsal 1/2x13-mm. Forward ventral 1x20-mm. Rear ventral 1x13-mm. Tail 1x20-mm.	12,320	68,000	21,000
(5) Junkers JU 88 A-4	LWM	4	2xJumo 211J 12 cyl. liquid-cooled—1335 HP	65'11"	291 at 14,000 ft.	490	Forward fuselage 1/2x7.9-mm and/or 1x20-mm. Dorsal 2x7.9-mm. Ventral 2x7.9-mm.	4,400	28,300	24,200
(6) Junkers JU 88 S	LWM	3	2xBMW 801 G-2 14 cyl. twin-row, air-cooled radial—1530 HP (est.)	65'11"	339 at 20,000 ft.	245	Forward fuselage 1x7.9-mm. Dorsal 1x13-mm.	1,980	26,400	30,000

BOMBERS—Continued

Aircraft Manufacturer and Model	Type	Normal Crew	Engines, Model, and Rated HP	Wing Span	Max. Speed MPH	Radius of Action (40% Normal Range) (Miles)	Typical Armament	Bomb or Freight Load (Pounds)	Normal Weight (Pounds)	Service Ceiling (Feet)
(7) Junkers JU 188 (Estimated performance)	LWM	4	2xJumo 213 A/1 12 cyl. liquid-cooled—1700 HP (est.)	72'6"	325 at 20,000 ft.	320	Forward fuselage 1x20-mm. Cockpit rear 1x13-mm. Dorsal turret 1x20-mm. Ventral 2x7.9-mm or 1x13-mm.	4,400		33/ 34,000
(8) Messerschmitt ME 110G	LWM	2	2xDB 605B, 12 cyl. liquid-cooled—1460 HP	53'11"	325 at 19,000 ft.	250	Forward fuselage 4x7.9-mm plus 2x20-or 30-mm. Dorsal 2x7.9-mm.	2,640	20,900	29,000
Four-Engine Focke-Wulf FW 200	LWM	5/7	4xBramo "FAFNIR" 323 R, 9 cyl. air-cooled radial—1,000 HP	107'7"	240 at 13,000 ft.	750	Dorsal forward 1x15-or 20-mm. Rear dorsal 1x13-mm. Lateral 2/4x7.9-mm or 2x13-mm. Forward ventral 1x15-or 20-mm. Rear ventral 1x7.9-, 13-, or 20-mm.	3,600	50,000	20,500

TRANSPORT AND GLIDER TUGS

Aircraft Manufacturer and Model	Type	Normal Crew	Engines, Model, and Rated HP	Wing Span	Max. Speed MPH	Radius of Action (40% Normal Range) (Miles)	Typical Armament	Bomb or Freight Load (Pounds)	Normal Weight (Pounds)	Service Ceiling (Feet)
(1) Arado AR 232 (performance and characteristics estimated)	HWM TT	3/4	2xBMW 801 A or L 14 cyl. twin-row, air-cooled radial—1595 HP	104'	210 at 18,000 ft.	350/400	*Forward fuselage* 1 MG *Lateral* 4 MGs	9,000	45,000	20,000
(2) Gotha GO 244 (Twin-engine powered version of GO 242 glider)	HWM TB	2	2xGnome-Rhone 14 m, 14 cyl. twin-row, air-cooled radial—800 HP	79'	169 at 10,000 ft.	145	*Forward fuselage* 1/2x7.9-mm. *Dorsal* 1x7.9-mm. *Lateral* 4x7.9-mm. *Tail* 1x7.9-mm.	4,400 or 23 men	17,500	19,000
(3) Junkers JU 52	LWM	3/4	3xBMW 132A A/T 9 cyl. air-cooled radial—660 HP	95'11"	165	210	*Forward fuselage* 1x7.9-mm. *Dorsal* 1x7.9-mm. *Lateral* 2x7.9-mm. *Ventral* 1x7.9-mm.	5,000 or 22 men	23,100	16,000
(4) Junkers JU 90	LWM	5	4xBMW 132 H 9 cyl. air-cooled radial—830 HP	115'	218 at 3,500 ft.	315	*Forward fuselage* 1x7.9-mm. *Dorsal* 1x13-mm. *Ventral* 1x7.9-mm.	9,000 or up to 70 men	51,000	15,000

TRANSPORT AND GLIDER TUGS—Continued

Aircraft Manufacturer and Model	Type	Normal Crew	Engines, Model, and Rated HP	Wing Span	Max. Speed MPH	Radius of Action (40% Normal Range) (Miles)	Typical Armament	Bomb or Freight Load (Pounds)	Normal Weight (Pounds)	Service Ceiling (Feet)
(5) Junkers JU 252	LWM	6	3xBMW 801 14 cyl. twin-row, air-cooled radial—1755 HP	111' (est.)	235 at 18,500 ft.	Unknown	*Dorsal* 1x13-or 20-mm. *Lateral* 2x7.9-mm. *Ventral* 1x13-mm. *Tail* 1x13-or 30-mm.	12,000 (est.) or 35 men	45,000 (est.)	26,000 (est.)
(6) Junkers JU 290	LWM TT	4/7	4xBMW 801 L-2 14 cyl. twin-row, air-cooled radial—1500 HP	138'	243 at 18,000 ft.	395	*Forward fuselage* 1x20-mm. *Dorsal* 1x15-or 20-mm. *Lateral* 4 or 6x7.9-mm or 2x13-mm. *Ventral* 1x13-mm, forward and 1x20-mm, rear *Tail* 1x20-mm.	19,000 or up to 90 men	90,000	19,000
(7) Messerschmitt ME 323	HWM	8/10	6xGnome-Rhone 14N 48/49, 14 cyl. twin-row, radial—965 HP	181'	195 at 13,000 ft.	255	*Fuselage* 2x7.9-mm, upper 2x7.9-mm, lower *Dorsal* 4x7.9-mm, forward plus 2x7.9-mm, rear *Lateral* 6x7.9-mm. *Ventral* 2x7.9-mm.	26,900 or 60/100 men	85,000	23,000

GLIDERS

Aircraft Manufacturer and Model	Type	Normal Crew	Engines, Model, and Rated HP	Wing Span	Max. Speed MPH	Radius of Action (40% Normal Range) (Miles)	Typical Armament	Bomb or Freight Load (Pounds)	Normal Weight (Pounds)	Service Ceiling (Feet)
(1) Gotha DFS 230	HWM	1 or 2	None	72'4"	Dependent on type of tug.		Light MG can be carried	2,800 or 10 men	4,700	
(2) Gotha GO 242	HWM TB	2	None	79'	Dependent on type of tug.		*Fuselage* 1 or 2x7.9-mm. *Dorsal* 1x7.9-mm. *Tail* 1x7.9-mm.	5,300 or 23 fully equipped troops	12,500	
(3) Messerschmitt ME 321 "GIGANT"	HWM	1 or 2	None	181'	Dependent on type of tug.		*Lateral* possibly 6x7.9-mm.	26,000 or 130 men	50,000	

RECONNAISSANCE AND ARMY COOPERATION

Aircraft Manufacturer and Model	Type	Normal Crew	Engines, Model, and Rated HP	Wing Span	Max. Speed MPH	Radius of Action (40% Normal Range) (Miles)	Typical Armament	Bomb or Freight Load (Pounds)	Normal Weight (Pounds)	Service Ceiling (Feet)
(1) Henschel HS 126	HWM	2	1xBramo "Fafnir" 323, 9 cyl. air-cooled radial— 1,000 HP	47'7"	230 at 15,000 ft.	210	*Forward fuselage* 1 or 2x7.9-mm. *Cockpit* 1x7.9-mm. *Dorsal* 2x7.9-mm.	220	7,250	27,000
(2) Fieseler FI 156	HWM	2 or 3	1xArgus As 10C/3, 8 cyl. air-cooled, inverted "V"— 240 HP	46'8"	110 at S.L.	95	*Dorsal* 1x7.9-mm.	220	2,250	15,000

NAVY TYPES

Aircraft Manufacturer and Model	Type	Normal Crew	Engines, Model, and Rated HP	Wing Span	Max. Speed MPH	Radius of Action (40% Normal Range) (Miles)	Typical Armament	Bomb or Freight Load (Pounds)	Normal Weight (Pounds)	Service Ceiling (Feet)
(1) Arado AR 196	LWM (Float)	2	1xBMW 132 K, 9 cyl. air-cooled radial—920 HP	41'	195 at S.L.	185	*Fuselage* 1x7.9-mm. *Forward wings* 2x20-m. *Dorsal* 2x7.9-mm.	220	6,600	21,500
(2) Blohm & Voss BV 138	HWM TB (Flying boat)	5 or 6	3xJumo 205 D 6 cyl. liquid-cooled Diesel 700 HP	88'7"	175 at S.L.	395	*Forward fuselage* 1x15-or 20-mm. *Dorsal* 1x13-mm. *Tail* 1x15-or 20-mm.	660	30,800	17,000
(3) Blohm & Voss BV 222 (Performance estimated)	HWM	10	6xBMW 801 A, 14 cyl. twin-row, air-cooled radial— 1595 HP	150'10"	200/240 at 15/ 17,000 ft.	1,400 to 1,800	*Forward fuselage* 1x13-or 15-or 20-mm. *Dorsal* 2x15-or 20-mm. *Lateral?*	45,000 (est.) up to 116 men	45,000	18,000
(4) Heinkel HE 115	MWM (Twin Floats)	3	2xBMW 132 K, 9 cyl. air-cooled radial—920 HP	72'6"	185 at S.L.	490	*Forward fuselage* 1x7.9-and 1x15-mm. *Engine nacelles* 2x7.9-mm. *Dorsal* 1x7.9-mm.	1,100	23,500	18,500

Figure 3.—FW 190 Single-Engine Fighter-Bomber with DB 603 Engine.

Figure 4.—ME 109 F Single-Engine Fighter-Bomber.

Figure 5.—DO 217 J Twin-Engine Night-Fighter.

Figure 6.—JU 88 C-6 Twin-Engine Fighter.

Figure 7.—ME 110's in action.

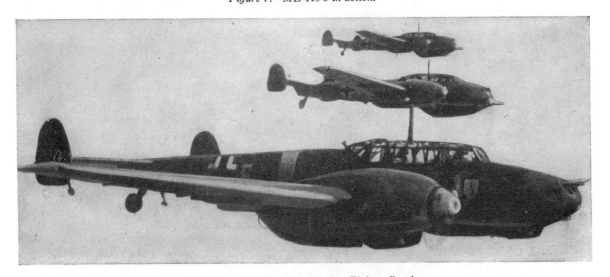

Figure 8.—ME 110 Twin-Engine Fighter-Bomber.

Figure 9.—ME 110 Twin-Engine Fighter-Bomber.

Figure 10.—ME 410 Twin-Engine Fighter-Bomber.

Figure 11.—JU 87 (Stuka) Twin-Engine Dive-Bomber.

Figure 12.—FW 190 Single-Engine Fighter-Bomber.

Figure 13.—DO 217 K-2 Twin-Engine Bomber.

Figure 14.—HE 111 Twin-Engine Bomber.

Figure 15.—HE 177 Twin "Doubled" Engine Bomber.

Figure 16.—JU 88 A-4 Twin-Engine Bomber.

Figure 17.—JU 88 S Twin-Engine Bomber.

Figure 18.—JU 188 Twin-Engine Bomber.

Figure 19.—FW 200 C Four-Engine Bomber.

Figure 20.—GO 244 Twin-Engine Transport.

Figure 21.—JU 52 Three-Engine Transport/Glider Tug.

Figure 22.—ME 323 Six-Engine Transport.

Figure 23.—JU 90 Four-Engine Transport/Glider Tug.

Figure 24.—DFS 230 Glider.

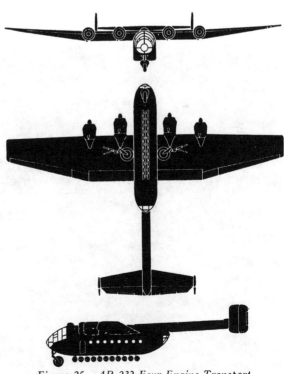

Figure 25.—AR 232 Four-Engine Transport.

Figure 26.—JU 290 Four-Engine Transport.

Figure 27.—GO 242 Glider.

Figure 28.—ME 321 "Gigant" Glider.

Figure 29.—HS 126 Single-Engine Army Cooperation.

Figure 30.—FI 156 "Storch" Single-Engine Army Cooperation.

Figure 31.—AR 196 Single-Engine Floatplane.

Figure 32.—BV 138 Three-Engine Flying Boat.

Figure 33.—BV 222 Six-Engine Flying Boat.

Figure 34.—HE 115 Twin-Engine Floatplane.

Figure 35.—ME 163 Liquid-Rocket Propelled Interceptor Fighter.

Figure 36.—ME 262 Jet-Propelled Turbine-Type Fighter.

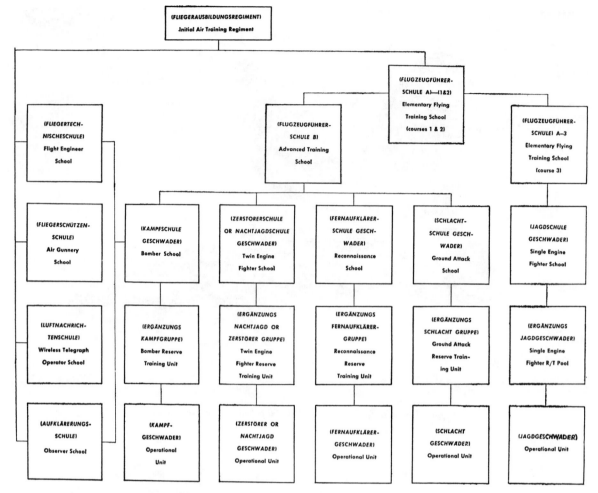

Figure 37.—German Air Force training program.

Section VI. TRAINING

1. General

Air Force training is the responsibility of the Air Ministry Training Inspectorate headed by the Air Officer for Training (*General der Fliegerausbildung*). Air Training Divisions control the assignment of recruits to training schools and assignment of trained pilots to operational units upon orders from the Air Ministry. At the individual flying schools all training is under the control of a Director of Instruction Courses (*Lehrgangsleiter*), who is also responsible for the maintenance of the training aircraft.

2. Recruit Training

All prospective Air Force personnel are sent to German Air Force Initial Training Regiments (*Fliegerausbildungsregimenter*), where for six weeks to three months they receive military or basic infantry training. Upon completion of Initial Training, pilot candidates enter Elementary Flying Training Schools. Personnel to be trained for the air crew positions of flight engineer, gunner, wireless operator, or observer are enrolled in their respective individual schools.

3. Elementary Flying Training

Pilot candidates proceed to and begin their actual flight training in the Elementary Flying Training Schools (*Flugzügführerschulen A*). All pupils take Course Number 1, a brief glider training course, and Course Number 2, (*Motor Auswahl*), a preliminary course in powered aircraft. Unsuitable trainees are eliminated, and those acceptable are assigned to bomber or fighter training upon determination of their qualifications. Students in single-engine, fighter-pilot training continue through Course Number 3 (*Jagdvorschule*), a branch of the Elementary Flying Training School, for preliminary instruction in fighter aircraft. This course includes aerobatics, cross-country, and formation flying.

4. Single-Engine Fighter Training

The single-engine fighter pilot progresses from Course Number 3 of Elementary Flying Training School to the specialized single-engine fighter school (*Jagdschule*) *Geschwader* where he learns to fly operational fighter types. He also receives instruction in gunnery, blind flying, and formation flying. He is next assigned to a Reserve Training Pool (*Ergänzungs Jagdgeschwader*) where he receives intensive combat training prior to joining an operational unit. The total time necessary to produce a single-engine fighter pilot is from 7 to 8 months, including flying time of from 107 to 112 hours.

5. Advanced Training or Conversion School

Upon completion of the Elementary Flying Training School (A) Course Number 2, the bomber, reconnaissance, ground-attack, and twin-engine fighter pilots are sent to an Advanced Training or Conversion School (*Flugzeugführerschule B*). Here they are instructed in the handling of multi-engine aircraft, in blind flying, link trainer, instrument flying, and the use of direction-finder apparatus. Two or three months are spent in this phase of training.

6. Specialized School *Geschwadern*

a. BOMBER TRAINING. From the Advanced Training or Conversion School the bomber pilot is sent to a Specialized Bomber School (*Kampfschule*) *Geschwader*, where pilots and members of their crews are assembled as units. This course includes formation flying and leading, torpedo and tactical bombing, high level and precision bombing, minelaying, and bomb ballistics. The total training period of a bomber pilot comprises about 9 months.

b. TWIN-ENGINE FIGHTER TRAINING. From the Advanced Training School, prospective twin-engine fighter pilots proceed to a Specialized Twin-Engine School *Geschwader*, either day (*Zerstörerschule*) or night (*Nachtjagdschule*). Here they are instructed in gunnery, blind flying, bad weather flying, mock attacks, and operational day and night flying. A twin-engine pilot spends from 6 to 7 months in training.

c. GROUND-ATTACK TRAINING. Upon completion of the Advanced Training School course, ground-attack students advance to a Specialized Ground-Attack School (*Schlachtschule*) *Geschwader*. Here the instruction includes dive bombing, strafing, aerobatics, rocket firing, and navigation. The total time required to produce a ground-attack pilot is about 5 months.

d. RECONNAISSANCE TRAINING. Proceeding from the Advanced Training School to a Specialized Reconnaissance School (*Fernaufklärerschule*) *Geschwader*, students training for reconnaissance pilots are instructed in aerial photography, visual reconnaissance, and navigation.

7. Reserve Training Units

After completion of instruction in their individual specialized school, *Geschwadern*—bomber, twin-engine, ground-attack, and reconnaissance—together with their assigned crews, are advanced to their respective Reserve Training Units (*Ergänzungs Kampfgruppe, Erzänzungs Nachtjagd* or *Zerstörer Gruppe, Ergänzungs Fernaufklärer Gruppe, Ergänzungs Schlacht Gruppe*). Here they are assigned to a non-operational *Gruppe* of a *Geschwader* until such time as vacancies occur in the operational *Gruppen* of the unit to which they are attached. Thus, training periods in this phase vary according to operational requirements. In such *Geschwadern* the crews receive intensive training under combat conditions in the specific tactics of the unit.

8. Air Crew Training

From the Initial Training Regiment prospective air crew members proceed to their respective specialist schools: Observer's School (*Aufklärungschule*); Wireless Telegraphy School (*Luftnachrichtenschule*); Air Gunnery School (*Fliegerschützenschule*); and Flight Engineer's School (*Fliegertechnisheschule*). Observer candidates spend 1 to 2 months learning map-making and reading, navigation, bombsights and bombing, meteorology, astro-navigation, and air gunnery. Students in wireless telegraphy undergo 1 to 2 months' intensive training in wireless transmitting and receiving, navigation, map reading, and radio direction-finding. Air gunners must complete a 1- to 2-months course, comprised of ground firing, camera-gun operation, air-to-air machine-gun firing, and elementary navigation. Students in flight engineering are given theoretical training in aircraft engines and aerodynamics. They also spend some time engaged in practical work on engines in an aircraft factory. Upon completion of their various courses, these specially trained personnel are assembled with pilots into crews for unit training in a specialized school *Geschwader*.

Section VII. TACTICS

I. General

In more than 5 years of warfare new tactics had to be perfected to take advantage of improvements or new developments in both German and Allied aircraft and armament. Other factors have been the German Air Force's loss of its original numerical superiority and the new problems arising in the defense of the homeland due to continually receding front lines. As a result, profound changes have and are still taking place in German Air Force tactics. In general, however, it may be said that through the last few years the German Air Force has been increasingly on the defensive. It has been unable to go on the offensive, except occasionally and on a limited scope. Thus, the German Air Force tactics were modified from one of bold attack to one of conservation of strength, assuming risks only when decisive results appeared obtainable. Within the limitations of such enforced caution the German Air Force has held to its basic concepts of surprise, concentrated attack and exploitation of the enemy's mistakes.

2. Long-Range Bombers

a. OPERATIONS EARLY IN THE WAR. The German Air Force never has had a heavy bomber force. Its long-range bomber force has consisted of medium bombers designed originally for close, as well as indirect, support. Typical of its intended purpose were the large-scale bombing attacks on airfields which initiated the German campaigns against Poland, France, and the Lowlands. The inadequacy of this bomber force for strategic operations was revealed in the Battle of Britain. The deficiency was never corrected, and thereafter the main employment of the long-range bomber force was as close support, a function which progressively declined as the German Air Force lost more and more its previous air superiority to the growing fighter forces of the Allies.

Units specializing in anti-shipping activities have comprised the most experienced and efficient branch of the bomber force during the war. They too eventually proved inadequate to their main mission when major Allied landings were made on the coasts of Europe.

b. RECENT TREND. In view of these factors, the German Air Force in the summer of 1944 substantially curtailed its bomber force. The relatively few units remaining operational are today engaged in the following operations:

(1) Level bombing from medium height, in dusk or dawn attacks by small formations on bridges, railroads, dock facilities, and targets of opportunity in the rear of battle areas.

(2) Mining of coastal waters and estuaries at night.

(3) Occasional torpedo attacks on shipping.

(4) Miscellaneous minor activities such as air launching of pilotless aircraft, "pick-a-back" attacks on shipping, docks and bridges, etc.

3. Ground Attack

a. "STUKAS." Ground attack is the extremely close support of ground forces in the battle area illustrated by the close teamwork of aircraft with advancing *Panzer* columns which was the basic formula of Germany's *Blitzkrieg*. The "Stuka" dive-bombing JU 87 was the air artillery which on short summons from the ground forces cleared road blocks and reduced opposition. It also roamed behind the enemy's line disrupting traffic and creating confusion. For such tactics, complete mastery of the air was a requirement. In the early campaigns, the skies were swept clear of opposition by sudden attacks on enemy airfields followed by destruction in the air of such aircraft as had escaped. Without such freedom from enemy fighter interception, the "Stuka" was too vulnerable and could not operate. This became apparent in the later stages of the Tunisian campaign. With the advent of appreciable Allied fighter strength, dive bombing in daytime continued only in areas where the enemy lacked fighter strength such as the Partisan sectors of the Balkans or where special front characteristics, such as the vastness of the Eastern Front, made their employment still possible. In the West, dive-bombing "Stukas" have been relegated to individual night sorties chiefly against troop concentrations, headquarters and other front-line objectives.

b. TWIN-ENGINE FIGHTERS. The German Air Force unsuccessfully experimented with heavily armored twin-engine fighters to fill the place left vacant by the obsolescence of the "Stuka". The HS 129 never proved satisfactory and is disappearing from the Eastern Front, its only sphere of operations.

c. SINGLE - ENGINE FIGHTER - BOMBERS. (1) The German Air Force then turned to the single-engine fighter to meet the ground-attack needs. The FW 190 equipped as a fighter-bomber proved satisfactory, and re-equipment of the *Schlacht* Units with this type apparently was intended.

(2) The fighter-bomber tactics are familiar. They consist of medium-height approach by small formations, ranging from a *Schwarm* of five planes to a half *Gruppe,* though occasionally concentration may be attempted. Troops, transport columns, and airfields are dive-bombed by each plane in turn, then strafed with the aircraft armament. Attacks against tanks or well defended sites are likely to be made from approaches at treetop level, and main reliance may be on cannon and machine-gun fire.

(3) Fighter-bombers, however, are still vulnerable to regular fighter attacks. It is therefore quite usual for them to be accompanied by a high cover of their own fighters, at least for the outward leg of their journey.

(4) The large numerical superiority of the Allied fighters on the Western Front after the Normandy landings prevented the German Air Force from giving adequate protection to its ground-attack aircraft and thus denied the possibility of any substantial close-support effort. On the Western Front today the fighter-bomber FW 190 is found in night harassing units, where it joins the JU 87 in attacks on headquarters, troop, communication and transportation systems. These night activities have been further augmented by assigning similar tasks to some of the twin-engine night fighters. These missions are generally individual free lance operations.

d. JET AIRCRAFT. Introduction of jet aircraft as ground-attack equipment is the latest German Air Force move in its endeavor to maintain close support by day for the German ground troops. Their tactics are based on the use of speed to escape antiaircraft defense fire or air interception. Jet aircraft attacks on airfields and troop concentrations have been made occasionally with anti-personnel bombs from great height in daytime. Most attacks, however, are at dusk, principally against bridges, dock facilities, railroads, etc, with small bombs. These attacks are made generally by single planes in dives from medium or low height. If attacking in pairs, one aircraft is likely to approach at medium height while the other follows at much lower level.

4. Fighter Tactics

a. MISSION. The mission of the fighter aircraft, be it day or night, single- or twin-engine, is the destruction of the enemy's air force and the protection of its bombers, ground-attack planes, etc., against enemy fighter action. As the development of the war forced Germany more and more on the defensive, the German Air Force fighters have been increasingly occupied with the interception of enemy bomber penetrations. Tactics have been continually revised to meet problems presented by new enemy equipment, greater fire power, new enemy defense formations, and increased enemy fighter cover. Only the most general principles can be outlined.

b. INTERCEPTION. (1) Against enemy day penetration, the German Air Force single-engine fighter tactic is to avoid if possible the fighter screen protecting the enemy bombers. Before the advent of Allied long-range fighters, the German fighters were wont to wait until the Allied bomber formations had reached a point beyond the range of their fighter cover. To insure such an unprotected period, the German Air Force sometimes made early attacks on enemy fighter cover to compel them to drop their auxiliary fuel tanks and thus shorten their protective flights. Always on the alert for opportunities, the German fighters would take quick advantage of gaps between successive fighter cover waves.

(2) Main tactics against the bomber formation have remained the concentrated attack against one particular group of the enemy bomber formation, preferably an outside or laggard one. Effort is made to bring the bombers to loosen their formation and thus lose much of their advantage of combined cross fire. Individual attacks are from the sun if possible, but the main consideration being the defensive fire power of the attacked bomber, approach will differ according to the type of aircraft faced. Single pass and mass attacks have both been employed.

(3) Twin-engine day fighters were used for a time, especially in rocket attacks, for the purpose of breaking enemy formations. The vulnerability of the twin-engine fighter to enemy fighters brought an end to these tactics as soon as the latter were able to accompany in force their bomber formation all the way to and from their target.

(4) Against other fighters, German Air Force single-engine fighter tactics follow whenever possible the usual basic principles of attack from the

sun, from above, and from behind. Speed and maneuverability remain as always the decisive factors. Tactics are based on the *"Rotte"* formation of 2 planes, number two flying wing man protection for his leader.

c. NIGHT FIGHTERS. Against enemy night penetration, the German Air Force night fighters have been equipped with both single- and twin-engine aircraft, but the latter has really been the basic equipment of the force. Two main night fighter-tactics have been the free lance, independent hunt, or the attack guided by radio from a ground control. In either case the attack is by single aircraft and target location is generally determined by airborne radar, though in some cases it is accomplished by visual sighting.

d. INTRUDER ATTACKS. Twin-engine fighters have carried out night intruder attacks. This consists of attacks against returning enemy bomber aircraft on or near their bases as they prepare to land as well as strafing attacks against the airfields.

5. Airborne Troops

a. ATTACK ON CRETE. In the early stages of the war Germany tried various methods of employing air-landing troops in the Lowlands, Norway, and the Balkans. Tactics for airborne combat became more clearly defined, however, in the combined attack on Crete, which was the first airborne invasion and capture of strongly defended territory across a body of water. The pattern established then consisted of the following:

(1) Short, intensive low and medium bombing and strafing of enemy positions in the intended landing area, immediately preceding or even simultaneous with the landing of glider-borne and parachute troops.

(2) As these troops proceeded, according to plan, to disrupt communications, silence local defenses, and seize airfields or other suitable landing grounds, areas surrounding their immediate objectives were subjected to continuous bombardment.

(3) With the arrival of the airborne infantry and engineer units closely followed by heavier elements, the parachute and other shock troops were reinforced and this combined force continued the task of attacking enemy communications from the rear, drawing off reserves, and clearing the area for the armored forces which were to follow.

b. OPERATIONS SINCE CRETE. (1) Since the capture of Crete, increasing transport commitments on all fronts and Allied air superiority have placed almost insurmountable difficulties in the way of such large scale ventures. The Germans have, however, dropped parachutists and landed glider troops in conjunction with land operations.

(2) In Russia, the Balkans, and the December 1944 counteroffensive in the Ardennes, units varying in strength from a platoon to a battalion have been landed behind enemy lines to disrupt communications, to seize such key points as railroads, roadheads, bridges, and power stations, and to engage in other sabotage activities. When such tactics are employed, the troops, whether they are parachuted from the JU 52 or landed by the DFS 230, usually hold their positions a limited time before being relieved by advancing ground forces or attempting to work their way back to their own lines.

6. Supply by Air

a. PURPOSES. As the complex of the war changes, sustained operations on several fronts forced the German Air Force to use defensively aircraft that had previously been envisioned as spearheading short, decisive victories. The supply situation has been so desperate on many occasions that the German Army has had to rely upon air transportation of personnel, supplies and equipment for its existence. This was evident in Russia, North Africa, and the Balkans first as an attempt to reinforce the *Wehrmacht;* when that failed, efforts were made to carry out evacuation by air. Although the JU 52 has been the mainstay in these operations, the German Air Force has employed nearly every type of its operational aircraft. Most recent application of the defensive mission of the German Air Force transports has been the supply of isolated garrisons in the Channel and Biscay ports and in other isolated localities. These landings or dropping of supplies are essentially emergency measures—carried on when all other means of supply are interrupted.

b. METHODS. A landing operation, accomplished by power-driven aircraft or by freight-carrying gliders, is the safest method of air supply if proper landing facilities are available. Glider landings may be made in good or bad weather after precise agreements on signals and markers have been reached. Power-driven aircraft have the additional asset of being able to carry off wounded and make other evacuations on the return trip. Supply-dropping operations have been necessary in other instances. T usually have been carried out by night, although some have taken place during the day. Whichever method is used, careful arrangements have to be made as to the time and locality of the dropping, and for the cessation of local defenses. Night missions, moreover, necessitate increasing the size of the dropping zone and more careful marking of the approach and target area with flares and other signals.

INDEX